Becoming a Teacher

FlexChoice Version

fifth edition

Becoming a Teacher

FlexChoice Version

Forrest W. Parkay
Washington State University

Beverly Hardcastle Stanford
Azusa Pacific University

Allyn and Bacon

Boston ■ London ■ Toronto ■ Sydney ■ Tokyo ■ Singapore

This book is dedicated to our students—their spirit continually renews us and inspires confidence in the future of teaching in America

Vice President, Editor-in-Chief	Paul A. Smith
Executive Editor and Publisher	Stephen D. Dragin
Senior Development Editor	Linda Bieze
Editorial Assistant	Barbara Strickland
Marketing Manager	Kathleen Morgan
Editorial Production Service	Omegatype Typography, Inc.
Photo Research	Helane M. Prottas/Posh Pictures
Composition Buyer	Linda Cox
Manufacturing Buyer	Suzanne Lareau
Cover Administrator	Linda Knowles
Text Designer	Debbie Schneck/Schneck-DePippo Graphics
Electronic Composition	Dayle Silverman/Silver Graphics
	Omegatype Typography, Inc.

Copyright © 2002, 2001, 1998 by Allyn & Bacon
A Pearson Education Company
75 Arlington Street
Boston, MA 02116

Internet: www.ablongman.com

Between the time Website information is gathered and published, some sites may have closed. Also, the transcription of URLs can result in typographical errors. The publisher would appreciate notification where these occur so that they may be corrected in subsequent editions.

Library of Congress Cataloging-in-Publication Data

Parkay, Forrest W.
    Becoming a teacher / Forrest W. Parkay, Beverly Hardcastle Stanford.—5th ed.,
FlexChoice version
        p. cm.
    Includes bibliographical references and index.
    ISBN 0-205-34987-0
    1. Teaching—Vocational guidance. 2. Education—Study and teaching—United States. 3.
Teachers—United States—Attitudes. 4. Teaching—Computer network resources. I.
Stanford, Beverly Hardcastle II. Title.

LB1775 .P28 2002
371.1'0023'73—dc21

                                                                                    2001045754

Printed in the United States of America
10 9 8 7 6 5 4 3 2 1   WEB   06 05 04 03 02 01

Contents

Part Two

Influences on the Professional Lives of Teachers 56

Dear Mentor 56

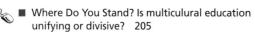

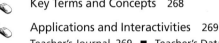

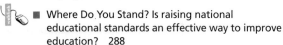

14 **Education Issues for the Twenty-First Century**   388

Preface

We hope that you share our belief that teaching is the world's most important profession. To facilitate your students' journey toward becoming professional teachers, the fifth edition of *Becoming a Teacher* emphasizes the concept of mentoring. For example, the **"Dear Mentor"** feature that opens each part provides practical advice from highly accomplished teachers for meeting the complex challenges of teaching. This popular feature presents the responses of experienced mentor teachers to questions and concerns raised by preservice teachers much like the students who will be using this book. In their responses, the mentors, including award-winning teachers and Teachers of the Year, provide practical and wise advice.

Throughout the fifth edition of *Becoming a Teacher,* we highlight **teacher leadership,** since today's teachers are assuming diverse leadership roles beyond the classroom. For instance, in Chapter 12, **"Teachers as Educational Leaders,"** readers learn about the exciting new leadership roles that await teachers.

Features of the New FlexChoice Version

The FlexChoice version of the fifth edition of *Becoming a Teacher* takes full advantage of the capabilities of the Internet to give students more opportunities for flexible, interactive learning. The FlexChoice version is

- **Shorter:** This affordable paperback textbook is 432 pages long (the hardback is 622), with most figures, tables, pedagogical features, and appendices moved to the open-access FlexChoice website and made interactive.
- **Assessment-rich:** Testing takes place both in the book and on the website. Students can complete Pre- and PostTests in the book, remove them, and submit them to you. On the FlexChoice website, assessment instruments including self-scoring, chapter-ending PostTests and quizzes appearing after selected features.
- **Interactive:** Both the book and the FlexChoice website involve the student in active learning. In addition to Pre- and PostTests, the book includes an in-text journaling feature on every page, plus numerous icons to point students to features that can be accessed on the FlexChoice website. The website includes interactive text features, assessment opportunities, audio, video, weblinks, and more.
- **Web-connected:** The technology component, delivered on an open-access website, provides not only the features excerpted from the larger hardbound text, but also mul-

timedia to make the material come alive for students with a variety of learning styles (auditory, visual, kinesthetic, etc.):

- Figures and tables, moved from the book to the FlexChoice website, are animated, make use of a variety of media, and include quizzes and essay questions on the content.
- All chapter pedagogical features—"Technology Highlights," "Where Do You Stand?," "Case to Consider," "Keepers of the Dream," and "Professional Reflection"—appear on the website, followed by essay questions.
- **Weblink icons** in the book are keyed to relevant sites on the World Wide Web and include Applications and Interactivities that require students to go to a variety of education-related sites, gather information, and apply analytical and critical thinking skills for better understanding of the material.
- **Key Terms** from the book appear on the website as visually appealing flashcards that allow for easier mastery of definitions and concepts.
- **Self-scoring PostTests** appear on the website to check students' grasp of each chapter's content.
- Students can forward their responses to quizzes, essay questions, and PostTests to you by e-mail.

Features of the Fifth Edition

An entirely new chapter, **"Teaching with Technology"** (Chapter 11), provides an up-to-date overview of how educational technologies are influencing schools and the profession of teaching. This chapter describes how teachers are using computer-assisted instruction (CAI); microcomputer-based laboratories (MBL); newsgroups, chat-rooms, and research assignments on the Internet; home-school communication systems; and high-quality hypermedia simulations. Also, each chapter has a new feature, **"Technology Highlights,"** that illustrates how educational technology is related to chapter content.

"Where Do You Stand?" and **"Case to Consider,"** two more new chapter features, give opportunities to reflect on the realities of teaching and on controversial trends and issues that have aroused public opinion and attracted media attention. Among the issues addressed in these features are violence in schools, vouchers and school choice, character education, psychological assessments of teaching candidates, school uniforms, and increased standardized testing.

Organization of the Book

The text has been extensively revised, based on feedback from students and instructors. To allow for expanded coverage of critical trends and issues in education, we have organized the book into four parts: "Part One: The Teaching Profession," "Part Two: Influences on the Professional Lives of Teachers," "Part Three: The Art of Teaching," and "Part Four: Your Teaching Future."

Chapters 1 and 2, which make up Part One, are on the theme of teachers and teaching. After reading these chapters, students will be better able to determine whether teaching is a good career choice for them. Among the topics we address are why people choose to teach, the challenges and realities of teaching, the knowledge and skills needed to become a teacher, and how to establish mentoring relationships.

Chapters 3–6 in Part Two take up the foundations of education, which every professional teacher needs to know. These foundational areas include the philosophical, historical, social, cultural, political, financial, and legal dimensions of U.S. education. Philosophical and historical foundations are treated in a new chapter, "Ideas and Events That Have Shaped Education in the United States" (Chapter 3).

Chapters 7–11, which make up Part Three, examine student characteristics and the worlds of the classroom and the school. Here, readers learn about characteristics of students at different stages of development, students as learners, the dynamics of classroom life, the curricula that are taught in schools, and teaching with technology.

Finally, in Part Four, Chapters 12–14 discuss issues and trends that will impact each student's quest to become an effective teacher, especially the expanding leadership role of teachers, planning for a successful first year of teaching, international education in a changing world, and the teacher's role in shaping the future of education.

Additional Features and Learning Aids

Included in *Becoming a Teacher* are many additional features we believe will help prepare students for rewarding futures as professional teachers. To guide study, "Focus Questions" at the beginning of each chapter reflect the questions posed in the main headings of the text. Opening scenarios present decision-making or problem-solving situations to reflect upon and resolve. These situations are referred to again in the chapter and give readers an opportunity to apply new learning in specific problem-solving contexts.

To inspire preservice teachers with the experiences of outstanding teachers, a web-based "Keepers of the Dream" feature for each odd-numbered chapter profiles an individual in education whose philosophies and professional contributions reflect a commitment to touching others' lives through teaching. A web-based "Professional Reflection" feature for each chapter gives readers an opportunity to reflect on their beliefs and values and on the issues teachers face. This feature is designed to give practice in the applied reflective inquiry that should characterize every teacher's professional life.

In addition, web-based chapter-ending material includes a "Teacher's Database" feature with online activities for using the vast resources of the World Wide Web and the Internet to facilitate professional growth. Cyberspace has transformed teaching and learning in many schools and classrooms, and advanced telecommunications will continue to change the way teachers teach and assess students' learning.

This edition of *Becoming a Teacher* continues the popular "Professional Portfolio" feature that will enable preservice teachers to document their growth and accomplishments over time. Each chapter includes web-based guidelines for creating a portfolio entry that readers can actually use when they begin teaching; in addition, students may wish to use selected portfolio entries during the process of applying for a first teaching position.

As a further study aid, "Key Terms and Concepts" are boldfaced in the text and listed on the FlexChoice website. An expanded "Glossary" at the end of the book helps readers quickly locate the definitions of key terms and concepts.

Other web-based end-of-chapter learning aids include a concise "Summary" and suggested "Applications and Interactivities." Applications and Interactivities include journal-writing opportunities in "Teacher's Journal" and field experiences in "Observations and Interviews." In "Teacher's Journal," we continue a feature that has proved useful and popular with instructors who ask students to keep a teacher's journal to encourage active reflection as they learn about teaching. The short, optional journal-writing activities are based on the "writing-to-learn" and "writing-across-the-curriculum" concepts.

A Teacher's Resource Guide, composed of appendice for 12 of 14 chapters, is located on the hardbound book's Companion Website (http://www.ablongman.com/parkay5e). It provides a rich and varied array of materials, sources, strategies, contacts, and data that beginning teachers can rely on for support. These materials—from a checklist for evaluating a school's effectiveness at integrating technology into the teaching-learning process to sample questions to ask during a job interview—will prove extremely valuable in preparing for, and beginning, a first teaching position.

Supplements for the Instructor

To help you get the most out of using *Becoming a Teacher* with your students, we have provided a number of useful supplements:

■ **Instructor's Resource Manual** in which, for each chapter of the text, a Chapter-at-a-Glance organizer correlates chapter outlines, learning objectives, and teaching supplements; an Annotated Lecture Outline provides examples, discussion questions, and student activities; suggestions for additional readings and media extend chapter learning; and handout masters provide additional lecture support materials.

- ■ **Test Bank** of more than 1,000 questions, including multiple-choice items, true/false items, essay questions, case studies, and authentic assessments, plus answer feedback keyed to the hardbound text.
- ■ **Computerized Testing Program,** an integrated suite of testing and assessment tools for Windows and Macintosh platforms.
- ■ **Allyn & Bacon Interactive Video for** *Becoming a Teacher,* **Fifth Edition,** featuring news reports from around the country on topics covered in the text.
- ■ **Allyn & Bacon Transparencies for Foundations of Education and Introduction to Teaching,** a set of one hundred acetate transparencies related to topics in the text.
- ■ **Allyn & Bacon Digital Media Archive for Education,** a CD-ROM containing PowerPoint lectures, images, video clips, and weblinks arranged topically to import into your own lectures and classroom presentations.

Acknowledgments

Many members of the Allyn and Bacon team provided expert guidance and support during the preparation of the fifth edition of *Becoming a Teacher.* Clearly, Linda Bieze, our developmental editor, heads the list. From suggestions for revision, feedback on draft manuscripts, and skillful coordination of the revision process from beginning to end, to coordination of the book's supplements, Linda's hard work is deeply appreciated. In addition, the authors benefited from excellent suggestions made by Steve Dragin, Executive Editor and Publisher. His extensive understanding of textbook publishing enriched the fifth edition immeasurably.

The authors extend a very special thanks to Paul A. Smith, Vice President and Editor-in-Chief; Kathleen Morgan, Marketing Manager; and Donna Simons, Production Administrator, who coordinated the FlexChoice Version.

The authors extend a special thanks to Steven Million of Winthrop University for writing the Test Bank and developing the new technology-based assessment component of the Test Bank. Thanks also go to mutindi ndunda and Diane Cudahy of College of Charleston for preparing the Instructor's Resource Manual and Handout Masters for this edition.

We are also grateful to the many people throughout the United States who have used the previous edition and provided suggestions and materials for this edition, including our students. We also wish to thank the following reviewers, who provided concise, helpful suggestions during the developmental stages of this book: Satnam Singh Bhugra, Lansing Community College; C. Lynn Davis, Plymouth State College; Ellen Eckman, Marquette University; Virden Evans, Florida A&M University; Frank Orlando, Rowan University; Lawrence H. Simon, Elon College; and Charles W. Smith, Ohio University.

Forrest W. Parkay appreciates the support of his family, friends, and colleagues during the intensive, months-long revision process. In particular, Judy N. Mitchell, Dean of the College of Education at Washington State University; Dennis Warner, Associate Dean; Donald B. Reed, Chair of the Department of Educational Leadership and Counseling Psychology; and the faculty, teaching assistants, and research assistants in the Department of Educational Leadership and Counseling Psychology gave him much-appreciated encouragement and support. In addition, the following colleagues provided Dr. Parkay with ideas, resources, and suggestions for this edition—Steve Casmar, Cindy Kaag, Merrill M. Oaks, Margaret Paden, Barbara Paulson, Nils Peterson, and Chris Sodorff, all of Washington State University; Robert Leahy, Stetson University; Ralph Karst, Northeastern Louisiana University; Satnam Singh Bhugra, Lansing Community College; Lyn Middleton, University of Wollongong, Australia; Liping Liu, Brevard College; Norma Bailey, Central Michigan University; and Soren Wheeler, American Association for the Advancement of Science. And, for demonstrating the power of professional inquiry, he owes a profound debt to a great teacher, mentor, and friend, Herbert A. Thelen, Professor Emeritus, University of Chicago.

Forrest W. Parkay

Beverly Hardcastle Stanford

Finally, the personal support Dr. Parkay received from his family was invaluable. During the revision process, the moments he spent with his daughters Anna, Catherine, and Rebecca were very special and brought much-needed balance back into his life. To Arlene, his wife, friend, and helper, he gives a deep thanks. She was always there to provide the support that made the fifth edition possible. Moreover, she made many valuable contributions to the project, not the least of which was obtaining and keeping track of letters of permission. Since the first edition of *Becoming a Teacher* was published in 1990, Arlene's encouragement, patience, and understanding have been remarkable.

Beverly Hardcastle Stanford thanks the many individuals who provided inspiration and assistance in the preparation of the fifth edition of this textbook. At Azusa Pacific University, the encouragement and support of President Richard Felix and Provost Patricia Anderson enable faculty to dream about and toil on projects such as this. Dr. Stanford is also grateful to Dean Alice Watkins for her ongoing practical and spiritual support. She appreciates her colleagues' sharing of insights on issues addressed in the text and gives special thanks to John Anderson, Nancy Brashear, Dave Harmeyer, Roger Harrell, Dennis Jacobsen, Ruth Kidd, Maria Pacino, Joe Rocha, and Lillian Wehmeyer. She pays tribute to her colleagues who teach creatively with this book: Nancy Brashear, Paul Flores, Dennis Jacobsen, and Mimi Zamary.

Dr. Stanford also appreciates the participation of Azusa Pacific University students who wrote the "Dear Mentor" letters: J. Casey Medlock, Elizabeth Acevedo, Darryl Hampton, and Sara Waltmire. She is grateful to school counselor DonnaLee Brown for writing the case study entitled "Help! Tell Me about This Kid!" She values the inspiration provided by the Keepers of the Dream, 1999 State Teachers of the Year, Peter White of New York and Mary L. Peacher of Oklahoma, and California administrator Marcia McVey. And she recognizes the fine contributions made by the expert teachers who wrote responses to the "Dear Mentor" letters; Andy Baumgartner, 1999 National Teacher of the Year; Diana Crim, Utah State Teacher of the Year; Joe Bacewicz, Connecticut Teacher of the Year; and Janice James, Kentucky Teacher of the Year.

Finally, Dr. Stanford thanks her students, from those beginning to teach to those leading schools as administrators. She continues to learn from and with them. Her greatest thanks in this endeavor go to her husband, Dick, for his ongoing support and enthusiasm for the project, from the days of the first edition to the present.

Forrest W. Parkay
Beverly Hardcastle Stanford

Becoming a Teacher

FlexChoice Version

The Teaching Profession

dear mentor

On Determining Whether Teaching Is the Right Profession for You

Dear Mentor,

As a new college graduate, I am searching for the right profession. Others have encouraged me to teach because I work well with children, but how might I truly know whether teaching is the right profession for me? I definitely desire to be a teacher, yet will my first year be the determining factor?

Sincerely,

J. Casey Medlock

D
ear Casey,

As a twenty-three year veteran teacher, I am always excited to share my experiences with those who are considering my profession for themselves. You are wise to ask whether teaching is right for you, but more important, you should ask whether you are right for teaching! An ability to work with students is certainly the most important characteristic of the teaching persona but many others are also important. Some other questions you might ask are

- Do I enjoy the company of children enough to spend most of my day with them?
- Do I have a limitless supply of energy?
- Do I possess a great deal of patience and perseverance?
- Do I enjoy learning and am I able to be a model of life-long learning for my students?
- Am I willing to learn from my students and use what they teach me to improve my ability as a teacher?
- Am I a person of strong convictions who can demonstrate those convictions in every aspect of my life?
- Can I focus on what is important and positive in my work while some around me seem to focus on negativism and dissension?
- Am I willing to be a strong advocate for the teaching profession, who is unwilling to accept the status quo and is prepared to fight to strengthen the profession, despite difficult odds?
- Can I always make the needs of my students the central reason for all that I do in teaching?

In response to your second question, whether your first year will be the determining factor in your success, the answer is both yes and no. I believe that the first year of any new experience has the potential to be a "make or break" year. This is one reason why I have chosen to teach kindergarten. Some children, like my son, find their kindergarten 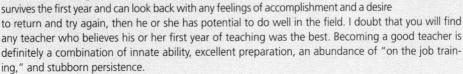 year such an abysmal experience that teachers and parents are never able to readjust their thinking and excite them about school. I have, therefore, made it my goal to ensure an enjoyable, productive kindergarten year for all of my students. What was true for my son in kindergarten seems also to be true for many new teachers—the first year sets the pattern for the rest. Furthermore, in education, the least experienced teachers have traditionally been placed in the most difficult situations. For some, this baptism by fire ignites a tenacity and strength that catapults them into "legendary teacher" status. But for too many, it either turns them away from teaching altogether or disillusions them, making them apathetic, ineffective teachers. I would say that if a teacher survives the first year and can look back with any feelings of accomplishment and a desire to return and try again, then he or she has potential to do well in the field. I doubt that you will find any teacher who believes his or her first year of teaching was the best. Becoming a good teacher is definitely a combination of innate ability, excellent preparation, an abundance of "on the job training," and stubborn persistence.

In a society that too often equates success with wealth and recognition, it is sometimes difficult for teachers to see themselves as successful, since they usually do not earn six figures and receive little acclaim for a job whose importance and responsibilities exceed those of almost all other professions. Those teachers who consider themselves successful have learned early in their careers to identify and celebrate their accomplishments! Helping one child is a reward in itself; helping many children is a measurement of great prosperity!

My twenty-three years of teaching have contained many peaks, plateaus, and valleys. But when I look into the faces of my students, I have never doubted the importance of my work. To teach is to impact directly the entire course of human destiny. It is an awesome responsibility, an incredible challenge, and a limitless opportunity for satisfaction and reward.

Sincerely,

Andy Baumgartner
1999 National Teacher of the Year

1

Teaching: Your Chosen Profession

My greatest satisfaction as a teacher has been helping young people learn to love history and instilling in them a personal desire to seek knowledge.

—Philip Bigler
1998 National Teacher of the Year
Thomas Jefferson High School for Science and Technology, Alexandria, Virginia

focus questions

1. Why do you want to teach?

2. What are the challenges of teaching?

3. What is teaching really like?

4. What does society expect of teachers?

5. How do good teachers view their work?

Your first interview for a job as a teacher is today, and you can hardly believe that it was only two years ago that you began to take courses to become a teacher. Several questions about your readiness for teaching occupy your mind while you walk from the faculty parking lot toward the school, which was just selected by the local newspaper as a "blue ribbon" school for its use of technology. "Am I ready? Do I have what it takes to become a good teacher? Can I handle the stress? Do I have sufficient skills to use educational technology in my classroom?"

AUDIO
Audio Clip 1.1

Approaching the main entrance, you look at the dozens of students playing on the open field next to the building. Their joyful, exuberant sounds this warm late-August morning remind you of your own school days. Some children are moving constantly, running in tight circles and zig-zags as they yell and motion to friends who are also on the move. Others stand near the entrance in groups of two or three, talking and milling about as they wait for the bell signaling the start of the first day of school.

At the bottom of the long stairs leading up to a row of green metal doors, you overhear the conversation of three students.

"It's a great movie. What time should we meet?" the taller of two girls asks. Before her friends can respond, she adds, "My aunt's going to pick me up at four o'clock, so I should be home by four-thirty."

"Let's meet at five o'clock," the other girl says. "I can be ready by then."

"Sí, pero no creo que pueda hacerlo para las cinco," the boy says. "Tengo que llevar a mi hermanita a la clinica. ¿Podermos hacerlo después?"

"Bueno, pero no muy tarde," the tall girl says, switching effortlessly to Spanish. "Tenemos que reunirnos con los otros chicos."

"Sí, además no quiero perder el comienzo de la película," says the other girl.

Reaching the top of the stairs, you open a door and walk through the vestibule out into a brightly lit hallway. The main office is directly in front of you. To the right of the office door is a bulletin board proclaiming in large red block letters, "Welcome back, students!" Beneath that greeting, in smaller black letters, is another message: "It's going to be a great year!"

Inside the office, you approach the counter on which sits a plastic sign that says "Welcome" in five languages: English, Spanish, Swahili, Chinese, and Russian. You introduce yourself to the school's head secretary. He remains seated behind a gray steel desk covered with loose papers.

"I have an appointment with Ms. Wojtkowski," you inform him. "It's about a replacement for Mr. Medina."

"Good. She's expecting you. Why don't you have a seat over there?" He motions for you to sit on the couch across from the teachers' mailboxes. "She's working with some teachers on setting up a meeting of our Site-Based Council. She ought to be finished in just a few minutes."

While waiting for Ms. Wojtkowski, you think about questions you might be asked. Why did you choose to become a teacher? What is your philosophy of education? How would you use technology in your classroom? What is your approach to classroom management? How would you meet the needs of students from different cultural and linguistic backgrounds? How would you set up a program in your major teaching area? How would you involve parents in the classroom? What are your strengths? Why should the district hire you?

Reflecting on these questions, you admit they are actually quite difficult. Your answers, you realize, could determine whether or not you get the job.

Name _____ Date _____

For each question, circle the letter of the answer you believe is correct. Then read the chapter to learn more about these topics.

1.1 The 1997 Gallup Poll of the Public's Attitudes toward the Public Schools indicated what percentage of the public would be willing to work as unpaid volunteers in local schools?
A. 19 percent.
B. 49 percent.
C. 39 percent.
D. 69 percent.

1.2 More than half of the student leaders who attended the 1999 United States Senate Youth Program reported which of the following as the biggest factor in their high school success?
A. A safe school environment.
B. Excellent teaching.
C. Support of peers.
D. Parental support.

1.3 All of the following statements about students and teachers with disabilities are true *except*
A. Approximately 10 percent of all children in public PreK–12 schools are receiving special education.
B. Information about the number of teachers with disabilities is incomplete.
C. Teachers with disabilities are rarely capable of being effective in classrooms.
D. There is an ongoing critical need for special education teachers.

1.4 A national survey of teachers indicates that when teachers are asked what they like most about their jobs, the most common response is that they enjoy the
A. Respect they receive from students.
B. Hours of the job.
C. Collaborative efforts between teachers and parents.
D. Opportunity to work with children and young adults.

1.5 Differences among students in regard to gender, race, ethnicity, culture, and socioeconomic status are often referred to as
A. Gender fairness.
B. Student variability.
C. Student diversity.
D. Cultural diversity.

1.6 Ms. Bradham has always enjoyed school and embraced the environment that encourages a high regard for education and the life of the mind. She probably chose teaching as a profession because of a love of the
A. Students.
B. Teaching life.
C. Teaching–learning process.
D. Salary and associated benefits.

1.7 Educational research supports the fact that those who become teachers are more influenced by their teachers as
A. People.
B. Coaches.
C. Subject-matter experts.
D. Disciplinarians.

1.8 All of the following are practical benefits of teaching *except*
A. Teachers' hours.
B. Rising salaries.
C. Generous vacation time.
D. Frequent promotions to administrative positions.

1.9 The percentage of teachers from minority groups is
A. Declining.
B. Increasing.
C. No longer considered an important consideration.
D. A direct reflection of community diversity.

1.10 Effective classroom management is difficult because of all of the following *except*
A. High teacher–student ratios.
B. Overcrowding.
C. Student-mobility rates.
D. Lack of administrative support.

Answers are available on the FlexChoice website at www.ablongman.com/parkayflex.

hough predictable, the interview questions just posed are surprisingly challenging. Why did you decide to become a teacher? How will you meet the needs of all students? What do you have to offer students? The answers to these and similar questions depend on the personality and experiences of the person responding. However, they are questions that professional teachers recognize as important and worthy of careful consideration.

The primary purpose of this book is to orient you to the world of education and to help you begin to formulate answers to such questions. In addition, this book will help you answer your own questions about the career you have chosen. What is teaching really like? What are the trends and issues in the profession? What problems can you expect to encounter in the classroom? What kind of rewards do teachers experience?

We begin this book by asking you to examine why you want to become a teacher because we believe that "good teachers select themselves" (Carmichael 1981, 113). They know why they want to teach and what subjects and ages they want to teach. They are active in the choosing process, aware of the options, informed about the attractions and obstacles in the field, and anxious to make their contributions to the profession.

Why Do You Want to Teach?

People are drawn to teaching for many reasons. For some, the desire to teach emerges early and is nurtured by positive experiences with teachers during the formative years of childhood. For others, teaching is seen as a way of making a significant contribution to the world and experiencing the joy of helping others grow and develop. And for others, life as a teacher is attractive because it is exciting, varied, and stimulating.

Desire to Work with Children and Young People

Figure 1.1

Figure 1.1, based on a national survey of more than 1,300 teachers, shows that most teachers say they began teaching because they wanted to work with young people. Though the conditions under which teachers work may be challenging, their salaries modest, and segments of their communities unsupportive, most teach simply because they care about students.

The day-to-day interactions between teachers and students build strong bonds. Daily contact also enables teachers to become familiar with the personal as well as the academic needs of their students, and this concern for students' welfare and growth outweighs the difficulties and frustrations of teaching. Like the following teachers, they know they can make a difference in students' lives:

> When I was struggling as a kid, one of my teachers was really there for me. She listened to me and supported me when nobody else believed in me. I want to pay her back by helping others like me (Zehm and Kottler 1993, 35).

> [Students] need someone to recognize their uniqueness and specialness and respect it and nurture it (Hansen 1995, 132).

Others, no doubt, love students because they appreciate the unique qualities of youth. They enjoy the liveliness, curiosity, freshness, openness, and trust of young children or the abilities, wit, spirit, independence, and idealism of adolescents. Like the following teacher, they want to be connected to their students: ". . . I now know that I teach so I can be involved in my students' lives, in their real life stories" (Henry et al. 1995, 69).

Teachers also derive significant rewards from meeting the needs of diverse learners. While students from the United States' more than one hundred racial and ethnic groups and students with special needs are increasing in number, effective teachers recognize that their classrooms are enriched by the varied backgrounds of students. To enable you to experience the satisfaction of helping all students learn, significant portions of this book are devoted to **student variability** (differences among students in regard to their developmental needs, interests, abilities, and disabilities) and **student diversity** (differences among students in regard to gender, race, ethnicity, culture, and socioeconomic status). An appreciation for such diversity, then, will help you to experience the rewards that come from enabling each student to make his or her unique contribution to classroom life.

The opportunity to work with young people, whatever their stage of development and whatever their life circumstances, is a key reason people are drawn to teaching and remain in the profession.

Love of Teaching

The Metropolitan Life Survey of the American Teacher, 1984–1995, *Old Problems, New Challenges* includes the following observation: ". . . teachers overwhelmingly agree with the statement, 'I love to teach.' This is true for teachers in urban as well as suburban and rural schools" (Louis Harris and Associates 1995). The survey, based on a nationally representative sample of 1,011 public school teachers interviewed in 1995, goes on to report that teachers express a great deal more personal satisfaction with teaching than they did in 1984, and they are more likely to say they would recommend teaching as a profession. Why do teachers find teaching so satisfying? What does it mean to *love* teaching?

Love of Subject   Some teachers who expressed a love of teaching may have meant that they love teaching in their discipline. The opportunity to continually learn more in one's profession and to share that knowledge with students is a definite attraction. Most of us can recall teachers who were so excited about their subjects that they were surprised when students were not equally enthusiastic. The affinity of such teachers toward their subjects was so great that we tended to see the two as inseparable—for instance, "Ms. Gilbert the French teacher" or "Mr. Montgomery the math teacher." Though other factors may draw teachers to their work, a love of subject is clearly one of them.

Love of the Teaching Life   For those teachers who always enjoyed school, it is often the life of a teacher that has appeal—to be in an environment that encourages a high regard for education and the life of the mind, and to have daily opportunities to see students become excited about learning. Albert Einstein, for example, regretted that he did not devote his career to the teaching life:

> Believe it or not, one of my deepest regrets [is that I didn't teach]. I regret this because I would have liked to have had more contact with children. There has always been something about the innocence and freshness of young children that appeals to me and brings me great enjoyment to be with them. And they are so open

to knowledge. I have never really found it difficult to explain basic laws of nature to children. When you reach them at their level, you can read in their eyes their genuine interest and appreciation (quoted in Bucky, 1992, 99).

Love of the Teaching–Learning Process   To love teaching can also mean to love the act of teaching and the learning that can follow. Many teachers, like the following high school special education teacher, focus on the process rather than on the subject or even the students: "I enjoy what I do. . . . I've been teaching long enough that when the fun stops . . . I'll get out. But it hasn't stopped yet, after thirty-four years. Every day is different. Every day is interesting" (Godar 1990, 244). Persons with this orientation are attracted by the live, spontaneous aspects of teaching and are invigorated by the need to think on their feet and to capitalize on teachable moments when they occur. "[T]hey possess a variety of schemata for seeing what is important, [and they] have a broad repertoire of moves with which to quickly and gracefully act on the situation that they see" (Eisner 1998, 200).

Influence of Teachers

It seems reasonable to assume that the process of becoming a teacher begins early in life. In fact, a Metropolitan Life Survey of 1,002 graduates who began teaching in a public school in 1990–91 reported that 52 percent decided to become teachers before college (Louis Harris and Associates 1990). Although it is not true that some people are born teachers, their early life experiences often encourage them to move in that direction. A teacher's influence during the formative years may have been the catalyst. In most cases, the adults who have the greatest influence on children—beyond their parents or guardians—are their teachers. For example, two University of Chicago researchers reported that 58 percent of the teenagers they interviewed said one or more teachers influenced them to become the kind of people they are (Csikszentmihalyi and McCormack 1986, 414–419).

Evidence also suggests that those who become teachers were often more influenced by their teachers as people than as subject-matter experts. "It is the human dimension that gives all teachers . . . their power as professional influencers" (Zehm and Kottler 1993, 2). Behind the decision to become a teacher is often the inspirational memory of earlier teachers to whom one continues to feel connected in a way that goes beyond the subjects they taught.

Desire to Serve

Many choose to teach because they want to serve others; they want the results of their labor to extend beyond themselves and their families. Some decide to select another major or leave teaching in order to earn more money elsewhere, only to return to teaching, confiding that they found the other major or work lacking in meaning or significance. Being involved in a service profession is their draw to the field.

For many teachers, the decision to serve through teaching was influenced by their experiences as volunteers. Nearly half of the teachers surveyed by the New York City School Volunteer Program, for example, reported that they had served as volunteers in an educational setting before deciding to become a teacher, and 70 percent of these teachers reported that this experience contributed to their decision to become a teacher (Educational Testing Service 1995). As one New York teacher said,

where do you stand?

Should psychological assessments be used to identify students who should not become teachers?

"I always wanted to be a teacher, and all of my volunteer experiences contributed to this career choice" (p. 8).

The desire to serve others and give something back to society is a key attraction of the **Teach for America** program developed in 1989 by Wendy Kopp as an outgrowth of her senior thesis at Princeton University. Teach for America volunteers, recent graduates from some of America's best colleges and universities, are assigned to teach for a minimum of two years in urban and rural school districts with severe shortages of science, math, and language arts teachers. Volunteers complete five weeks of intensive training at the Teach for America Institute in Houston. After two years of teaching, being monitored by state and school authorities, and taking professional development courses, Teach for America teachers can earn regular certification. Upon completion of their two-year assignment, volunteers then return to their chosen careers in other fields, though more than half remain in education as teachers, principals, and educational administrators (Teach for America 1999).

Explore more deeply your reasons for becoming a teacher. The following Professional Reflection feature focuses on several characteristics that may indicate your probable satisfaction with teaching as a career.

 Assessing your reasons for choosing to teach

Practical Benefits of Teaching

Not to be overlooked as attractions to teaching are its practical benefits. Teachers' hours and vacations are widely recognized as benefits. Though the number of hours most teachers devote to their work goes far beyond the number of hours they actually spend at school, their schedules do afford them a measure of flexibility not found in other professions. For example, teachers with school-age children can often be at home when their children are not in school, and nearly all teachers, regardless of their years of experience, receive the same generous vacation time: holiday breaks and a long summer vacation. On the other hand, with the continued growth of year-round schools—2,800 schools in forty-one states were on year-round schedules in 1997–98—many teachers have three or four "mini vacations" throughout the year and welcome the flexibility of being able to take vacations during off-peak seasons (National Association for Year-Round Education 1999).

Salaries and Benefits   Although intangible rewards represent a significant attraction to teaching, teachers are demanding that the public acknowledge the value and professional standing of teaching by supporting higher salaries. As a result, teacher earnings

Table 1.1

have increased steadily since the 1980s—for example, the average salaries (in 1997 constant dollars) of all teachers in 1980–81 was $32,711 (National Center for Education Statistics 1999); for 1998–99, the average was $40,582 (National Education Association 1999). In 1996–97, 40 school districts serving the nation's 100 largest cities had maximum salaries exceeding $50,000; Yonkers had the highest maximum salary ($74,854) followed by Jersey City ($73,175), Rochester ($68,863), Pittsburgh ($62,200), and Anchorage ($60,775) (American Federation of Teachers 1998). Table 1.1 shows a state-by-state ranking of salaries for public school teachers for 1998–99.

Though the general consensus is still that teachers are underpaid, teacher salaries are becoming more competitive with other occupations; in fact, salaries are becoming one of the attractions for the profession. For example, based on the fact that 884 teachers were paid more than $70,000 during 1997–98 in New Jersey, John Challenger, a job placement specialist and CEO, predicted that New Jersey would see its first $100,000 teacher before the next millennium. According to Challenger, occupations typically stereotyped as moderate-to-low paying will experience a "windfall" in the twenty-first century. As private businesses invest in public schools to help develop tomorrow's skilled workforce, teachers will be "able to contract their skills and wares to the highest corporate bidder, yet remain on the payroll at their school" (United Press International 1998).

When we are comparing teacher salaries state-by-state, it is important to remember that higher salaries are frequently linked to a higher **cost of living,** a more experienced teaching force, and a more desirable location. For example, the National Center for Education Statistics found a $23,000 difference between the highest and lowest average state teachers' salaries in 1995; after using a regional cost-of-living index, however, the difference narrowed to about $14,000 (National Center for Education Statistics 1995). Another study by economists at North Carolina State University found that New Hampshire, which ranked twenty-fifth among states in actual salaries for 1995, jumped to ninth in the ranking adjusted for cost of living, while Indiana dropped from sixteenth to thirty-eighth (*Education Week,* January 10, 1996a, 16).

Teachers' salaries are typically determined by years of experience and advanced training as evidenced by graduate credit hours or advanced degrees. Additional duties, such as coaching an athletic team, producing the yearbook and school newspaper, sponsoring clubs, or directing the band, bring extra pay for many teachers. Most districts offer at least limited summer employment for teachers who wish to teach summer school or develop curriculum materials. Additionally, about one-fourth of the nation's two million public school teachers **"moonlight"** (i.e., hold a second job) to increase their earnings.

Teachers also receive various **fringe benefits,** such as medical insurance and retirement plans, which are usually given in addition to base salary. These benefits vary from district to district and are determined during collective bargaining sessions. When considering a school district for your first position, carefully examine the fringe benefits package as well as the salary schedule and opportunities for extra pay.

Job Security and Status   Compared to workers in other sectors of U.S. society who experienced increasing layoffs during the first half of the 1990s, teachers enjoyed a higher level of job security during the same period. Technological advances, corporate mergers and breakups, and a need to cut costs to remain competitive in a global economy led to huge layoffs in the early 1990s. Not surprisingly, 77 percent of teachers surveyed in 1995 rated job security as better in teaching than in other occupations they had considered (Louis Harris and Associates 1995). In addition, the widespread practice of **tenure** (job security granted to teachers after satisfactory performance for a specified period, usually two to five years) contributes to job security for teachers.

As a result of what researchers call a demographic "echo" of the baby boom, America's school-age population in 2002 is expected to be double what it was in 1986. This enrollment increase, plus the fact that about one-third of teachers are 50 years of age or older and nearing retirement, means many job opportunities for teachers in the near future (American Federation of Teachers 1999b). A 1998 *Education Week* article, "New Teachers Are Hot Commodity," reported that schools would need to hire two million new teachers during the next decade and that competition for teachers was leading some school districts to offer bonuses, housing assistance, and higher starting salaries. For example, the Baltimore school system raised starting salaries by $3,000 and offered teachers an incentive package that included on-the-job mentoring, $5,000 toward closing costs on a home, and $1,200 for relocation expenses (Bradley 1998).

Perhaps the most accurate view of the status accorded teachers comes from the teachers themselves. In 1984, 47 percent of the 1,981 teachers responding to *The Metropolitan Life Survey of the American Teacher* agreed with the statement, "As a teacher, I feel respected in today's society." According to the 1995 survey of 1,011 teachers, the number of teachers agreeing with the statement had increased to 53 percent (Louis Harris and Associates 1995, 16). In addition, it should be noted that teachers, as members of the "professional middle class," are accorded status "based on education, rather than on the ownership of capital or property" (Ehrenreich 1989, 12). As a result, "many teachers and school administrators now are thought to be of a more elite social class than the majority of the population in the United States" (Parker and Shapiro 1993, 42).

Job Opportunities for Teachers from Diverse Groups   During the first part of the twenty-first century, there will be exceptional job opportunities for teachers from diverse racial and ethnic backgrounds and for teachers with disabilities. Clearly, students from diverse racial, ethnic, and cultural backgrounds and students with disabilities benefit from having role models with whom they can easily identify. In addition, teachers from diverse groups and teachers with disabilities may have, in some instances, an enhanced understanding of student diversity and student variability that they can share with other teachers.

Data released in 1998 by the National Center for Education Statistics indicated the following percentages for enrollment in public elementary through secondary schools: 70.4 percent white, 16.1 percent African American, 9.9 percent Hispanic, 2.8 percent Asian or Pacific Islander, and 0.9 percent Native American/Native Alaskan. When contrasted with the diverse mosaic of student enrollments, the backgrounds of today's teachers reveal less diversity, a situation that has been labeled a "crisis" (King 1993). A 1997 survey by Recruiting New Teachers, Inc., found that 92 percent of the largest urban districts reported an immediate need for teachers from minority races and ethnic groups, and *Education Week* reported that only 20 percent of undergraduate teacher education students were minority-group members in 1998.

Table 1.2 shows the actual numbers of teachers in public and private schools by race and ethnicity. These data provide the basis for calculating the respective percentages of public and private school teachers from minority groups: African American, 7.4 percent in public schools and 3.1 percent in private schools; Hispanic, 4.2 percent and 3.2 percent; Asian American/Pacific Islander, 1.0 percent and 1.4 percent; and Native American 0.8 percent and 0.4 percent. Furthermore, the percentage of teachers from minority groups is declining, perhaps as a result of increased opportunities in other professional fields for people from diverse backgrounds.

Research indicates that people with disabilities can be effective educators (Anderson, Keller, and Karp 1998; Karp and Keller 1998). "They hold positions in a variety

Table 1.2

of educational professions, such as all types of teaching, counseling, administration, and speech therapy, and have a variety of disabilities, such as learning disabilities, physical disabilities, visual impairments, deafness and hearing loss, medical conditions, and brain injuries" (Keller, Anderson, and Karp 1998, 8).

The percentage of children with disabilities receiving special education in public preK–12 schools is approximately 10 percent (Hardman, Drew, and Egan 1999), and the current critical need for special education teachers is expected to continue well into the twenty-first century. Nevertheless, there is an apparent lack of information on the number of educators with disabilities—a situation that leads Keller, Anderson, and Karp (1998, 8) to suggest that our need to "approach the question of how many educators have disabilities so tentatively and circumspectly is perhaps telling."

What Are the Challenges of Teaching?

Like all professions, teaching has undesirable or difficult aspects. As one high school social studies teacher put it: "Teaching is not terrible. It's great. I love it. It just feels terrible sometimes" (Henry et al. 1995, 119).

Prospective teachers need to consider the problems as well as the pleasures they are likely to encounter. You need to be informed about what to expect if you are to make the most of your professional preparation program. With greater awareness of the realities of teaching, you can more purposefully and meaningfully (1) reflect on and refine your personal philosophy of education, (2) acquire teaching strategies and leadership techniques, and (3) develop a knowledge base of research and theory to guide your actions. In this manner, you can become a true professional—free to savor the joys and satisfactions of teaching and confident of your ability to deal with its frustrations and challenges. Table 1.3 shows that teachers must deal with a variety of problems in the schools.

Table 1.3

Classroom Management and Increasing School Violence

For three of the five years from 1994 to 1998, the public ranked lack of discipline as the most important problem facing the schools in the annual Gallup Polls of the Public's Attitudes toward the Public Schools. For the other two years, the public ranked fighting, violence, and gangs as the most important. Not surprisingly, discipline and increased crime and violence among youth are strong concerns for education majors. Before teachers can teach they must manage their classrooms effectively. Even when parents and the school community are supportive and problems are relatively minor, dealing with discipline can be a disturbing, emotionally draining aspect of teaching. Moreover, the last few years of the 1990s were marked by frequent reports of random, horrific violence in and around schools. Thirty-six percent of parents in 1998 feared for their oldest child's safety while at school; in 1977, only 25 percent of parents had such fears (Rose and Gallup 1998). Several communities previously immune to such tragedies were thrust into the national spotlight as a result of violent incidents: Littleton, Colorado; Paducah, Kentucky; Moses Lake, Washington; Springfield, Oregon; and Jonesboro, Arkansas, to name a few. Though such acts of violence in schools are rare, the possibility of experiencing such events can cause additional job-related stress for teachers.

In addition, many schools have high **teacher–student ratios,** which can make classroom management more difficult. Feeling the press of overcrowding and valiantly resisting the realization that they cannot meet the needs of all their students, teachers may try to work faster and longer to give their students the best possible education. All too often, however, they learn to put off, overlook, or otherwise attend inadequately to many students each day. The problem of high teacher–student ratios becomes even more acute when complicated by the high **student-mobility rates** in many schools. In such situations, teachers have trouble not only in meeting students' needs but also in recognizing students and remembering their names! As you will see, developing a leadership plan, a learning environment, and communication skills will help you face the challenges of classroom management.

Social Problems That Impact Students

Many social problems affect the lives and learning of many children and youth, such as substance abuse, teen pregnancy, homelessness, poverty, family distress, child abuse and neglect, violence and crime, suicide, and health problems such as HIV/AIDS and fetal alcohol syndrome. The social problems that place students at risk of school failure are not always easy to detect. Students' low productivity, learning difficulties, and attitude problems demand teacher attention; yet teachers may be unaware of the source of those difficulties. Even when teachers do recognize the source of a problem, they may lack the resources or expertise to offer help. Teachers feel frustrated by the wasted potential they observe in their students. In addition, when the public calls for schools to curb or correct social problems, that expectation can increase the stress teachers experience.

Need for Family and Community Support

Support from parents and the community can make a significant difference in the teacher's effectiveness in the classroom. Increasingly, there has been a realization that school, parents, and community must work together so that children and youth develop to their maximum potential academically, socially, emotionally, and physically. For example, 53 percent of the student leaders who attended the 1999 United States Senate Youth Program said "parental support" was the biggest factor in their success at high school (William Randolph Hearst Foundation 1999). Parents who talk with their children, help with homework, read to them, monitor their television viewing, and attend meetings of the Parent Teacher Organization (PTO) and school open houses can enhance their children's ability to succeed in school (Henry 1996; Moore 1992; Fuligni and Stevenson 1995). Similarly, communities can support schools by providing essential social, vocational, recreational, and health support services to students and their families. While teachers in suburban and rural schools believe that parental and community support has increased since 1984 (see Figure 1.2), teachers in inner-city schools have seen an alarming decrease in support. Also, among teachers who seriously considered leaving teaching in 1995, "lack of respect/support from parents" was identified by 14 percent as a major factor (Louis Harris and Associates 1995, 60).

Figure 1.2

A low rate of parental participation in their children's schooling is reflected in the 1994 Gallup Poll of the Public's Attitudes toward the Public Schools, which reported that less than 50 percent of the parents of public school students attended a PTA (Parent-Teacher Association) meeting during the academic year, and in the 1995 poll, which reported that only 38 percent of parents attended a school board meeting during the past school year. Nevertheless, the 1997 poll revealed that 69 percent of the public would be willing to work as an unpaid volunteer in local schools—a significant increase compared to 1992, when 59 percent indicated their willingness to volunteer.

Audio Clip 1.2

Long Working Hours and Job Stress

The official working hours for teachers are attractive, but the real working hours are another matter. Not built into contracts are the after-hours or extra assignments found at all levels of teaching—from recess duty and parent conferences to high school club sponsorships and coaching. Also not obvious are the hours of preparation that occur before and after school—frequently late into the night and over the weekend. Over 90 percent of teachers work more than forty hours per week, with the largest percentage working more than 55 hours per week (Louis Harris and Associates 1995).

The need to complete copious amounts of paperwork, including record keeping, may be the most burdensome of the teacher's nonteaching tasks. On average, teachers spend ten hours per week on school-related responsibilities not directly related to teaching (Louis Harris and Associates 1995, 68). Other nonteaching tasks include supervising student behavior on the playground, at extracurricular events, and in the halls, study halls, and lunchrooms; attending faculty meetings, parent conferences, and open houses; and taking tickets or selling at concessions for athletic events. Individually, such assignments and responsibilities may be enjoyable; too many of them at once, however, become a burden and consume the teacher's valuable time.

In addition to long working hours, factors such as students' lack of interest, conflicts with administrators, public criticism, overcrowded classrooms, lack of resources, and isolation from other adults cause some teachers to experience high levels of stress. Unchecked, acute levels of stress can lead to job dissatisfaction, emotional and physical exhaustion, and an inability to cope effectively—all classic symptoms of teacher **burnout**. To cope with stress and avoid burnout, teachers report that activities in seven areas are beneficial: social support, physical fitness, intellectual stimulation, entertainment, personal hobbies, self-management, and supportive attitudes (Gmelch and Parkay 1995, 46–65).

Gaining Professional Empowerment

In an interview with journalist Bill Moyers, noted Harvard educator Sara Lawrence Lightfoot eloquently describes why teachers desire **professional empowerment:**

> [Teachers are] saying, "I haven't had the opportunity to participate fully in this enterprise." Some teachers are speaking about the politics of teachers' voice. They're saying, "We want more control over our lives in this school." Some of them are making an even more subtle point—they're talking about voice as knowledge. "We know things about this enterprise that researchers and policy makers can never know. We have engaged in this intimate experience, and we have things to tell you if you'd only learn how to ask, and if you'd only learn how to listen" (Moyers 1989, 161).

Although some teachers may experience frustration in their efforts to gain professional empowerment, efforts to empower teachers and to "professionalize" teaching are leading to unprecedented opportunities for today's teachers to extend their leadership roles beyond the classroom. In fact, "teachers in the U.S. today are developing leadership skills to a degree not needed in the past . . . the continuing professional

Weblink 1.1

development of teaching as a profession requires that teachers exercise greater leadership at the school level and beyond" (Parkay et al. 1999, 20–21).

What Is Teaching Really Like?

In this section we examine six basic **realities of teaching** that illustrate why teaching is so demanding and why it can be so exciting, rewarding, and uplifting. And when we say that teaching is demanding, we mean more than the fact that Mr. Smith's third-period plane geometry students just can't seem to learn how to compute the area of a triangle; or that Ms. Ellis's sixth-grade composition class can't remember whether to use *there* or *their;* or even that 35 percent of teachers in 1995 reported they were "under great stress" almost every day or several days a week (Louis Harris and Associates 1995, 55). Although there are many frustrating, stressful events with which teachers must cope, the difficulty of teaching goes much further, or deeper, than these examples suggest.

Reality 1: The Unpredictability of Outcomes

The outcomes of teaching, even in the best of circumstances, are neither predictable nor consistent. Any teacher, beginner or veteran, can give countless examples of how the outcomes of teaching are often unpredictable and inconsistent. Life in most classrooms usually proceeds on a fairly even keel—with teachers able to predict, fairly accurately, how their students will respond to lessons. Adherence to the best laid lesson plans, however, may be accompanied by students' blank stares, yawns of boredom, hostile acting out, or expressions of befuddlement. On the other hand, lack of preparation on the teacher's part does not necessarily rule out the possibility of a thoroughly exciting class discussion, a real breakthrough in understanding for an individual student or the entire class, or simply a good, fast-paced review of previously learned material. In short, teachers are often surprised at students' reactions to classroom activities.

Students' Responses Contrary to the popular notion that teaching consists entirely of specific competencies or observable behaviors that have predetermined effects on students, the reactions of students to any given activity cannot be guaranteed. Furthermore, teachers, unlike other professionals, cannot control all the results of their efforts.

One example of the unpredictability of teaching is given in a teacher intern's description of setting up an independent reading program in his middle-school classroom. Here we see how careful room arrangement and organization of materials do not ensure desired outcomes and how a teacher learned to adjust to one reality of teaching.

> I wanted everything looking perfect. For two more hours, I placed this here and stuffed that in there. . . . There were stacks of brand-new books sitting on three odd shelves and a metal display rack. . . . I coded the books and arranged them neatly on the shelves. I displayed their glossy covers as if the room was a B. Dalton store.

A few weeks after setting up the reading program, however, this teacher observes that

> The orderly environment I thought I had conceived was fraught with complications. For example, the back rows of the classroom were inaccessible regions from which paper and pencil pieces were hurled at vulnerable victims, and there were zones where, apparently, no teacher's voice could be heard. . . . The books . . . remained in chaos. Novels turned up behind shelves, on the sidewalks outside, and in the trash can. And still, at least once a week, I dutifully arranged them until I was satisfied. But something was happening. It was taking less and less for me to be satisfied. . . . [I] loosened up (Henry et al. 1995, 73–76).

Contrary to the preceding example, unpredictability in the classroom is not always bad. Another teacher intern describes her unexpected success at setting up a writing workshop at an urban middle school with a large population of at-risk students. One day she began by telling her students that

> "We're going to be starting something new these six weeks. . . . We will be transforming this classroom into a writing workshop." What was I trying to do here? They're not writers. . . . Raymond stared down at *Where's Waldo*. Michael was engrossed in an elaborate pencil drum solo. Edwina powdered her nose and under her eyes.

> "Listen to me, you guys," I said, trying not to lose it before we even started. "We're starting something completely different, something you never get a chance to do in your other classes."

> A few heads turned to face me. Veronica slugged Edwina, and Edwina slid her compact into her back pocket.

In what ways must this classroom teacher face the reality of unpredictable outcomes? What are five other basic realities that all teachers face in their work?

"What, Miss... chew gum?"

In spite of her initial reservations, this teacher made the following observations the next day—the first day of the writing workshop.

Today, it's all clicking.

"Aw, man, I told you I don't understand that part. Why does that guy in your story. . . Chris. . . say that it's too early to rob the store?" David pleads. "It doesn't make sense."

Raymond tips his desk forward and smiles. "It's too early because they want to wait until the store's almost closed."

"Well, then, you've got to say that. Right, Miss?"

I lean against the door frame and try not to laugh. I listen to the conversations around me. Yes, they're loud and they're talking and they're laughing. But they're learning. My students are involved in their writing, I say to myself and shake my head (Henry et al. 1995, 54–55).

Philip Jackson describes the unpredictability of teaching in his well-known book *Life in Classrooms:* "[As] typically conducted, teaching is an opportunistic process. . . . Neither teacher nor students can predict with any certainty exactly what will happen next. Plans are forever going awry and unexpected opportunities for the attainment of educational goals are constantly emerging" (Jackson 1990, 166).

Results in the Future   Teachers strive to effect changes in their students for the future as well as for the here and now. In *Life in Classrooms,* Jackson labels this the preparatory aspect of teaching. In addition to having students perform better on next Monday's unit exam or on a criterion-referenced test mandated by the state, teachers expect students to apply their newly acquired skills and knowledge at some indeterminate, usually distant, point in the future.

Just as months or years may pass before the results of teaching become clear, teachers may wait a long time before receiving positive feedback from students. The following comment by a kindergarten teacher illustrates the delayed satisfaction that can characterize teaching:

About a month ago I had a 22-year-old boy knock on the door. He said, "Miss R?" I said, "Yes." He is now in England, an architect; he's married and has a little girl. I thought, "This is not happening to me. I had you in kindergarten." If you teach high school and a kid comes back and he's married in two or three years, that's expected, but 16 years or 18 years—first year in kindergarten. It's rewarding. . . be it one year, or ten years down the road. . . . There are daily satisfactions—"She got it!"—that's a reward in itself, but I think it's a little bit down the road that you get your satisfaction (Cohn and Kottkamp 1993, 42–43).

Reality 2: The Difficulty of Assessing Students' Learning

It is difficult to assess what students learn as a result of being taught. The ultimate purpose of teaching is to lead the student to a greater understanding of the things and ideas of this world. But, as even the most casual appraisal of human nature will confirm, it is very difficult, perhaps impossible, to determine precisely what another human being does or does not understand. Although the aims or intentions of teaching may be specified with exacting detail, one of the realities of teaching, as the following junior high school teacher points out, is that some of what students learn may be indeterminate and beyond direct measurement:

> There is no clear end result. . . . That frustrates me. I want so badly for my joy [of teaching] to be neatly tied up so that I can look at it admiringly. . . . I want so badly to *see* my successes—I don't know, give me certificates or badges or jelly beans. Then I can stack them up, count them, and rate myself as a teacher (Henry et al. 1995, 68–69).

In spite of state-by-state efforts to institute standardized tests of basic skills and thereby hold teachers accountable, the conventional wisdom among teachers is that they are often uncertain about just what their students learn. We have miles of computer printouts with test data, but very little knowledge of what lies behind a child's written response, little understanding of how the child experiences the curriculum. As one educational researcher concludes: "The inaccessibility of data is similar both in science and in learning. We cannot directly 'see' subatomic particles, nor can we 'see' the inner-workings of the mind and emotions of the child. Both are inferential: both are subject to human interpretation" (Costa 1984, 202).

On the one hand, then, teachers must recognize their limited ability to determine what students actually learn; on the other, they must continuously work to become aware of the latest approaches to assessing students' learning. Figure 1.3 presents a set of guiding principles for teachers to follow in developing a student-centered approach to classroom assessment.

Figure 1.3

Reality 3: The Need for Teacher–Student Partnership

The teacher's ability to influence student behavior is actually quite limited. The very fact that we refer to the teaching–learning process indicates the extent to which classroom events are "jointly produced" (Doyle 1986, 395) and depend upon a teacher–student partnership. According to Arthur Combs (1979, 234–35) in a book aptly titled *Myths in Education: Beliefs That Hinder Progress and Their Alternatives*:

> A teacher's influence on all but the simplest, most primitive forms of student behavior, even in that teacher's own classroom, cannot be clearly established. The older children get, the less teachers can influence even those few, primitive forms of behavior. The attempt to hold teachers responsible for what students do is, for all practical purposes, well nigh impossible.

At best, a teacher tries to influence students so that they make internal decisions to behave in the desired manner—whether it be reading the first chapter of *The Pearl* by Friday or solving ten addition problems during a mathematics lesson. Teaching is a uniquely demanding profession, therefore, because the work of teachers is evaluated not in terms of what teachers do but in terms of their ability "to help the students become more effective as learners," to "become active seekers after new development" (Joyce and Weil 2000, 408, 399). This reality underscores the need for a partnership between teacher and learners, including learners who are culturally diverse.

Video 1.1

Reality 4: The Impact of Teachers' Attitudes

With the role of teacher also comes the power to influence others by example. Educational psychologist Anita E. Woolfolk (1998, 223) states that "teachers serve as models for a vast range of behaviors, from pronouncing vocabulary words to reacting to the seizure of an epileptic student, to being enthusiastic about learning." Clearly, students learn much by imitation, and teachers are models for students. In the primary grades, teachers are idolized by their young students. At the high school level, teachers have the potential to inspire students' emulation and establish the classroom tone by modeling expected attitudes and behaviors.

In *The Tact of Teaching: The Meaning of Pedagogical Thoughtfulness,* Max van Manen (1991, 167) states the importance of teachers' attitudes toward students:

> An educator needs to believe in children. Specifically he or she needs to believe in the possibilities and goodness of the particular children for whom he or she has responsibility. My belief in a child strengthens that child—provided of course that the child experiences my trust as something real and as something positive.

A high school social studies teacher expresses the same idea in this manner: "[The] relationship between teachers and students is becoming one of the most important aspects of teaching. [In] a world of broken homes and violence, the encouragement of their teachers may be the only thing students can hold onto that makes them feel good about themselves" (Henry et al. 1995, 127).

Teachers also model attitudes toward the subjects they teach and show students through their example that learning is an ongoing, life-enriching process that does not end with diplomas and graduations. Their example confirms the timeless message of Sir Rabindranath Tagore that is inscribed above the doorway of a public building in India: "A teacher can never truly teach unless he is still learning himself. A lamp can never light another lamp unless it continues to burn its own flame."

Reality 5: The Drama and Immediacy of Teaching

Audio Clip 1.3

Interactive teaching is characterized by events that are rapid-changing, multidimensional, and irregular. We have already discussed how the outcomes of teaching are unpredictable and inconsistent. Yet the challenges of teaching go beyond this. The face-to-face interactions teachers have with students—what Jackson (1990, 152) has termed **interactive teaching**—are themselves rapid-changing, multidimensional, and irregular. "Day in and day out, teachers spend much of their lives 'on stage' before audiences that are not always receptive . . . teachers must orchestrate a daunting array of interpersonal interactions and build a cohesive, positive climate for learning" (Gmelch and Parkay 1995, 47).

When teachers are in the **preactive teaching** stages of their work—preparing to teach or reflecting on previous teaching—they can afford to be consistently deliberate and rational. Planning for lessons, grading papers, reflecting on the misbehavior of a student—such activities are usually done alone and lack the immediacy and sense of urgency that characterize interactive teaching. While actually working with students, however, you must be able to think on your feet and respond appropriately to complex, ever-changing situations. You must be flexible and ready to deal with the unexpected. During a discussion, for example, you must operate on at least two levels. On one level, you respond appropriately to students' comments, monitor other students for signs of confusion or comprehension, formulate the next comment or question, and be alert for signs of misbehavior. On another level, you ensure that participation is evenly distributed among students, evaluate the content and quality of students' contributions, keep the discussion focused and moving ahead, and emphasize major content areas.

How do teacher's attitudes affect students' learning? In what ways are teachers significant role models for students?

weblink

Figure 1.4

During interactive teaching, the awareness that you are responsible for the forward movement of the group never lets up. Teachers are the only professionals who practice their craft almost exclusively under the direct, continuous gaze of up to thirty or forty clients. Jackson (1990, 119) sums up the experience: "The *immediacy* of classroom events is something that anyone who has ever been in charge of a roomful of students can never forget."

Reality 6: The Uniqueness of the Teaching Experience

Teaching involves a unique mode of being between teacher and student—a mode of being that can be experienced but not fully defined or described. On your journey to become a teacher, you will gradually develop your capacity to listen to students and to convey an authentic sense of concern for their learning. Unfortunately, there is no precise, easy-to-follow formula for demonstrating this to students. You will have to take into account your personality and special gifts to discover your own best way for showing this concern.

One reason it is difficult to describe teaching is that an important domain of teaching, **teachers' thought processes,** including professional reflection, cannot be observed directly. Figure 1.4 shows how the unobservable domain of the teacher's "interior reflective thinking" interacts with and is influenced by the observable domain of the teacher's "exterior reflective action." Teachers' thought processes include their theories and beliefs about students and how they learn, their plans for teaching, and the decisions they make while teaching. Thought processes and actions can be constrained by the physical setting of the classroom or external factors such as the curriculum, the principal, or the community. On the other hand, teachers' thought processes and actions may be influenced by unique opportunities, such as the chance to engage in curriculum reform or school governance. The model also illustrates a further complexity of teaching—namely, that the relationships between teacher behavior, student behavior, and student achievement are reciprocal. What teachers do is influenced not only by their thought processes before, during, and after teaching but also by student behavior and student achievement. This complexity contributes to the uniqueness of the teaching experience.

What Does Society Expect of Teachers?

The prevailing view within our society is that teachers are public servants accountable to the people. As a result, society has high expectations of teachers—some would say too high. Entrusted with our nation's most precious resource, its children and youth, today's teachers are expected to have advanced knowledge and skills and high academic and ethical standards. Although promoting students' academic progress has always been their primary responsibility, teachers are also expected to further students' social, emotional, and moral development and to safeguard students' health and well-being.

Increasingly, the public calls on teachers and schools to address social problems and risk factors that affect student success.

The Public Trust

Teaching is subject to a high degree of public scrutiny and control. The level of trust that the public extends to teachers as professionals varies greatly. The public appears to have great confidence in the work that teachers do. Because of its faith in the teaching profession, the public invests teachers with considerable power over its children. For the most part, parents willingly allow their children to be influenced by teachers and expect their children to obey and respect teachers. However, the public trust increases and decreases in response to social and political changes that lead to waves of educational reform.

In the 1970s, for example, teachers were portrayed as incompetent, unprofessional, unintelligent, and generally unable to live up to the public's expectations. Calls for higher standards and minimum competency testing were an expression of diminished public trust. Further professionalization of teaching has been the response. During the 1980s, the image of teachers was battered by ominous sounding commission reports, a negative press, and public outcries for better schools. National reports, such as *A Nation at Risk,* declared that U.S. education was shockingly inadequate, if not a failure.

In the 1990s, however, deliberate efforts were made to restore dignity to the profession of teaching. To highlight the important work of teachers, public and commercial television stations aired programs with titles such as "Learning in America: Schools That Work," "America's Toughest Assignment: Solving the Education Crisis," "The Truth about Teachers," "Why Do These Kids Love School?", "Liberating America's Schools," and "America's Education Revolution: A Report from the Front." The Learning Channel began to air *Teacher TV,* a news-style program that explores education trends and issues and features teachers, schools, and communities around the country. Many national corporations initiated award programs to recognize excellence among teachers. Disney Studios, for example, initiated Disney's American Teacher Awards in 1991. As a tribute to countless outstanding teachers, a major media campaign to recruit new teachers in the early 1990s was formed around the slogan, "Be a Teacher. Be a Hero." Table 1.4 shows how people rated their public schools in selected years between 1983, just after the release of *A Nation at Risk,* and 1999.

Table 1.4

Teacher Competency and Effectiveness

Society believes that competent, effective teachers are important keys to a strong system of education. Accordingly, teachers are expected to be proficient in the use of instructional strategies, curriculum materials, advanced educational technologies, and classroom management techniques. They are also expected to have a thorough understanding of the developmental levels of their students and a solid grasp of the content they teach. To maintain and extend this high level of skill, teachers are expected to be informed of exemplary practices and to demonstrate a desire for professional development.

Teacher competency and effectiveness includes the responsibility to help all learners succeed. Though today's students come from a diverse array of backgrounds, society expects teachers to hold strong beliefs about the potential for all children. Regardless of their students' ethnicity, language, gender, socioeconomic status, family backgrounds and living conditions, abilities, or disabilities, teachers have a responsibility to ensure that all students develop to their fullest potential. To accomplish this, teachers are expected to have a repertoire of instructional strategies and resources to create meaningful learning experiences that promote students' growth and development.

Teacher Accountability

Teachers must "be mindful of the social ethic—their public duties and obligations—embodied in the practice of teaching . . ." (Hansen 1995, 143). Society agrees that teachers are primarily responsible for promoting students' learning, though it is not always in agreement about what students should learn. In any case, society expects teachers to understand how factors such as student backgrounds, attitudes, and learning styles can affect achievement; and it expects that teachers will create safe and effective learning environments. Society also believes that teachers and schools should be accountable for equalizing educational opportunity and maintaining high professional standards.

　　Teacher accountability also means meeting high standards of conduct. Teachers are no longer required to sign statements such as the following, taken from a 1927 contract: "I promise to sleep at least eight hours a night, to eat carefully, and to take every precaution to keep in the best of health and spirits, in order that I may be better able to render efficient service to my pupils" (Waller 1932, 43). Nevertheless, society does expect teachers to hold high standards of professional ethics and personal morality and to model behaviors that match those standards.

How Do Good Teachers View Their Work?

Teachers' overall satisfaction with their careers has increased steadily since 1981 (National Education Association 1997). Figure 1.5 shows that 62.6 percent of all teachers say they "certainly" or "probably would" become a teacher again—a proportion that compares favorably to the level of satisfaction reported by members of other professions.

　　Good teachers derive greatest satisfaction when they are effective in promoting students' learning—when they "make a difference" in students' lives. When you recall your most effective teachers, you probably think of particular individuals, not idealizations of the teacher's many roles. What good teachers do can be described in terms of five **modes of teaching,** which are more general and significant than a discussion of roles. You may recognize these modes in your observations of teachers and in the writings of gifted teachers when they reflect on their work. You may even acknowledge these modes of teaching as deeper reasons for becoming a teacher.

Figure 1.5

A Way of Being

In becoming a teacher, you take on the role and let it become a part of you. Increasingly, the learning of facts can be achieved easily with good books, good TV, CD-ROMs, and access to the Internet. What cannot be done in these ways is teaching styles of life, teaching what it means to be, to grow, to become actualized, to become complete. The only way a teacher can teach these qualities is to possess them. "They become living examples for their students, showing that what they say is important enough for them to apply to their own lives. They are attractive models who advertise, by their very being, that learning does produce wondrous results" (Zehm and Kottler 1993, 16).

A Creative Endeavor

Teaching is a creative endeavor in which teachers are continually shaping and reshaping lessons, events, and the experiences of their students. In *The Call to Teach*, David Hansen (1995, 13) describes the creative dimensions of teaching this way: "In metaphorical terms, teaching is. . . more than carrying brick, mortar, and shovel. Rather, it implies being the architect of one's classroom world."

With careful attention to the details of classroom life, effective teachers artistically develop educative relationships with their students; they "read" the myriad events that emerge while teaching and respond appropriately. One high school teacher, identified as highly successful by her principal, reported: "I have to grab the kids that don't want to do math at all and somehow make them want to do this work. I'm not sure how I do it, but kids just want to do well in my class. For some mysterious reason, and I don't care why, they really want to do well."

A Live Performance

Teaching is a live performance with each class period, each day, containing the unpredictable. Further, teachers are engaged in live dialogues with their classes and individual students. The experience of teaching is thus an intense, attention-demanding endeavor—an interactive one that provides minute-to-minute challenges.

Some teachers embrace the live performance aspect of teaching more than others, believing that within it lies true learning. They recognize that teaching ". . . is full of surprises; classroom lessons that lead to unexpected questions and insights; lessons that fail despite elaborate planning; spur-of-the-moment activities that work beautifully and that may change the direction of a course; students who grow and learn; students who seem to regress or grow distant" (Hansen 1995, 12).

A Form of Empowerment

Power is the dimension of teaching most immediately evident to the new teacher. It is recognized in the first-grader's awed "Teacher, is this good?" on through the

What are the modes of teaching that define the essence of good teaching and distinguish gifted teachers? Which mode of teaching might this photo represent?

keepers of the
dream

weblink

Caroline Bitterwolf
National Board Certified Teacher

"I was amazed at what I found."

high school senior's "How much will this paper count?" Customarily, teachers get respect, at least initially; the deference derives from their power to enhance or diminish their students' academic status and welfare.

Even in the most democratic classrooms, teachers have more influence than students because they are responsible for what happens when students are with them, establishing the goals, selecting the methods, setting the pace, evaluating the progress, and deciding whether students should pass or fail. How you use this power is critical. As you know, students at any level can be humiliated by teachers who misuse their power or convey negative expectations to students. A student teacher in a fifth-grade class comments on the impact negative expectations can have on students:

> They [students] can sense how a teacher feels, especially how she feels about them personally. Students often find themselves locked into a role that they have played for so long they don't know how to get out of it. Students deserve the right to have an education. They should not have to worry about what negative comments their teachers are saying about them (Rand and Shelton-Colangelo 1999, 107).

An Opportunity to Serve

To become a teacher is to serve others professionally—students, the school, the community, and the country, depending on how broad the perspective is. Most who come to teaching do so for altruistic reasons. The altruistic dimension of teaching is at the heart of the motivation to teach. The paycheck, the public regard, and the vacations have little holding power compared to the opportunity to serve. As the authors of *On Being a Teacher* observe:

> Very few people go into education in the first place to become rich or famous. On some level, every teacher gets a special thrill out of helping others. . . . [The] teachers who flourish, those who are loved by their students and revered by their colleagues, are those who feel tremendous dedication and concern for others— not just because they are paid to do so, but because it is their nature and their ethical responsibility (Zehm and Kottler 1993, 8–9).

Whatever form the altruistic rewards of teaching take, they ennoble the profession and remind teachers of the human significance of their work.

As Keepers of the Dream

Many of our country's most talented youth and dedicated veterans in the teaching field retain the desire to teach. In part, the desire endures because teachers have been positively influenced by one or more teachers of their own, who enriched, redirected, or significantly changed their lives. The desire also endures because teachers recognize the many joys and rewards the profession offers.

Reflecting on dedicated teachers and their contributions to our lives, we are guided to teaching for the benefit it brings to others. In doing so, we become keepers of a part of the American dream—the belief that education can improve the quality of life. That dream, more powerful than all our images of teachers, is alive throughout the country in classrooms where outstanding teachers work. This textbook acknowledges these teachers in selected chapters in a special feature called *Keepers of the Dream*.

SUMMARY

Why Do You Want to Teach? (p. 6)

What Are the Challenges of Teaching? (p. 12)

What Is Teaching Really Like? (p. 15)

What Does Society Expect of Teachers? (p. 20)

How Do Good Teachers View Their Work? (p. 22)

KEY TERMS AND CONCEPTS

Go to the website for interactive flashcards.

APPLICATIONS AND INTERACTIVITIES

Go to the website for interactive assignments in the following areas:

Teacher's Journal

Teacher's Database

Observations and Interviews

Professional Portfolio

Weblink 1.2

Name _____ **Date** _____

For each question, write in the blank the answer you believe is correct.

1.1 Many choose to teach because they want to serve _____.

1.2 In considering a career in teaching, its _____ benefits should not be overlooked.

1.3 Teachers' earnings have _____ steadily since the 1980s.

1.4 In 1995, 77 percent of teachers surveyed rated job _____ as better in teaching than in other occupations.

1.5 Research (Anderson, Keller, and Karp 1998) indicates that people with disabilities can be _____ educators.

1.6 For three of the five years from 1994 to 1998, the public ranked lack of _____ as the most important problem facing the schools in the annual Gallup Poll of the Public's Attitudes toward the Public Schools.

1.7 Over _____ percent of teachers work more than forty hours per week.

1.8 It is difficult to assess what students _____ as a result of being taught.

1.9 _____ teaching is characterized by events that are rapid-changing, multidimensional, and irregular.

1.10 Society expects teachers to understand how factors such as student backgrounds, attitudes, and learning styles can affect _____.

Answers are available on the FlexChoice website at www.ablongman.com/parkayflex.

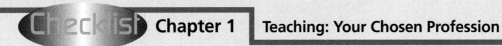

Name _____

Keep this checklist at your computer as a reminder to read and complete the chapter features and activities located on the FlexChoice website at www.ablongman.com/parkayflex.

**Date
Completed**

_____ ❑ **PreTest with Answers**

_____ ❑ **Audio Clip 1.1:** Thinking Over the Opening Vignette

_____ ❑ **Figure 1.1:** Why Do Teachers Teach?

_____ ❑ **Where Do You Stand?:** Should psychological assessments be used to identify students who should not become teachers?

_____ ❑ **Professional Reflection:** Assessing your reasons for choosing to teach

_____ ❑ **Table 1.1:** Average salaries of public school teachers, 1998–99

_____ ❑ **Table 1.2:** Teachers in public and private elementary and secondary schools, by gender and race/ethnicity, 1993–94

_____ ❑ **Table 1.3:** Teacher's perceptions of the frequency of discipline problems

_____ ❑ **Figure 1.2:** Percentage of teachers who believe parental support is "excellent" or "good," 1984, 1995, and 1998

_____ ❑ **Audio Clip 1.2:** Sources of Stress

_____ ❑ **Technology Highlights:** Will I be prepared to teach in a digital age?

_____ ❑ **Weblink 1.1:** National Council for Accreditation of Teacher Education

_____ ❑ **Figure 1.3:** The principles of sound assessment: a critical blend

_____ ❑ **Video 1.1:** Teacher's Attitudes

_____ ❑ **Audio Clip 1.3:** The Immediacy of Teaching

_____ ❑ **Figure 1.4:** A model of reflective action in teaching

_____ ❑ **Table 1.4:** Ratings given the local public schools (in percent)

_____ ❑ **Figure 1.5:** Percentage of teachers who would choose teaching again

_____ ❑ **Keepers of the Dream:** Caroline Bitterwolf

_____ ❑ **Summary**

_____ ❑ **Key Terms and Concepts**

_____ ❑ **Applications and Interactivities:** Teacher's Journal

_____ ❑ **Applications and Interactivities:** Teacher's Database

_____ ❑ **Weblink 1.2:** Allyn &Bacon website for *Becoming a Teacher*, www.ablongman.com/parkay5e

_____ ❑ **Applications and Interactivities:** Observations and Interviews

_____ ❑ **Applications and Interactivities:** Professional Portfolio

_____ ❑ **PostTest with Answers**

2

Learning to Teach

Teaching ultimately requires judgment, improvisation, and conversation about means and ends. Human qualities, expert knowledge and skill, and professional commitment together compose excellence in this craft.

—National Board for Professional Teaching Standards

AUDIO)))
Audio Clip 2.1

focus questions

1. What essential knowledge do you need to teach?

2. What are five ways of viewing the teacher knowledge base?

3. How do reforms in teacher education affect you?

4. What can you learn from observing in classrooms?

5. How can you gain practical experience for becoming a teacher?

6. How can you develop your teaching portfolio?

7. How can you benefit from mentoring relationships?

8. What opportunities for continuing professional development will you have?

The room was filled with the chatter of writing workshop. Nat puzzled over two crayons in his hand, one of them blue: "Mrs. Hankins, ain't you had you a blue bicycle when you was a little-girl-teacher?" Nat had a way of naming me for what I was: always a teacher—or was it always a little girl? I answered Nat's present question, remembering my past blue bicycle and a childhood story about it that I had shared with the children recently.

Perhaps it was one of those "tell-me-about-when-you-were-little" moments that brought writing memoirs to the forefront of my teaching journal. Perhaps it was the need to make some sense of the cacophonous days with my three special students, Nat, Loretta, and Rodney, who had all been damaged in utero by crack cocaine or alcohol. The original impetus for these writings is lost to me now, but, as Lucy Calkins (1991, 169) says, writing memoirs "has everything to do with rendering the ordinariness of our lives so that it becomes significant." The past seemed to wrap itself around my present-day questions, and as the number of memoirs grew, my journal became a place for uncovering the significant. . . .

I wrote up a study of Nat, Loretta, and Rodney's journey through kindergarten and presented parts of the study at a conference. After the presentation, I wrote the following reflection in my journal:

So, I keep this journal. It was easier when no one else knew or cared that I wrote. It's a teaching journal. It's a personal journal. It's a research journal. It's both a personal and teaching journal because John Dewey first and Lucy Calkins later taught me to reflect on my day and my life in the same breath. It's both a teaching and research journal because I no longer believe that teaching can be separated from research. (Perhaps it CAN be but it shouldn't be.) The question is . . . I guess . . . Can it be both personal and research journal? That's what people really want me to defend. But how can I tell people what my heart and head do together in my classroom? (journal entry, April)

I wrote at nap time, while waiting for faculty meetings to begin, during the last ten minutes before turning out the light each night, and on the backs of church bulletins or napkins in restaurants. I had never heard of field notes at the time. I read recently a definition of ethnographic field notes as "the systematic ways of writing what one observes and learns while participating in the daily rounds of the lives of others" (Emerson, Fretz, and Shaw 1995, 18). As the year progressed, I fell into a system of sorts as I recorded the "lives of others." My journal served, then, as the field notes of a teacher. Mine were records of what Emerson et al. (1995) call "headnotes"—mental notes—"hard notes"—direct observations—and "heartnotes"—my feelings and reflections. . . .

When I began seriously listening to my life, my teaching life, I also began to listen to my students' lives at a different level. . . . I became more tolerant of those who were different from me. When I began to stop and examine the flashes of memory that jolted me, I became a more patient teacher. I more often saw the students and their parents as people; people walking in and out of pain, in and out of joy, in and out of socially constructed prisons (Hankins 1998, 81, 83, 93).*

*Source: Excerpts from Karen Hale Hankins, "Cacophony to Symphony: Memoirs in Teacher Research," Harvard Educational Review, 68:1 (Spring 1998), pp. 80–95. Copyright © 1998 by the President and Fellows of Harvard College. All rights reserved.

Name _____ Date _____

For each question, circle the letter of the answer you believe is correct. Then read the chapter to learn more about these topics.

2.1 All of the following are goals adopted by The Holmes Partnership *except*
A. Simultaneous renewal of public K–12 schools and pre- and in-service education.
B. Scholarly inquiry.
C. Maintenance of policy to promote stability.
D. Equity, diversity, and cultural competence.

2.2 What does the National Board for Professional Teaching Standards (1994) mean when they use the phrase "pedagogical content knowledge"?
A. The possession of broad general knowledge.
B. Advanced understanding of the nature of learners and learning.
C. A thorough founding in the knowledge of the academic discipline one plans to teach.
D. A joint product of wisdom about teaching, learning, students, and content.

2.3 In understanding the characteristics of students, all of the following are considered important *except*
A. Aptitudes.
B. Learning styles.
C. Religious affiliation.
D. Talents.

2.4 Teachers' expectations of students directly affect
A. Student achievement.
B. Developmental patterns.
C. Diagnostic labeling of students.
D. Parental attitudes.

2.5 Teacher education programs that focus on demonstrations of learning are considered
A. Standardized.
B. Outcome-based.
C. Traditional.
D. Assessment-based.

2.6 The procedure a school district would likely use to determine the knowledge and skills needed for a job would be
A. Personal reflection.
B. Porfolio development.
C. A job analysis.
D. Self-assessment.

2.7 Ms. Wong has been identified as a "star" urban teacher. According to the research, Ms. Wong most likely has all of the following characteristics *except* a
A. Belief that education will provide students with a chance to "make it" in life.
B. Teaching style that is modeled on coaching.
C. View of success based on effort rather than ability.
D. Quiet, soft-spoken style of teaching.

2.8 All of the following are standards developed by the National Board for Professional Teaching Standards *except*
A. Teachers must obtain a master's degree to be certified as a "master" teacher.
B. Teachers should think systematically about their practice and learn from experience.
C. Teachers are members of learning communities.
D. Teachers are committed to students and their learning.

2.9 Schools that are linked to colleges or universities and provide opportunities for the development of new teaching methods and collaboration on research projects are called
A. Holmes Schools.
B. Learning communities.
C. Laboratory schools.
D. Professional development schools.

2.10 The organization that was created to issue certificates to teachers who meet specified high standards is
A. The Educational Reform Movement Association.
B. The National Board for Professional Teaching Standards.
C. The Interstate New Teacher Assessment and Support Consortium.
D. The National Education Association.

Answers are available on the FlexChoice website at www.ablongman.com/parkayflex.

In the preceding excerpt from her article in the *Harvard Educational Review,* Karen Hale Hankins, a first-grade teacher at Whit Davis Elementary School in Athens, Georgia, describes how reflective journal writing enabled her to see significant connections between her personal history and her present experiences in the classroom. By purposely examining her "mental notes," "direct observations," and "feelings and reflections," Hankins learned how to "reach and teach" the students with whom she once felt she had little in common. Her ability to reflect upon her experiences in the classroom and her appreciation for the interconnectedness of teaching and research are the hallmarks of a professional teacher. Furthermore, her reflections are reminders that teaching is a complex act—one that requires thoughtfulness, insight into the motivations of others, and good judgment.

What Essential Knowledge Do You Need to Teach?

Students preparing to become teachers must have three kinds of knowledge before they can manage effectively the complexities of teaching: knowledge of self and students, knowledge of subject, and knowledge of educational theory and research. It is to this essential knowledge that we now turn.

Self-Knowledge

Effective teachers are aware of themselves and sensitive to the needs of their students. Although it is evident that teachers should understand their students as fully and deeply as possible, it is less evident that this understanding depends on their level of self-knowledge. If teachers are knowledgeable about their needs (and, most important, able to take care of those needs), they are better able to help their students. As Arthur Jersild (1955, 3), one of the first educators to focus attention on the connection between the teacher's personal insight and professional effectiveness, pointed out, a teacher's self-understanding and self-acceptance are prerequisites for helping students to know and accept themselves.

Teachers' self-evaluations often are influenced by emotions that teachers may experience when they teach, such as anxiety or loneliness. Promoting anxiety are the realities of teaching outlined in Chapter 1. For example, three conditions that cloud teachers' efforts are (1) the interminable nature of teaching (i.e., their work is never completed), (2) the intangible and often unpredictable characteristics of teaching results, and (3) the inability to attribute learning results to specific teachers' instruction. Unlike architects, lawyers, and doctors, teachers can never stand back and admire their work. If a student does well, that success rightfully belongs to the student.

Teachers thus need to develop the ability to tolerate ambiguities and to reduce their anxieties about being observably effective. Without this ability, a teacher "can feel that one is 'wrong,' 'missing something,' a 'bad fit' with students and with teaching itself. One can feel that one's circumstances are unfair, that one is giving but not receiving. One can feel helpless, not knowing what to do, not even knowing how to get the frustration out of mind let alone how to resolve it in practice" (Hansen 1995, 60).

Teachers can also experience loneliness or psychological isolation, since most of their time is spent interacting with children and youth, not adults. Though increased opportunities for professional collaboration and networking are reducing teacher isolation, teachers are behind classroom doors most of the day, immersed in the complexities of teaching and trying to meet the diverse needs of their students. Most teachers would welcome more interaction with their colleagues, especially time to observe one another. Without opportunities to receive feedback from one's peers, teachers are deprived of an important catalyst for professional growth. As Elliot Eisner puts it: "The result of professional isolation is the difficulty that teachers encounter in learning what they themselves do in their own classrooms when they teach. [How] can a teacher learn that he or she is talking too much, not providing sufficient time for student reflection, raising low-order questions, or is simply boring students? Teachers unaware of such features of their own performance are in no position to change them" (1998, 160–61). Additionally, by observing how a colleague responds to the challenges of teaching, the observer has an opportunity to reflect on his or her approaches to meeting those same challenges. For example, a fourth-grade teacher came to the following insight as a result of observing his teaching partner: "Being a teacher is so much more than an extensive repertoire of strategies and techniques. [To] be a teacher is to find a way to live within an environment filled with dilemmas" (Hole 1998, 419).

Knowledge of Students

Knowledge of students is also important. Student characteristics such as their aptitudes, talents, learning styles, stage of development, and their readiness to learn new material are among the essential knowledge teachers must have. The importance of this knowledge is evident in comments made by an intern at a middle school: "To teach a kid well you have to know a kid well. . . . teaching middle school takes a special breed of teachers who understand the unique abilities and inabilities . . . [of] those undergoing their own metamorphosis into teenagers" (Henry et al. 1995, 124–25). Teachers gain this kind of knowledge through study, observation, and constant interaction. Without considerable understanding of children and youth, teachers' efforts to help students learn and grow can be inappropriate and, in some cases, counterproductive. Teachers' expectations of students directly affect student achievement. The following Professional Reflection activity is designed to guide you in reflecting on opportunities you have already had to acquire knowledge about learners.

 **Professional Reflection** **Inventorying your knowledge of children and youth**

Which type of knowledge do teachers need more—subject-matter knowledge or professional knowledge?

Knowledge of Subject

With the title of *teacher* comes an assumption of knowledge. Those outside the field of education expect a teacher to be a ready reference for all sorts of information. Clearly, teachers who have extensive knowledge of their subjects are better equipped to help their students learn. However, knowledge of subject matter does not translate into an understanding of *how* to share that knowledge with students—a point illustrated in a case study conducted by a team of researchers at the National Center for Research on Teacher Learning. The case focused on "Mary," an undergraduate literature major enrolled in a teacher education program at a major university. By any standards, Mary was a subject-matter expert—she was valedictorian of a large, urban high school; had straight A's in the literature courses she had taken; and had a sophisticated understanding of literature, especially poetry. The case study revealed that Mary had little understanding of classroom activities that would show her students *how* to read with sophistication and concluded that "some prospective teachers may come to teacher education unaware of how they have learned the processes they use and that render them expert. Unaided by their disciplines in locating the underpinnings of their expertise, these skilled, talented, and desirable recruits may easily become, ironically, those who can *do* but who cannot *teach*" (Holt-Reynolds 1999, 43).

Extensive knowledge of subject matter, as the National Board for Professional Teaching Standards (1994, 19–20) puts it, "entails more than being able to recite lists of dates, multiplication tables, or rules of grammar. [Accomplished] teachers possess what is sometimes called **'pedagogical content knowledge.'** Such understanding is the joint product of wisdom about teaching, learning, students and content. It includes knowledge of the most appropriate ways to present the subject matter to students through analogies, metaphors, experiments, demonstrations and illustrations."

Knowledge of Methods for Applying Educational Theory and Research

Theories about learners and learning guide the decision making of professional teachers. Not only do such teachers know that a certain strategy works, but they also know *why* it works. Because they recognize the importance of theories, they have at their disposal a greater range of options for problem solving than teachers who have not developed their repertoire of theories. Your ultimate goal as a professional is to apply theoretical knowledge to the practical problems of teaching.

To illustrate the usefulness of research on students' learning, we present six teaching strategies that Barak Rosenshine (1995, 267) recommends, based on his and others' research on cognitive processing, studies of teachers whose students have higher achievement gains than students of other teachers, and research on cognitive strategies.

1. Present new material in small steps so that the working memory does not become over-loaded.
2. Help students develop an organization for the new material.
3. Guide student practice by (a) supporting students during initial practice and (b) providing for extensive student processing.
4. When teaching higher level tasks, support students by providing them with cognitive strategies.
5. Help students to use cognitive strategies by providing them with procedural prompts (e.g., questions students ask themselves while learning new material—"who," "what," "why," "when," etc.) and modeling the use of procedural prompts.
6. Provide for extensive student practice.

What kinds of basic knowledge and skills do teachers need to do their jobs well? How will you acquire and develop knowledge and skills in these areas?

Research on students' learning is not intended to set forth, in cookbook fashion, exactly what teachers should do to increase students' learning. Instead, it may be helpful to think of educational research as providing teachers with rules of thumb to guide their practice. For example, Rosenshine, Meister, and Chapman (1996, 198) point out that, in spite of extensive research on the effectiveness of procedural prompts, "at the present time, developing procedural prompts appears to be an art. [It] is difficult to derive any prescriptions on how to develop effective procedural prompts for cognitive strategies in reading, writing, and subject matter domains." Finally, noted educational psychologist Lee Cronbach (quoted in Eisner, 1998, 112) may have put it best when he said "[educational research] is to help practitioners use their heads."

What Are Five Ways of Viewing the Teacher Knowledge Base?

Just as people hold different expectations for schools and teachers, there are different views on the knowledge and abilities teachers need to teach well. The complexities of teaching make it difficult to describe in exact detail the **knowledge base** on which teaching as a profession rests. This difficulty results, in part, because there is no universally accepted definition of what good teaching is. Educational researchers are still learning *what* good teachers know and *how* they use that knowledge. Five widespread views of teachers' knowledge and abilities are portrayed in Figure 2.1.

Figure 2.1

A Personal Development View

One view of what teachers need to know and be able to do places primary emphasis on who the teacher is as a person. According to this view, teachers should be concerned with developing themselves as persons so that they may learn to use themselves more effectively. The importance of personal development is described as follows by the authors of *On Being a Teacher:* ". . . teachers who appear in charge of their own lives, who radiate power, tranquility, and grace in their actions, are going to command attention and respect. People will follow them anywhere. . . . What we are saying is that you have not only the option, but also the imperative, to develop the personal dimensions of your functioning, as well as your professional skills" (Zehm and Kottler 1993, 15).

What this approach requires, then, is that teachers continually develop their powers of observation and reflection so that they can most effectively respond to the needs of students. Teaching becomes an authentic, growth-oriented encounter between teacher and students. An important dimension of this **personal development view** is the teacher's need for self-knowledge, particularly in regard to oneself as a learner.

Research-Based Competencies

Since the late 1980s, several states and a few large cities have developed their own lists of **research-based competencies** that beginning teachers must demonstrate. These competencies are derived from educational research that has identified what effective teachers do. Typically, the states have developed *behavioral indicators* for each competency, which trained observers from universities and school districts use to determine to what extent teachers actually exhibit the target behaviors in the classroom.

The Florida Performance Measurement System (FPMS) was the first research-based performance system to be implemented on a statewide basis. Beginning teachers in Florida must now demonstrate behaviors in six domains: planning, management of student conduct, instructional organization and development, presentation of subject matter, verbal and nonverbal communication, and testing (student preparation, administration, and feedback). Appendix 2.1 presents the Summative Observation Instrument for the FPMS and the "effective" and "ineffective" behavioral indicators for four of those domains.

Appendix 2.1

State Standards

In addition to sets of research-based competencies for evaluating practicing teachers, several states have developed performance-based standards for what new teachers should know and be able to do. Known as **outcome-based** or **performance-based teacher education,** the new approach is based on several assumptions:

- Outcomes are demonstrations of learning rather than a list of teaching specializations, college courses completed, or concepts studied.
- Outcomes are performances that reflect the richness and complexity of the teacher's role in today's classrooms—not discrete, single behaviors.
- Demonstrations of learning must occur in authentic settings—that is, settings similar to those within which the teacher will teach.
- Outcomes are culminating demonstrations of what beginning teachers do in real classrooms.

Typically, outcome-based standards are developed with input from teachers, teacher educators, state department of education personnel, and various professional associa-

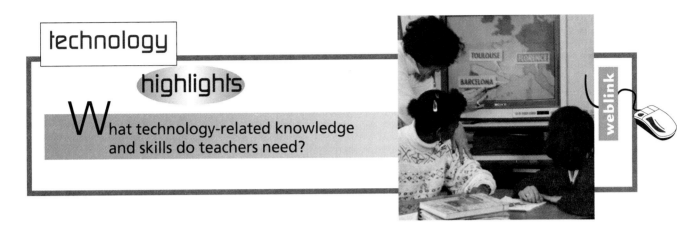

tions. To illustrate state standards for teacher preparation, we present standards from Kentucky in Appendix 2.2.

Appendix 2.2

A Job-Analysis Approach

Another view of what teachers need to know and be able to do is based on the job analyses that some school districts conduct. Typically, a **job analysis** begins with a review of existing job descriptions and then proceeds to interviews with those currently assigned to the job and their supervisors regarding the activities and responsibilities associated with the job. These data are then analyzed to identify the dimensions of the job. Finally, interview questions based on the dimensions are developed and used by district personnel responsible for hiring.

To illustrate the job-analysis view of the knowledge, skills, and attitudes needed by teachers, we present the thirteen dimensions used for selecting "star" urban teachers. By comparing the behaviors and beliefs of outstanding urban teachers with those of quitters and failures, Martin Haberman (1995, 779–80) and his colleagues at the University of Wisconsin, Milwaukee, identified thirteen characteristics of successful teachers of low-income urban students. These characteristics, identified by principals, supervisors, other teachers, parents, and the teachers themselves, include the following:

- *Persistence*
- *Protecting learners and learning*—Star teachers see protecting and enhancing students' involvement in learning activities as their highest priority. . . .
- *Application of generalizations*—[Stars are] able to take principles and concepts from a variety of sources (i.e., courses, workshops, books, and research) and translate them into practice.
- *Approach to students "at-risk"*—Star teachers believe that, regardless of the life conditions their students face, they as teachers bear a primary responsibility for sparking their students' desire to learn.
- *Professional versus personal orientation to students*—[Stars] use such terms as *caring, respect,* and *concern,* and they enjoy the love and affection of students when it occurs naturally. But they do not regard it as a prerequisite for learning.
- *Burnout: its causes and cures*—[Star teachers] recognize that even good teachers will eventually burn out if they are subjected to constant stress, so they learn how to protect themselves. . . .
- *Fallibility*—[Stars] can accept their own mistakes.

The remaining six dimensions are *organizational ability, physical/emotional stamina, teaching style* modeled on coaching, *explanation of success* based on students' effort rather than ability, *rapport* with students, and *readiness* to believe that education will provide students with the best chance of "making it" in American society.

Professional Views

Various professional associations have outlined what teachers should know and be able to do. The **National Board for Professional Teaching Standards (NBPTS)**, established in 1987 as an outgrowth of the Carnegie Forum report *A Nation Prepared: Teachers for the 21st Century*, has developed the following five general standards on which voluntary national teacher certification will be based; specific standards are also being developed in more than thirty certification areas.

- Teachers are committed to students and their learning.
- Teachers know the subjects they teach and how to teach those subjects to students.
- Teachers are responsible for managing and monitoring student learning.
- Teachers think systematically about their practice and learn from experience.
- Teachers are members of learning communities (National Board for Professional Teaching Standards 1994, 13–14).

By the end of 1999, the NBPTS had set the national standard for excellence in teaching, and almost 2,000 teachers held Board certification. The goal of the NBPTS is to have 100,000 Board certified teachers by 2006.

Standards proposed by the **Interstate New Teacher Assessment and Support Consortium (INTASC)**, also established in 1987, reflect a trend toward performance-based or outcome-based assessment of essential knowledge and abilities for teachers. In other words, such standards describe what teachers should know and be able to do rather than list courses that teachers need in order to receive a license to teach. To enhance collaboration among states for the initial licensing of teachers, INTASC proposed in early 1993 ten principles that are compatible with the standards proposed by the NBPTS (see Appendix 2.3). Specific statements for essential "knowledge," "dispositions," and "performances" were also developed for each principle.

In light of the five differing views of what teachers ought to know and be able to do, it seems clear that becoming a teacher is complex and demanding. We believe that effective teachers use five kinds of knowledge and skills to meet the challenges of the profession. As Figure 2.2 shows, effective teachers are guided by **reflection** and a **problem-solving orientation**. On the basis of reflection and problem solving, they use knowledge of self and students (including cultural differences), knowledge of subject matter, and knowledge of educational theory and research to create optimum conditions.

weblink
Appendix 2.3

weblink
Figure 2.2

How Do Reforms in Teacher Education Affect You?

Since the publication in 1983 of *A Nation at Risk: The Imperative for Educational Reform*, the United States has experienced an unprecedented push for reform in education. During that time, numerous commissions were established and scores of reports were written outlining what should be done to improve America's schools. Most of these reports called for changes in the education of teachers. In fact, the preparation program you are now involved in probably has been influenced by this **educational reform movement.** Calls for reform in teacher education have emphasized increased academic preparation, an expanded role for schools, and a national board for teacher certification.

Increased Academic Preparation

One call for the reform of teacher education was made by the **Holmes Group,** named after Henry W. Holmes, dean of the Harvard Graduate School of Education during the 1920s. The Holmes Group was initially made up of ninety-six major universities. In *Tomorrow's Teachers*, a 1986 report written by thirteen deans of education and one college president, the Holmes Group recommended that all teachers have a bachelor's degree in an academic field and a master's degree in education. Although the Holmes Group viewed additional academic preparation as a means of enhancing the professional status of teachers, critics maintained that students' education would be delayed and be more expensive, with no assurance that students who spent five years obtaining a teaching certificate would be paid more.

The Holmes Group held an action summit in 1993 to develop a comprehensive plan for redesigning the schools of education at Holmes Group member institutions. The plan outlined steps for creating Tomorrow's School of Education (TSE)—an institution that has put into practice the Holmes Group agenda for the reform of teacher education. In early 1995, the Holmes Group released the TSE plan, which recommended that teacher educators become more involved with schools and that students move through a five-year program in cohorts. The report also urged colleges of education to establish **professional development schools** (PDSs) that are linked to colleges or universities and operate on the same principle as teaching hospitals. Students act as intern teachers, and college faculty and school staff develop new teaching methods and collaborate on educational research projects.

In 1996, after a decade of what it described as "uneven progress" in the reform of teacher education and a realization that "the reform of professional education is so complicated and difficult that it has not yielded to any one reform group's efforts to improve it," the Holmes Group joined with other professional organizations—including the National Board for Professional Teaching Standards, the National Education Association, and the American Federation of teachers—to create the **Holmes Partnership.** The Holmes Partnership adopted six principal goals: high quality professional preparation; simultaneous renewal (of public K–12 schools and pre- and in-service education); equity, diversity, and cultural competence; scholarly inquiry and programs of research; faculty development; and policy initiation (Holmes Partnership 1999).

Expanded Role for Schools

Based on his study of teacher education programs around the country, noted educator John Goodlad set forth his plan for the simultaneous renewal of schools and teacher preparation programs in his 1994 book, *Educational Renewal: Better Teachers, Better Schools.* To improve teacher preparation, Goodlad recommended the creation of Centers of Pedagogy that would operate according to a specific set of principles. These centers would take the place of current teacher education departments, and they would be staffed by a team of teacher educators, liberal arts professors, and educators from local schools. In addition, Goodlad recommended that school districts and universities create jointly operated partner schools. Selected teachers at the partner school would divide their time between teaching students at the school and supervising beginning teachers. Partner schools would thus become centers for the renewal of education as well as laboratory schools for the professional development of beginning teachers.

National Certification

The National Board for Professional Teaching Standards (NBPTS) was created to issue certificates to teachers who meet the Board's high standards. The NBPTS is governed by a sixty-three member board of directors, the majority of whom are active classroom teachers. In 1995, five nationally certified teachers were elected to the board.

The NBPTS encourages school districts and states to pay its certification fee ($2,000 for 1998–99) on behalf of teachers who seek board certification. Candidates first submit portfolios documenting their performance over several months; then they complete a series of exercises at an assessment center. Examples of NBPTS portfolio activities and assessment center activities for the early childhood/generalist and early adolescence/ English language arts are presented in Appendix 2.4 and in the Teacher's Resource Guide section "NBPTS Assessment Center Activities" on this book's website.

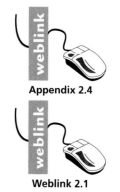

Appendix 2.4

Weblink 2.1

State Standards Boards

To regulate and improve the professional practice of teachers, administrators, and other education personnel, states have established **professional standards boards.** In some states, standards boards have the authority to implement standards; in others, they serve in an advisory capacity to educational policymakers. In Washington state, for example, the Washington Advisory Board for Professional Teaching Standards recently made a recommendation to the State Board of Education calling for a three-level teacher certification system. Candidates, on completion of an approved program, would receive a Residency Certificate. With demonstration of successful teaching and a recommendation from the employing school district, a candidate then would be eligible for a renewable, five-year Professional Certificate. Finally, persons who hold national certification from the National Board for Professional Teaching Standards or who hold a combination of advanced degrees, experience, and proficiency in performance-based standards would be eligible for the optional Professional Career Certificate.

In the wake of national reports such as *What Matters Most: Teaching for America's Future* (National Commission on Teaching and America's Future 1996) and *Quality Counts 2000: Who Should Teach? (Education Week* 2000), which highlighted the common practice of teachers teaching "out-of-field," professional standards boards in many states have launched extensive reviews of their teacher certification standards. Also, some standards boards have addressed whether education students' subject matter preparation should continue to be separate from professional preparation and whether alternative routes to certification such as school district-controlled internship programs should be encouraged.

What Can You Learn from Observing in Classrooms?

Classroom observations are a vital element of many **field experiences.** Students report that these experiences aid them greatly in making a final decision about entering the teaching field. Most become more enthusiastic about teaching and more motivated to learn the needed skills; a few decide that teaching is not for them. Recognizing the value of observations, many teacher education programs are increasing the amount of field experiences and placing such fieldwork earlier in students' programs. For example, at Washington State University (WSU), students preparing to become elementary teachers complete one week of classroom observations as part of their first education course. Later in their program, WSU students participate in "Schools First!", a three-week, full-day practicum (or field experience) at a school. In addition, as part of a required methods course, the WSU program is piloting an "advanced" practicum that spans eight weeks and requires several hours of classroom observation each week.

Technology and Classroom Observations

Currently, many universities and school districts are cooperating on the use of two-way interactive compressed video technology to enable preservice teachers on campus to observe live coverage in school classrooms off campus. Compressed video can be transmitted over existing telephone lines or the Internet in a relatively inexpensive, unobtrusive, and time-efficient way. **Distance learning**—the use of technology such as video transmissions that enables students to receive instruction at multiple, often remote sites—now enables teacher education programs to use the power of models for learning how to teach. For example, distance learning enables students at Texas A & M University and the University of Memphis to observe inner-city classrooms and afterwards to discuss their observations with the teachers. One of the designers of the interactive video program at Memphis comments on its benefits: "Previously everyone visited different schools and saw very different things. [This] shared clinical experience will lead to a more focused discussion of teaching methods" (University of Memphis 1994/95, 2).

Focused Observations

Observations are more meaningful when they are focused and conducted with clear purposes. Observers may focus on the students, the teacher, the interactions between the two, the structure of the lesson, or the setting. More specifically, for example, observers may note differences between the ways boys and girls or members of different ethnic groups communicate and behave in the classroom. They may note student interests and ability levels, study student responses to a particular teaching strategy, or analyze the question and response patterns in a class discussion.

Observations may also be guided by sets of questions related to specific areas. For instance, since beginning teachers are frequently frustrated by their lack of success in interesting their students in learning, asking questions specifically related to motivation can make an observation more meaningful and instructive. Figure 2.3 presents a helpful set of focused questions on motivation. Similar questions can be generated for

Figure 2.3

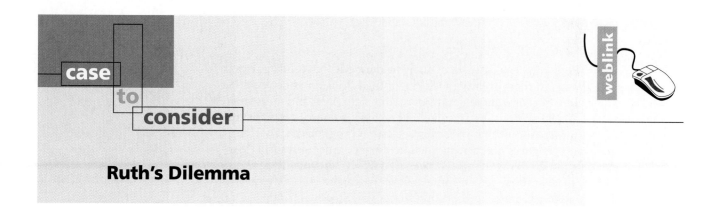

Ruth's Dilemma

other focus areas such as classroom management, student involvement, questioning skills, evaluation, and teacher–student rapport.

Observation Instruments

Weblink 2.2

A wide range of methods can be used to conduct classroom observations, ranging from informal, qualitative descriptions to formal, quantitative checklists. With reform efforts to improve education in the United States has come the development of instruments to facilitate the evaluation of teacher performance, a task now widely required of school administrators. Students preparing to teach can benefit by using these evaluative instruments in their observations. An example is the "Formative Observation of Effective Teaching Practices Instrument" on this book's website.

How Can You Gain Practical Experience for Becoming a Teacher?

A primary aim of teacher education programs is to give students opportunities to experience, to the extent possible, the real world of the teacher. Through field experiences and carefully structured experiential activities, preservice teachers are given limited exposure to various aspects of teaching. Observing, tutoring, instructing small groups, analyzing video cases, operating instructional media, performing student teaching, and completing various noninstructional tasks are among the most common experiential activities.

Classroom Experiences

Because of the need to provide opportunities to put theory into practice before student teaching, many teacher education programs enable students to participate in microteaching, teaching simulations, analyses of video cases, field-based practica and clinical experiences, and classroom aide programs.

Microteaching   Introduced in the 1960s, **microteaching** was received enthusiastically and remains a popular practice. The process calls for students to teach brief, single-concept lessons to a small group of students (five to ten) while concurrently practicing a specific teaching skill, such as positive reinforcement. Often the microteaching is video-taped for later study.

As originally developed, microteaching includes the following six steps.

1. Identify a specific teaching skill to learn about and practice.
2. Read about the skill in one of several pamphlets.
3. Observe a master teacher demonstrate the skill in a short movie or on videotape.
4. Prepare a three- to five-minute lesson to demonstrate the skill.
5. Teach the lesson, which is videotaped, to a small group of peers.
6. Critique, along with the instructor and student peers, the videotaped lesson.

Simulations   As an element of teacher training, **teaching simulations** provide opportunities for vicarious practice of a wide range of teaching skills. In simulations, students analyze teaching situations that are presented in writing, on audiotape, in short films, or on videotape. Typically, students are given background information about a hypothetical school or classroom and the pupils they must prepare to teach. After this orientation, students role-play the student teacher or the teacher who is confronted with the problem situation. Following the simulation, participants discuss the appropriateness of solutions and work to increase their problem-solving skills and their understanding of the teacher's multifaceted role as a decision maker.

With recent advances in computer technology, some teacher education programs now use computer-based simulations that enable students to hone their classroom planning and decision-making skills. Students at Nova Southwestern University in Florida, for example, learn to diagnose learning disabilities among children and youth by analyzing computer-simulated cases (Brown 1994). In addition, continuing progress in the development of virtual reality technology suggests that preservice teachers soon will be able to practice their skills with computer-simulated students who "learn" by interacting with humans (VanLehn et al. 1994; Sigalit and VanLehn 1995).

Video Cases   Teacher education students who view, analyze, and then write about video cases have an additional opportunity to appreciate the ambiguities and complexities of real-life classrooms, to learn that "there are no clear-cut, simple answers to the complex issues teachers face" (Wasserman 1994, 606). Viewing authentic video cases enables students to see how "teaching tradeoffs and dilemmas emerge in the video 'text' as do the strategies teachers use, the frustrations they experience, the brilliant and less-brilliant decisions they make" (Grant, Richard, and Parkay 1996, 5).

Practica   A **practicum** is a short-term field-based experience (usually about two weeks long) that allows teacher education students to spend time observing and assisting in classrooms. Though practica vary in length and purpose, students are often able to begin instructional work with individuals or small groups. For example, a cooperating teacher may allow a practicum student to tutor a small group of students, read a story to the whole class, conduct a spelling lesson, monitor recess, help students with their homework, or teach students a song or game.

Classroom Aides   Serving as a teacher's aide is another popular means of providing field experience before student teaching. A teacher aide's role depends primarily on the unique needs of the school and its students. Generally, aides work under the supervision of a certified teacher and perform duties that support the teacher's instruction. Assisting teachers in classrooms familiarizes college students with class schedules, record-keeping procedures, and students' performance levels, and provides ample opportunity for observations. In exchange, the classroom teacher receives much needed assistance.

Student Teaching

The most extensive and memorable field experience in teacher preparation programs is the period of student teaching. As *The Student Teacher's Handbook* points out, student teaching "is the only time in a teaching career that one is an apprentice under the close guidance of an experienced mentor" (Schwebel et al. 1996, 4). States require students to have a five-week to semester-long student teaching experience in the schools before certifying them as teachers. The nature of student teaching varies considerably among teacher education programs. Typically, a student is assigned to a cooperating (or master) teacher in the school, and a university supervisor makes periodic visits to observe the student teacher. Some programs even pay student teachers during the student teaching experience.

Student teaching is a time of responsibility. As one student teacher put it, "I don't want to mess up [my students'] education!" It is also an opportunity for growth, a chance to master critical skills. According to data gathered from 902 teacher education institutions in the United States, about 60 percent of the student teacher's time is actually spent teaching (Johnson and Yates 1982). The remaining time is devoted to observing and participating in classroom activities. The amount of time one actually spends teaching, however, is not as important as one's willingness to reflect carefully on the student teaching experience. Two excellent ways to promote reflection during student teaching are journal writing and maintaining a reflective teaching log.

Student Teacher Journal Writing   Many supervisors require student teachers to keep a journal of their classroom experiences so that they can engage in reflective teaching and begin the process of criticizing and guiding themselves. The following two entries —the first written by a student teacher in a fourth-grade classroom, the second by a student teacher in a high school English class—illustrate how journal writing can help student teachers develop strategies for dealing with the realities of teaching.

> Today I taught a lesson on the geography of the Northeast, and the kids seemed so bored. I called on individuals to read the social studies text, and then I explained it. Some of them really struggled with the text. Mr. H. said I was spoon-feeding them too much. So tomorrow I am going to put them into groups and let them answer questions together rather than give them the answers. This ought to involve the students in the learning a bit more and enable some of the better readers to help out those who have difficulty, without the whole class watching. I feel bad when I see those glazed looks on their faces. I need to learn how to be more interesting (Pitton 1998, 120).

> I had good feedback on small groups in their responses to questions on *Of Mice and Men*. They were to find a paragraph that might indicate theme and find two examples of foreshadowing. We found five!

> The short story unit was awful during fourth hour. The kids just didn't respond. I quickly revamped my approach for the next hour. Fifth hour did seem to go better. (Mostly though, I think it was just that I was more prepared, having had one class to try things out.) I can see how experience really helps. Now that I've tried the story "The Tiger or the Lady," I would use the same material, but I would know HOW to use it more effectively! (Pitton 1998, 143).

Relatively unstructured, open-ended journals, such as the ones from which these entries were selected, provide student teachers with a medium for subjectively exploring the student teaching experience.

Reflective Teaching Logs   To promote the practice of reflecting more analytically, some supervisors ask their student teachers to use a more directed and structured form of journal keeping, the **reflective teaching log.** In this form a student lists and briefly describes the daily sequence of activities, selects a single episode to expand on, analyzes the reason for selecting it and what was learned from it, and considers the possible future application of that knowledge.

To illustrate the reflective teaching approach to keeping a log, we share here a partial entry for one episode that was recounted and critiqued by a college student tutoring a student in Spanish. The entry is of particular interest because it provides us with a glimpse of a college student's first experience with a pupil's difficulty in understanding subject matter.

Log #1: February 14, 1991 (10:00–10:30am)

Sequence of Events: Worked with Richy on his Spanish

Episode: Because I wasn't sure of Richy's level, I asked him a few questions to see what he knew. His homework exercises involved work like reflexives, irregular verbs, and vocabulary. But when he and I started reviewing, he didn't remember the very basics of conjugation. He said, "I know this stuff, I just need review." We reviewed the conjugation of regular verbs. I set up a chart of *ar*, *er* and *ir* endings and had him fill in the correct forms. He kept saying, "I just don't remember," or "Oh yeah, I knew that." His facial expressions reflected concentration and perhaps frustration. At times, he would just stare at the page until I gave him a hint. His forehead was scrunched up and he fidgeted a bit with his hands and legs. After working on the regular endings, he wanted to get a drink. I told him to go ahead. . . .

What strategies can you use to make your student teaching experience truly valuable to you in becoming a teacher? In what sense will you remain a student teacher throughout your career?

Analysis: I guess that I was just shocked at how little Richy knew. What we went over was the most simple form of Spanish grammar and in a way he was acting as if he had no idea what we were doing. I was surprised, like I said, but only on the inside. I just helped him along, showing him why the concepts made sense. I had no idea how we were going to do his homework assignments since they were considerably more difficult . . . (Posner 1993, 116–117).

Though student teaching will be the capstone experience of your teacher education program, the experience should be regarded as an *initial* rather than a terminal learning opportunity—your first chance to engage in reflection and self-evaluation for a prolonged period.

Gaining Experiences in Multicultural Settings

The enrollment in schools in the United States of students from diverse cultural backgrounds will continue to increase dramatically during the twenty-first century. As this trend continues, it is vitally important that those entering the teaching profession achieve an understanding of children's differing backgrounds. For example, students in Washington State University's teacher education program must document how they have met the following "administrative code" for teacher certification: "All candidates for teacher certification must demonstrate in their field experience their ability to work effectively with students of various backgrounds

Video 2.1

including (1) students from racial and or ethnic populations other than the candidate's, and (2) students with exceptional needs (i.e., those with handicapping conditions and the highly capable)."

As a teacher you can be assured that you will teach students from backgrounds that differ from your own—including students from the more than 100 racial and ethnic groups in the United States and students who are poor, gifted, or have disabilities. You will have the challenge of reaching out to all students and teaching them that they are persons of worth and can learn. You will also be confronted with the difficult challenge of being sensitive to differences among students while at the same time treating all equally and fairly. To prepare for these realities of teaching, you should make every effort to gain experiences in multicultural settings.

Induction and Internship Programs

In response to widespread efforts to improve education, many states and local school districts, often in collaboration with colleges and universities, have begun teacher induction and/or internship programs. Among the programs that have received national attention are the Florida Beginning Teacher Program, the California Mentor Teacher Program, the Virginia Beginning Teacher Assistance Program, and the Kentucky Beginning Teacher Internship Program.

Induction programs provide beginning teachers with continued assistance at least during the first year. **Internship programs** also provide participants with support, but they are usually designed primarily to provide training for those who have not gone through a teacher education program. In some instances, however, the terms *induction* and *internship* are used interchangeably.

Most induction and internship programs serve a variety of purposes:

1. To improve teaching performance
2. To increase the retention of promising beginning teachers during the induction years
3. To promote the personal and professional well-being of beginning teachers by improving teachers' attitudes toward themselves and the profession
4. To satisfy mandated requirements related to induction and certification
5. To transmit the culture of the system to beginning teachers (Huling-Austin 1990, 539).

To accomplish these purposes, induction programs offer resources such as workshops based on teacher-identified needs, observations by and follow-up conferences with individuals not in a supervisory role, support from mentor (or buddy) teachers, and support group meetings for beginning teachers.

School-Based Teacher Education

A new model of teacher preparation that provides students with extensive practical field experiences is known as **school-based teacher education.** In most instances, school-based programs are designed for students who have received a bachelor's degree and then wish to obtain teacher certification. Two examples are the school-based teacher education programs in Texas and the Teachers for Chicago Program.

Since 1985, completion of a school-based program has been one path to teacher certification in Texas. Candidates complete a year-long paid internship at a school, during which they undertake intensive practical study of teaching. Interns are mentored by the supervisor of the district's teacher education program, the district's curriculum specialist, the principal, the assistant principal, and, in some cases, a university supervisor. Area universities deliver courses specifically designed for the interns. At the end of the year, interns take district- and/or state-adopted tests of content and pedagogy to become eligible for standard certification.

To select, train, and retain effective teachers for Chicago's schools, a group of schools, the Chicago Teachers Union, deans of education at area universities, and the Golden Apple Foundation for Excellence in Teaching created the Teachers for Chicago Program. Candidates, selected through a rigorous interview process, enroll in a graduate education program at one of nine area colleges and universities. After a summer of coursework, they begin a two-year paid internship under the guidance of a mentor teacher. Interns fill vacant teacher positions in the schools and are responsible for the academic progress of their students. On completion of the program, interns have earned a master's degree and have met state certification requirements.

Substitute Teaching

On completion of a teacher education program and prior to securing a full-time teaching assignment, many students choose to gain additional practical experience in classrooms by **substitute teaching**. Others, unable to locate full-time positions, decide to substitute, knowing that many districts prefer to hire from their pool of substitutes when full-time positions become available. Substitute teachers replace regular teachers who are absent due to illness, family responsibilities, personal reasons, or professional workshops and conferences.

Each day, thousands of substitutes are employed in schools across the United States. For example, during one school year at the fifteen high schools in a large urban district, the total number of absences for 1,200 regular teachers equaled 14,229 days. Multiplying this figure by five (the number of classes per day for most high school teachers) yields 71,145 class periods taught by substitutes that year (St. Michel 1995).

Qualifications for substitutes vary from state to state and district to district. An area with a critical need for subs will often relax its requirements to provide classroom coverage. In many districts, it is possible to substitute teach without regular certification. Some districts have less stringent qualifications for short-term, day-to-day substitutes and more stringent ones for long-term, full-time ones. In many districts, the application process for substitutes is the same as that for full-time applicants; in others, the process may be somewhat briefer. Often, substitutes are not limited to working in their area of certification; however, schools try to avoid making out-of-field assignments. If you decide to substitute teach, contact the schools in your area to learn about the qualifications and procedures for hiring substitutes.

In spite of the significant role substitutes play in the day-to-day operation of schools, ". . . research tells us that they receive very little support, no specialized training, and are rarely evaluated. . . . In short, the substitute will be expected to show up to each class on time, maintain order, take roll, carry out the lesson, and leave a note for the regular teacher about the classes and events of the day without support, encouragement, or acknowledgement" (St. Michel 1995, 6–7). While working conditions such as these are certainly challenging, substitute teaching can be a rewarding, professionally fulfilling experience. Figure 2.4 presents several advantages and disadvantages of substitute teaching.

Figure 2.4

How Can You Develop Your Teaching Portfolio?

Now that you have begun your journey toward becoming a teacher, you should acquire the habit of assessing your growth in knowledge, skills, and attitudes. Toward this end, you may wish to collect the results of your reflections and self-assessment in a **professional portfolio.** A professional portfolio is a collection of work that documents an individual's accomplishments in an area of professional practice. An artist's portfolio, for example, might consist of a résumé, sketches, paintings, slides and photographs of exhibits, critiques of the artist's work, awards, and other documentation of achievement. Recently, new approaches to teacher evaluation have included the professional portfolio. The National Board for Professional Teaching Standards, for example, uses "portfolios [and] other evidence of performance prepared by the candidate" (National Board for Professional Teaching Standards 1994, 55) as one way of assessing whether teachers have met the high standards for Board certification. Teacher education programs at several universities now use portfolios as one means of assessing the competencies of candidates for teacher certification. Also, many school districts are beginning to ask applicants to submit portfolios that document their effectiveness as teachers.

Portfolio Contents

What will your portfolio contain? Written materials might include the following: lesson plans and curriculum materials, reflections on your development as a teacher, journal entries, writing assignments made by your instructor, sample tests you have prepared, critiques of textbooks, evaluations of students' work at the level for which you

What questions might you ask a mentor teacher about developing your professional portfolio?

are preparing to teach, sample letters to parents, and a résumé. Nonprint materials might include video- and audiotapes featuring you in simulated teaching and role-playing activities, audiovisual materials (transparencies, charts, or other teaching aids), photographs of bulletin boards, charts depicting room arrangements for cooperative learning or other instructional strategies, sample grade book, certificates of membership in professional organizations, and awards.

Your portfolio should represent your *best work* and give you an opportunity to become an advocate of *who you are* as a teacher. Because a primary purpose of the professional portfolio is to stimulate reflection and dialogue, you may wish to discuss what entries to make in your portfolio with your instructor or other teacher education students. In addition, the following questions from *How to Develop a Professional Portfolio: A Manual for Teachers* (Campbell et al. 1996) can help you select appropriate portfolio contents:

> Would I be proud to have my future employer and peer group see this? Is this an example of what my future professional work might look like? Does this represent what I stand for as a professional educator? If not, what can I revise or rearrange so that it represents my best efforts? (p. 5).

Using a Portfolio

In addition to providing teacher education programs with a way to assess their effectiveness, portfolios can be used by students for a variety of purposes. Campbell et al. (1996, 7–8) suggest that a portfolio may be used as

1. A way to establish a record of quantitative and qualitative performance and growth over time.
2. A tool for reflection and goal setting as well as a way to present evidence of your ability to solve problems and achieve goals.
3. A way to synthesize many separate experiences; in other words, a way to get the "big picture."
4. A vehicle for you to use to collaborate with professors and advisors in individualizing instruction.
5. A vehicle for demonstrating knowledge and skills gained through out-of-class experiences, such as volunteer experiences.
6. A way to share control and responsibility for your own learning.
7. An alternative assessment measure within the professional education program.
8. A potential preparation for national, regional, and state accreditation.
9. An interview tool in the professional hiring process.
10. An expanded résumé to be used as an introduction during the student teaching experience.

How Can You Benefit from Mentoring Relationships?

When asked "What would have been most helpful in preparing you to be a teacher?" a majority of respondents to the 1991 Metropolitan Life Survey of the American Teacher said, "a skilled, experienced teacher assigned to provide [me] with advice and assistance" (Louis Harris and Associates 1991, 15). Like the following first-year suburban high school teacher, the teachers surveyed realized the value of a mentor: "I wish I had

Weblink 2.3

Audio Clip 2.2

Table 2.1

one [a mentor] here. . . . There are days that go by and I don't think I learn anything about my teaching, and that's too bad. I wish I had someone" (Dollase 1992, 138).

In reflecting on how a mentor contributed to his professional growth, Forrest Parkay defined **mentoring** as

> . . . an intensive, one-to-one form of teaching in which the wise and experienced mentor inducts the aspiring protégé [one who is mentored] into a particular, usually professional, way of life. . . . [T]he protégé learns from the mentor not only the objective, manifest content of professional knowledge and skills but also a subjective, nondiscursive appreciation for *how* and *when* to employ these learnings in the arena of professional practice. In short, the mentor helps the protégé to "learn the ropes," to become socialized into the profession (Parkay 1988, 196).

An urban middle school intern's description of how his mentor helped him develop effective classroom management techniques exemplifies "learning the ropes": "'You've got to develop your own sense of personal power,' [my mentor] kept saying. 'It's not something I can teach you. I can show you what to do. I can model it. But I don't know, it's just something that's got to come from within you'" (Henry et al. 1995, 114).

Those who have become highly accomplished teachers frequently point out the importance of mentors in their preparation for teaching. A mentor can provide moral support, guidance, and feedback to students at various stages of professional preparation. In addition, a mentor can model for the protégé an analytical approach to solving problems in the classroom. Table 2.1 shows several problem-solving approaches a mentor can demonstrate to a novice teacher.

What Opportunities for Continuing Professional Development Will You Have?

Professional development is a life-long process; any teacher, at any stage of development, has room for improvement. Many school systems and universities have programs in place for the continuing professional development of teachers. Indeed, teachers are members of a profession that provides them with a " . . . continuous opportunity to grow, learn, and become more expert in their work" (Lieberman 1990, viii).

Self-Assessment for Professional Growth

Self-assessment is a necessary first step in pursuing opportunities for professional growth. A teacher comments on the importance of self-assessment after being certified by the National Board for Professional Teaching Standards: "Serious reflection and self-examination [were necessary] as I gauge[d] my skills and knowledge against objective, peer-developed, national standards in specific teaching areas" (National Board for Professional Teaching Standards 1995, 13).

Several questions can help you make appropriate choices as a teacher: In which areas am I already competent? In which areas do I need further development? How will I acquire the knowledge and skills I need? How will I apply new knowledge and practice new skills? Answers to such questions will lead you to a variety of sources for professional growth: teacher workshops, teacher centers, professional development schools, the opportunity to supervise and mentor student teachers, and graduate programs. Figure 2.5 illustrates the relationship of these professional development experiences to your teacher education program.

Figure 2.5

Teacher Workshops

The quality of **inservice workshops** is uneven, varying with the size of school district budgets and the imagination and knowledge of the administrators and teachers who arrange them. It is significant that the most effective inservice programs tend to be the ones that teachers request—and often design and conduct.

Some workshops focus on topics that all teachers (regardless of subject or level) can benefit from: classroom management, writing-across-the-curriculum, multicultural education, and strategies for teaching students with learning disabilities in the general education classroom, for example. Other workshops have a sharper focus and are intended for teachers of a subject at a certain level—for example, whole-language techniques for middle school students, discovery learning for high school science students, and student-centered approaches to teaching literature in the high school classroom.

Teacher Centers

Teacher centers provide opportunities for teachers "to take the lead in the decision making and implementation of staff development programs based on the needs of teachers. [They] provide the structure for teachers to take charge of their own professional growth" (Teacher Centers of New York State 1999). In contrast to inservice programs, these are more clearly initiated and directed by teachers. Some centers cooperate with a local or neighboring college of education and include members of the faculty on their planning committees.

Many teachers find teacher centers stimulating because they offer opportunities for collegial interaction in a quiet, professionally oriented setting. The busy, hectic pace of life in many schools, teachers often find, provides little time for professional dialogue with peers. Furthermore, in the teacher center, teachers are often more willing to discuss openly areas of weakness in their performance. As one teacher put it:

> At the teacher center I can ask for help. I won't be judged. The teachers who have helped me the most have had the same problems. I respect them, and I'm willing to learn from them. They have credibility with me.

Professional Development Schools

Professional development schools (PDSs) have emerged recently as a way to link school restructuring and the reform of teacher education in America. These school–university partnerships offer teachers the following opportunities:

- Fine learning programs for diverse students
- Practical, thought-provoking preparation for novice teachers
- New understanding and professional responsibilities for experienced educators
- Research projects that add to all educators' knowledge about how to make schools more productive (Holmes Group n.d., 1).

For example, a teacher at a PDS might team with a teacher education professor and teach a university-level course, participate in a collaborative research project, offer a professional development seminar for other teachers, arrange for the teacher educator to demonstrate instructional strategies in his or her classroom, or jointly develop relevant field experiences for prospective teachers.

Supervision and Mentoring of Student Teachers

After several years in the classroom, teachers may be ready to stretch themselves further by supervising student teachers. Some of the less obvious benefits of doing so are that teachers must rethink what they are doing so that they can explain and sometimes justify their behaviors to someone else, learning about themselves in the process. Furthermore, because they become a model for their student teachers, they continually strive to offer the best example. In exchange, they gain an assistant in the classroom—another pair of eyes, an aid with record keeping—and more than occasionally, fresh ideas and a spirit of enthusiasm.

Graduate Study

A more traditional form of professional development is to do graduate study. With the recent reforms, most states now require teachers to take some graduate courses to keep their certifications and knowledge up to date. Some teachers take only courses that are of immediate use to them; others use their graduate study to prepare for new teaching or administrative positions; and still others pursue doctoral work in order to teach prospective teachers or others in their discipline at the college level.

Study on the Internet

Weblink 2.4

If you have access to the **Internet,** you can locate many possibilities for continuing professional development. Teachers use the Internet to exchange ideas and experiences and to acquire additional expertise in teaching or to share their expertise with others. See the Teacher's Resource Guide section "Professional Development Opportunities on the Internet" on this book's website. If you decide to visit any of these sites, remember that websites are frequently changed or withdrawn from the Internet. The web addresses given throughout this book were active at the time of printing. Also, because it is estimated that 10,000 websites are added each day, you should periodically use key words related to education and your favorite search engine to gather the latest information and resources.

SUMMARY

What Essential Knowledge Do You Need to Teach? (p. 32)

What Are Five Ways of Viewing the Teacher Knowledge Base? (p. 35)

KEY TERMS AND CONCEPTS

Go to the website for interactive flashcards.

APPLICATIONS AND INTERACTIVITIES

Go to the website for interactive assignments in the following areas:

Teacher's Journal

Teacher's Database

Observations and Interviews

Professional Portfolio

Name _____ **Date** _____

For each question, write in the blank the answer you believe is correct.

2.1 Effective teachers are aware of _____ and sensitive to the needs of their students.

2.2 Teachers' _____ of students directly affect student achievement.

2.3 Suggesting the design of "Tomorrow's School of Education," including a plan for more involvement with schools and a five-year teacher education program was the work of the _____ Group.

2.4 The National _____ for Professional Teaching Standards was created to issue certificates to teachers who meet high standards.

2.5 The use of technology to receive instruction at multiple, often remote sites is known as _____ learning.

2.6 The process known as _____ calls for students to teach brief, single-concept lessons to a small group of students while concurrently practicing a specific teaching skill.

2.7 _____ programs provide beginning teachers with continued assistance at least during the first year.

2.8 A professional _____ is a collection of work documenting an individual's accomplishments in an area of professional practice.

2.9 The process through which an experienced teacher offers a beginning teacher intense, one-on-one advice and guidance about professional matters is known as _____.

2.10 Workshops for teachers focused on issues of direct interest to them and normally sponsored by school districts are known as _____ workshops.

Answers are available on the FlexChoice website at www.ablongman.com/parkayflex.

Name _____

Keep this checklist at your computer as a reminder to read and complete the chapter features and
activities located on the FlexChoice website at www.ablongman.com/parkayflex.

**Date
Completed**

_____ ❏ **PreTest with Answers**
_____ ❏ **Audio Clip 2.1:** Thinking Over the Opening Vignette
_____ ❏ **Professional Reflection:** Inventorying your knowledge of children and youth
_____ ❏ **Where Do You Stand?:** Which type of knowledge do teachers need more—subject-matter knowledge or professional knowledge?
_____ ❏ **Figure 2.1:** Five views of the teacher knowledge base
_____ ❏ **Appendix 2.1:** Florida Performance Measurement System Screening/Summative Observation Instrument
_____ ❏ **Technology Highlights:** What technology-related knowledge and skills do teachers need?
_____ ❏ **Appendix 2.2:** Models of Professional Standards: Kentucky's New Teacher Standards
_____ ❏ **Appendix 2.3:** Interstate New Teacher Assessment and Support Consortium Standards
_____ ❏ **Figure 2.2:** Essential knowledge and skills for the professional teacher
_____ ❏ **Appendix 2.4:** Sample NBPTS Portfolio Exercise
_____ ❏ **Weblink 2.1:** NBPTS Assessment Center Activities
_____ ❏ **Figure 2.3:** Guiding questions for observing motivation
_____ ❏ **Case to Consider:** Ruth's Dilemma
_____ ❏ **Weblink 2.2:** Formative Observation of Effective Teaching Practices Instrument
_____ ❏ **Video 2.1:** Gaining Real World Experience
_____ ❏ **Figure 2.4:** Advantages and disadvantages of substitute teaching
_____ ❏ **Weblink 2.3:** The Metropolitan Life Survey of the American Teacher
_____ ❏ **Audio Clip 2.2:** Mentoring
_____ ❏ **Table 2.1:** Problem-solving approaches used by a mentor
_____ ❏ **Figure 2.5:** Professional development: From teacher education student to practitioner
_____ ❏ **Weblink 2.4:** Professional Development Opportunities on the Internet
_____ ❏ **Summary**
_____ ❏ **Key Terms and Concepts**
_____ ❏ **Applications and Interactivities:** Teacher's Journal
_____ ❏ **Applications and Interactivities:** Teacher's Database
_____ ❏ **Applications and Interactivities:** Observations and Interviews
_____ ❏ **Applications and Interactivities:** Professional Portfolio
_____ ❏ **PostTest with Answers**

Influences on the Professional Lives of Teachers

dear mentor

On Keeping Up with a Rapidly Changing Profession

Dear Mentor:

With all we see in the news media about modernizing and changing education to fit today's political agenda, how can educators be sure they are teaching students the "right" curriculum? How can I, as a teacher, be sure that I can keep up with the rapidly changing times? Is it possible that I can find the answers to these questions by studying the history, philosophy, and governance of education?

Sincerely,

Elizabeth Acevedo

Dear Elizabeth:

The questions you pose concerning curriculum and the rapidly changing times and forces in education today are probably among the most difficult for educators to deal with, but at the same time they are part of what makes education so exciting in this era of technology and the information age. I suggest you start with the curriculum that virtually every school system in the United States has today. This curriculum is based on values and knowledge that are grounded in the history of education and in the education philosophies that have been developed through study and research. These values are also the foundation on which you should build your personal teaching style and philosophy.

I think it is also important to recognize that curricula are not static. They are not rigidly bound to just tradition and accepted values. A good curriculum has to be a vibrant, almost living device that allows us to teach the basic ideas, theories, and learning strategies, as well as to incorporate today's growing body of knowledge which is expanding exponentially because of computers and technology. I think that this makes education particularly exciting. To cite just one example, the amount of research done in the past decade concerning the brain and learning is revolutionizing the way we teach today. As educators we have to keep up with this research and use it in the best way possible to educate our students.

This leads me to your second question: How can a teacher be sure to keep up with the rapidly changing times? I think we should take the medical profession as a good example of how and why we must keep up with our ever-changing field. Just as a good doctor follows the advancements made in medicine by reading professional journals, attending professional conferences, and sharing practices and ideas with colleagues, we as educators have to do the same. We must realize that as professional educators, we have a responsibility to our students to provide them with the best education possible, and we cannot do this unless we are constantly learning, and studying, and improving our profession. We have to make a commitment to learning and incorporate it into our professional development, as well as to instill it into our students' thinking. After all, I think a good teacher would want to be a learner for life and would want to encourage his or her students to be lifelong learners, too.

I hope these thoughts will help you in your quest to become a good teacher. Your questions already indicate that you possess the reflective abilities that all good educators must have. Best of luck to you in the future.

Sincerely,

Joe Bacewicz
1999 Connecticut Teacher of the Year

3

Ideas and Events That Have Shaped Education in the United States

Educational philosophy is a way not only of looking at ideas, but also of learning how to use ideas in better ways.

—Howard A. Ozmon and Samuel M. Craver
Philosophical Foundations of Education,
6th ed., 1999

Y ou are having an animated conversation in the teacher's lounge with four colleagues, Mary, Juan, Karen, and Hal, about educational reform and the changes sweeping across our nation's schools. The discussion was sparked by a television special everyone watched last night about new approaches to teaching and assessing students' learning.

AUDIO
Audio Clip 3.1

"I was really glad to see teachers portrayed in a professional light," you say. "The message seemed to be 'Let's get behind teachers and give them the support and resources they need to implement new ideas and technologies. Effective schools are important to our nation's well-being.'"

"I think it's just a case of schools trying to jump on the bandwagon," Hal says. "All this talk about restructuring schools, developing partnerships with the community, and using technology—they're supposed to be the silver bullets that transform education. These ideas just take time away from what we should be doing, and that's teaching kids how to read, write, and compute. If we don't get back to what really matters, our country is going to become a second-rate power in the world . . . that's my educational philosophy."

"But times have changed; the world is a different place," Mary says. "Look at how the Internet has changed things in just a few years. We can't return to the 'good old days.' Students need to learn how to learn; they need to learn how to solve problems that we can't even imagine today."

"Just a minute," Juan interjects. "I don't think the 'good old days' ever were. That's a nostalgia trap. What kids need is to see how education is the key to understanding themselves and others. If we can't get along as human beings on this planet, we're in trouble. Look at the ethnic cleansing in Kosovo, the killing in Rwanda, Angola, Northern Ireland. . . . Sure, we've got the Internet and all this technology, but as a species we haven't evolved at all."

"Of course we can't return to the past," Karen says, "but we can learn a lot from it. That's one of the main purposes of education . . . to see how the great ideas can help us improve things. Like I tell my students, there isn't one problem today that Shakespeare didn't have tremendous insights into 400 years ago—racism, poverty, war."

"Well, all I know is that when I started teaching thirty years ago, we taught the basics," Hal says. "It was as simple as that. We were there to teach, and the kids, believe it or not, were there to learn. Nowadays, we have to solve all of society's problems—eliminate poverty, racism, crime, or whatever."

Hal pauses a moment and then turns his attention to you. "It all changed in the 1980s and 1990s; we got involved in all this reform stuff . . . restructuring schools, empowering teachers, developing partnerships—I don't know where it's all going. What do you think . . . what's your educational philosophy?"

What do you say?

Name _____ Date _____

For each question, circle the letter of the answer you believe is correct. Then read the chapter to learn more about these topics.

3.1 What teachers believe students are like is based on
A. Their unique life experiences.
B. The views of teaching peers.
C. School district policies.
D. Their views of their own children.

3.2 Which of the following is an example of a metaphysical question?
A. What is real?
B. What values are worthy of possession?
C. How do we know?
D. What is value?

3.3 Axiology highlights the fact that teachers have an interest not only in how much students learn, but also in
A. The quality of life that comes from knowledge.
B. The nature of reality.
C. The origin of student learning.
D. The depth of student understanding.

3.4 Perennialism views truth as
A. Relativistic.
B. Beyond human comprehension.
C. Constant.
D. In a state of constant change.

3.5 John Dewey (1859–1952) believed that
A. Effective teaching is based on the notion of the constancy of human nature and truth.
B. Public school curriculum should derive from students' interests and needs.
C. Curricula in public schools should emphasize the Great Books of Western Civilization.
D. Learning is essentially passive.

3.6 The idea that every individual first exists and then decides what that existence means is most closely associated with
A. John Dewey.
B. Robert Hutchins.
C. Mortimer Adler.
D. Jean-Paul Sarte.

3.7 John B. Watson (1878–1958) and B. F. Skinner (1904–1990) are most closely associated with which branch of psychology?
A. School.
B. Humanistic.
C. Behavioristic.
D. Reverse.

3.8 Constructivists believe all of the following *except*
A. Learners make sense out of activities.
B. Student knowledge is little influenced by previous experience.
C. Learning is active.
D. Teachers must understand students' understanding.

3.9 During the late nineteenth and early twentieth centuries, the diversity of America's school population increased dramatically. The goal of immigrant education at this time was
A. Slow social integration designed to promote cultural diversity.
B. Promotion of the use of non-English languages in public schools.
C. Maintenance of ethnic identity and cultural integrity.
D. Rapid assimilation into an English-speaking society.

3.10 The National Defense Education Act of 1958 sponsored all of the following *except*
A. Research and innovation in social studies.
B. Research and innovation in modern foreign languages.
C. Research and innovation in mathematics.
D. Research and innovation in science.

Answers are available on the FlexChoice website at www.ablongman.com/parkayflex.

Mary is correct when she says we cannot return to the past, to the "good old days." On the other hand, Karen is also correct when she says we should learn from the past. We cannot understand schools today without a look at what they were yesterday. The current system of public and private education in the United States is an ongoing reflection of its philosophical and historical foundations and of the aspirations and values brought to this country by its founders and generations of settlers. Developing an appreciation for the ideas and events that have shaped education in the United States is an important part of your education as a professional.

Still, you may wonder, what is the value of knowing about the philosophy and history of U.S. education? Will that knowledge help you to be a better teacher? First, knowledge of the ideas and events that have influenced our schools will help you evaluate more effectively current proposals for change. You will be in a better position to evaluate changes if you understand how schools have developed and how current proposals might relate to previous change efforts. Second, awareness of ideas and events that have influenced teaching is a hallmark of professionalism in education.

The first half of this chapter presents several basic philosophical concepts that will help you answer five important questions that teachers must consider as they develop an educational philosophy:

- What should the purposes of education be?
- What is the nature of knowledge?
- What values should students adopt?
- What knowledge is of most worth?
- How should learning be evaluated?

The second half presents brief overviews of six periods of education in the United States. For each period, we discuss the philosophical concepts, social forces, events, and persons that, in our judgment, have had the greatest impact on education in our country.

What Determines Your Educational Philosophy?

In simplest terms, **educational philosophy** consists of what you believe about education—the set of principles that guides your professional action. Every teacher, whether he or she recognizes it, has a philosophy of education—a set of beliefs about how human beings learn and grow and what one should learn in order to live the good life. Teachers differ, of course, in regard to the amount of effort they devote to the development of their personal philosophy or educational platform. Some feel that philosophical reflections have nothing to contribute to the actual act of teaching. (This stance, of course, is itself a philosophy of education.) Other teachers recognize that teaching, because it is concerned with *what ought to be,* is basically a philosophical enterprise.

Your behavior as a teacher is strongly connected to your personal beliefs and your beliefs about teaching and learning, students, knowledge, and what is worth knowing (see Figure 3.1). Regardless of where you stand in regard to these five dimensions of teaching, you should be aware of the need to reflect continually on *what* you believe and *why* you believe it.

Figure 3.1

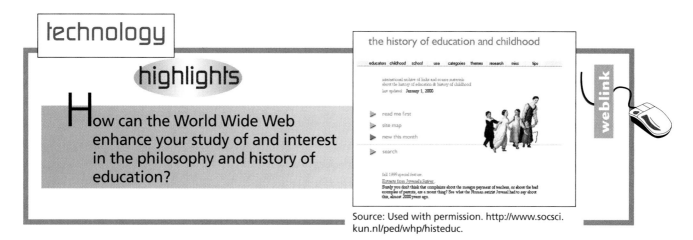

Source: Used with permission. http://www.socsci. kun.nl/ped/whp/histeduc.

Beliefs about Teaching and Learning

One of the most important components of your educational philosophy is how you view teaching and learning. In other words, what is the teacher's primary role? Is the teacher a subject matter expert who can efficiently and effectively impart knowledge to students? Is the teacher a helpful adult who establishes caring relationships with students and nurtures their growth in needed areas? Or is the teacher a skilled technician who can manage the learning of many students at once?

Some teachers emphasize the individual student's experiences and cognitions. Others stress the student's behavior. Learning, according to the first viewpoint, is seen as the changes in thoughts or actions that result from personal experience; that is, learning is largely the result of internal forces within the individual. In contrast, the other view defines learning as the associations between various stimuli and responses. Here, learning results from forces that are external to the individual.

Weblink 3.1

Beliefs about Students

Your beliefs about students will have a great influence on how you teach. Every teacher formulates an image in his or her mind of what students are like—their dispositions, skills, motivation levels, and expectations. What you believe students are like is based on your unique life experiences, particularly your observations of young people and your knowledge of human growth and development.

Negative views of students may promote teacher–student relationships based on fear and coercion rather than on trust and helpfulness. Extremely positive views may risk not providing students with sufficient structure and direction and not communicating sufficiently high expectations. In the final analysis, the truly professional teacher—the one who has a carefully thought-out educational philosophy—recognizes that, although children differ in their predispositions to learn and grow, they all *can* learn.

Beliefs about Knowledge

How a teacher views knowledge is directly related to how he or she goes about teaching. If teachers view knowledge as the sum total of small bits of subject matter or discrete facts, their students will most likely spend a great deal of time learning that information in a straightforward, rote manner.

Other teachers view knowledge more conceptually, that is, as consisting of the big ideas that enable us to understand and influence our environment. Such teachers would want students to be able to explain how legislative decisions are made in the state capital, how an understanding of the eight parts of speech can empower the writer and vitalize one's writing, and how chemical elements are grouped according to their atomic numbers.

Finally, teachers differ in their beliefs as to whether students' increased understanding of their own experiences is a legitimate form of knowledge. Knowledge of self and one's experiences in the world is not the same as knowledge about a particular subject, yet personal knowledge is essential for a full, satisfying life.

Beliefs about What Is Worth Knowing

As we saw in this chapter's opening scenario, teachers have different ideas about what should be taught. Hal believes it is most important that students learn the basic skills of reading, writing, and computation. These are the skills they will need to be successful in their chosen occupations, and it is the school's responsibility to prepare students for the world of work. Karen believes that the most worthwhile content is to be found in the classics or the Great Books. Through mastering the great ideas from the sciences, mathematics, literature, and history, students will be well prepared to deal with the world of the future. Mary is most concerned with students learning how to reason, communicate effectively, and solve problems. Students who master these cognitive processes will have learned how to learn—and this is the most realistic preparation for an unknown future. Last, Juan is concerned with developing the whole child and teaching students to become self-actualizing. Thus, the curriculum should be meaningful and contribute to the student's efforts to become a mature, well-integrated person.

What Are the Branches of Philosophy?

To provide you with further tools to formulate and clarify your educational philosophy, this section presents brief overviews of six areas of philosophy that are of central concern to teachers: metaphysics, epistemology, axiology, ethics, aesthetics, and logic. Each area focuses on one of the questions that have concerned the world's greatest philosophers for centuries: What is the nature of reality? What is the nature of knowledge and is truth ever attainable? According to what values should one live? What is good and what is evil? What is the nature of beauty and excellence? What processes of reasoning will yield consistently valid results?

Metaphysics

Metaphysics is concerned with explaining, as rationally and as comprehensively as possible, the nature of reality (in contrast to how reality *appears*). What is reality? What is the world made of? These are metaphysical questions. Metaphysics also is concerned with the nature of being and explores questions such as, What does it mean to exist? What is humankind's place in the scheme of things? Metaphysical questions such as these are at the very heart of educational philosophy. As two educational philosophers put it: "Our ultimate preoccupation in educational theory is with the most primary of all philosophic problems: metaphysics, the study of ultimate reality" (Morris and Pai 1994, 28).

Metaphysics has important implications for education because the school curriculum is based on what we know about reality. And what we know about reality is driven by the kinds of questions we ask about the world. In fact, any position regarding what schools should teach has behind it a particular view of reality, a particular set of responses to metaphysical questions.

Epistemology

The next major set of philosophical questions that concerns teachers is called **epistemology.** These questions focus on knowledge: What knowledge is true? How does knowing take place? How do we know that we know? How do we decide between opposing views of knowledge? Is truth constant, or does it change from situation to situation? What knowledge is of most worth?

How you answer the epistemological questions that confront all teachers will have significant implications for your teaching. First, you will need to determine what is true about the content you will teach; then you must decide on the most appropriate means of conveying this content to students. Even a casual consideration of epistemological questions reveals that there are many ways of knowing about the world, at least five of which are of interest to teachers:

1. *Knowing Based on Authority*—for example, knowledge from the sage, the poet, the expert, the ruler, the textbook, or the teacher.
2. *Knowing Based on Divine Revelation*—for example, knowledge in the form of supernatural revelations from the sun god of early peoples, the many gods of the ancient Greeks, or the Judeo-Christian god.
3. *Knowing Based on Empiricism (Experience)*—for example, knowledge acquired through the senses, the informally gathered empirical data that direct most of our daily behavior.
4. *Knowing Based on Reason and Logical Analysis*—for example, knowledge inferred from the process of thinking logically.
5. *Knowing Based on Intuition*—for example, knowledge arrived at without the use of rational thought.

Axiology

The next set of philosophical problems concerns values. Teachers are concerned with values because "school is not a neutral activity. The very idea of schooling expresses a set of values. [We] educate and we are educated for some purpose we consider good. We teach what we think is a valuable set of ideas. How else could we construct education? (Nelson, Carlson, and Palonsky 2000, 304).

Among the axiological questions teachers must answer for themselves are: What values should teachers encourage students to adopt? What values raise humanity to our highest expressions of humaneness? What values does a truly educated person hold?

Axiology highlights the fact that the teacher has an interest not only in the *quantity* of knowledge that students acquire but also in the *quality* of life that becomes possible because of that knowledge. Extensive knowledge may not benefit the individual if he or she is unable to put that knowledge to good use. This point raises additional questions: How do we define quality of life? What curricular experiences contribute most to that quality of life? All teachers must deal with the issues raised by these questions.

Ethics   While axiology addresses the question "What is valuable?", **ethics** focuses on "What is good and evil, right and wrong, just and unjust?"

A knowledge of ethics can help the teacher solve many of the dilemmas that arise in the classroom. Frequently, teachers must take action in situations where they are unable to gather all of the relevant facts and where no single course of action is totally right or wrong. For example, a student whose previous work was above average plagiarizes a term paper: Should the teacher fail the student for the course if the example of swift, decisive punishment will likely prevent other students from plagiarizing? Or should the teacher, following her hunches about what would be in the student's long-term interest, have the student redo the term paper and risk the possibility that other students might get the mistaken notion that plagiarism has no negative consequences? Another ethical dilemma: Is an elementary mathematics teacher justified in trying to increase achievement for the whole class by separating two disruptive girls and placing one in a mathematics group beneath her level of ability?

Aesthetics   The branch of axiology known as **aesthetics** is concerned with values related to beauty and art. Although we expect that teachers of music, art, drama, literature, and writing regularly have students make judgments about the quality of works of art, we can easily overlook the role that aesthetics ought to play in *all* areas of the curriculum.

Aesthetics can also help the teacher increase his or her effectiveness. Teaching, because it may be viewed as a form of artistic expression, can be judged according to artistic standards of beauty and quality. In this regard, the teacher is an artist whose medium of expression is the spontaneous, unrehearsed, and creative encounter between teacher and student.

What might this teacher want her students to learn about aesthetics? How were aesthetic values reflected in the K–12 curricula you experienced?

Logic   **Logic** is the area of philosophy that deals with the process of reasoning and identifies rules that will enable the thinker to reach valid conclusions. The two kinds of logical thinking processes that teachers most frequently have students master are *deductive* and *inductive* thinking. The deductive approach requires the thinker to move from a general principle or proposition to a specific conclusion that is valid. By contrast, inductive reasoning moves from the specific to the general. Here, the student begins by examining particular examples that eventually lead to the acceptance of a general proposition. Inductive teaching is often referred to as discovery teaching—by which students discover, or create, their own knowledge of a topic.

Perhaps the best-known teacher to use the inductive approach to teaching was the Greek philosopher Socrates (ca. 470–399 B.C.). His method of teaching, known today as the Socratic method, consisted of holding philosophical conversations (dialectics) with his pupils. The legacy of Socrates lives in all teachers who use his questioning strategies to encourage students to think for themselves. Figure 3.2 presents guidelines for using **Socratic questioning** techniques in the classroom.

Socrates
(ca. 470–399 B.C.)

Figure 3.2

What Are Five Modern Philosophical Orientations to Teaching?

Five major philosophical orientations to teaching have been developed in response to the branches of philosophy we have just examined. These orientations, or schools of thought, are perennialism, essentialism, progressivism, existentialism, and social reconstructionism. The following sections present a brief description of each of these orientations, moving from those that are teacher-centered to those that are student-centered (see Figure 3.3).

Figure 3.3

Perennialism

Perennialism, as the term implies, views truth as constant, or perennial. The aim of education, according to perennialist thinking, is to ensure that students acquire knowledge of unchanging principles or great ideas. Like Karen, whom you met briefly in this chapter's opening scenario, perennialists believe that the great ideas continue to have the most potential for solving the problems of any era.

The curriculum, according to perennialists, should stress students' intellectual growth in the arts and sciences. To become "culturally literate," students should encounter in these areas the best, most significant works that humans have created. Thus, a high school English teacher would require students to read Melville's *Moby Dick* or any of Shakespeare's plays rather than a novel on the current best-seller list. Similarly, science students would learn about the three laws of motion or the three laws of thermodynamics rather than build a model of the space shuttle.

Perennialist Educational Philosophers   Two of the best known advocates of the perennialist philosophy have been Robert Maynard Hutchins (1899–1977) and, more recently, Mortimer Adler. As president of the University of Chicago from 1929 to 1945, Hutchins (1963) developed an undergraduate curriculum based on the study of the Great Books and discussions of these classics in small seminars. Noted educational philosopher Mortimer Adler, along with Hutchins, was instrumental in organizing the Great Books of the Western World curriculum. Through focusing study on over 100 enduring classics, from Plato to Einstein, the Great Books approach aims at the major

Robert Maynard
Hutchins (1899–1977)

perennialist goal of teaching students to become independent and critical thinkers. It is a demanding curriculum, and it focuses on the enduring disciplines of knowledge rather than on current events or student interests.

Essentialism

William C. Bagley
(1874–1946)

Essentialism, which has some similarities to perennialism, is a conservative philosophy of education originally formulated as a criticism of progressive trends in schools by William C. Bagley (1874–1946), a professor of education at Teachers College, Columbia University. Essentialists, like Hal whom you met in this chapter's opening scenario, believe that human culture has a core of common knowledge that schools are obligated to transmit to students in a systematic, disciplined way. Unlike perennialists, who emphasize a set of external truths, essentialists stress what they believe to be the essential knowledge and skills (often termed "the basics") that productive members of our society need to know.

According to essentialist philosophy, schooling should be practical and provide children with sound instruction that prepares them to live life; schools should not try to influence or set social policies. Critics of essentialism, however, charge that such a tradition-bound orientation to schooling will indoctrinate students and rule out the possibility of change. Essentialists respond that, without an essentialist approach, students will be indoctrinated in humanistic and/or behavioral curricula that run counter to society's accepted standards and need for order.

How might you explain what is happening in this classroom from the perspective of progressivism? From the perspective of perennialism? From the perspective of essentialism?

Progressivism

Progressivism is based on the belief that education should be child-centered rather than focused on the teacher or the content area. The writing of John Dewey (1859–1952) in the 1920s and 1930s contributed a great deal to the spread of progressive ideas. Briefly, Deweyan progressivism is based on three central assumptions:

1. The content of the curriculum ought to be derived from students' interests rather than from the academic disciplines.
2. Effective teaching takes into account the whole child and his or her interests and needs in relation to cognitive, affective, and psychomotor areas.
3. Learning is essentially active rather than passive.

Progressive Strategies   The progressive philosophy also contends that knowledge that is true in the present may not be true in the future. Hence, the best way to prepare students for an unknown future is to equip them with problem-solving strategies that will enable them to discover meaningful knowledge at various stages of their lives.

Educators with a progressive orientation give students a considerable amount of freedom in determining their school experiences. Contrary to the perceptions of many, though, progressive education does not mean that teachers do not provide structure or that students are free to do whatever they wish. Progressive teachers begin where students are and, through the daily give-and-take of the classroom, lead students to see that the subject to be learned can enhance their lives.

In a progressively oriented classroom, the teacher serves as a guide or resource person whose primary responsibility is to facilitate student learning. The teacher helps students learn what is important to them rather than passing on a set of so-called enduring truths. Students have many opportunities to work cooperatively in groups, often solving problems that the group, not the teacher, has identified as important.

John Dewey
(1859–1952)

Existentialism

Existential philosophy is unique in that it focuses on the experiences of the individual. Other philosophies are concerned with developing systems of thought for identifying and understanding what is common to *all* reality, human existence, and values. Existentialism, on the other hand, offers the individual a way of thinking about *my* life, what has meaning for *me*, what is true for *me*. In general, existentialism emphasizes creative choice, the subjectivity of human experiences, and concrete acts of human existence over any rational scheme for human nature or reality.

The writings of Jean-Paul Sartre (1905–1980), well-known French philosopher, novelist, and playwright, have been most responsible for the widespread dissemination of existential ideas. According to Sartre (1972), every individual first exists and then he or she must decide what that existence is to mean. The task of assigning meaning to that existence is the individual's alone; no preformulated philosophical belief system can tell one who one is. It is up to each of us to decide who we are.

Life, according to existential thought, has no meaning, and the universe is indifferent to the situation humankind finds itself in. Moreover, "existententialists [believe] that too many people wrongly emphasize the optimistic, the good, and the beautiful —all of which create a false impression of existence" (Ozmon and Craver 1999, 253). With the freedom that we have, however, each of us must commit him- or herself to assign meaning to his or her *own* life. As Maxine Greene, an eminent philosopher of education whose work is based on existentialism, states: "We have to know about our lives, clarify our situations if we are to understand the world from our shared standpoints . . ." (1995, 21). The human enterprise that can be most helpful in promoting this personal quest for meaning is the educative process. Teachers, therefore, must allow students freedom of choice and provide them with experiences that will help them find the meaning of their lives. This approach, contrary to the belief of many, does not mean that students may do whatever they please; logic indicates that freedom has rules, and respect for the freedom of others is essential.

Existentialists judge the curriculum according to whether or not it contributes to the individual's quest for meaning and results in a level of personal awareness that Greene (1995) terms "wide-awakeness." The ideal curriculum is one that provides students with extensive individual freedom and requires them to ask their own questions, conduct their own inquiries, and draw their own conclusions.

AUDIO
Audio Clip 3.2

Jean-Paul Sartre
(1905–1980)

Maxine Green
(b. 1917)

Social Reconstructionism

As the name implies, **social reconstructionism** holds that schools should take the lead in changing or reconstructing society. Theodore Brameld (1904–1987), acknowledged

What Are Five Modern Philosophical Orientations to Teaching? **69** as the founder of social reconstructionism, based his philosophy on two fundamental premises about the post-World War II era: (1) We live in a period of great crisis, most evident in the fact that humans now have the capability of destroying civilization overnight, and (2) humankind also has the intellectual, technological, and moral potential to create a world civilization of "abundance, health, and humane capacity" (Brameld 1959, 19). In this time of great need, then, social reconstructionists like Juan, whom we met in this chapter's opening scenario, believe that schools should become the primary agent for planning and directing social change. Schools should not only *transmit* knowledge about the existing social order; they should seek to *reconstruct* it as well.

Social Reconstructionism and Progressivism   Social reconstructionism has clear ties to progressive educational philosophy. Both provide opportunities for extensive interactions between teacher and students and among students themselves. Furthermore, both place a premium on bringing the community, if not the entire world, into the classroom. Student experiences often include field trips, community-based projects of various sorts, and opportunities to interact with people beyond the four walls of the classroom.

According to Brameld and social reconstructionists such as George Counts, who wrote *Dare the School Build a New Social Order?* (1932), the educative process should provide students with methods for dealing with the significant crises that confront the world: war, economic depression, international terrorism, hunger, inflation, and ever-accelerating technological advances. The logical outcome of such education would be the eventual realization of a world-wide democracy (Brameld 1956). Unless we actively seek to create this kind of world through the intelligent application of present knowledge, we run the risk that the destructive forces of the world will determine the conditions under which humans will live in the future.

George Counts
(1889–1974)

What Psychological Orientations Have Influenced Teaching Philosophies?

In addition to the five philosophical orientations to teaching described in previous sections of this chapter, several schools of psychological thought have formed the basis for teaching philosophies. These psychological theories are comprehensive world views that serve as the basis for the way many teachers approach teaching practice. Psychological orientations to teaching are concerned primarily with understanding the conditions that are associated with effective learning. In other words, what motivates students to learn? What environments are most conducive to learning? Chief among the psychological orientations that have influenced teaching philosophies are humanistic psychology, behaviorism, and constructivism.

Humanistic Psychology

Humanistic psychology emphasizes personal freedom, choice, awareness, and personal responsibility. As the term implies, it also focuses on the achievements, motivation, feelings, actions, and needs of human beings. The goal of education, according to this orientation, is individual self-actualization.

Humanistic psychology is derived from the philosophy of **humanism,** which developed during the European Renaissance and Protestant Reformation and is based on the belief that individuals control their own destinies through the application of their intelligence and learning. People "make themselves." The term "secular humanism" refers to the closely related belief that the conditions of human existence relate to human nature and human actions rather than to predestination or divine intervention.

In the 1950s and 1960s, humanistic psychology became the basis of educational reforms that sought to enhance students' achievement of their full potential through self-actualization (Maslow 1954, 1962; Rogers 1961). According to this psychological orientation, teachers should not force students to learn; instead, they should create a climate of trust and respect that allows students to decide what and how they learn, to question authority, and to take initiative in "making themselves." Teachers should be what noted psychologist Carl Rogers calls "facilitators," and the classroom should be a place "in which curiosity and the natural desire to learn can be nourished and enhanced" (1982, 31). Through their nonjudgmental understanding of students, humanistic teachers encourage students to learn and grow.

Behaviorism

Behaviorism is based on the principle that desirable human behavior can be the product of design rather than accident. According to behaviorists, it is an illusion to say that humans have a free will. Although we may act as if we are free, our behavior is really *determined* by forces in the environment that shape our behavior. "We are what we are and we do what we do, not because of any mysterious power of human volition, but because outside forces over which we lack any semblance of control have us caught in an inflexible web. Whatever else we may be, we are not the captains of our fate or the masters of our soul" (Power 1982, 168).

Founders of Behavioristic Psychology   John B. Watson (1878–1958) was the principal originator of behavioristic psychology and B. F. Skinner (1904–1990) its best-known promoter. Watson first claimed that human behavior consisted of specific stimuli that resulted in certain responses. In part, he based this new conception of learning on the classic experiment conducted by Russian psychologist Ivan Pavlov (1849–1936). Pavlov had noticed that a dog he was working with would salivate when it was about to be given food. By introducing the sound of a bell when food was offered and repeating this several times, Pavlov discovered that the sound of the bell alone (a conditioned stimulus) would make the dog salivate (a conditioned response). Watson came to believe that all learning conformed to this basic stimulus-response model (now termed classical or type S conditioning).

B. F. Skinner
(1904–1990)

Skinner went beyond Watson's basic stimulus-response model and developed a more comprehensive view of conditioning known as operant (or type R) conditioning. Operant conditioning is based on the idea that satisfying responses are conditioned, unsatisfying ones are not. In other words, "The things we call pleasant have an energizing or strengthening effect on our behaviour" (Skinner 1972, 74). Thus the teacher can create learners who exhibit desired behaviors by following four steps:

1. Identify desired behaviors in concrete (observable and measurable) terms.
2. Establish a procedure for recording specific behaviors and counting their frequencies.
3. For each behavior, identify an appropriate reinforcer.
4. Ensure that students receive the reinforcer as soon as possible after displaying a desired behavior.

Constructivism

In contrast to behaviorism, constructivism focuses on processes of learning rather than on learning behavior. According to **constructivism,** students use cognitive processes to *construct* understanding of the material to be learned—in contrast to the view that they *receive* information transmitted by the teacher. Constructivist approaches support student-centered rather than teacher-centered curriculum and instruction. The student is the key to learning.

Unlike behaviorists who concentrate on directly observable behavior, constructivists focus on the mental processes and strategies that students use to learn. Our understanding of learning has been extended as a result of advances in **cognitive science**—the study of the mental processes students use in thinking and remembering. By drawing from research in linguistics, psychology, anthropology, neurophysiology, and computer science, cognitive scientists are developing new models for how people think and learn.

Teachers who base classroom activities on constructivism know that learning is an active, meaning-making process, that learners are not passive recipients of information. In fact, students are continually involved in making sense out of activities around them. Thus the teacher must *understand students' understanding* and realize that students' learning is influenced by prior knowledge, experience, attitudes, and social interactions.

How Can You Develop Your Educational Philosophy?

As you read the preceding brief descriptions of five educational philosophies and three psychological orientations to teaching, perhaps you felt that no single philosophy fit perfectly with your image of the kind of teacher you want to become. Or, there may have been some element of each approach that seemed compatible with your own emerging philosophy of education. In either case, don't feel that you need to identify a single educational philosophy around which you will build your teaching career. In reality, few teachers follow only one educational philosophy, and, as Figure 3.4 shows, educational philosophy is only one determinant of the professional goals a teacher sets.

Figure 3.4

Weblink 3.2

Most teachers develop an *eclectic* philosophy of education, which means they develop their own unique blending of two or more philosophies. To help you identify the philosophies most consistent with your beliefs and values about educational goals, curriculum, and teachers' and students' roles in learning, complete the Philosophic Inventory found on this book's website. The self-knowledge you glean from completing the inventory and the philosophical constructs presented in the first half of this chapter provide a useful framework for studying the six periods in the historical development of schools that follow. For example, you will be able to see how philosophical orientations to education waxed and waned during each period—whether it was the perennialism and essentialism that characterized colonial schools, the progressivism of the 1920s and 1930s, the essentialism of the 1950s and 1980s, the humanism and social reconstructionism of the 1960s, or the constructivism of the 1990s.

What Were Teaching and Schools Like in the American Colonies (1620–1750)?

Education in colonial America had its primary roots in English culture. The settlers of our country initially tried to develop a system of schooling that paralleled the British

These children are active learners in a real or relevant context, and they are constructing their own meanings through direct experience. How might this lesson be seen as an eclectic blend of progressive, existential, and constructivist ideals?

two-track system. If students from the lower classes attended school at all it was at the elementary level for the purpose of studying an essentialist curriculum of reading, writing, and computation and receiving religious instruction. Students from the upper classes had the opportunity to attend Latin grammar schools, where they were given a college-preparatory education that focused on perennialist subjects such as Latin and Greek classics.

Above all, the colonial curriculum stressed religious objectives. Generally, no distinction was made between secular and religious life in the colonies. The religious motives that impelled the Puritans to endure the hardships of settling in a new land were reflected in the schools' curricula. The primary objective of elementary schooling was to learn to read so that one might read the Bible and religious catechisms and thereby receive salvation.

Colonial Schools

In the New England colonies (Massachusetts Bay, New Hampshire, and Connecticut), there was a general consensus that church, state, and schools were interrelated. As a result, town schools were created throughout these colonies to teach children the basics of reading and writing so they could learn the scriptures. The Puritan view of the child included the belief that people are inherently sinful. Even natural childhood play was seen as devil-inspired idleness. The path to redemption lay in learning to curb one's natural instincts and behave like an adult as quickly as possible.

The middle colonies (New York, New Jersey, Pennsylvania, and Delaware) were more diverse, and groups such as the Irish, Scots, Swedes, Danes, Dutch, and Germans established **parochial schools** based on their religious beliefs. Anglicans, Lutherans, Quakers, Jews, Catholics, Presbyterians, and Mennonites in the Middle Colonies tended to establish their own schools. In the largely Protestant southern colonies (Virginia, Maryland, Georgia, and North and South Carolina), wealthy plantation owners believed the primary purpose of education was to promote religion and to prepare their children to attend colleges and universities in Europe. The vast majority of small farmers received no formal schooling and the children of African slaves received only the training they needed to serve their masters.

No one type of schooling was common to all the colonies. The most common types, however, were the dame schools, the reading and writing schools, and the Latin grammar schools. **Dame schools** provided initial instruction for boys and, often, the only schooling for girls. These schools were run by widows or housewives in their homes and supported by modest fees from parents. Classes were usually held in the kitchen, where children learned only the barest essentials of reading, writing, and arithmetic during instruction lasting for a few weeks to one year. Females might also be taught sewing and basic homemaking skills. Students often began by learning the alphabet from a **horn book.** Developed in medieval Europe, the horn book was a copy of the alphabet covered by a thin transparent sheet made from a cow's horn. The alphabet and the horn covering were attached to a paddle-shaped piece of wood.

Reading and writing schools offered boys an education that went beyond what their parents could teach them at home or what they could learn at a dame school. Reading lessons were based on the Bible, various religious catechisms, and the *New England Primer,* first printed in 1690. The **Primer** introduced children to the letters of the alphabet through the use of illustrative woodcuts and rhymed couplets. The first couplet began with the pronouncement that

> In Adam's fall
> We sinned all.

And the final one noted that

> Zaccheus he
> Did climb the Tree
> His Lord to see.

The *Primer* also presented children with large doses of stern religious warnings about the proper conduct of life.

The **Latin grammar school,** comparable to today's secondary school, was patterned after the classical schools of Europe. Boys enrolled in the Latin grammar schools at

What do these two pages from a 1727 edition of *The New England Primer* suggest about the curriculum and aims of education in early schools in the United States?

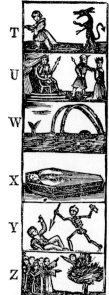

the age of seven or eight, whereupon they began to prepare to enter Harvard College (established in 1636). Following graduation from Harvard, they would assume leadership roles in the church.

The Origins of Mandated Education

Universal compulsory education had its origins in the **Massachusetts Act of 1642.** Prior to this date, parents could decide whether they wished their children to be educated at home or at a school. Church and civic leaders in the colonies, however, decided that education could no longer remain voluntary. They saw that many children were receiving inadequate training. Moreover, they realized that organized schools would serve to strengthen and preserve Puritan religious beliefs.

The Puritans decided to make education a civil responsibility of the state. The Massachusetts General Court passed a law in 1642 that required each town to determine whether young people could read and write. Parents and apprentices' masters whose children were unable "to read and understand the principles of religion and the capital laws of the country" (Rippa 1997, 36) could be fined and, possibly, lose custody of their children.

Although the Act of 1642 did not mandate the establishment of schools, it did make it clear that the education of children was a direct concern of the local citizenry. In 1648, the Court revised the 1642 law, reminding town leaders that "the good education of children is of singular behoof and benefit to any commonwealth" and that some parents and masters were still "too indulgent and negligent of their duty" (Cohen 1974, 394–95). As the first educational law in this country, the Massachusetts Act of 1642 was a landmark.

The **Massachusetts Act of 1647,** often referred to as the Old Deluder Satan Act (because education was seen as the best protection against the wiles of the devil), mandated the establishment and support of schools. In particular, towns of fifty households or more were to appoint a person to instruct "all such children as shall resort to him to write and read." Teachers were to "be paid either by the parents or masters of such children, or by the inhabitants in general" (Rippa 1997, 36).

Education for African Americans and Native Americans

At the close of the American Revolution, nearly all of the half million African Americans were slaves who could neither read nor write (Button and Provenzo 1989). In most cases, those who were literate had been taught by their masters or through small, church-affiliated programs. Literate Native Americans and Mexican Americans usually had received their training at the hands of missionaries. One of the first schools for African Americans was started by Elias Neau in New York City in 1704. Sponsored by the Church of England, Neau's school taught African and Native Americans how to read as part of the Church's efforts to convert students.

Other schools for African and Native Americans were started by the Quakers, who regarded slavery as a moral evil. Though Quaker schools for African Americans existed as early as 1700, one of the best known was founded in Philadelphia in 1770 by Anthony Benezet, who believed that African Americans were ". . . generously sensible, humane, and sociable, and that their capacity is as good, and as capable of improvement as that of white people" (Button and Provenzo 1989, 45). Schools modeled on the Philadelphia African School opened elsewhere in the Northeast, and "Indian schools" also were founded as philanthropic enterprises.

From the seventeenth to the late-twentieth centuries, schools were segregated by race. The first recorded official ground for school segregation dates back to a decision of the Massachusetts Supreme Court in 1850. When the Roberts family sought to send their daughter Sarah to a white school in Boston, the court ruled that "equal, but separate" schools were being provided and that the Roberts therefore could not claim an injustice (*Roberts v. City of Boston* 1850). From the beginning, however, schools were not equal, and students did not have equal educational opportunity.

What Were the Goals of Education during the Revolutionary Period (1750–1820)?

Education in the United States during the Revolutionary period was characterized by a general waning of European influences on schools. Though religious traditions that had their origins in Europe continued to affect the curriculum, the young country's need to develop agriculture, shipping, and commerce also exerted its influence on the curriculum. By this time, the original settlers who had emigrated from Europe had been replaced by a new generation whose most immediate roots were in the new soil of the United States. This new, exclusively American, identity was also enhanced by the rise of civil town governments, the great increase in books and newspapers that addressed life in the new country, and a turning away from Europe toward the unsettled west. The colonies' break with Europe was most potently demonstrated in the American Revolution of 1776.

Following independence, many leaders were concerned that new disturbances from within could threaten the well-being of the new nation. To preserve the freedoms that had been fought for, a system of education became essential. Through education, people would become intelligent, participating citizens of a constitutional democracy. Among these leaders were Benjamin Franklin, Sarah Pierce, Thomas Jefferson, and Noah Webster.

Benjamin Franklin's Academy

Benjamin Franklin
(1706–1790)

Benjamin Franklin (1706–1790) designed and promoted the Philadelphia Academy, a private secondary school, which opened in 1751. This school, which replaced the old Latin grammar school, had a curriculum that was broader and more practical and also focused on the English language rather than Latin. The academy was also a more democratically run institution than previous schools had been. Though **academies** were largely privately controlled and privately financed, they were secular and often supported by public funds. Most academies were public in that anyone who could pay tuition could attend, regardless of church affiliation (Rippa 1997, 65).

In his *Proposals Relating to the Education of Youth in Pennsylvania,* written in 1749, Franklin noted that "the good Education of youth has been esteemed by wise men in all ages, as the surest foundation of the happiness both of private families and of commonwealths" (Franklin 1931, 151).

Franklin's proposals for educating youth called for a wide range of subjects that reflected perennialist and essentialist philosophical orientations: English grammar, composition, and literature; classical and modern foreign languages; science; writing and drawing; rhetoric and oratory; geography; various kinds of history; agriculture and gardening; arithmetic and accounting; and mechanics.

Sarah Pierce's Female Academy

English **academies,** often called people's colleges, multiplied across the country, reaching a peak of 6,185 in 1855, with an enrollment of 263,096 (Spring 1997, 22). Usually, these academies served male students only; a notable exception was Sarah Pierce's Litchfield Female Academy in Litchfield, Connecticut. Pierce (1767–1852) began her academy in the dining room of her home with two students; eventually, the academy grew to 140 female students from nearly every state and from Canada (Button and Provenzo 1989, 87).

For the most part, however, girls received little formal education in the seventeenth and eighteenth centuries and were educated for entirely different purposes than were boys. As the following mission statement for Pierce's Academy suggests, an essentialist, rather than perennialist, curriculum was appropriate for girls:

> Our object has been, not to make learned ladies, or skillful metaphysical reasoners, or deep read scholars in physical science: there is a more useful, tho' less exalted and less brilliant station that woman must occupy, there are duties of incalculable importance that she must perform: that station is home; these duties, are the alleviation of the trials of her parents; the soothing of the labours & fatigues of her partner; & the education for time and eternity of the next generation of immortal beings . . . (Button and Provenzo 1989, 88).

Some women enrolled in **female seminaries,** first established in the early nineteenth century to train women for higher education and public service outside of the home. Educational opportunities for women expanded in conjunction with social reform movements that gradually led to greater political equality for women, including the right to vote in the twentieth century. For example, Troy Seminary, founded in 1821 by educator and poet Emma Willard (1787–1870), became one of the first women's colleges in the country.

Emma Willard
(1787–1870)

Thomas Jefferson's Philosophy

Thomas Jefferson (1743–1826), author of the Declaration of Independence, viewed the education of common people as the most effective means of preserving liberty. As historian S. Alexander Rippa put it, "Few statesmen in American history have so vigorously strived for an ideal; perhaps none has so consistently viewed public education as the indispensable cornerstone of freedom" (1997, 55).

For a society to remain free, Jefferson felt, it must support a continuous system of public education. He proposed to the Virginia legislature in 1779 his Bill for the More General Diffusion of Knowledge. This plan called for state-controlled elementary schools that would teach, with no cost to parents, three years of reading, writing, and arithmetic to all white children. In addition, twenty state grammar schools would be created in which selected poor students would be taught free for a maximum period of six years.

Jefferson was unsuccessful in his attempt to convince the Virginia House of Burgesses of the need for a uniform system of public schools as outlined in his bill. Jefferson

Thomas Jefferson
(1743–1826)

was, however, able to implement many of his educational ideas through his efforts to found the University of Virginia. He devoted the last years of his life to developing the university, and he lived to see the university open with forty students in March 1824, one month before his eighty-first birthday.

Noah Webster's Speller

In the years following the Revolution, several textbooks were printed in the United States. Writers and publishers saw the textbook as an appropriate vehicle for promoting democratic ideals and cultural independence from England. Toward this end, U.S. textbooks were filled with patriotic and moralistic maxims. Among the most widely circulated books of this type were Noah Webster's *Elementary Spelling Book* and *The American Dictionary*.

Webster (1758–1843) first introduced his speller in 1783 under the cumbersome title, *A Grammatical Institute of the English Language*. Later versions were titled the *American Spelling Book* and the *Elementary Spelling Book*. Webster's speller earned the nickname "the old blue-back" because early copies of the book were covered in light blue paper and later editions covered with bright blue paper.

In the introduction to his speller, Webster declared that its purpose was to help teachers instill in students "the first rudiments of the language, some just ideas of religion, morals and domestic economy" (Button and Provenzo 1989, 65). Throughout, the little book emphasized patriotic and moralistic virtues. Short, easy-to-remember maxims taught pupils to be content with their lot in life, to work hard, and to respect the property of others.

Noah Webster
(1758–1843)

How Was the Struggle Won for State-Supported Common Schools (1820–1865)?

The first state-supported high school in the United States was the Boston English Classical School, established in 1821. The opening of this school, renamed English High School in 1824, marked the beginning of a long, slow struggle for state-supported **common schools** in this country. Those in favor of free common schools tended to be city residents and nontaxpayers, democratic leaders, philanthropists and humanitarians, members of various school societies, and working people. Those opposed were rural residents and taxpayers, members of old aristocratic and conservative groups, owners of private schools, members of conservative religious sects, Southerners, and non-English-speaking residents. By far the most eloquent and effective spokesperson for the common school was Horace Mann.

where do you stand?

weblink

Should school attendance beyond the elementary level become voluntary?

Horace Mann's Contributions

Horace Mann (1796–1859) was a lawyer, Massachusetts senator, and the first secretary of a state board of education. He is best known as the champion of the common school movement, which has led to the free, public, locally controlled elementary schools we know today. Mann worked tirelessly to convince people that their interests would be well served by a system of universal free schools for all:

Horace Mann
(1796–1859)

> It [a free school system] knows no distinction of rich and poor, of bond and free, or between those, who, in the imperfect light of this world, are seeking, through different avenues, to reach the gate of heaven. Without money and without price, it throws open its doors, and spreads the table of its bounty, for all the children of the State (Mann 1868, 754).

Improving Schools   In 1837, Mann accepted the position of Secretary of the Massachusetts State Board of Education. At the time, conditions in Massachusetts schools were deplorable, and Mann immediately began to use his new post to improve the quality of schools. Through the twelve annual reports he submitted while secretary and through *The Common School Journal,* which he founded and edited, Mann's educational ideas became widely known in this country and abroad.

In his widely publicized *Fifth Report* (published in 1841), Mann told the moneyed conservative classes that support of common public schools would provide them "the cheapest means of self-protection and insurance." Where could they find, Mann asked, "any police so vigilant and effective, for the protection of all the rights of person, property and character, as such a sound and comprehensive education and training, as our system of Common Schools could be made to impart?" (Rippa 1997, 95).

In his *Seventh Report* (published 1843), Mann extolled the virtues of schools he had visited in Prussia that implemented the humanistic approaches of noted Swiss educator Johann Heinrich Pestalozzi (1746–1827). "I heard no child ridiculed, sneered at, or scolded, for making a mistake," Mann wrote (Rippa 1997, 96).

The Normal School   During the late 1830s, Mann put forth a proposal that today we take for granted. Teachers, he felt, needed more than a high school education to teach; they should be trained in professional programs. The French had established the *école normale* for preparing teachers, and Mann and other influential educators of the period, such as Catherine Beecher (1800–1878), whose sister, Harriet Beecher Stowe (1811–1896), wrote *Uncle Tom's Cabin,* believed that a similar program was needed in the United States. Through her campaign to ensure that women had access to an education equal to that of men and her drive to recruit women into the teaching profession, Beecher contributed significantly to the development of publicly funded schools for training teachers (Holmes and Weiss 1995).

The first public **normal school** in the United States opened in Lexington, Massachusetts, on July 3, 1839. The curriculum consisted of general knowledge courses plus courses in pedagogy (or teaching) and practice teaching in a model school affiliated with the normal school. In 1849, Electa Lincoln Walton (1824–1908), an 1843 graduate of the normal school, became acting head administrator and the first woman to administer a state normal school. Walton was energetic and determined to succeed, as her journal reveals:

> Many people think women can't do much. I'd like to show them that they can keep a Normal School and keep it well too . . . I will succeed . . . I will never be pointed at as an example of the incompetency of woman to conduct a large establishment well" (Holmes and Weiss 1995, 42).

When Mann resigned as secretary in 1848, his imprint on education in the United States was broad and deep. As a result of his unflagging belief that education was the "great equalizer of the conditions of men—the balance wheel of the social machinery" (Mann 1957, 87), Massachusetts had a firmly established system of common schools and led the way for other states to establish free public schools.

Reverend W. H. McGuffey's Readers

Reverend William Holmes McGuffey (1800–1873) had perhaps the greatest impact on what children learned in the new school. Far exceeding Noah Webster's speller in sales were the famous **McGuffey readers.** It has been estimated that 122 million copies of the six-volume series were sold after 1836. The six readers ranged in difficulty from the first-grade level to the sixth grade level. Through such stories as "The Wolf," "Meddlesome Matty," and "A Kind Brother," the readers emphasized virtues such as hard work, honesty, truth, charity, and obedience.

Absent from the McGuffey readers were the dour, pessimistic views of childhood so characteristic of earlier primers. Nevertheless, they had a religious, moral, and ethical influence over millions of American readers. Through their reading of the "Dignity of Labor," "The Village Blacksmith," and "The Rich Man's Son," for example, readers learned that contentment outweighs riches in this world. In addition to providing explicit instructions on right living, the McGuffey readers also taught countless children and adults how to read and study.

Justin Morrill's Land-Grant Schools

The common school movement and the continuing settlement of the West stimulated the development of public higher education. In 1862, the **Morrill Land-Grant Act,** sponsored by Congressman Justin S. Morrill (1810–1898) of Vermont, provided federal land for states either to sell or to rent in order to raise funds for the establishment of colleges of agriculture and mechanical arts. Each state was given a land subsidy of 30,000 acres for each representative and senator in its congressional delegation. Eventually, seven and a half million dollars from the sale of over seventeen million acres was given to land-grant colleges and state universities. The Morrill Act of 1862 set a precedent for the federal government to take an active role in shaping higher education in the United States. A second Morrill Act in 1890 provided even more federal funds for land-grant colleges.

How Did Compulsory Education Change Schools and the Teaching Profession (1865–1920)?

From the end of the Civil War to the end of World War I, publicly supported common schools steadily spread westward and southward from New England and the Middle Atlantic states. Beginning with Massachusetts in 1852, compulsory education laws were passed in thirty-two states by 1900 and in all states by 1930.

Because of compulsory attendance laws, an ever-increasing proportion of children attended school. In 1869–70, only 64.7 percent of five- to seventeen-year-olds attended public school. By 1919–20, this proportion had risen to 78.3 percent; and in 1995–96, it was 91.7 percent (National Center for Education Statistics 1999, 50). The growth in enrollment on the high school level was exceptional. Historical data from the National Center for Education Statistics (1999) enable us to determine that between 1880 and 1920, the population in the United States increased 108 percent, and high school enrollment increased 1,900 percent!

As common schools spread, school systems began to take on organizational features associated with today's schools: centralized control; increasing authority for state, county, and city superintendencies; and a division of labor among teachers and administrators at the individual school site. Influenced by the work of Frederick W. Taylor (1856–1915), an engineer and the founder of **scientific management,** school officials undertook reforms based on management principles and techniques from big business. For example, they believed that top-down management techniques should be applied to schools as well as factories.

Higher Education for African Americans

In *Up from Slavery,* Booker T. Washington (1856–1915) recounts how he walked part of the 500 miles from his home in West Virginia to attend the Hampton Normal and Agricultural Institute of Virginia, one of the country's first institutions of higher education for African Americans. Four years after graduating from Hampton, Washington returned to be the school's first African American instructor.

Washington had a steadfast belief that education could improve the lives of African Americans just as it had for white people: "Poverty and ignorance have affected the black man just as they affect the white man. But the day is breaking, and education will bring the complete light" (Rippa 1997, 122). In 1880, Washington helped to found the Tuskegee Institute, an industrial school for African Americans in rural Alabama. According to Washington, the Institute would play a key role in bringing about racial equality:

> The Tuskegee idea is that correct education begins at the bottom, and expands naturally as the necessities of the people expand. As the race grows in knowledge, experience, culture, taste, and wealth, its wants are bound to become more and more diverse; and to satisfy these wants there will be gradually developed within our ranks—as already has been true of the whites—a constantly increasing variety of professional and business men and women (Button and Provenzo 1989, 274).

Not all African Americans shared Washington's philosophy and goals. William E. Burghardt DuBois (1868–1963), the first African American to be awarded a Ph.D. and one of the founders of the National Association for the Advancement of Colored People (NAACP), challenged Booker T. Washington's views on education. In his book *The Souls of Black Folks,* DuBois criticized educational programs that seemed to imply that African Americans should accept inferior status and develop manual skills. DuBois called for the education of the most "talented tenth" of the African American population to equip them for leadership positions in society as a whole.

The Kindergarten

Early childhood education also spread following the Civil War. Patterned after the progressive, humanistic theories of the German educator Friedrich Froebel

(1782–1852), the **kindergarten,** or "garden where children grow," stressed the motor development and self-activity of children before they began formal schooling at the elementary level. Through play, games, stories, music, and language activities, a foundation beneficial to the child's later educational and social development would be laid. After founding the first kindergarten in 1837, Froebel developed child-centered curriculum materials that were used in kindergartens in the the United States and throughout the world.

Margarethe Schurz (1832–1876), a student of Froebel, opened the first U.S. kindergarten in her home at Watertown, Wisconsin, in 1855. Her small neighborhood class was conducted in German. In 1860, Elizabeth Palmer Peabody (1804–1891), sister-in-law of Horace Mann and the American writer Nathaniel Hawthorne, opened the first private English-speaking kindergarten in this country in Boston. Initially, kindergartens were privately supported, but in St. Louis in 1873, Susan Blow (1843–1916) established what is commonly recognized as the first successful public kindergarten in the United States. She patterned her kindergarten after one she visited while in Germany. So successful was her kindergarten that by 1879, a total of 131 teachers were working in fifty-three kindergarten classes (Button and Provenzo 1989, 169). The United States Bureau of Education recorded a total of twelve kindergartens in the country in 1873, with seventy-two teachers and 1,252 students. By 1997, enrollments had mushroomed to 2,847,000 in public kindergartens and 575,000 in private kindergartens (National Center for Education Statistics 1999, 61).

Margarethe Schurz
(1832–1876)

The Professionalization of Teaching

During the later 1800s, professional teacher organizations began to have a great influence on the development of schools in America. The National Education Association (NEA), founded in 1857, and the American Federation of Teachers (AFT), founded in 1916, labored diligently to professionalize teaching and to increase teachers' salaries and benefits.

By the early 1900s, the demand for teachers had grown dramatically. An increasing number of women entered the teaching field at this time, beginning a trend often referred to as the "feminization of teaching." Female teachers were given less respect from the community than their male predecessors, though they were still more highly regarded than women who worked in factories or as domestics. In addition, they were expected to be of high moral character. They were subjected to a level of public scrutiny hard to imagine today, as illustrated by the following Professional Reflection.

Margaret Haley

Professional Reflection   **Reflecting on changes in the image of teachers**

Women became influential in shaping educational policies during the early 1900s, in part through the women's suffrage movement that led to the right to vote. Women such as Ella Flagg Young (1845–1918), superintendent of Chicago schools from 1909 to 1915, and Catherine Goggin and Margaret Haley, leaders of the Chicago Teachers Federation, played important roles in the governance of Chicago schools (Holmes and Weiss 1995; Button and Provenzo 1989). Another Chicagoan and visionary educational leader, Jane Addams (1860–1935), founded Hull House, a social and educational center for poor immigrants. In *Democracy and Social Ethics* (published in 1902), Addams drew from her training as a social worker and developed a philosophy of socialized education that linked schools with other social service agencies and institutions in the city. At the ceremony to present her the Nobel Peace Prize in 1931, Addams was described as "the foremost woman of her nation" (Rippa 1997, 142).

What Were the Aims of Education during the Progressive Era (1920–1945)?

The philosophy of progressivism had a profound influence on the character of education in the United States from the end of World War I to the end of World War II. During the late nineteenth and early twentieth centuries, supporters of the **progressive movement** were intent on social reform to improve the quality of American life. As pointed out earlier, educational progressives believed that the child's interests and practical needs should determine the focus of schooling. In 1919, the Progressive Education Association was founded and went on to devote the next two decades to implementing progressive theories in the classroom that they believed would lead to the improvement of society.

Teachers in progressive schools functioned as guides rather than taskmasters. They first engaged students through providing activities related to their natural interests, and then they moved students to higher levels of understanding. To teach in this manner was demanding: "Teachers in a progressive school had to be extraordinarily talented and well educated; they needed both a perceptive understanding of children and a wide knowledge of the disciplines in order to recognize when the child was ready to move through an experience to a new understanding, be it in history or science or mathematics or the arts" (Ravitch 1983, 47).

Audio Clip 3.3

What hallmarks of progressive education are evident in this photograph of one of the first classrooms in the country operated according to Dewey's philosophy? How would a progressive classroom look today?

John Dewey's Laboratory School

As pointed out earlier in this chapter, progressive educational theories were synthesized most effectively and eloquently by John Dewey (1859–1952). Born in the year that Darwin's *Origin of Species* was published, Dewey graduated from the University of Vermont when he was twenty. He later earned a doctorate at Johns Hopkins University, where his thinking was strongly influenced by the psychologist William James.

From 1894 to 1904, Dewey served as head of the departments of philosophy, psychology, and pedagogy at the University of Chicago. From 1904 until he retired in 1930, Dewey was a professor of philosophy at Columbia University. Dewey's numerous writings have had a profound impact on U.S. schools. In his best known works, *The School and Society* (1900) and *The Child and the Curriculum* (1902), Dewey states that school and society are connected and that teachers

must begin with an understanding of the child's world, the psychological dimension, and then progress to the logical dimension represented by the accumulated knowledge of the human race.

While at the University of Chicago, Dewey and his wife, Alice, established a Laboratory School for testing progressive principles in the classroom. The school opened in 1896 with two instructors and sixteen students and by 1902 had grown to 140 students with twenty-three teachers and ten university graduate students as assistants. The children, four to fourteen years old, learned traditional subjects by working cooperatively in small groups of eight to ten on projects such as cooking, weaving, carpentry, sewing, and metalwork (Rippa 1997).

Maria Montessori's Method

While Dewey's ideas provided the basis for the development of progressive education in the United States, progressive educators in Europe were similarly developing new approaches that would also impact American education. Chief among these was Maria Montessori (1870–1952), an Italian physician who was influenced by Rousseau and believed that children's mental, physical, and spiritual development could be enhanced by providing them with developmentally appropriate educational activities.

At Montessori's school for poor preschool-age children in Rome, teachers created learning environments based on students' levels of development and readiness to learn new material. According to the **Montessori method,** prescribed sets of materials and physical exercises are used to develop students' knowledge and skills, and students are allowed to use or not use the materials as they see fit. The materials arouse students' interest, and the interest motivates them to learn. Through highly individualized instruction, students develop self-discipline and self-confidence. Montessori's ideas spread throughout the world; by 1915, almost 100 Montessori schools were operating in the United States (Webb, Metha, and Jordan 1999). Today, Montessorian materials and activities are a standard part of the early childhood and elementary curricula in public schools throughout the nation.

Maria Montessori
(1870–1952)

Education of Immigrants and Minorities

The diversity of America's school population increased dramatically during the late nineteenth and early twentieth centuries. Latin Americans, Eastern Europeans, and Southern Europeans followed earlier waves of Western- and Northern-European immigrants such as the Irish and Germans. As with Native American education, the goal of immigrant education was rapid assimilation into an English-speaking Anglo-European society that did not welcome racially or ethnically different newcomers.

Also at stake was the preservation or loss of traditional culture. In some areas, school policies included the punishment of Cuban and Puerto Rican children, for example, for speaking Spanish in school, and children learned to mock their unassimilated parents. In other areas, efforts were made to exclude certain groups, such as Asians, and ethnic enclaves established separate schools for the purpose of preserving, for example, traditional Chinese culture.

By the time Native Americans were granted U.S. citizenship in 1924, confinement on reservations and decades of forced assimilation had devastated Native American cultures and provided few successful educational programs. In 1928, a landmark report titled *The Problem of Indian Administration* recommended that Native American education be restructured. Among the recommendations were the building of day schools in Native American communities and the reform of boarding schools for Native American children. In addition, the report recommended that school curricula be revised to reflect tribal cultures and the needs of local tribal communities. Another fifty years passed before the recommendations began to be implemented.

How Did Education Change during the Modern Postwar Era (1945–2000)?

Throughout the twentieth century, many long-standing trends in U.S. education continued. These trends may be grouped and summarized in terms of three general patterns, shown in Figure 3.5. At the same time, the decades since the end of World War II have seen a series of profound changes in U.S. education. These changes have addressed three as yet unanswered questions: (1) How can full and equal educational opportunity be extended to all groups in our culturally pluralistic society? (2) What knowledge and skills should be taught in our nation's schools?(3) How should knowledge and skills be taught?

Figure 3.5

The 1950s: Defense Education and School Desegregation

Teachers and education were put in the spotlight in 1957 when the Soviet Union launched the first satellite, named Sputnik, into space. Stunned U.S. leaders immediately blamed the space lag on inadequacies in the education system. The Soviet Union was first into space, they maintained, because the progressive educational philosophy had undermined academic rigor. For example, students in the United States were taught less science, mathematics, and foreign language than their European counterparts.

Video 3.1

The federal government appropriated millions of dollars over the next decade for educational reforms that reflected the essentialist educational philosophy. Through provisions of the **National Defense Education Act of 1958,** the U.S. Office of Education sponsored research and innovation in science, mathematics, modern foreign languages, and guidance. Out of their work came the new math; new science programs; an integration of anthropology, economics, political science, and sociology into new social studies programs; and renewed interest and innovations in foreign language instruction. Teachers were trained in the use of new methods and materials at summer workshops, schools were given funds for new equipment, and research centers were established. In 1964, Congress extended the act for three years and expanded Title III of the act to include money for improving instruction in reading, English, geography, history, and civics.

The end of World War II also saw the beginning of school **desegregation.** On May 17, 1954, the United States Supreme Court rejected the "separate but equal" doctrine that had been used since 1850 as a justification for excluding African Americans from attending school with whites. In response to a suit filed by the National Association

keepers of the
dream

Marion Wright Edelman
Founder of Children's Defense Fund

"You never ever forget."

for the Advancement of Colored People (NAACP) on behalf of a Kansas family, Chief Justice Earl Warren declared that to segregate school children "from others of similar age and qualifications solely because of their race generates a feeling of inferiority as to their status in the community that may affect their hearts and minds in a way unlikely ever to be undone" (***Brown v. Board of Education of Topeka*** 1954).

The Supreme Court's decision did not bring an immediate end to segregated schools. Though the court one year later ordered that desegregation proceed with "all deliberate speed," opposition to school integration arose in school districts across the country. Some districts, whose leaders modeled restraint and a spirit of cooperation, desegregated peacefully. Other districts became battlegrounds, characterized by boycotts, rallies, and violence.

The 1960s:
The War on Poverty and the Great Society

The 1960s, hallmarked by the Kennedy administration's spirit of action and high hopes, provided a climate that supported change. Classrooms were often places of pedagogical experimentation and creativity reminiscent of the progressive era. The open-education movement, team teaching, individualized instruction, the integrated-day concept, flexible scheduling, and nongraded schools were some of the innovations that teachers were asked to implement. These structural, methodological, and curricular changes implied the belief that teachers were capable professionals.

The image of teachers in the 1960s was enhanced by the publication of several books by educators who were influenced by the progressivist educational philosophy and humanistic psychology. A. S. Neill's *Summerhill* (1960), Sylvia Ashton-Warner's *Teacher* (1963), John Holt's *How Children Fail* (1964), Herbert Kohl's *36 Children* (1967), James Herndon's *The Way It Spozed to Be* (1969), and Jonathan Kozol's *Death at an Early Age* (1967)—a few of the books that appeared at the time—gave readers inside views of teachers at work and teachers' perceptions of how students learn.

The administrations of Presidents Kennedy and Johnson funneled massive amounts of money into a War on Poverty. Education was seen as the key to breaking the transmission of poverty from generation to generation. The War on Poverty developed methods, materials, and programs such as subsidized breakfast and lunch programs, Head Start, Upward Bound, and the Job Corps that would be appropriate to children who had been disadvantaged due to poverty.

The War on Poverty has proved much more difficult to win than imagined, and the results of such programs nearly forty years later have been mixed. The three- to six-year-olds who participated in Head Start did much better when they entered public schools; however, academic gains appeared to dissolve over time. Although the Job Corps enabled scores of youth to avoid a lifetime of unemployment, many graduates returned to the streets where they eventually became statistics in unemployment and crime records. The education of low-income children received a boost in April 1965 when Congress passed the **Elementary and Secondary Education Act.** As part of President Johnson's Great Society program, the act allocated funds on the basis of the number of poor children in school districts. Thus schools in poverty areas that frequently had to cope with such problems as low achievement, poor discipline, truancy, and high teacher turnover rates received much needed assistance in addressing their problems.

In 1968, the Elementary and Secondary Education Act was amended with Title VII, the Bilingual Education Act. This act provided federal aid to low-income children "of limited English-speaking ability." The act did not spell out clearly what bilingual education might mean other than to say that it provided money for local school districts to "develop and carry out new and imaginative elementary and secondary school programs" to meet the needs of non-English-speaking children. Since the passing of Title VII, debate over the ultimate goal of bilingual education has been intense: Should it help students to make the *transition* to regular English-speaking classrooms, or should it help such students *maintain* their non-English language and culture?

The 1970s:
Accountability and Equal Opportunity

The 1970s was a mixed decade for U.S. education, marked by drops in enrollment, test scores, and public confidence, as well as progressive policy changes that promoted a more equal education for all in the United States. Calls for "back to basics" and teacher accountability drives initiated by parents, citizens groups, and politicians who were unhappy with the low academic performance level of many students dominated this troubled decade at the height of the Vietnam conflict. For the first time in polling history, more than half of the U.S. adults polled in 1975 reported that they regarded themselves as better educated than the younger generation (Gallup 1975).

Financial difficulties also confronted the schools. National Center for Education Statistics data reveal that, instead of increasing as it had since 1940, the enrollment of children in prekindergarten through grade 8 in public and private schools declined by nearly five million during the 1970s (National Center for Education Statistics 1999, 12). Schools found themselves with a reduction in state aid, which was determined on the basis of pupil attendance figures. Financial problems were exacerbated by reduced support from local taxpayers, who resisted tax increases for the schools because they were stressed by their own economic problems, or had lost confidence in the schools, or because fewer of them had children in school. Consequently, this further reduced the ability to meet the needs of students.

Many parents responded to the crisis by becoming education activists, seeking or establishing alternative schools, or joining the home education movement led by John Holt, who by then had given up on reforming schools. These parents held a poor image of teachers and schools; they believed that they could provide a better

What impact has Title IX had on the education of females? What does equal educational opportunity for female and male students really mean?

education for their children than public school teachers could. Those who kept their children in the public schools demanded teacher **accountability,** which limited teachers' instructional flexibility and extended their evaluation paperwork. Basal readers and teacher-proof curricular packages descended on teachers, spelling out with their cookbook directions the deeper message that teachers were not to be trusted to teach on their own. Confidence in teachers reached a low point.

In addition, during the late 1960s and early 1970s increasing numbers of young people questioned what the schools were teaching and how they were teaching it. Thousands of them mobilized in protest against an establishment that, in their view, supported an immoral, undeclared war in Vietnam and was unconcerned with the oppression of minorities at home. In their search for reasons why these and other social injustices were allowed to exist, many militant youth groups singled out the schools' curricula. From their perspective, the schools taught subjects irrelevant to finding solutions to pressing problems.

Responding in good faith to their critics' accusations, schools greatly expanded their curricular offerings and instituted a wide variety of instructional strategies. In making these changes, however, school personnel gradually realized that they were alienating other groups: taxpayers who accused schools of extravagant spending; religious sects who questioned the values that children were being taught; **back-to-basics** advocates who charged that students were not learning how to read, write, and compute; and citizens who were alarmed at steadily rising school crime, drugs, and violence.

Despite the siege on teachers and schools, however, the reforms of the 1960s and 1970s did result in a number of improvements that have lasted into the present. More young people graduate from high school now than in previous decades, more teachers have advanced training, school buildings are better equipped, and instructional methods and materials are both more relevant to learners and more diverse.

For those people who had been marginalized by the educational system, the federal acts that were passed in the 1970s brought success and encouragement: the Title IX Education Amendment prohibiting sex discrimination (1972), the Indian Education Act (1972), the Education for All Handicapped Children Act (1975), and the Indochina Migration and Refugee Assistance Act (1975).

Title IX of the Education Amendments Act, which took effect in 1975, stated that "no person in the United States shall, on the basis of sex, be excluded from participation in, be denied the benefits of, or be subjected to discrimination under any education program or activity receiving Federal financial assistance."

The **Education for All Handicapped Children Act** (Public Law 94–142), passed by Congress in 1975, extended greater educational opportunities to children with disabilities. This act (often referred to as the **mainstreaming** law) specifies extensive due process procedures to guarantee that children with special needs will receive a free, appropriate education in the least restrictive educational environment. Through the act's provisions, parents are involved in planning educational programs for their children.

The 1980s: A Great Debate

The first half of the 1980s saw a continuation, perhaps even an escalation, of the criticisms aimed at the schools during the two previous decades. With the publication in 1983 of the report by the National Commission on Excellence in Education, *A Nation at Risk: The Imperative for Educational Reform,* a great national debate was begun on how to improve the quality of schools. *A Nation at Risk* and dozens of other national reports on U.S. schools gave evidence to some that the schools were failing miserably to achieve their goals.

Responses included more proposals for curriculum reform. Mortimer Adler's *Paideia Proposal* (1982) called for a perennialist core curriculum based on the Great Books. *High School: A Report on Secondary Education in America* (1983), written by Ernest Boyer for the Carnegie Foundation for the Advancement of Teaching, suggested strengthening the academic core curriculum in high schools, a recommendation that was widely adopted. In 1986, former Secretary of the U.S. Department of Education William Bennett advocated a perennialist high-school curriculum that he described in *James Madison High* (1987). Educators at the middle-school level began to create small learning communities, eliminate tracking, and develop new ways to enhance student self-esteem as a result of the Carnegie Council on Adolescent Development report *Turning Points: Preparing American Youth for the 21st Century* (1989). These and other reform reports that swept the nation during the 1980s made a lasting imprint on education in the United States.

The 1990s and into the Twenty-First Century: Teacher Leadership

The push to reform schools begun in the 1980s has continued into the twenty-first century, and teaching is being transformed in dramatic ways. In response to challenges such as greater diversity, greater international competition, less support for public education, and decentralization and deregulation of schools, innovative approaches to teaching and learning are being developed throughout the United States (see Figure 3.6). Teachers are going beyond the classroom and assuming leadership roles in school restructuring and educational reform—roles that we examine more fully in Chapters 12 and 13. Through collaborative relationships with students, principals, parents, and the private sector, teachers are changing the nature of their profession. As one high school teacher said in the late 1990s: "I see it [change] happening. Not overnight, but I think it's going to. When I first started teaching in the early sixties, I would never have envisioned things changing as much as they have" (Grant and Murray 1999, 212).

Figure 3.6

SUMMARY

What Determines Your Educational Philosophy? (p. 62)

weblink

KEY TERMS AND CONCEPTS

Go to the website for interactive flashcards.

APPLICATIONS AND INTERACTIVITIES

Go to the website for interactive assignments in the following areas:

Teacher's Journal

Teacher's Database

Observations and Interviews

Professional Portfolio

Name _____ Date _____

For each question, write in the blank the answer you believe is correct.

3.1 In simplest terms, educational _____ consists of what you believe about education.

3.2 What one believes about students is based on his or her unique life _____.

3.3 That branch of philosophy concerned with explaining the nature of reality is known as _____.

3.4 _____ is that branch of philosophy concerned with the nature of knowledge.

3.5 Teachers who are concerned with values are likely interested in that branch of philosophy known as _____.

3.6 _____ is that aspect of philosophy that focuses on good and evil as well as right and wrong.

3.7 The branch of axiology known as _____ is concerned with the values of beauty and art.

3.8 The area of philosophy that deals with the process of reasoning and identifies rules that enable the thinker to reach valid conclusions is known as _____.

3.9 The belief that education's aim should be to ensure student acquisition of knowledge of unchanging principles or great ideas is indicative of the philosophical orientation to education known as _____.

3.10 Teachers who believe that education should be child-centered and focused on problem solving are likely allied with the philosophical orientation known as _____.

Answers are available on the FlexChoice website at www.ablongman.com/parkayflex.

 www.ablongman.com/parkayflex

weblink

Name _____

Keep this checklist at your computer as a reminder to read and complete the chapter features and activities located on the FlexChoice website at www.ablongman.com/parkayflex.

**Date
Completed**

_____ ❑ **PreTest with Answers**

_____ ❑ **Audio Clip 3.1:** Thinking Over the Opening Vignette

_____ ❑ **Figure 3.1:** The influence of the teacher's educational beliefs on teaching behavior

_____ ❑ **Technology Highlights:** How can the World Wide Web enhance your study of and interest in the philosophy and history of education?

_____ ❑ **Weblink 3.1:** The history of education and childhood

_____ ❑ **Figure 3.2:** The spirit and principles of Socratic questioning

_____ ❑ **Figure 3.3:** Five philosophical orientations to teaching

_____ ❑ **Audio Clip 3.2:** Existentialism

_____ ❑ **Figure 3.4:** The relationship of philosophy to educational practice

_____ ❑ **Weblink 3.2:** Philosophic Inventory

_____ ❑ **Where Do You Stand?:** Should school attendance beyond the elementary level become voluntary?

_____ ❑ **Professional Reflection:** Reflecting on changes in the image of teachers

_____ ❑ **Audio Clip 3.3:** The Progressive Movement

_____ ❑ **Figure 3.5:** Three general patterns of trends in American education

_____ ❑ **Video 3.1:** School desegregation

_____ ❑ **Keepers of the Dream:** Marian Wright Edelman

_____ ❑ **Figure 3.6:** The 1990s: A sampler of trends in education

_____ ❑ **Summary**

_____ ❑ **Key Terms and Concepts**

_____ ❑ **Applications and Interactivities:** Teacher's Journal

_____ ❑ **Applications and Interactivities:** Teacher's Database

_____ ❑ **Applications and Interactivities:** Observations and Interviews

_____ ❑ **Applications and Interactivities:** Professional Portfolio

_____ ❑ **PostTest with Answers**

4

Social Realities Confronting Today's Schools

The educational system is part of the common life and cannot escape suffering the consequences that flow from the conditions prevailing outside the school building.

—John Dewey
"Introduction," *The Use of Resources in Education*

focus questions

1. What are the aims of education today?

2. How can schools be described?

3. What are schools like as social institutions?

4. What characteristics distinguish successful schools?

5. What social problems affect schools and place students at risk?

6. What are schools doing to address societal problems?

J eff Banks, a history teacher at Southside High School, enters the faculty lunchroom and sees his friends, Sue Anderson, Nancy Watkins, and Bret Thomas, at their usual table in the corner. Southside is located in a medium-size city in the Southeast. The school, in the center of a low- to middle-income area known as Lawndale, has an enrollment of almost 1,900 students. About 70 percent of these self-identify as Anglo-European Americans, with the remaining 30 percent about evenly divided between African Americans and Mexican Americans. Southside has a reputation for being a "good" school—for the most part, students are respectful of their teachers. Parents, many of whom work in the several small factories found in Lawndale, generally support the school and are involved in school activities in spite of their heavy work schedules. The consensus among teachers is that most Southside parents recognize that education is the key if their children are to "better themselves" and move out of Lawndale.

As soon as Jeff is within earshot of his friends, he knows they are talking about last week's tragic shooting at a high school in Colorado. During a rampage that lasted several hours at the school, two boys killed twelve fellow students, one teacher, and then themselves.

"It's so scary," Sue says, "Who knows, something like that could happen right here at Southside. We have no idea what kids have to deal with today."

AUDIO)))
Audio Clip 4.1

"Yeah, we have no idea who might snap," says Bret. "With a lot of these school shootings lately, it seems to be a kid that no one would have expected. Quiet, polite, good student—you just never know."

"In some cases, that's true," Jeff says, placing his lunch tray on the table and then sitting down between Sue and Bret. "But a lot of time there are signs. A lot of these kids are loners and outcasts; they're into violent video games, cults, drugs, guns, you name it."

"What I want to know," says Sue, "is how we can prevent something like that from happening here? Since the Colorado shootings, there have been bomb scares, threats, guns confiscated at dozens of schools around the country."

"Well, I don't think metal detectors, more police in schools, and stiffer penalties for kids who bring guns to school are necessarily the answers," says Bret. "The question is, Why are kids doing this?"

"Right, how can we prevent things like this?" says Jeff.

"If we're going to change things," says Sue, "we've got to figure out ways to identify and help kids who feel so desperate that they turn to violence."

"Well, that's all well and good," says Nancy with a sigh. "But I don't see where all of this is going to lead. Our responsibility as teachers is to educate our kids. We're not psychiatrists or social workers. We can't change society. Besides, we've got youth agencies, centers for families in crisis, and all kinds of social service agencies."

What is the role of schools at the start of the twenty-first century? Should teachers play a role in addressing social problems such as violence in our society? What would you say to a teacher who expresses views such as Nancy's?

Name _____ Date _____

For each question, circle the letter of the answer you believe is correct. Then read the chapter to learn more about these topics.

4.1 Between 1972 and 1996, the school dropout rate for African American students
A. Declined significantly.
B. Was lower than that for their white peers.
C. Increased significantly.
D. Was higher than that for Latino students.

4.2 All of the following are strategies for reducing the impact of gang activities on schools *except*
A. Quickly removing visible evidence of gang activity from school property.
B. Identification of gang members.
C. Retaining graffiti on school property as a symbol of gang destructiveness.
D. Implementing dress codes that ban styles of dress identified with gangs.

4.3 In 1999, the American Psychological Association reviewed research concluding that television violence *alone*
A. Was solely responsible for aggressive behavior by children and youth.
B. Contributed little to aggressive behavior by children and youth.
C. Was responsible for nearly 50 percent of all aggressive behavior by children and youth.
D. Was responsible for up to 15 percent of all aggressive behavior by children and youth.

4.4 All of the following are true of female and male involvement in suicide *except*
A. Latino students are twice as likely as white students to attempt suicide.
B. Male students are more likely to actually end their lives through suicide.
C. Students in grade twelve are the most likely to attempt suicide.
D. Female students are twice as likely to attempt suicide.

4.5 The award-winning Salome Urena Middle Academy in New York state is a full-service school characterized by all of the following *except*
A. Modest increase in test scores.
B. Increase in attendance.
C. Growing misbehavior among students.
D. Lower per-pupil expenditures.

4.6 In response to the need to make the United States "internationally competitive," the National Education Goals were developed, placing a high priority on
A. Acquisition of a foreign language by students.
B. Higher level of problem-solving skills.
C. Student achievement in English, mathematics, science, history, and geography.
D. Student achievement in fine arts.

4.7 The most universally agreed-upon goal for schools is
A. Discipline.
B. Socialization.
C. Achievement.
D. Moral development.

4.8 The Hernandez family just moved to a new neighborhood. Within their school system, they are able to make choices as to what school to attend based on the specialization offered at the school. They have chosen Murray Elementary because of the focus on environmental education. This is an example of
A. Model schools.
B. Magnet schools.
C. Outcome-based schools.
D. Performance focused schools.

4.9 According to Jean Anyon, schools that focus on developing students' analytical intellectual powers are usually
A. Working-class schools.
B. Middle-class schools.
C. Executive elite schools.
D. Magnet schools.

4.10 Groups that see the school as a means of perpetuating their preferred way of life include all of the following *except*
A. Religious schools.
B. Public schools.
C. Private schools.
D. Parochial schools.

Answers are available on the FlexChoice website at www.ablongman.com/parkayflex.

The discussion among Jeff and his fellow teachers highlights the expectation of much of the public that schools (and teachers) have a responsibility to address problems that confront modern society. Those who agree with Nancy's point of view tend to believe that schools should teach only content to students. Others, however, believe that teachers have an obligation to address domestic social problems. Underlying both positions are conflicting views on the aims of education.

What Are the Aims of Education Today?

In the United States, people agree that the purpose of schools is to educate. Unlike other institutions in society, schools have been developed exclusively to carry out that very important purpose. That we are not always in agreement about what the aims of education should be, however, is illustrated by the fact that we disagree about what it means to be an educated person. Is a person with a college degree educated? Is the person who has overcome, with dignity and grace, extreme hardships in life educated?

Debate about the **aims of education** is not new. Fourth century B.C. philosopher Aristotle, for example, expressed the dilemma this way: "The existing practice [of education] is perplexing; no one knows on what principle we should proceed—should the useful in life, or should virtue, or should the higher knowledge, be the aim of our training; all three opinions have been entertained" (1941, 1306). Definitive answers to Aristotle's questions have not been achieved; instead, each generation has developed its own response to what the aims of education should be.

Education for National Goals

In 1994, President Clinton signed into law the **Goals 2000: Educate America Act,** a comprehensive funding program to help schools achieve a set of eight national goals (see following), six of which were developed at a 1989 educational summit meeting convened by President Bush for the fifty state governors. The goals place a high priority on increasing student achievement in English, mathematics, science, history, and geography; creating more effective learning environments in the nation's schools; providing for teachers' professional development; and increasing parental involvement.

By the year 2000, the following goals were to be accomplished:

1. *School readiness*—All children in the United States will start school ready to learn.
2. *School completion*—The high school graduation rate will increase to at least 90 percent.
3. *Student achievement and citizenship*—All students will leave grades 4, 8, and 12 having demonstrated competency in challenging subject matter, including English, mathematics, science, foreign languages, civics and government, economics, arts, history, and geography; and every school in the United States will ensure that all students learn to use their minds well, so they may be prepared for responsible citizenship, further learning, and productive employment in our nation's modern economy.

4. *Mathematics and science*—United States students will be first in the world in mathematics and science achievement.

5. *Adult literacy and lifelong learning*—Every adult in the United States will be literate and will possess the knowledge and skills necessary to compete in a global economy and to exercise the rights and responsibilities of citizenship.

6. *Safe, disciplined, and alcohol- and drug-free schools*—Every school in the United States will be free of drugs, violence, and the unauthorized presence of firearms and alcohol and will offer a disciplined environment conducive to learning.

7. *Teacher education and professional development*—The nation's teaching force will have access to programs for the continued improvement of their professional skills and the opportunity to acquire the knowledge and skills needed to instruct and prepare all U.S. students for the next century.

8. *Parental participation*—Every school will promote partnerships that will increase parental involvement and participation in promoting the social, emotional, and academic growth of children.

In February 1999, the National Education Goals Panel acknowledged that the goals would not be met and passed a resolution to rename the National Education Goals as "America's Education Goals" and to continue striving to meet the goals "beyond the year 2000 without a specific deadline for their achievement." Although some states reached some goals by 2000, none achieved all eight. Schools in North Carolina, South Carolina, California, Colorado, and Texas showed the most signs of improvement during the 1990s. Though the goals were not met, the panel pointed out that America's Education Goals made significant contributions in the following areas: launching and supporting the academic standards movement, legitimizing "benchmarking" and state and international comparisons, increasing the attention paid to early childhood education, and focusing and sustaining educational reform (National Education Goals Panel 1999).

Education for Prosocial Values

Although there is widespread debate about what academic content the schools should teach, the public agrees that schools should teach **prosocial values** such as honesty, patriotism, fairness, and civility. The well-being of any society requires support of such values; they enable people from diverse backgrounds to live together peacefully. One poll of the public, for example, revealed that 90 percent or more of the public believed that the following values should be taught in public schools: respect for others, industry or hard work, persistence or the ability to follow through, fairness in dealing with others, compassion for others, and civility and politeness (Elam, Rose, and Gallup 1994). The strong support for these prosocial values reflects the public's belief that the schools should play a key role in promoting the democratic ideal of equality for all.

Education for Socialization

Schools are places where the young become socialized—where they learn to participate intelligently and constructively in the nation's society. This purpose is contained in the national educational goal that calls for schools to prepare students for "responsible citizenship, further learning, and productive employment in our nation's modern economy." Table 4.1 shows the percentage of the public in 1998 who believed that the

Table 4.1

practice of good citizenship was a "very important" measure of school effectiveness, even more important than going on to postsecondary education, getting a job, or scoring well on standardized tests.

Additionally, schools, more than any other institution in our society, assimilate persons from different ethnic, racial, religious, and cultural backgrounds and pass on the values and customs of the majority. The Los Angeles Unified School District, for example, recently reported that its students represented nine major language groups and 171 languages. It is through the schools that persons from such diverse backgrounds learn English and learn about the importance Americans attach to the Fourth of July or Veterans Day; about the contributions of George Washington, Abraham Lincoln, or Dr. Martin Luther King, Jr.; and about the basic workings of capitalism and democracy.

Education for Achievement

Of the various aims that the schools have, achievement is the most universally agreed on. For most people, the primary purpose of schools is to impart to students the academic knowledge and skills that will prepare them either for additional schooling or for the world of work. Regardless of political ideology, religious beliefs, and cultural values, people want their schools to teach academic content. When asked whether they favor establishing national standards for measuring the academic performance of public schools, 77 percent of respondents in a public poll said they favored such a measure (Rose, Gallup, and Elam 1997).

Education for Personal Growth

Society places great value on the dignity and worth of the individual. Accordingly, one aim of schools is to enable the young to become all that they are capable of becoming. Unlike socialization or achievement, the emphasis on personal growth puts the individual first, society second. According to this view, the desired outcomes of education go beyond achievement to include the development of a positive self-concept and interpersonal skills, or what psychologist Daniel Goleman has termed **"emotional intelligence."** According to Goleman (1997, 1998), schools should emphasize five dimensions of emotional intelligence: self-awareness, handling emotions, motivation, empathy, and social skills. Emotional intelligence is essential for achievement in school, job success, marital happiness, and physical health; it enables students to live independently and to seek out the "good" life according to their own values, needs, and wants. The knowledge and skills students acquire at schools are seen as enabling them to achieve personal growth and self-actualization.

Education for Social Change

Schools also provide students with the knowledge and skills to improve society and the quality of life and to adapt to rapid social change. Naturally, there exists a wide range of opinion about how society might be improved. Some teachers, like Jeff, Sue, and Bret in this chapter's opening scenario, believe that one purpose of schooling is to address social problems such as violence in society; while other teachers, such as their friend, Nancy, believe schools should teach academic content and not try to change society. Less controversial have been efforts to prepare students to serve others through volunteerism and to participate actively in the political life of the nation. During the early 1990s, some high schools began to direct every student to complete a service requirement to help students see that they are not only autonomous individuals but also members of a larger community to which they are accountable. Other schools began to introduce service-learning activities into their curricula. **Service learning** provides students with opportunities to deliver service to their communities while engaging in reflection and study on the meaning of those experiences. Service learning brings young people into contact with the elderly, the sick, the poor, and the homeless, as well as acquaints them with neighborhood and governmental issues.

Education for Equal Educational Opportunity

Ample evidence exists that certain groups in U.S. society are denied equality of opportunity economically, socially, and educationally. For example, if we look at the percentage of children three to four years old who participate in early childhood programs such as Head Start, nursery school, and prekindergarten—experiences that help children from less advantaged backgrounds start elementary school on an equal footing with other children—we find that children from lower-income families are less likely to have such opportunities (see Table 4.2). In addition, there is a positive relationship between parents' educational attainment and their children's enrollment in early childhood programs; also, Latino children are less likely to be enrolled than white or African American children.

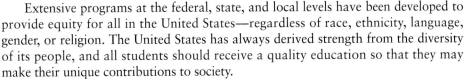

Table 4.2

Extensive programs at the federal, state, and local levels have been developed to provide equity for all in the United States—regardless of race, ethnicity, language, gender, or religion. The United States has always derived strength from the diversity of its people, and all students should receive a quality education so that they may make their unique contributions to society.

The goal of providing equal educational opportunity for all has long distinguished education in the United States from that found in most other countries. Since the 1850s, schools in the United States have been particularly concerned with providing children from diverse backgrounds the education they need to succeed in our society. As James Banks (1999, 4) suggests, "Education within a pluralistic society should affirm and help students understand their home and community cultures. [To] create and maintain a civic community that works for the common good, education in a democratic society should help students acquire the knowledge, attitudes, and skills needed to participate in civic action to make society more equitable and just."

How Can Schools Be Described?

Given the wide variation in schools and their cultures, many models have been proposed for describing the distinguishing characteristics of schools. Schools can be categorized according to the focus of their curricula; for example, high schools may be college prep, vocational, or general. Another way to view schools is according to their organizational structure; for example, open schools or magnet schools. A **magnet school** allows students from an entire district to attend a school's specialized program. Some magnet schools are organized around specific academic disciplines such as science, mathematics, or the basic skills; others focus on the performing and visual arts, health professions, computers, or international studies and languages.

Metaphors for Schools

Other models view schools metaphorically; that is, what is a school like? Some schools, for example, have been compared to factories; students enter the school as raw material, move through the curriculum in a systematic way, and exit the school as finished products. Terrence Deal and Kent Peterson (1999, 21) have suggested that exemplary schools "become like tribes or clans, with deep ties among people and with values and traditions that give meaning to everyday life." Others have suggested that schools are like banks, gardens, prisons, mental hospitals, homes, churches, families, and teams.

In the school-as-family metaphor, for example, the effective school is a caring community of adults who attend to the academic, emotional, and social needs of the children and youth entrusted to their care.

Schools and Social Class

In spite of a general consensus that schools should promote social change and equal opportunity, some individuals believe that schools "reproduce" the existing society by presenting different curricula and educational experiences to students from different socioeconomic classes. Students at a school in an affluent suburb, for example, may study chemistry in a well-equipped lab and take a field trip to a high-tech industry to see the latest application of chemical research, while students at a school in an impoverished inner-city neighborhood learn chemistry from out-of-date texts, have no lab in which to conduct experiments, and take no field trips because the school district has no funds. Schools, in effect, preserve the stratification within society and maintain the differences between the "haves" and the "have-nots." As Joel Spring puts it: "the affluent members of U.S. society can protect the educational advantages and, consequently, economic advantages, of their children by living in affluent school districts or by using private schools. [T]heir children will attend the elite institutions of higher education, and their privileged educational background will make it easy for them to follow in the footsteps of their parent's financial success" (Spring 1999, 290–91).

A useful way to talk about the relationship between schooling and social class in the United States is suggested by the four categories of schools Jean Anyon (1996) found in her study of several elementary schools in urban and suburban New Jersey. Anyon maintains that schools reproduce the existing society by presenting different curricula and educational experiences to students from different socioeconomic classes.

Anyon studied a small group of schools in one metropolitan area and her criteria are linked almost exclusively to socioeconomic status. Few schools actually fit the categories in all ways.

The first kind of school she calls the *working-class school*. In this school, the primary emphasis is on having students follow directions as they work at rote, mechanical activities such as completing dittoed worksheets. Students are given little opportunity to exercise their initiative or to make choices. Teachers may make negative, disparaging comments about students' abilities and, through subtle and not-so-subtle means, convey low expectations to students. Additionally, teachers at working-class schools may spend much of their time focusing on classroom management, dealing with absenteeism, and keeping extensive records.

The *middle-class school* is the second type identified by Anyon. Here, teachers emphasize to students the importance of getting right answers, usually in the form of words, sentences, numbers, or facts and dates. Students have slightly more opportunity to make decisions, but not much. Most lessons are textbook based. Anyon points out that "while the teachers spend a lot of time explaining and expanding on what the textbooks say, there is little attempt to analyze how or why things happen. . . . On the occasions when creativity or self-expression is requested, it is peripheral to the main activity or it is 'enrichment' or 'for fun'" (Anyon 1996, 191).

The *affluent professional school,* unlike the previous two types of schools, gives students the opportunity to express their individuality and to make a variety of choices. Fewer rules govern the behavior of students in affluent professional schools, and teacher and student are likely to negotiate about the work the student will do.

Anyon provides the following definition of the fourth type of school she identified, the *executive elite school:*

> In the executive elite school, work is developing one's analytical intellectual powers. Children are continually asked to reason through a problem, to produce intellectual products that are both logically sound and of top academic quality (Anyon 1996, 196).

In the affluent professional and executive elite schools, teacher–student relationships are more positive than those in the working-class and middle-class schools. Teachers are polite to their students, seldom give direct orders, and almost never make sarcastic or nasty remarks. However schools are categorized, it seems clear that they reflect the socioeconomic status of the communities they serve.

What Are Schools Like as Social Institutions?

Schools are social institutions. An **institution** is an organization established by society to maintain and improve its way of life. Schools are the institutions our society has established for the purpose of educating the young. For the last 200 years, American schools have developed complex structures, policies, and curricula to accomplish this mission. "The Institutional Structure of Education in the United States" is shown in Figure 4.1.

Figure 4.1

The School as a Reflection of Society

As you might expect, schools mirror the national culture and the surrounding local culture and other special interests. Private, parochial, and religious schools, for example, are often maintained by groups that see the school as a means of perpetuating their preferred way of life. One example of how schools reflect contemporary priorities in life in the United States is the growing number of public schools located in shopping malls. In commenting on his experiences at a school located in the Landmark Shopping Mall in Northern Virginia, a student is able to say that the goal of countless students around the country is his reality: "As well as getting an education, I get a job" (Spring 1996, 4). Nevertheless, as Mary Henry (1993, 29) points out, "Schools are . . . not simply puppets of the dominant mainstream society. They have their own unique concerns and their own 'poetry' of people and events. Whether public or private, all schools are not the same."

Rural, Suburban, and Urban Schools

Schools also reflect their location. Schools in rural, urban, and suburban settings often have significantly different cultures. Rural schools are often the focal point for community life and reflect values and beliefs that tend to be more conservative than those associated with urban and suburban schools. While the small size of a rural school may contribute to the development of a family-like culture, its small size may also make it difficult to provide students with an array of curricular experiences equal to that found at larger schools in more populated areas. In contrast, large suburban or urban schools may provide students with more varied learning experiences, but these schools may lack the cohesiveness and community focus of rural schools.

Schools and Community Environments

The differences among the environments that surround schools can be enormous. Urban schools found in or near decaying centers of large cities often reflect the social problems of the surrounding area, such as drug abuse, crime, and poverty. One of the most serious problems confronting education in the United States is the quality of such schools. Across the country—in Chicago, New York, Los Angeles, St. Louis, Detroit, and Cleveland—middle-class families who can afford to, move away from urban centers or place their children in private schools. As a result, students in urban school districts are increasingly from low-income backgrounds.

In *Savage Inequalities,* Jonathon Kozol documents the startling contrast between the neighborhoods that surround impoverished inner-city schools and those that surround affluent suburban schools. In comparing New Trier High School in affluent Winnetka, Illinois, and Chicago's DuSable High School, an inner-city school at which the first author of this textbook taught for eight years, Kozol points out that New Trier is in a neighborhood of "circular driveways, chirping birds and white-columned homes" (1991, 62). In contrast, DuSable's surroundings are "almost indescribably despairing"; across the street from the school is "a line of uniform and ugly 16-story buildings, the Robert Taylor Homes, which constitute . . . the city's second-poorest neighborhood" (1991, 68, 71).

Though some communities may impact their schools in undesirable ways, many teachers at such schools find their work professionally stimulating and growth-enhancing. As one teacher said:

> I taught in two different environments—middle school in an inner city and high school in a more rural area. I think that combination was the experience that made me

In what ways do schools reflect their communities and the wider American society? What difference might the community make for this school? for the students who attend it? for the teachers who work there?

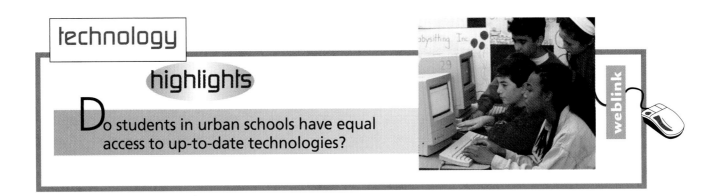

technology

highlights

Do students in urban schools have equal access to up-to-date technologies?

weblink

become a teacher. When I did my student teaching, I enjoyed it so much, and I realized I had a knack for it. When recruiters looked at my résumé, they were impressed that I had two different experiences I could draw from and elaborate on. I know that's how I got my job (Sallie Mae Corporation 1995, 8).

The Culture of the School

Although schools are very much alike, each school is unique. Each has a culture of its own—a network of beliefs, values and traditions, and ways of thinking and behaving that distinguishes it from other schools.

Much like a community, a school has a distinctive culture—a collective way of life. Terms that have been used to describe **school culture** include *climate, ethos, atmosphere,* and *character.* Some schools may be characterized as community-like places where there is a shared sense of purpose and commitment to providing the best education possible for all students. Other schools lack a unified sense of purpose or direction and drift, rudderless, from year to year. Still others are characterized by internal conflict and divisiveness and may even reflect what Deal and Peterson (1999) term a "toxic" school culture; students, teachers, administrators, and parents may feel that the school is not sufficiently meeting their needs. The following excerpt from the mission statement of an award-winning school in the high desert of Northern Arizona illustrates several qualities of a school culture that nurtures students:

> The Ganado Primary School's mission is to provide opportunities for children to make sense of their world, to respect themselves and others, to respect their environment, and to appreciate and understand their cultural and linguistic heritage. [Our] mission is to help everyone [children, teachers, and administrators] negotiate their experiences with the content of the classroom, instructional style, and the social, emotional, physical and professional interactions of school life. We believe that a relaxed atmosphere [characterized by] surprise, challenge, hard work, celebration, humor, satisfaction, and collegiality is the natural order of the day for all (Deal and Peterson 1999, 17).

The Physical Environment The physical environment of the school both reflects and helps to create the school's overall culture. "Whether school buildings are squeezed between other buildings or located on sprawling campuses, their fenced-in area or other physical separation distinguishes them from the community-at-large" (Ballantine 1997, 210). Some schools are dreary places or, at best, aesthetically bland. The tile floors, concrete block walls, long, straight corridors, and rows of fluorescent lights often found in these schools contribute little to their inhabitants' sense of beauty, concern for others, or personal comfort.

Other schools are much more attractive. They are clean, pleasant, and inviting; and teachers and students take pride in their building. Overall, the physical environment has a positive impact on those who spend time in the school; it encourages learning and a spirit of cohesiveness.

Formal Practices of Schools   The formal practices of schools are well known to anyone who has been educated in U.S. schools. With few exceptions, students attend school from six years of age through sixteen at least, and usually to eighteen, Monday through Friday, September through May, for twelve years. For the most part, students are assigned to grade level on the basis of age rather than ability or interest. Assignment to individual classes or teachers at a given grade level, however, may be made on the basis of ability or interest.

Teachers and students are grouped in several ways in the elementary school and in one dominant pattern in junior and senior high school. At the elementary school level, the **self-contained classroom** is the most traditional and prevalent arrangement. In this type of classroom, one teacher teaches all or nearly all subjects to a group of about twenty-five children, with the teacher and students remaining in the same classroom for the entire day. Often art, music, physical education, and computer skills are taught in other parts of the school, so students may leave the classroom for scheduled periods. Individual students may also attend special classes for remedial or advanced instruction, speech therapy, or instrumental music and band lessons.

In **open-space schools,** students are free to move among various activities and learning centers. Instead of self-contained classrooms, open-space schools have large instructional areas with movable walls and furniture that can be rearranged easily. Grouping for instruction is much more fluid and varied. Students do much of their work independently, with a number of teachers providing individual guidance as needed.

In middle schools and junior and senior high schools, students typically study four or five academic subjects taught by teachers who specialize in them. In this organizational arrangement, called **departmentalization,** students move from classroom to classroom for their lessons. High school teachers often share their classrooms with other teachers and use their rooms only during scheduled class periods.

School Traditions   **School traditions** are those elements of a school's culture that are handed down from year to year. The traditions of a school reflect what students, teachers, administrators, parents, and the surrounding community believe is important and valuable about the school. One school, for example, may have developed a tradition of excellence in academic programs; another school's traditions may emphasize the performing arts; and yet another may focus on athletic programs. Whatever a school's traditions, they are usually a source of pride for members of the school community.

Ideally, traditions are the glue that holds together the diverse elements of a school's culture. They combine to create a sense of community, identity, and trust among people affiliated with a school. Traditions are maintained through stories that are handed down, rituals and ceremonial activities, student productions, and trophies and artifacts that have been collected over the years. For example, Joan Vydra, now principal of Briar Glen Elementary School in Wheaton, Illinois, initiated Care Week as part of the fall tradition at her former school, Hawthorne Elementary. Influenced by the work of Nel Noddings (featured as the "Keeper of the Dream" in Chapter 9), Vydra believed that a tradition of care would nurture student success. On the first day of Care Week, students learned the importance of caring for themselves; on Tuesdays, caring for their families; on Wednesdays, caring for each other; on Thursdays, caring for the school; and on Fridays, caring for those served by local charities (Deal and Peterson 1999).

The Culture of the Classroom

Just as schools develop their unique cultures, each classroom develops its own culture or way of life. The culture of a classroom is determined in large measure by the manner in which teacher and students participate in common activities. In addition, "the environment of the classroom and the inhabitants of that environment—students and teachers—are constantly interacting. Each aspect of the system affects all others" (Woolfolk 1998, 440).

The quality of teacher–student interactions is influenced by the physical characteristics of the setting (classroom, use of space, materials, resources, etc.) and the social dimensions of the group (norms, rules, expectations, cohesiveness, distribution of power and influence). These elements interact to shape **classroom culture.** Teachers who appreciate the importance of these salient elements of classroom culture are more likely to create environments that they and their students find satisfying and growth-promoting. For example, during the second month of student teaching in the second grade, "Miss Martin" reflects on her efforts to create classroom culture characterized by positive teacher–student interactions:

> I started off with a big mistake. I tried to be their friend. I tried joining with them in all the jokes and laughter that cut into instruction time. When this didn't work, I overcompensated by yelling at them when I needed them to quiet down and get to work. I wasn't comfortable with this situation. I did not think it was like me to raise my voice at a child. I knew I needed to consider how they felt. I realized that if I were them, I'd hate me, I really would. In desperation, I turned to my education textbooks for advice.

> This was a huge help to me, but a book can only guide you. It can't establish a personality for you or even manage your classroom for you. You have to do that yourself and as lovingly and effectively as possible. But I had so much trouble finding a middle ground: love them, guide them, talk to them, manage them, but don't control them (Rand and Shelton-Colangelo 1999, 8–9).

Similarly, a beginning teacher at an experimental school describes the classroom culture she wants to create: "What I'm trying to get to in my classroom is that they have power. I'm trying to allow students to have power—to know what their knowledge is and to learn to create their own ideas as opposed to my being the one who is the only holder of ideas in the universe. I want to transfer the authority back to them" (Dollase 1992, 101). The efforts of this teacher to create an empowering classroom culture were supported by the culture of the school itself: "Because her comments reflect the prevailing view of this small, neo-progressive public school, she is able to implement her philosophy in her upper-level middle school classroom. [T]he structure of the school and the organization of the school day, which permits more personalization and more time with each class, are school variables that allow her a chance to succeed in redefining the authority relationships in her class" (Dollase 1992, 101).

What Characteristics Distinguish Successful Schools?

Like Miss Martin referenced above, you may be uncertain at this point in your professional education of your ability to develop a positive classroom climate at a school. However, a great many schools in all settings and with all kinds of students are highly successful, including inner-city and isolated rural schools and schools that serve pupils of all socioeconomic, racial, and ethnic backgrounds. What are the characteristics of these schools? Do they have commonalities that account for their success?

Measures of Success

First, we must define what we mean by a *successful school*. One measure of success, naturally, is that students at these schools achieve at a high level and complete requirements for graduation. Whether reflected in scores on standardized tests or other documentation of academic learning gains, students at these schools are learning. They are achieving literacy in reading, writing, computation, and computer skills. They are learning to solve problems, think creatively and analytically, and, most importantly, they are learning to learn.

Another valid measure of success for a school is that it achieves results that surpass those expected from comparable schools in comparable settings. The achievement of students goes beyond what one would expect. In spite of surrounding social, economic, and political forces that impede the educative process at other schools, these schools are achieving results.

Finally, **successful schools** are those that are improving, rather than getting worse. School improvement is a slow process, and schools that are improving—moving in the right direction rather than declining—are also successful.

Research on School Effectiveness

During the 1980s and early 1990s, much research was conducted to identify the characteristics of successful (or effective) schools. The characteristics of successful schools were described in different ways in several research projects. The following is a synthesis of those findings.

- *Strong leadership*—Successful schools have strong leaders—individuals who value education and see themselves as educational leaders, not just as managers or bureaucrats. They monitor the performance of everyone at the school—teachers, staff, students, and themselves. These leaders have a vision of the school as a more effective learning environment, and they take decisive steps to bring that about.
- *High expectations*—Teachers at successful schools have high expectations of students. These teachers believe that all students, rich or poor, can learn, and they communicate this to students through realistic, yet high, expectations.
- *Emphasis on basic skills*—Teachers at successful schools emphasize student achievement in the basic skills of reading, writing, and mathematical computation.
- *Orderly school environment*—The environments of successful schools are orderly, safe, and conducive to learning. Discipline problems are at a minimum, and teachers are able to devote greater amounts of time to teaching.
- *Frequent, systematic evaluation of student learning*—The learning of students in successful schools is monitored closely. When difficulties are noticed, appropriate remediation is provided quickly.
- *Sense of purpose*—Those who teach and those who learn at successful schools have a strong sense of purpose. From the principal to the students, everyone at the school is guided by a vision of excellence.
- *Collegiality and a sense of community*—Teachers, administrators, and staff at successful schools work well together. They are dedicated to creating an environ-

ment that promotes not only student learning but also their own professional growth and development.

Research has also focused on strategies for making schools more effective. Since the early 1990s, school districts across the nation have been participating in **school restructuring** that changes the way students are grouped, uses of classroom time and space, instructional methods, and decision making. A synthesis of research (Newmann and Wehlage 1995) conducted between 1990 and 1995 on restructuring schools identified four characteristics of successful schools:

- *Focus on student learning*—Planning, implementation, and evaluation focus on enhancing the intellectual quality of student learning. All students are expected to achieve academic excellence.
- *Emphasis on authentic pedagogy*—Students are required to think, to develop in-depth understanding, and to apply academic learning to important, realistic problems. Students might, for example, conduct a survey on an issue of local concern, analyze the results, and then present their findings at a town council meeting.
- *Greater school organizational capacity*—The ability of the school to strive for continuous improvement through professional collaboration is enhanced. For example, teachers exchange ideas to improve their teaching; they seek feedback from students, parents, and community members; and they attend conferences and workshops to acquire new materials and strategies.
- *Greater external support*—The school receives critical financial, technical, and political support from outside sources.

In short, the cultures of effective schools encourage teachers to grow and develop in the practice of their profession.

What Social Problems Affect Schools and Place Students at Risk?

A complex and varied array of social issues impact schools. These problems often detract from the ability of schools to educate students according to the seven aims discussed at the beginning of this chapter: national goals, prosocial values, socialization, achievement, personal growth, social change, and equal opportunity. Furthermore, schools are often charged with the difficult (if not impossible) task of providing a front-line defense against such problems.

One of the most vocal advocates of the role of schools in solving social problems was George S. Counts, who said in his 1932 book *Dare the School Build a New Social Order?* that "If schools are to be really effective, they must become centers for the building, and not merely the contemplation, of our civilization" (p. 12). Many people, however, believe that schools should not try to build a new social order. They should be concerned only with the academic and social development of students—not with solving society's problems. Nevertheless, the debate over the role of schools in regard to social problems will continue to be vigorous. For some time, schools have served in the battle against social problems by offering an array of health, education, and social service programs. Schools provide breakfasts, nutritional counseling, diagnostic services related to health and family planning, after-school child care, job placement, and sex and drug education, to name a few. In the following sections we examine several societal problems that directly influence schools, teachers, and students.

Identifying Students at Risk

An increasing number of young people live under conditions characterized by extreme stress, chronic poverty, crime, and lack of adult guidance. As James Garbarino (1999, 19) points out in *Lost Boys: Why Our Sons Turn Violent and How We Can Save Them*: "In almost every community in America, growing numbers of kids live in a socially toxic environment." Frustrated, lonely, and feeling powerless, many youths escape into music with violence-oriented and/or obscene lyrics, violent video games, cults, movies and television programs that celebrate gratuitous violence and sex, and cruising shopping malls or "hanging out" on the street. Others turn also to crime, gang violence, promiscuous sex, or substance abuse. Not surprisingly, these activities place many young people at risk of dropping out of school. In fact, it is estimated that the following percentages of fourteen-year-olds are likely to exhibit one or more at-risk behaviors (substance abuse, sexual behavior, violence, depression, or school failure) and to experience serious negative outcomes as a result: 10 percent at very high risk, 25 percent at high risk, 25 percent at moderate risk, 20 percent at low risk, and 20 percent at no risk (Dryfoos 1998).

Table 4.3

Grouped by race/ethnicity or family income, students drop out of school at varying rates. Table 4.3, for example, shows that between 1972 and 1996, the dropout rate for Latinos has been consistently higher than the rates for other groups. Also, while the dropout rate for African American students declined significantly during that period, African American students were still more likely overall to drop out of school than their white peers. Lastly, the data reveal that students from low-income families are more likely to drop out than their counterparts from middle- and high-income families. **Students at risk** of dropping out tend to get low grades, perform below grade level academically, are older than the average student at their grade level because of previous retention, and have behavior problems in school.

Many youth take more than the typical four years to complete high school, or they eventually earn a high school equivalency certificate (GED). If these alternative routes to high school completion are considered, however, there are still significant differences among racial/ethnic groups. For example, in 1997, 92.9 percent of whites between the ages of 25 and 29 had completed high school, compared to 86.9 percent of African Americans and 61.8 percent of Latinos (National Center for Education Statistics 1998a).

Many children in the United States live in families that help them grow up healthy, confident, and skilled, but many do not. Instead, their life settings are characterized by problems of alcoholism or other substance abuse, family or gang violence, unemployment, poverty, poor nutrition, teenage parenthood, and a history of school failure. Such children live in communities and families that have many problems and frequently become dysfunctional, unable to provide their children with the support and guidance they need. According to *Kids Count Data Book, 1999*, "13 percent, or 9.2 million, of our children are growing up with a collection of disadvantages that could curtail, if not scuttle, their chances to become productive adult participants in the mainstream of America's future" (Annie E. Casey Foundation 1999, 1).

Children who experience the negative effects of poverty are from families of all ethnic and racial groups. As Marian Wright Edelman (November 9, 1997, B5), founder and president of the Children's Defense Fund, said:

> Since 1973, families headed by someone younger than 30 have suffered a collapse in the value of their incomes, a surge in poverty, and a stunning erosion of employer-provided health benefits for their children. . . . Virtually every category of young families with young children has suffered major losses in median incomes: whites

(22 percent), Hispanics (28 percent), and blacks (46 percent). . . . Low-income children are two or three times more likely to suffer from health problems, including infant death, iron deficiency, stunted growth, severe physical or mental disabilities, and fatal accidental injuries . . . the risk of students falling behind in school goes up by 2 percentage points for every year spent in poverty.

The life experiences of students who are at risk of dropping out can be difficult for teachers to imagine; and, as the following comments by a student teacher in an inner-city third-grade classroom illustrate, encountering the realities of poverty for the first time can be upsetting:

> Roughly 85 percent of [students are] living in poverty. The entire school population is eligible for free or reduced lunch. I was horrified. I guess I was a little ignorant of other people's situations.

> [Some] students came in wearing the same clothes for a week. Others would come in without socks on. No pencils, crayons, scissors, or glue. Some without breakfast, lunch, or a snack. My heart bled every day. I found myself becoming upset about their lives. I even found myself thinking about them at night and over the weekend. [I] noticed that they were extremely bright students, but their home life and economic status hindered them from working to their potential. Some of my students couldn't even complete their homework because they had no glue, scissors, or crayons at home (Molino 1999, 55).

Children and Poverty

Although the United States is one of the richest countries in the world, it has by no means achieved an enviable record in regard to poverty among children. According to the U.S. Census Bureau, 21 percent of children under eighteen years of age, or 14.7 million, lived in families below the poverty line in 1998 (see Figure 4.2). In the District of Columbia, 40 percent lived in poverty; 32 percent in Louisiana; and 30 percent in New Mexico and Mississippi (Annie E. Casey Foundation 1999).

Figure 4.2

Despite the healthy economy during the last half of the 1990s, it was estimated that every night about 600,000 people, 15 percent of whom are children, were homeless (Department of Health and Human Services, 1999). And, not surprisingly, the incidence of child abuse, poor health, underachievement in school, and attendance problems is higher among these children than it is among children with homes.

Family Stress

The stress placed on families in a complex society is extensive and not easily handled. For some families, such stress can be overwhelming. The structure of families who are experiencing the effects of financial problems, substance abuse, or violence, for example, can easily begin to crumble.

The National Clearinghouse on Child Abuse and Neglect (NCCAN) reported that state Child Protective Service (CPS) agencies investigated an estimated two million reports of alleged child maltreatment, involving approximately three million children in 1996. Of these children, CPS determined that almost one million were victims of substantiated or indicated abuse or neglect, an increase of approximately 18 percent since 1990 (National Clearinghouse on Child Abuse and Neglect 1998). Clearly, the burden of having to cope with such abuse in the home environment does not prepare a child to come to school to learn.

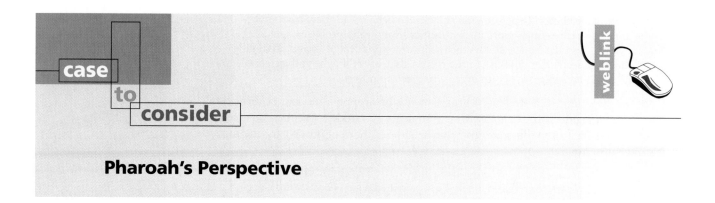

case to consider

Pharoah's Perspective

Figure 4.2

Stress within the family can have a significant negative effect on students and their ability to focus on learning while at school. Such stress is often associated with health and emotional problems, failure to achieve, behavioral problems at school, and dropping out of school.

With the high rise in divorce and women's entry into the workforce, family constellations have changed dramatically. No longer is a working father, a mother who stays at home, and two or three children the only kind of family in the United States. The number of single-parent families, stepparent families, blended families, and extended families has increased dramatically during the last decade. Figure 4.2 shows that one in three families with children was headed by a single parent in 1998.

Just as there is diversity in the composition of today's families, so, too, there is diversity in the styles with which children are raised in families. Because of the number of working women and single-parent homes, an alarming number of children are unsupervised during much of the day. It has been estimated that there may be as many as five million such **latchkey children** between the ages of five and fourteen (Child Care Bureau 1997). To meet the needs of latchkey children, many schools offer before- and after-school programs.

In addition, many middle-class couples are waiting longer to have children. Although children of such couples may have more material advantages, they may be "impoverished" in regard to the reduced time they spend with their parents. To maintain their life-style, these parents are often driven to spend more time developing their careers. As a result, the care and guidance their children receive is inadequate, and "Sustained bad care eventually leads to a deep-seated inner sense of insecurity and inadequacy, emotional pain, and a troublesome sense of self" (Comer 1997, 83). To fill the parenting void that characterizes the lives of an increasing number of children from all economic classes, schools and teachers are being called on to play an increased role in the socialization of young people.

Substance Abuse

Video 4.1

One of the most pressing social problems confronting today's schools is the abuse of illegal drugs, tobacco, and alcohol. Though drug abuse by students moved from the top-ranked problem facing local schools according to the 1996 Gallup Poll of public's attitudes toward the public schools to the fourth-ranked problem in the 1998 poll, drug use among students actually increased during the 1990s. The National Education Goals

Panel reported that the percentage of tenth graders who reported using illicit drugs increased from 24 percent in 1991 to 40 percent in 1997, and the percentage reporting that someone offered to sell or give them an illegal drug at school during the previous year rose from 18 percent in 1992 to 33 percent in 1997 (National Education Goals Panel 1998, 15). Table 4.4 (see p. 145) shows the percentages of eighth, tenth, and twelfth graders who reported using alcohol or drugs between 1991 and 1997.

Table 4.4

The use of drugs among young people varies from community to community and from year to year, but overall it is disturbingly high. Mind-altering substances used by young people include the easily acquired glue, white correction fluid, and felt marker, as well as marijuana, amphetamines, and cocaine. The abuse of drugs not only poses the risks of addiction and overdosing, but is also related to problems such as HIV/AIDS, teenage pregnancy, depression, suicide, automobile accidents, criminal activity, and dropping out of school.

For an alarming number of young people, drugs are seen as a way of coping with life's problems.

Violence and Crime

While the nation experienced a decline in serious violent crimes during the 1990s, crime rates among adolescents rose during the same period. Nearly one million adolescents between the ages of twelve and nineteen are victims of violent crimes each year (Hamburg 1997), and since World War II, there has been a sevenfold increase in serious assaults by juveniles in the United States (Garbarino 1999). Each year, almost 5 percent of high school seniors report being injured with a weapon during the previous twelve months, 13 percent threatened with a weapon, and 12 percent injured without a weapon (National Center for Education Statistics 1998a). Figure 4.3 shows the extent of criminal incidents in public schools by seriousness of crimes, instructional level, and location.

Figure 4.3

In addition, the U.S. Department of Justice estimates that there are more than 30,500 gangs and approximately 816,000 gang members (Moore and Terrett, 1999). An eleven-city survey of eighth graders found that 9 percent were currently gang members, and 17 percent said they had belonged to a gang at some point in their lives (Esbensen and Osgood 1997). Gang membership is perceived by many youth as providing them with several advantages: a sense of belonging and identity, protection from other gangs, opportunities for excitement, or a chance to make money through selling drugs or participating in other illegal activities. Though few students are gang members, a small number of gang-affiliated students can disrupt the learning process, create disorder in a school, and cause others to fear for their physical safety. Strategies for reducing the effect of gang activities on schools include the identification of gang members, implementing dress codes that ban styles of dress identified with gangs, and quickly removing gang graffiti from the school.

The nation's concern about school crime and safety heightened as a result of a string of school shootings between 1996 and 1999. Among the communities that had to cope with such tragic incidents were Moses Lake, Washington (1996); Pearl, Mississippi (1997); West Paducah, Kentucky (1997); Jonesboro, Arkansas (1998); Springfield, Oregon (1998); and Littleton, Colorado (1999).

Alarmed by the rise in school violence, President Clinton asked the U.S. Departments of Justice and Education to begin preparing an *Annual Report on School Safety*, the first of which was released in 1998. In addition, shortly after the killings in

Figure 4.4

Video 4.2

Appendix 4.1

Colorado, Clinton convened a White House conference on youth violence that included representatives from the gun manufacturing, television, movie, and video games industries. Since the recurring question after each instance of horrific school violence was why, there was a renewed effort to understand the origins of youth violence. Indeed, the entire nation debated gun control measures; the influence of violence in television, movies, and point-and-shoot video games; and steps that parents, schools, and communities could take to curb school crime and violence. Figure 4.4 shows the percentage of schools reporting various types of security measures.

The increased use of guns by children and youth to solve conflicts is one consequence of the "gun culture" in the United States, in which it is estimated that nearly 40 percent of homes have at least one gun (Garbarino 1999). On the issue of television violence, the American Psychological Association reviewed research studies and concluded that television violence *alone* is responsible for up to 15 percent of all aggressive behavior by children and youth (Garbarino 1999). Lastly, David Grossman, a military psychologist, and his colleague pointed out that violent point-and-shoot video games are similar to those used to "desensitize" soldiers to shoot at human figures (Grossman and Siddle 1999).

As a result of the school shootings listed earlier and the public's concern with school crime and violence, many schools developed crisis management plans to cope with violent incidents on campus. Schools also reviewed their ability to provide students, faculty, and staff with a safe environment for learning; for example, Appendix 4.1 presents a "School Safety Checklist" excerpted from the National Education Association's *School Safety Check Book*. Additionally, to help troubled youth *before* they commit violence, educators familiarized themselves with research-identified risk factors for violence such as the following: economic and social deprivation, family history of substance abuse and/or crime, lack of effective parenting and parental rejection, victimization by physical or sexual abuse, observation of domestic violence, early conduct problems, academic failure, substance abuse, gang affiliation, and possessing of guns (Washington State Department of Health, Non-Infectious Disease and Conditions Epidemiology Section 1994).

Professional Reflection   **Identifying the factors behind youth violence**

Teen Pregnancy

Each year more than one million U.S. teenagers (one in nine women between the ages of fifteen and nineteen) become pregnant, and about 85 percent of these pregnancies are unintended. This figure includes about 18 percent of all African American women ages fifteen to nineteen, 16 percent of Latina women, and 8 percent of Anglo-European women (Alan Guttmacher Institute 1999). Indeed, most teachers of adolescents today may expect to have at least some students who are, or have been, pregnant.

Since peaking in 1990, the teenage pregnancy, birth, and abortion rates have declined 17 percent; about 20 percent of this decrease is the result of decreased sexual activity and 80 percent the result of more effective contraceptive practices among sexually active teenagers (Alan Guttmacher Institute 1999). Nevertheless, teen pregnancies remain a serious problem in society. Because the physical development of girls in adolescence may not be complete, complications can occur during pregnancy and in the birthing process. Also, adolescents are less likely to receive prenatal care in the crucial first trimester; they tend not to eat well-balanced diets; and are not free of harmful substances such as alcohol, tobacco, and drugs, which are known to be detrimental to

Should metal detectors be installed in schools?

a baby's development. These young mothers "are at risk for chronic educational, occupational, and financial difficulties, and their offspring are also at risk for medical, educational, and behavioral problems" (Durlak 1995, 66). Because most teen mothers drop out of school, forfeiting their high school diplomas and limiting their access to decent, higher-paying job opportunities, they and their children stay at the bottom of the economic ladder.

Students with HIV/AIDS

One of the most challenging social problems confronting the schools is providing for the education of children who have HIV/AIDS (human immunodeficiency virus/ acquired immune deficiency syndrome). With AIDS, nearly always fatal, the body is no longer able to defend itself against disease. Many school districts have been involved in litigation over the right of children with HIV/AIDS to attend school, and the condom-distribution programs that a few school systems have initiated to stem the spread of the HIV virus have been challenged in the courts.

According to the Centers for Disease Control and Prevention (CDC), the number of AIDS cases continues to increase at an alarming rate. During 1998, 48,269 persons were reported with AIDS, bringing the total number of persons reported with AIDS since the beginning of the epidemic to 688,200. In 1998, the World Health Organization reported that, worldwide, as many as 42 million people had been infected with HIV since the epidemic began, and that each day 16,000 more become infected and 1,600 babies are born with HIV.

Increasingly, states are beginning to require that schools provide information on HIV/AIDS and how to avoid the disease. The CDC reported in 1998 that about 87 percent of states required a separate health education course between grades six and twelve, and that HIV education was a part of almost all of those required courses. In addition, the CDC found that more than half of schools had a written policy on HIV infection and students and school staff (Centers for Disease Control and Prevention 1998a). To promote the development and implementation of HIV education programs for school-age populations, the CDC funds an HIV education coordinator in each state.

Suicide among Children and Youths

The increase in individual and multiple suicides is alarming. The National Institute for Mental Health (1999) reported that suicide is the third leading cause of death among youth ages fifteen to twenty-four and accounts for more than 4,000 deaths yearly for this group. The Institute also estimated that there are eight to twenty-five attempted suicides for one completion. According to the Centers for Disease Control and Prevention (1998b), about 21 percent of high school students seriously considered committing suicide in 1997; about 16 percent made a specific suicide plan; about 8 percent

Audio Clip 4.2

actually attempted suicide; and about 3 percent required medical attention as a result of their suicide attempt.

Although female students are almost two times more likely than male students to have seriously considered attempting suicide during the preceding twelve months, about six times as many male students as females actually commit suicide. Latino students are about two times more likely than white students to attempt suicide, and students in grade nine are about four times more likely than students in grade twelve to make a suicide attempt that requires medical attention (Centers for Disease Control and Prevention 1998b). Also, lesbian and gay youth are two to three times more likely to attempt suicide than their heterosexual peers, and they account for up to 30 percent of all completed suicides among youth (Besner and Spungin 1995).

What Are Schools Doing to Address Societal Problems?

Responding to the needs of at-risk students will be a crucial challenge for schools, families, and communities during the twenty-first century. Since most children attend school, it is logical that this pre-existing system be used for reaching large numbers of at-risk children (and, through them, their families). During the last decade, many school districts have taken innovative steps to address societal problems that impact students' lives.

Though programs that address social problems are costly, the public believes that schools should be used for the delivery of health and social services to students and their families. According to the 1995 Gallup Poll of the Public's Attitudes toward the Public Schools, for example, 91 percent of respondents said that "serving the emotional and health needs of students" is "very important" or "somewhat important" (Elam and Rose 1995, 44). However, there is some disagreement about the extent to which school facilities should be used for anything but meeting students' educational needs. For example, in a publication titled *Putting Learning First,* the Committee for Economic Development (1994, 1) stated, "Schools are not social service institutions; they should not be asked to solve all our nation's social ills and cultural conflicts." In isolated instances, community groups and school boards have resisted school-based services such as family planning clinics and mental health services. Meanwhile, increases in state funding and foundation support to provide school-based health, mental health, and social services have tended to dissipate most of this resistance (Dryfoos 1998).

Intervention Programs

Under pressure to find solutions to increasing social problems among children and adolescents, educators have developed an array of intervention programs. In general, the aim of these programs is to address the behavioral, social, and academic adjustment of at-risk children and adolescents so they can receive maximum benefit from their school experiences.

In the following sections, we briefly review several comprehensive strategies that have proven effective in addressing academic, social, and behavioral problems among children and adolescents; these approaches to intervention are peer counseling, full-service schools, and school-based interprofessional case management. Chapter 14 presents additional information about recent, innovative steps schools are taking for the *prevention* of the effects of social problems on students. Also see Appendix 4.2 for "Selected Resources for Meeting Needs of Students Placed at Risk"—a list of publications, organizations, and online locations that are good sources of information on the problems children and youth may encounter.

Appendix 4.2
Weblink 4.1
Weblink 4.2
Weblink 4.3
Weblink 4.4
Weblink 4.5

Peer Counseling   To address the social problems that affect students, some schools have initiated student-to-student **peer counseling** programs—usually monitored by a school counselor or other specially trained adult. In peer counseling programs, students can address problems and issues such as low academic achievement, interpersonal problems at home and at school, substance abuse, and career planning. Evidence indicates that both peer counselors and students experience increased self-esteem and greater ability to deal with problems.

When peer counseling is combined with cross-age tutoring, younger students can learn about drugs, alcohol, premarital pregnancy, delinquency, dropping out, HIV/AIDS, suicide, and other relevant issues. Here the groups are often college-age students meeting with those in high school, or high school students meeting with those in junior high school or middle school. In these preventative programs, older students sometimes perform dramatic episodes that portray students confronting problems and model strategies for handling the situations presented.

Full-Service Schools   In response to the increasing number of at-risk students, many schools are serving their communities by integrating educational, medical, social and/or human services. **Full-service schools** tend to be in low-income urban areas

What approach to the education of students at risk does the scene in this photograph represent? What other risk factors affect children and youths? What are some other effective approaches for helping students at risk to succeed in school?

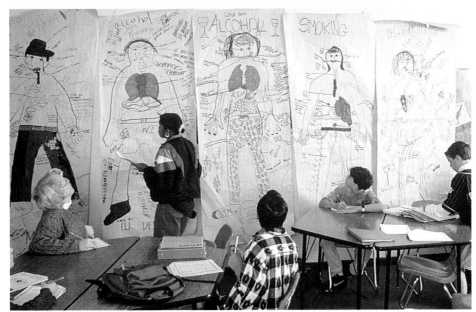

Weblink 4.6

and involve collaborative partnerships among school districts, departments of public health, hospitals, and various nonprofit organizations. At full-service schools, students and their families can receive health screening, psychological counseling, drug prevention counseling, parent education, and family planning information. See the Teacher's Resource Guide section "Family Needs Assessment" on this book's website.

One example of a full-service school is award-winning Salome Urena Middle Academy (SUMA), a middle school serving a Dominican community in Washington Heights, New York. Open six days per week, fifteen hours per day, year round, SUMA offers before-school and after-school child care. Through seventy-five partnerships with various community groups and agencies, SUMA offers a comprehensive, integrated array of programs and services to children and their families. Students may enroll in their choice of four academies—business; community service; expressive arts; and mathematics, science, and technology. A Family Institute offers English as a second language, Spanish, aerobics, and entrepreneurial skills. At a Family Resource Center, social workers, paraprofessionals, parents, and other volunteers offer help with immigration, employment, and housing. Next to the Family Resource Center, a clinic provides dental, medical, and mental health services. Each year, the school's more than 1,200 students, their parents, and siblings are served at a cost significantly less than the per-pupil expenditures in most suburban schools. Moreover, according to an evaluation conducted by Fordham University, the school has realized a significant increase in attendance, a major reduction in misbehavior, and a modest increase in test scores (Dryfoos 1994, 1998; Karvarsky 1994).

School-Based Interprofessional Case Management In responding to the needs of at-risk students, it has been suggested that schools "will need to reconceptualize the networks of community organizations and public services that might assist, and they will need to draw on those community resources" (Edwards and Young 1992, 78). One such approach to forming new home/school/community partnerships is known as **school-based interprofessional case management.** The approach uses professionally trained case managers who work directly with teachers, the community, and the family to coordinate and deliver appropriate services to at-risk students and their families. The case management approach is based on a comprehensive service delivery network of teachers, social agencies, and health service agencies.

One of the first case-management programs in the country is operated by the Center for the Study and Teaching of At-Risk Students (C-STARS) and serves 20 school districts in the Pacific Northwest. Center members include Washington State University, the University of Washington, a community-based organization, and Washington State's Department of Social and Health Services. Working with teachers and other school personnel, an interprofessional case management team fulfills seven functions to meet the needs of at-risk students: assessment, development of a service plan, brokering with other agencies, service implementation and coordination, advocacy, monitoring and evaluation, and mentoring. Program evaluation data have shown significant measurable improvements in student's attendance, academic performance, and school behavior.

Compensatory Education

To meet the learning needs of at-risk students, several federally funded **compensatory education programs** for elementary and secondary students have been developed, the largest of which is Title I. Launched in 1965 as part of the Elementary and Secondary Education Act (ESEA) and President Lyndon Johnson's Great Society education program, Title I (called Chapter I between 1981 and 1994) was designed to improve the basic skills (reading, writing, and mathematics) of low-ability students from low-income families. Each year, more than five million students (about 10 percent of enrollments) in nearly all school districts benefit from Title I programs. The Educational Excellence for All Children Act of 1999, President Clinton's plan for reauthorizing the Elementary and Secondary Education Act, including Title I, called for dramatic new steps to improve education for at-risk students. The $8 billion program called for an end to "social promotion" in schools and higher standards for teacher quality and training. Moreover, school districts would be required to show by 2002 that their Title I schools are treated the same as their other schools regarding staff qualifications, curricula, and the condition and safety of school buildings (*Education Week* 1999c).

Students who participate in Title I programs are usually taught through "pull-out" programs, in which they leave the regular classroom to receive additional instruction individually or in small groups. Title I teachers, sometimes assisted by an aide, often have curriculum materials and equipment not available to regular classroom teachers.

Research on the effectiveness of Title I programs has been inconclusive, with some studies reporting achievement gains not found in other studies. Recent research has found positive effects on students' achievement in the early grades, but these gains tend to dissipate during the middle grades. The pattern of short-lived gains is strongest for students attending urban schools that serve a high proportion of families in poverty (Levine and Levine 1996). Some critics of Title I and other compensatory education programs such as Head Start for preschool children, Success for All for preschool and elementary children, and Upward Bound for high school students argue that they are stopgap measures at best. Instead, they maintain, social problems such as poverty, the breakdown of families, drug abuse, and crime that contribute to poor school performance should be reduced.

Alternative Schools and Curricula

To meet the needs of students whom social problems place at risk, many school districts have developed alternative schools and curricula. Usually, an **alternative school** is a small, highly individualized school separate from the regular school; in other cases, the alternative school is organized as a **school-within-a-school.** Alternative school programs usually provide remedial instruction, some vocational training, and individualized counseling. Since they usually have much smaller class sizes, alternative school teachers can monitor students' progress more closely and, when problems do arise, respond more quickly and with greater understanding of student needs.

One exemplary alternative school is the Buffalo Alternative High School serving at-risk seventh to twelfth grade students in the Buffalo, New York, Public School District. To reach students who are not successful at regular schools, the Buffalo program offers individualized instruction, small class sizes, and various enrichment programs delivered in what school staff describe as a "supportive, noncoercive, nontraditional setting." Most students are expected to return to their regular schools after a minimum of four weeks. Students must earn 600 "points" (based on attendance, punctuality, attitude, behavior, and performance) to return to their regular school.

In addition, the Buffalo Alternative High School operates eight satellite schools in nonschool buildings throughout Buffalo. Among these programs are:

- *SAVe (Suspension Avoidance Vehicle)*—a two-week program students complete before returning to their sending school or enrolling in the Alternative High School
- *City-as-School*—students serve as interns in the public and private sectors and earn academic credit
- *SMART (Students Moving Ahead Through Remediation Testing)*—seventh- and eighth-grade students held behind can qualify for promotion to the appropriate grade
- *Bilingual Satellite*—educational services provided to Spanish-speaking students

While they don't work in alternative school settings, many highly effective regular teachers have developed alternative curricula to meet the unique learning needs of students at risk. Many teachers, for example, link students' learning to the business, civic, cultural, and political segments of their communities. The rationale is that connecting at-risk students to the world beyond their schools will enable them to see the relevance of education.

SUMMARY

What Are the Aims of Education Today? (p. 98)

How Can Schools Be Described? (p. 101)

What Are Schools Like as Social Institutions? (p. 103)

What Characteristics Distinguish Successful Schools? (p. 107)

What Social Problems Affect Schools and Place Students at Risk? (p. 109)

What Are Schools Doing to Address Social Problems? (p. 116)

KEY TERMS AND CONCEPTS

Go to the website for interactive flashcards.

APPLICATIONS AND INTERACTIVITIES

Go to the website for interactive assignments in the following areas:

Teacher's Journal

Teacher's Database

Observations and Interviews

Professional Portfolio

Handout Master M4.1
Handout Master M4.2

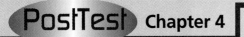

Name _____ **Date** _____

For each question, write in the blank the answer you believe is correct.

4.1 In addition to training the intellect, schools are places where young people are _____—where they learn to participate intelligently and constructively in society.

4.2 Although schools have many aims, _____ is the most universally accepted among them.

4.3 Efforts to provide equal educational _____ for all has long distinguished education in the United States from that found in most other countries.

4.4 Terms like *climate, ethos, atmosphere,* and *character* have been used to describe school _____.

4.5 The self-contained classroom is the most traditional and prevalent arrangement at the _____ school level.

4.6 Schools seeking to improve the way students are grouped, uses of classroom time and space, instructional methods, and decision making are said to be engaged in school _____.

4.7 Students who are likely to drop out of school, earn low grades, and exhibit behavior problems are said to be at _____.

4.8 Children living in homes where they are unsupervised for much of the day are sometimes known as _____children.

4.9 Although twice as many female students have seriously considered suicide, about _____ times as many male students actually commit suicide.

4.10 Some schools serving large numbers of at-risk students have begun integrating educational, medical, social, and/or human services on the school campus. Such schools are known as _____-service schools.

Answers are available on the FlexChoice website at www.ablongman.com/parkayflex.

Name _____

Keep this checklist at your computer as a reminder to read and complete the chapter features and activities located on the FlexChoice website at www.ablongman.com/parkayflex.

**Date
Completed**

_____ ❑ **PreTest with Answers**

_____ ❑ **Audio Clip 4.1:** Thinking Over the Opening Vignette

_____ ❑ **Table 4.1:** What are the most important criteria for measuring school effectiveness?

_____ ❑ **Table 4.2:** Percentage of three- and four-year-olds enrolled in early childhood programs by selected student characteristics: 1991, 1993, 1995, and 1996

_____ ❑ **Figure 4.1:** The institutional structure of education in the United States

_____ ❑ **Technology Highlights:** Do students in urban schools have equal access to up-to-date technologies?

_____ ❑ **Table 4.3:** Event dropout rates for those in grades ten through twelve, ages fifteen to twenty-four, by race/ethnicity and family income: October 1972–96

_____ ❑ **Figure 4.2:** Percentage of children with certain risks

_____ ❑ **Case to Consider:** Pharoah's Perspective

_____ ❑ **Video 4.1:** Substance Abuse

_____ ❑ **Table 4.4:** Percentage of students who reported using alcohol or drugs any time during the previous thirty days, by type of drug and grade: School years 1991–97

_____ ❑ **Figure 4.3:** Percentage of public schools reporting one or more criminal incidents to police and number of incidents reported per 1,000 students by seriousness of crimes, instructional level, and urbanicity: 1996-97

_____ ❑ **Figure 4.4:** Security measures

_____ ❑ **Video 4.2:** Guns in Schools

_____ ❑ **Appendix 4.1:** School Safety Checklist

_____ ❑ **Professional Reflection:** Identifying the factors behind youth violence

_____ ❑ **Where Do You Stand?:** Should metal detectors be installed in schools?

_____ ❑ **Audio Clip 4.2:** Teen Suicide

_____ ❑ **Appendix 4.2:** Selected Resources for Meeting Needs of Students Placed at Risk

_____ ❑ **Weblink 4.1:** American Red Cross

_____ ❑ **Weblink 4.2:** Center for Research on the Education of Students Placed at Risk

_____ ❑ **Weblink 4.3:** Children's Defense Fund

_____ ❑ **Weblink 4.4:** The Family Resource Coalition of America

_____ ❑ **Weblink 4.5:** National Institute on the Education of At-Risk Students

_____ ❑ **Weblink 4.6:** Family Needs Assessment

_____ ❑ **Summary**

_____ ❑ **Key Terms and Concepts**

_____ ❑ **Applications and Interactivities:** Teacher's Journal

_____ ❑ **Applications and Interactivities:** Teacher's Database

_____ ❑ **Applications and Interactivities:** Observations and Interviews

_____ ❑ **Handout Master M4.1:** Observing Characteristics of Effective Schools

_____ ❑ **Handout Master M4.2:** Analyzing Impacts of Social Problems on Schools

_____ ❑ **Applications and Interactivities:** Professional Portfolio

_____ ❑ **PostTest with Answers**

5

Struggles for Control of Schools in the United States

In the late 1990s, we asked teachers to estimate the current status of the teacher empowerment reform effort at their school. . . . Two-thirds of the teachers responded that the reforms had been incorporated either in a robust and major way or in a partial but still significant way.

—Gerald Grant and Christine E. Murray
Teaching in America: The Slow Revolution

1. Who is involved in the struggles for control of schools in the United States?

2. What is the role of the local community in school governance?

3. What powers and influence do states have in governing schools?

4. What assistance do regional education agencies provide?

5. How does the federal government influence education?

6. How are schools financed in the United States?

7. What are some trends in funding for equity and excellence?

O n entering the teachers' lounge during your planning period, you can tell immediately that the four teachers in the room are having a heated discussion.

"I don't see how you can say that teachers have much control over the schools," says Kim, a language arts teacher who came to the school three years ago. "It's all so political. The feds, our legislators, the school board—it's the politicians who really control the schools. This April all my kids have to take a test based on the new state standards—we didn't write the standards, it was the politicians. They exploit the schools just so they can get elected."

"If you want to know who *really* controls the schools," Enrique, a mathematics teacher, says, "it's big business. The politicians are actually their pawns. Big business is concerned about international competition—so, they exert tremendous pressure on the politicians who, in turn, lean on the teachers. And then. . ."

"Just a minute," says Frank, raising his hand to silence Enrique. Frank is one of the school's lead teachers and chair of the site-based council. "Maybe that's the way things were in the past, but things *are* changing. I'm not saying that politics or big business doesn't influence the schools, but we have a lot of influence over what we teach and how. Look at our site-based council and all the decisions we've made during the last two years—block scheduling, teaching teams, a common planning time, and integrated curricula."

"Right, teaching really is changing," says Roberta, a science teacher and multimedia coordinator for the school. She motions for you to have a seat at the table. Feeling a bit uncomfortable at the intensity of the discussion, but anxious to fit in with your new colleagues, you take a seat. "When I first started teaching ten years ago," Roberta continues, "I never thought I'd see as many changes as I've seen in the last few years."

"Name one change," says Kim. "Things are still top-down. The politicians, the governor, the school board, the superintendent, the principal—they all tell us what to do."

"Well, like Frank said, look at all the decisions our site-based council has made," Roberta answers. "Plus, just think about the National Board for Professional Teaching Standards—now we've got the option of becoming board certified, just like lawyers have the bar exam and architects have their licensing exam. Also, the majority of the board is made up of teachers, and they helped to develop the standards."

"Good example," Frank says. "Already there's a few thousand board-certified teachers, and there's supposed to be more than 100,000 by 2005. I'm working on my portfolio so I can apply next year."

"It's just a matter of time before board-certified teachers come to have more leverage in controlling the schools," says Roberta. "With more and more districts moving to some sort of school choice, the school that has more board-certified teachers is going to attract more students. So, teachers with board certification will be able to set the conditions under which they work. The market value of board certification is going to rise."

"Exactly," says Frank. "Right now in North Carolina, board-certified teachers get a 12 percent increase in pay."

"Well, I don't quite share your optimism about how teachers are going to have all this influence," says Kim. "Look at every presidential election—the Democrats and Republicans always try to exploit education. So, they talk about all the changes they'd make . . . higher standards, more accountability for teachers, more input for parents, and so on. Plus all politicians—whether they're running for president, governor, or whatever—they use education to build their political careers, and teachers are the ones who have to implement their utopian ideas."

"I agree to some extent," says Roberta. "Politicians will always use education for their own ends. But that's just rhetoric; what's really happening, bit by bit, is that teachers are becoming much more influential."

"Let's just ask this new teacher here," says Frank as he smiles and nods in your direction. "Don't you think teachers have a lot of influence over how schools are run? During the rest of your career, you'll be involved in school governance, won't you?"

Frank, Roberta, Enrique, and Kim look at you, awaiting your response. What do you say?

Name _____ **Date** _____

For each question, circle the letter of the answer you believe is correct. Then read the chapter to learn more about these topics.

5.1 The responsibility for managing schools is primarily a function of the
A. U.S. Department of Education.
B. Federal government.
C. Intermediate region.
D. States.

5.2 Ensuring that schools operate in accordance with federal and state guidelines is the responsibility of the
A. School board.
B. Professional education association.
C. State board of education.
D. Superintendent.

5.3 An approach to school improvement in which teachers, principals, students, parents, and community members manage individual schools and share in the decision-making process is known as
A. The entitlement process.
B. Equity for Students (EFS).
C. Indirect governance.
D. School-based management.

5.4 The body that determines how taxes will be used to support schools, what will or will not be taught, and the length of the school day and year is the
A. Governor's cabinet.
B. Federal government.
C. State legislature.
D. School board.

5.5 All of the following are responsibilities of the chief state school officer *except*
A. Supervising superintendents throughout the state.
B. Selecting state department of education personnel.
C. Reporting on the status of education to the governor.
D. Ensuring compliance with state school laws and policies.

5.6 An intermediate or regional unit may provide all of the following services *except*
A. Education for students with disabilities.
B. Educational technology.
C. Site-based administrative services.
D. Education for students who are gifted.

5.7 An influential and extensive federal education program signed into law by President Roosevelt in 1944 was the
A. Civil Rights Act.
B. Old Deluder Satan Law.
C. Education for All Handicapped Children Law.
D. G.I. Bill of Rights.

5.8 The majority of funding for schools is provided by
A. Private sector.
B. Federal government.
C. States.
D. Intermediate level.

5.9 Programs in which states set the same per-pupil expenditure level for all schools and districts are called
A. Equal tax levy programs.
B. Full-funding programs.
C. Redistricting.
D. Block grants.

5.10 State-appropriated funds to cover the costs of educating students with special needs are known as
A. Block grants.
B. Categorical aid.
C. Entitlements.
D. Title IX.

Answers are available on the FlexChoice website at www.ablongman.com/parkayflex.

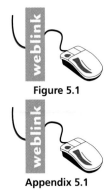

Figure 5.1

Appendix 5.1

Who Is Involved in the Struggles for Control of Schools in the United States?

Professional teachers recognize the need to understand the many complex political forces that currently influence schools in the United States (see Figure 5.1). For example, the opening scenario for this chapter illustrates how teachers and various political interest groups seek to influence policies related to school governance. Clearly, teachers have much to gain from becoming politically involved; and, as the title of a guide to political action for teachers suggests, *You Can Make a Difference* (Keresty, O'Leary, and Wortley 1998). (Appendix 5.1 presents "Guidelines for Teachers to Think and Act Politically" and "25 Ways to Become Involved.")

During the twenty-first century, struggles for control of schools in the United States will continue. Among the groups that will continue to have a keen concern for shaping educational policies, at least nine can be identified:

1. *Parents*—Concerned with controlling local schools so that quality educational programs are available to their children
2. *Students*—Concerned with policies related to freedom of expression, dress, behavior, and curricular offerings
3. *Teachers*—Concerned with their role in school reform, improving working conditions, terms of employment, and other professional issues
4. *Administrators*—Concerned with providing leadership so that various interest groups, including teachers, participate in the shared governance of schools and the development of quality educational programs
5. *Taxpayers*—Concerned with maintaining an appropriate formula for determining local, state, and federal financial support of schools
6. *State and federal authorities*—Concerned with the implementation of court orders, guidelines, and legislative mandates related to the operation of schools
7. *Minorities and women*—Concerned with the availability of equal educational opportunity for all and with legal issues surrounding administrative certification, terms of employment, and evaluation
8. *Educational theorists and researchers*—Concerned with using theoretical and research-based insights as the bases for improving schools at all levels
9. *Businesses and corporations*—Concerned with receiving from the schools graduates who have the knowledge, skills, attitudes, and values to help an organization realize its goals

Out of the complex and often turbulent interactions of these groups, school policies are developed. And, as strange as it may seem, no one of these groups can be said to control today's schools. As Seymour Sarason (1997, 36), author of several books on the complexities of educational change, points out, education in the United States *"is a system in which accountability is so diffused that no one is accountable"* (italics in original). Those who we might imagine control schools—principals, superintendents, and boards of education—are in reality responding to shifting sets of conditions created by those who have an interest in the schools. In addition, schools are influenced by several out-of-school factors—what sociologists have termed *environmental press*. Because schools reflect the society they serve, they are influenced directly and indirectly by factors such as those illustrated in Figure 5.1.

Clearly, it is difficult to untangle the web of political forces that influence schools. Figure 5.2 shows graphically how school authorities are confronted with the difficult task of funneling the input from various sources into unified, coherent school programs. In the next four sections of this chapter, we examine the many political forces that

Figure 5.2

impinge on the schools by looking at how they are influenced at the local, state, federal, and regional levels.

What Is the Role of the Local Community in School Governance?

The Constitution does not address the issue of public education, but the Tenth Amendment is used as the basis for giving states the responsibility for the governance of education, that is, the legal authority to create and manage school systems. In addition, as seen in Figure 5.2, various individuals and groups, though not legally empowered, do exercise local control over schools by trying to influence those legally entitled to operate the schools.

The Tenth Amendment gives to the states all powers not reserved for the federal government and not prohibited to the states. The states have, in turn, created local school districts, giving them responsibility for the daily operation of public schools. As a result of efforts to consolidate districts, the number of local public school districts has declined from 119,001 in 1937–38 to 14,841 in 1996–97 (National Center for Education Statistics 1998a, 97).

Local School District

Local school districts vary greatly in regard to demographics such as number of school-age children; educational, occupational, and income levels of parents; operating budget; number of teachers; economic resources; and number of school buildings. Some serve ultrawealthy communities, others impoverished ghetto neighborhoods or rural areas. Their operations include 487 one-teacher elementary schools in this country (National Center for Education Statistics 1999) as well as scores of modern, multibuilding campuses in heavily populated areas. The largest school districts are exceedingly complex operations with multimillion-dollar-a-year operating budgets (see Table 5.1) The largest—the New York City school system—has more than a million pupils (from 190 countries), more than 57,000 teachers (a number that exceeds the number of *students* in Cincinnati; Minneapolis; Portland, Oregon; Sacramento; Seattle; and St. Louis), 1,100 schools, and total annual expenditures of almost $9 billion. The New York system, overseen by a Schools Chancellor, consists of 32 community school districts, each with its own superintendent.

School districts also differ in regard to their organizational structures. Large urban systems, which may contain several districts, tend to have more complex distribution of roles and responsibilities than do smaller districts. Appendix 5.2 presents a typical organizational structure for a school district of about 20,000 pupils, while the Teacher's Resource Guide section "New York City Board of Education"on this book's website presents the organizational structure for the New York City Board of Education.

weblink

Table 5.1

weblink

Appendix 5.2

weblink

Weblink 5.1

School Board

A **school board,** acting as a state agent, is responsible for the following important activities: approving the teachers, administrators, and other school personnel hired by the superintendent; developing organizational and educational policies; and determining procedures for the evaluation of programs and personnel.

In most communities, school board members are elected in general elections. In some urban areas, however, board members are selected by the mayor. Board members typically serve a minimum of three to five years, and their terms of office are usually staggered. School boards usually range in size from five to fifteen members, with five or seven frequently suggested as the optimum size. Board members in urban areas usually are paid, but in most other areas are not.

A national survey of school board members revealed that women constituted 39.1 percent of school boards and men 54.1 percent (nonresponses and rounding account for the other 6.8 percent). The survey also revealed that minority membership on school boards was 10.9 percent. School board members were somewhat atypical of the general population in other ways: They were older (46.6 percent were between forty-one and fifty years old, with another 24.2 percent between fifty-one and sixty), and they were more affluent—the family income of 45.3 percent of 1998 board members was over $80,000, and over $100,000 for 28 percent (*American School Board Journal* 1998, A15).

Nearly all school board meetings are open to the public; in fact, many communities even provide radio and television coverage. Open meetings allow parents and interested citizens an opportunity to express their concerns and to get more information about problems in the district.

Criticism of school boards has increased recently, with some critics suggesting that school boards should focus more on removing barriers to student learning (Mental Health in Schools Center 1998). Other critics have pointed out that school boards often

- fail to provide far-reaching or politically risky leadership for reform;
- have become another level of administration, often micromanaging districts;
- are so splintered by members' attempts to represent special interests or meet their individual political needs that boards cannot govern effectively;
- are not spending enough time on educating themselves about issues or about education policy making; and
- exhibit serious problems in their capacity to develop positive and productive, lasting relationships with superintendents (Danzberger 1994a, 369).

Some states have taken steps to reform school boards. For example, West Virginia implemented legislation in 1994 to restructure school boards "so that they become well-informed, responsive, policy-making bodies." Board members now serve for four years rather than six, and they must complete training focused on "boardmanship and governing effectiveness" (Danzberger 1994b, 394).

Audio Clip 5.2

Superintendent of Schools

Though school boards operate very differently, the **superintendent** is invariably the key figure in determining a district's educational policy. The superintendent is the chief administrator of the school district, the person charged with the responsibility of seeing to it that schools operate in accord with federal and state guidelines as well as policies set by the local school board. Though the board of education delegates broad powers to the superintendent, his or her policies require board approval.

How the superintendent and his or her board work together appears to be related to the size of the school district, with superintendents and school boards in larger districts more likely to be in conflict. School boards in smaller districts, however, are more effective when they do oppose the superintendent. In large districts, the board's

keepers of the
dream

Marcia McVey
School District Superintendent

"...getting involved in the community..."

own divisiveness makes it less likely that the board will successfully oppose the superintendent (Wirt and Kirst 1997).

Superintendents must have great skill to respond appropriately to the many external political forces that demand their attention, and conflict is inevitable. Effective superintendents demonstrate that they are able to play three roles simultaneously: politician, manager, and teacher. It is a demanding position, and turnover is high; for example, between 1980 and 1995, the New York City school system had ten chancellors (Hurwitz, April 1999).

The Role of Parents

Parents may not be involved legally in the governance of schools, but they do play an important role in education. One characteristic of successful schools is that they have developed close working relationships with parents. Additionally, children whose parents or guardians support and encourage school activities have a definite advantage in school.

Through participation on school advisory and site-based councils, parents are making an important contribution to restructuring and school reform efforts around the country. In addition, groups such as the Parent-Teacher Association (PTA), Parent-Teacher Organization (PTO), or Parent Advisory Council (PAC) give parents the opportunity to communicate with teachers on matters of interest and importance to them. Through these groups, parents can become involved in the life of the school in a variety of ways—from making recommendations regarding school policies to providing much-needed volunteer services, or to initiating school-improvement activities such as fund-raising drives.

Many parents are also influencing the character of education through their involvement with the growing number of private, parochial, for-profit, and charter schools. In addition, many parents are activists in promoting school choice, voucher systems, and the home schooling movement. In their effort to influence schools in the United States, some parents even join well-funded conservative think tanks that launch sophisticated national campaigns to remove from public schools practices and materials that they believe have links to secular humanist or New Age beliefs. According to a book titled *School Wars: Resolving Our Conflicts over Religion and Values*, educational reform initiatives targeted by activist parents have included "outcome-based education, the whole language approach [to teaching reading], thinking skills programs, imagery techniques, self-esteem programs, the teaching of evolution, global education and multiculturalism, and sex education" (Gaddy, Hall, and Marzano 1996, 93).

School Restructuring

At many schools across the country exciting changes are taking place in regard to how schools are controlled locally. To improve the performance of schools, to decentralize the system of governance, and to enhance the professional status of teachers, some districts are **restructuring** their school systems. Restructuring goes by several names: shared governance, administrative decentralization, teacher empowerment, professionalization, bottom-up policymaking, school-based planning, school-based management, and shared decision making. What all these approaches to school governance have in common is allowing those who know students best—teachers, principals, aides, custodians, librarians, secretaries, and parents—greater freedom in deciding how to meet students' needs.

In a synthesis of research on school restructuring at more than 1,500 schools, the Center on Organization and Restructuring of Schools at the University of Wisconsin found that the following structural conditions enhance a school's "professional community" and increase students' learning:

- Shared governance that increases teachers' influence over school policy and practice
- Interdependent work structures, such as teaching teams, which encourage collaboration
- Staff development that enhances technical skills consistent with school missions for high-quality learning
- Deregulation that provides autonomy for schools to pursue a vision of high intellectual standards
- Small school size, which increases opportunities for communication and trust
- Parent involvement in a broad range of school affairs (Newmann and Wehlage 1995, 52).

School-Based Management

One of the most frequently used approaches to restructuring schools is **school-based management (SBM).** Most SBM programs have three components in common:

1. Power and decisions formerly made by the superintendent and school board are delegated to teachers, principals, parents, community members, and students at local schools. At SBM schools, teachers can become directly involved in making decisions about curriculum, textbooks, standards for student behavior, staff development, promotion and retention policies, teacher evaluation, school budgets, and the selection of teachers and administrators.
2. At each school, a decision-making body (known as a board, cabinet, site-based team, or council)—made up of teachers, the principal, and parents—implements the SBM plan.
3. SBM programs operate with the whole-hearted endorsement of the superintendent of schools.

Chicago School Reform A pioneer in school-based management has been the City of Chicago Public Schools. For years, the Chicago Public School System has been beset by an array of problems: low student achievement, periodic teacher strikes, budget crises, a top-heavy central bureaucracy, and schools in the decaying inner city that seemed beyond most improvement efforts. In response to these problems, the late Mayor Harold Washington appointed a fifty-five-member committee of business, education, and com-

munity leaders to develop a school reform proposal. Among the group's recommendations was
the creation of a **local school council (LSC)** for
each of the city's more than 550 schools, with
the majority of council members being parents
of schoolchildren.

In December 1988, the Illinois state legislature passed the Chicago School Reform Act, "an
undertaking of enormous scope" (Bryk et al.
1998, 28) and believed by some to be "the most
fundamental restructuring since the early part
of the twentieth century" (Moore 1992, 153).
Among the provisions of the act were the following:

■ School budgets would be controlled by a
local school council made up of six parents,
two community members, two school
employees, and the principal.

■ The council had the authority to hire and fire
the principal.

What are the goals of school restructuring? In school-based management, who participates in the governance and management of
schools? How is school-based management different from the
school board model of local governance?

■ The council, with input from teachers and
the principal, had the authority to develop an
improvement plan for the local school.

■ New teachers would be hired on the basis
of merit, not seniority.

■ Principals could remove teachers forty-five days after serving them official notice
of unsatisfactory performance.

■ A Professional Personnel Advisory Committee of teachers would have advisory
responsibility for curriculum and instruction.

The first six years of the Chicago Reform Act produced few concrete improvements. In 1995, frustrated with the district's chronic fiscal problems and inability
to increase student achievement, the Illinois legislature gave Mayor Richard M. Daley
control over Chicago's schools. Daley created a five-member "reform board of
trustees" and appointed a chief executive officer (CEO) who advocated "a balance
between local control and central-office control" (Hendrie, May 5, 1999).

By many accounts, the Chicago reform efforts during the last half of the 1990s were
a continuing "struggle about how to improve an urban school system" (Hendrie,
May 5, 1999). Friction between the mayor's management team and the parent-
dominated LSCs intensified with each report that an LSC member had abused his or
her authority. As a former chairwoman of a high school council said, "I've seen LSC
members who had personal agendas, and I have seen them destroy schools" (Hendrie,
May 5, 1999). In response to these allegations, Mayor Daley introduced a bill to
allow recourse to principals fired by their LSCs, an action that the director of the Chicago Association of Local School Councils described as "just the first attempt at destroying local school councils" (Hendrie, May 5, 1999).

To date, the overall effectiveness of the Chicago program has been mixed. While
the Reform Act called for all Chicago schools to reach national norms within five years,
this goal was not reached (Bryk et al. 1994; Walberg and Niemiec 1994; 1996). Eight
years after the reform effort was launched, the CEO of Chicago schools even admitted that "not a lot of progress has been made. . . . the bottom line is only 77 of the
[557] schools have more than half of the kids at or above national averages" (Hendrie,

May 5, 1999). However, "of the schools most in need of change—schools where student achievement had been well below national norms—one third had developed strong democratic support and participation within their school communities [and] were following a systemic approach toward reform. Another third displayed some of these characteristics but were not as far along in implementing change" (Hess 1995, 111). Though it has yet to result in increased student achievement, the Chicago experiment is clearly one of the more dramatic efforts to empower parents and make them full partners in the educative process.

What Powers and Influence Do States Have in Governing Schools?

Above the level of local control, states have a great influence on the governance of schools. Throughout the 1990s, the influence of the state on educational policy increased steadily. In fact, by the end of the 1990s, many states were exerting unprecedented control over public school classrooms, causing one expert in school finance to comment: "I don't think the public realizes the sea change that's occurred in who's responsible for schools. While we talk about local control, what we have is anything but local control" (*Education Week* 1999b). For example, forty-eight states had statewide academic standards in 1999 (Iowa and Nebraska were the exceptions), and thirty-nine had mandated tests aligned to those standards; also, nineteen states required high school exit exams, while eight others were considering exit exams. Moreover, twenty-three states had passed legislation allowing them to take over academically failing school districts (eleven states had done so by 1999), and ten states allowed takeovers of individual schools that were failing (*Education Week* 1999b).

In response to criticisms of U.S. education, many of which pointed to the nation's frequent low ranking in international comparisons of achievement, many states launched extensive initiatives to improve education, such as the following:

- Increased academic standards
- Greater accountability for teachers
- Testing students in teacher education programs prior to graduation
- Frequent assessments of students' mastery of basic skills
- Professional development as a criterion for continued employment of teachers
- Recertification of experienced teachers

As mentioned previously, the Tenth Amendment to the Constitution allows the states to organize and to administer education within their boundaries. To meet the responsibility of maintaining and supporting schools, the states have assumed several powers:

- The power to levy taxes for the support of schools and to determine state aid to local school districts
- The power to set the curriculum and, in some states, to identify approved textbooks
- The power to determine minimum standards for teacher certification
- The power to establish standards for accrediting schools
- The power to pass legislation necessary for the proper maintenance and support of schools

To carry out the tasks implied by these powers, the states have adopted a number of different organizational structures. Most states, however, have adopted a hierarchical structure similar to that presented in the Teacher's Resource Guide section, "Organizational Structure of a Typical State School System" on this book's website.

Weblink 5.2

The Roles of State Government in Education

Various people and agencies within each state government play a role in operating the educational system within that state. Though state governments differ in many respects, the state legislature, the state courts, and the governor have a direct, critical impact on education in their state.

The Legislature   In nearly every state, the legislature is responsible for establishing and maintaining public schools and for determining basic educational policies within the state. To accomplish these ends, the legislature has the power to enact laws related to education. Among the policies that the state legislature may determine are the following:

- How the state boards of education will be selected and what their responsibilities will be
- How the chief state school officer will be selected and what his or her duties will be
- How the state department of education will function
- How the state will be divided into local and regional districts
- How higher education will be organized and financed
- How local school boards will be selected and what their powers will be

In addition, the legislature may determine how taxes will be used to support schools, what will or will not be taught, the length of the school day and school year, how many years of compulsory education will be required, and whether or not the state will have community colleges and/or vocational/technical schools. Legislatures may also make policies that apply to such matters as pupil attendance, admission, promotion, teacher certification, teacher tenure and retirement, and collective bargaining.

The Courts   From time to time, state courts are called on to uphold the power of the legislature to develop laws that apply to schools. The state courts must determine, however, that this power does not conflict with the state or federal constitution. It is important to remember, too, that the role of state courts is not to develop laws but to rule on the reasonableness of laws that apply to specific educational situations.

Perhaps no state court had a greater impact on education during the first half of the 1990s than the Kentucky Supreme Court. In 1989, the Court ruled that the state's entire school system was "inadequate." Naming the state superintendent and the state education agency as part of the problem and pointing out that Kentucky schools were ineffective and inequitable, the Court labeled the school system "unconstitutional." The Court called on the governor and the legislature to develop an entirely new system of education for the state. A twenty-two-member task force, appointed by the governor and the legislature, then developed the 906-page **Kentucky Education Reform Act (KERA)** passed in 1990. KERA required each school to form a school-based management council by 1996 with authority to set policy in eight areas: curriculum, staff time, student assignment, schedule, school space, instructional issues, discipline, and extracurricular activities. Three teachers, two parents (elected by their peers), and the principal comprised each council.

Almost ten years after its adoption, KERA had dramatically equalized funding across the state, and some school districts made substantial gains in funding for students. Though variations among district spending on education still existed, these were no longer based on "the traditional determinants of educational financing . . . local income and property wealth. Now districts with low incomes or little property value per student are just as likely to have high educational spending as are wealthy districts" (Hoyt 1999, 36). In addition, teacher salaries and student/teacher ratios improved compared to national averages. However, student achievement, as measured by test score gains or graduation rates, had not improved (Hoyt 1999).

The Governor   Though the powers of governors vary greatly from state to state, a governor can, if he or she chooses, have a far-reaching impact on education within the state. The governor may appoint and/or remove educators at the state level, and in some states the governor may even appoint the chief state school officer. Furthermore, in every state except North Carolina, the governor may use his or her veto power to influence the legislature to pass certain laws related to education. Governors are also extremely influential because they make educational budget recommendations to legislatures, and, in many states, they may elect to use any accumulated balances in the state treasury for education. Governors can also have a significant impact on matters related to curriculum and instruction within the state and, indeed, across the nation. For example, in the mid-1990s, Roy Romer, governor of Colorado, was instrumental in organizing ACHIEVE, an effort by U.S. governors and corporate leaders to raise academic standards and develop accountability systems for schools. In addition, the **National Governors' Association (NGA)** is active in teacher education and school reforms.

State Board of Education

The **state board of education,** acting under the authority of the state legislature, is the highest educational agency in a state. Every state, with the exception of Wisconsin, has a state board of education. In most states there are two separate boards, one responsible for elementary through secondary education, the other for higher education.

The method of determining board members varies from state to state. In some states, the governor appoints members of the state board; in other states, members are selected through general elections. Two states have *ex officio* members who, by virtue of the positions they hold, automatically serve on the board. Most states have either seven- or nine-member boards.

People disagree on which is better: electing or appointing board members. Some believe that election to the state board may cause members to be more concerned with politics than with education. Others argue that elected board members are more aware of the wishes of the public whom the schools are supposed to serve. People in favor of appointing members to the state board suggest that appointment increases the likelihood that individuals will be chosen on the basis of merit rather than politics.

The regulatory and advisory functions generally held by state boards are as follows:

- Ensuring that local school districts adhere to legislation concerning educational policies, rules, and regulations
- Setting standards for issuing and revoking teaching and administrative certificates
- Establishing standards for accrediting schools
- Managing state monies appropriated for education

■ Developing and implementing a system for collecting educational data needed for reporting and program evaluation
■ Advising the governor and/or the state legislature on educational issues
■ Identifying both short- and long-range educational needs in the state and developing plans to meet those needs
■ Hearing all disputes arising from the implementation of its educational policies

State Department of Education

The educational program of each state is implemented by the state's department of education, under the leadership of the chief state school officer. State departments of education have a broad set of responsibilities, and they affect literally every school, school district, and teacher education program in a state. In general, the state board of education is concerned with policymaking, the **state department of education** with the day-to-day implementation of those policies. Perhaps the greatest boost for the development of state departments of education came with the federal government's Elementary and Secondary Education Act of 1965 (see Chapter 3). This act and its subsequent amendments required that local applications for federal funds to be used for innovative programs and for the education of disadvantaged, disabled, bilingual, and migrant students first receive approval from state departments of education.

Today, the responsibilities of state departments of education include (1) certifying teachers, (2) distributing state and federal funds to school districts, (3) reporting to the public the condition of education within the state, (4) ensuring that school districts adhere to state and federal guidelines, (5) accrediting schools, (6) monitoring student transportation and safety, and (7) sponsoring research and evaluation projects to improve education within the state.

Perhaps the most significant index of the steady increase in state control since the 1980s is the fact that the states now supply the majority of funding for schools. During the twenty-first century, the power and influence of state departments of education will continue to be extensive.

Chief State School Officer

The **chief state school officer** (known as the commissioner of education or superintendent of public instruction in many states) is the chief administrator of the state department of education and the head of the state board of education. In twenty-five states, the state board of education appoints the chief state school officer; in fifteen, the office is filled through a general election; and in the remaining ten, the governor appoints an individual to that position (personal communciation, Council of Chief State School Officers June 7, 1999).

Though the specific responsibilities of the chief state school officer vary from state to state, most individuals in this position hold several responsibilities in common:

1. Serving as chief administrator of the state department of education and state board of education
2. Selecting state department of education personnel
3. Recommending educational policies and budgets to the state board
4. Interpreting state school laws and state board of education policies
5. Ensuring compliance with state school laws and policies
6. Mediating controversies involving the operation of schools within the state

7. Arranging for studies, committees, and task forces to address educational problems and recommend solutions
8. Reporting on the status of education to the governor, legislature, state board, and public

What Assistance Do Regional Education Agencies Provide?

When one thinks of how schools are governed and the sources of political pressure applied to them, one typically thinks of influences originating at three levels: local, state, and federal. There is, however, an additional source of control—the regional, or intermediate, unit. The intermediate unit of educational administration, or the **Regional Educational Service Agency (RESA)**, is the least understood branch of the state public school system. Through the intermediate unit, local school districts can receive supportive services that, economically and logistically, they could not provide for themselves.

Presently, about half of the states have some form of intermediate or regional unit. The average unit is made up of twenty to thirty local school districts and covers a fifty-square-mile area. The intermediate or regional unit has many different names: educational service district (in Washington), county education office (in California), education service center (in Texas), intermediate school district (in Michigan), multi-county educational service unit (in Nebraska), and board of cooperative educational services (in New York).

The primary role of the intermediate unit is to provide assistance directly to districts in the areas of staff development, curriculum development, instructional media, and program evaluation. Intermediate or regional units also help school districts with their school improvement efforts by providing help in targeted areas such as bilingual education, vocational education, educational technology, and the education of gifted and talented students and students with disabilities. Although intermediate units do monitor local school districts to see that they follow state educational guidelines, local districts, in fact, exert great influence over RESAs by identifying district-level needs that can be met by the intermediate unit.

How Does the Federal Government Influence Education?

Since the birth of the United States, the federal government has played a major role in shaping the character of schools. This branch of government has always recognized that the strength and well-being of the country are directly related to the quality of its schools. The importance of a quality education, for example, has been highlighted by many U.S. Supreme Court rulings supporting the free speech rights of teachers and students under the First Amendment and the right of all citizens to equal educational opportunity under the Fourteenth Amendment. During the twenty-first century it is clear that the nation will face unprecedented levels of both global competition and the need for greater international cooperation. A rapidly changing, increasingly complex society will require a better-educated workforce to compete and cooperate successfully.

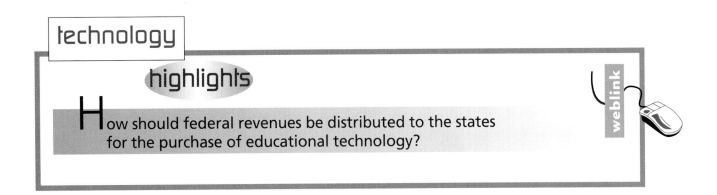

technology

highlights

How should federal revenues be distributed to the states for the purchase of educational technology?

weblink

The federal government has taken aggressive initiatives to influence education at several points in U.S. history, such as the allocation of federal money to improve science, mathematics, and foreign language education after Russia launched the world's first satellite. During World War II, the federal government funded several new educational programs. One of these, the Lanham Act (1941), provided funding for (1) the training of workers in war plants by U.S. Office of Education personnel, (2) the construction of schools in areas where military personnel and workers on federal projects resided, and (3) the provision of child care for the children of working parents.

Another influential and extensive federal program in support of education was the Servicemen's Readjustment Act, popularly known as the **G.I. Bill of Rights.** Signed into law by President Franklin D. Roosevelt in 1944, the G.I. Bill has provided millions of veterans with payments for tuition and room and board at colleges and universities and at technical schools. Similar legislation was later passed to grant educational benefits to veterans of the Korean and Vietnam conflicts. Not only did the G.I. Bill stimulate the growth of colleges and universities in the United States, but it also opened higher education to an older and nontraditional student population.

The executive, legislative, and judicial branches of the federal government influence education in four ways:

1. *Exert moral suasion*—develop a vision and promote educational goals for the nation; for example, William Bennett, Secretary of Education during the Reagan administration, referred to the "Bully Pulpit" he used to promote policies and programs
2. *Provide categorical aid*—assist school systems with funding if they adopt federally endorsed programs, methods, or curricula
3. *Regulate*—withhold federal funds if a school system fails to follow legal statutes related to equal educational opportunity
4. *Fund educational research*—identify and then fund research projects related to federal goals for education

The Impact of Presidential Policies

Presidential platforms on education often have a profound effect on education. Ronald Reagan's two terms of office (1980–1988) and George Bush's term (1988–1992), for example, saw a significant shift in the federal government's role in education. In general, these two administrations sought to scale back what some viewed as excessive

"To meet our responsibility to create twenty-first century schools for all our children, we have to do a far, far better job of spending the $15 billion in federal aid we send to our schools every year." (White House press briefing, May 19, 1999.)

federal involvement in education. During Bill Clinton's two terms of office (1992–2000), the federal government assumed a more active role in ensuring equal educational opportunity. As President Clinton (1999) said of the "Educational Excellence for All Children Act of 1999," his proposal to reauthorize the Elementary and Secondary Education Act (ESEA):

> [T]his legislation strengthens accountability for results. It says that states and school districts that choose to accept federal aid must take responsibility for turning around failing schools, or shutting them down. It says they must give parents report cards not just on their children, but on the children's schools. It says school districts must have strong discipline codes that are fair, consistent, and focused on prevention. It says they must make sure that teachers actually know the subjects they are teaching. It says they must stop the practice of social promotion, not by holding students back, but by making sure they have the support to meet the higher standards.

U.S. Department of Education

In addition to supporting educational research, disseminating the results of research, and administering federal grants, the U.S. Department of Education advises the president on setting a platform for his educational agenda. For example, Secretary of Education Richard Riley and President Clinton promoted the following educational initiatives for fiscal year 1999:

1. All students will read independently and well by the end of third grade.
2. All students will master challenging mathematics, including the foundations of algebra and geometry, by the end of eighth grade.
3. By eighteen years of age, all students will be prepared for and able to afford college.
4. All states and schools will have challenging and clear standards of achievement and accountability for all children, and effective strategies for teaching those standards.
5. There will be a talented, dedicated, and well-prepared teacher in every classroom.
6. Every classroom will be connected to the Internet by 2000 and all students will be technologically literate.
7. Every school will be strong, safe, drug-free, and disciplined.

weblink

Professional Reflection   **Examining the tension between federal and state roles in education**

How Are Schools Financed in the United States?

To provide free public education to all school-age children in the United States is a costly undertaking. Schools must provide services and facilities to students from a wide range of ethnic, racial, social, cultural, linguistic and individual backgrounds. Expenditures for these services and facilities have been rising rapidly and are expected to continue rising through 2008 (see Figure 5.3). Total expenditures for public elementary and secondary schools in 1997–98 were $351 billion, and the total **expenditure per pupil** was $7,502 (in constant 1997-98 dollars) (National Center for Education Statistics 1999, 35). Figure 5.4 shows how the budget for a typical school district is allocated.

Financing an enterprise as vast and ambitious as the United States system of free public schools has not been easy. It has proved difficult both to devise a system that equitably distributes the tax burden for supporting schools and to provide equal educational services and facilities for all students. And, "rather than one national education system [in the United States], there are fifty state systems that raise revenues from local, state, and federal sources. Dollars are distributed quite unequally across the states, districts, and schools. And only a small fraction of the education dollar supports regular classroom instruction—significant proportions are spent in schools, but outside of the classroom" (Odden and Busch 1998, 4). Moreover, there has been a tendency for the financial support of schools to be outpaced by factors that continually increase the cost of operating schools, such as inflation, rising enrollments, and the need to update aging facilities. According to the 1999 Gallup Poll of the public's attitudes toward the public schools, lack of financial support/funding/money was seen as the number three problem (after lack of discipline/more control and fighting/violence/gangs) confronting local schools. Moreover, "finances/funding" topped the list of what the public views as the "main obstacle" to improving schools in their communities.

A combination of revenues from local, state, and federal sources is used to finance public elementary and secondary schools in the United States. As Table 5.2 shows, schools received almost half of their 1995–96 funding from the state, 45.9 percent from local and other sources, and 6.6 percent from the federal government. Since 1980, schools have received almost equal funding from local and state sources; prior to that date, however, schools received most of their revenues from local sources, and early in the twentieth century, nearly all school revenues were generated from local property taxes. The 1998 Gallup Poll revealed that the public is undecided about the best way to finance schools: 21 percent believed local property taxes should provide funding; 33 percent, state taxes; and 37 percent, federal taxes.

Revenues for education are influenced by many factors, including the apportionment of taxes among the local, state, and federal levels; the size of the tax base at each level; and competing demands for allocating funds at each level. In addition, funding for education is influenced by the following factors:

- The rate of inflation
- The health of the national economy
- The size of the national budget deficit
- Taxpayer revolts to limit the use of property taxes to raise money, such as Proposition 13 in California and Oregon's property tax limitation
- Changes in the size and distribution of the population

Figure 5.3

Figure 5.4

Table 5.2

■ School-financed lawsuits to equalize funding and ensure educational opportunity. (As of 1999, the systems of school finance in eighteen states had been overturned by court rulings, and more than twenty lawsuits seeking reform of state financing of K–12 education were pending [*Education Week* 1999b]).

Local Funding

At the local level, most funding for schools comes from **property taxes** that are determined by the value of property in the school district. Property taxes are assessed against real estate and, in some districts, also against personal property such as cars, household furniture and appliances, and stocks and bonds. Increasing taxes to meet the rising costs of operating local schools or to fund needed improvements is often a heated issue in many communities.

Although property taxes provide a steady source of revenue for local school districts, there are inequities in the ways in which taxes are determined. By locating in areas where taxes are lowest, for example, businesses and industries often avoid paying higher taxes while continuing to draw on local resources and services. In addition, the fair market value of property is often difficult to assess, and groups within a community sometimes pressure assessors to keep taxes on their property as low as possible. Most states specify by law the minimum property tax rate for local school districts to set. In many districts, an increase in the tax rate must have the approval of voters. Some states place no cap, or upper limit, on tax rates, and other states set a maximum limit.

State Funding

Video 5.1

Table 5.3

Most state revenues for education come from sales taxes and income taxes. Sales taxes are added to the cost of items such as general goods, gasoline, amusements, alcohol, and insurance. Income taxes are placed on individuals (in many states) and on business and industry.

As mentioned previously, states contribute nearly 50 percent of the resources needed to operate the public schools. The money that a state gives to its cities and towns is known as **state aid**. Table 5.3 compares selected states on the percent of education funds received from federal, state, local and intermediate, and private sources in relation to total expenditures for 1995–96. The table also shows how total expenditures may vary widely from state to state as well as the per-pupil amount retained for the administration of state education agencies.

Federal Funding

The role of the federal government in providing resources for education has been limited. As Table 5.2 shows, the federal share of funding for public elementary and secondary schools peaked in 1979–80 at 9.8 percent and had declined to 6.6 percent by 1995–96. Prior to 1980 the federal government had in effect bypassed the states and provided funding for local programs that were administered through various federal agencies, such as the Office of Economic Opportunity (Head Start, migrant education, and Follow Through) and the Department of Labor (Job Corps and the Comprehensive Employment Training Act [CETA]). Since the Reagan administration (1980–88), federal aid has increasingly been given directly to the states in the form of **block grants**, which a state or local education agency may spend as it wishes with few limitations. The 1981 **Education Consolidation and Improvement Act (ECIA)** gave the states a broad range of choices in spending federal money. The ECIA significantly reduced federal aid to education, however, thus making state aid to education even more critical.

Though a small proportion of the funds for schools comes from the federal level, the federal government has enacted supplemental programs to help meet the educational needs of special student populations. Such programs are often referred to collectively as **entitlements.** The most significant is the Elementary and Secondary Education Act of 1965. Title I of the act allocates a billion dollars annually to school districts with large numbers of students from low-income families. Among the other funded entitlement programs are the Vocational Education Act (1963), the Manpower Development and Training Act (1963), the Economic Opportunity Act (1964), the Bilingual Education Act (1968), the Indian Education Act (1972), and the Education for All Handicapped Children Act (1975).

How does federal funding influence schools at the local level? How does federal funding help to reduce inequities among schools?

The federal government also provides funding for preschool programs such as Project Head Start. Originally started under the Economic Opportunity Act of 1964 to provide preschool experiences to poor children, Head Start was later made available to children whose parents were above the poverty level. Under the Clinton administration, funding for Head Start more than doubled, increasing from $2.2 billion in fiscal year 1992 to $4.66 billion in 1999. Reauthorized by Congress in 1998, Head Start served an estimated 830,000 children and their families that year. The Head Start Act Amendments of 1994 also established the Early Head Start program, designed to serve pregnant women and children under three from low-income families. In fiscal year 1998, Early Head Start funding totaled $279 million, and 39,000 children were served by the program (U.S. Department of Health and Human Services October 27, 1998).

What Are Some Trends in Funding for Equity and Excellence?

The fact that schools have had to rely heavily on property taxes for support has resulted in fiscal inequities for schools. Districts with higher property wealth are able to generate more money per pupil than districts with lower property values. The degree of inequity between the wealthiest and the poorest districts, therefore, can be quite large. In some states, for example, the ability of one district to generate local property tax revenues may be several times greater than another district's. Moreover, unequal educational funding in the United States makes it one of the most inequitable countries in the world (Odden and Busch 1998).

Audio Clip 5.3

In *Savage Inequalities: Children in America's Schools*, noted educator Jonathan Kozol (1991) presents a compelling analysis of the inequities in school funding. He found that the amount of money spent on each school age child ranged from $1,500 to $15,000, depending on where the child lived. Disputing those who claim that parental values, not high spending on education, determines how much children learn, Kozol points out that high spending on education in affluent districts does coincide with high achievement.

Tax Reform and Redistricting

To correct funding inequities, several court suits were initiated during the 1970s. In the 1971 *Serrano v. Priest* case in California, it was successfully argued that the relationship between spending and property wealth violated the state's obligation to provide equal protection and education. The California Supreme Court ruled in a six-to-one decision that the quality of a child's education should not be dependent on the "wealth of his parents and neighbors." The court also recognized that communities with a poor tax base could not be expected to generate the revenues of more affluent districts. Nevertheless, the Court did not forbid the use of property taxes to fund education.

Then, in 1973, the U.S. Supreme Court decided in *San Antonio Independent School District v. Rodriguez* that fiscal inequities stemming from unequal tax bases did not violate the Constitution. That court's decision reversed a lower court's ruling claiming that school financing on the basis of local property taxes was unconstitutional.

Regardless of the mixed outcomes of court challenges, many state legislatures have enacted school finance equity reforms during the last fifteen years. A few states (California, Hawaii, New Mexico, Washington, and West Virginia, for example) have led the way by developing programs to ensure statewide financial equality. These states have **full-funding programs** in which the state sets the same per-pupil expenditure level for all schools and districts.

Other states have adopted new funding formulas to try to broaden their revenue base. Level funding augmented by sales taxes, cigarette taxes, state lottery revenues, property taxes on second homes, and school-choice plans are among the solutions tried. One of the most dramatic changes in educational funding occurred in Michigan in 1993 with the passage of Proposal A, a plan that greatly reduced school funding from local property taxes and increased funding from the state's sales tax.

Since each state has been free to determine the number of districts within its boundaries—the number varied from 1,043 in Texas to 1 in Hawaii in 1996–97 (National Center for Education Statistics 1999, 98)—a common approach to achieving equal funding is **redistricting,** redrawing school district boundaries to reduce the range of variation in the ability of school districts to finance education. Redistricting not only equalizes funding; it can also reduce the cost of maintaining and operating schools if smaller districts are combined. The per-pupil cost of instruction, supplies, and equipment is usually lower in large districts. In addition, greater resources often allow larger districts to offer a broader curriculum and higher salaries to attract more qualified teachers.

Vertical Equity

Other states have developed various mechanisms for providing **vertical equity,** that is, for allocating funds according to legitimate educational needs. Thus, additional support is given to programs that serve students from low-income backgrounds; those with limited English proficiency, or special gifts and talents; and those who need special education or vocational programs.

Additional state-appropriated funds to cover the costs of educating students with special needs are known as **categorical aid.** Funding adjustments are also made to compensate for differences in costs within a state—higher expenses due to rural isolation or the higher cost of living in urban areas, for example. Some states even conduct periodic regional cost-of-living analyses, which are then used to determine adjustments in per-pupil funding.

School Choice

One of the most bitter struggles for control of schools in the United States during the last half of the 1990s centered around **school choice,** the practice of allowing parents to choose the schools their children attend. According to the 1999 Phi Delta Kappa/Gallup Poll of the public's attitudes toward the public schools, 51 percent were in favor of allowing parents to send their school-age children to any public, private, or church-related school they choose, with the government paying all or part of the tuition (Rose and Gallup 1999, 53).

Debate continues about whether school choice programs will, in fact, promote equity and excellence. Advocates of school choice believe that giving parents more options will force public schools to adjust to free-market pressures—low-performing schools would have to improve or shut down. Moreover, they contend that parents whose children must now attend inferior, and sometimes dangerous, inner-city schools would be able to send their children elsewhere. In addition, some supporters see choice as a way to reduce the influence of top-heavy school bureaucracies and teachers' unions—as Florida's governor stated in defense of his school choice proposal: "We must dismantle the bureaucracy and make our schools parent–oriented and performance-driven" (National Governor's Association 1998).

On the other hand, opponents believe that school choice would have disastrous consequences for public schools and lead to students being sorted by race, income, and religion. School choice, they argue, would subsidize the wealthy by siphoning money away from the public schools and further widen the gap between rich and poor districts. Moreover, opponents point out that research does not indicate that school choice would improve education (Smith and Meier 1995), nor would it promote educational equity:

> Since poor parents lack the supplemental resources that rich people have for helping their children, it is foolish to argue that [school choice] would help to equalize educational opportunities. (For example, rich parents can afford the extra costs for transportation, clothing, and educational supplies when they send their children to a distant, private school; poor parents cannot) (Berliner and Biddle 1995, 175).

Other critics contend that school choice could lead to the creation of segregated schools and schools that would be more committed to competing for education dollars and the most able, manageable students. Still others point out that, while school choice is offered as a solution to the U.S. education crisis (Chubb and Moe 1990), our nation's school system is not failing, it is *perceived* as failing. As David Berliner and Bruce Biddle (1995, 4) point out in *The Manufactured Crisis: Myths, Fraud, and the Attack on America's Public Schools,* "When one actually *looks* at the evidence [for a failing school system], one discovers that most of the claims of the Manufactured Crisis are, indeed, myths, half-truths, and sometimes outright lies."

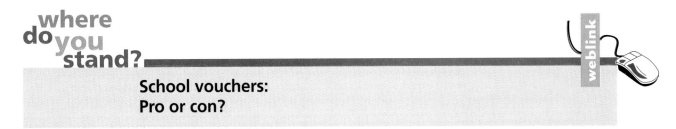

where do you stand?

weblink

School vouchers: Pro or con?

Voucher Systems

One approach to providing educational equity that has generated considerable controversy is the **voucher system** of distributing educational funds. Although various plans have been proposed, one of the most common would give states the freedom to distribute money directly to parents in the form of vouchers. Parents would then use the vouchers to enroll their children in schools of their choice. The most controversial voucher proposals would allow parents to choose from among public as well as private (secular, parochial, for-profit, and charter) schools; others would limit parents' choice to public schools.

Half of the respondents to the 1999 Phi Delta Kappa/Gallup Poll were asked if they favored vouchers that would pay *full tuition* at private or church-related schools—47 percent favored such a voucher system, 48 percent opposed it, and 5 percent said they "don't know." The other half of respondents were asked if they favored vouchers that would pay *partial tuition*—52 percent were in favor, 45 percent were opposed, and 3 percent said they didn't know (Rose and Gallup 1999, 53–54).

In the late 1990s, debates about vouchers regularly made the national news. New Mexico's provoucher governor clashed with the state's legislature over private school vouchers (*Education Week* 1999a). After months of contentious debate, Florida became the first state to offer state-paid tuition to children in failing public schools to attend a public, private, or religious school of choice (*The Miami Herald*, 1999). And, for months, the media covered New York City Schools Chancellor Rudolph Crew's opposition to Mayor Rudolph W. Giuliani's plan to "give poorer parents the same opportunity to make choices about their children's education that the richest and most affluent parents in new York City have" (*Education Week* 1999e).

It is clear that the debate over school choice will continue for the foreseeable future. Gradually, support for school choice appears to be increasing—as of 1999, twenty states allowed some form of "interdistrict" transfer, which would allow students to attend public schools outside of their home district, and an equal number of states were considering choice plans. In fact, Grant and Murray (1999, 235) suggest that "It is conceivable that by 2020 as many as a quarter of all students could be enrolled in some 'school of choice,' whether private or public."

Corporate-Education Partnerships

To develop additional sources of funding for equity and excellence, many local school districts have established partnerships with the private sector. Businesses may contribute funds or materials needed by a school, sponsor sports teams, award scholarships, provide cash grants for pilot projects and teacher development, and even construct school buildings. One example of a corporate-education partnership is Thomas Jefferson High School for Science and Technology, a college preparatory magnet school in Alexandria, Virginia. Twenty-five local and multinational businesses, including AT&T, Mobil, Boeing, Honeywell, and Exxon, raised almost a million dollars for the school. State-of-the-art facilities include a $600,000 telecommunications lab with a television studio, radio station, weather station, and a satellite earth station. The school has a biotech laboratory for genetic engineering experiments in cloning and cell fission as well as labs for research on energy and computers.

Corporate contributions to education total more than $2 billion annually, with about 9 percent going to elementary and secondary education and the rest to colleges, including grants to improve teacher preparation. A survey of Fortune 500 and Service 500 companies found that 78 percent contributed money to education, 64 percent contributed materials or equipment, 26 percent offered teachers summer employment, and 12 percent provided executives-on-loan to schools (Hopkins and Wendel 1997, 15).

If schools in the United States are to succeed in meeting the challenges of the twenty-first century, they will need to be funded at a level that provides quality educational experiences to students from a diverse array of backgrounds. Though innovative approaches to school funding have been developed, much remains to be done before both excellence and equity characterize all schools in the United States.

SUMMARY

Who Is Involved in the Struggles for Control of Schools in the United States? (p. 128)

What Is the Role of the Local Community in School Governance? (p. 129)

What Powers and Influence Do States Have in Governing Schools? (p. 134)

What Assistance Do Regional Education Agencies Provide? (p. 138)

How Does the Federal Government Influence Education? (p. 138)

How Are Schools Financed in the United States? (p. 141)

What Are Some Trends in Funding for Equity and Excellence? (p. 143)

KEY TERMS AND CONCEPTS

Go to the website for interactive flashcards.

APPLICATIONS AND INTERACTIVITIES

Go to the website for interactive assignments in the following areas:

Teacher's Journal

Teacher's Database

Observations and Interviews

Professional Portfolio

Handout Master M5.1
Handout Master M5.2

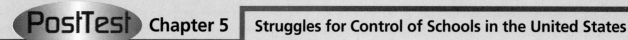

Name _____ **Date** _____

For each question, write in the blank the answer you believe is correct.

5.1 Regardless of the organizational or operational patterns of school districts, the _____ is commonly the key figure in determining a district's educational policy.

5.2 In nearly every state, the _____ is responsible for establishing and maintaining public schools and for determining educational policy in the state.

5.3 The least understood branch of the state public school system is the regional or intermediate unit known as the Regional Educational _____ Agency.

5.4 Signed into law by President Franklin D. Roosevelt in 1944, the G.I. Bill of _____ is a federal program designed to support the education of military veterans.

5.5 Generally, public schools receive about half of their funding from state government and about half from _____ sources.

5.6 Local funding for public schools comes principally from _____ taxes.

5.7 Money given in support of public schools by states is known as state _____.

5.8 The federal government's role in supporting education when compared to the contributions of state and local governments is _____.

5.9 Federal government support of public schools is most often offered in the form of _____.

5.10 The process of redrawing school district boundaries to reduce the range of variation in the ability of school districts to finance education is known as _____.

Answers are available on the FlexChoice website at www.ablongman.com/parkayflex.

Name _____

Keep this checklist at your computer as a reminder to read and complete the chapter features and activities located on the FlexChoice website at www.ablongman.com/parkayflex.

**Date
Completed**

_____ ❏ **PreTest with Answers**

_____ ❏ **Audio Clip 5.1:** Thinking Over the Opening Vignette

_____ ❏ **Figure 5.1:** Political influences on the schools

_____ ❏ **Appendix 5.1:** Guidelines for Teachers to Think and Act Politically

_____ ❏ **Figure 5.2:** School politics

_____ ❏ **Table 5.1:** Selected data for the ten largest public school systems, 1996–97

_____ ❏ **Appendix 5.2:** Typical Organizational Structure for a Medium-Size School District (20,000 pupils)

_____ ❏ **Weblink 5.1:** New York City Board of Education

_____ ❏ **Audio Clip 5.2:** The Superintendent vs. the School Board

_____ ❏ **Keepers of the Dream:** Marcia McVey

_____ ❏ **Weblink 5.2:** Organizational Structure of a Typical State School System

_____ ❏ **Technology Highlights:** How should federal revenues be distributed to the states for the purchase of educational technology?

_____ ❏ **Professional Reflection:** Examining the tension between federal and state roles in education

_____ ❏ **Figure 5.3:** Current expenditures of public schools (in constant 1995–96 dollars), with alternative projections: 1982–83 to 2007–08

_____ ❏ **Figure 5.4:** Average allocation of the 1996–97 school district operating budget

_____ ❏ **Table 5.2:** Revenues for public elementary and secondary schools, by source of funds: 1919–20 to 1995–96

_____ ❏ **Video 5.1:** The Politics of State Funding

_____ ❏ **Table 5.3:** Revenues for public elementary and secondary schools by source and per-pupil funds retained for administration of state education agencies for selected states and the District of Columbia

_____ ❏ **Audio Clip 5.3:** Equality in Funding

_____ ❏ **Where Do You Stand?:** School vouchers: Pro or con?

_____ ❏ **Summary**

_____ ❏ **Key Terms and Concepts**

_____ ❏ **Applications and Interactivities:** Teacher's Journal

_____ ❏ **Applications and Interactivities:** Teacher's Database

_____ ❏ **Applications and Interactivities:** Observations and Interviews

_____ ❏ **Handout Master M5.1:** Observing Community-Based Decision Making on Education

_____ ❏ **Handout Master M5.2:** Observing School-Based Decision Making

_____ ❏ **Applications and Interactivities:** Professional Portfolio

_____ ❏ **PostTest with Answers**

6

Ethical and Legal Issues in Education in the United States

Teachers [must] balance public obligations with their personal beliefs and purposes in teaching.

—David T. Hansen
The Call to Teach

1. Why do you need a professional code of ethics?

2. What are your legal rights as a teacher?

3. Do student teachers have the same rights?

4. What are your legal responsibilities as a teacher?

5. What are the legal rights of students and parents?

6. What are some issues in the legal rights of school districts?

The day has ended and you are grading papers while waiting to meet with Cassandra, one of your fifth-grade students, and her mother. Cassandra's mother called you at home yesterday to arrange the meeting. When you asked her about the purpose of the meeting, she was vague and offered only that Cassandra had recently had "some trouble" with one of her classmates, Robert.

Audio Clip 6.1

A quick glance at the clock tells you they should arrive at any moment. To prepare for the meeting, you stop grading papers and reflect on what you know about the situation between Cassandra and Robert.

Because he was held back in the third grade, Robert is almost two years older than his classmates. Though physically more mature than the other boys in your class, Robert's social skills are less developed. Although he acts silly and immature from time to time, Robert has not been a behavior problem . . . at least not until a week ago, when Cassandra told you what happened on the playground.

Last Monday at the end of the day, Cassandra told you that Robert had "talked mean" to her during recess on the playground. When you questioned Cassandra to find out exactly what Robert said, her answers were hard to follow. At first, it seemed that, whatever words were exchanged, they were not unlike the taunts boys and girls hurl back and forth daily on playgrounds across the country. As you continued to press for details, however, Cassandra began to talk, again vaguely, about how Robert had "talked dirty" to her. Further questioning of Cassandra still failed to give you a clear picture of what happened on the playground.

Based on what you learned from talking with Cassandra, you decided to give Robert a stern reminder about appropriate ways of talking to other people. The following morning you did just that.

Robert listened respectfully and seemed genuinely contrite. He promised to leave Cassandra alone while they were on the playground. The conversation ended with you telling Robert that his behavior on the playground and in the classroom would be monitored closely.

During the following week, it appeared that the friction between Robert and Cassandra had ended. As far as you could tell, the matter was over.

When Cassandra and her mother entered the room, you knew immediately that both were upset. Cassandra looked like she was on the verge of tears, and her mother looked angry.

"Tell your teacher what you told me," Cassandra's mother began, as she and her daughter seated themselves at two student desks in front of your desk.

"Well," Cassandra began slowly, almost whispering, "Robert bothered me on the playground yesterday." Cassandra started breathing more deeply as she struggled to continue. "He came over to me and. . . ." Cassandra stared at the top of her desk while searching for additional words to express what she wanted to say.

"What she means to tell you," said Cassandra's mother, "is that Robert rubbed up against her and said he wanted to have sex with her. She was sexually harassed."

On hearing what Robert is alleged to have done, you are shocked. What should you do? How does a teacher tell the difference between sexual harassment and the teasing and name calling that are an inescapable part of growing up? Should you try to determine the truth of the allegations before involving the principal? What are your responsibilities to Cassandra and her mother? What are your responsibilities to Robert? How should your school handle the matter?

Name _____ Date _____

For each question, circle the letter of the answer you believe is correct. Then read the chapter to learn more about these topics.

6.1 According to the tenure laws, a teacher may be dismissed for
   A. Threatening to organize a strike by faculty members.
   B. Using obscene or racist language in the presence of students.
   C. Being gay or lesbian.
   D. Living unmarried with a member of the opposite sex.

6.2 The process through which school boards negotiate contracts with teacher organizations is known as
   A. Collective bargaining.
   B. Academic freedom.
   C. Grievance process.
   D. Affirmative action.

6.3 In 1999, the National Home Education Research Institute reported all of the following *except*
   A. More than sixty percent of the states have home-schooling statutes or regulations.
   B. Most home school teachers are as well qualified academically as licensed teachers.
   C. Four out of five states have no minimum academic requirements for parents who decide to home school their children.
   D. Half of all states require that home-schooled children participate in standardized testing.

6.4 When establishing home pages on the Internet, teachers should be careful not to include information that would
   A. Identify the school district.
   B. Identify children in the class.
   C. Identify the particular school.
   D. Identify the teachers' names.

6.5 A "site license" is a commercial software agreement that permits installation
   A. On the computers of those who frequently visit the licensed site.
   B. On any computers designated by the owner of the license.
   C. On one and only one computer.
   D. On any and all computers owned by the institution specified in the license.

6.6 Behavioral indicators of child abuse and neglect among students include all of the following *except*
   A. Fear of going home after school.
   B. Aggressiveness.
   C. Refusal to cooperate.
   D. Withdrawal.

6.7 Which of the following statements best describes application of the principle of "academic freedom"?
   A. This principle is no longer applicable to public school teaching.
   B. A U.S. District Court (*Murray v. Pittsburgh Board of Public Education* 1996) ruled that a teacher could not claim academic freedom in using a teaching methodology rejected by the school board.
   C. The Supreme Court (*Morrison v. State Board of Education* 1969) ruled that teachers have little or no academic freedom in matters related to reading assignments for junior- and senior-level students, even when those readings are consistent with the approved curriculum.
   D. It is a solemn privilege that is never violated, giving teachers essentially unbridled freedom in classrooms.

6.8 Teachers often have to take action in situations in which all the facts are not known or for which no single course of action can be called right or wrong. These situations are often referred to as
   A. Ethical dilemmas.
   B. Moral destruction.
   C. Risk management.
   D. Management and discipline.

6.9 Henry has just graduated from a teacher education program and meets all of the state requirements for initial certification. Under what circumstances could Henry be denied certification?
   A. Henry has a GPA that is considered below average.
   B. Henry received some unsatisfactory ratings in student teaching.
   C. Henry is blind.
   D. Henry cannot be denied a certificate.

6.10 All of the following represent good advice for student teachers *except*
   A. Document problems with students.
   B. The best time to learn emergency procedures is when an emergency occurs.
   C. Know what controls the district has placed on the curriculum.
   D. Read the teacher's handbook.

Answers are available on the FlexChoice website at www.ablongman.com/parkayflex.

The preceding scenario, based partially on actual events that culminated with the filing of a lawsuit against a school board *(Davis v. Monroe County Board of Education* 1999) and a U.S. Supreme Court ruling in 1999, highlights the role that legal issues can play in the lives of teachers and students. In this instance, a fifth-grade Georgia girl said she endured a five-month "barrage of sexual harassment and abuse" from a classmate. The boy allegedly touched the girl's breasts, rubbed against her suggestively, and repeatedly said he wanted to have sex with her. The lawsuit claimed that the girl's mother reported each incident to school officials but the boy was never disciplined; as a result, the girl's grades fell and she became mentally and emotionally upset. The sharply divided Supreme Court (five majority and four dissenting) ruled that school districts can be sued under Title IX in cases involving student-on-student sexual harassment, if the district acts with "deliberate indifference" to the harassment. (Title IX prohibits discrimination on the basis of sex in programs that receive federal money.)

In this chapter we examine significant ethical and legal issues that affect the rights and responsibilities of teachers, administrators, students, and parents. Teachers must act in accordance with a wide range of federal and state legislation and court decisions. As a teacher, you may need to deal with such legal issues as the teacher's responsibility for accidents, discriminatory employment practices, freedom of speech, desegregation, student rights, and circumstances related to job termination or dismissal. Without knowledge of the legal dimensions of such issues, you will be ill-equipped to protect your rights and the rights of your students.

Why Do You Need a Professional Code of Ethics?

The actions of professional teachers are determined not only by what is legally required of them, but also by what they know they *ought* to do. They do what is legally right, and they *do the right thing.* A specific set of values guides them. A deep and lasting commitment to professional practice characterizes their work. They have adopted a high standard of professional ethics and they model behaviors that are in accord with that code of ethics.

At present, the teaching profession does not have a uniform **code of ethics** similar to the Hippocratic oath, which all doctors are legally required to take when they begin practice. However, the largest professional organization for teachers, the National Education Association (NEA) has a code of ethics for its members (see Appendix 6.1) that includes the following statement: "The educator accepts the responsibility to adhere to the highest ethical standards."

Appendix 6.1

Ethical Teaching Attitudes and Practices

Teaching is an ethical enterprise—that is, a teacher has an obligation to act ethically, to follow what he or she knows to be the most appropriate professional action to take. The best interests of students, not the teacher, provide the rule of thumb for determining what is ethical and what is not. Behaving ethically is more than a matter of following the rules or not breaking the law—it means acting in a way that promotes the learning and growth of students and helps them realize their potential.

Unethical acts break the trust and respect on which good student–teacher relationships are based. An example of unethical conduct would be to talk publicly about Cassandra's allegations against Robert (described in this chapter's opening scenario). Other examples would be using grades as a form of punishment, expressing rage in the classroom, or intentionally tricking students on tests. You could no doubt think of other examples from your own experience as a student.

Ethical Dilemmas in Classroom and School

Teachers routinely encounter **ethical dilemmas** in the classroom and in the school. They often have to take action in situations in which all the facts are not known or for which no single course of action can be called right or wrong. At these times it can be quite difficult to decide what an ethical response might be. Dealing satisfactorily with ethical dilemmas in teaching often requires the ability to see beyond short-range consequences to consider long-range consequences.

Consider, for example, the following three questions based on actual case studies. On the basis of the information given, how would you respond to each situation?

1. Should the sponsor of the high school literary magazine refuse to print a well-written story by a budding writer if the piece appears to satirize a teacher and a student?
2. Is a reading teacher justified in trying to increase achievement for an entire class by separating two disruptive students and placing one in a reading group beneath his reading level?
3. Should a chemistry teacher punish a student (on the basis of circumstantial, inconclusive evidence) for a laboratory explosion if the example of decisive, swift punishment will likely prevent the recurrence of a similar event and thereby ensure the safety of all students?

What ethical dilemmas might this experiment pose for a teacher? How might you respond? On what moral or ethical grounds would you base your response? What legal concerns might be involved?

What Are Your Legal Rights as a Teacher?

It is frequently observed that with each freedom comes a corresponding responsibility to others and to the community in which we live. As long as there is more than one individual inhabiting this planet, there is a need for laws to clarify individual rights and responsibilities. This necessary balance between rights and responsibilities is perhaps more critical to teaching than to any other profession. As education law experts Martha McCarthy, Nelda Cambron-McCabe, and Stephen Thomas (1998, 309) point out: "Although public educators do not shed their constitutional rights as a condition of public employment, under certain circumstances restrictions on these freedoms are justified by overriding governmental interests."

While schools do have limited "power over" teachers, teachers' rights to **due process** cannot be violated. Teachers, like all citizens, are protected from being treated arbitrarily by those in authority. A principal who disagrees with a teacher's methods cannot suddenly fire that teacher. A school board cannot ask a teacher to resign merely by claiming that the teacher's political activities outside of school are "disruptive" of the

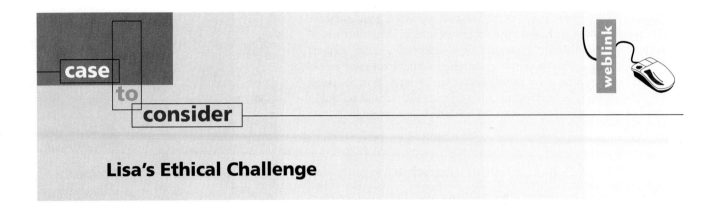

Lisa's Ethical Challenge

educational process. A teacher cannot be dismissed for "poor" performance without ample documentation that the performance was, in fact, poor and without sufficient time to meet clearly stated performance evaluation criteria.

Certification

Karla Brown is a junior high school English teacher and lives in a state with a law specifying that a teacher must show proof of five years of successful teaching experience for a teaching certificate to be renewed. Last year was Karla's fifth year of teaching, and her principal gave her an unsatisfactory performance rating. Karla's principal told her that her teaching certificate cannot be renewed. Is the principal correct?

Karla's principal is mistaken about the grounds for nonrenewal of a teaching certificate. According to the state's law, *unsuccessful* performance, or a failure to complete the school year, is grounds for nonrenewal of a certificate—not performance that is judged to be *unsatisfactory*. Because state laws vary and unsuccessful performance is defined differently in different states, however, Karla's principal might have been correct if she taught in another state.

No teacher who meets all of a state's requirements for initial certification can arbitrarily be denied a certificate. And once obtained, a certificate may not be revoked without due process of law. For a certificate to be revoked, the reason must be job-related and demonstrably impair the teacher's ability to perform satisfactorily. In this regard, the case of a California teacher whose certificate was revoked because someone admitted to having a homosexual relationship with the teacher is often cited. The court determined that the teacher's homosexual conduct was not an impairment to the teacher's performance and ordered the certificate restored (*Morrison v. State Board of Education* 1969). When courts have upheld the refusal to hire and the right to terminate homosexual teachers, these decisions have been influenced by factors such as sexual involvement with students or public acts of indecency (McCarthy, Cambron-McCabe, and Thomas 1998). Several states (California, Connecticut, Hawaii, Massachusetts, Minnesota, New Jersey, and Wisconsin) and the District of Columbia have laws that prohibit discrimination on the basis of sexual orientation in regard to employment, housing, and education. In states that have such antidiscrimination laws, "it will be difficult, if not impossible . . . to uphold the denial of employment or the discharge of homosexuals with respect to teaching positions in the public schools" (LaMorte 1999, 213).

Teachers' Rights to Nondiscrimination

Harold Jones has met all the qualifications for teaching but is denied certification because he has a prison record. Several years ago he was convicted of a felony. Harold claims he is being discriminated against because of his past. Is he right?

States may impose certain limitations on initial certification as long as those limitations are not discriminatory in regard to race, religion, ethnic origin, sex, or age. Nearly all the states, for example, require that applicants for a teaching certificate pass a test that covers basic skills, professional knowledge, or academic subject areas. Qualifications for initial certification may also legally include certain personal qualities. The case of Harold Jones at the beginning of this section, for example, is based on an Oregon case involving a man who had successfully completed a teacher training program but was denied a certificate because he had once been found guilty of a felony and served a term in prison. The Oregon State Board of Education raised some legitimate questions regarding the moral character of the applicant. The court held that a criminal conviction is proof of bad moral character, and his character flaw is irremediable regardless of the passage of time and subsequent legal behavior. As a result, he was unable to obtain the teaching certificate he needed to be hired as a teacher (*Application of Bay v. State Board of Education* 1963).

The right to **nondiscrimination** in regard to employment is protected by Title VII of the Civil Rights Act of 1964, which states:

It shall be an unlawful employment practice for an employer (1) to fail or refuse to hire or to discharge any individual, or otherwise to discriminate against any individual with respect to his compensation, terms, conditions, or privileges of employment, because of such individual's race, color, religion, sex, or national origin; or (2) to limit, segregate, or classify his employees or applicants for employment in any way which would deprive or tend to deprive any individual of employment opportunities or otherwise adversely affect his status as an employee, because of such individual's race, color, religion, sex, or national origin.

Teaching Contracts

A **teaching contract** represents an agreement between the teacher and a board of education. For a contract to be valid, it must contain these five basic elements:

1. *Offer and acceptance*—The school board has made a formal offer and the employee has accepted the contract terms.
2. *Competent parties*—The school board is not exceeding the authority granted to it by the state and the teacher meets the criteria for employment.
3. *Consideration*—Remuneration is promised to the teacher.
4. *Legal subject matter*—The contract terms are neither illegal nor against public policy.
5. *Proper form*—The contract adheres to state contract laws.

Before you sign a teaching contract, it is important that you read it carefully and be certain that it is signed by the appropriate member(s) of the board of education or board of trustees. Ask for clarification of any sections you don't understand. It is preferable that any additional nonteaching duties be spelled out in writing rather than left to an oral agreement. Because all board of education policies and regulations will be part of your contract, you should also read any available teacher handbook or school policy handbook.

The importance of carefully reading a contract and asking for clarification is illustrated in the following case:

Victor Sanchez had just begun his first year as an English teacher at a high school in a city of about 300,000. Victor became quite upset when he learned that he had been assigned by his principal to sponsor the poetry club. The club was to meet once a week after school. Victor refused to sponsor the club, saying that the contract he had signed referred only to his teaching duties during regular school hours. Could Victor be compelled to sponsor the club?

Certain assignments, though not specified in a contract, may be required of teachers in addition to their regular teaching load, as long as there is a reasonable relationship between the teacher's classroom duties and the additional assignment. Furthermore, such assignments can include supervision of school events on weekends as well. Though Victor's contract did not make specific reference to club sponsorship, such a duty would be a reasonable addition to his regular teaching assignment.

When school authorities have assigned teachers to additional duties not reasonably related to their teaching, the courts have tended to rule in favor of teachers who file suit. For example, a school's directive to a tenured teacher of American history to assume the additional role of basketball coach was not upheld by a court of appeals (*Unified School Dist. No. 241 v. Swanson* 1986).

Due Process in Tenure and Dismissal

Tenure is a policy that provides the individual teacher with job security by (1) preventing his or her dismissal on insufficient grounds and (2) providing him or her with due process in the event of dismissal. Tenure is granted to teachers by the local school district after a period of satisfactory teaching, usually two to five years. In most cases, tenure may not be transferred from one school district to another.

The following case highlights the importance of tenure to a teacher's professional career:

A teacher was dismissed from his teaching position by the school board after it learned that the teacher was a homosexual. The teacher filed suit in court, claiming that his firing was arbitrary and violated the provisions of tenure that he had been granted. The school board, on the other hand, maintained that his conduct was inappropriate for a teacher. Was the school board justified in dismissing the teacher?

The events in this case were actually heard by a court, which ruled that the teacher was unfairly dismissed (*Burton v. Cascade School Dist. Union High School No. 5* 1975). The court said that the board violated the teacher's rights as a tenured employee by failing to show "good and just cause" for dismissal. The teacher was awarded the balance due under his contract and an additional one-half year's salary. In a similar case, however, a court upheld the dismissal of a teacher whose sexual orientation was the target of parents' complaints and students' comments. The court ruled that the teacher could no longer effectively carry out his teaching duties (*Gaylord v. Tacoma School District No. 10* 1977).

The practice of providing teachers with tenure is not without controversy. Some critics point out that tenure policies make it too difficult to dismiss incompetent teachers and that performance standards are high in many other fields that do not provide employees with job security. Generally, however, the courts have held the position that tenure is a property right "from which students ultimately benefit" (Essex 1999, 179).

Just about every state today has a tenure law that specifies that a teacher may be dismissed with good cause; what counts as a good cause varies from state to state. The courts have ruled on a variety of reasons for **dismissal:** (1) insubordination, (2) incompetence or inefficiency, (3) neglect of duty, (4) conduct unbecoming a teacher, (5) subversive activities, (6) retrenchment or decreased need for services, (7) physical and/or mental health, (8) age, (9) causing or encouraging disruption, (10) engaging in illegal activities, (11) using offensive language, (12) personal appearance, (13) sex-related activities, (14) political activities, and (15) use of drugs or intoxicants.

For a tenured teacher to be dismissed, a systematic series of steps must be followed so that the teacher receives due process and his or her constitutionally guaranteed rights are not violated. Due process involves a careful, step-by-step examination of the charges brought against a teacher. Most states have outlined procedures that adhere to the following nine steps:

1. The teacher must be notified of the list of charges.
2. Adequate time must be provided for the teacher to prepare a rebuttal to the charges.
3. The teacher must be given the names of witnesses and access to evidence.
4. The hearing must be conducted before an impartial tribunal.
5. The teacher has the right to representation by legal counsel.
6. The teacher (or legal counsel) can introduce evidence and cross-examine adverse witnesses.
7. The school board's decision must be based on the evidence and findings of the hearing.
8. A transcript or record must be maintained of the hearing.
9. The teacher has the right to appeal an adverse decision.

These steps notwithstanding, it should be noted that "the definition [of due process] in each instance depends largely on a combination of the specific facts in a situation, the law governing the situation, the particular time in history in which judgment is being rendered, and the predilections of the individual judge(s) rendering the decision" (LaMorte 1999, 6), as the following case illustrates:

> Near the start of his fifth year of teaching at an elementary school in a small city, and two years after earning tenure, Mr. Mitchell went through a sudden and painful divorce. A few months later a woman whom he had met around the time of his divorce moved into the house he was renting.
>
> For the remainder of the school year he and the woman lived together. During this time, he received no indication that his lifestyle was professionally unacceptable, and his teaching performance remained satisfactory.
>
> At the end of the year, however, Mr. Mitchell was notified that he was being dismissed because of immoral conduct; that is, he was living with a woman he was not married to. The school board called for a hearing and Mr. Mitchell presented his side of the case. The board, nevertheless, decided to follow through with its decision to dismiss him. Was the school board justified in dismissing Mr. Mitchell?

Though at one time teachers could readily be dismissed for living, unmarried, with a member of the opposite sex, a lifestyle such as Mr. Mitchell's is not that unusual today. Because the board had not shown that Mr. Mitchell's alleged immoral conduct had a negative effect on his teaching, his dismissal would probably not hold up in court, unless the community as a whole was upset by his behavior. Moreover, Mr. Mitchell could charge that his right to privacy as guaranteed by the Ninth Amendment to the

Constitution had been violated. Overall, it appears that the decision to dismiss Mr. Mitchell was arbitrary and based on the collective bias of the board. Nevertheless, teachers should be aware that courts frequently hold that teachers are role models, and the local community determines "acceptable" behavior both in school and out of school.

Teachers also have the right to organize and to join teacher organizations without fear of dismissal. In addition, most states have passed **collective bargaining** laws that require school boards to negotiate contracts with teacher organizations. Usually, the teacher organization with the most members in a district is given the right to represent teachers in the collective bargaining process.

An important part of most collective bargaining agreements is the right of a teacher to file a **grievance,** a formal complaint against his or her employer. A teacher may not be dismissed for filing a grievance, and he or she is entitled to have the grievance heard by a neutral third party. Often, the teachers' union or professional association that negotiated the collective bargaining agreement will provide a teacher who has filed a grievance with free legal counsel.

One right that teachers are not granted by collective bargaining agreements is the right to strike. Like other public employees, teachers do not have the legal right to strike in most states. Although teachers have a limited right to strike in a few states, "extensive restrictions have been placed on its use" (McCarthy, Cambron-McCabe, and Thomas 1998, 433). Teachers who do strike run the risk of dismissal (*Hortonville Joint School District No. 1 v. Hortonville Education Association* 1976), though when teacher strikes occur a school board cannot possibly replace all the striking teachers.

Academic Freedom

A teacher of at-risk students at an alternative high school used a classroom management/motivational technique called "Learnball." The teacher divided the class into teams, allowed students to elect team leaders and determine class rules and grading exercises, and developed a system of rewards that included listening to the radio and shooting baskets with a foam ball in the classroom. The school board ordered the teacher not to use the Learnball approach. Did the teacher have the right to continue using this teaching method?

This case is based on actual events involving a teacher in Pittsburgh. The teacher brought suit against the board to prevent it from imposing a policy that banned Learnball in the classroom. The teacher cited the principle of **academic freedom** and claimed that teachers have a right to use teaching methods and materials to which school officials might object. A U.S. District Court, however, upheld the school board policy against Learnball (*Murray v. Pittsburgh Board of Public Education* 1996).

Although the courts have held that teachers have the right to academic freedom, it is not absolute and must be balanced against the interests of society. In fact, education law expert Michael LaMorte (1999, 189–90) suggests that the concept of academic freedom "is no longer as strong a defense as it once was"; for this defense to prevail "it must be shown that the teacher did not defy legitimate state and local curriculum directives; followed accepted professional norms for that grade level and subject matter; discussed matters which were of public concern; and acted professionally and in good faith when there was no precedent or policy."

Famous Cases   A landmark case involving academic freedom focused on John Scopes, a biology teacher who challenged a Tennessee law in 1925 that made it illegal to teach in a public school "any theory which denies the story of the Divine Creation of man as taught in the Bible, and to teach instead that man is descended from a lower order of animals." Scopes maintained that Darwin's theory about human origins had scientific merit and that the state's requirement that he teach the biblical account of creation violated his academic freedom.

Scopes's trial, which came to be known as the Monkey Trial, attracted national attention. Prosecuting Scopes was the "silver-tongued" William Jennings Bryan, a famous lawyer, politician, and presidential candidate. The defending attorney was Clarence Darrow.

Scopes believed strongly in academic freedom and his students' right to know about scientific theories. He expressed his views in his memoirs, *Center of the Storm*:

> Especially repulsive are laws restricting the constitutional freedom of teachers. The mere presence of such a law is a club held over the heads of the timid. Legislation that tampers with academic freedom is not protecting society, as its authors piously proclaim. By limiting freedom they are helping to make robot factories out of schools; ultimately, this produces nonthinking robots rather than the individualistic citizens we desperately need—now more than ever before (1966, 277).

The Monkey Trial ended after eleven days of heated, eloquent testimony. Scopes was found guilty of violating the Butler Act and was fined $100. The decision was later reversed by the Tennessee Supreme Court on a technicality.

Since the Scopes trail, controversy has continued to surround the teaching of evolution. In many states during the 1980s, for example, religious fundamentalists won rulings that required science teachers to give equal time to both creationism and evolutionism in the classroom. The Supreme Court, however, in *Edwards v. Aguillard* (1987) ruled that such "balanced treatment" laws were unconstitutional. In the words of the Court: "Because the primary purpose of the [Louisiana] Creationism Act is to advance a particular religious belief, the Act endorses religion in violation of the First Amendment." In 1996, controversy over evolution again emerged in Tennessee when lawmakers defeated, by a 20 to 13 vote, legislation that would allow districts to dismiss teachers for "insubordination" if they taught evolution as fact.

Another case suggesting that a teacher's right to academic freedom is narrow and limited is *Krizek v. Cicero-Stickney Township High School District No. 201* (1989). In this instance, a District Court ruled against a teacher whose contract was not renewed because she showed her students an R-rated film *(About Last Night)* as an example of a modern-day parallel to Thornton Wilder's play *Our Town*. Although the teacher told her students that they would be excused from viewing the film if they or their parents objected, she did not communicate directly with their parents. The teacher's attempt to consider the objections of students and parents notwithstanding, the Court concluded that

> . . . the length of the film indicates that its showing was more than an inadvertent mistake or a mere slip of the tongue, but rather was a planned event, and thus indicated that the teacher's approach to teaching was problematic. . . .

Though concerned more with the right of a school to establish a curriculum than with the academic freedom of teachers per se, other cases have focused on the teacher's use of instructional materials. In *Mozert v. Hawkins County Board of Education* (1987, 1988), for example, a group of Tennessee parents objected to "secular humanist" reading materials used by their children's teachers. In *Smith v. Board of School Commissioners of Mobile County* (1987), 624 parents and teachers initiated a court suit alleging that forty-four history, social studies, and home economics texts used in the Mobile County, Alabama, public schools encouraged immorality, undermined parental authority, and were imbued with the "humanist" faith. In both cases, the courts supported the right of schools to establish a curriculum even in the face of parental disapproval. In *Smith v. Board of School Commissioners of Mobile County* (1987) the Eleventh Circuit Court stated that "[i]ndeed, given the diversity of religious views in this country, if the standard were merely inconsistency with the beliefs of a particular religion there would be very little that could be taught in the public schools. . . ."

States' Rights   The preceding cases notwithstanding, the courts have not set down specific guidelines to reconcile the teacher's freedom with the state's right to require teachers to follow certain curricular guidelines. The same federal court, for example, heard a similar case regarding a high school teacher who wrote a vulgar word for sexual intercourse on the blackboard during a discussion of socially taboo words. The court actually sidestepped the issue of academic freedom and ruled instead that the regulations authorizing teacher discipline were unconstitutionally vague and, therefore, the teacher could not be dismissed. The court did, however, observe that a public school teacher's right to traditional academic freedom is "qualified," at best, and the "teacher's right must yield to compelling public interests of greater constitutional significance." In reviewing its decision, the court also said, "Nothing herein suggests that school authorities are not free after they have learned that the teacher is using a teaching method of which they disapprove, and which is not appropriate to the proper teaching of the subject, to suspend him [or her] until he [or she] agrees to cease using the method" (*Mailloux v. Kiley* 1971).

Although some teachers have been successful in citing academic freedom as the basis for teaching controversial subjects, others have been unsuccessful. Teachers have been dismissed for ignoring directives regarding the teaching of controversial topics related to sex, polygamy, race, and religion. Though the courts have not been able to clarify just where academic freedom begins and ends, they have made it clear that the state does have a legitimate interest in what is taught to impressionable children.

 **Professional Reflection**   **Evaluating statements about academic freedom**

Do Student Teachers Have the Same Rights?

Do student teachers have the same legal status as certified teachers? Read the following case:

> Meg Grant had really looked forward to the eight weeks she would spend as a student teacher in Mrs. Walker's high school English classes. Meg knew that Mrs. Walker was one of the best supervising teachers she might have been paired with, and she was anxious to do her best.

> In Mrs. Walker's senior class, Meg planned to teach *Brave New World*. Mrs. Walker pointed out to Meg that this book was controversial and some parents might object. She asked Meg to think about selecting an additional title that students could read if their parents objected to *Brave New World*. Meg, however, felt that Mrs. Walker was bowing to pressure from conservative parents, so she decided to go ahead and teach the book.

> Two weeks later Meg was called down to the principal's office where she was confronted by an angry father who said, "You have no right to be teaching my daughter this Communist trash; you're just a student teacher." What should Meg do? Does she have the same rights as a fully certified teacher?

In some states, a student teacher such as Meg might have the same rights and responsibilities as a fully certified teacher; in others, her legal status might be that of an unlicensed visitor. The most prudent action for Meg to take would be to apologize to the father and assure him that if any controversial books are assigned in the future, alternative titles would be provided. In addition, Meg should learn how important it is for a student teacher to take the advice of his or her supervising teacher.

The exact status of student teachers has been the subject of controversy in many states. In fact, one study found that the authority of student teachers to teach was established by law in only forty states, and no state had a statutory provision regulating the dismissal of a student teacher, the assignment of a student teacher, or the denial of the right to student teach (Morris and Curtis 1983). Nevertheless, student teachers should be aware that a potential for liability exists with them just as it does with certified teachers.

One area of debate regarding student teachers is whether they can act as substitutes for their cooperating teachers or even other teachers in a school building. Unfortunately, many school districts have no policy regarding this practice. Depending on statutes in a particular state, however, a student teacher may substitute under the following conditions:

- A substitute teacher is not immediately available.
- The student teacher has been in that student teaching assignment for a minimum number of school days.
- The supervising teacher, the principal of the school, and the university supervisor agree that the student teacher is capable of successfully handling the teaching responsibilities.
- A certificated classroom teacher in an adjacent room or a member of the same teaching team as the student teacher is aware of the absence and agrees to assist the student teacher if needed.
- The principal of the school or the principal's representative is readily available in the building.
- The student teacher is not paid for any substitute service (Shoop and Dunklee 1992, 98).

Given the ambiguous status of student teachers, it is important that you begin your student teaching assignment with a knowledge of the legal aspects of teaching and a clear idea of your rights and responsibilities. To accomplish this, read the "NEA Bill of Rights for Student Teachers" in Appendix 6.2 and follow the recommendations in Figure 6.1 made by school law experts Julie Mead and Julie Underwood.

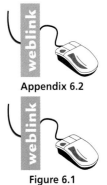

weblink
Appendix 6.2

weblink
Figure 6.1

What Are Your Legal Responsibilities as a Teacher?

Teachers are, of course, responsible for meeting the terms of their teaching contracts. As noted previously, teachers are responsible for duties not covered in the contract if they are reasonably related to teaching. Among these duties may be club sponsorship; lunchroom, study hall, or playground duty; academic counseling of students; and record keeping.

Teachers are also legally responsible for the safety and well-being of students assigned to them. Although it is not expected that a teacher be able to control completely the behavior of young, energetic students, a teacher can be held liable for any injury to a student if it is shown that the teacher's negligence contributed to the injury.

Avoiding Tort Liability

An eighth-grade science teacher in Louisiana left her class for a few moments to go to the school office to pick up some forms. While she was gone, her students continued to do some laboratory work that involved the use of alcohol-burning devices. Unfortunately, one girl was injured when she tried to relight a defective burner. Could the teacher be held liable for the girl's injuries?

The events described above actually occurred in 1974 *(Station v. Travelers Insurance Co.)*. The court that heard the case determined that the teacher failed to provide adequate supervision while the students were exposed to dangerous conditions. Considerable care is required, the court observed, when students handle inherently dangerous objects, and the need for this care is magnified when students are exposed to dangers they don't appreciate.

At times, teachers may have concerns about their liability for damages as a result of their actions. The branch of law concerned with compensating an individual who suffers losses resulting from another's negligence is known as tort law. "A tort is a civil wrong in which one suffers loss as a result of the improper conduct of another" (LaMorte 1999, 384). The harm inflicted on the injured party may be the result of "intentional wrongdoing, recklessness, or simple carelessness" (Imber and van Geel 1993, 575). According to **tort liability** law, an individual who is negligent and at fault in the exercise of his or her legal duty may be required to pay monetary damages to an injured party. Generally, the standard of behavior applied by the courts is that the injury "must be avoidable by the exercise of reasonable care" (McCarthy, Cambron-McCabe, and Thomas 1998, 436). However, teachers are held to a higher standard than ordinary citizens, and certain teachers (e.g., physical education and chemistry teachers) are held to an even higher standard because of the increased risk of injury involved in the classes they teach. Table 6.1 presents several examples of cases in which students were injured and educators were found to have breached their duty of care.

Table 6.1

Should this teacher/coach have any concerns about tort liability? How might this teacher reduce the risk of liability?

Negligence   In contrast to the decision reached by the Louisiana court mentioned earlier, the courts have made it clear that there are many accidents that teachers cannot reasonably foresee that do result in student injuries. For example, a teacher on playground duty was found to be not negligent when a student threw a rock that struck another student in the eye. After the teacher walked past a group of boys, one boy threw a small rock that hit a larger rock on the ground and then bounced up to hit the other boy in the eye. The court ruled that "[w]here the time between an act of a student and injury to a fellow student is so short that the teacher had no opportunity to prevent injury, it cannot be said that negligence of the teacher is a proximate cause of the injury" *(Fagen v. Summers* 1972). In another case, the court ruled that a New York teacher could not have anticipated that the paper bag she asked a student to pick up contained a broken bottle upon which the student cut herself (*West v. Board of Education of City of New York* 1959). In two almost identical cases, the courts ruled that a teacher of a class with a good behav-

ior record could not reasonably be expected to anticipate that a student would be injured by a pencil thrown by a classmate while the teacher was momentarily out of the room attending to her usual duties (*Ohman v. Board of Education* 1950; *Simonetti v. School District of Philadelphia* 1983).

When a court considers a case involving tort liability, evidence is examined to determine whether the responsible party (the school district, the administrator, or the teacher) acted negligently. For a school official to be considered liable, the following must be shown to be present:

1. A legal duty to conform to a standard of conduct for the protection of others
2. A failure to exercise an appropriate standard of care
3. A causal connection, often referred to as "proximate cause," between the conduct and the resultant injury
4. Actual loss or damage as a result of the injury (LaMorte 1999, 400–01)

As a teacher, you should be especially alert when conditions exist that might lead to accidental injury of one or more students. You will have a duty in regard to your pupils, and you could be held liable for injuries that students incur as a result of your **negligence.** This does not mean, however, that your liability extends to any and all injuries your students might suffer; only if you fail to provide the same degree of care for pupils that a reasonable and prudent person would have shown in similar circumstances can you be held liable. Our review of court cases involving the tort liability of teachers suggests that most cases involve at least one of the following:

- Inadequate supervision
- Inadequate instruction
- Lack of or improper medical treatment of pupils
- Improper disclosure of defamatory information concerning pupils—for example, release of school records that contain negative statements about a student

Teachers' concern about their potential monetary liability for failing to act reasonably and prudently in preventing injury to their students has been lessened by the availability of liability insurance. Many professional organizations for teachers offer liability coverage as part of their membership benefits, and teachers may also purchase individual liability insurance policies. In addition, some states that provide school districts with full or partial immunity from tort liability are considering extending the same protection to school employees. Georgia, for example, has extended immunity to teachers and principals (LaMorte 1999).

Educational Malpractice   Since the mid-1970s several plaintiffs have charged in their **educational malpractice** suits that schools should be responsible for a pupil whose failure to achieve is significant. In the first of such cases, the parents of Peter W. Doe charged that the San Francisco Unified School District was negligent because it allowed him to graduate from high school with a fifth-grade reading level and this handicap would not enable him to function in adult society. In particular, they charged that the "defendant school district, its agents and employees, negligently and carelessly failed to provide plaintiff with adequate instruction, guidance, counseling and/or supervision in basic academic skills such as reading and writing, although said school district had the authority, responsibility, and ability [to do so]." They sought $500,000 for the negligent work of the teachers who taught Peter.

In evaluating the claim of Peter W. Doe and his parents, the court pointed out that the alleged injury was not within the realm of tort law and that many factors beyond a school's responsibility or control can account for lack of achievement. The court did not hold the school responsible for Peter's lack of achievement and made it clear that to do so would be to set a precedent with potentially drastic consequences: "To hold [schools] to an actionable duty of care, in the discharge of their academic functions, would expose them to the tort claims—real or imagined—of disaffected students and parents in countless numbers. . . . The ultimate consequences, in terms of public time and money, would burden them—and society—beyond calculation" (*Peter Doe v. San Francisco Unified School District* 1976).

Reporting Child Abuse

Table 6.2

Teachers, who are now *required* by law to report any suspected child abuse, are in positions to monitor and work against the physical, emotional, and sexual abuse and the neglect and exploitation of children. Teachers' professional journals and information from local, state, and federal child welfare agencies encourage teachers to be more observant of children's appearance and behavior in order to detect symptoms of child abuse. Such sources often provide lists of physical and behavioral indicators of potential child abuse, similar to that shown in Table 6.2. Many communities, through their police departments or other public and private agencies, provide programs adapted for children to educate them about their rights in child-abuse situations and to show them how to obtain help.

Schools usually have a specific process for dealing with suspected abuse cases, involving the school principal and nurse as well as the reporting teacher. Because a child's physical welfare may be further endangered when abuse is reported, caution and sensitivity are required. Teachers are in a unique position to help students who are victims of child abuse, both because they have daily contact with them and because children learn to trust them.

Observing Copyright Laws

The continuing rapid development of technology has resulted in a new set of responsibilities for teachers in regard to observing **copyright laws** pertaining to the use of photocopies, videotapes, and computer software programs. In 1976 Congress revised the Copyright Act by adding the doctrine of **fair use.** Although the fair use doctrine cannot be precisely defined, it is generally interpreted as it was in *Marcus v. Rowley* (1983)—that is, one may "use the copyrighted material in a reasonable manner without [the copyright holder's] consent" as long as that use does not reduce the demand for the work or the author's income.

With the vast amount of material (in text, audio, video, and graphic formats) now distributed in digital form over the Internet, teachers must consider copyright laws and restrictions that apply to the use of this material. Unfortunately, the Copyright Act does not provide guidelines for the use of intellectual property found on the Internet. In any case, teachers should understand that ". . . when [their] computer displays a home page on the Internet, [the] computer is presenting a copy of the page that 'exists' on a remote computer. . . . [They] are viewing a published copy of an original document" (Schwartz and Beichner 1999, 199), and the doctrine of fair use applies to the use of such materials.

Photocopies   To clarify the fair use doctrine as it pertained to teachers photocopying instructional materials from books and magazines, Congress endorsed a set of guidelines developed by educators, authors, and publishers. These guidelines allow teachers

technology

highlights

What ethical and legal issues will you face regarding the use of computer software?

to make single copies of copyrighted material for teaching or research but are more restrictive regarding the use of multiple copies. The use of multiple copies of a work must meet the tests of brevity, spontaneity, and cumulative effect.

- *Brevity* means that short works can be copied. Poems or excerpts cannot be longer than 250 words, and copies of longer works cannot exceed 1,000 words or 10 percent of the work (whichever is less). Only one chart or drawing can be reproduced from a book or an article.
- The criterion of *spontaneity* means that the teacher doing the copying would not have time to request permission from the copyright holder.
- The criterion of *cumulative effect* limits the use of copies to one course and limits the material copied from the same author, book, or magazine during the semester. Also, no more than nine instances of multiple copying per class are allowed during a semester.

Videotapes   Guidelines for the use of videotapes made by teachers of television broadcasts were issued by Congress in 1981 (see the Teacher's Resource Guide section "Guidelines for Off-Air Recordings" on this book's website). Videotaped material may be used in the classroom only once by the teacher within the first ten days of taping. Additional use is limited to reinforcing instruction or evaluation of student learning, and the tape must be erased within forty-five days.

Weblink 6.1

Computer Software   Computer software publishers have become concerned about the abuse of their copyrighted material. Limited school budgets and the high cost of computer software have led to the unauthorized reproduction of software. To address the problem, the Copyright Act was amended in 1980 to apply the fair use doctrine to software. Accordingly, a teacher may now make one backup copy of a program. If a teacher were to make multiple copies of software, the fair use doctrine would be violated because the software is readily accessible for purchase and making multiple copies would substantially reduce the market for the software. Software publishers have several different options for licensing their software to schools (see Table 6.3), and teachers should be aware of the type of license that has been purchased with each software program they use.

Table 6.3

The increased practice of networking computer programs—that is, storing a copy of a computer program on a network file server and serving the program to a computer on the network—is also of concern to software publishers. As yet, the practice has not yet been tested in the courts. As more public schools develop computer networks, however, the issue of networked software will most likely be debated in the courts.

Electronic Mail and the Internet   With the huge increase in the transmission of documents via electronic mail (e-mail) and the Internet, copyright laws have been extended to cyberspace. Material "published" online may include a statement by the author(s) that the material is copyright protected and may not be duplicated without permission. In other cases, the material may include a statement such as the following: "Permission is granted to distribute this material freely through electronic or by other means, provided it remains completely intact and unaltered, the source is acknowledged, and no fee is charged for it." If the material is published without restrictions on the Internet, one may assume that the author waives copyright privileges; however, proper credit and a citation should accompany the material if it is reproduced.

Publishing on the Internet   Thousands of teachers and their students around the globe are publishing material at their home pages on the Internet. Teacher- and student-produced materials can be copyright protected by including a statement that the materials may not be duplicated without permission. In addition, teachers should be careful not to include information that would enable someone to identify children in a class. Children's last names should never be published, nor should photos of children be published with any identifying information.

What Are the Legal Rights of Students and Parents?

As a prospective teacher, you have an obligation to become familiar with the rights of students. Since the 1960s students have increasingly confronted teachers and school districts with what they perceived to be illegal restrictions on their behavior. In this section we discuss briefly some of the major court decisions that have clarified students' rights related to freedom of expression, suspension and expulsion, search and seizure, privacy, and nondiscrimination.

Freedom of Expression

Video 6.1

The case of *Tinker v. Des Moines Independent Community School District* (1969) is perhaps the most frequently cited case concerning students' **freedom of expression.** The Supreme Court ruled in *Tinker* that three students, ages thirteen, fifteen, and sixteen, had been denied their First Amendment freedom of expression when they were suspended from school for wearing black arm bands in protest of the Vietnam War. The court ruled that neither teachers nor students "shed their rights to freedom of speech or expression at the schoolhouse gate." In addition, the court found no evidence that the exercise of such a right interfered with the school's operation.

Censorship   One area of student expression that has generated frequent controversy is that of student publications. Prior to 1988, the courts generally made it clear that student literature enjoyed constitutional protection, and it could only be regulated if it posed a substantial threat of school disruption, if it was libelous, or if it was judged vulgar or obscene *after publication.* However, school officials could use "prior **censorship**" and require students to submit literature before publication if such controls were necessary to maintain order in the school.

Within these guidelines, students frequently successfully defended their right to freedom of expression. For example, the right of high school students to place in the school newspaper an advertisement against the war in Vietnam was upheld (*Zucker v. Panitz* 1969). Students were also upheld in their right to distribute information on birth control and on laws regarding marijuana (*Shanley v. Northeast Independent School District* 1972). And other cases upheld the right of students to publish literature that was critical of teachers, administrators, and other school personnel (*Scoville v. Board of Education of Joliet Township High School District 204* 1971; *Sullivan v. Houston Independent School District* 1969).

In January of 1988, however, the Supreme Court, in a five-to-three ruling in *Hazelwood School District v. Kuhlmeier,* departed from the earlier *Tinker* decision and gave public school officials considerable authority to censor school-sponsored student publications. The case involved a Missouri high school principal's censorship of articles in the school newspaper, the *Spectrum,* on teenage pregnancy and the impact of divorce on students. The principal believed the articles were inappropriate because they might identify pregnant students and because references to sexual activity and birth control were inappropriate for younger students. Several students on the newspaper staff distributed copies of the articles on their own and later sued the school district, claiming that their First Amendment rights had been violated.

Writing for the majority in *Hazelwood School District v. Kuhlmeier* Justice Byron White (who had voted with the majority in *Tinker*) said school officials could bar "speech that is ungrammatical, poorly written, inadequately researched, biased or prejudiced, vulgar or profane, or unsuitable for immature audiences." White also pointed out that *Tinker* focused on a student's right of "personal expression," and the Missouri case dealt with school-sponsored publications that were part of the curriculum and bore the "imprimatur of the school." According to White, "Educators do not offend the First Amendment by exercising editorial control over the style and content of student speech in school-sponsored expressive activities so long as their actions are reasonably related to legitimate pedagogical concerns."

A case involving an attempt to regulate an "underground" student newspaper entitled *Bad Astra,* however, had a different outcome. Five high school students in Renton, Washington, produced a four-page newspaper at their expense, off school property, and without the knowledge of school authorities. *Bad Astra* contained articles that criticized school policies, a mock poll evaluating teachers, and several poetry selections. The students distributed 350 copies of the paper at a senior class barbecue held on school grounds.

After the paper was distributed, the principal placed letters of reprimand in the five students' files, and the district established a new policy whereby student-written, non-school-sponsored materials with an intended distribution of more than ten were subject to predistribution review. The students filed suit in federal district court, claiming a violation of their First Amendment rights. The court, however, ruled that the new policy was "substantially constitutional." Maintaining that the policy was unconstitutional, the students filed an appeal in 1988 in the Ninth Circuit Court and won. The court ruled that *Bad Astra* was not "within the purview of the school's exercise of reasonable editorial control" (*Burch v. Barker* 1987, 1988).

Dress Codes   Few issues related to the rights of students have generated as many court cases as have dress codes and hairstyles. The demand on the courts to hear such cases prompted Supreme Court Justice Hugo L. Black to observe that he did not believe "the federal Constitution imposed on the United States Courts the burden of supervising the length of hair that public school students should wear" (*Karr v. Schmidt* 1972). In line with Justice Black's observation, the Supreme Court has repeatedly refused to review the decisions reached by the lower courts.

In general, the courts have suggested that schools may have dress codes as long as such codes are clear, reasonable, and students are notified. However, when the legality of such codes has been challenged, the rulings have largely indicated that schools may not control what students wear unless it is immodest or is disruptive of the educational process.

Students in private schools, however, do not have First Amendment protections provided by *Tinker v. Des Moines Independent Community School District* because private schools are not state affiliated. As a result, students at private schools can be required to wear uniforms, and "[d]isagreements over 'student rights' . . . are generally resolved by applying contract law to the agreement governing the student's attendance" (LaMorte 1999, 98).

At one time, educators' concerns about student appearance may have been limited to hairstyles and immodest dress; however, today's educators, as Michael LaMorte (1996, 93) points out, may be concerned about "T-shirts depicting violence, drugs (e.g., marijuana leaves), racial epithets, or characters such as Bart Simpson; ripped, baggy, or saggy pants or jeans; sneakers with lights; colored bandannas, baseball or other hats; words shaved into scalps, brightly colored hair, distinctive haircuts or hairstyles, or ponytails for males; exposed underwear; Malcolm X symbols; Walkmen, cellular phones, or beepers; backpacks; tatoos, unusual-colored lipstick, pierced noses, or earrings; and decorative dental caps."

Since gangs, hate groups, and violence in and around public schools have become more prevalent during the last decade, rulings that favor schools are becoming more common when the courts "balance the First Amendment rights of students to express themselves against the legitimate right of school authorities to maintain a safe and disruption-free environment" (LaMorte 1999, 147). This balance is clearly illustrated in *Jeglin v. San Jacinto Unified School District* (1993). In this instance, a school's dress code prohibiting the wearing of clothing with writing, pictures, or insignia of professional or college athletic teams was challenged on the grounds that it violated students' freedom of expression. The court acknowledged that the code violated the rights of elementary and middle school students, but not those of high school students. Gangs, known to be present at the high school, had intimidated students and faculty in connection with the sports-oriented clothing. The court ruled that the curtailment of students' rights did not "demand a certainty that disruption will occur, but only the existence of facts which might reasonably lead school officials to forecast substantial disruption."

After the Colorado high school shootings in 1999, which left fouteen students and a teacher dead—including the two gunmen who were members of a clique called the "Trench Coat Mafia"—many school districts made their rules for student dress more restrictive. Ten days after the shootings, a federal judge who upheld a school's decision to suspend a student for wearing a T-shirt that said "Vegan" (a vegetarian who doesn't eat animal products), said "gang attire has become particularly troubling since two students wore trench coats in the Colorado shooting." And, in Jonesboro, Arkansas, where four students and a teacher were shot and killed the previous year, a group of boys and girls identifying themselves as the "Blazer Mafia" were suspended for ten days (Portner, May 12, 1999).

To reduce disruption and violence in schools, some school districts and policy makers have considered requiring students to wear uniforms. During his last term in office, President Clinton frequently expressed his support for school uniforms; for example, during a conversation with high school students in Alexandria, Virginia, two days after the Colorado shootings, he had this to say about the effects of the nation's first mandatory school uniform policy in Long Beach, California: "it [the uniform policy] distinguished [students] from the gangs, which created a safety problem . . . it made all the kids safe. And it lowered dropouts, it increased attendance, it reduced discipline problems" (1999). The U.S. Department of Education, which has developed guidelines for schools that wish to implement a uniform policy, reported in 1998 that 4 percent of public elementary schools and 4 percent of middle schools required students to wear uniforms.

Due Process in Suspension and Expulsion

In February and March of 1971, a total of nine students received ten-day suspensions from the Columbus, Ohio, public school system during a period of citywide unrest. One student, in the presence of his principal, physically attacked a police officer who was trying to remove a disruptive student from a high school auditorium. Four others were suspended for similar conduct. Another student was suspended for his involvement in a lunchroom disturbance that resulted in damage to school property. All nine students were suspended in accordance with Ohio law. Some of the students and their parents were offered the opportunity to attend conferences prior to the start of the suspensions, but none of the nine was given a hearing. Asserting that their constitutional rights had been denied, all nine students brought suit against the school system.

In a sharply divided five-to-four decision, the Supreme Court ruled that the students had a legal right to an education, and that this "property right" could be removed only through the application of procedural due process. The court maintained that suspension is a "serious event" in the life of a suspended child and may not be imposed by the school in an arbitrary manner (*Goss v. Lopez* 1975).

As a result of cases such as *Goss v. Lopez*, every state has outlined procedures for school officials to follow in the suspension and expulsion of students. In cases of short-term suspension (defined by the courts as exclusion from school for ten days or less), the due process steps are somewhat flexible and determined by the nature of the infraction and the length of the suspension. As Figure 6.2 shows, however, long-term suspension (more than ten days) and expulsion require a more extensive due process procedure. The disciplinary transfer of a disruptive student to an alternative school, designed to meet his or her needs, is not considered an expulsion (LaMorte 1999).

Figure 6.2

In response to an increase of unruly students who disrupt the learning of others, a few districts and states have granted teachers the authority to suspend students for up to ten days. Teachers in Cincinnati and Dade County, Florida, for example, have negotiated contracts that give them authority to remove disruptive students from their classrooms; however, district administrators decide how the students will be disciplined. In 1995, Indiana became the first state to grant teachers the power to suspend students, and the following year New York's governor proposed legislation to allow teachers to remove students from their classrooms for up to ten days for "committing an act of violence against a student, teacher, or school district employee; possessing or

where do you stand?

Should schools require students to wear uniforms?

threatening to use a gun, knife, or other dangerous weapon; damaging or destroying school district property; damaging the personal property of teachers or other employees; or defying an order from a teacher or administrator to stop disruptive behavior" (Lindsay 1996, 24).

Reasonable Search and Seizure

As a teacher you have reason to believe that a student has drugs, and possibly a dangerous weapon, in his locker. Do you have the right to search the student's locker and seize any illegal or dangerous items? According to the Fourth Amendment, citizens are protected from **search and seizure** conducted without a search warrant. With the escalation of drug use in schools and school-related violence, however, cases involving the legality of search and seizure in schools have increased. These cases suggest guidelines that you can follow if confronted with a situation such as that described here.

The case of *New Jersey v. T.L.O.* (1985) involved a fourteen-year-old student (T.L.O.) whom a teacher found smoking a cigarette in a rest room. The teacher took the student to the principal's office, whereupon the principal asked to see the contents of her purse. On opening the purse, the principal found a pack of cigarettes and what appeared to be drug paraphernalia and a list titled "People who owe me money." T.L.O. was arrested and later found guilty of delinquency charges.

After being sentenced to one year's probation, T.L.O. appealed, claiming that the evidence found in her purse was obtained in violation of the Fourth Amendment and that her confession to selling marijuana was tainted by an illegal search. The United States Supreme Court found that the search had been reasonable. The Court also developed a two-pronged test of "reasonableness" for searches: (1) A school official must have a reasonable suspicion that a student has violated a law or school policy and (2) the search must be conducted using methods that are reasonable in scope.

Another case focused on the use of trained dogs to conduct searches of 2,780 junior and senior high school students in Highland, Indiana. During a two-and-a-half- to three-hour period, six teams with trained German shepherds sniffed the students. The dogs alerted their handlers a total of 50 times. Seventeen of the searches initiated by the dogs turned up beer, drug paraphernalia, or marijuana. Another eleven students singled out by the dogs, including thirteen-year-old Diane Doe, were strip searched in the nurse's office. It turned out that Diane had played with her dog, who was in heat, that morning and that the police dog had responded to the smell of the other dog on Diane's clothing.

Diane's parents later filed suit, charging that their daughter was searched illegally. The court ruled that the use of dogs did not constitute an unreasonable search, nor did holding students in their homerooms constitute a mass detention in violation of the Fourth Amendment. The court did, however, hold that the strip searches of the students were unreasonable. The court pointed out that the school personnel did not have any evidence to suggest that Diane possessed contraband because, prior to the strip search, she had emptied her pockets as requested. Diane was awarded $7,500 in damages (*Doe v. Renfrow* 1980, 1981).

Court cases involving search and seizure in school settings have maintained that school lockers are the property of the schools, not students, and may be searched by school authorities if reasonable cause exists. In addition, students may be sniffed by police dogs if school authorities have a reasonable suspicion that illegal or dangerous items may be found. Lastly, courts have tended not to allow strip searches; however, as *Cornfield v. Consolidated High School District No. 230* (1993) illustrates, strip searches may be constitutional depending upon the circumstances giving rise to the search, the age of the student, and the severity of the suspected infraction. In *Cornfield,* the court allowed a strip search of a 16-year-old student suspected of "crotching" drugs. The court's decision was influenced by "allegations of several recent prior incidents such as dealing in drugs, testing positive for marijuana, possession of drugs, having 'crotched' drugs during a police raid at his mother's house, failing a urine analysis for cocaine, unsuccessful completion of a drug rehabilitation program, and a report by a bus driver that there was a smell of marijuana where the student sat on the bus" (LaMorte 1999, 144–45).

In general, the courts have tried to balance the school's need to obtain information and the student's right to privacy. To protect themselves from legal challenges related to searches, educators should follow guidelines that have been suggested by school law experts:

■ Inform students and parents at the start of the school year of the procedures for conducting locker and personal searches.
■ Base any search on "reasonable suspicion."
■ Conduct any search with another staff member present.
■ Avoid strip searches or mass searches of groups of students.
■ Require that police obtain a search warrant before conducting a search in the school.

What are students' rights with regard to their persons, lockers, personal property, and records in school and on school grounds? How are school districts' rights of search and seizure decided? In what ways have students' rights to privacy been upheld?

Some schools use drug testing as a requirement for either attendance or interscholastic participation, including sports competition, or as a means of discipline. A 1988 court case upheld a urinalysis drug test for randomly selected student athletes because those who tested positively were suspended only from participating in sports for a period of time and no disciplinary or academic penalties were imposed (*Schaill v. Tippecanoe School Corporation* 1988). Similarly, the U.S. Supreme Court reversed a lower court's ruling and stated that a school district's desire to reduce drug use justified the degree of intrusion required by random tests of student athletes' urine (*Acton v. Vernonia School District* 1995). A few school districts have attempted to implement mandatory drug testing of teachers. So far the courts have upheld the decision rendered in *Patchogue-Medford Congress of Teachers v. Board of Education of Patchogue-Medford Union Free School District* (1987) that drug testing of teachers violates the Fourth Amendment's prohibition of unreasonable searches.

Privacy

Prior to 1974 students and parents were not allowed to examine school records. On November 19, 1974, Congress passed the Family Educational Rights and Privacy Act (FERPA), which gave parents of students under eighteen and students eighteen and older the right to examine their school records. Every public or private educational institution must adhere to the law, known as the **Buckley Amendment,** or lose federal money.

Under the Buckley Amendment, schools must do the following:

1. Inform parents or eligible students of their rights.
2. Facilitate access to records by parents or eligible students by providing information on the types of educational records that exist and the procedures for gaining access to them.

3. Permit parents or eligible students to review educational records, request changes, request a hearing if the changes are disallowed, and add their own statement by way of explanation, if necessary.
4. Ensure that the institution does not give out personally identifiable information without the prior written, informed consent of a parent or an eligible student.
5. Allow parents and eligible students to see the school's record of disclosures (Fischer and Sorenson 1996, 89).

The Buckley Amendment actually sets forth the minimum requirements that schools must adhere to, and many states and school districts have gone beyond these minimum guidelines in granting students access to their records. Most high schools, for example, now grant students under eighteen access to their educational records, and all students in Virginia, elementary through secondary, are guaranteed access to their records.

A number of exceptions are allowed by the Buckley Amendment. The teacher's gradebook, psychiatric or treatment records, notes or records written by the teacher for his or her exclusive use or to be shared with a substitute teacher, or the private notes of school law enforcement units, for example, are not normally subject to examination (Fischer and Sorenson 1996).

Students' Rights to Nondiscrimination

Schools are legally bound to avoid discriminating against students on the basis of race, sex, religion, disability, marital status, or infection with a noncommunicable disease such as HIV/AIDS. One trend that has confronted schools with the need to develop more thoughtful and fair policies has been the epidemic in teenage pregnancies.

In regard to students who are married, pregnant, or parents, the courts have been quite clear: Students in these categories may not be treated differently. A 1966 case in Texas involving a sixteen-year-old mother established that schools may provide separate classes or alternative schools on a *voluntary* basis for married and/or pregnant students. However, the district may not *require* such students to attend separate schools, nor may they be made to attend adult or evening schools (*Alvin Independent School District v. Cooper* 1966).

The courts have made an about-face in their positions on whether students who are married, pregnant, or parents can participate in extracurricular activities. Prior to 1972 participation in these activities was considered a privilege rather than a right, and restrictions on those who could participate were upheld. In 1972, however, cases in Tennessee, Ohio, Montana, and Texas established the right of married students (and, in one case, a divorced student) to participate (*Holt v. Sheldon* 1972; *Davis v. Meek* 1972; *Moran v. School District No. 7* 1972; and *Romans v. Crenshaw* 1972). Since then, restrictions applicable to extracurricular activities have been universally struck down.

Since the mid-1980s, many school districts have become embroiled in controversy over the issue of how to provide for the schooling of young people with HIV/AIDS and whether school employees with HIV/AIDS should be allowed to continue working. As one observer put it:

> Public schools now face the difficulty of balancing two equal and opposing rights: the right of a student with AIDS to an education and the right of students who are not infected with HIV to be protected against infection. The latter right is fueled by fear that one can be infected with HIV through casual contact, even though no medical evidence has found or remotely suggested that HIV can be transmitted

through casual contact. The practical result of attempts to balance those rights has been to open a floodgate to discrimination against students infected with this insidious virus (Alali 1995, 3).

In rulings on HIV/AIDS-related cases, the courts have sided with the overwhelming medical evidence that students with AIDS pose no "significant risk" of spreading the disease. "To date, courts have revealed a high degree of sensitivity to students with HIV or AIDS and to their being included in the public school mainstream" (LaMorte 1999, 338). In 1987, for example, a judge prevented a Florida school district from requiring that three hemophiliac brothers who were exposed to HIV/AIDS through transfusions be restricted to homebound instruction (*Ray v. School District of DeSoto County* 1987).

To stem the spread of HIV/AIDS, school systems in many large cities—New York, Los Angeles, San Francisco, and Seattle, to name a few—have initiated programs to distribute condoms to high school students. According to a 1994 poll by Public Agenda, 55 percent of Americans believe it is appropriate to allow schools to distribute condoms to students, while 43 percent oppose it (Public Agenda 1994, 28).

New York's condom-distribution program, which initially did not require parental consent, was challenged in 1993 (*Alfonso v. Fernandez*). The court ruled that the program was a "health issue" and that the district could not dispense condoms without prior parental approval. The court maintained that the program violated parents' due process rights under the Fourteenth Amendment to raise their children as they see fit; however, the program did not violate parents' or students' freedom of religion. Three years later, however, the U.S. Supreme Court declined to review a Massachusetts high court ruling that upheld a school board's decision to place condom machines in high school restrooms and allow junior- and senior-level students to request condoms from the school nurse (*Curtis v. School Committee of Falmouth* 1996).

What Are Some Issues in the Legal Rights of School Districts?

Clearly, the law touches just about every aspect of education in the United States today. Daily, the media remind us that ours is an age of litigation; no longer are school districts as protected as they once were from legal problems. Corporal punishment, sexual harassment, religious expression, and home schooling are among the issues in the legal rights of school districts.

Corporal Punishment

The practice of **corporal punishment** has had a long and controversial history in education in the United States. Currently, policies regarding the use of corporal punishment vary widely from state to state, and even from district to district.

Video 6.2

Critics believe that corporal punishment "is neither a necessary nor an effective response to misbehavior in school" (Slavin 2000, 391), and some believe the practice is "archaic, cruel, and inhuman and an unjustifiable act on the part of the state" (LaMorte 1999, 129). In spite of such arguments against its effectiveness, corporal punishment continues to be widespread. Nevertheless, almost half of the states and many school districts currently ban corporal punishment, and many others restrict its use (LaMorte 1999).

The most influential Supreme Court case involving corporal punishment is *Ingraham v. Wright,* decided in 1977. In Dade County, Florida, in October 1970, junior high school students James Ingraham and Roosevelt Andrews were paddled with a wooden paddle. Both students received injuries as a result of the paddlings, with Ingraham's being the most severe. Ingraham, who was being punished for being slow to respond to a teacher's directions, refused to assume the "paddling position" and had to be held over a desk by two assistant principals while the principal administered twenty "licks." As a result, Ingraham "suffered a hematoma requiring medical attention and keeping him out of school for several days."

The court had two significant questions to rule on in *Ingraham:* Does the Eighth Amendment's prohibition of cruel and unusual punishment apply to corporal punishment in the schools? And, if it does not, should the due process clause of the Fourteenth Amendment provide any protection to students before punishment is administered? In regard to the first question, the Court, in a sharply divided five-to-four decision, ruled that the Eighth Amendment was not applicable to students being disciplined in school, only to persons convicted of crimes. On the question of due process, the Court said, "We conclude that the Due Process clause does not require notice and a hearing prior to the imposition of corporal punishment in the public schools, as that practice is authorized and limited by the common law." The Court also commented on the severity of the paddlings in *Ingraham* and said that, in such cases, school personnel "may be held liable in damages to the child and, if malice is shown, they may be subject to criminal penalties."

Though the Supreme Court has upheld the constitutionality of corporal punishment, many districts around the country have instituted policies banning its use. Where corporal punishment is used, school personnel are careful to see that it meets criteria that have emerged from other court cases involving corporal punishment:

1. It is consistent with the existing statutes.
2. It is a corrective remedy for undesirable behavior.
3. It is neither cruel nor excessive.
4. There is no permanent or lasting injury.
5. Malice is not present.
6. The punishment is suitable for the age and sex of the child.
7. An appropriate instrument is used (O'Reilly and Green 1983, 144–45).

Sexual Harassment

Though few victims report it, sexual harassment affects about four out of every five teenagers in schools across the nation, according to a survey of eighth- through eleventh-graders sponsored by the American Association of University Women (1993). Students' responses were based on the following definition: "Sexual harassment is unwanted and unwelcome sexual behavior which interferes with your life" (American Association of University Women 1993, 6). Although most teens report that they are harassed by their schoolmates, one-fourth of the girls and one-tenth of the boys said they had been harassed by school employees. Figure 6.3 shows the percentage of students reporting various types of **sexual harassment.** In addition, the survey indicated that only 7 percent of the victims told the school about the sexual harassment, and more than half didn't even know whether their school had a policy on sexual harassment.

Data from the AAUW study were further analyzed by four University of Michigan researchers who came to the surprising conclusion that "the large majority of

Figure 6.3

adolescents who experience harassment have also harassed someone else during their school life. Over half of all students, equivalent by gender, have experienced harassment both as victim and perpetrator" (Lee, Chen, and Smerdon 1996, 399–400). They also concluded that "we cannot say which came first, harassing others or being harassed" and that their findings "run counter to any explanation of sexual harassment based solely on differential social or power status" (399). To address the alarming problem of sexual harassment in schools, the University of Michigan team recommended the following:

- The discussion of sexuality, both wanted and unwanted, should be included in the formal and informal curriculum.
- Helping students understand, recognize, and address their own ambivalence about sexual harassment (indeed, about sexuality generally) should be a meaningful component of every secondary school's curriculum.
- Adults in schools should serve as models for respectful cross-status relations (Lee, Chen, and Smerdon 1996, 410).

As our discussion of this chapter's opening scenario pointed out, a landmark Supreme Court Case (*Davis v. Monroe County Board of Education* 1999) ruled by a narrow 5 to 4 margin that educators can be held liable if they fail to take steps to end peer sexual harassment. In their majority opinion, five justices disagreed with the claim by the other four justices that "nothing short of expulsion of every student accused of misconduct involving sexual overtones would protect school systems from liability or damages." Instead, their ruling was intended "only for harassment that is so severe, pervasive, and objectively offensive that it effectively bars the victim's access to an educational opportunity or benefit."

The dissenting justices, however, expressed concern about the "avalanche of liability now set in motion" and the "potentially crushing financial liability" for schools.

> A female plaintiff who pleads only that a boy called her offensive names, that she told a teacher, that the teacher's response was unreasonable, and that her school performance suffered as a result, appears to state a successful claim. . . . After today, Johnny will find that the routine problems of adolescence are to be resolved by invoking a federal right to demand assignment to a desk two rows away.

To highlight their concern about the effects of the ruling, the dissenting Justices also noted that shortly after a U.S. Department of Education warning that schools could be liable for peer sexual harassment, a North Carolina school suspended a six-year-old boy who kissed a female classmate on the cheek.

In addition to harassment by the opposite sex, same-sex harassment, usually against gay and lesbian students, is a problem at some schools. Since the mid-1990s, several school districts have faced lawsuits filed by gay and lesbian students who claimed that school officials failed to protect them from verbal and physical antigay harassment. For example, in 1999 six gay and lesbian teenagers in Morgan Hill, California, filed a complaint in a U.S. District Court charging that school officials failed to protect them from years of antigay harassment. One of the complainants alleged that teachers regularly witnessed the harassment but did nothing to stop it: "Most [teachers] just don't want the hassle; others will acknowledge that they are homophobic, that they just don't like gays and lesbians." Moreover, the student found that administrators also refused to get involved: "Taking these things [i.e., complaints about antigay harassment] to the administrators and having them, my protectors, say 'Go back to class and stop talking about it' affected me more than anything. I learned that teachers won't do anything for you if they don't get any backup from the administration" (Ruenzel 1999). A 1996 verdict awarding almost $1 million to a gay student by a U.S. District Court was the first time a federal jury found school officials responsible for antigay harassment committed by students (Jacobson, November 22, 1996). Currently, at least five states and several school districts have education policies that prohibit discrimination based on sexual orientation.

Increased reports of sexual harassment of students by educators and a Supreme Court ruling in 1992 *(Franklin v. Gwinnett County Public Schools)* that students could sue and collect damages for harassment under Title IX of the Education Act of 1972 are causing some teachers to be apprehensive about working closely with students, and a small number of teachers even report that they fear being falsely accused by angry, disgruntled students. As a school superintendent put it, "There's no question but that the attitudes of personnel in schools are changing because of the many cases [of sexual harassment] that have come up across the country. I think all of us are being extremely cautious in how we handle students and in what we say and do with students and employees" (*Spokesman Review* 1993, 1A). To address the problem, many school districts have suggested guidelines that teachers can follow to show concern for students, offer them encouragement, and congratulate them for their successes.

Religious Expression

Conflicts over the proper role of religion in schools are among the most heated in the continuing debate about the character and purposes of education in the United States. Numerous school districts have found themselves embroiled in legal issues related to school prayer, Bible reading, textbooks, creationism, singing of Christmas carols, distribution of religious literature, New Age beliefs, secular humanism, religious holidays, use of school buildings for religious meetings, and the role of religion in moral education, to name a few. On the one hand, conservative religious groups wish to restore prayer and Christian religious practices to the public schools; on the other, secular liberals see religion as irrelevant to school curricula and maintain that public schools should not promote religion. In addition, somewhere between these two positions are those who believe that, while schools should not be involved in the *teaching of* religion, they should *teach about* religion.

During the last fifty years, scores of court cases have addressed school activities related to the First Amendment principle of separation of church and state. As Michael Imber and Tyll van Geel put it: "By far the most common constitutional objection raised against a school program in the latter half of the twentieth century is that it fails to respect the wall of separation between church and state" (1993, 88). In one of these landmark cases (*Engel v. Vitale* 1962), the United States Supreme Court ruled that recitation of a prayer said in the presence of a teacher at the beginning of each school day was unconstitutional and violated the First Amendment which states: "Congress shall make no law respecting an establishment of religion, or prohibiting the free exercise thereof." Justice Hugo Black, who delivered the opinion of the Court, stated ". . . it is no part of the business of government to compose official prayers for any group of the American people to recite as a part of a religious program carried on by government."

The following year, the U.S. Supreme Court ruled that Bible reading and reciting the Lord's Prayer in school were unconstitutional (*School District of Abington Township v. Schempp* 1963). In response to the district's claim that unless these religious activities were permitted a "religion of secularism" would be established, the Court stated that "We agree of course that the State may not establish a 'religion of secularism' in the sense of affirmatively opposing or showing hostility to religion, thus 'preferring those who believe in no religion over those who do believe.' We do not agree, however, that this decision in any sense has that effect."

To determine whether a state has violated the separation of church and state principle, the courts refer to the decision rendered in *Lemon v. Kurtzman* (1971). In this instance, the U.S. Supreme Court struck down an attempt by the Rhode Island legislature to provide a 15 percent salary supplement to teachers of secular subjects in nonpublic schools and Pennsylvania legislation to provide financial supplements to nonpublic schools through reimbursement for teachers' salaries, texts, and instructional materials in certain secular subjects. According to the three-part test enunciated in *Lemon v. Kurtzman,* governmental practices "must (1) reflect a clearly secular purpose; (2) have a primary effect that neither advances nor inhibits religion; and (3) avoid excessive entanglement with religion" (LaMorte 1999, 39). Though criticized vigorously by several Supreme Court justices since 1971, the so-called **Lemon test** has not been overruled.

During the mid-1990s, the courts heard several cases addressing the question of whether parents' right to direct their children's upbringing meant they could demand curricula and learning activities that were compatible with their religious beliefs. Without exception, the courts have rejected "parent-rights" cases against the schools; those rights, according to a U.S. Court of Appeals ruling in support of a schoolwide assembly on HIV/AIDS, "do not encompass a broad-based right to restrict the flow of information in the public schools" (*Brown v. Hot, Sexy and Safer Productions, Inc.* 1996). In a similar case, parents objected to a Massachusetts school district's policy of distributing condoms to junior and senior high school students who requested them. The state's Supreme Judicial Court rejected the parental rights argument and their argument that the program infringed on their First Amendment right to free exercise of religion: "Parents have no right to tailor public school programs to meet their individual religious or moral preferences" (*Curtis v. School Committee of Falmouth* 1996).

Home Schooling

One spinoff of the public's heightened awareness of the problems that schools face has been the decision by some parents to educate their children in the home. While most home-schoolers view home schooling as an opportunity to provide their children with a curriculum based on religious values, "a new breed of home-schooler is emerging, motivated not by religious doctrine but by more practical concerns ranging from school violence to poor academic quality to overzealous peer pressure" (Schnaiberg 1996, 24). Estimates of the number of school-age children being taught at home vary; however, the National Home Education Research Institute (NHERI) estimated that about 1.5 million students were home schooled in 1999.

Home schooling is legal in all the states and the District of Columbia; however, how it is regulated, and whether resources are allocated, vary greatly. In 1999, NHERI reported that forty-one states had no minimum academic requirements for parents who decided to home-school their children. More than 60 percent of the states have home-schooling statutes or regulations, and half of the states require that home-schooled students participate in standardized testing (LaMorte 1999). In most states, home-schoolers must demonstrate that their instruction is "equivalent" to that offered in the public schools, a standard set in *New Jersey v. Massa* (1967).

Legal support for home schools has been mixed. In 1994, home-schoolers in Maine defeated legislative attempts to require that home schools be visited monthly by public school officials. In 1993 and 1994, legislation to require home-school teachers to be state certified were defeated in South Dakota and Kansas, and similar laws were overturned in Iowa and North Dakota. However, a federal district court upheld a West Virginia statute making children ineligible for home schooling if their standardized test scores fell below the 40th percentile (*Null v. Board of Education* 1993). In Iowa, mandatory home-schooling reports to the state were upheld in *State v. Rivera* (1993); home-schoolers in that state must submit course outlines, weekly lesson plans, and provide the amount of time spent on areas of the curriculum. And, a Maryland law requiring the state's monitoring of home schooling was upheld despite a parent's claim that the state's curriculum promoted atheism, paganism, and evolution (*Battles v. Anne Arundel County Board of Education* 1996).

Table 6.4

Table 6.4 lists chronologically and summarizes the key legislation and court decisions affecting educators that are discussed in this chapter.

As the preceding cases related to home schooling show, school law is not static—instead, it is continually evolving and changing. In addition, laws pertaining to education vary from state to state. Therefore, it is important for the beginning teacher to become familiar with current publications on school law in his or her state.

SUMMARY

Why Do You Need a Professional Code of Ethics? (p. 154)

What Are Your Legal Rights as a Teacher? (p. 155)

Do Student Teachers Have the Same Rights? (p. 162)

What Are Your Legal Responsibilities as a Teacher? (p. 163)

What Are the Legal Rights of Students and Parents? (p. 168)

What Are Some Issues in the Legal Rights of School Districts? (p. 175)

KEY TERMS AND CONCEPTS

Go to the website for interactive flashcards.

APPLICATIONS AND INTERACTIVITIES

Go to the website for interactive assignments in the following areas:

Teacher's Journal

Teacher's Database

Observations and Interviews

Handout Master M6.1
Handout Master M6.2

Professional Portfolio

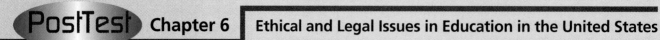

Name _____ **Date** _____

For each question, write in the blank the answer you believe is correct.

6.1 In establishing limitations on initial _____, states may prescribe standards as long as they are not discriminatory in regard to race, religion, ethnic origin, sex, or age.

6.2 An agreement between a teacher and a board of education specifying conditions of employment is known as a teaching _____.

6.3 _____ is a policy providing individual teachers with job security by preventing dismissal in the absence of sufficient cause and guaranteeing access to due process.

6.4 Most states have passed collective _____ laws that require school boards to negotiate contracts with teacher organizations.

6.5 An important aspect of many collective bargaining agreements is the right of a teacher to file a _____.

6.6 According to _____ liability law, an individual who is negligent and at fault in exercising his or her legal duty may be required to pay monetary damages to an injured party.

6.7 Teachers are required by law to report any suspected cases of child _____.

6.8 In 1976 Congress revised the Copyright Act by adding the doctrine of fair _____.

6.9 The famous Supreme Court ruling known as *Tinker v. Des Moines Independent Community School District* is often cited in connection with students' freedom of _____.

6.10 An act of Congress passed in 1974 specified the minimum requirements concerning access to school records that must be followed by schools. This law is known today as the _____ Amendment—named for one of its authors.

Answers are available on the FlexChoice website at www.ablongman.com/parkayflex.

weblink

Name _____

Keep this checklist at your computer as a reminder to read and complete the chapter features and activities located on the FlexChoice website at www.ablongman.com/parkayflex.

Date
Completed

_____	❏ **PreTest with Answers**
_____	❏ **Audio Clip 6.1:** Thinking Over the Opening Vignette
_____	❏ **Appendix 6.1:** NEA Code of Ethics for Teachers
_____	❏ **Case to Consider:** Lisa's Ethical Challenge
_____	❏ **Professional Reflection:** Evaluating statements about academic freedom
_____	❏ **Appendix 6.2:** NEA Bill of Rights for Student Teachers
_____	❏ **Figure 6.1:** Legal advice for student teachers
_____	❏ **Table 6.1:** Selected court decisions in which school personnel were found negligent for failure to meet a "standard of care"
_____	❏ **Table 6.2:** Physical and behavioral indicators of child abuse and neglect
_____	❏ **Technology Highlights:** What ethical and legal issues will you face regarding the use of computer software?
_____	❏ **Weblink 6.1:** Guidelines for Off-Air Recordings
_____	❏ **Table 6.3:** Common types of commercial software licenses
_____	❏ **Video 6.1:** Freedom of Expression
_____	❏ **Figure 6.2:** Due process in suspension and expulsion
_____	❏ **Where Do You Stand?:** Should schools require students to wear uniforms?
_____	❏ **Video 6.2:** Corporal Punishment
_____	❏ **Figure 6.3:** Teen sexual harassment
_____	❏ **Table 6.4:** Educators' rights and responsibilities
_____	❏ **Summary**
_____	❏ **Key Terms and Concepts**
_____	❏ **Applications and Interactivities:** Teacher's Journal
_____	❏ **Applications and Interactivities:** Teacher's Database
_____	❏ **Applications and Interactivities:** Observations and Interviews
_____	❏ **Handout Master M6.1:** Identifying Ethical Dilemmas in Teaching
_____	❏ **Handout Master M6.2:** Analyzing Teachers' Responses to Ethical Dilemmas
_____	❏ **Applications and Interactivities:** Professional Portfolio
_____	❏ **PostTest with Answers**

part three

The Art
of Teaching

d ear mentor

On Becoming a Master Teacher

Dear Mentor,

I have been a student at California State University—
Los Angeles for two years. I would like to find out how
to become a master teacher. What is the profile of a
master teacher?

Sincerely,

Darryl Hampton

Dear Darryl,

Congratulations on being a second-year university student with the goal of becoming a teacher. Teaching is a valuable profession and one that will require your heart, talent, and energy.

Regarding how to become a master teacher, I think you've taken an important first step by asking the question. Look for master teachers and observe them. Keep in mind what good teaching looks like. Seek a mentor and make time for the relationship.

As you begin your career, it is important that you know and use the academic standards for your subject area—whether is it elementary education, middle school math, or high school English. Your lesson plans should show how you will teach students the learning strategies they will need to meet those standards. Join the academic professional organization in your subject area. The members can become an expert support group.

Also, take time to observe and learn about your school's culture. Seek to understand the school's community. From there, decide how you can be a positive contributor to both your school and community.

Believe in your ability to teach. When a challenge faces you, use your problem-solving skills. For example, in your class there could be a student who is reading below grade level. Use a variety of instructional methods to engage the student, and continue to explore other approaches to teaching reading skills. Read articles, attend professional development classes, or consult with your school district's or university's reading specialists. For, you see, as a teacher, your learning is ever-growing.

But most important of all, believe in your students' desire to learn. That has become my driving force. My students motivate and inspire me to become a better teacher for them. As the professional in the classroom, a teacher must provide a safe and caring environment that encourages learning and effort. It is not enough to instill high dreams. We must equip our students with academic skills so that they have the tools to reach those dreams.

Incorporate your talents and interests into your teaching. That's one way to show your students a connection between what they learn in school and the real world.

In closing, I want to share with you some advice for new teachers that my second and third graders gave: "I would suggest patience and thoughtfulness, and make them laugh a little." "If a student needs help don't tell them the answer; just help them with the problem." So Darryl, you see, students really want a teacher's help.

Above all, remember to celebrate successes, because encouragement is never wasted.

Sincerely,

Janice James
1999 Kentucky Teacher of the Year

7

Teaching Diverse Learners

Prejudice is a burden which confuses the past, threatens the future, and renders the present inaccessible.

—Maya Angelou

focus questions

1. How is diversity embedded in the culture of the United States?

2. What does equal educational opportunity mean?

3. What is meant by bilingual education?

4. What is multicultural education?

5. How is gender a dimension of multicultural education?

Today I strolled into Sojourner Truth High School with a bit of concern. I had been student teaching for the spring semester at the same high school I had attended myself as a teenager and was really enjoying the experience, looking forward to it every day. Since February, I have been responsible for teaching five freshman world history classes to a group of inner-city students. The classes are made up of mostly African Americans like myself as well as a small percentage of Caribbean, Hispanic, Asian, and Polish American students. I care for these students and am committed to making a difference in their lives.

AUDIO
Audio Clip 7.1

Ms. Callaway, my cooperating teacher, puts a lot of faith and trust in my approach to teaching. She told me that the students sorely need African American males in positions of authority who can relate to their problems. She stressed that the students look up to me and enjoy my innovative lessons.

I know that I have in fact reached some of the students, and I am proud of my teaching successes. The students seem to be really learning by relating history to their everyday lives. I have spent many long hours trying to make history come alive for them. I want the students to see history as *theirs,* and I believe that I am meeting with much success, at least on the academic front.

But my zeal and eagerness are nevertheless starting to wear down. My growing lack of enthusiasm, I have realized, is due to the daily blatant disregard and disrespect that students have for themselves and others.

I find it difficult to teach a lesson without constantly reminding my class, "Watch your mouth!" "Take your hat off, please," and "Please be respectful of other folks' differences." All day long, in and out of class, I directly and indirectly hear conversations heavily laced with profanity, disrespect, and insults. I know that this kind of talk will not help my students advance themselves in the outside world. I know that for them to succeed, I need to help them gain self-esteem and to project a better image to others.

At first, I thought that maybe if I set a good example each and every day by using proper speech, not wearing my hat in the building, and respecting my peers and all of the students, I could help. After all, I had graduated from this same school and could serve as a role model of someone who had gone to college and gained a profession. But without fail, there was little improvement.

My failure to reach my students has caused me many sleepless nights. I worry that knowledge and love for history is not enough. So much is stacked against my students that they need every edge they can get. I remember Ms. Jefferson, a teacher at this very school, now retired, who inspired me to make profound changes in my own life. I want to do for my students what Ms. Jefferson did for me, but I feel that I am reaching a dead end.

One day, out of frustration, I simply asked the students, "Why do you think that it is so necessary to use profanity in the classroom?"

I listened to their answers: "It's a habit!" "It's the way I express myself!" "I can't help it!" "I don't know; it's the way I talk!"

So I went on to ask, "Why do guys wear their hats in the building?" They pretty much all agreed that it was done "to be cool" and as a "habit."

"But how," I responded, "are you guys going to go to college if you are trying so hard to be cool all the time and can't control your mouths or your dress?"

They said they liked the way they talked and dressed and didn't need college.

Then I asked, "Well, why do you think that it's a must to insult or hurt someone's feelings?"

Everyone agreed that it was done because "it's fun."

"But what happens when someone's feelings are really hurt or the insults get out of hand?" I persisted.

"Well, I guess I got to kick his #@@###**!" was the only response.

Deep down inside, I know there must be some hope for these kids, but I do not know where to begin or what else to do. I feel helpless. (Curtis Parker quoted in Rand and Shelton-Colangelo, 1999, 87–88).

Name _____ Date _____

For each question, circle the letter of the answer you believe is correct. Then read the chapter to learn more about these topics.

7.1 Using two languages as the medium of instruction is
A. Language diversity.
B. Bilingual education.
C. Dual instruction.
D. Immersion.

7.2 Individuals within a larger culture who share a self-defined racial or cultural identity and a set of beliefs, attitudes, and values are members of
A. An ethnic group.
B. A bilingual group.
C. A pluralistic group.
D. A bicultural group.

7.3 Age, racial identity, exceptionalities, language, gender, sexual orientation, income level, and beliefs and values are elements that shape
A. Bilingual culture.
B. Ethnicity.
C. Cultural identity.
D. Race.

7.4 Which of the following is *not* a purpose of bilingual education?
A. Help students maintain their ethnic identity.
B. Encourage assimilation into the mainstream culture.
C. Eliminate the use of the home language.
D. Integrate the home language and culture with a new one.

7.5 Concerning student language patterns, researchers have found that children from working-class backgrounds
A. Tend to have no unique language patterns.
B. Tend to develop language patterns unrelated to standard English.
C. Tend to develop more "elaborated" language patterns.
D. Tend to develop "restricted" language patterns.

7.6 According to the U.S. Bureau of the Census (1998), which of these states has the lowest percentage of five-to seventeen-year-olds who speak a non-English language at home?
A. North Carolina.
B. West Virginia.
C. Wyoming.
D. Alaska.

7.7 Students at Indiana University can choose to student teach in all of the following settings *except*
A. On a Native American reservation.
B. In an inner-city school.
C. Overseas.
D. On the Rio Grande border.

7.8 Ms. Bird has developed "cultural immersion" experiences within several cultures to develop an increased understanding and appreciation for others. This is an example of
A. Service learning.
B. Multiculturalism.
C. Bilingual education.
D. Cultural identity.

7.9 Which of the following statements is *not* true?
A. People can be classified into as many as 300 races.
B. Every person belongs to at least one ethnic group.
C. Many Americans favor the addition of a "mixed race" category to the census.
D. There is no distinction between ethnicity and race.

7.10 All of the following statements are true about students from minority groups *except*
A. They are disproportionately represented among students who have not mastered minimum competencies in the "basics."
B. They are expelled or suspended from school more often than nonminority students.
C. They are more likely to drop out of high school than other students.
D. There has been a steady increase in the academic achievement of minority students since 1990.

Answers are available on the FlexChoice website at www.ablongman.com/parkayflex.

The above reflections by Curtis Parker on his student teaching experience highlight how important it is for teachers to be able to communicate with students from diverse cultural backgrounds. Although Curtis is momentarily discouraged by his inability to get his students to stop using profanity and to improve their behavior, he may actually be influencing his students more than he realizes. It is possible, for example, that some of Curtis's students really do understand the important lesson in life he is trying to teach them; however, their strong need not to risk disapproval of their peers prevents them from changing their behavior at this time. At the very least, Curtis's students know that he cares genuinely about their education, that he wants to learn about their lives, and, though he disapproves of some of their behavior, he does not disapprove of them. Finally, as Curtis notes, his students are "relating history to their everyday lives" and he is "meeting with much success"—two solid indicators that he is building positive relationships with his students and will continue to become an increasingly influential role model in their lives.

This chapter looks at cultural diversity in the United States and the challenges of equalizing educational opportunity for all students. Professional teachers, such as Curtis is well on his way toward becoming, see cultural diversity as an asset to be preserved and valued, not a liability. The United States has always derived strength from the **diversity** of its people, and *all* students should receive a high-quality education so that they may make their unique contributions to society.

How Is Diversity Embedded in the Culture of the United States?

Audio Clip 7.2

The percentage of ethnic minorities in the United States has been growing steadily since the end of World War II. According to the U.S. Census Bureau, there were more than 25 million foreign-born people living in the United States in 1999, and there was a net increase of one international migrant every 30 seconds. Twenty percent of U.S. senators are grandchildren of immigrants, a claim that can be made by no other nation in the world about its leading legislative body (Wirt and Kirst 1997). In addition, the Census Bureau estimates that

- By 2010, blacks and Hispanics will equal the number of whites.
- By 2025, half of U.S. youth will be white and half "minority."
- By 2050, no one group will be a majority among adults.

Figure 7.1

As a result, the number of students from diverse cultural backgrounds is increasing in most schools in the United States (see Figure 7.1). The District of Columbia now has minority group enrollments of 96.0 percent; Hawaii, 76.5 percent; New Mexico, 56.9 percent; and Mississippi, 56.1 percent (National Center for Education Statistics 1999). Most students in urban school districts are members of groups traditionally thought of as minorities. Among the urban school districts where non-Hispanic white students currently number less than 20 percent are Atlanta, Baltimore, Chicago, Detroit, Houston, Los Angeles, Miami, New Orleans, Oakland, Richmond, and San Antonio (National Center for Education Statistics 1999).

Clearly, the increasing diversity of U.S. society has extensive implications for schools. There is, for example, an increased demand for bilingual programs and teachers. All but a few school districts face a critical shortage of minority teachers. And, there is a need to develop curricula and strategies that address the needs and backgrounds of all students—regardless of their social class, gender, sexual orientation, or ethnic, racial, or cultural identity.

The Meaning of Culture

As we pointed out in Chapter 4's discussion of the aims of education, one mission of schools is to maintain the culture of the United States. But what is the U.S. culture? Is there a single culture to which everyone in the country belongs? Before we can answer that question we must define the term *culture*. Simply put, **culture** is *the way of life* common to a group of people. It consists of the values, attitudes, and beliefs that influence their traditions and behavior. It is also a way of interacting with and looking at the world. Though at one time it was believed that the United States was a "melting pot" in which ethnic cultures would melt into one, ethnic and cultural differences have remained very much a part of life in the United States. A "salad-bowl" analogy captures more accurately the **cultural pluralism** of U.S. society. That is, the distinguishing characteristics of cultures are to be preserved rather than blended into a single culture.

Dimensions of Culture Within our nation's boundaries, we find cultural groups that differ according to other distinguishing factors, such as religion, politics, economics, and geographic region. The regional culture of New England, for example, is quite different from that of the Southeast. Similarly, Californians are culturally different from Iowans.

However, everyone in the United States does share some common dimensions of culture. James Banks, an authority on multicultural education, has termed this shared culture the "national macroculture" (Banks 1999). In addition to being members of the national macroculture, people in the United States are members of ethnic groups. An ethnic group is made up of individuals within a larger culture who share a self-defined racial or cultural identity and a set of beliefs, attitudes, and values. Members of an ethnic group distinguish themselves from others in the society by physical and social attributes. In addition, you should be aware that the composition of ethnic groups can change over time, and that there is often as much variability within groups as between them.

Cultural Identity In addition to membership in the national macroculture, each individual participates in an array of subcultures, each with its customs and beliefs. Collectively, these subcultures determine an individual's **cultural identity,** an overall sense of who one is. Other possible elements that might shape a person's cultural identity include age, racial identity, exceptionalities, language, gender, sexual orientation, income level, and beliefs and values. These elements have different significances for different people. For example, the cultural identity of some people is most strongly determined by their occupations; for others by their ethnicity; and for others by their religious beliefs.

Students in today's classrooms have diverse cultural identities. As a teacher, what steps will you take to integrate *all* students into the classroom?

Remember that your future students will have their own complex cultural identities, which are no less valid for being different. For some of them, these identities may make them feel "disconnected" from the attitudes, expectations, and values conveyed by the school. For example,

> Students who come from homes where languages other than English are the medium of communication, who share customs and beliefs unique to their cultural community and/or home countries, or who face the range of challenges posed by economic insecurity will not often find much of their family, community, or national existence reflected in the school setting. Often these students feel that school is itself foreign, alienating, and unrelated to their beliefs and concerns (Rice and Walsh 1996, 9).

As a teacher, you will be challenged to understand the subtle differences in cultural identities among your students and to create a learning environment that enables all students to feel comfortable in school and "connected to" their school experiences.

Language and Culture   Culture is embedded in language, a fact that has resulted in conflict among different groups in our society. Some groups, although they support the preservation of ethnic cultures, believe that members of non-English-speaking groups must learn English if they are to function in U.S. society. There is also conflict between those who wish to preserve linguistic diversity and those who wish to establish English as a national language.

Much of the debate has focused on **bilingual education,** that is, using two languages as the medium of instruction. Bilingual education is designed to help students maintain their ethnic identity and become proficient in both English and the language of the home, to encourage assimilation into the mainstream culture and integrate the home language and culture with a new one. Some people are staunchly opposed to any form of bilingual education, and others support it as a short-term way to teach English to students.

Language diversity is an important dimension of U.S. cultural diversity regardless. Many students come from homes where English is not spoken. The National Clearinghouse for Bilingual Education reported that there were nearly 3.5 million **limited English proficient (LEP)** students—those with limited ability to understand, read, or speak English and who have a first language other than English—in public and non-public schools in 1998, or about 7.4 percent of the total enrollment (Macías et al. 1998). Currently, one in seven U.S. residents speaks a language other than English at home, most frequently Spanish; and in eleven states, 15 or more percent of five- to seventeen-year-olds speak a non-English language at home (see Table 7.1).

Table 7.1

Students differ among themselves not only regarding the first language spoken in the home, but also in the *language patterns* they acquire from the culture within which they are raised. Researchers have found that children from working-class backgrounds tend to develop "restricted" language patterns with their use of English, while children from middle-class backgrounds tend to develop more "elaborated" language patterns (Bernstein 1996; Heath 1983). In many cases, children encounter a mismatch between the language patterns used in the home and those they are expected to use in school, and this mismatch can be "a serious stumbling block for working-class and nonwhite pupils" (MacLeod 1995, 18).

Students' language patterns became a topic of national debate in late 1996 when the Oakland, California, school district passed a resolution on "ebonics" (a blend of the words *ebony* and *phonics),* also known as "black English." The resolution, which recognized ebonics as the "primary language" of many of the district's 28,000 African

American students, called for them to be taught in their primary language and suggested that some students might be eligible for state and federal bilingual education or ESL money. Critics of the resolution, including U.S. Secretary of Education Richard W. Riley, pointed out that "black English" is a nonstandard form of English or a dialect of English and not a foreign language. Other critics were concerned that students and teachers would be taught ebonics. In the midst of intense national debate, the district revised the resolution so that it no longer called for students to be taught in their "primary language"; instead, the district would implement new programs to move students from the language patterns they bring to school toward proficiency in standard English. Other dialects of English and their use in the classroom have been debated from time to time—for example, "Chicano English," "Cajun English," or Hawaiian Creole English (more popularly known as "pidgin English").

The Concept of Multiculturalism **Multiculturalism** is a set of beliefs based on the importance of seeing the world from different cultural frames of reference and on recognizing and valuing the rich array of cultures within a nation and within the global community. For teachers, multiculturalism affirms the need to create schools where differences related to race, ethnicity, gender, disability, and social class are acknowledged and all students are viewed as valuable members and as human resources for enriching the teaching–learning process. Furthermore, a central purpose of teaching, according to the multiculturalist view, is to prepare students to live in a culturally pluralistic world—a world that "contrasts sharply with cultural assimilation, or 'melting pot' images, where ethnic minorities are expected to give up their traditions and blend in or be absorbed by the mainstream society or predominant culture" (Bennett 1999, 11).

For teachers, multiculturalism also means actively seeking out experiences within other cultures that lead to increased understanding of and appreciation for those ways of life. To provide such cross-cultural experiences for their students, several teacher education programs have developed "cultural immersion" experiences that enable prospective teachers to live in their students' neighborhoods and communities while student teaching. The University of Alaska-Fairbanks Teachers for Alaska Program, for example, enables students to live in remote Alaskan Native villages during their year-long student teaching experience. In the Urban Education Program of the Associated Colleges of the Midwest, prospective teachers live in a former convent in a multiracial, economically diverse neighborhood in Chicago. There the students teach and participate in structured activities that take them into the city's other ethnic neighborhoods. Students at Indiana University can choose among three unique student teaching experiences: the Native American Reservation Project, the Overseas Project, and the Bilingual/Bicultural Project. Through student teaching on a reservation, in another country, or on the Rio Grande border, students have a life-altering cultural immersion experience. As a student who participated in the Native American Reservation Project and now teaches high school in Indianapolis put it: "Before we went to the reservation, people [came] back to IU who said that it would change your life. We thought, 'Oh yeah, sure.' But it really does. A day doesn't go by when I don't think of those students, of that place" (Indiana University 1999).

Ethnicity and Race

Your understanding of the distinction between ethnicity and race will enable you to provide students with educational experiences that reflect ethnic and racial diversity in meaningful ways. **Ethnicity** refers to "a shared feeling of common identity, a sense of peoplehood, and a shared sense of interdependence of fate. These feelings derive, in part, from a common ancestral origin, a common set of values, and a common set of experiences" (Banks 1999, 71).

On the other hand, **race** is a subjective concept that is used to distinguish among human beings on the basis of biological traits and characteristics. Numerous racial categories have been proposed, but because of the diversity among humans and the mixing of genes that has taken place over time, no single set of racial categories is universally accepted. Since many genetic factors are invisible to the naked eye (DNA, for example), noted anthropologist Ashley Montagu has suggested that there could be as few as three "races" (Negroid, Caucasoid, and Mongoloid) or as many as 300, depending on the kind and number of genetic features chosen for measurement. In his classic book, *Man's Most Dangerous Myth: The Fallacy of Race,* Montagu pointed out that

> It is impossible to make the sort of racial classification which some anthropologists and others have attempted. The fact is that all human beings are so . . . mixed with regard to origin that between different groups of individuals . . . "overlapping" of physical traits is the rule (1974, 7).

To reflect the realities of racial identities in the United States, the questionnaire for Census 2000 was changed so that people with a "mixed race" background could select "one or more races" for their racial identity. In addition, the "Spanish/Hispanic/Latino" category allowed respondents to choose among the following: Mexican, Mexican American, and Chicano; Puerto Rican; Cuban; and "other" Spanish/Hispanic/Latino. Similarly, respondents who self-identified as "Asian or Pacific Islander" had the following choices: Asian Indian, Chinese, Filipino, Japanese, Korean, Vietnamese, "other" Asian, Native Hawaiian, Guamanian or Chamorro, Samoan, and "other" Pacific Islander.

There are many ethnic groups in U.S. society, and everyone belongs to at least one. However, as James Banks points out:

> an individual American is ethnic to the extent that he or she functions within ethnic subsocieties and shares their values, behavioral styles, and cultures. An individual, however, may have a low level of ethnicity or psychological identification with his or her ethnic group or groups (1997, 9).

It is also clear that racial and ethnic identities in the United States are becoming more complex. We now know that "racial and ethnic identities derive their meanings from social and historical circumstances, that they can vary over time, and that they can sometimes even be slipped on and off like a change of clothing" (Coughlin 1993, A7). For example, a third-generation descendent of a Japanese immigrant may choose to refer to him- or herself as a Japanese American, an American, or an Asian American. Furthermore, it is evident that "specific racial categories acquire and lose meaning over time" (Coughlin 1993, A7), and the use of ethnic and racial labels and expressions of group membership is largely self-selected and arbitrary.

The Concept of Minorities

To understand the important concept of **minorities,** it may help to remember that even though the term *minority* technically refers to any *group* numbering less than half of the total population, in certain parts of the country "minorities" are actually the majority. However, more important than the numbers themselves is an appreciation of how many groups of people have continuously struggled to obtain full educational, economic, political, and social opportunities in society. Along with minority racial and ethnic groups, others who have traditionally lacked power in U.S. public life are immigrants, the poor, children and the elderly, non-English speakers, members of minority religions, and women. Groups that have been most frequently discriminated against in terms of the quality of education they have received include African Americans, Spanish-speaking Americans, Native Americans, Asian Americans, exceptional learners, people with disabilities, and females. There is mounting evidence that many students from these groups continue to receive a substandard education that does not meet their needs or help empower them to participate fully and equally in life in the United States.

Minority Groups and Academic Achievement   Minority-group students are disproportionately represented among students who have failed to master minimum competencies in reading, writing, and mathematics. It has been estimated that ethnic minority students are two to four times more likely than others to drop out of high school. In addition, "in many schools across the nation, racial and language minority students are overrepresented in special education and experience disproportionately high rates of suspension and expulsion" (Bennett 1999, 15). Nevertheless, there has been a trend of "modest growth in achievement among students from minority groups and from 'less advantaged' backgrounds" (Berliner and Biddle 1995, 27).

When we consider the lower achievement levels of minority students, it is important to note the much higher incidence of poverty among minority families and the research showing that socioeconomic status—not race, language, or culture—contributes most strongly to students' achievement in school (Coleman et al. 1966; National Center for Education Statistics 1980; Jencks et al. 1972; Jencks and Phillips 1998). Understandably, it is difficult for poor children to learn well if they endure the stress of living in crime-ridden neighborhoods, dwelling in dilapidated homes, or going to school hungry.

Language Minorities   According to the 1990 census, one in seven U.S. residents aged five years or older spoke a language other than English at home. Various bilingual education programs have been developed to meet the special needs of **language-minority students,** those whose language of the home is a language other than English, and students with limited English proficiency (LEP). Figure 7.2 shows LEP enrollment growth from 1986–87 to 1996–97. Though most bilingual education programs serve Spanish-speaking students, there are bilingual education programs for the more than ninety other language groups in the United States.

Figure 7.2

Stereotyping and Racism

Although teachers should expand their knowledge of and appreciation for the diverse cultural backgrounds of their students, they should also guard against forming stereotypes or overgeneralizations about those cultures. **Stereotyping** is the process of attributing behavioral characteristics to all members of a group. In some cases, stereotypes are formed on the basis of limited experiences with and information about the group being stereotyped, and the validity of these stereotypes is not questioned.

Within any cultural group that shares a broad cultural heritage, however, considerable diversity exists. For example, two Puerto Rican children who live in the same community and attend the same school may appear alike to their teachers when, in reality, they are very different. One may come from a home where Spanish is spoken and Puerto Rican holidays are observed; the other child may know only a few words of Spanish and observe only the holidays of the majority culture.

In addition to being alert for stereotypes they and others may hold, teachers should learn to recognize **individual racism,** the prejudicial belief that one's ethnic or racial group is superior to others, and **institutional racism,** "established laws, customs, and practices which systematically reflect and produce racial inequalities in American society . . . whether or not the individuals maintaining those practices have racist intentions" (Jones 1981, 118).

In light of the arbitrariness of the concept of race, James A. Banks points out, "In most societies, *the social significance of race is much more important than the presumed physical differences among groups*" (1997, 74, italics in original). Unfortunately, many people attach great importance to the concept of race. If you believe "that human groups can be validly grouped on the basis of their biological traits and that these identifiable groups inherit certain mental, personality, and cultural characteristics that determine their behavior" (Banks 1997, 78) then you hold racist beliefs. When people use such beliefs as a rationale for oppressing other groups, they are practicing racism. Appendix 7.1 presents a checklist for a small-group activity that can help you become more aware of individual and institutional racism.

As a teacher, you will not be able to eliminate stereotypic thinking or racism in society. However, you have an obligation to all your students to see that your curriculum and instruction are free of any forms of stereotyping or racism. The following Professional Reflection will help you examine, and possibly reassess, your cultural attitudes and values and determine whether you have stereotypes about other cultural groups.

Appendix 7.1

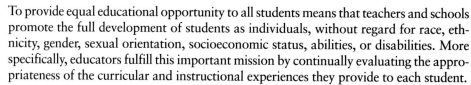

Professional Reflection   **Reflecting on your cultural identity**

What Does Equal Educational Opportunity Mean?

Audio Clip 7.3

Video 7.1

To provide equal educational opportunity to all students means that teachers and schools promote the full development of students as individuals, without regard for race, ethnicity, gender, sexual orientation, socioeconomic status, abilities, or disabilities. More specifically, educators fulfill this important mission by continually evaluating the appropriateness of the curricular and instructional experiences they provide to each student.

In the following sections, we review the progress that has been made to provide students from diverse groups with equal educational opportunity, and we focus on strategies for teaching in diverse classrooms. The strategies we present for each group draw from research that suggests that particular learning styles *may be* associated with specific ethnic groups in U.S. society (Shade 1982; Hale-Benson 1986; Bennett 1999). These strategies should not lead you to assume, however, that *all* students from a certain group learn in a particular way. As Christine I. Bennett, an expert on multicultural education, points out:

> The notion that certain learning styles are associated with different ethnic groups is both promising and dangerous. Promise lies in the realization that low academic achievement among some ethnic minorities may sometimes be attributed to conflicts between styles of teaching and learning, not low intelligence. This leads to the possibility that teachers will alter their own instructional styles to be more responsive to the learning needs of students. Danger lies in the possibility that new ethnic stereotypes will develop while old ones are reinforced, as in "Blacks learn aurally," "Asians excel in math," "Mexican American males can't learn from female peer tutors," and "Navajos won't ask a question or participate in a discussion" (Bennett 1999, 63).

We omit Anglo-European Americans from our review, not because students from this very diverse group always have had equal educational opportunities, but because this group represents the historically dominant culture. To a great extent, it has determined the curricular and instructional practices found in schools.

Like the groups we discuss, however, "Anglo-European American" is not a single, monolithic culture. Americans whose ethnic heritage is English, Polish, German, Italian, Irish, Czechoslovakian, Russian, or Swedish, for example, often differ greatly in religious and political traditions, beliefs, and values. Their individual ethnic identity may or may not be strengthened by recent immigrants from their country of origin. European ethnics have, nevertheless, assimilated into the mainstream U.S. society more completely than others.

Education and African Americans

Of the more than 273 million persons living in the United States, approximately 13 percent are African Americans. According to U.S. Census Bureau projections, the African American population in the United States is expected to increase from 36 million (13 percent of the total population) in 2001 to 45 million (14 percent of the total) in 2020, and then to 55 million (15 percent of the total) in 2040. The incidence of social problems such as unemployment, crime, drug abuse, poverty, inadequate housing, and school dropouts is proportionally greater for African Americans than for whites. The struggle of African Americans to improve their quality of life after the end of slavery has been hampered for generations by persistent racism, discrimination, poverty, crime, unemployment, and underemployment.

The civil rights movement of the 1960s and 1970s made it clear that African Americans had been denied full access to many aspects of U.S. life, including the right to a good education. A 1976 report by the United States Commission on Civil Rights, for example, revealed that a Southern school district in the 1930s spent nearly eighteen times as much for the education of white pupils as it did for the education of African Americans.

What is the legacy of school desegregation today? What are some outcomes of education research and curriculum reform related to the African American experience?

The Desegregation Era Perhaps the most blatant form of discrimination against African Americans has been school segregation and unequal educational opportunity. As you learned in Chapter 3, the attempt was made to justify segregation by the idea of separate-but-equal schools. It was not until the National Association for the Advancement of Colored People (NAACP) brought suit on behalf of a Kansas family (*Brown v. Board of Education of Topeka, Kansas*) in 1954 that the concept of separate-but-equal schools was decidedly struck down.

The parents of Linda Brown felt that the education their fourth-grader was receiving in the segregated Topeka schools was inferior. When their request that she be transferred to a white school was turned down, they filed suit. In a landmark decision, the U.S. Supreme Court ruled that segregated schools are "inherently unequal" and violate the equal protection clause of the Fourteenth Amendment. U.S. citizens, the justices asserted, have a right to receive an equal opportunity for education.

As a result of opportunities created during the civil rights movement, a substantial number of African Americans are now members of the middle class. Affirmative action programs have enabled many African Americans to attain high-ranking positions in the business, medical, legal, and educational professions. Such gains lead James Banks to point out that

> [A]ny accurate and sophisticated description of the status of African Americans on the threshold of the twenty-first century must describe not only the large percentage of Blacks who are members of the so-called underclass, but also the smaller and significant percentage of African Americans who have entered the middle and upper classes and who function in the mainstream society. Many of the children of the new middle class are not only unacquainted with poverty, but also have been socialized in mainstream middle- and upper-class communities. They have little first-hand experience with traditional African American culture (Banks and Banks 1997, 228–29).

Resegregation of Schools in the United States   As the United States continues to become more ethnically and racially diverse, there is evidence that schools have been "resegregating" during the last ten years, according to *Resegregation in American Schools,* a Harvard University report released in June 1999 (Orfield and Yun 1999). The report included the following findings:

Figure 7.3

- Latinos attend the most severely segregated schools (see Figure 7.3).
- Since the late 1980s, schools in the South have been resegregating.
- As African Americans and Latinos move to the suburbs, they are attending segregated schools, especially in urban areas.
- States with a high proportion of African American students made progress toward desegregation in the 1970s; however, all showed increases in school segregation between 1980 and 1996.
- Segregated schools, with the exception of those for white students, tend to have a high concentration of poverty, which has a negative influence on student achievement.

One reason for the trend back to resegregation has been Supreme Court rulings that removed judicial supervision of school districts' efforts to desegregate—for example, *Board of Education of Oklahoma City Public Schools v. Dowell,* 1991 and *Freeman v. Pitts,* 1992. In addition, the Supreme Court ruled in *Missouri v. Jenkins,* 1995, that Kansas City schools did not have to maintain desegregation through a magnet school approach until actual benefits for African American students were shown. Such rulings by the Supreme Court prompted the filing of many lawsuits to end desegregation in several large school districts.

The Learning Needs of African American Students   Research on factors related to students' success in school suggests that schools are monoethnic and do not take into account the diverse needs of ethnic minority-group students (Bennett 1999). In the case of African American students, the failure of the school curriculum to address their learning needs may contribute to high dropout rates and below-average achievement. For example, research indicates that teaching strategies that emphasize cooperation—not competition—often result in higher achievement among African American (and Mexican American) students (Aronson and Gonzalez 1988). In addition, it has been suggested that because many African Americans have grown up in an oral tradition, they may learn better through oral/aural activities—for example, reading aloud and listening to audiotapes (Bennett 1999). However, one should not assume that all African Americans learn better aurally.

Afrocentric Schools To address the educational inequities that African American and other minority-group students may experience as a result of segregation, many communities have tried to create more ethnically and racially diverse classrooms through the controversial practice of busing students to attend schools in other neighborhoods. Also, some African Americans have recently begun to call for **Afrocentric schools**—that is, schools that focus on African American history and cultures for African American pupils. Proponents believe that the educational needs of African American students can be met more effectively in schools that offer Afrocentric curricula.

Private Afrocentric schools, or "black academies," have sprung up across the country in recent years, many supported by the growing number of African Americans who practice Islam, a religion based on the teachings of the prophet Mohammed. Curricula in these schools emphasize the people and cultures of Africa and the history and achievements of African Americans. Teaching methods are often designed for culture-based learning styles, such as choral response, learning through movement, and sociality.

Education and Latino and Hispanic Americans

Hispanic Americans, the fastest growing minority group in the United States, account for about 10 percent of the population, and it has been estimated that an additional five million illegal aliens who speak Spanish may be in the country. By 2010, the Hispanic population is expected to be 14 percent, surpassing African Americans as the nation's largest minority group. The U.S. Census Bureau estimates that the Hispanic American population in the United States will increase from 32 million (12 percent of the total population) in 2001 to 52 million (16 percent of the total) in 2020, and then to 80 million (22 percent of the total) in 2040.

Included in the category of Hispanic Americans are people who call themselves Latinos and Chicanos and who report their ancestry as Mexican, Puerto Rican, Cuban, Central American, or South American. Five states have populations that are more than 10 percent Hispanic: California, Texas, New Mexico, Arizona, and Colorado. Many states have passed English-only laws and made efforts to restrict Hispanic immigrants' access to education. Prior to 1983, six states had English-language laws; however, efforts by political action groups such as U.S. English, founded by the late Senator S.I. Hayakawa of California in 1983, were instrumental in getting English-only laws passed in 25 states by 1999, including California and Colorado. Arizona's 1988 Official English amendment was overturned by the Arizona State Supreme Court in 1998. In addition, California voters approved Proposition 187 in 1994, which prevents public schools from educating the children of illegal aliens.

Socioeconomic Factors Although some Spanish-speaking immigrants come to the United States hoping to escape a life of poverty in their home country, many others come because they have relatives in the United States or they wish to take advantage of business opportunities in this country. For those Spanish-speaking immigrants who lack job skills and have little education, however, adjusting to the complexities and demands of life in the United States may be difficult.

Socioeconomic factors affect the education of some Hispanics, such as the children of migrant farm workers. Among the estimated one million or so migrant farm workers in this country, more than 70 percent are Spanish-speaking. The dropout rate among all migrant workers is 90 percent, and 50 percent leave school before finishing the ninth grade (Bennett 1999). Migrant children are handicapped by the language barrier, deprivation resulting from poverty, and irregular school attendance. Some states have educational intervention programs in place for reaching this group.

The Learning Needs of Spanish-Speaking Students   What can easily happen to Spanish-speaking learners if they are taught by teachers who are not sensitive to their learning needs is illustrated in Christine I. Bennett's portrait of Jesús, a student with limited English proficiency (LEP):

> Jesús Martinez was a bright, fine-looking six-year old when he migrated with his family from Puerto Rico to New York City. At a time when he was ready to learn to read and write his mother tongue, Jesús was instead suddenly thrust into an English-only classroom where the only tool he possessed for oral communication (the Spanish language) was completely useless to him. Jesús and his teacher could not communicate with each other because each spoke a different language and neither spoke the language of the other. Jesús felt stupid, or retarded; his teacher perceived him to be culturally disadvantaged and beyond her help. However, she and the school officials agreed to allow him to "sit there" because the law required that he be in school (Bennett 1999, 7).

Bennett also captures well the dilemma that many Spanish-speaking LEP students find themselves in: "Students with limited English proficiency are often caught up in conflicts between personal language needs—for example, the need to consolidate cognitive skills in the native language—and a sociopolitical climate that views standard English as most desirable and prestigious" (Bennett 1999, 387). The degree to which students from Spanish-speaking backgrounds are motivated to learn English varies from group to group. Mexican American students who live in the southwest may retain the Spanish language to maintain ties with family and friends in Mexico. Recently arrived Cubans, on the other hand, may have a stronger motivation to learn the language of their new country. In regard to what they wish to learn, children take their cues from the adults around them. If their parents or guardians and friends and relatives have learned English and are bilingual, then they will be similarly motivated. Many Hispanic Americans who value assimilation over their traditional culture favor English-only education.

However, the limited English proficiencies of many children raised in native Spanish-speaking families contribute significantly to the difficulties they have in school. To address the needs of these students, federally funded bilingual-bicultural programs encourage teachers to view bicultural knowledge as a bridge to the school's curriculum. Bilingual education is examined in detail later in this chapter.

Video 7.2

Education and Asian Americans and Pacific Islanders

Asian Americans and Pacific Islanders represent about 3 percent of the total population of the United States. The U.S. Census Bureau estimates that the Asian and Pacific Islander population in the United States will increase from 11.6 million (4 percent of the total population) in 2001 to 19.6 million (6 percent of the total) in 2020, and then to 29 million (8 percent of the total) in 2040. This group, comprising at least 34 ethnic groups that speak more than 300 languages and dialects (Asian Americans/Pacific Islanders in Philanthropy 1997), is tremendously diverse and includes people from South Asia, primarily Bangladesh, India, and Pakistan; Southeast Asia, including Indochina (Laos, Thailand, Indonesia, Malaysia, and Vietnam) and the Philippines; East Asia, including China, Hong Kong, Japan, Korea, and Taiwan; and the Pacific Islands, including Hawaii, Guam, and Samoa. About 55 percent of the total Asian American and Pacific Islander population lives in the western United States, compared to 22 percent of the total population (U.S. Census Bureau 1999).

Historical, Cultural, and Socioeconomic Factors   The three largest Asian American groups are Chinese (23.8 percent of Asian Americans), Filipinos (20.4 percent), and Japanese (12.3 percent) (U.S. Census Bureau 1998). Although these groups differ significantly, each "came to the United States seeking the American dream, satisfied important labor needs, and became victims of an anti-Asian movement designed to prevent their further immigration to the United States. [They] also experienced tremendous economic, educational, and social mobility and success in U.S. society" (Banks 1997, 438).

The California gold rush of 1849 brought the first immigrants from Asia, Chinese men who worked in mines, on railroads, and on farms, and who planned to return to their families and homeland. Early Chinese immigrants encountered widespread discrimination in their new country, with anti-Chinese riots occurring in San Francisco, Los Angeles, and Denver between 1869 and 1880. In 1882, Congress passed the Immigration Act, which ended Chinese immigration until 1902. The Chinese were oriented toward maintaining traditional language and religion and established tight-knit urban communities, or "Chinatowns." Recently, many upwardly mobile, professional Chinese Americans have been assimilated into suburban communities, while newly arrived, working-class immigrants from China and Hong Kong are settling in redeveloped Chinatowns.

Japanese immigrants began to arrive in Hawaii and the U.S. mainland in the late 1800s; most worked in agriculture, fisheries, the railroads, or industry and assimilated rapidly despite racial discrimination. The San Francisco Board of Education, for example, began to segregate all Japanese students in 1906, and the Immigration Act of 1924 ended Japanese immigration until 1952. During World War II, the United States was at war with Japan. In response to war hysteria over the "yellow peril," the United States government interned 110,000 Japanese Americans, most of them American-born, in ten detention camps from 1942 to 1946. Since World War II, Japan has developed into one of the world's leading economic and technological powers—an accomplishment that has contributed, no doubt, to a recent decline in Japanese immigration to the United States.

Filipinos began to immigrate to Hawaii and the mainland as field laborers during the 1920s. They, too, encountered racism; in 1934 Congress passed the Tydings-McDuffie Act, which limited Filipino immigration to the United States to 50 persons annually. The following year, President Franklin Roosevelt signed the Repatriation Act, which provided free transportation to Filipinos willing to return to the Philippines. While most early Filipino immigrants had little education and low income, recent immigrants have tended to be professional, technical workers who hope to obtain employment in the United States more suitable for their education and training than they could in the Philippines (Banks 1997).

Teachers' Concerns about Asian American Students   Asian Americans are frequently stereotyped as hard-working, conscientious, and respectful of authority, what Sue and Sue (1999) term a "model minority." In fact, 42.2 percent of Asian Americans 25 years and over have a bachelor's degree or more, compared to 23.9 percent of the total population (U.S. Census Bureau 1999). The unreliability of such stereotypes notwithstanding, Asian American parents do tend to require their children to respect authority and value education. However, "for many Asian American students, this image is a destructive myth," according to a report titled *An Invisible Crisis: The Educational Needs of Asian Pacific American Youth*. "As their schools fail them, these children become increasingly likely to graduate with rudimentary language skills, to drop out of school, to join gangs, or to find themselves in the low-paying occupations and on the margins of American life" (Asian Americans/Pacific Islanders in Philanthropy 1997). Families often pressure children to be successful academically through sacrifice and hard work. At the same time, there has been an increase in the number of Asian American youth who are in conflict with their parents' way of life. Leaders in Asian American communities have expressed concern about increases in dropout rates, school violence, and declining achievement. Some Indochinese Americans, for example, face deep cultural conflict in schools. Values and practices that are accepted in U.S. culture, such as dating and glorification of the individual, are sources of conflict between many Indochinese students and their parents.

Teachers need to be sensitive to cultural conflicts that may contribute to problems in school adjustment and achievement for Asian American students and realize that

> Stereotypes about Asian "whiz kids" and jealousy over the relatively high percentages of Asian Americans in the nation's colleges and universities may blind some non-Asian parents, fellow students, and teachers to the deep cultural conflict many Southeast Asian Americans face in our schools (Bennett 1999, 150).

To help Asian American students adjust to the U.S. culture, Qiu Liang offers teachers the following advice based on his school experiences as a Chinese immigrant:

> They [teachers] should be more patient [with an immigrant child] because it is very difficult for a person to be in a new country and learn a new language. Have patience.
>
> If the teacher feels there is no hope in an immigrant child, then the child will think, "Well, if the teacher who's helping me thinks that I can't go anywhere, then I might as well give up myself" (Igoa 1995, 99–100).

Similarly, Dung Yoong offers these recommendations based on her educational experiences as a Vietnamese immigrant:

> Try to get them to talk to you. Not just everyday conversation, but what they feel inside. Try to get them to get that out, because it's hard for kids. They don't trust—I had a hard time trusting and I was really insecure because of that.
>
> [P]utting an immigrant child who doesn't speak English into a classroom, a regular classroom with American students, is not very good. It scares [them] because it is so different. [Teachers] should start [them] slowly and have special classes where the child could adapt and learn a little bit about American society and customs (Igoa 1995, 103).

Education and Native Americans and Alaskan Natives

Native Americans and Alaskan Natives peopled the Western hemisphere more than 12,000 years ago. Today, they represent less than 1 percent of the total U.S. population, or about 2 million people (U.S. Census Bureau 1999). This group consists of 517 federally recognized and 365 state-recognized tribes, each with its own language, religious beliefs, and way of life. The four largest groups are the Cherokee Nation of Oklahoma, over 308,000 members; the Navajo Nation, 219,000; the Chippewa Nation, 104,000; and the Sioux Nation of the Dakotas, 103,000 (U.S. Census Bureau 1993).

Approximately 760,000 Native Americans live on 275 reservations located primarily in the West. More than half of the Native American and Alaskan Native population lives in six states: Alaska, Arizona, California, New Mexico, Oklahoma, and Washington (Manning and Baruth 1996). Though most Native Americans live in cities, many are establishing connections with reservation Indians as a means of strengthening their cultural identities.

Native Americans are an example of the increasing ambiguity of racial and ethnic identities in the United States. For example, controversy exists over who is Native American. "Some full-blooded native people do not regard a person with one-quarter native heritage to qualify, while others accept $^1/_{128}$" (Bennett 1999, 132). While most Native Americans consider a person with one-quarter or more tribal heritage to be a member, the U.S. Census Bureau considers anyone who claims native identity to be a member. An expert on Native Americans and Alaskan Natives, Arlene Hirschfelder, points out that fifty-two legal definitions of Native Americans have been identified (Hirschfelder 1986). Native Americans were declared U.S. citizens in 1924, and native nations have been recognized as independent, self-governing territories since the 1930s (Bennett 1999).

Historical, Cultural, and Socioeconomic Factors Perhaps more than any other minority group, Native Americans have endured systematic long-term attempts to eradicate their languages and cultures. Disease, genocide, confinement on reservations, and decades of forced assimilation have devastated Native American cultures. In 1492, native people used 2 billion acres of land; currently, they own about 94 million acres of land, or about 5 percent of U.S. territory (Bennett 1999). Today, the rates of unemployment, poverty, and lack of educational attainment among Native Americans are among the nation's highest. Since the 1970s, however, there has been a resurgence of interest in preserving or restoring traditional languages, skills, and land claims.

There are hundreds of Native American languages, which anthropologists have attempted to categorize into six major language families (Banks 1999). Older tribal members fluent in the original tribal language and younger members often speak a form of so-called "reservation English." The challenge of educating Native Americans from diverse language backgrounds is further complicated by the difference in size of various Native American populations. These range from the more than 300,000 Cherokee to the 200 or so Supai of Arizona. As a result of the extreme diversity among Native Americans, it has even been suggested that "There is no such thing as an 'Indian' heritage, culture, or value system. [N]avajo, Cherokee, Sioux, and Aleut children are as different from each other in geographic and cultural backgrounds as they are from children growing up in New York City or Los Angeles" (Gipp 1979, 19).

Education for Native American children living on reservations is currently administered by the federal government's Bureau of Indian Affairs (BIA). The **Indian Education Act of 1972** and its **1974 amendments** supplement the BIA's educational programs and provide direct educational assistance to tribes. The act seeks to improve Native American education by providing funds to school districts to meet the special needs of Native American youth, to Indian tribes and state and local education agencies to improve education for youth and adults, to colleges and universities for the purpose of training teachers for Indian schools, and to Native American students to attend college.

Research on Native American Ways of Knowing Considerable debate has occurred over the best approaches for educating Native Americans. For example, Banks points out that "since the 1920s, educational policy for Native Americans has vacillated between strong assimilationism to self-determination and cultural pluralism" (Banks

What factors contribute to below-average achievement levels of Native American children? How do forces toward assimilation and cultural preservation coexist in the Native American experience?

1999, 22). In any case, the culture-based learning styles of many Native Americans and Alaskan Natives differ from that of other students. The traditional upbringing of Native American children generally encourages them to develop a view of the world that is holistic, intimate, and shared. "They approach tasks visually, seem to prefer to learn by careful observation which precedes performance, and seem to learn in their natural settings experientially" (Swisher and Deyhle 1987, 350). Bennett suggests the following guideline to ensure that the school experiences of Native American students are in harmony with their cultural backgrounds: "An effective learning environment for Native Americans is one that does not single out the individual but provides frequent opportunities for the teacher to interact privately with individual children and with small groups, as well as opportunities for quiet, persistent exploration" (Bennett 1999, 206).

Increasingly, Native Americans are designing multicultural programs to preserve their traditional cultures and ways of knowing. Although these programs are sometimes characterized as emphasizing separatism over assimilation, for many Native Americans they are a matter of survival. The Heart of the Earth Survival School in Minneapolis, for example, was created to preserve the languages and cultures of the northern Plains Indians. Native American teachers at the school provide bilingual instruction in Ojibwe and Dakota. Students are encouraged to wear traditional dress and practice traditional arts, such as drumming and dancing.

Cultural preservation is also the primary concern at Alaskan Native schools in remote parts of western Alaska and Cherokee schools in the Marietta Independent School District of Stillwell, Oklahoma. In Alaska, elders come into the classroom to teach children how to skin a seal, an education that few Alaskan Native children receive today at home. In Oklahoma, schools try to keep alive the diverse languages of peoples forced to relocate to reservations there from the Southwestern United States in the last century. Students of mixed Cherokee, Creek, and Seminole descent become fluent and literate in the Cherokee language.

What Is Meant by Bilingual Education?

Bilingual education programs are designed to meet the learning needs of students whose first language is not English by providing instruction in two languages. Regardless of the instructional approach used, one outcome for all bilingual programs is for students to become proficient in English. Additionally, students are encouraged to become **bicultural,** that is, able to function effectively in two or more linguistic and cultural groups.

In 1968, Congress passed the Bilingual Education Act, which required that language-minority students be taught in both their native language and English. In response to the Act, school districts implemented an array of bilingual programs that varied greatly in quality and effectiveness. As a result, many parents filed lawsuits, claiming that bilingual programs were not meeting their children's needs. In 1974, the Supreme Court heard a class action suit *(Lau v. Nichols)* filed by 1,800 Chinese students in San Francisco who charged that they were failing to learn because they could not understand English. The students were enrolled in all-English classes and received no special assistance in learning English. In a unanimous ruling, the Court asserted that federally funded schools must "rectify the language deficiency" of students who "are certain to find their classroom experiences wholly incomprehensible." That same year, Congress adopted the Equal Educational Opportunity Act (EEOA), which stated in part that a school district must "take appropriate action to overcome language barriers that impede equal participation by its students in its instructional programs."

Bilingual programs, most of which serve Latino and Hispanic American students, are tremendously varied and reflect "extreme differences in student composition, program organization, teaching methodologies and approaches, and teacher backgrounds and skills" (Griego-Jones 1996, 115). Generally, however, four types of bilingual education programs are currently available to provide special assistance to the 3.5 million language-minority students in the United States (see Figure 7.4). Only about 315,000 students actually participate in some kind of bilingual program.

Video 7.3

Figure 7.4

Research and Debate on Bilingual Programs

Research on the effectiveness of bilingual programs is mixed (Rothstein 1998). Some who have examined the research conclude that bilingual programs have little effect on achievement (Rossell 1990; Baker 1991). Others have found that well-designed bilingual programs do increase students' achievement and are superior to monolingual programs (Willig 1987; Schmidt 1991; Cziko 1992; Nieto 1992; Trueba, Cheng, and Kenji 1993).

Considerable debate surrounds bilingual programs in the United States. Those in favor of bilingual education make the following points:

- Students are better able to learn English if they are taught to read and write in their native language.
- Bilingual programs allow students to learn content in their native language rather than delaying that learning until they master English.
- Further developing competencies in students' native languages provides important cognitive foundations for learning English and academic content.
- Second-language learning is a positive value and should be as valid for a Spanish-speaker learning English as for an English-speaker learning Spanish.
- Bilingual programs support students' cultural identity, social context, and self-esteem.

On the other hand, those opposed to bilingual programs make the following points:

- Public schools should not be expected to provide instruction in all the first languages spoken by their students, nor can schools afford to pay a teacher who might teach only a few students.
- The cost of bilingual education is high. Bilingual programs divert staff and resources away from English-speaking students.

where do you stand?

Is multicultural education unifying or divisive?

- If students spend more time exposed to English, they will learn English more quickly.
- Bilingual programs emphasize differences among and barriers between groups; they encourage separateness rather than assimilation and unity.
- Bilingual education is a threat to English as the nation's first language.

Advice for Monolingual Teachers

Although the future of bilingual education in the United States is uncertain, teachers must continue to meet the needs of language-minority students. These needs are best met by teachers who speak their native language as well as English. However, this is often not possible, and monolingual teachers will find increasing numbers of LEP students in their classrooms. See the Teacher's Resource Guide sections "Creating Classroom Environments That Support Second-Language Learners" and "Strategies for Enhancing the Learning and Literacy of Second-Language Learners" on this book's website. Developed by bilingual/ESL education expert Gisela Ernst and her colleagues, these strategies can be used whether or not a teacher is bilingual.

Weblink 7.1
Weblink 7.2

Audio Clip 7.4

What Is Multicultural Education?

Multicultural education is committed to the goal of providing all students—regardless of socioeconomic status, gender, sexual orientation or ethnic, racial, or cultural backgrounds—with equal opportunities to learn in school. Multicultural education is also based on the fact that students do not learn in a vacuum—their culture predisposes them to learn in certain ways. And finally, multicultural education recognizes that current school practices have provided, and continue to provide, some students with greater opportunities for learning than students who belong to other groups. The suggestions in the Teacher's Resource Guide referenced above are examples of multicultural education in practice.

As multiculturalism has become more pervasive in U.S. schools, controversy over the need for multicultural education and its purposes has emerged (see Where Do You Stand? feature). Carl Grant has identified as "myths" the following six arguments against multicultural education: "(1) It is both divisive and so conceptually weak that it does little to eliminate structural inequalities; (2) it is unnecessary because the United States is a melting pot; (3) multiculturalism—and by extension multicultural education—and political correctness are the same thing; (4) multicultural education rejects the notion of a common culture; (5) multicultural education is a 'minority thing'; and (6) multicultural education will impede learning the basic skills" (Grant 1994, 5). Though multicultural education is being challenged by those who promote these beliefs, we believe that public dialogue and debate about how schools can more effectively address diversity is healthy—an indicator that our society is making real progress toward creating a culture that incorporates the values of diverse groups.

Dimensions of Multicultural Education

According to James A. Banks, "Multicultural education is a complex and multidimensional concept" (Banks 1999, 13). More specifically, Banks suggests that multicultural education may be conceptualized as consisting of five dimensions: (1) content integration, (2) knowledge construction, (3) prejudice reduction, (4) an equity pedagogy, and

keepers of the dream

Peter White: Opportunity Creator
1999 National Teacher of the Year Finalist

"I have journeyed with my students . . ."

(5) an empowering school culture (see Figure 7.5). As you progress through your teacher-education program and eventually begin to prepare curriculum materials and instructional strategies for your multicultural classroom, remember that integrating content from a variety of cultural groups is just one dimension of multicultural education. Multicultural education is not "something that is done at a certain time slot in the school day where children eat with chopsticks or listen to Peruvian music . . . [it is] something that is infused throughout the school culture and practiced daily" (Henry 1996, 108).

Figure 7.5

Multicultural education promotes students' positive self-identity and pride in their heritage, acceptance of people from diverse backgrounds, and critical self-assessment. In addition, multicultural education can prompt students, perhaps with guidance from their teachers, to take action against prejudice and discrimination within their school. Indeed, as Joel Spring says, "multicultural education should create a spirit of tolerance and activism in students. An understanding of other cultures and of differing cultural frames of reference will . . . spark students to actively work for social justice" (Spring 1998, 163). For example, students might reduce the marginalization of minority-group students in their school by inviting them to participate in extracurricular and after-school activities.

Multicultural Curricula

As a teacher you will teach students who historically have not received full educational opportunity—students from the many racial and ethnic minority groups in the United States, students from low-income families or communities, students with exceptional abilities or disabilities, students who are gay or lesbian, and students who are male or female. You will face the challenge of reaching out to all students and teaching them that they are persons of worth who can learn.

In your diverse classroom your aim is not to develop a different curriculum for each group of students—that would be impossible and would place undue emphasis on differences among students. Rather, your curriculum should help increase students' awareness and appreciation of the rich diversity in U.S. culture. A **multicultural curriculum** addresses the needs and backgrounds of all students regardless of their cultural identity. As Banks suggests, the multicultural curriculum "enable[s] students to derive valid generalizations and theories about the characteristics of ethnic groups and to learn how they are alike and different, in both their past and present experiences. . . . [It] focus[es] on a range of groups that *differ* in their racial characteristics, cultural experiences, languages, histories, values, and current problems" (Banks 1997, 15). Teachers who provide multicultural education recognize the importance of asking questions such as those posed by Valerie Ooka Pang: "Why is a child's home language important to keep? What strengths does culture give children? What impact does culture have on learning? What does racism, sexism, or classism look like in schools?" (Pang 1994, 292).

In developing a multicultural curriculum, you should be sensitive to how your instructional materials and strategies can be made more inclusive so that they reflect cultural perspectives, or "voices," that previously have been silent or marginalized in discussions about what should be taught in schools and how it should be taught. "Nondominant groups representing diversity in the school whose voices traditionally have not been heard include those defined by race, language, gender, sexual orientation, alternative family structures, social class, disability, bilingualism, and those with alien or refugee status" (Henry 1996, 108). Effective teachers attend to these previously unheard voices not as an act of tokenism but with a genuine desire to make the curriculum more inclusive and to "create space for alternative voices, not just on the periphery but in the center" (Singer 1994, 286).

Multicultural Instructional Materials and Strategies

Weblink 7.3

To create classrooms that are truly multicultural, teachers must select instructional materials that are sensitive, accurately portray the contributions of ethnic groups, and reflect diverse points of view. (See the Teacher's Resource Guide section "Selected Resources for Multicultural Education" on this book's website.) Teachers must also recognize that "[s]ome of the books and other materials on ethnic groups published each year are insensitive, inaccurate, and written from mainstream and insensitive perspectives and points of view" (Banks 1997, 124). Some guidelines for selecting multicultural instructional materials follow:

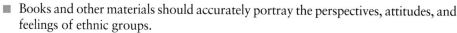

- Books and other materials should accurately portray the perspectives, attitudes, and feelings of ethnic groups.
- Fictional works should have strong ethnic characters.
- Books should describe settings and experiences with which all students can identify and yet should accurately reflect ethnic cultures and lifestyles.
- The protagonists in books with ethnic themes should have ethnic characteristics but should face conflicts and problems universal to all cultures and groups.
- The illustrations in books should be accurate, ethnically sensitive, and technically well done.
- Ethnic materials should not contain racist concepts, clichés, phrases, or words.
- Factual materials should be historically accurate.
- Multiethnic resources and basal textbooks should discuss major events and documents related to ethnic history (Banks 1997, 125–26).

Yvonne Wilson, a first-grade teacher in Talmoon, Minnesota, and an Ojibwe Indian, points out that a teacher's willingness to learn about other cultures is very important to students and their parents:

People in the community know if you are trying to understand their culture. Students also see it. Becoming involved—going to a powwow or participating in other cultural events—shows people that here is a teacher who is trying to learn about our culture.

Figure 7.6

Participating wholeheartedly in cross-cultural experiences will help you to grow in the eight areas outlined in Figure 7.6 as essential for successful teaching in a diverse society.

How Is Gender a Dimension of Multicultural Education?

Though it may be evident that gender affects students' learning in many ways, it may not be evident that gender is an important dimension of multicultural education. However, as Tozer, Violas, and Senese point out:

> Traditional definitions of culture have centered around the formal expression of a people's common existence—language, art, music, and so forth. If culture is more broadly defined to include such things as ways of knowing, ways of relating to others, ways of negotiating rights and privileges, and modes of conduct, thought, and expression, then the term "culture" applies not only to ethnic groups but to people grouped on the basis of gender. [G]ender entails cultural as well as physiological dimensions (Tozer, Violas, and Senese 1993, 310).

Gender Differences

Cultural differences between males and females are partially shaped by society's traditional expectations of them. Through **sex role stereotyping** families, the media, the schools, and other powerful social forces condition boys and girls to act in certain ways regardless of abilities or interests. As we mentioned in Chapter 4, one of the aims of schools is to socialize students to participate in society. One dimension of the **sex role socialization** process conveys to students certain expectations about the way boys and girls are "supposed" to act. Girls are supposed to play with dolls, boys with trucks. Girls are supposed to be passive, boys active. Girls are supposed to express their feelings and emotions when in pain, boys to repress their feelings and deny pain.

Students may be socialized into particular gender-specific roles as a result of the curriculum materials they use at school. By portraying males in more dominant, assertive ways and portraying females in ways that suggest that they are passive and helpless, textbooks can subtly reinforce expectations about the way girls and boys "should" behave. Within the last few decades, though, publishers of curriculum materials have become more vigilant about avoiding these stereotypes.

Gender and Education

As noted in Chapter 3, it was not until Title IX of the Education Amendments Act was passed in 1972 that women were guaranteed equality of educational opportunity

Audio Clip 7.5

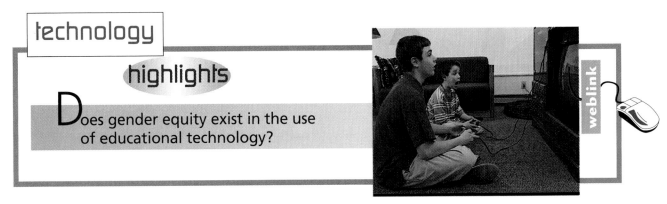

technology highlights

Does gender equity exist in the use of educational technology?

weblink

in educational programs receiving federal assistance. Title IX has had the greatest impact on athletic programs in schools; for example, in 1973, 800,000 girls played high school sports; and in 1997, 2.5 million girls participated (*Health* 1999). The law requires that both sexes have equal opportunities to participate in and benefit from the availability of coaches, sports equipment, resources, and facilities. For contact sports such as football, wrestling, and boxing, sports that were not open to women, separate teams are allowed.

The right of females to equal educational opportunity was further enhanced with the passage of the **Women's Educational Equity Act (WEEA)** of 1974. This act provides the following opportunities:

- Expanded math, science, and technology programs for females
- Programs to reduce sex-role stereotyping in curriculum materials
- Programs to increase the number of female educational administrators
- Special programs to extend educational and career opportunities to minority, disabled, and rural women
- Programs to help school personnel increase educational opportunities and career aspirations for females
- Encouragement for more females to participate in athletics

Despite reforms stemming from WEEA, several reports in the early 1990s criticized schools for subtly discriminating against girls in tests, textbooks, and teaching methods. Research on teacher interactions in the classroom seemed to point to widespread unintentional gender bias against girls. Two of these studies, *Shortchanging Girls, Shortchanging America* (1991) and *How Schools Shortchange Girls* (1992), both commissioned by the American Association of University Women (AAUW), claimed that girls were not encouraged in math and science and that teachers favored boys' intellectual growth over that of girls.

What impact has civil rights legislation had on the education of females? Why and in what ways does gender bias persist in many U.S. classrooms and schools?

In the mid-1990s, however, some gender equity studies had more mixed findings. In their analysis of data on achievement and engagement of 9,000 eighth-grade boys and girls, University of Michigan researchers Valerie Lee, Xianglei Chen, and Becky A. Smerdon concluded that "the pattern of gender differences is inconsistent. In some cases, females are favored; in others males are favored" (Lee, Chen, and Smerdon 1996). Similarly, University of Chicago researchers Larry Hedges and Amy Nowell found in their study of thirty-two years of mental tests given to boys and girls that, while boys do better than girls in science and mathematics, they were "at a rather profound disadvantage" in writing and scored below girls in reading comprehension (Hedges 1996, 3).

Additional research and closer analyses of earlier reports on gender bias in education were beginning to suggest that boys, not girls, were most "shortchanged" by the schools (Sommers, 1996). Numerous articles as well as a 1999 PBS series that began with a program titled "The War on Boys" challenged the conclusions of the earlier AAUW report, *How Schools Shortchange Girls*. Other commentary discounted gender bias in the schools as a fabrication of radical feminism; among the first to put forth this view was Christina Hoff Sommers' (1994) controversial book, *Who Stole Feminism? How Women Have Betrayed Women*; and, more recently, Judith Kleinfeld's (1998) *The Myth*

That Schools Shortchange Girls: Social Science in the Service of Deception and Cathy Young's (1999) *Ceasefire!*

To examine gender issues in the public schools, the 1997 Metropolitan Life Survey of the American Teacher surveyed 1,306 students in grades 7–12 and interviewed 1,035 teachers in grades 6–12. The analysis of data indicated that:

> (1) contrary to the commonly held view that boys are at an advantage over girls in school, girls appear to have an advantage over boys in terms of their future plans, teachers' expectations [see Figure 7.7], everyday experiences at school and interactions in the classroom; (2) minority girls [African Americans and Hispanics only] hold the most optimistic views of the future and are the group most likely to focus on education goals; (3) minority boys are the most likely to feel discouraged about the future and the least interested in getting a good education; and (4) teachers nationwide view girls as higher achievers and more likely to succeed than boys. [These] findings appear to contradict those from other studies which conclude that girls have lower expectations than boys, feel less confident, perceive competitiveness as a barrier to learning and believe that society discourages them from pursuing their goals (Louis Harris and Associates 1997, 3).

Figure 7.7

To shed light on gender differences in academic achievement, Warren Willingham and Nancy Cole (1997) conducted a seminal study of the scores of 15 million students in the fourth, eighth, and twelfth grades on hundreds of standardized exams used by schools and college placement exams such as the SAT. Contrary to long-standing assumptions that there are pronounced differences between the performance of males and females on standardized tests, their study found that "There is not a dominant picture of one gender excelling over the other and, in fact, the average performance difference across all subjects is essentially zero." Boys and girls, Willingham and Cole found, were fairly evenly matched in verbal and abstract reasoning, math computation, and the social sciences. The superiority of boys in math and science was found to be surprisingly slight and "significantly smaller than 30 years ago." Boys were found to have a clear advantage in mechanical and electronic ability and knowledge of economics and history, while girls had a clear advantage in language skills, especially writing, and a "moderate edge" in short-term memory and perceptual speed. Furthermore, the authors concluded that gender differences in test scores are not the result of bias in the exams; instead, the differences are genuine and would be reflected also in more carefully designed tests.

Gender-Fair Classrooms and Curricula

Although research and debate about the bias boys and girls encounter in school will no doubt continue, it is clear that teachers must encourage girls and boys to develop to the full extent of their capabilities and provide them an education that is free from **gender bias**—subtle favoritism or discrimination on the basis of gender.

Following is a list of basic guidelines for creating a **gender-fair classroom.** Adherence to these guidelines will help teachers "address the inequities institutionalized in the organizational structure of schools, the curriculum selected to be taught, the learning strategies employed, and their ongoing instructional and informal interactions with students" (Stanford 1992, 88).

- Become aware of differences in interactions with girls and boys.
- Promote boys' achievement in reading and writing and girls' achievement in mathematics and science.
- Reduce young children's self-imposed sexism.

Weblink 7.4

- Teach about sexism and sex role stereotyping.
- Foster an atmosphere of collaboration between girls and boys.

See the Teacher's Resource Guide section "Selected Resources for Achieving Gender Equity" on this book's website.

Sexual Orientation   In addition to gender bias, some students experience discrimination on the basis of their sexual orientation. To help all students realize their full potential, teachers should acknowledge the special needs of gay, lesbian, and bisexual students for "there is an invisible gay and lesbian minority in every school, and the needs of these students [a]re often unknown and unmet" (Besner and Spungin 1995, xi). One study of 120 gay and lesbian students ages fourteen to twenty-one found that only one-fourth said they were able to discuss their sexual orientation with school counselors, and less than one in five said they could identify someone who had been supportive of them (Tellijohann and Price 1993). Moreover, a similar study of lesbian and gay youth reported that 80 percent of participants believed their teachers had negative attitudes about homosexuality (Sears 1991).

Based on estimates that as much as 10 percent of society may be homosexual, a high school with an enrollment of 1,500 might have as many as 150 gay, lesbian, and bisexual students (Besner and Spungin 1995; Stover 1992). The National Education Association, the American Federation of Teachers, and several professional organizations have passed resolutions urging members and school districts to acknowledge the special needs of these students.

The nation's first dropout prevention program targeting gay, lesbian, and bisexual students was implemented in the Los Angeles school system. Known as Project 10, the program focuses on education, suicide prevention, dropout prevention, creating a safe environment for homosexual students, and HIV/AIDS education (Uribe and Harbeck 1991). In 1993, Massachusetts became the first state to adopt an educational policy prohibiting discrimination against gay and lesbian students and teachers. At one Massachusetts high school, gay and straight students created the Gay-Straight Alliance (GSA), a school-sanctioned student organization that gives students a safe place to discuss sexual orientation issues (Bennett 1997).

Homosexual students can experience school-related problems and safety risks. The hostility gay, lesbian, and bisexual youth can encounter may cause them to feel confused, isolated, and self-destructive (Alexander 1998; Jordan, Vaughan, and Woodworth 1997; Edwards 1997; Anderson, 1997). Teachers and other school personnel can provide much-needed support. Informed, sensitive, and caring teachers can play an important role in helping all students develop to their full potential. Such teachers realize the importance of recognizing diverse perspectives, and they create inclusive classroom environments that encourage students to respect differences among themselves and others and to see the contributions that persons from all groups have made to society.

SUMMARY

How Is Diversity Embedded in the Culture of the United States? (p. 190)

What Does Equal Educational Opportunity Mean? (p. 196)

What Is Meant by Bilingual Education? (p. 204)

What Is Multicultural Education? (p. 206)

How Is Gender a Dimension of Multicultural Education? (p. 209)

KEY TERMS AND CONCEPTS

Go to the website for interactive flashcards.

APPLICATIONS AND INTERACTIVITIES

Go to the website for interactive assignments in the following areas:

Teacher's Journal

Teacher's Database

Observations and Interviews

Professional Portfolio

Name _____ **Date** _____

For each question, write in the blank the answer you believe is correct.

7.1. Seeing the world from different cultural frames of reference and recognizing and valuing the rich array of cultures within a nation and within the global community defines the concept known as _____.

7.2 _____ refers to shared feelings of common identity, community, and an interdependent destiny.

7.3 The practice of attributing behavioral characteristics to all members of a particular group is known as _____.

7.4 _____ education programs are designed to meet the learning needs of students whose first language is not English by providing instruction in two languages.

7.5 The "sex role _____" process conveys to boys and girls certain expectations about the way they are to behave regardless of individual differences.

7.6 The right of females to equal educational opportunity was enhanced with passage of the _____ Educational Equity Act of 1974.

7.7 The 1997 Metropolitan Life Survey of the American Teacher found that minority girls hold the most optimistic views of the _____, and are the group most likely to focus on education goals.

7.8 When compared to the academic skills of boys, girls were found to have a clear advantage in _____ skills and a moderate advantage in short-term memory and perceptual speed.

7.9 In addition to gender bias, some students experience discrimination based on their _____ orientation.

7.10 In 1993, Massachusetts became the first state to adopt an educational policy prohibiting _____ against homosexual students and teachers.

Answers are available on the FlexChoice website at www.ablongman.com/parkayflex.

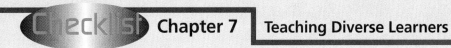

Name _____

Keep this checklist at your computer as a reminder to read and complete the chapter features and activities located on the FlexChoice website at www.ablongman.com/parkayflex.

Date
Completed

_____ ❏ **PreTest with Answers**
_____ ❏ **Audio Clip 7.1:** Thinking Over the Opening Vignette
_____ ❏ **Audio Clip 7.2:** The Changing Ethnic Population
_____ ❏ **Figure 7.1:** Changing school population
_____ ❏ **Table 7.1:** Fifty languages with greatest number of speakers in the United States after English
_____ ❏ **Figure 7.2:** LEP enrollment growth from 1986–87 to 1996–97
_____ ❏ **Appendix 7.1:** Can You Recognize Racism?
_____ ❏ **Professional Reflection:** Reflecting on your cultural identity
_____ ❏ **Audio Clip 7.3:** The Learning Styles of Asians and Native Americans
_____ ❏ **Video 7.1:** Sensitivity to Cultural Values
_____ ❏ **Figure 7.3:** Percent of African American and Latino students in 50–100% minority schools, 1968–96
_____ ❏ **Video 7.2:** Asian Immigrants
_____ ❏ **Video 7.3:** Immersion
_____ ❏ **Figure 7.4:** Four types of bilingual education programs
_____ ❏ **Video 7.4:** Bilingual Classrooms
_____ ❏ **Where Do You Stand?:** Is multicultural education unifying or divisive?
_____ ❏ **Weblink 7.1:** Creating Classroom Environments That Support Second-Language Learners
_____ ❏ **Weblink 7.2:** Strategies for Enhancing the Learning and Literacy of Second-Language Learners
_____ ❏ **Audio Clip 7.4:** Promoting Multiculturalism
_____ ❏ **Keepers of the Dream:** Peter White: Opportunity Creator
_____ ❏ **Figure 7.5:** Banks's dimensions of multicultural education
_____ ❏ **Weblink 7.3:** Selected Resources for Multicultural Education
_____ ❏ **Figure 7.6:** Essential knowledge and skills for successful teaching in a diverse society
_____ ❏ **Audio Clip 7.5:** Sex Stereotypes
_____ ❏ **Technology Highlights:** Does gender equity exist in the use of educational technology?
_____ ❏ **Figure 7.7:** Teachers' opinions on who aims higher: boys or girls
_____ ❏ **Weblink 7.4:** Selected Resources for Achieving Gender Equity
_____ ❏ **Summary**
_____ ❏ **Key Terms and Concepts**
_____ ❏ **Applications and Interactivities:** Teacher's Journal
_____ ❏ **Applications and Interactivities:** Teacher's Database
_____ ❏ **Applications and Interactivities:** Observations and Interviews
_____ ❏ **Applications and Interactivities:** Professional Portfolio
_____ ❏ **PostTest with Answers**

8

Addressing Learners' Individual Needs

I was . . . fortunate that I chose theoretical physics, because it is all in the mind. So my disability has not been a serious handicap.

—Stephen W. Hawking
A Brief History of Time: From the Big Bang to Black Holes

1. How do students' needs change as they develop?

2. How do students vary in intelligence?

3. How do students vary in ability and disability?

4. What are special education, mainstreaming, and inclusion?

5. How can you teach all learners in your inclusive classroom?

focus questions

It's late Friday afternoon, the end of the fourth week of school, and you've just finished arranging your classroom for the cooperative learning groups you're starting on Monday. Leaning back in the chair at your desk, you survey the room and imagine how things will go on Monday. Your mental image is positive, with one possible exception—eleven-year-old Rick. Since the first day of school, he's been very disruptive. His teacher last year described him as "loud, aggressive, and obnoxious."

Since school began, Rick has been belligerent and noncompliant. For the most part, he does what he wants, when he wants. As far as you know, he has no close friends; he teases the other kids constantly and occasionally gets into fights.

Rick's parents divorced when he was in the second grade. His father was given custody of Rick and his younger sister. Two years later, Rick's father married a woman with three children of her own. You've heard that Rick's two new half-brothers, thirteen and fifteen years old, are "out of control," and the family has been receiving counseling services from the local mental health clinic.

Rick's school records indicate that other teachers have had trouble with him in the past. Academically, he's below his classmates in all subjects except physical education and art. Comments from two of his previous teachers suggest Rick has a flair for artwork. Last year, Rick was diagnosed with mild learning and behavior disorders.

Mr. Chavez, the school psychologist, and Ms. Tamashiro, the school's inclusion facilitator, have been working with you on developing an individualized education program (IEP) for Rick. In fact, before school on Monday, you're meeting with Ms. Tamashiro to discuss how to involve Rick in the cooperative learning groups. You're anxious to get her suggestions, and you're confident that with her help and Mr. Chavez's, you can meet Rick's learning needs.

Name _____ **Date** _____

For each question, circle the letter of the answer you believe is correct. Then read the chapter to learn more about these topics.

8.1 Hardman, Drew, and Egan (1999) suggest that a "disability" is all of the following *except*
A. Poor social adjustment.
B. Limitations imposed on the individual by environmental demands.
C. Difficulty in learning.
D. Loss of physical functioning.

8.2 All of the following may be early indicators of learning disabilities *except*
A. Highly developed social skills.
B. Hyperactive behavior, exhibited through excessive movement.
C. Difficulty in listening, speaking, reading, writing, reasoning, or computing.
D. Impulsiveness.

8.3 Feldhusen (1997) suggests that teachers of gifted students should possess which of the following characteristics?
A. Narrow, focused knowledge of academic matters.
B. Possession of average intelligence.
C. Interest in cultural and intellectual matters.
D. Participation in sports activities.

8.4 Kohlberg's theory of moral development includes all of the following *except*
A. Preconventional level.
B. Postconventional level.
C. Formal operations.
D. Conventional level.

8.5 Children who require special education services to realize their full potential are referred to as
A. Mainstreamed students.
B. Exceptional students.
C. Handicapped students.
D. Gifted and talented students.

8.6 Instruction that is designed to meet the needs of exceptional children is known as
A. Remedial education.
B. Age-appropriate education.
C. Special education.
D. Developmental education.

8.7 Mr. Onofrio is a ninth grade English teacher and a member of a team that is developing an Individualized Education Program (IEP) for Karen, a student with visual impairments. All of the following are mandated to be part of the IEP team *except*
A. The county social worker.
B. Karen's mother.
C. A special education teacher.
D. Mr. Onofrio's principal.

8.8 In 1975, Congress passed the Education for All Handicapped Children Act. This act guaranteed
A. An education for children with disabilities only at public schools.
B. A free and appropriate education for all children with disabilities between the ages of three and eighteen.
C. An education for children with mild disabilities.
D. An education for children with disabilities not exceeding $10,000 per student.

8.9 A student must be mainstreamed into a general education classroom whenever such integration is feasible and appropriate. This is called
A. Special education initiative.
B. Diversity.
C. Least restrictive environment.
D. Due process.

8.10 What was the name Erikson gave his postulated ninth stage in the human life cycle?
A. Transescence.
B. Transitory.
C. Hypotransitional.
D. Gerotranscendence.

Answers are available on the FlexChoice website at www.ablongman.com/parkayflex.

As the preceding scenario about Rick suggests, teachers must understand and appreciate students' unique learning and developmental needs. They must be willing to learn about students' abilities and disabilities and to explore the special issues and concerns of students at three broad developmental levels—childhood, early adolescence, and late adolescence. The need to learn about the intellectual and psychological growth of students at the age level you plan to teach is obvious. In addition, understanding how their interests, questions, and problems will change throughout their school years will better equip you to serve them in the present. In this chapter, we look at how students' needs change as they develop and how their needs reflect various intelligences, abilities, and disabilities.

How Do Students' Needs Change as They Develop?

Development refers to the predictable changes that all human beings undergo as they progress through the life span—from conception to death. Although developmental changes "appear in orderly ways and remain for a reasonably long period of time" (Woolfolk 1998, 24), it is important to remember that students develop at different rates. Within a given classroom, for example, some students will be larger and physically more mature than others; some will be socially more sophisticated; and some will be able to think at a higher level of abstraction.

As humans progress through different **stages of development,** they mature and learn to perform the tasks that are a necessary part of daily living. There are several different types of human development. For example, as children develop physically, their bodies undergo numerous changes. As they develop cognitively, their mental capabilities expand so that they can use language and other symbol systems to solve problems. As they develop socially, they learn to interact more effectively with other people—as individuals and in groups. And, as they develop morally, their actions come to reflect a greater appreciation of principles such as equity, justice, fairness, and altruism.

Because no two students progress through the stages of cognitive, social, and moral development in quite the same way, teachers need perspectives on these three types of development that are flexible, dynamic, and, above all, useful. By becoming familiar with models of cognitive, social, and moral development, teachers at all levels, from preschool through college, can better serve their students. Three such models are Piaget's theory of **cognitive development,** Erikson's stages of **psychosocial development,** and Kohlberg's stages of **moral reasoning.**

Piaget's Model of Cognitive Development

Jean Piaget
(1896–1980)

Jean Piaget (1896–1980), the noted Swiss biologist and epistemologist, made extensive observational studies of children. He concluded that children reason differently from adults and even have different perceptions of the world. Piaget surmised that children learn through actively interacting with their environments, much as scientists do, and proposed that a child's thinking progresses through a sequence of four cognitive stages (see Figure 8.1). According to Piaget's theory of cognitive development, the rate of progress through the four stages varies from individual to individual.

1. **Sensorimotor Intelligence (birth to 2 years):**
Behavior is primarily sensory and motor. The child does not yet "think" conceptually; however, "cognitive" development can be observed.

2. **Preoperational Thought (2–7 years):**
Development of language and rapid conceptual development are evident. Children begin to use symbols to think of objects and people outside of their immediate environment. Fantasy and imaginative play are natural modes of thinking.

3. **Concrete Operations (7–11 years):**
Children develop ability to use logical thought to solve concrete problems. Basic concepts of objects, number, time, space, and causality are explored and mastered. Through use of concrete objects to manipulate, children are able to draw conclusions.

4. **Formal Operations (11–15 years):**
Cognitive abilities reach their highest level of development. Children can make predictions, think about hypothetical situations, think about thinking, and appreciate the structure of language as well as use it to communicate. Sarcasm, puns, argumentation, and slang are aspects of adolescents' speech that reflect their ability to think abstractly about language.

Figure 8.1

Piaget's stages of cognitive growth

During the school years, students move through the **preoperational stage,** the **concrete operations stage,** and the **formal operations stage;** yet, because of individual interaction with the total environment, each student's perceptions and learning will be unique. According to Piaget,

> The principal goal of education is to create [learners] who are capable of doing new things, not simply repeating what other generations have done—[learners] who are creative, inventive, and discoverers. [We] need pupils who are active, who learn early to find out by themselves, partly by their own spontaneous activity and

Figure 8.2

Table 8.1

Erik Erikson
(1902–1994)

partly through material we set up for them; who learn early to tell what is verifiable and what is simply the first idea to come to them (quoted in Ripple and Rockcastle 1964, 5).

Figure 8.2 presents guidelines for teaching children at the preoperational stage, the concrete operations stage, and the formal operations stage.

Erikson's Model of Psychosocial Development

Erik Erikson's model of psychosocial development delineates eight stages, from infancy to old age (see Table 8.1). For each stage a **psychosocial crisis** is central in the individual's emotional and social growth. Erikson expresses these crises in polar terms; for instance, in the first stage, that of infancy, the psychosocial crisis is trust versus mistrust. Erikson explains that the major psychosocial task for the infant is to develop a sense of trust in the world but not to give up totally a sense of distrust. In the tension between the poles of trust and mistrust, a greater pull toward the more positive pole is considered healthy and is accompanied by a virtue. In this case, if trust prevails, the virtue is hope. Shortly before his death in 1994 at the age of 91, Erikson postulated a ninth stage in the human life cycle, *gerotranscendence*, during which some people mentally transcend the reality of their deteriorating bodies and faculties. In the final chapter of an extended version of Erikson's *The Life Cycle Completed*, first published in 1982, his wife and lifelong colleague, Joan M. Erikson (1901–1997), described the challenge of the ninth stage:

> Despair, which haunts the eighth stage, is a close companion in the ninth, because it is almost impossible to know what emergencies and losses of physical ability are imminent. As independence and control are challenged, self-esteem and confidence weaken. Hope and trust, which once provided firm support, are no longer the sturdy props of former days. To face down despair with faith and appropriate humility is perhaps the wisest course (Erikson 1997, 105–6).

When we examine the issues and concerns of students in childhood and early and late adolescence later in this chapter, we will return to Erikson's model of psychosocial development. For further information on this significant and useful theory of development, we recommend that you read Erikson's first book, *Childhood and Society* (1963).

Audio Clip 8.2

Table 8.2

Kohlberg's Model of Moral Development

According to Lawrence Kohlberg (1927–1987), the reasoning process people use to decide what is right and wrong evolves through three levels of development. Within each level, Kohlberg has identified two stages. Table 8.2 shows that at Level I, the preconventional level, the individual decides what is right on the basis of personal needs and rules developed by others. At Level II, the conventional level, moral decisions reflect a desire for the approval of others and a willingness to conform to the expectations of family, community, and country. At Level III, the postconventional level, the individual has developed values and principles that are based on rational, personal choices that can be separated from conventional values.

Kohlberg suggests that "over 50 percent of late adolescents and adults are capable of full formal reasoning [i.e., they can use their intelligence to reason abstractly, form hypotheses, and test these hypotheses against reality], but only 10 percent of these adults

where do you stand?

Is character education an effective way to improve society?

display principled (Stages 5 and 6) moral reasoning" (2000, 138–39). In addition, Kohlberg found that maturity of moral judgment is not highly related to IQ or verbal intelligence.

Some individuals have criticized Kohlberg's model as being too systematic and sequential, limited because it focuses on moral reasoning rather than actual behavior, or biased because it tends to look at moral development from a male perspective (Bracey 1993). Carol Gilligan, for example, suggests that male moral reasoning tends to address the rights of the individual while female moral reasoning addresses the individual's responsibility to other people. In her book, *In a Different Voice: Psychological Theory and Women's Development* (1993), Gilligan refers to women's principal moral voice as the "ethics of care," which emphasizes care of others over the more male-oriented "ethics of justice." Thus, when confronted with a moral dilemma, females tend to suggest solutions based more on altruism and self-sacrifice than on rights and rules (Gilligan 1993).

The question remains, can moral reasoning be taught? Can teachers help students develop so that they live according to principles of equity, justice, caring, and empathy? Kohlberg suggests the following three conditions that can help children internalize moral principles:

Weblink 8.1
Weblink 8.2
Weblink 8.3
Weblink 8.4
Weblink 8.5

1. Exposure to the next higher stage of reasoning
2. Exposure to situations posing problems and contradictions for the child's current moral structure, leading to dissatisfaction with his [her] current level
3. An atmosphere of interchange and dialogue combining the first two conditions, in which conflicting moral views are compared in an open manner (Kohlberg 2000, 144).

One approach to teaching values and moral reasoning is known as **character education,** a movement that stresses the development of students' "good character." According to *A Nation of Spectators,* a 1998 report by the National Commission on Civic Renewal, the need for character education to make a "comeback" in our society is clear:

> On the eve of the twenty-first century, America is prosperous, secure, and free. [But] when we assess our country's civic and moral condition, we are deeply troubled. Neighborhood and community ties have frayed. Many of our streets and public spaces have become unsafe. Our character-forming institutions are enfeebled. Much of our popular culture is vulgar, violent, and mindless. Much of our public square is coarse and uncivil. Political participation is at depressed levels last seen in the 1920s. Public trust in our leaders and institutions has plunged (National Commission on Civic Renewal 1998).

There is no single way for teachers to develop students' character; however, in comments made shortly after the shooting deaths of fourteen students and a teacher at

Lawrence Kohlberg
(1927–1987)

Figure 8.3

Columbine High School in Colorado, well-known sociologist and organizer of several White House conferences on character education Amitai Etzioni said, "What schools should help youngsters develop—if schools are going to help lower the likelihood of more Columbines—are two crucial behavior characteristics: the capacity to channel impulses into prosocial outlets, and empathy with others" (Etzioni 1999). In addition, Figure 8.3 illustrates twelve strategies Thomas Lickona suggests teachers can use to create moral classroom communities.

Some teachers, such as those at Dry Creek Elementary School in Clovis, California, Alexander Dumas School (K–8) in Chicago, and Allen Elementary School in inner-city Dayton, Ohio, emphasize specific moral values in their curricula. At Franklin Elementary School, a charter school near Boston, teachers and students focus on a virtue a month as well as a virtue a week. The parents who founded the school organized the curriculum around the four cardinal virtues of the ancient Greeks: fortitude, justice, temperance, and prudence (Lickona 1998).

Maslow's Model of a Hierarchy of Needs

Figure 8.4

Students' developmental levels also vary according to how well their biological and psychological needs have been satisfied. Psychologist Abraham Maslow (1908–1970) formulated a model of a **hierarchy of needs** (see Figure 8.4) that suggests that people are motivated by basic needs for survival and safety first. When these basic needs have been met sufficiently, people naturally seek to satisfy higher needs, the highest of which is self-actualization—the desire to use one's talents, abilities, and potentialities to the fullest. Students whose needs for safety have been fairly well satisfied will discover strong needs for friendship, affection, and love, for example. If efforts to satisfy the various needs are thwarted, the result can be maladjustment and interruption or delay in the individual's full and healthy development.

The hierarchy of needs model has particular relevance for teachers because students differ markedly in terms of where they are on Maslow's hierarchy of needs. Many families lack the resources to provide adequately for children's basic needs. Children from families that are concerned with day-to-day survival may not receive the support that could help them succeed in school. They come to school tired and hungry and may have trouble paying attention in class. Others may be well fed and clothed but feel unsafe, alien, or unloved; they may seek to protect themselves by withdrawing emotionally from activities around them.

Developmental Stresses and Tasks of Childhood

During Erikson's school-age stage, children strive for a sense of industry and struggle against feelings of inferiority. If successful, they gain the virtue of competence, believing in their abilities to do things. If children find evidence that they are inferior to others, if they experience failure when they try new tasks, and if they struggle without ever gaining a sense of mastery, then they feel incompetent.

Children gain the sense of industry needed at this age by playing seriously, mastering new skills, producing products, and being workers. When they first go to school they are oriented toward accomplishing new things (some kindergartners expect to learn to read on their first day of school and are disappointed when they don't). For young schoolchildren, the idea of work is attractive; it means that they are doing something grown-up.

Is childhood a time of carefree play or a period of stress? Certainly the answer depends on the life circumstances and personality of the individual child. In a study of stressful events in the lives of more than 1,700 children in the second through the ninth grades in six countries, Karou Yamamoto and his associates found that the most stressful events "threaten[ed] one's sense of security and occasion[ed] personal denigration and embarrassment" (Yamamoto et al. 1996, 139). Other studies have shown that serious stress is experienced by latchkey children, for example, who are left on their own or in each others' care for part or all of the day.

Developmental Stresses and Tasks of Adolescence

Many psychologists believe that adolescence contains two distinct stages: an early period covering the ages of ten to twelve through the ages of fourteen to sixteen, and a late period from approximately fifteen to sixteen through nineteen. Although a continuity exists in each individual's life, the psychosocial issues of adolescence—coping with change and seeking identity—vary in form and importance as individuals progress through the transition from childhood to adulthood.

What needs must this child satisfy for healthy development? What childhood stresses does she face? What developmental tasks must she accomplish in her psychosocial development? What needs, stresses, and developmental tasks will affect this child as an adolescent? Why is information about development important to teachers?

In Erik Erikson's model of the eight stages of humans, identity versus role diffusion is the psychosocial crisis for the adolescent years. Although the quest for identity is a key psychosocial issue for both early and late adolescence, many believe that Erikson's identity-versus-role diffusion stage fits best for early adolescence. During this time, young adolescents, using their new thinking abilities, begin integrating a clearer sense of personal identity. Erikson's role diffusion refers to the variety of roles that adolescents have available to them.

According to Erikson's theory, when adolescents identify themselves with a peer group, with a school, or with a cause, their sense of fidelity—the "virtue" of this stage—is clear and strong. At this stage adolescents are loyal and committed, sometimes to people or ideas that may dismay or alarm their parents, sometimes to high ideals and dreams.

In late adolescence, the quest for identity shifts from relying on others to self-reliance. Young people continue to work on strengthening their sense of identity in late adolescence, but as they do so they draw less on the reactions of their peers and more on their own regard for what matters. Although late adolescents possess an array of interests, talents, and goals in life, they share a desire to achieve independence. More like adults than children, late adolescents are anxious to use newly acquired strengths, skills, and knowledge to achieve their own purposes, whether through marriage, parenthood, full-time employment, education beyond high school, a career, or military service.

The vulnerability of today's adolescents is portrayed graphically in *Great Transitions: Preparing Adolescents for a New Century,* a report by the Carnegie Council on Adolescent Development: "Altogether, nearly half of American adolescents are at high or moderate risk of seriously damaging their life chances. The damage may be near-term and vivid, or it may be delayed, like a time bomb set in youth" (Carnegie Council on Adolescent Development 1995). The list of alarming concerns in adolescence includes academic failure and retention, accidents, anorexia, assaultive behavior, criminal activity, cultism, depression, discipline problems, dropouts, drug abuse, homicides, incest, prostitution, runaways, school absenteeism, suicide, teenage pregnancy, vandalism, and the contraction of sexually transmitted diseases.

What can teachers do to help children and adolescents develop to their full potential? To help prevent the problems that place them at risk, an energetic, creative, and multifaceted approach is necessary. Figure 8.5 presents several strategies for helping students develop competence, positive self-concepts, and high esteem and for intervening to prevent or address problems that place them at risk.

Figure 8.5

How Do Students Vary in Intelligence?

In addition to developmental differences, students differ in terms of their intellectual capacity. Unfortunately, test scores, and sometimes intelligence quotient (IQ) scores, are treated as accurate measurements of students' intellectual ability because of their convenience and long-time use. What is intelligence and how has it been redefined to account for the many ways in which it is expressed? Though many definitions of intelligence have been proposed, the term has yet to be completely defined. One view is that **intelligence** is the ability to learn. As David Wechsler, the developer of the most widely used intelligence scales for children and adults, said: "Intelligence, operationally defined, is the aggregate or global capacity to act purposefully, to think rationally, and to deal effectively with the environment" (Wechsler 1958, 7). Other definitions of intelligence that have been proposed are the following:

- Goal-directed adaptive behavior
- Ability to solve novel problems
- Ability to acquire and think with new conceptual systems
- Problem-solving ability
- Planning and other metacognitive skills
- Memory access speed
- What people think intelligence is
- What IQ tests measure
- The ability to learn from bad teaching (Woolfolk 1998, 109)

Intelligence Testing

The intelligence tests that we now use can be traced to the 1905 Metrical Scale of Intelligence designed by French psychologists Alfred Binet and Theodore Simon, who were part of a Paris-based commission that wanted a way to identify children who would need special help with their learning. Binet revised the scale in 1908, which was adapted for American children in 1916 by Lewis Terman, a psychologist at Stanford University. Terman's test was, in turn, further adapted, especially by the U.S. Army, which transformed it into a paper-and-pencil test that could be administered to large groups. The use of such intelligence tests has continued throughout the years. Approximately 67 percent of the population have an IQ between 85 and 115—the range of normal intelligence.

Individual intelligence tests are presently valued by psychologists and those in the field of special education because they can be helpful in diagnosing a student's strengths and weaknesses. However, group intelligence tests given for the purpose of classifying students into like-score groups have received an increasing amount of criticism.

The most significant and dramatic criticism of group IQ tests has been that test items and tasks are culturally biased, drawn mostly from white middle-class experience. Thus the tests are more assessments of how informed students are about features in a specific class or culture than of how intelligent they are in general. This complaint became a formal, legal challenge when, on the basis of their IQ test scores, a group of African American children were put into special classes for mentally retarded children. Their parents brought the complaint to the courts in 1971 and persisted with it all the way to the federal appellate court, where a decision was eventually made in their favor in 1984. In that well-known case, *Larry P. v. Riles* (1984), the court decided that IQ tests were discriminatory and culturally biased. However, in another case, *PASE v. Hannon* (1980), an Illinois district court ruled that when IQ tests were used in conjunction with other forms of assessment, such as teacher observation, they were not discriminatory for placement purposes. Although the criticism continues, a number of psychometricians are seeking other solutions by attempting to design culture-free intelligence tests.

Multiple Intelligences

Many theorists believe that intelligence is a basic ability that enables one to perform mental operations in the following areas: logical reasoning, spatial reasoning, number ability, and verbal meaning. However, "the weight of the evidence at the present time is that intelligence is multidimensional, and that the full range of these dimensions is not completely captured by any single general ability" (Sternberg 1996, 11). Howard Gardner, for example, believes that human beings possess at least eight separate forms of intelligence; "each intelligence reflects the potential to solve problems or to fashion products that are valued in one or more cultural settings. [Each] features its own distinctive form of mental representation" (Gardner 1999, 71–72). Drawing on the theories of others and research findings on savants, prodigies, and other exceptional individuals, Gardner originally suggested in *Frames of Mind* (1983) that human beings possessed seven human intelligences: logical-mathematical, linguistic, musical, spatial, bodily-kinesthetic, interpersonal, and intrapersonal. In the mid-1990s, he identified an eighth intelligence, that of the naturalist; and in his most recent book, *The Disciplined Mind,* he suggests that "it is possible that human beings also exhibit a ninth, existential intelligence—the proclivity to pose (and ponder) questions about life, death, and ultimate realities" (Gardner 1999, 72). According to Gardner, every person possesses the eight intelligences (see Figure 8.6), yet each person has his or her particular blend of the intelligences.

Gardner's theory of **multiple intelligences** is valuable for teachers. As Robert Slavin suggests, "Teachers must avoid thinking about children as smart or not smart because there are many ways to be smart" (Slavin 2000, 130). Some students are talented in terms of their interpersonal relations and exhibit natural leadership abilities. Others seem to have a high degree of what Peter Salovey and David Sluyter (1997) term *emotional intelligence*—awareness of and ability to manage their feelings. Differences in musical, athletic, and mechanical abilities can be recognized by even the minimally informed observer. Because these intelligences are not tested or highlighted, they may go unnoticed and possibly wasted.

Figure 8.6

However, keep in mind Gardner's "reflections" twelve years after the publication of *Frames of Mind* (Gardner 1995, 206):

> MI [multiple intelligence] theory is in no way an educational prescription. [E]ducators are in the best position to determine the uses to which MI theory should be put. . . .

Learning Styles

Students vary greatly in regard to **learning styles,** the approaches to learning that work best for them. These differences have also been called *learning style preferences* or *cognitive styles* (Woolfolk 1998). The National Task Force on Learning Style and Brain Behavior suggests that there is a "consistent pattern of behavior and performance by which an individual approaches educational experiences. It is the composite of characteristic cognitive, affective, and physiological behaviors that serve as relatively stable indicators of how a learner perceives, interacts with, and responds to the learning environment."

Students' learning styles are determined by a combination of hereditary and environmental influences. Some more quickly learn things they hear; others learn faster when they see material in writing. Some need a lot of structure; others learn best when they can be independent and follow their desires. Some learn best in formal settings; others learn best in informal, relaxed environments. Some need almost total silence to concentrate; others learn well in noisy, active environments. Some are intuitive learners; some prefer to learn by following logical, sequential steps.

There is no one "correct" view of learning styles to guide teachers in their daily decision making. Culture-based differences in learning styles are subtle, variable, and difficult to describe; and learning styles change as the individual matures. Moreover, critics maintain that there is little evidence to support the validity of dozens of conceptual models for learning styles and accompanying assessment instruments. Nevertheless, you should be aware of the concept of learning styles and realize that any given classroom activity may be more effective for some students than for others. Knowledge of your own and your students' learning styles will help you to individualize instruction and motivate your students.

 **Professional Reflection**   **Identifying your learning style preferences**

How Do Students Vary in Ability and Disability?

Students also differ according to their special needs and talents. Some enter the world with exceptional abilities or disabilities; others encounter life experiences that change their capabilities significantly, and still others struggle with conditions that medical scientists have yet to understand. Where possible, all children and youth with exceptionalities are given a public education in the United States.

Exceptional Learners

Children "who require special education and related services if they are to realize their full human potential" (Hallahan and Kauffman 2000, 7) are referred to as **excep-**

tional learners. They are taught by special education teachers and by regular teachers into whose classrooms they have been integrated or *included*. Among the many exceptional children that teachers may encounter in the classroom are students who have physical, mental, or emotional disabilities and students who are gifted or talented.

Special-needs students are often referred to synonymously as *handicapped* or *disabled*. However, it is important for teachers to understand the following distinction between a disability and a handicap:

> A disability . . . results from a loss of physical functioning (e.g., loss of sight, hearing, or mobility) or from difficulty in learning and social adjustment that significantly interferes with normal growth and development. A handicap is a limitation imposed on the individual by environmental demands and is related to the individual's ability to adapt or adjust to those demands (Hardman, Drew, and Egan 1999, 3).

For example, Stephen W. Hawking, the gifted physicist who provides the epigraph for this chapter, has amyotrophic lateral sclerosis (also known as Lou Gehrig's disease), which requires him to use a wheelchair for mobility and a speech synthesizer to communicate. If Hawking had to enter a building accessible only by stairs, or if a computer virus infected his speech synthesizer program, his disability would then become a handicap.

In addition, teachers should know that current language use emphasizes the concept of "people first." In other words, a disabling condition should not be used as an adjective to describe a person. Thus, one should say "a child with a visual impairment," not a "blind child" or even a "visually impaired child."

Teachers should also realize that the definitions for disabilities are generalized, open to change, and significantly influenced by the current cultural perception of normality. For example, the American Association on Mental Retardation (AAMR) has changed its definition of mental retardation seven times since 1950 to reflect shifting views of people with cognitive disabilities.

Cautions about labeling should also apply to gifted and talented students. Unfortunately, people commonly have a negative view of gifted and talented youngsters. Like many ethnic groups, gifted students are "different" and thus have been the target of many myths and stereotypes. However, a landmark study of 1,528 gifted males and females begun by Lewis Terman (Terman, Baldwin, and Bronson 1925; Terman and Oden 1947, 1959) in 1926 and to continue until 2010 has "exploded the myth that high-IQ individuals [are] brainy but physically and socially inept. In fact, Terman found that children with outstanding IQs were larger, stronger, and better coordinated than other children and became better adjusted and more emotionally stable adults" (Slavin 2000, 428).

Students with Disabilities

Table 8.3 shows that the percentage of all students participating in federally supported education programs for **students with disabilities** increased from 8.33 percent in 1976–77 to 12.98 percent in 1996–97. More than 5.9 million students participated in these programs in 1997 (National Center for Education Statistics 1999).

Various tests and other forms of assessment are used to identify persons in the categories of disability listed in Table 8.3. The following brief definitional characteristics of these categories are based on the Individuals with Disabilities Education Act (IDEA) and definitions used by professional organizations dedicated to meeting the needs of persons in each category.

Table 8.3

1. *Specific learning disabilities (LD)*—Learning is significantly hindered by difficulty in listening, speaking, reading, writing, reasoning, or computing

2. *Speech or language impairments*—Significant difficulty in communicating with others as a result of speech or language disorders
3. *Mental retardation*—Significant limitations in cognitive ability
4. *Serious emotional disturbance (SED)*—Social and/or emotional maladjustment that significantly reduces the ability to learn
5. *Hearing impairments*—Permanent or fluctuating mild to profound hearing loss in one or both ears
6. *Orthopedic impairments*—Physically disabling conditions that affect locomotion or motor functions
7. *Other health impairments*—Limited strength, vitality, or alertness caused by chronic or acute health problems
8. *Visual impairments*—Vision loss that significantly inhibits learning
9. *Multiple disabilities*—Two or more interrelated disabilities
10. *Deaf-blindness*—Vision and hearing disability that severely limits communication
11. *Autism and other*—Significantly impaired communication, learning, and reciprocal social interactions

Figure 8.7

As Figure 8.7 shows, students with learning disabilities account for about 51 percent of all students ages six through twenty-one with disabilities. Since the term **learning disability (LD)** was first introduced in the early 1960s, there has been no universally accepted definition. The National Joint Committee on Learning Disabilities states that

Learning disabilities is a general term that refers to a heterogeneous group of disorders manifested by significant difficulties in the acquisition and use of listening, speaking, reading, writing, reasoning, or mathematical skills. These disorders are intrinsic to the individual, presumed to be due to central nervous system dysfunction, and may occur across the life span. Problems in self-regulatory behaviors, social perception, and social interaction may exist with learning disabilities but do not, by themselves, constitute a learning disability (National Joint Committee on Learning Disabilities 1997).

Imagine that you are concerned about two of your new students—Mary and Bill. Mary has an adequate vocabulary and doesn't hesitate to express herself, but her achievement in reading and mathematics doesn't add up to what you believe she can do. Often, when you give the class instructions, Mary seems to get confused about what to do. In working with her one-on-one, you've noticed that she often reverses letters and numbers the way much younger children do—she sees a *b* for a *d* or a 6 for a 9. Mary may have a learning disability, causing problems in taking in, organizing, remembering, and expressing information. Like Mary, students with learning disabilities often show a significant difference between their estimated intelligence and their actual achievement in the classroom.

Bill presents you with a different set of challenges. He is obviously bright, but he frequently seems to be "out of sync" with classroom activities. He gets frustrated when he has to wait for his turn. He sometimes blurts out answers before you've even asked a question. He can't seem to stop wiggling his toes and tapping his pencil, and he often comes to school without his backpack and homework. Bill may have **attention deficit hyperactivity disorder (ADHD),** one of the most commonly diagnosed disabilities among children. Students with ADHD have difficulty remaining still so they can concentrate. Students with an **attention deficit disorder (ADD)** have difficulty focusing their attention long enough to learn well. Children with ADD/ADHD do not qualify for special education unless they also have another disability in a federally defined category.

Treatment for students with ADD/ADHD includes behavior modification and medication. Since the early 1980s, Ritalin has become the most commonly prescribed drug for ADD/ADHD, and more than one million American children are currently estimated to take Ritalin to increase their impulse control and attention span.

By being alert for students who exhibit several of the following characteristics, teachers can help in the early identification of students with learning disabilities so they can receive the instructional adaptations or special education services they need.

- Significant discrepancy between potential and academic achievement
- Distractibility or inability to pay attention for as long as peers do
- Hyperactive behavior, exhibited through excessive movement
- Inattentiveness during lectures or class discussions
- Impulsiveness
- Poor motor coordination and spatial relation skills
- Inability to solve problems
- Poor motivation and little active involvement in learning tasks
- Overreliance on teacher and peers for class assignments
- Evidence of poor language and/or cognitive development
- Immature social skills
- Disorganized approach to learning
- Substantial delays in academic achievement (Smith 1998, 139)

Students Who Are Gifted and Talented

You are concerned about the poor performance of Paul, a student in your eighth-period high school class. Paul is undeniably bright. When he was ten, he had an IQ of 145 on the Stanford-Binet. Last year, when he was sixteen, he scored 142. Paul's father is a physician, and his mother is a professor. Both parents clearly value learning and are willing to give Paul any needed encouragement and help.

Throughout elementary school, Paul had an outstanding record. His teachers reported that he was brilliant and very meticulous in completing his assignments. He entered high school amid expectations by his parents and teachers that he would continue his outstanding performance. Throughout his first two years of high school, Paul never seemed to live up to his promise. Now, halfway through his junior year, Paul is failing English and geometry. Paul seems to be well adjusted to the social side of school. He has a lot of friends and says he likes school. Paul explains his steadily declining grades by saying that he doesn't like to study.

Paul may be gifted. **Gifted and talented students,** those who have demonstrated a high level of attainment in intellectual ability, academic achievement, creativity, or visual and performing arts, are evenly distributed across all ethnic and cultural groups and socioeconomic classes. Although you might think it is easy to meet the needs of gifted and talented students, you will find that this is not always the case. "Students with special gifts or talents often challenge the system of school, and they can be verbally caustic. Their superior abilities and unusual or advanced interests demand teachers who are highly intelligent, creative, and motivated" (Hallahan and Kauffman 2000, 497). The ability of such students to challenge the system is reflected in a recent U.S. Department of Education study that found that gifted and talented elementary schoolchildren have mastered 35 percent to 50 percent of the grade curriculum in five basic subject areas *before* starting the school year.

There are many forms that giftedness may take; Joseph S. Renzulli (1998), Director of the National Research Center on the Gifted and Talented at the University of Connecticut, for example, suggests two kinds of giftedness: "schoolhouse giftedness [which]

Gifted and talented students benefit from accelerated and enriched learning experiences. What are some forms of acceleration and enrichment that you will offer your students?

might also be called test-taking or lesson-learning giftedness" and "creative-productive giftedness." The trend during the last few decades has been to broaden our view of what characterizes giftedness.

Drawing from the work of Renzulli and his colleagues, Woolfolk (1998) defines *giftedness* "as a combination of three basic characteristics: above-average general ability, a high level of creativity, and a high level of task commitment or motivation to achieve in certain areas. Truly gifted children are not the students who simply learn quickly with little effort. The work of gifted students is original, extremely advanced for their age, and potentially of lasting importance" (Woolfolk 1998, 126).

Variations in criteria used to identify gifted and talented students are especially evident in the reported incidence of giftedness from state to state; for example, North Dakota identifies only 1.0 percent of its students as gifted and talented, while Wisconsin identifies 15.0 percent (National Center for Education Statistics 1999, 67). Depending on the criteria used, estimates of the number of gifted and talented students range from 3 to 5 percent of the total population.

Strategies for teaching students who are gifted and talented begin with effective teachers. Educational psychologist Anita Woolfolk suggests that "Teaching methods for gifted students should encourage abstract thinking (formal-operational thought), creativity, and independence, not just the learning of greater quantities of facts. In working with gifted and talented students, a teacher must be imaginative, flexible, and unthreatened by the capabilities of these students. The teacher must ask, What does this child need most? What is she or he ready to learn? Who can help me to challenge them?" (Woolfolk 1998, 129).

Research indicates that effective teachers of the gifted and talented have many of the same characteristics as their students (Davis and Rimm 1998; Piirto 1999). In fact, Feldhusen (1997) suggests that teachers of gifted students should be gifted themselves and should possess the following characteristics:

- Be highly intelligent
- Have cultural and intellectual interests
- Strive for excellence and high achievement
- Be enthusiastic about talent
- Relate well to talented people
- Have broad general knowledge

Several innovative approaches exist for meeting the educational needs of gifted students.

Acceleration—Accelerated programs for intellectually precocious students have proven successful. For example, an analysis of 314 studies of the academic, psychological, and social effects of acceleration practices at the elementary and secondary levels found "generally positive academic effects for most forms of acceleration" and no negative effects on socialization or psychological adjustment (Rogers 1991). In addition, the analysis identified the following acceleration options as the most beneficial at different grade levels:

- *Elementary school*—early entrance, grade-skipping, nongraded classes, and curriculum compacting (modifying the curriculum to present it at a faster pace).
- *Junior high school*—grade-skipping, grade telescoping (shortening the amount of time to complete a grade level), concurrent enrollment in a high school or college, subject acceleration, and curriculum compacting.
- *Senior high school*—concurrent enrollment, subject acceleration, advanced placement (AP) classes, mentorships, credit by examination, and early admission to college.

One example of acceleration is a suburban Chicago alternative school where high-potential at-risk students work at their own pace in high-tech classrooms. They engage in "integrative accelerative learning," which offers advanced curricula and encourages individual creativity, positive reinforcement, and relaxation. At the National Research Center on Gifted and Talented Education, teachers in experimental classrooms practice thematic "curriculum compacting," which encourages brighter students to forge ahead in the regular curriculum while all students work to their strengths and less able students still get the time and attention they need. Also, many colleges and universities now participate in accelerated programs whereby gifted youth who have outgrown the high school curriculum may enroll in college courses.

Self-directed or independent study—For some time, self-directed or independent study has been recognized as an appropriate way for teachers to maintain the interest of gifted students in their classes. Gifted students usually have the academic backgrounds and motivation to do well without constant supervision and the threat or reward of grades.

Individual education programs—Since the passage of PL 94-142 and the mandating of Individual Education Programs (IEPs) for special education students, IEPs have been promoted as an appropriate means for educating gifted students. Most IEPs for gifted students involve various enrichment experiences, self-directed study, and special, concentrated instruction given to individuals or small groups in pull-out programs. For example, at Columbia Teachers College in New York, economically disadvantaged students identified as gifted participate in Project Synergy, which pairs students with mentors who nurture their talents and guide them through advanced academic content.

Alternative or magnet schools—Several large-city school systems have developed magnet schools organized around specific disciplines, such as science, mathematics, fine arts, basic skills, and so on. The excellent programs at these schools are designed to attract superior students from all parts of the district. Many of these schools offer outstanding programs for gifted and talented youth. Gary Davis and Sylvia Rimm, experts in education for the gifted and talented, say that such schools "are indeed relevant, and they do meet students' needs" (Davis and Rimm 1998, 137).

What Are Special Education, Mainstreaming, and Inclusion?

Prior to the twentieth century, children with disabilities were usually segregated from regular classrooms and taught by teachers in state-run and private schools. Today, an array of programs and services in general and special education classrooms is aimed at developing the potential of exceptional students. Three critical concepts to promote the growth, talents, and productivity of exceptional students are special education, mainstreaming, and inclusion.

Special education refers to "specially designed instruction that meets the unusual needs of an exceptional student" (Hallahan and Kauffman 2000, 12). Teachers who are trained in special education become familiar with special materials, techniques, and equipment and facilities for students with disabilities. For example, children with visual impairment may require reading materials in large print or Braille; students with hearing impairment may require hearing aids and/or instruction in sign language; those with physical disabilities may need special equipment; those with emotional disturbances may need smaller and more highly structured classes; and children with special gifts or talents may require access to working professionals. "Related services—special transportation, psychological assessment, physical and occupational therapy, medical treatment, and counseling—may be necessary if special education is to be effective" (Hallahan and Kauffman 1997, 14).

Special Education Laws

Until 1975, the needs of students with disabilities were primarily met through self-contained special education classes within regular schools. That year, however, Congress passed the **Education for All Handicapped Children Act (Public Law 94-142).** This act guaranteed to all children with disabilities a free and appropriate public education. The law, which applied to every teacher and every school in the country, outlined extensive procedures to ensure that exceptional students between the ages of three and eighteen were granted due process in regard to identification, placement, and educational services received. As a result of PL 94-142, the participation of students with disabilities in all classrooms and school programs became routine.

In 1990, PL 94-142 was replaced by the **Individuals with Disabilities Education Act (IDEA).** IDEA included the major provisions of PL 94-142 and extended the availability of a free, appropriate education to youth with disabilities between the ages of three and twenty-one years of age. IDEA, which is one of the most important and far-reaching pieces of educational legislation ever passed in this country, has several provisions with which all teachers should be familiar. In 1997, the **Amendments to the Individuals with Disabilities Education Act (IDEA 97)** were passed. IDEA 97, which went beyond IDEA's focus on public school *access* for students with disabilities to emphasize educational *outcomes,* modified eligibility requirements, IEP guidelines, public and private placements, student discipline guidelines, and procedural safeguards.

Least restrictive environment—IDEA requires that all children with disabilities be educated in the **least restrictive environment.** In other words, a student must be mainstreamed into a general education classroom whenever such integration is feasible and appropriate and the child would receive educational benefit from such placement. Figure 8.8 shows the educational service options for students with disabilities, from the least restrictive to the most restrictive. About 95 percent of students with disabilities receive their education in general education classes, with the remaining 5 percent in a residential facility, day school, or hospital/homebound program (U.S. Department of Education 1998).

Individualized education plan—Every child with a disability is to have a written **individualized education plan (IEP)** that meets the child's needs and specifies educational goals, methods for achieving those goals, and the number and quality of special educational services to be provided. A sample IEP is shown in Appendix 8.1. The IEP must be reviewed annually by five parties: (1) a parent or guardian, (2) the child, (3) a teacher, (4) a professional who has recently evaluated the child, and (5) others, usually the principal or a special-education resource person from the school district.

Related services—IDEA 97 ensures that students with disabilities receive any related services, including "transportation, and such developmental, corrective, and other

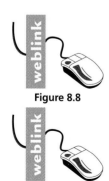

Figure 8.8

Appendix 8.1

supportive services as may be required to assist a child with a disability to benefit from special education" (Amendments to IDEA 97).

Confidentiality of records—IDEA also ensures that records on a child are kept confidential. Parental permission is required before any official may look at a child's records. Moreover, parents can amend a child's records if they feel information in it is misleading, inaccurate, or violates the child's rights.

Due process—IDEA gives parents the right to disagree with an IEP or an evaluation of their child's abilities. If a disagreement arises, it is settled through an impartial due process hearing presided over by an officer appointed by the state. At the hearing, parents may be represented by a lawyer, give evidence, and cross-examine, and are entitled to receive a transcript of the hearing and a written decision on the case. If either the parents or the school district disagree with the outcome, the case may then be taken to the civil courts.

Meeting the Mainstreaming Challenge

To help teachers satisfy the provisions of IDEA, school districts across the nation have developed inservice programs designed to acquaint classroom teachers with the unique needs of students with disabilities. In addition, colleges and universities with preservice programs for educators have added courses on teaching students with special educational needs.

The guidelines for IDEA suggest that schools must make a significant effort to include, or mainstream, *all* children in the classroom. However, it is not clear how far schools must go to meet this **mainstreaming** requirement. For example, should children with severe disabilities be included in general education classrooms if they are unable to do the academic work? Recent court cases have ruled that students with severe disabilities must be included if there is a potential benefit for the child, if the class would stimulate the child's language development, or if other students could act as appropriate role models for the child. In one case, the court ordered a school district to place a child with an IQ of 44 in a regular second-grade classroom and rejected as exaggerated the district's claim that the placement would be prohibitively expensive (*Board of Education, Sacramento City Unified School District v. Holland*, 1992). In another case, the court rejected a school district's argument that inclusion of a child with a severe disability would be so disruptive as to significantly impair the learning of the other children (*Oberti v. Board of Education of the Borough of Clementon School District*, 1992).

To meet the mainstreaming challenge, teachers must have knowledge of various disabilities and the teaching methods and materials appropriate for each. Since teachers with negative attitudes toward students with special needs can convey these feelings to all students in a class and thereby reduce the effectiveness of mainstreaming (Lewis and Doorlag 1999), general education teachers must have positive attitudes toward students receiving special education. An accepting, supportive climate can significantly enhance the self-confidence of students with disabilities.

In addition, Hallahan and Kauffman suggest that all teachers should be prepared to participate in the education of exceptional learners. Teachers should be willing to do the following:

1. Make maximum effort to accommodate individual students' needs
2. Evaluate academic abilities and disabilities
3. Refer [students] for evaluation [as appropriate]
4. Participate in eligibility conferences [for special education]
5. Participate in writing individualized education programs
6. Communicate with parents or guardians

7. Participate in due process hearings and negotiations
8. Collaborate with other professionals in identifying and making maximum use of exceptional students' abilities (Hallahan and Kauffman 2000, 20–22)

The Debate Over Inclusion

While mainstreaming refers to the application of the least restrictive environment clause of PL 94-142, **inclusion** goes beyond mainstreaming to integrate all students with disabilities into general education classes and school life with the active support of special educators and other specialists and service providers, as well as **assistive technology** and adaptive software. Advocates of inclusion believe that "if students cannot meet traditional academic expectations, then those expectations should be changed. They reject the mainstreaming assumption that settings dictate the type and intensity of services and propose instead the concept of inclusion" (Friend and Bursuck 1999, 4).

Full inclusion goes even further and calls for "the integration of students with disabilities in the general education classrooms at all times regardless of the nature or severity of the disability" (Friend and Bursuck 1999, 4). According to the full-inclusion approach, if a child needs support services, these are brought *to the child*; the child does not have to participate in a pull-out program to receive support services. Advocates of full inclusion maintain that pull-out programs stigmatize participating students because they are separated from their general-education classmates, and pull-out programs discourage collaboration between general and special education teachers. Those who oppose full inclusion maintain that classroom teachers, who may be burdened with large class sizes and be assigned to schools with inadequate support services, often lack the training and instructional materials to meet the needs of all exceptional students.

In addition, some parents of children with disabilities believe that full inclusion could mean the elimination of special education as we know it along with the range of services currently guaranteed by federal special education laws. Full inclusion, they reason, would make them depend upon individual states, not the federal government, to meet their children's needs. Moreover, some parents believe that special education classes provide their children with important benefits. For example, in 1994, parents of exceptional children attending Vaughn Occupational High School in Chicago protested a decision by the Chicago Board of Education to include the children in neighborhood schools. The Chicago Board was responding to the Illinois State Board of Education's threat to withhold state and federal funds from the school if students were not included in regular classrooms. In response, the parents picketed a Chicago Board of Education meeting with signs reading "The board's inclusion is exclusion." One parent expressed concern that inclusion would deny her son essential vocational training: "I know [my son] won't go to college so I don't expect that, just for him to learn everyday living and work skills" (Spring 1998, 140).

The general public also has reservations about full inclusion. According to the 1998 Phi Delta Kappa/Gallup Poll of the Public's Attitudes toward the Public Schools, 65 percent believed exceptional students should be educated in special classes of their own; 26 percent believed they should be put in the same classes with regular students; and 9 percent said they "don't know" (Rose and Gallup 1998, 53). Nevertheless, the trend toward full inclusion continues.

How do classroom teachers feel about inclusion? Lin Chang, an eighth-grade teacher, addresses the concerns general education teachers may have about the availability of resources to help them be successful in inclusive classrooms.

At first I was worried that it would all be my responsibility. But after meeting with the special education teacher, I realized that we would work together and I would have additional resources if I needed them (Vaughn, Bos, and Schumm 1997, 18).

In addition, the following comments by Octavio Gonzalez, a ninth-grade English teacher who has three students with disabilities in two of his five sections of English, express the satisfaction that teachers can experience in inclusive classrooms:

At first I was nervous about having students with disabilities in my class. One of the students has a learning disability, one student has serious motor problems and is in a wheelchair, and the third student has vision problems. Now I have to say the adaptations I make to meet their special learning needs actually help all of the students in my class. I think that I am a better teacher because I think about accommodations now (Vaughn, Bos, and Schumm 1997, 18).

Equal Opportunity for Exceptional Learners

Like many groups in our society, exceptional learners have often not received the kind of education that most effectively meets their needs. Approximately 10 percent of the population aged three to twenty-one is classified as exceptional; that is, "they require special education because they are markedly different from most children in one or more of the following ways: They may have mental retardation, learning disabilities, emotional or behavioral disorders, physical disabilities, disorders of communication, autism, traumatic brain injury, impaired hearing, impaired sight, or special gifts or talents" (Hallahan and Kauffman 2000, 7).

Just as there are no easy answers for how teachers should meet the needs of students from diverse cultural backgrounds, there is no single strategy for teachers to follow to ensure that all exceptional students receive an appropriate education. The key, however, lies in not losing sight of the fact that *the most important characteristics of exceptional children are their abilities*" (Hallahan and Kauffman 2000, 6).

To build on students' strengths, classroom teachers must work cooperatively and collaboratively with special education teachers, and students in special education programs must not become isolated from their peers. In addition, teachers must understand how some people can be perceived as "different" and presumed to be "handicapped" because of their appearance or physical condition. Evidence suggests, for example, that people who are short, obese, or unattractive are often victims of discrimination, as are people with conditions such as AIDS, cancer, multiple sclerosis, or epilepsy. Significantly, many individuals with clinically diagnosable and classifiable impairments or disabilities do not perceive themselves as *handicapped*. The term itself means permanently unable to be treated equally.

Officially labeling students has become a necessity with the passage of the laws that provide education and related services for exceptional students. The classification labels help determine which students qualify for the special services, educational programs, and individualized instruction provided by the laws, and they bring to educators' attention many exceptional children and youth whose educational needs could be overlooked, neglected, or inadequately served otherwise. Detrimental aspects include the fact that classification systems are imperfect and have arbitrary cutoff points that sometimes lead to injustices. Also, labels tend to evoke negative expectations, which can cause teachers to avoid and underteach these students, and their peers to isolate or reject them, thereby stigmatizing individuals, sometimes permanently. The most serious detriment, however, is that students so labeled are taught to feel inadequate, inferior, and limited in terms of their options for growth.

How Can You Teach All Learners in Your Inclusive Classroom?

Teachers have a responsibility to address all students' developmental, individual, and exceptional learning needs. Although addressing the range of student differences in the inclusive classroom is challenging, it can also be very rewarding. Consider the comments of three first-year teachers who reflect on their successes with diverse learners:

> I taught a boy with ADD. His first-grade teacher segregated him from other students, but I had him stay with his peer group. Soon, I heard from other teachers that he was not being a troublemaker anymore. By year's end, he had published his own booklet for a writing project.

> I had a troubled student who dropped out of school mid-year after I had spent a considerable amount of time working with him. He went to court over a trespassing charge, so I went to court with him. His mother wrote me a letter saying I had been such a positive influence on him and she was very grateful. It was the relationships I was able to establish with these kids that meant so much to me. The opportunity to take kids with disciplinary problems and make them your kids—to get them to trust you and do what they need to do—is the most rewarding part of teaching.

> One little girl in my kindergarten class had neurological problems, but all the children joined together in helping her. By the end of the year, she was kicking and screaming, not because she had to come to school, but because she had to leave! (Sallie Mae Corporation 1994, 5, 11).

Though it is beyond the scope of this book to present in-depth instructional strategies to address students' diverse learning needs, Appendix 8.2 presents "Examples of Instructional Strategies for Teaching All Learners." See the Teacher's Resource Guide section "Selected Resources for Including Exceptional Learners" on this book's website. In addition, attention to three key areas will enable you to create a truly inclusive classroom: collaborative consultation, partnerships with parents, and assistive technology for special learners.

weblink
Appendix 8.2

weblink
Weblink 8.6

Collaborative Consultation with Other Professionals

One approach to meeting the needs of all students is known as **collaborative consultation,** an approach in which a classroom teacher meets with one or more other professionals (a special educator, school psychologist, or resource teacher, for example) to focus on the learning needs of one or more students. The following first-year teacher describes how collaborative consultation enabled her to meet the needs of a special student.

> I taught a Down's syndrome child who was very frustrated. I convened a meeting that included district experts, his parent, and a resource teacher, suggesting a change in educational strategy. All agreed to pilot the plan, and things have worked more smoothly ever since. It was a very rewarding experience (Sallie Mae Corporation 1995, 11).

Collaborative consultation is based on mutuality and reciprocity (Hallahan and Kauffman 1994), and participants assume equal responsibility for meeting students' needs. Friend and Bursuck (1999) make the following suggestions for working with a consultant:

1. **Do your homework.** Working with a consultant should be an intervention you seek only after you have attempted to identify and resolve the problem by analyzing

the situation yourself, talking about it with parents, presenting it at a grade-level meeting, and so on.

2. **Demonstrate your concern with documentation.** At your initial meeting with a consultant, bring samples of student work, notes recounting specific incidents in the classroom, records of correspondence with parents, and other concrete information.

3. **Participate actively.** If you clearly describe the problem, contribute specific information about your expectations for how the situation should change, offer your ideas on how best to intervene to resolve the problem, implement the selected strategy carefully, and provide your perception of the effectiveness of the strategy, you will find consultation very helpful.

4. **Carry out the consultant's suggestions carefully and systematically.**

5. **Contact the consultant if problems occur** (Friend and Bursuck 1996, 96).

To enhance the educational experiences of their students with disabilities, general education teachers are often assisted by special educators and other support professionals. The following professionals are among those who consult and/or collaborate with general education teachers:

> *Consulting teacher*—A special educator who provides technical assistance such as arranging the physical setting, helping to plan for instruction, or developing approaches for assessing students' learning
>
> *Resource-room teacher*—A special educator who provides instruction in a resource room for students with disabilities
>
> *School psychologist*—Consults with the general education teacher and arranges for the administration of appropriate psychological, educational, and behavioral assessment instruments; may observe a student's behavior in the classroom
>
> *Speech and language specialist*—Assesses students' communication abilities and works with general education teachers to develop educational programs for students with speech and/or language disorders
>
> *Physical therapist*—Provides physical therapy for students with physical disabilities
>
> *Occupational therapist*—Instructs students with disabilities to prepare them for everyday living and work-related activities

Working with Parents

In addition to working with education professionals to meet the learning needs of all students, effective teachers develop good working relationships with parents. Parents of exceptional children can be a source of valuable information about the characteristics, abilities, and needs of their children; they can be helpful in securing necessary services for their children; and they can assist you by reviewing skills at home and praising their children for their learning. The power of partnerships with parents is evident, for instance, in three examples from the U.S. Department of Education's *Schools with IDEAs That Work* (1999b), state-by-state descriptions of schools that work closely with parents to implement IDEA.

Video 8.1

- *O'Loughlin Elementary School*—At this award-winning school in Hays, Kansas, parents pay for after school programs such as Young Astronauts and O'Loughlin Singers; and students lead the four parent-teacher conferences per year.
- *Sudduth Elementary School*—Since this rural school of approximately 1,000 students in Starkville, Mississippi, has limited fiscal and human resources, parent

case to consider

Help! Tell Me about This Kid!

volunteers come and go throughout the day; during the first eight weeks of school one year, parents had 1,129 contacts with the school.

- *Mirror Lake Middle School*—At this school in Chugiak, Alaska, parents volunteer in the office, classroom, and other areas of the school; and frequently they help teach lessons and serve as guest speakers in classrooms.

Assistive Technology for Special Learners

The ability of teachers to create inclusive classrooms has increased dramatically as a result of many technological advances that now make it easier for exceptional students to learn and communicate. For example, computer-based word processing and math tutorials can greatly assist students with learning disabilities in acquiring literacy and computational skills. Students with hearing impairments can communicate with other students by using telecommunications equipment, and students with physical disabilities can operate computers through voice commands or with a single switch or key. Among the recent developments in assistive technology are the following:

1. talking word processor
2. speech synthesizer
3. touch-sensitive computer screens
4. computer screen image enlarger
5. teletypewriter (TTY) (connects to telephone and types a spoken message to another TTY)

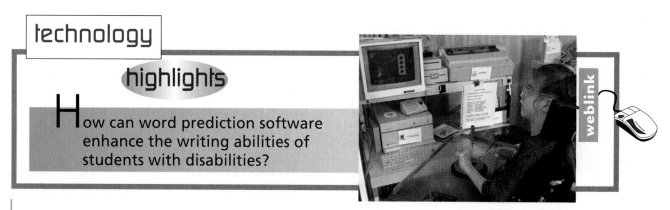

technology highlights

How can word prediction software enhance the writing abilities of students with disabilities?

6. customized computer keyboards
7. ultrasonic head controls for computers
8. voice-recognition computers
9. television closed captioning
10. Kurzweil reading machine (scans print and reads it aloud)

In addition, assistive technology includes devices to enhance the mobility and everyday activities of people with disabilities (wheelchairs, lifts, adaptive driving controls, scooters, laser canes, feeders).

Many technology-related special education resources and curriculum materials are available on the Internet. One of these sites, The National Center to Improve Practice in Special Education through Technology, Media, and Materials, also maintains discussion forums for teachers of students with disabilities. Clearly, the dazzling revolution in microelectronics will continue to yield new devices to enhance the learning of all students.

The IEP for this student with multiple disabilities provides for assistive technology, which enables her to create and respond to language.

SUMMARY

How Do Students' Needs Change as They Develop? (p. 220)

How Do Students Vary in Intelligence? (p. 226)

How Do Students Vary in Ability and Disability? (p. 228)

What Are Special Education, Mainstreaming, and Inclusion? (p. 233)

How Can You Teach All Learners in Your Inclusive Classroom? (p. 238)

KEY TERMS AND CONCEPTS

Go to the website for interactive flashcards.

APPLICATIONS AND INTERACTIVITIES

Go to the website for interactive assignments in the following areas:

Teacher's Journal

Teacher's Database

Observations and Interviews

Professional Portfolio

Handout Master M8.1
Handout Master M8.2

Name _____ Date _____

For each question, write in the blank the answer you believe is correct.

8.1 Jean _____ (1896–1980) was a Swiss biologist and epistemologist who determined that children reason differently from adults and even have different perceptions of the world.

8.2 According to Piaget's theory of cognitive development, children progress through four stages, which he named _____, preoperational, concrete operations, and formal operations.

8.3 It was Erik _____ (1902–1994) who developed a model of psychosocial development within which crisis is central to the individual's emotional and social growth.

8.4 The theory of Lawrence _____ (1927–1987) suggests that the reasoning process people use to decide what is right and wrong evolves through three levels of development.

8.5 Psychologist Abraham _____ (1908–1970) conceived a model of a hierarchy of needs, suggesting that people are motivated by basic needs for survival and safety before other less fundamental requirements.

8.6 The most pervasive criticism of group IQ tests has been that test items and tasks are _____ biased, drawn mostly from white middle-class experience.

8.7 Howard _____ has formulated a theory suggesting that humans possess multiple intelligences.

8.8 Students vary greatly in their preferences for particular learning _____, the approaches to learning that work best for them.

8.9 One of the most commonly diagnosed disabilities among children is known as attention deficit _____ disorder, characterized by difficulty in remaining still and inability to concentrate.

8.10 In 1975, Congress passed the Education for All _____ Children Act (Public Law 94-142) that guaranteed a free and appropriate public education to all children with disabilities.

Answers are available on the FlexChoice website at www.ablongman.com/parkayflex.

Name _____

Keep this checklist at your computer as a reminder to read and complete the chapter features and activities located on the FlexChoice website at www.ablongman.com/parkayflex.

**Date
Completed**

_____ ❑ **PreTest with Answers**
_____ ❑ **Audio Clip 8.1:** Thinking Over the Opening Vignette
_____ ❑ **Figure 8.2:** Guidelines for teaching school-age children at Piaget's three stages of cognitive growth
_____ ❑ **Table 8.1:** Erikson's eight stages of psychosocial development
_____ ❑ **Audio Clip 8.2:** Kohlberg's Stages of Moral Development
_____ ❑ **Table 8.2:** Kohlberg's theory of moral reasoning
_____ ❑ **Where Do You Stand?:** Is character education an effective way to improve society?
_____ ❑ **Weblink 8.1:** National Association of Elementary School Principals
_____ ❑ **Weblink 8.2:** Boston University Center for Advancement of Character and Ethics
_____ ❑ **Weblink 8.3:** Center for Research on Ethics and Values
_____ ❑ **Weblink 8.4:** Character Education Partnership
_____ ❑ **Weblink 8.5:** International Center for Character Education
_____ ❑ **Figure 8.3:** A comprehensive approach to values and character education
_____ ❑ **Figure 8.4:** Maslow's Hierarchy of Needs
_____ ❑ **Figure 8.5:** What teachers can do to help children and adolescents develop
_____ ❑ **Figure 8.6:** The eight intelligences
_____ ❑ **Professional Reflection:** Identifying your learning style preferences
_____ ❑ **Audio Clip 8.3:** Identifying Exceptional Learners
_____ ❑ **Table 8.3:** Percent of children 0–21 years old in federal programs for students with disabilities, 1976–77 to 1996–97
_____ ❑ **Figure 8.7:** Number of children ages 6–21 served under IDEA by disability
_____ ❑ **Figure 8.8:** Educational service options for students with disabilities
_____ ❑ **Appendix 8.1:** A Sample Individualized Education Plan
_____ ❑ **Appendix 8.2:** Examples of Instructional Strategies for Teaching All Learners
_____ ❑ **Weblink 8.6:** Selected Resources for Including Exceptional Learners
_____ ❑ **Video 8.1:** Parent–Teacher Collaboration
_____ ❑ **Case to Consider:** Help! Tell Me about This Kid!
_____ ❑ **Technology Highlights:** How can word prediction software enhance the writing abilities of students with disabilities?
_____ ❑ **Summary**
_____ ❑ **Key Terms and Concepts**
_____ ❑ **Applications and Interactivities:** Teacher's Journal
_____ ❑ **Applications and Interactivities:** Teacher's Database
_____ ❑ **Applications and Interactivities:** Observations and Interviews
_____ ❑ **Handout Master M8.1:** Who Are the Students in the Classroom?
_____ ❑ **Handout Master M8.2:** Conversations with Students in the School
_____ ❑ **Applications and Interactivities:** Professional Portfolio
_____ ❑ **PostTest with Answers**

9

Creating a Community of Learners

Teacher-oriented, passive-student approaches to instruction are outdated . . . we cannot effectively conduct our classes as if students were sponges who sit passively and absorb attentively.

—A middle school mathematics teacher, quoted in Burden and Byrd (1999, 103)

focus questions

1. What determines the culture of the classroom?

2. How can you create a positive learning environment?

3. What are the keys to successful classroom management?

4. What teaching methods do effective teachers use?

5. What are some characteristics of effective teaching?

September 26

I set up a classroom library. We don't use the reading textbook. What for? Grown-ups don't read textbooks unless they're forced. I told them we could read real books so long as they don't steal any. I make a big show of counting the books at the end of the day. The kids sigh audibly when they're all there. They look beautiful, like a bookstore, facing out in a big wooden display my uncle made for me. Plus, it covers the bullet-riddled window that never was repaired.

We don't call the subjects the old-fashioned names in Room 211. Math is "Puzzling," science is "Mad Scientist Time," social studies is "T.T.W.E." which stands for "Time Travel and World Exploring," language arts is "Art of Language," and reading is "Free Reading Time." I did this because I figured kids at this age come to me with preconceived notions of what they are good at. This way, a kid who thinks she's no good in math might turn out to be good at Puzzling, and so on.

In the morning, three things happen religiously. I say good morning, real chipper, to every single child and make sure they say good morning back. Then I collect "troubles" in a "Trouble Basket," a big green basket into which the children pantomime unburdening their home worries so they can concentrate on school. Sometimes a kid has no troubles. Sometimes a kid piles it in, and I in turn pantomime bearing the burden. This way, too, I can see what disposition the child is in when he or she enters. Finally, before they can come in, they must give me a word, which I print on a piece of tagboard and they keep in an envelope. It can be any word, but preferably one that they heard and don't really know or one that is personally meaningful. A lot of times the kids ask for *Mississippi,* just to make me spell it. We go over the words when we do our private reading conferences. I learned this from reading *Teacher* by Sylvia Ashton-Warner, who taught underprivileged Maori children in New Zealand. She says language should be an organic experience. I love her approach.

It takes a long time to get in the door this way, but by the time we are in, I know every kid has had and given a kind greeting, has had an opportunity to learn something, and has tried to leave his or her worries on the doorstep. Some kids from other classrooms sneak into our line to use the Trouble Basket or to get a word card.

Then the national anthem blares over the intercom. The kids sing with more gusto now that we shout "Play ball!" at the end. We do Puzzling until 10:30, then we alternate Mad Sciencing with T.T.W.E., lunch, reading aloud, Free Reading and journaling, and Art of Language.

At the end of the day, as the kids exit, they fill in the blanks as I call out, "See you in the _____ [morning!]." "Watch out for the _____ [cars!]." Don't say _____ [shut up!]." I love _____ [you!]." This is a game I played with my father at bedtime growing up. It gives the day a nice closure (Codell 1999, 29–31).

Name _____   **Date** _____

For each question, circle the letter of the answer you believe is correct. Then read the chapter to learn more about these topics.

9.1 Educational psychologist Anita Woolfolk suggests all of the following "necessary conditions" to increase student learning through positive interactions *except*
A. Learning tasks that are authentic.
B. Teachers who are patient and supportive and who never embarrass students for making mistakes.
C. Classrooms that are free and open, allowing students to set the tone.
D. Work that is challenging but reasonable.

9.2 According to the Praxis framework, teachers must be proficient in all of the following *except*
A. Structuring classroom environments.
B. Treating all students similarly without regard to individual characteristics.
C. Planning and preparation.
D. Structuring instruction.

9.3 The manner in which teachers and students participate in common activities determines
A. Classroom ability groups.
B. The culture of the classrooms.
C. The time on task.
D. Group sanctions.

9.4 Asking students to work with partners on an assignment is an example of
A. Homogeneous grouping.
B. No interdependence.
C. Negative interdependence.
D. Positive interdependence.

9.5 According to a study by Walberg, students tend to learn more if they perceive their classroom morale as all of the following *except*
A. Friendly.
B. Goal-directed.
C. Controlling.
D. Challenging.

9.6 A model of teaching that can strengthen students' interpersonal skills is
A. Nondirective teaching.
B. Cooperative learning.
C. Behavior modification.
D. Theory into practice.

9.7 Several researchers have shown that learning is directly related to
A. The educational resources that are available.
B. The gender of the child.
C. The competence of the teacher.
D. Time on task.

9.8 The way teachers structure their learning environments to prevent, or minimize, behavior problems is called
A. Discipline.
B. Classroom control.
C. Environmental control.
D. Classroom management.

9.9 The key to successful classroom management is
A. Responding swiftly and decisively to misbehavior in the classroom.
B. Accurately identifying misbehaving students.
C. Seat arrangement.
D. Preventing problems before they occur.

9.10 In regard to teaching strategies, effective teachers usually
A. Choose a method endorsed by the administration.
B. Are consistent in using one method.
C. Have developed a repertoire of teaching strategies.
D. Use one style with high achievers, a different style with low achievers.

Answers are available on the FlexChoice website at www.ablongman.com/parkayflex.

The opening scenario for this chapter, taken from *Educating Esmé: Diary of a Teacher's First Year,* by Esmé Raji Codell, a fifth-grade teacher in Chicago, illustrates how one teacher organized her classroom to create a positive learning environment. Sensitivity to the elements that combine to give a day in the classroom a "nice closure" is the hallmark of a professional, reflective teacher. For teacher education students such as you, making the transition between the study of teaching and actual teaching can be a challenge. The more you understand how "the classroom learning environment develops gradually, in response to the teacher's communication of expectations, modeling of behavior, and approach to classroom management" (Good and Brophy 1997, 129), the better prepared you will be to make the transition smoothly.

What Determines the Culture of the Classroom?

As you learned in Chapter 7, one definition of *culture* is the way of life common to a group of people. In much the same way, each classroom develops its own culture. The culture of a classroom is determined by the manner in which teachers and students participate in common activities.

The activities that teachers and students engage in are influenced by several factors. As a teacher, you will make countless decisions that will shape the physical and social milieus of your classroom. From seating arrangement, to classroom rules and procedures, to the content and relevance of the curriculum, you will have a strong influence on the culture that emerges in your classroom. You will have many methodological choices to make—when to shift from one activity to another, when to use discussion rather than lecture, or whether to make one requirement rather than another.

Classroom Climate

Part of the environment of the classroom is **classroom climate**—the atmosphere or quality of life in a classroom. The climate of your classroom will be determined by how you interact with your students and "by the manner and degree to which you exercise authority, show warmth and support, encourage competitiveness or cooperation, and allow for independent judgment and choice" (Borich 1996, 470).

Video 9.1

In addition to promoting learning, the classroom climate should make students feel safe and respected. In light of the finding in the 1996 Metropolitan Life Survey of the American Teacher, *Students Voice Their Opinions on: Their Education, Teachers and Schools,* that 42 percent of students would give their teachers a grade of "C" or worse on "treating students with respect," it is important that your classroom fosters respect for others and be a place where students feel supported while learning.

Classroom climates are complex and multidimensional; their character is determined by a wide array of variables, many of which are beyond the teacher's control. Nevertheless, our observations of high-performing teachers have confirmed that they take specific steps to create classroom climates with the following eight characteristics:

- A productive, task-oriented focus
- Group cohesiveness
- Open, warm relationships between teacher and students

- Cooperative, respectful interactions among students
- Low levels of tension, anxiety, and conflict
- Humor
- High expectations
- Frequent opportunities for student input regarding classroom activities

These dimensions of classroom climates are within teachers' spheres of influence and are promoted, consciously or unconsciously, by their styles of communicating and treating students. As the following reflections by a student teacher indicate, creating a classroom climate characterized by these eight dimensions is not easy; teachers must make moment-to-moment judgments about what actions will enhance students' motivation to learn.

The next day, as I was going over the instructions for a science experiment I noticed Sheila and Devon leaning over and whispering. I immediately stopped my presentation and said, "Sheila and Devon, you need to turn around in your seats and stop whispering while I am talking." Both girls rolled their eyes and slowly turned their bodies around in their seats. Neither of them made eye contact with me as I continued the lesson. Although the class was now quiet, I felt uncomfortable myself. As the students gathered the science materials they needed to carry out the experiment in their cooperative learning groups, I noticed that Theresa was passing a note to Sheila. Trying to hide my anger and frustration, I said, "Theresa, you need to get rid of that note now. You can come up and put it in the wastebasket. It is time to be working on science, not note passing." Although singling out the girls worked in the short term, to tell the truth I did not feel comfortable dealing with the situation as I did.

I didn't want to feel as if I was spending half the time handling misbehavior, but that's just what I was doing. I had learned in school to reach for student strengths, so I am trying to practice the strategy of giving the students a better attitude about themselves through praise. I explained to them that by correcting their behavior I was just trying to create a climate in which they could learn. I am trying to be a supportive teacher who still corrects misbehavior—always with the goal of redirecting students toward meaningful classroom work.

That same afternoon, I began to gather the students together for literature circles. I had four groups reading different novels. Today I was planning to have the students discuss their reactions to the first chapter and make predictions about the rest of the book. For the first five minutes or so, the groups were very productive, and I felt a surge of hope that all would go well. Just then, I noticed Devon lean back in her chair to pass a note to Theresa, who was in a different group. I wanted to shout across the room at them, but I kept my calm and tried to figure out what I should do now (Rand and Shelton-Colangelo 1999, 10–11).

What words would you use to describe the apparent climate of this classroom? In what ways does this classroom appear to be an effective learning environment? What would you look for to determine if this is a caring classroom?

How would you describe this classroom climate using the eight dimensions listed earlier? What changes in the student teacher's behavior could transform the overall climate?

Although teachers influence the classroom climate by the way they regard and treat students, they also shape it by their instructional decisions. David Johnson and Roger Johnson, two researchers in the area of classroom communication and dynamics, delineate three types of interactions promoted by instructional decisions: cooperative or positive interdependence, competitive or negative interdependence, and individualistic or no interdependence (Johnson and Johnson 1999). To illustrate the three types, Johnson and Johnson suggest that a group project to measure classroom furniture would promote cooperative interdependence; a race to be the first student to measure the furniture would call for competitive interdependence; and having a student measure the furniture independently would be an example of no interdependence. Johnson and Johnson believe that teachers should use strategies that foster all three forms of interactions, depending on their instructional goals, but that, ideally, the emphasis should be on furthering cooperative interdependence.

Classroom Dynamics

Interactions between teachers and students are the very core of teaching. The quality of these interactions reveals to students how the teacher feels about them. Teachers who empathize with students, genuinely respect them, and expect them to learn are more likely to develop a classroom climate free of management problems. In classrooms with positive group dynamics, teachers and students work toward a common goal—learning. In classrooms with negative interactions, the energy of teachers and students may be channeled into conflict rather than into learning.

There is no precise formula to guarantee success in the classroom; however, educational psychologist Anita Woolfolk (1998, 427) suggests four "necessary conditions" to increase student learning through positive interactions:

1. The classroom must be relatively organized and free from constant interruptions and disruptions.
2. The teacher must be a patient, supportive person who never embarrasses students for mistakes.
3. The work must be challenging but reasonable.
4. The learning tasks must be authentic.

Teacher Communication   Successful teachers possess effective communication skills. They express themselves verbally and nonverbally (and in writing) in a manner that is clear, concise, and interesting. They "are able to communicate clearly and directly to their students without wandering, speaking above students' levels of comprehension, or using speech patterns that impair the clarity of what is being presented" (Borich 1996, 11). In addition, they are good listeners. Their students feel that not only are they heard, they are understood.

Effective teachers relish the live, thinking-on-your-feet dimensions of classroom communication. Their communication skills enable them to respond appropriately to events that could sabotage the plans of less effective teachers: a student's clowning, announcements on the public address system, interruptions by other teachers or parents, students' private arguments or romances, or simply the mood of the class at that particular time.

Student Interaction   In addition to engaging in positive, success-oriented interactions with their students, effective teachers foster positive, cooperative interactions among students. As a result, students feel supported by their peers and free to devote their attention to learning. Richard Schmuck and Patricia Schmuck (1997) describe the climate of such classrooms as "mature" and "self-renewing." Their research on classroom group processes has led them to identify the four sequential stages of group development portrayed in Figure 9.1.

Figure 9.1

During Stage 1 of a class's group development, students are on their best behavior. Teachers who are aware of this "honeymoon period" use it to their advantage; they discuss and teach classroom rules and procedures, outline their goals, and deliberately set the classroom tone and standards they want. During Stage 2, teachers seeking to promote group development are advised to encourage student participation and communication and to discourage the formation of cliques.

Groups that have met the requirements of the preceding stages move into Stage 3, which lasts for the majority of the expected life of the group (i.e., the semester or the school year). This stage is characterized by the group's willingness to set clear goals, share tasks, and agree on deadlines. At Stage 4, the final stage, group members fully accept responsibility for the group's quality of life, and they continuously strive to improve it.

In addition, teachers who effectively orchestrate group processes in their classrooms recognize that, for good or ill, students as well as teachers exert leadership in classrooms. Wise teachers quickly identify student leaders and develop ways to focus their leadership abilities on the attainment of goals that benefit the entire class. Teachers should also encourage their students to develop leadership skills.

How Can You Create a Positive Learning Environment?

A positive classroom climate and positive classroom dynamics are prerequisites for a good learning environment. Creating and then maintaining a positive learning environment is a multidimensional challenge. While no single set of strategies will ensure success in all situations, educational researchers have identified teacher behaviors that tend to be associated with high levels of student learning. Effective teachers also know how to use these behaviors and *for what purposes* they are best suited. The following sections address three important dimensions of positive learning environments: the caring classroom, the physical classroom environment, and classroom organization, including procedures for grouping students for instruction and managing time.

The Caring Classroom

At this point in your preparation to become a teacher, you may feel uncertain of your ability to create a positive classroom climate and to orchestrate the complex dynamics of the classroom so that you and your students become a cohesive, productive, and mutually supportive group. In your quest to achieve these aims, it will help to remember that an authentic spirit of caring is at the heart of an effective learning environment. "[C]aring interactions between teachers, students, and parents often make the difference between positive school experiences and frustration or alienation" (Chaskin and Rauner 1995, 667–68).

How do teachers establish a **caring classroom?** First, teachers demonstrate caring through their efforts to help all students learn to their fullest potential. "Teachers display genuine caring for students when they find out about students' abilities and motivations. They continue this pervasive caring by providing all their students with the appropriate amount of support, structure, and expectations they need in order to be self-directed, responsible learners" (Zehm and Kottler 1993, 54). In addition, teachers realize that how they speak and listen to students determines the extent to which students believe their teachers care about them. In a synthesis of research on classroom environments that enhance students' learning, Herbert Walberg and Rebecca Greenberg (1997, 46) found that "students learn more when their classes are satisfying, challenging, and friendly and they have a voice in decision making. [When] classes are unfriendly, cliquish, and fragmented, they leave students feeling rejected and therefore impede learning." Table 9.1, based on Walberg and Greenberg's work, presents fifteen dimensions of classroom life and how each influences students' learning at the junior and senior high levels.

Table 9.1

While students learn best in caring classrooms, Nel Noddings has suggested that students also must learn to care for others. Toward this end, she recommends reorganizing the school curriculum around "themes of care" and points out that "educators must recognize that caring for students is fundamental in teaching and that developing people with a strong capacity for care is a major objective of responsible education" (Noddings 1995, 678).

The Classroom as a Physical Environment

When you become a teacher, the physical environment you work in will probably be similar to that of schools you attended. However, we encourage you, with the help of your students, to make your surroundings as safe, pleasant, and convenient as possible. Fresh air; plants; clean, painted walls; displays of students' work; a comfortable reading or resource area; and a few prints or posters can enhance the quality of teacher–student relationships. Seating arrangements and the placement of other classroom furniture also do much to shape the classroom environment. Although seating by rows may be very appropriate for whole-group instruction or examinations, other arrangements may be more beneficial for other activities. For example, you can enhance small-group activities by moving desks into small clusters in different parts of the room. Figure 9.2 shows the arrangement of a classroom at an exemplary elementary school. The room is designed to encourage students to learn through discovery at learning centers located around the room.

Figure 9.2

However you design your classroom, take care to ensure that seating arrangements do not reduce the opportunity of some students to learn. For example, students in some classrooms receive more attention if they are seated in the "action zone," the middle front-row seats and seats on the middle aisle. Teachers often stand near this area and unknowingly give students seated there more opportunities to speak.

Classroom Organization

A factor in positive learning environments is **classroom organization**—the way teachers and students are grouped for instruction, the way learning tasks are structured, and other resources used. The following sections focus on these aspects of classroom organization.

 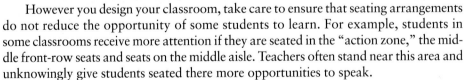

Grouping Students by Ability Two common approaches for grouping students on the basis of shared characteristics are between-class ability grouping, often called tracking, and within-class ability grouping. Students who attend schools where **between-class ability** grouping is practiced are assigned to classes on the basis of ability or achievement (usually determined by scores on standardized tests). Another form of between-class ability grouping, especially at the high school level, is based on students' goals after graduation. Many high schools, for example, have a college preparatory track, a vocational track, and a business education track.

Research suggests that, for the most part, between-class ability grouping does not contribute to greater achievement (Good and Brophy 2000). Supporters nevertheless claim that teachers are better able to meet the needs of students in homogeneous groupings. Among the alternatives to between-class ability grouping are heterogeneous (or mixed-ability) grouping, regrouping by subject area, the Joplin Plan (regrouping students for reading instruction by ability across grade levels), and cooperative learning.

Within-class ability grouping often is used for instruction in reading and mathematics within a class, where a teacher instructs students in homogeneous, small groups. Within-class grouping is used widely in elementary classrooms. Perhaps you can recall learning to read in a small group with a name such as the Eagles, the Redbirds, or the Mustangs. Like tracking, within-class ability grouping can heighten preexisting differences in achievement between groups of students, especially if teachers give high-achieving groups more attention. Also, once students are grouped, they tend not to be regrouped, even when differences in achievement are reduced.

At best, evidence to support student groupings is mixed. Whether students are grouped on the basis of ability, curricular interests, or disabling condition, there is a danger that some group labels can evoke negative expectations, causing teachers to "underteach" certain students, and their peers to isolate or reject them. The most serious consequence, of course, is that students so labeled are taught to feel inadequate, inferior, and limited in their options for growth.

Grouping Students for Cooperative Learning Cooperative learning is an approach to teaching in which students work in small groups, or teams, sharing the work and helping one another complete assignments. Student-Team-Learning, for example, is a cooperative approach teachers use to increase the basic skills achievement of at-risk students. In cooperative learning arrangements, students are motivated to learn in small groups through rewards that are made available to the group as a whole and to individual members of the group. Cooperative learning includes the following key elements:

- Small groups (four to six students) work together on learning activities.
- Assignments require that students help one another while working on a group project.
- In competitive arrangements, groups may compete against one another.
- Group members contribute to group goals according to their talents, interests, and abilities.

In addition, cooperative learning is an instructional method that can strengthen students' interpersonal skills. When students from different racial, ethnic, and cultural backgrounds and mainstreamed special-needs students all contribute to a common group goal, friendships increase and group members tend to view one another as more equal in status and worth. The contribution that cooperative learning can make to the culture of the classroom is supported by research that indicates that, under cooperative learning arrangements, "African American, Mexican American, and White

keepers of the dream

Nel Noddings
Leader in the Challenge to Care

"Keep reflecting on everything you do. . . ."

students develop more positive racial attitudes and choose more friends from outside racial groups" (Banks 1999, 47). In addition, cooperative learning has "a positive effect on the academic achievement of students of color" (Banks 1999, 48).

Cooperative learning also enables students to learn a variety of roles and responsibilities, as the following comments by a fifth-grade science teacher indicate:

> I have the class divided into groups of five students and each group works as a team. The job duties are as follows: principal investigator (PI), materials manager (MM), reader, recorder, and reporter. The PI is the leader of the group and helps mediate when problems occur. The PI is the only student who can come to me with questions during the actual procedure. This rule enables me to monitor the groups and also teaches the group to work independently.

> Students change job duties within their group [for] each activity and every six weeks students change groups. This plan gives each student the experience of working with different classmates as well as learning the responsibility of group participation through performing the different job duties.

Delivering Instruction   The delivery of instruction is a key element in creating positive learning environments. What the teacher does and what students do have powerful influences on learning and on the quality of classroom life. A common activity format in elementary schools consists of students doing seatwork on their own or listening to their teachers and participating in whole-class recitations. In addition, students participate in reading groups, games, and discussions; take tests; check work; view films; give reports; help clean up the classroom; and go on field trips.

A teacher must answer the question "What activity will enable me to accomplish my instructional goals?" Teachers also must realize that learning activities should meet *students'* goals; that is, the activities must be meaningful and authentic for students. **Authentic learning tasks** enable students to see the connections between classroom learning and the world beyond the classroom—both now and in the future. To understand how authentic learning tasks can motivate students to learn, reflect upon your own school experiences. Do you recall memorizing facts only because they would appear on a test? Did you ever wonder why a teacher asked you to complete a learning task? Did you ever feel that a teacher asked you to do "busywork"? What kinds of learning tasks motivated you the most?

Herbert A. Thelen (1981, 86) contends that authenticity is "the first criterion all educational activity must meet." According to Thelen, an activity is authentic for a person if he or she "feels emotionally 'involved' and mentally stimulated . . . is aware of choices and enjoys the challenge of making decisions," and feels he or she "has something to bring to the activity and that its outcome will be important" (Thelen 1981,

86). A comprehensive nationwide study of successfully restructured schools reported that "authentic pedagogy" helps students to (1) "construct knowledge" through the use of higher-order thinking, (2) acquire "deep knowledge" (relatively complex understandings of subject matter), (3) engage in "substantive conversations" with teachers and peers, and (4) make connections between substantive knowledge and the world beyond the classroom (Newmann and Wehlage 1995; Newmann et al. 1996). In addition, as Figure 9.3 shows, high authentic pedagogy classes boost achievement for students at all grade levels. The following Professional Reflection illustrates the differences between high and low authentic pedagogy.

Figure 9.3

Professional Reflection **How do low and high authentic pedagogy differ?**

Structuring the Use of Time How teachers use time affects student learning. **Allocated time** is the time teachers allocate for instruction in various areas of the curriculum. Teachers vary widely in their instructional use of time. Educational researchers Tom Good and Jere Brophy report, for example, that "some students [may receive] as much as four times more instructional time in a given subject than other students in the same grade" (Good and Brophy 1997, 29–30).

Audio Clip 9.3

Researchers have shown that **time on task**—the amount of time students are actively engaged in learning activities—is directly related to learning. As anyone who has ever daydreamed while appearing to pay attention can confirm, time on task is difficult to measure. In response to this difficulty, researchers have introduced the concept of **academic learning time**—the amount of time a student spends working on academic tasks with a high level of success (80 percent or higher) Not surprisingly, learning time, like allocated time, varies greatly from classroom to classroom. For example, Figure 9.4 shows how the more than 1,000 hours most states mandate for instruction at the elementary level actually result in about 300 hours during which students are truly engaged in meaningful, appropriate tasks.

Figure 9.4

An additional concept that is proving useful in understanding teachers' use of time in the classroom is known as **opportunity to learn** (OTL). OTL is based on the premise that teachers should use time to provide all students with challenging content through appropriate instruction. Many states are developing OTL standards for how teachers should use time in the classroom.

To increase the time available for active learning, many high schools have implemented block scheduling arrangements. **Block scheduling** uses longer blocks of time each class period, with fewer periods each day. Longer blocks of time allow more in-depth coverage of subject matter and lead to deeper understanding and higher-level applications. Block scheduling also gives teachers more time to present complex concepts and students more time to practice applying those concepts to authentic problems.

What Are the Keys to Successful Classroom Management?

For most new teachers, classroom management is a primary concern. How can you prevent discipline problems from arising and keep students productively engaged in learning activities? While effective **classroom management** cannot be reduced to a cookbook recipe, there are definite steps you can take to create an effective learning environment in your classroom. First, it is important to understand that classroom management refers to how teachers structure their learning environments to prevent, or minimize, behavior problems; *discipline* refers to the methods teachers use *after* students misbehave. *Classroom management* is prevention-oriented, while *discipline* is control-oriented. Second, it is important to recognize that "the key to good management is use of techniques that elicit student cooperation and involvement in activities and thus *prevent* problems from emerging in the first place" (Good and Brophy 1997, 129). In addition, sound classroom management techniques are based on the guidelines for creating an effective learning environment presented previously in this chapter—in other words, (1) creating a caring classroom, (2) organizing the physical classroom environment, (3) grouping students for instruction, (4) providing authentic learning tasks, and (5) structuring the use of time to maximize students' learning. Positive leadership and preventive planning thus are central to effective classroom management.

The Democratic Classroom

Research findings suggest that teachers who allow students to participate in making decisions about the physical classroom environment, classroom rules and procedures, modifications to the curriculum, and options for learning activities also have fewer discipline problems. Students in **democratic classrooms** have both more power and more responsibility than students in conventional classrooms. On the premise that if students are to live in a democracy, they must learn to manage freedom responsibly, teachers model democracy by giving their students some choices and some control over classroom activities. William Glasser, well-known psychiatrist and author of *Quality School* (1998a), *The Quality School Teacher* (1998b), *Choice Theory* (1998c), and (with Karen Dotson) *Choice Theory in the Classroom* (1998), recommends that teachers develop "quality" classrooms based on democratic principles. According to Glasser, many teachers struggle with classroom management because their actions are guided by stimulus-response theory; that is, they try to coerce students through rewards or punishment, or what many teachers term "logical consequences." Instead, Glasser maintains that teachers should establish "quality' environments in the classroom by following *choice theory*—that is, recognizing that human beings make choices that enable them to create "quality worlds" that satisfy four needs: the need to belong, the need for power, the need for freedom, and the need for fun. From a **choice theory** perspective, misbehavior in the classroom arises when students' learning experiences do not enable them to create quality worlds for themselves. Therefore, teachers "must give up bossing and turn to 'leading'" (Glasser 1997, 600). We follow leaders, Glasser says, because we believe they are concerned about our welfare. To persuade students to do quality schoolwork, teachers must establish warm, noncoercive relationships with students; teach students meaningful skills rather than ask them to memorize information; enable them to experience satisfaction and excitement by working in small teams; and move from teacher evaluation to student self-evaluation.

Preventive Planning

In what other ways can teachers prevent discipline problems from occurring? The key to prevention is excellent planning and an understanding of life in classrooms. In addition, teachers who have mastered the essential teaching skills have fewer discipline problems because students recognize that such teachers are prepared, well organized, and have a sense of purpose. They are confident of their ability to teach all students, and their task-oriented manner tends to discourage misbehavior.

In a seminal study of how teachers prevent discipline problems, Jacob Kounin looked at two sets of teachers: those who managed their classrooms smoothly and productively with few disruptions and those who seemed to be plagued with discipline problems and chaotic working conditions. He found that the teachers who managed their classrooms successfully had certain teaching behaviors in common: (1) they displayed the proverbial eyes-in-the-back-of-the-head, a quality of alertness Kounin referred to as *withitness,* (2) they used individual students and incidences as models to communicate to the rest of the class their expectations for student conduct—Kounin's *ripple effect,* (3) they supervised several situations at once effectively, and (4) they were adept at handling transitions smoothly (Kounin 1970). In addition to the principles of effective classroom management that emerge from Kounin's study, two key elements of preventive planning are establishing rules and procedures and organizing and planning for instruction.

Establishing Rules and Procedures Educational researchers have found that effective classroom managers have carefully planned rules and procedures, which they teach early in the year using clear explanations, examples, and practice (Evertson et al. 1997; Good and Brophy 1997). Your classroom rules should be clear, concise, reasonable, and few in number. For example, five general rules for elementary-age students might include: (1) be polite and helpful; (2) respect other people's property; (3) listen quietly while others are speaking; (4) do not hit, shove, or hurt others; and (5) obey all school rules. Rules for the secondary level might stipulate the following: (1) bring all needed materials to class; (2) be in your seat and ready to work when the bell rings; (3) respect and be polite to everyone; (4) respect other people's property; (5) listen and stay seated while someone else is speaking; and (6) obey all school rules (Evertson et al. 1997).

It is important to enforce classroom rules consistently and fairly. "Consistency is a key reason why some rules are effective while others are not. Rules that are not enforced or that are not applied evenly and consistently over time result in a loss of prestige and respect for the person who has created the rules and has the responsibility for carrying them out" (Borich 1996, 364).

Procedures—the routines your students will follow as they participate in learning activities—also are essential for smooth classroom functioning and minimizing opportunities for misbehavior. How will homework be collected? How will supplies be distributed? How will housekeeping chores be completed? How will attendance be taken? How do students obtain permission to leave the classroom? Part of developing classroom rules and procedures is to decide what to do when students do not follow them. Students must be made aware of the consequences for failing to follow rules or procedures. For example, consequences for rule infractions can range from an expression of teacher disapproval to penalties such as loss of privileges, detention after school, disciplinary conference with a parent or guardian, or temporary separation from the group.

Organizing and Planning for Instruction The ability to organize instructional time, materials, and activities so that classes run smoothly are skills that will enable you to keep your students engaged in learning, thereby reducing the need for discipline. Time spent planning authentic learning activities that are appropriate to students' needs, interests, and abilities will enable you to enjoy the professional satisfaction that comes from having a well-managed classroom.

In the following, a remedial algebra teacher in an urban school tells how organization and planning helped her effectively teach a class of twenty-seven students, grades 9 through 12, who enrolled in the class "for a myriad of reasons, [including] absenteeism, learning disabilities, failure in college prep classes, unwillingness to do required work in college prep classes, personal problems, nonconformity, and a need for credits":

> I am consistently rewarded by the creative thinking and quickness of these students when they are asked to do something other than listen to my thinking, take notes, and copy examples from the board. I have learned that planning meaningful activities, choosing engaging tasks, organizing small groups and pair problem-solving experiences, valuing thinking, and carefully assessing understanding promote an improved classroom atmosphere where learning is the objective for everyone (Schifter 1996, 75–76).

Effective Responses to Student Behavior

When student misbehavior does occur, effective teachers draw from a repertoire of problem-solving strategies. These strategies are based on their experience and common sense, their knowledge of students and the teaching–learning process, and their knowledge of human psychology. There are many structured approaches to classroom management; some are based on psychological theories of human motivation and behavior, while others reflect various philosophical views regarding the purposes of education. None of these approaches, however, is appropriate for all situations or for all teachers or for all students, and the usefulness of a given method depends, in part, on the teacher's individual personality and leadership style and ability to analyze the complex dynamics of classroom life. In addition, what works should not be the only criterion for evaluating structured or "packaged" approaches to discipline; what they teach students about their self-worth, acting responsibly, and solving problems is also important (Curwin and Mendler 1988, 1989).

Severity of Misbehavior   Your response to student misbehavior will depend, in part, on whether an infraction is mild, moderate, or severe and whether it is occurring for the first time or is part of a pattern of chronic misbehaviors. For example, a student who throws a wad of paper at another student might receive a warning for the first infraction, while another student who repeatedly throws objects at other students might receive an after-school detention. Definitions of the severity of misbehavior vary from school to school and from state to state. Table 9.2 presents one classification of examples of mild, moderate, and severe misbehaviors and several alternative responses.

Table 9.2

Constructive Assertiveness   The effectiveness of your responses to students' misbehavior will depend, in part, on your ability to use "constructive assertiveness" (Evertson et al. 1997). Constructive assertiveness "lies on a continuum of social response between aggressive, overbearing pushiness and timid, ineffectual, or submissive responses that allow some students to trample on the teacher's and other students' rights. Assertiveness skills allow you to communicate to students that you are serious about teaching and about maintaining a classroom in which everyone's rights are respected" (Evertson et al, 1997 139). Communication based on constructive assertiveness is neither hostile, sarcastic, defensive, nor vindictive; it is clear, firm, and concise.

Evertson and colleagues (1997) suggest that constructive assertiveness has three basic elements:

- A clear statement of the problem or concern
- Body language that is unambiguous (e.g., eye contact with student, erect posture, facial expressions that match the content and tone of corrective statements)
- Firm, unwavering insistence on appropriate behavior

Lee Cantor developed an approach to discipline based on teacher assertiveness. The approach calls on teachers to establish firm, clear guidelines for student behavior and to follow through with consequences for misbehavior. Cantor (1989, 58) comments on how he arrived at the ideas behind assertive discipline: "I found that, above all, the master teachers were assertive; that is, they *taught* students how to behave. They established clear rules for the classroom, they communicated those rules to the students, and they taught students how to follow them." **Assertive discipline** requires teachers to do the following:

1. Make clear that they will not tolerate anyone preventing them from teaching, stopping learning, or doing anything else that is not in the best interest of the class, the individual, or the teacher.
2. Instruct students clearly and in specific terms about what behaviors are desired and what behaviors are not tolerated.
3. Plan positive and negative consequences for predetermined acceptable or unacceptable behaviors.
4. Plan positive reinforcement for compliance. Reinforcement includes verbal acknowledgment, notes, free time for talking, and, of course, tokens that can be exchanged for appropriate rewards.
5. Plan a sequence of steps to punish noncompliance. These range from writing a youngster's name on the board to sending the student to the principal's office (Mac-Naughton and Johns 1991, 53).

Teacher Problem Solving   When a teacher's efforts to get a student to stop misbehaving are unsuccessful, a problem-solving conference with the student is warranted. A problem-solving conference may give the teacher additional understanding of the situation, thus paving the way for a solution. A conference also helps teacher and student understand the other's perceptions better and begin to build a more positive relationship.

The goal of a problem-solving conference is for the student to accept responsibility for his or her behavior and make a commitment to change it. While there is no "right way" to conduct a problem-solving conference, Glasser's choice theory lends itself to a conferencing procedure that is flexible and appropriate for most situations. Students will usually make good choices (i.e., behave in an acceptable manner) if they experience success and know that teachers care about them. The following steps are designed to help misbehaving students see that the choices they make may not lead to the results they want.

1. Have the misbehaving student evaluate and take responsibility for his or her behavior. Often, a good first step is for the teacher to ask "What are you doing?" and then "Is it helping you?"
2. Have the student make a plan for a more acceptable way of behaving. If necessary, the student and the teacher brainstorm solutions. Agreement is reached on how the student will behave in the future and the consequences for failure to follow through.
3. Require the student to make a commitment to follow the plan.
4. Don't accept excuses for failure to follow the plan.
5. Don't use punishment or react to a misbehaving student in a punitive manner. Instead, point out to the student that there are logical consequences for failure to follow the plan.
6. Don't give up on the student. If necessary, remind the student of his or her commitment to desirable behavior. Periodically ask "How are things going?"

Developing Your Own Approach to Classroom Management   No approach to classroom management is effective with all students at all times. How you respond to misbehavior in your classroom will depend on your personality, value system, and beliefs about children and will range along a continuum from the "minimum power" of giving students nonverbal cues to the "maximum power" of physical intervention.

Classroom management expert Charles Wolfgang points out that teachers usually present one of three "faces" (or attitudes) to students who misbehave:

1. The *relationship-listening* "face" involves the use of minimum power. This reflects a view that the student has the capabilities to change his or her own behavior, and that if the student is misbehaving, it is because of inner emotional turmoil, flooded behavior, or feelings of inner inadequacy.
2. The *confronting-contracting* "face" is one of "I am the adult. I know misbehavior when I see it and will confront the student to stop this behavior. I will grant the student the power to decide how he or she will change, and encourage and contract with the student to live up a mutual agreement for behavioral change."
3. The *rules and consequences* "face" is one that communicates an attitude of "This is the rule and behavior that I want and I will set out assertively to get this action" (Wolfgang 1999, 5–6).

Weblink 9.1

See the Teacher's Resource Guide section "Beliefs about Discipline Inventory" on this book's website, so you can determine which "face of discipline" best fits your personality.

In your journey toward becoming a professional teacher, you will develop a repertoire of strategies for classroom management; then, when you encounter a discipline problem in the classroom, you can analyze the situation and respond with an effective strategy. The ability to do so will give you confidence, like the following beginning teacher:

> I went into the classroom with some confidence and left with lots of confidence. I felt good about what was going on. I established a comfortable rapport with the kids and was more relaxed. Each week I grew more confident. When you first go in you are not sure how you'll do. When you know you are doing OK, your confidence improves.

What Teaching Methods Do Effective Teachers Use?

As we pointed out in our discussion of educational philosophy in Chapter 3, beliefs about teaching and learning, students, knowledge, and what is worth knowing influence the instructional methods a teacher uses. In addition, instruction is influenced by variables such as the teacher's style, learners' characteristics, the culture of the school and surrounding community, and the resources available. All of these components contribute to the "model" of teaching the teacher uses in the classroom. A model of teaching provides the teacher with rules of thumb to follow to create a particular kind of learning environment, or, as Bruce Joyce, Marsha Weil, and Emily Calhoun point out in *Models of Teaching* (2000, 13), a model of teaching is "a description of a learning environment." Table 9.3 presents brief descriptions of four widely used models of teaching.

Table 9.3

Effective teachers use a repertoire of teaching models and assessment strategies, depending upon their situations and the goals and objectives they wish to attain. Your teaching strategies in the classroom will most likely be eclectic, that is, a combination of several models and assessment techniques. Also, as you gain classroom experience and acquire new skills and understanding, your personal model of teaching will evolve, enabling you to respond appropriately to a wider range of teaching situations.

Methods Based on Learning New Behaviors

Many teachers use instructional methods that have emerged from our greater understanding of how people acquire or change their behaviors. **Direct instruction,** for example, is a systematic instructional method that focuses on the transmission of knowledge and skills from the teacher (and the curriculum) to the student. Direct instruction is organized on the basis of observable learning behaviors and the actual products of learning. Generally, direct instruction is most appropriate for step-by-step knowledge acquisition and basic skill development but not appropriate for teaching less structured, higher-order skills such as writing, the analysis of social issues, and problem solving.

Extensive research was conducted in the 1970s and 1980s on the effectiveness of direct instruction (Gagné 1974, 1977; Good and Grouws 1979; Rosenshine 1988; Rosenshine and Stevens 1986). The following eight steps are a synthesis of research on direct instruction and may be used with students ranging in age from elementary to senior high school.

1. Orient students to the lesson by telling them what they will learn.
2. Review previously learned skills and concepts related to the new material.
3. Present new material, using examples and demonstrations.
4. Assess students' understanding by asking questions; correct misunderstandings.
5. Allow students to practice new skills or apply new information.
6. Provide feedback and corrections as students practice.
7. Include newly learned material in homework.
8. Review material periodically.

A direct instruction method called **mastery learning** is based on two assumptions about learning: (1) virtually all students can learn material if given enough time and taught appropriately and (2) students learn best when they participate in a structured, systematic program of learning that enables them to progress in small, sequenced steps (Carroll 1963; Bloom 1981):

1. Set objectives and standards for mastery.
2. Teach content directly to students.
3. Provide corrective feedback to students on their learning.
4. Provide additional time and help in correcting errors.
5. Follow a cycle of teaching, testing, reteaching, and retesting.

In mastery learning, students take diagnostic tests and then are guided to do corrective exercises or activities to improve their learning. These may take the form of programmed instruction, workbooks, computer drill and practice, or educational games. After the corrective lessons, students are given another test and are more likely to achieve mastery.

Methods Based on Child Development

As you learned in Chapter 8, children move through stages of cognitive, psychosocial, and moral development. Effective instruction includes methods that are developmentally appropriate, meet students' diverse learning needs, and recognize the importance of learning that occurs in social contexts. For example, one way that students reach higher levels of development is to observe and then imitate their parents, teachers, and peers, who act as models. As Woolfolk (1998, 229) points out:

> Modeling has long been used, of course, to teach dance, sports, and crafts, as well as skills in subjects such as home economics, chemistry, and shop. Modeling

can also be applied deliberately in the classroom to teach mental skills and to broaden horizons—to teach new ways of thinking. Teachers serve as models for a vast range of behaviors, from pronouncing vocabulary words, to reacting to the seizure of an epileptic student, to being enthusiastic about learning.

Effective teachers also use **modeling** by "thinking out loud" and following three basic steps of "mental modeling" (Duffy and Roehler 1989):

1. Showing students the reasoning involved
2. Making students conscious of the reasoning involved
3. Focusing students on applying the reasoning

In this way, teachers can help students become aware of their learning processes and enhance their ability to learn.

Since the mid-1980s, several educational researchers have examined how learners *construct* understanding of new material. "Constructivist views of learning, therefore, focus on how learners make sense of new information—how they construct meaning based on what they already know" (Parkay and Hass 2000, 168). Teachers with this constructivist view of learning focus on students' thinking about the material being learned and, through carefully orchestrated cues, prompts, and questions, help students arrive at a deeper understanding of the material. The common elements of **constructivist teaching** include the following:

- The teacher elicits students' prior knowledge of the material and uses this as the starting point for instruction.
- The teacher not only presents material to students, but he or she also responds to students' efforts to learn the material. While teaching, the teacher must *learn about students' learning*.
- Students not only absorb information, but they also actively use that information to construct meaning.
- The teacher creates a social milieu within the classroom, a community of learners, that allows students to reflect and talk with one another as they construct meaning and solve problems.

Constructivist teachers provide students with support, or "scaffolding," as they learn new material. By observing the child and listening carefully to what he or she says, the teacher provides **scaffolding** in the form of clues, encouragement, suggestions, or other assistance to guide students' learning efforts. The teacher varies the amount of support given on the basis of the student's understanding—if the student understands little, the teacher gives more support; conversely, the teacher gives progressively less support as the student's understanding becomes more evident. Overall, the teacher provides just enough scaffolding to enable the student to "discover" the material on his or her own.

The concept of scaffolding is based on the work of L. S. Vygotsky, a well-known Soviet psychologist. Vygotsky (1978, 1980) coined the term *zone of proximal development* to refer to the point at which students need assistance in order to continue learning. The effective teacher is sensitive to the student's zone of development and ensures that instruction neither exceeds the student's current level of understanding nor underestimates the student's ability.

Methods Based on the Thinking Process

Some instructional methods are derived from the mental processes involved in learning, thinking, remembering, problem solving, and creativity. **Information processing,** for example, is a branch of cognitive science concerned with how people use their long- and short-term memory to access information and solve problems. The computer is often used as an analogy for information-processing views of learning:

> Like the computer, the human mind takes in information, performs operations on it to change its form and content, stores the information, retrieves it when needed, and generates responses to it. Thus, processing involves gathering and representing information, or *encoding;* holding information, or *storage;* and getting at the information when needed, or *retrieval.* The whole system is guided by *control processes* that determine how and when information will flow through the system (Woolfolk 1998, 249-50).

Although several systematic approaches to instruction are based on information processing—teaching students how to memorize, think inductively or deductively, acquire concepts, or use the scientific method, for example—they all focus on how people acquire and use information. Table 9.4 presents general teaching guidelines based on ideas from information processing.

In **inquiry learning** and **discovery learning** students are given opportunities to inquire into subjects so that they "discover" knowledge for themselves. When teachers ask students to go beyond information in a text to make inferences, draw conclusions, or form generalizations; and when teachers do not answer students' questions, preferring instead to have students develop their own answers, they are using methods based on inquiry and discovery learning. These methods are best suited for teaching concepts, relationships, and theoretical abstractions, and for having students formulate and test hypotheses. The following example shows how inquiry and discovery learning in a first-grade classroom fostered a high level of student involvement and thinking.

Table 9.4

> The children are gathered around a table on which a candle and jar have been placed. The teacher, Jackie Wiseman, lights the candle and, after it has burned brightly for a minute or two, covers it carefully with the jar. The candle grows dim, flickers, and goes out. Then she produces another candle and a larger jar, and the exercise is repeated. The candle goes out, but more slowly. Jackie produces two more candles and jars of different sizes, and the children light the candles, place the jars over them, and the flames slowly go out. "Now we're going to develop some ideas about what has just happened," she says. "I want you to ask me questions about those candles and jars and what you just observed" (Joyce, Weil, and Calhoun 2000, 3).

Methods Based on Peer-Mediated Instruction

Student peer groups can be a deterrent to academic performance (Steinberg et al. 1996), but they can also motivate students to excel. Because school learning occurs in a social setting, **peer-mediated instruction** provides teachers with options for increasing students' learning. Cooperative learning, described earlier in this chapter, is an example of peer-mediated instruction. Another example is **group investigation,** in which the teacher's role is to create an environment that allows students to determine what they will study and how. Students are presented with a situation to which they "react and discover basic conflicts among their attitudes, ideas, and modes of perception. On the basis of this information, they identify the problem to be investigated, analyze the roles required to solve it, organize themselves to take these roles, act, report, and evaluate these results" (Thelen 1960, 82).

The teacher's role in group investigation is multifaceted; he or she is an organizer, guide, resource person, counselor, and evaluator. The method is very effective in increasing student achievement (Sharan and Sharan 1989/90, 17–21), positive attitudes toward learning, and the cohesiveness of the classroom group. The model also allows students to inquire into problems that interest them and enables each student to make a meaningful, authentic contribution to the group's effort based on his or her experiences, interests, knowledge, and skills.

Other common forms of peer-mediated instruction include peer tutoring and cross-age tutoring. In **peer-tutoring** arrangements, students are tutored by other pupils in the same class or the same grade. **Cross-age tutoring** involves, for example, sixth-grade students tutoring second-grade students in reading. Research clearly shows that with proper orientation and training, cross-age tutoring can greatly benefit both "teacher" and learner (Henriques 1997; Schneider and Barone 1997; Utay and Utay 1997; Zukowski 1997). Pilot programs pairing students at risk of dropping out of school with younger children and with special-needs students have proved especially successful.

What Are Some Characteristics of Effective Teaching?

The *outcomes* of effective teaching are relatively easy to enumerate: (1) students acquire an understanding of the subject at hand; (2) they can apply what they have learned to new situations; and (3) they have a desire to continue learning. However, if we wish to identify the *characteristics* of effective teaching, we find ourselves confronted with a more difficult task.

What do effective teachers do when they are teaching? How do they communicate with students? How do they manage classroom activities? What models of teaching do they use? As the previous discussions of classroom cultures, learning environments, classroom management, and teaching methods suggest, answers to questions such as these are not easy to formulate. However, one broad helpful view of the characteristics that underlie all effective teaching is the "Framework for Teaching," developed as part of the Praxis Series: Professional Assessments for Beginning Teachers. According to the Praxis framework, teachers must be proficient in four domains: planning and preparation, structuring classroom environment, instruction, and professional responsibilities. Teachers must be effective within these domains while taking into account individual, developmental, and cultural differences among students and differences among subjects. Figure 9.5 shows the tasks teachers should be able to perform within the four domains.

Figure 9.5

Establishing Goals

One characteristic of successful teachers is that they focus on the outcomes—the results or consequences of their teaching. Regardless of the instructional method used, with clear goals to provide guidance, teachers can make good decisions about classroom activities to select or develop.

Goals are general statements of purpose that guide schools and teachers as they develop instructional programs. **Instructional goals** can be derived from the curriculum or content being taught; or, as you saw in Chapter 3, they can be derived from various educational philosophies. Goals range from very broad statements of purpose that apply to a large number of students to those that apply to students in a particular classroom. In addition, teachers evaluate their teaching by how well students master certain objectives. **Learning objectives** are specific, measurable outcomes of learning that students are to demonstrate. For example, "Students will identify the structural elements of cells and explain their functions" might be a specific objective toward a larger goal of "understanding biological concepts and principles."

Successful teachers also realize that the quality of their teaching depends on what students can *do*, not only on what they *know*. To evaluate their effectiveness in this area, teachers assess students' mastery of performance tasks in which they apply their learning to a new problem. Figure 9.6 illustrates two different approaches to lesson planning that take into account targeted goals, objectives, and performance tasks.

Figure 9.6

Linking Assessment with Instruction

In assessing students' learning, teachers make judgments about the performance of students and about their own performance as teachers. Successful teachers use **assessment** to evaluate the effectiveness of their teaching because they recognize that how well students learn depends on how well they teach.

To assess students' learning, teachers use measurement and evaluation techniques. **Measurement** is the gathering of quantitative data related to the knowledge and skills students have acquired. Measurement yields scores, rankings, or ratings that teachers can use to compare students. **Evaluation** involves making judgments about or assigning a value to those measurements. **Formative evaluation** occurs when the teacher measures students' learning for instruction. **Summative evaluation** is used by teachers to determine grades at the end of a unit, semester, or year and to decide whether students are ready to proceed to the next phase of their education.

Authentic assessments (sometimes called *alternative assessments*) require students to use higher-level thinking skills to perform, create, or solve real-life problems—not just choose one of several designated responses as on a multiple-choice test. The authentic assessments a teacher might use include evaluating the quality of individual and small-group projects, videotaped demonstrations of skills, or participation in community-based activities. In science, for example, students might design and conduct an experiment; in mathematics, they might explain in writing how they solved a problem. Authentic assessments require students to solve problems or to work on tasks that approximate as much as possible those they will encounter beyond the classroom. **Portfolio assessment** is based on a collection of student work

From this photo, what can you tell about this teacher's proficiency in planning and preparation, structuring classroom environment, instruction, and professional responsibilities?

Should the use of standardized testing be increased?

that "tell[s] a story of a learner's growth in proficiency, long-term achievement, and significant accomplishments in a given academic area" (Tombari and Borich 1999, 164). For students, an important part of portfolio assessment is clarifying the criteria used to select work to be included in the portfolio. **Performance assessment** is used to determine what students can do as well as what they know. In some cases, the teacher observes and then evaluates an actual performance or application of a skill; in others, the teacher evaluates a product created by the student.

Examples of Effective Teachers

This chapter concludes with comments by several effective teachers in which they describe strategies that help them create communities of learners. As you read the teachers' comments, identify how each has put into practice many of the concepts discussed in this chapter. In addition, reflect on the degree to which that teacher's approach would "fit" your personality and value system.

Laurie Robben, Fourth Grade Teacher, Greenwich, Connecticut[*]   I am extremely proud of the positive rapport that I have with my students. One way that I instill mutual respect is through classroom meetings. Every Friday, I set aside at least fifteen minutes for a class meeting. We all sit together on the floor, including myself, to show that no one's ideas are more important than another's.

Classroom meetings provide a time for students to share their feelings openly about their school experience, and issues can be positive or negative. An important rule is that if someone wants to say something negative about a particular student, the class is not allowed to talk about that conversation outside the confines of our meeting. This is to prevent a student from being badgered.

One example is Alex, a nine-year old who desperately wants peer attention but resorts to behaving like a clown. In a recent meeting, students told him they were not comfortable with his clowning and wished that he would stop. I asked the class to share times when they enjoyed being with Alex, and they encouraged him to practice those behaviors more frequently. At the end of the meeting, Alex asked his peers, "Could you help me be better and tell me when I'm bugging you?" We talked about how to tell Alex. The class concluded that a person is more likely to respond if you ask nicely ("Alex, this is an example of something that bugs me. Please stop."). Improvement has been apparent since that meeting.

[*]From Paul Burden and David Byrd, *Methods for Effective Teaching*, 2nd ed. Copyright © 1999 by Allyn and Bacon, p. 120. Reprinted by permission.

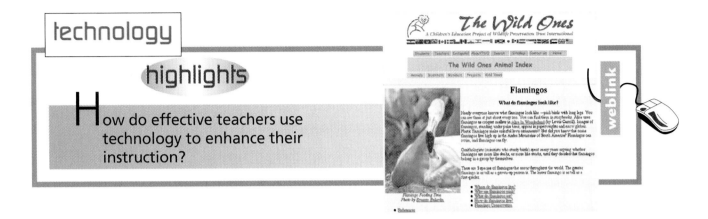

technology

highlights

How do effective teachers use technology to enhance their instruction?

Since we regularly have class meetings, the students will give me updates on past issues, such as "Lunch is better now. Adam doesn't show us the food in his mouth anymore!"

Class meetings show the class that I care about them outside of the traditional academic areas. It also encourages them to listen to one another. And it allows me to use peer influence to encourage behavioral changes. We all win!

Terri Jenkins, Eighth-Grade Middle School Language-Arts Teacher, Hephzibah, Georgia[*]   Four years ago, I was teaching in an inner city school with 99 percent minority enrollment. From the beginning, I was convinced that all these children could learn. My goal each day was to provide material and present in such a way that ensured every student would experience some degree of success. I will never forget one particular series of lessons.

We began reading "The Graduation" by Maya Angelou, which recounts her own graduation and valedictory address. We then learned the Negro spiritual, "We Shall Overcome." The story and song were inspirational, but they weren't enough. I wanted to make the entire experience personal. I told the class that one day someone sitting in that very classroom would be responsible for giving a valedictory address at his or her own graduation, and that their next assignment was to prepare a speech and present it in class. The speeches were wonderful as I introduced each and every one of them as the valedictorian of that year. As they spoke, I could hear a new determination in their voices; I could see a new pride in their posture.

Three weeks ago, there was a soft tap on my classroom door and a welcomed face appeared. Immediately I recognized Carol, one of those students who had given her valedictory address in my eighth grade classroom almost five years ago. After a big smile and a warm hug, she quietly spoke. "I just had to come by and personally invite you to my graduation on June 5. I'll be giving the valedictory address, and I want you to be there." With that, an irrepressible smile burst across her face. After much earned congratulations, she looked at the tears in my eyes and said, "I did it just for you." Carol had become a believer in her dreams, a believer in herself.

Self-esteem and belief in oneself are essential. I firmly believe that self-esteem must be built through real achievement. I still strive to provide lessons designed to maximize

[*]From Paul Burden and David Byrd, *Methods for Effective Teaching*, 2nd ed. Copyright © 1999 by Allyn and Bacon. Reprinted by permission.

student success and ensure achievement, and I continually verbalize my own convictions that they all can be winners. I make every effort to personalize success in the classroom. I realize that I cannot assure success for every student in my classroom, but I now know that I truly can make a difference.

James P. Anderson, Barbara Floisand, David Martinez, and Dalmar P. Robinson, Alternative High School Teachers, Salt Lake City, Utah[*]   We believe that schools should be democratic institutions. We are a service organization and live in the neighborhood as fellow citizens. Our priorities are as follows: students first, teachers second, classified staff third, and administrators fourth. Above all, every student must be treated fairly and with dignity. We tell students: "You can't pick your parents or where or when you are born. It is perfectly natural to want to belong, to be acknowledged, to succeed, regardless of your circumstances."

Most high school students who find themselves at [our school] have not been successful in the regular school setting. Their self-esteem may be low. They may feel alienated from their peers. Some may believe that society has set them up for failure. [Our] task is to provide a supportive environment that motivates and allows students to recognize windows of opportunity and to reach their educational and career goals.

[*]Anderson, J. P.; Floisand, B.; Martinez, D.; and Robinson, D. P. (1997). Horizonte—where students come first. *Educational Leadership, 54*(7), p. 51.

SUMMARY

What Determines the Culture of the Classroom? (p. 248)

How Can You Create a Positive Learning Environment? (p. 251)

What Are the Keys to Successful Classroom Management? (p. 255)

What Teaching Methods Do Effective Teachers Use? (p. 260)

What Are Some Characteristics of Effective Teaching? (p. 264)

KEY TERMS AND CONCEPTS

Go to the website for interactive flashcards.

APPLICATIONS AND INTERACTIVITIES

Go to the website for interactive assignments in the following areas:

Teacher's Journal

Teacher's Database

Observations and Interviews

Professional Portfolio

Weblink 9.2
Weblink 9.3
Weblink 9.4
Weblink 9.5
Weblink 9.6
Weblink 9.7
Weblink 9.8
Weblink 9.9
Weblink 9.10

Name _____ **Date** _____

For each question, write in the blank the answer you believe is correct.

9.1 Classroom _____ are complex and multidimensional; their natures are determined by a wide range of variables, many of which are beyond the control of teachers.

9.2 Among her four conditions to increase student learning through positive interactions, Anita Woolfolk suggests that teachers must ensure that the learning tasks they present to students are _____.

9.3 Students learn best in _____ classrooms.

9.4 Grouping students for instruction and structuring learning tasks are examples of classroom _____.

9.5 An approach to teaching in which students work in small groups, or teams, sharing the work and helping one another complete assignments is known as _____ learning.

9.6 _____ learning tasks enhance the likelihood that students will see the connections between classroom learning and the world beyond the school.

9.7 The amount of time a student spends working on academic tasks with high success rates is known as _____ learning time.

9.8 Nontraditional classrooms in which students have greater power and responsibility are known as _____ classrooms.

9.9 Cantor developed an approach to classroom discipline based on firm, clear guidelines for student behavior and unambiguous consequences of misconduct known as _____ discipline.

9.10 _____ instruction is a systematic instructional method focused on transmitting knowledge and skills from the teacher to the student.

Answers are available on the FlexChoice website at www.ablongman.com/parkayflex.

Name _____

Keep this checklist at your computer as a reminder to read and complete the chapter features and activities located on the FlexChoice website at www.ablongman.com/parkayflex.

**Date
Completed**

_____ ❏ **PreTest with Answers**
_____ ❏ **Audio Clip 9.1:** Thinking Over the Opening Vignette
_____ ❏ **Video 9.1:** A Positive Environment
_____ ❏ **Figure 9.1:** Characteristics of groups at four stages of development
_____ ❏ **Table 9.1:** Fifteen dimensions of classroom environment
_____ ❏ **Figure 9.2:** Learning centers in an elementary classroom
_____ ❏ **Audio Clip 9.2:** Cooperative Learning
_____ ❏ **Keepers of the Dream:** Nel Noddings
_____ ❏ **Figure 9.3:** Level of authentic student performance for students who experience low, average, and high authentic pedagogy in restructuring elementary, middle, and high schools
_____ ❏ **Professional Reflection:** How do low and high authentic pedagogy differ?
_____ ❏ **Audio Clip 9.3:** Time on Task
_____ ❏ **Figure 9.4:** How much time is there, anyway?
_____ ❏ **Table 9.2:** Mild, moderate, and severe misbehaviors and some alternative responses
_____ ❏ **Weblink 9.1:** Beliefs about Discipline Inventory
_____ ❏ **Table 9.3:** Four instructional models
_____ ❏ **Table 9.4:** Using information processing ideas in the classroom
_____ ❏ **Figure 9.5:** The Praxis framework for teaching
_____ ❏ **Figure 9.6:** Two approaches to planning lessons
_____ ❏ **Where Do You Stand?:** Should the use of standardized testing be increased?
_____ ❏ **Technology Highlights:** How do effective teachers use technology to enhance their instruction?
_____ ❏ **Summary**
_____ ❏ **Key Terms and Concepts**
_____ ❏ **Applications and Interactivities:** Teacher's Journal
_____ ❏ **Applications and Interactivities:** Teacher's Database
_____ ❏ **Weblink 9.2:** American Educational Research Journal
_____ ❏ **Weblink 9.3:** Contemporary Educational Psychology
_____ ❏ **Weblink 9.4:** Journal of Educational Psychology
_____ ❏ **Weblink 9.5:** Review of Educational Research
_____ ❏ **Weblink 9.6:** Educational Researcher
_____ ❏ **Weblink 9.7:** Review of Research in Education
_____ ❏ **Weblink 9.8:** Social Psychology of Education
_____ ❏ **Weblink 9.9:** ERIC Clearinghouse on Assessment and Evaluation
_____ ❏ **Weblink 9.10:** CRESST
_____ ❏ **Applications and Interactivities:** Observations and Interviews
_____ ❏ **Applications and Interactivities:** Professional Portfolio
_____ ❏ **PostTest with Answers**

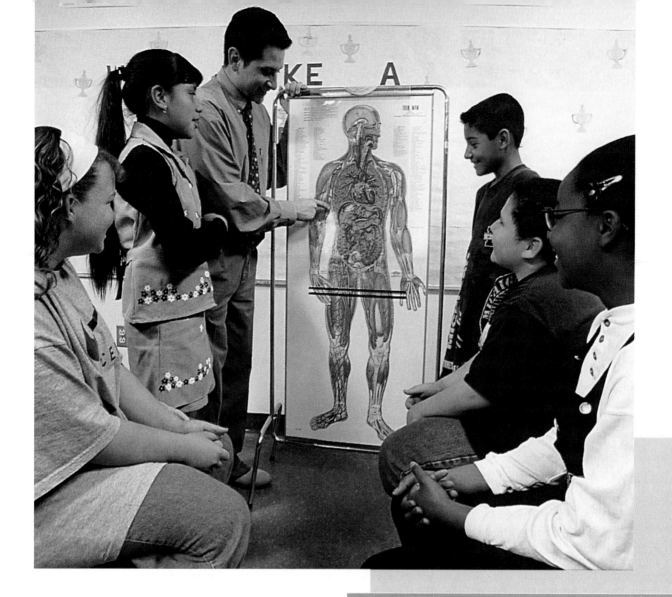

10

Developing and Implementing the Curriculum

An educator is entrusted with the most serious work that confronts humankind: the development of curricula that enable new generations to contribute to the growth of human beings and society.

—William H. Schubert
Curriculum: Perspective, Paradigm, and Possibility

1. What is taught in schools?

2. How is the school curriculum developed?

3. What reform efforts have affected the curriculum?

4. What are some current subject-area trends?

As a beginning teacher, you are attending your school's open house held one evening during the early fall. From 7:30 to 9:00, teachers stay in their classrooms and visit with parents as they drop by. Several parents have already visited your classroom and heard you explain your curriculum. Judging by their comments and questions, you think they appear to be pleased with what their children are learning.

AUDIO

Audio Clip 10.1

Shortly before 9:00, the parents of one of your students enter the room. After greeting them, you start to outline the goals and objectives of your curriculum. They listen attentively; the father even jots down a few notes on the cover of the open house program he was given at the orientation session in the auditorium.

"My curriculum is organized around an integrated, thematic approach," you say. "Each theme addresses a key concept—how animals have influenced the lives of human beings on earth, for example. As kids explore each theme, they learn relevant skills from areas such as language, reading, mathematics, science, art, and music."

To illustrate the thematic approach, you direct the parents' attention to a nearby bulletin board display titled "How Do Animals Influence Our

Lives?" The bulletin board features children's drawings that are clustered into categories such as "Companionship," "Transportation," "Food," "Work," and "Recreation."

After a brief pause, you continue. "Overall, one of the main goals of my curriculum is for students to go beyond the basics. I want them to know how to use the material they learn, how to solve problems. The curriculum should be a unified whole, rather than separate, disconnected parts."

At this point, your student's mother says, "I'm not sure I agree. The purpose of the curriculum should be to learn the basics. We want our child to do well on the state's test of basic skills. If the curriculum is organized around themes, how can we be sure the kids master the basics?"

"Right," her husband says. "If kids don't do well on the test, they're less likely to continue their education. To focus on anything other than the basics is to emphasize needless frills. That may sound harsh, but that's the way I feel."

How do you justify your curriculum to these parents?

Name _____ Date _____

For each question, circle the letter of the answer you believe is correct. Then read the chapter to learn more about these topics.

10.1 Concerning the push to move schools in the United States "back to the basics," John Goodlad reports that
A. Nonessential courses have assumed curricular dominance.
B. English/language arts and mathematics are especially underemphasized.
C. Far too little emphasis is placed on core academic subjects in today's schools.
D. Developing reading, writing, and arithmetical operations pervades instruction.

10.2 Across all aspects of school curriculum, which academic area has held the most insecure position?
A. Language arts.
B. Social studies.
C. Mathematics.
D. Arts.

10.3 All of the following are true of students who have studied the arts *except*
A. Early exposure to the arts can help "wire" children's brains for successful learning.
B. Students who study the arts for four years or more tend to earn higher math scores than others.
C. Students who study the arts for four years or more tend to earn higher verbal scores on the SAT.
D. Students who study the arts for four years or more tend to do less well in "academic" subjects.

10.4 The authors' definition of curriculum is
A. All the educational experiences with the exception of the extracurricular program.
B. The experiences, both planned and unplanned, that affect the education and growth of the child.
C. The academic offerings of the school.
D. All the experiences in a child's life.

10.5 The curriculum that a school intends to teach students is called the
A. Functional curriculum.
B. Implicit curriculum.
C. Null curriculum.
D. Explicit curriculum.

10.6 Sophie is captain of the volleyball team, president of the student council, and plays trombone for the school band. According to educational research, it is more likely that Sophie
A. Has a positive self-concept.
B. Is an "A" student.
C. Comes from a low socioeconomic background.
D. Is an overachiever.

10.7 In the United States, most school curricula emphasize
A. Higher order thinking skills.
B. Problem solving skills.
C. Functional skills.
D. Reading, writing, and arithmetic.

10.8 Mr. Chen, a high school teacher, is chairperson of the Curriculum Development Committee in Math. His focus is on providing the facts, laws, and principles of math. He will most likely be advocating
A. A student-centered curriculum.
B. An integrated curriculum.
C. A college curriculum.
D. A subject-centered curriculum.

10.9 All of the following are examples of factors that influence curricular decisions except
A. Community pressures.
B. Social issues.
C. Salary level of teachers.
D. Test results of students.

10.10 The philosophy that students should be involved in activities that parallel those found in society characterizes the
A. Core curriculum.
B. Inquiry-based curriculum.
C. Progressive curriculum.
D. Relevancy-based curriculum.

Answers are available on the FlexChoice website at www.ablongman.com/parkayflex.

Think back to your experiences as a student at the elementary, middle, junior, and secondary schools you attended. What things did you learn? Certainly, the curriculum you experienced included reading, computation, penmanship, spelling, geography, and history. In addition to these topics, though, did you learn something about cooperation, competition, stress, football, video games, computers, popularity, and the opposite sex? Or, perhaps, did you learn to love chemistry and to hate English grammar?

What Is Taught in Schools?

The countless things you learned in school make up the curriculum that you experienced. Curriculum theorists and researchers have suggested several different definitions for **curriculum,** with no one definition universally accepted. Here are some definitions in current use.

1. A course of study, derived from the Latin *currere,* meaning "to run a course"
2. Course content, the information or knowledge that students are to learn
3. Planned learning experiences
4. Intended learning outcomes, the *results* of instruction as distinguished from the *means* (activities, materials, etc.) of instruction
5. All the experiences that students have while at school

No one of these five is in any sense the "right" definition. The way we define curriculum depends on our purposes and the situation we find ourselves in. If, for example, we were advising a high school student on the courses he or she needed to take in order to prepare for college, our operational definition of curriculum would most likely be "a course of study." However, if we were interviewing sixth-grade students for their views on the K–6 elementary school they had just graduated from, we would probably want to view curriculum as "all the experiences that students have while at school." Let us posit an additional definition of curriculum: *Curriculum refers to the experiences, both planned and unplanned, that enhance (and sometimes impede) the education and growth of students.*

Kinds of Curriculum

Elliot Eisner, a noted educational researcher, has said that "schools teach much more—and much less—than they intend to teach. Although much of what is taught is explicit and public, a great deal is not" (1994, 87). For this reason, we need to look at the four curricula that all students experience. The more we understand these curricula and how they influence students, the better we will be able to develop educational programs that do, in fact, educate.

Explicit Curriculum   The explicit, or overt, curriculum refers to what a school intends to teach students. This curriculum is made up of several components: (1) the goals, aims, and learning objectives the school has for all students, (2) the actual courses that make up each student's course of study, and (3) the specific knowledge, skills, and attitudes that teachers want students to acquire. If we asked a principal to describe the educational program at his or her school, our inquiry would be in reference to the explicit curriculum. Similarly, if we asked a teacher to describe what he or she wished to accomplish with a particular class, we would be given a description of the explicit curriculum.

In short, the **explicit curriculum** represents the publicly announced expectations the school has for its students. These expectations range from learning how to read, write, and compute to learning to appreciate music, art, and cultures other than one's own. In most instances, the explicit curriculum takes the form of written plans or guides for the education of students. Examples of such written documents are course descriptions, curriculum guides that set forth the goals and learning objectives for a school or district, texts and other commercially prepared learning materials, and teachers' lesson plans. Through the instructional program of a school, then, these curricular materials are brought to life.

Hidden Curriculum   The hidden, or implicit, curriculum refers to the behaviors, attitudes, and knowledge the culture of the school unintentionally teaches students (Parkay and Hass 2000). In addition, the **hidden curriculum** addresses "aspects of schooling that are recognized only occasionally and remain largely unexamined, particularly the schools' pedagogical, organizational, and social environments, and their interrelations" (Cornbleth 1990, 48). For example, one study of an "effective" inner-city elementary school revealed that students had "learned" that grades depended as much or more on their attitudes and behavior as on their academic ability. When asked "How do you earn grades for your report card?" the responses of fifth- and sixth-grade students included the following (Felsenthal 1982, 10):

> If you want to earn good grades you got to hand in your work on time. You got to sit up straight and don't talk to no one.

> You have to be quiet, be a nice student and know how to write and read and stuff.

As a result of the hidden curriculum of schools, students learn more than their teachers imagine. Although teachers cannot directly control what students learn through the hidden curriculum, they can increase the likelihood that what it teaches will be positive. By allowing students to help determine the content of the explicit curriculum, by inviting them to help establish classroom rules, and by providing them with challenges appropriate for their stage of development, teachers can ensure that the outcomes of the hidden curriculum are more positive than negative.

Null Curriculum   Discussing a curriculum that cannot be observed directly is like talking about dark matter or black holes, unseen phenomena in the universe whose existence must be inferred because their incredible denseness and gravitational fields do not allow light to escape. In much the same way, we can consider the curriculum that we *do not* find in the schools; it may be as important as what we *do* find. Elliot Eisner has labeled the intellectual processes and content that schools do not teach "the **null curriculum**—the options students are not afforded, the perspectives they may never know about, much less be able to use, the concepts and skills that are not a part of their intellectual repertoire" (1994, 106–7).

For example, the kind of thinking that schools foster among students is largely based on manipulations of words and numbers. Thinking that is imaginative, subjective, and poetic is stressed only incidentally. Also, students are seldom taught anthropology, sociology, psychology, law, economics, filmmaking, or architecture.

Eisner points out that "certain subject matters have been traditionally taught in schools not because of a careful analysis of the range of other alternatives that could be offered but rather because they have traditionally been taught. We teach what we teach largely out of habit, and in the process neglect areas of study that could prove to be exceedingly useful to students" (1994, 103).

Professional Reflection — Identifying kinds of curriculum

Extracurricular/Cocurricular Programs   The curriculum includes school-sponsored activities—music, drama, special interest clubs, sports, student government, and honor societies, to name a few—that students may pursue in addition to their studies in academic subject areas. When such activities are perceived as additions to the academic curriculum, they are termed *extracurricular*. When these activities are seen as having important educational goals—and not merely as extras added to the academic curriculum—they are termed *cocurricular*. To reflect the fact that these two labels are commonly used for the same activities, we use the term *extracurricular/cocurricular* activities.

Though **extracurricular/cocurricular programs** are most extensive on the secondary level, many schools at the elementary, middle, and junior high levels also provide their students with a broad assortment of extracurricular/cocurricular activities. For those students who choose to participate, such activities provide an opportunity to use social and academic skills in many different contexts.

Research shows that the larger a school is, the less likely it is that a student will take part in extracurricular/cocurricular activities. At the same time, those who do participate tend to have higher self-concepts than those who do not (Coladarci and Cobb 1996). The actual effects that extracurricular/cocurricular activities have on students' development, however, are not entirely clear. Although it is known that students who participate in extracurricular/cocurricular activities tend to receive higher grades than nonparticipants and are more frequently identified as gifted (Jordan and Nettles 1999; Modi, Konstantopoulos, and Hedges 1998; Gerber 1996), it is not known whether participation influences achievement, or whether achievement influences participation. However, research has shown that participation has a positive influence on the decision to remain in school (Mahoney and Cairns 1997), educational aspirations (Modi, Konstantopoulos, and Hedges 1998), and the occupation one aspires to and eventually attains (Holland and Andre 1987; Brown, Kohrs, and Lanzamo 1991). Furthermore, students themselves tend to identify extracurricular/cocurricular activities as a high point in their school careers.

It is also clear that students who might benefit the most from participating in extracurricular/cocurricular activities—those below the norm in academic achievement and students at risk—tend not to participate. In addition, students from low socioeconomic backgrounds participate less often. Table 10.1, for example, indicates that low-socioeconomic-status tenth-grade students had a lower rate of participation in eight out of nine areas of extracurricular/cocurricular activities.

Table 10.1

Curriculum Content

Table 10.2

The nation's schools teach what the larger society believes young people should learn. For example, Table 10.2, based on a survey by Public Agenda, shows several curriculum content areas that the public believes are "absolutely essential." Like the parents featured in this chapter's opening scenario, the public believes that the "basics" of reading, writing, and mathematics plus the development of good work habits should be the heart of the curriculum. Additional support for these curriculum goals comes from employers and college professors who deal with students after they graduate from high school. For example, when asked whether public school graduates have the skills needed to succeed "in the work world" or "in college," only 32 percent of employers surveyed and 39 percent of professors believe students have the skills (Public Agenda 1999). The following comments by two parents who participated in an earlier Public Agenda survey typify the concern many people have about the position of the basic skills in the school curriculum:

> Education is becoming more about social issues as opposed to reading, writing, and arithmetic. Some of it's fine, but I think schools need to stay with the basics. . . . You can't get by in the business world on social issues if you can't add and subtract.

> They all talk all the time about this "whole child educational process". . . . It's not your business to make a "whole child." Your business is to teach these students how to read, how to write, and give them the basic skills to balance their checkbook. It's not to make new Emersons out of them (Johnson and Immerwahr 1994, 13)

Although much of the public is concerned about a perceived lack of emphasis on the basics in the curriculum, evidence suggests that it may be incorrect to assume that schools need to "get *back* to the basics." As John Goodlad noted of the data reported in *A Place Called School*, a landmark study of 129 elementary, 362 junior high, and 525 senior high classrooms around the country, schools teach the basic skills with remarkable uniformity:

> Our data, whatever the source, reveal not only the curricular dominance of English/language arts and mathematics but also the consistent and repetitive attention to basic facts and skills. Developing "the ability to read, write, and handle basic arithmetical operations" pervades instruction from the first through the ninth grades and the lower tracks of courses beyond (Goodlad 1983a, 14–15).

How Is the School Curriculum Developed?

Although there is no easy-to-follow set of procedures for developing curriculum, Ralph Tyler has provided four fundamental questions that must be answered in developing any curriculum or plan of instruction. These four questions, known as the **Tyler rationale**, are as follows (Tyler 1949, 1):

1. What educational purposes should the school seek to attain?
2. What educational experiences can be provided that are likely to attain these purposes?
3. How can these educational experiences be effectively organized?
4. How can we determine whether these purposes are being attained?

Tyler's classic work has been used by a great number of school systems to bring some degree of order and focus to the curriculum development process.

The Focus of Curriculum Planning

In discussing curriculum development, it is helpful to clarify the focus of curriculum planning. Figure 10.1 illustrates two dimensions of this planning process: the target and the time orientation. The target of curriculum planning may be at the macro- or the

Figure 10.1

micro-level. At the macro-level, decisions about the content of the curriculum apply to large groups of students. The national goals for education and state-level curriculum guidelines are examples of macro-level curricular decisions. At the micro-level, curriculum decisions are made that apply to groups of students in a particular school or classroom. To some extent, all teachers are micro-level curriculum developers—that is, they make numerous decisions about the curricular experiences they provide students in their classrooms.

Another dimension of curriculum planning is the time orientation—does the planning focus on the present or the future? In addition to the national goals and state-level curriculum guidelines, the semester-long or monthly plans or unit plans that teachers make are examples of future-oriented curriculum planning. Present-oriented curriculum planning usually occurs at the classroom level and is influenced by the unique needs of specific groups of students. The daily or weekly curriculum decisions and lesson plans that teachers make are examples of present-oriented curriculum planning.

Student-Centered versus Subject-Centered Curricula

A key concern in curriculum development is whether greater emphasis should be given to the requirements of the subject area or to the needs of the students. It is helpful to imagine where a school curriculum might be placed on the following continuum.

Student-Centered Curriculum ←————→ Subject-Centered Curriculum

Although no course is entirely subject- or student-centered, curricula vary considerably in the degree to which they emphasize one or the other. The **subject-centered curriculum** places primary emphasis on the logical order of the discipline students are to study. The teacher of such a curriculum is a subject-matter expert and is primarily concerned with helping students understand the facts, laws, and principles of the discipline. Subject-centered curricula are more typical of high school education.

Some teachers develop curricula that reflect greater concern for students and their needs. Though teachers of the **student-centered curriculum** also teach content, they emphasize the growth and development of students. This emphasis is generally more typical of elementary school curricula.

The Integrated Curriculum

The opening scenario for this chapter is based on the integrated approach to developing the school curriculum. Used most frequently with elementary-age students, the **integrated curriculum** draws from several different subject areas and focuses on a theme or concept rather than on a single subject. Early childhood education expert Suzanne Krogh (2000, 340) suggests that an integrated approach based on thematic "webs" is a more "natural" way for children to learn:

> [Children] do not naturally learn through isolating specific subjects. These have been determined by adult definition. Children's natural learning is more likely to take place across a theme of interest: building a fort, exploring a sandbox, interacting with the first snow of winter. Teachers can create a good deal of their curriculum by building webs made up of these themes of interest. Done with

knowledge and care, a web can be created that incorporates most, or even all, of the required and desired curriculum.

According to a national survey of elementary teachers' views on the integrated curriculum, 89 percent believed that integration was the "most effective" way to present the curriculum. As one teacher who was surveyed said, "I'm not interested in presenting isolated facts which children seem to memorize and forget. I want to help students put each lesson in perspective" (Boyer 1995, 83). In *The Basic School: A Community for Learning*, the late Ernest Boyer suggested that the elementary school curriculum should be integrated according to eight themes or "core commonalities": The Life Cycle, The Use of Symbols, Membership in Groups, A Sense of Time and Space, Response to the Aesthetic, Connections to Nature, Producing and Consuming, and Living with Purpose (Boyer 1995).

Who Plans the Curriculum?

Slightly more than 34 percent of public school teachers in the country believe they have "a good deal of influence" over establishing the curriculum (National Center for Education Statistics 1998a). However, Figure 10.2, based on Boyer's survey of elementary teachers, shows that most teachers believe "groups of teachers working together" should control the curriculum.

Figure 10.2

Various agencies and people outside the school are involved in curriculum planning. Textbook publishers, for example, influence what is taught because many teachers use textbooks as curriculum guides. The federal government contributes to curriculum planning by setting national education goals, and state departments of education develop both broad aims for school curricula and specific minimum competencies for students to master.

Within a given school, the curriculum-planning team and the classroom teacher plan the curriculum that students actually experience. As a teacher you will draw from a reservoir of curriculum plans prepared by others, thus playing a vital role in the curriculum-planning process. Whenever you make decisions about what material to include in your teaching, how to sequence content, and how much time to spend teaching certain material, you are planning the curriculum.

What Influences Curricular Decisions?

From the earliest colonial schools to schools of the twenty-first century, curricula have been broadly influenced by a variety of religious, political, and utilitarian agendas. Figure 10.3 illustrates the influence of community pressures, court decisions, students' life situations, testing results, national reports, teachers' professional organizations, research results, and other factors. The inner circle of the figure represents factors that have a more direct influence on curriculum development (such as students' needs and school district policies). The outer circle represents factors that are more removed from the school setting or have less obvious effects on the curriculum. Individual schools respond to all these influences differently, which further affects their curricula. Let us examine some of these influences in greater detail.

Figure 10.3

Social Issues and Changing Values Values that affect curriculum planning include prevailing educational theories and teachers' educational philosophies. In addition, curriculum planners respond to social issues and changing values in the wider society. As a result, current social concerns find their way into textbooks, teaching aids, and lesson plans. Often curriculum changes are made in the hope that changing what students learn will help solve social problems or achieve local, statewide, or national goals.

Because the United States is so culturally diverse, proposed curriculum changes also reflect divergent interests and values. This divergence then leads to controversies over curriculum content and conflicting calls for reform. Recall, for example, the discussion in Chapter 6 of legal issues surrounding the demands of some groups that Christian teachings and observances be included in the public school curricula or that materials regarded as objectionable on religious grounds be censored or banned; or the discussion in Chapter 7 of the trend for states to pass English-only laws and the controversy that erupted in California around the teaching of "ebonics" or "black English." Additional curriculum controversies have arisen over calls for the elimination of all activities or symbols that have their origins in organized religion, including even secularized or commercialized ones such as Halloween and the Easter bunny. Curriculum changes to promote greater social integration or equity among racial or ethnic groups may draw complaints of irrelevancy or reverse discrimination. Traditionalists may object to curriculum changes that reflect feminist views.

As you can imagine, consensus on many curriculum reform issues is never achieved. However, because of their public accountability, schools must consider how to respond to those issues. One survey revealed that during a one-year period, half the school districts in Florida received complaints about curriculum content. Included were complaints claiming that the schools were undermining family values, overemphasizing globalism, underemphasizing patriotism, permitting profanity and obscenity, and teaching taboo subjects such as satanism and sex (Sheuerer and Parkay 1992, 112–18). In the end, the creative and evaluative tasks of choosing and developing curriculum materials are a source of both empowerment and frustration for teachers. Budget constraints, social and legal issues, and state and local curriculum mandates often determine curriculum choices.

Textbook Publishing Textbooks greatly influence the curriculum. According to one study, "with nearly 95 percent of classroom instruction in grades K–8 and 90 percent of homework time derived from printed materials, textbooks predominate the school day" (Venezky 1992, 444). In addition, textbook publishers influence school curricula by providing teaching objectives, learning activities, tests, audiovisual aids, and other supplements to assist their customers.

Like curriculum planners, textbook authors and publishers are influenced by trends in education and by social issues. In response to criticism, for example, publishers now tend to avoid bias in terms of gender, religion, class, race, and culture. However, because the goal of business is profit, publishers are most responsive to market trends and customer preferences. They are often reluctant to risk losing sales by including subjects that are controversial or that may be offensive to their bigger customers. They may also modify textbooks to appeal to decision makers in populous states that make statewide adoptions of textbooks, such as California and Texas. About half the states have statewide adoption policies that school districts must follow in selecting textbooks. In addition, California and Texas are among several states that systematically review state-approved textbooks for accuracy. Texts with too many errors are dropped from state-approved lists, and publishers are levied fines for failing to correct errors (Manzo 1999).

Educators have criticized textbooks for inoffensiveness to the point of blandness, for artificially lowered reading levels (called "dumbing down"), and for pedagogically

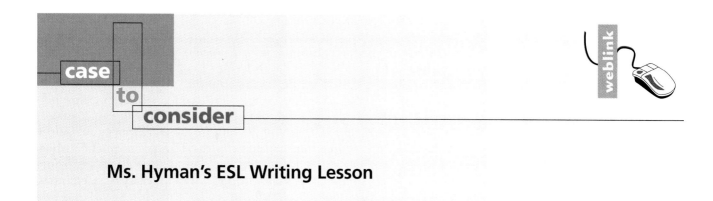

Ms. Hyman's ESL Writing Lesson

questionable gimmicks to hold students' attention. "The quality problem [with textbooks also] encompasses [f]actors such as poor writing, poor content 'coverage,' and failure to engage students in the skills needed to create the knowledge contained in a particular area of study" (Sowell 1996, 158). Although the publishing industry continually responds to such criticisms, you would be wise to follow systematic guidelines in evaluating and selecting textbooks and other curriculum materials.

What Reform Efforts Have Affected the Curriculum?

The content of the curricula in America's schools has changed frequently since the colonial period. These modifications came about as the goals of the schools were debated, additional needs of society became evident, and the characteristics of student populations shifted. The following list is a sampling of goals the schools have set for themselves at different times in our history:

■ Prepare students to carry out religious and family responsibilities
■ Provide employers with a source of literate workers
■ Desegregate society
■ Reduce crime, poverty, and injustice
■ Help our country maintain its competitive edge in the world economy
■ Provide the scientists needed to keep our country strong
■ Educate students for intelligent participation in a democracy

Forrest W. Parkay and Glen Hass (2000, 51) suggest that three interrelated "social forces" influence the school curriculum: "[An] appropriately developed school program— from preschool through the graduate level—must enhance [the student's] ability to accomplish developmental tasks in three areas: *vocation, citizenship, and self-fulfillment.*" The timeline presented in Figure 10.4 shows how school curricula have shifted in their degree of emphasis on these three demands since 1620.

Figure 10.4

Church, Nation, and School

From 1620 to 1760, the primary aim of the curriculum was to train students in religious beliefs and practices. It was only later that a distinction was made between civil and religious life. Basic skills were taught for the purpose of learning religious catechisms and reading prayers. In addition to taking courses with religious content, students also studied such practical subjects as surveying, navigation, bookkeeping, architecture, and agriculture.

From 1770 to 1860 the development of citizenship provided the curriculum's major focus. The United States had just won its independence from England, and many policymakers believed that literacy was essential to the preservation of freedom. Accordingly, students were taught history, geography, health, and physical training, as well as the basic skills of reading, writing, and computation. In 1821, the nation's first public high school was opened in Boston, and two years later the first private normal school for teachers opened in Concord, Vermont. The first English-speaking kindergarten, taught by Elizabeth Peabody, opened in Boston in 1860.

By the beginning of the Civil War, the basic skills of reading, writing, and mathematics were well established in the curriculum. Various types of schools had been incorporated into state systems, and in 1852 the first compulsory school attendance law was passed in Massachusetts. Parents in every section of the country wanted more and better opportunities for their children. Through a curriculum that stressed individual virtue, literacy, hard work, and moral development, reformers wished to improve social conditions and to provide more opportunities for the poor.

The development of citizenship continues to influence school life and school curricula. All students, for example, are required to study U.S. history and the U.S. Constitution at some time during their school career. Presidents' birthdays and national holidays are built into the school year calendar. Issues concerning civil liberties and the expression of patriotism often become educational issues, as in controversies during the last decades over treatment of the American flag and the recitation of the Pledge of Allegiance in schools.

Children and School

Vocational goals for the curriculum were most prominent from 1860 to 1920. The turn of the century brought with it many changes that profoundly influenced the curriculum. The dawning of the machine age altered the nature of industry, transportation, and communication. The growth of cities and the influx of millions of immigrants resulted in new functions for all social institutions, and home life was forever changed. As a result, curricula came to be based on vocationally oriented social and individual need rather than on subject-matter divisions. Subjects were judged by the criterion of social utility rather than by their ability to develop the intellect.

During this period, several national committees met for the purpose of deciding what should be taught in elementary and secondary schools. Initially, these committees espoused goals formed by educators at the college and private secondary school levels—that is, uniform curricula with standardized methods of instruction. Gradually, though, these appointed groups began to recommend curricula that were more flexible and based on the needs of children. This shift is seen clearly in the recommendations made by three of the more influential committees during this period: the Committee of Ten, the Committee of Fifteen, and the Commission on Reorganization of Secondary Education.

The Committee of Ten   During 1892–93, the directors of the National Education Association appropriated $2,500 for a **Committee of Ten** to hold nine conferences that focused on the following subjects in the high school curriculum: (1) Latin; (2) Greek;

(3) English; (4) other modern languages; (5) mathematics; (6) physics, astronomy, and chemistry; (7) natural history (biology, botany, and zoology); (8) history, civil government, and political science; and (9) geography (physical geography, geology, and meteorology). The group's members decided that the primary function of high schools was to take intellectually elite students and prepare them for life. Their recommendations stressed mental discipline in the humanities, languages, and science.

The Committee of Fifteen   The report of the Committee of Ten sparked such discussion that in 1893 the National Education Association appointed the **Committee of Fifteen** to examine the elementary curriculum. In keeping with the view that high schools were college preparatory institutions, the committee's report, published in 1895, called for the introduction of Latin, the modern languages, and algebra into the elementary curriculum. In addition, the curriculum was to be organized around five basic subjects: grammar, literature, arithmetic, geography, and history.

The Reorganization of Secondary Education   In 1913 the National Education Association appointed the Commission on the **Reorganization of Secondary Education.** The commission's report, *Cardinal Principles of Secondary Education,* was released in 1918 and called for a high school curriculum designed to accommodate individual differences in scholastic ability. Seven educational goals were to provide the focus for schooling at all levels: health, command of fundamental processes (reading, writing, and computation), worthy home membership, vocation, citizenship, worthy use of leisure time, and ethical character.

Standards and the Schools

From 1920 to the present, schools have become increasingly accountable for providing all students with curricular experiences based on high standards. The following comments made by Roy Romer, former governor of Colorado and a vocal national advocate for higher standards, for example, reflects the nation's concern about current standards in schools (2000, 314–15):

> Setting standards, raising expectations, and assessing student progress in a meaningful way gives students the tools they need to thrive in the twenty-first century and the tools parents and teachers need to help them. [Content] standards are a compilation of specific statements of what students should know or be able to do. They do not represent the totality of what students should learn at school. They are not curriculum. When standards are well conceptualized and written, they can focus the education system on common, explicit goals; ensure that rigorous academic content is taught by all teachers in all classrooms and raise expectations for all students.

To meet these demands for higher standards, schools have undertaken numerous curricular reforms over the years and used more sophisticated methods for measuring the educational outcomes of these reforms.

The Push for Mass Education   Since 1920, schools have been expected to provide educational opportunities for all Americans. During this period, curricula have been developed to meet the needs and differences of many diverse student groups: disabled, bilingual, gifted, delinquent, and learning-disabled students, for example. Moreover, these curricula have been used not only in public schools but also in schools that provide alternatives to public education: religious and nonsectarian private schools; night schools; boarding schools; schools without walls; continuation schools; magnet schools; and schools for students who are African American, Native American, or members of other ethnic and racial groups. According to the National Center for Education Statistics, more than 360,000 teachers taught at almost 28,000 private and/or alternative schools in 1998. And, near the end of 1999, researchers at the University of California at Berkeley and Stanford University reported that nearly one-fourth of all children, about 8 million students nationwide, attended alternatives to the nearest public school. So remarkable was the growth in alternative schools during the 1990s, that one of the researchers asserted that "Anyone who claims there is a public school monopoly out there is about 20 years behind" (Fuller et al. 1999).

The Progressive Curriculum   The concern in this country for educating all our youth has drawn much of its initial energy from the progressive education movement. During the 1920s, the Progressive Education Association reacted against the earlier emphasis on the mental disciplines and called for elementary schools to develop curricula based on the needs and interests of all students. Throughout the 1930s, progressive ideas were promoted on the secondary level as well.

Though there was no single set of beliefs that united all Progressives, there was general agreement that students should be involved in activities that parallel those found in society. Furthermore, those activities should engage students' natural interests and contribute to their self-fulfillment. With these guidelines in mind, the progressive education movement expanded the curriculum to include such topics as home economics, health, family living, citizenship, and wood shop. The spirit of the progressive education movement is expressed well in a statement made in 1926 by the Director of the School of Organic Education in Fairhope, Alabama (Johnson 1926, 350–51):

> We believe that education is life, growth; that the ends are immediate; that the end and the process are one. We believe that all children should have the fullest opportunity for self-expression, for joy, for delight, for intellectual stimulus through subject matter, but we do not believe that children should be made self-conscious or externalized by making subject matter an end. Our constant thought is not what do the children learn or do, but what are the "learning" and the "doing" doing to them. . . .

> We believe that society owes all children guidance, control, instruction, association, and inspiration—right conditions of growth—throughout the growing years until physical growth is completed. No child may know failure—all must succeed. Not "what do you know" but "what do you need," should be asked, and the nature of childhood indicates the answer.

The Eight-Year Study   One of the most ambitious projects of the progressive education movement was the **Eight-Year Study,** which ran from 1932 to 1940. During this period, thirty public and private high schools were given the opportunity to restructure their educational programs according to progressive tenets and without regard for college and university entrance requirements. Over 300 colleges and universities then agreed to accept the graduates of these schools. The aim of the study, according to its director, was "to develop students who regard education as an enduring quest for meanings rather than credit accumulation" (Aiken 1942, 23). The curricula developed by these schools emphasized problem solving, creativity, self-directed study, and more extensive counseling and guidance for students.

Ralph Tyler evaluated the Eight-Year Study by matching nearly 1,500 graduates of the experimental schools who went on to college with an equal number of college freshmen who graduated from other high schools. He found that students in the experimental group received higher grades in every subject area except foreign languages and had slightly higher overall grade point averages. Even more significant, perhaps, was the finding that the experimental group had higher performance in such areas as problem solving, inventiveness, curiosity, and motivation to achieve. Unfortunately, the Eight-Year Study failed to have any lasting impact on American education—possibly because World War II overshadowed the study's results.

The Push for Excellence   Concern with excellence in our schools ran high during the decade that spanned the late 1950s to the late 1960s. The Soviet Union's launching of the satellite Sputnik in 1957 marked the beginning of a great concern in this country over the content of the schools' curricula. Admiral Hyman G. Rickover was a leading proponent of an academically rigorous curriculum and urged the public to see that our strength as a nation was virtually linked to the quality of our educational system. He wrote in his 1959 book *Education and Freedom* (188):

> The past months have been a period of rude awakening for us. Our eyes and ears have been assaulted by the most distressing sort of news about Russia's giant strides in technology, based on the extraordinary success she has had in transforming her educational system. All but in ruins twenty-five years ago, it is today an efficient machine for producing highly competent scientists and engineers—many more than we can hope to train through our own educational system which we have so long regarded with pride and affection.
>
> We are slowly thinking our way through a thicket of bitter disappointment and humiliating truth to the realization that America's predominant educational philosophy is as hopelessly outdated today as the horse and buggy. Nothing short of a complete reorganization of American education, preceded by a revolutionary reversal of educational aims, can equip us for winning the educational race with the Russians.

Fueled by arguments like Rickover's, many curriculum reform movements were begun in the 1950s and 1960s. The federal government became involved and poured great sums of money into developing curricula in mathematics, the sciences, modern languages, and, to a lesser extent, English and history. Once again, the focus of the curriculum was on the mental disciplines and the social and psychological needs of children were secondary. Testing and ability grouping procedures were expanded in an effort to identify and to motivate academically able students.

The Inquiry-Based Curriculum   The prevailing view of what should be taught in the schools during this period was influenced significantly by Jerome Bruner's short book, *The Process of Education.* A report on a conference of scientists, scholars, and educators at Woods Hole, Massachusetts, in 1959, Bruner's book synthesized current ideas about intelligence and about how to motivate students to learn. Bruner believed that students should learn the "methods of inquiry" common to the academic disciplines. For example, in an **inquiry-based curriculum,** instead of learning isolated facts about chemistry, students would learn the principles of inquiry common to the discipline of chemistry. In short, students would learn to think like chemists; they would be able to use principles from chemistry to solve problems independently.

Bruner's ideas were used as a rationale for making the curriculum more rigorous at all levels. As he pointed out in an often-quoted statement in *The Process of Education,* "Any subject can be taught effectively in some intellectually honest form to any child at any stage of development" (1960, 33). Bruner advocated a spiral curriculum

Is raising national educational standards an effective way to improve education?

wherein children would encounter the disciplines at ever-increasing levels of complexity as they progressed through school. Thus elementary students could be taught physics in a manner that would pave the way for their learning more complex principles of physics in high school.

The Relevancy-Based Curriculum The push for a rigorous academic core curriculum was offset in the mid-1960s by a call for a **relevancy-based curriculum.** Many educators, student groups, and political activists charged that school curricula were unresponsive to social issues and significant changes in our culture. At some schools, largely high schools, students actually demonstrated against educational programs they felt were not relevant to their needs and concerns. In response to this pressure, educators began to add more courses to the curriculum, increase the number of elective and remedial courses offered, and experiment with new ways of teaching. This concern with relevancy continued until the back-to-basics movement began in the mid-1970s.

The Core Curriculum In the early 1980s, the public was reminded anew that the country's well-being depended on its system of education, and once again the schools were found lacking in excellence. Several national reports claimed that curriculum standards had eroded. The 1983 report by the National Commission on Excellence in Education asserted, for example, that secondary school curricula had become "homogenized, diluted, and diffused." And even Admiral Rickover, in his characteristically terse, hard-hitting manner, pointed out in 1983 that school curricula had become less rigorous (Rickover 1983):

> Student performance is lower than in 1957 at the time of Sputnik, when many so-called reforms were initiated. Some curricula involve expensive gimmicks, trivial courses and quick fixes of dubious value. Teachers are often poorly trained and misused on nonacademic tasks. Many students have settled for easy, so-called relevant and entertaining courses. They and their parents are deceived by grade inflation. And the lack of national standards of performance blinds everyone to how poor our education system is.

The push for excellence in the high school curriculum received a boost at the end of 1987 when U.S. Secretary of Education William J. Bennett proposed an academically rigorous **core curriculum** for all high school students. In a U.S. Department of Education booklet entitled *James Madison High School: A Curriculum for American Students,* Bennett described what such a curriculum might look like for an imaginary high school. His course of study called for four years of English consisting of four year-long literature courses; three years each of science, mathematics, and social studies; two years of foreign language; two years of physical education; and one semester each of art and music history. Twenty-five percent of his program would be available for students to use for electives.

Performance-Based Education   One approach to reforming the curriculum to ensure that all students learn and perform at higher levels is known as **performance-based** or **outcome-based education.** The performance-based approach focuses on assessing students' mastery of a set of rigorous learning goals or outcomes. Opponents to performance-based education have expressed concern about the content of the outcomes, who determines them, and how they will be assessed. By 2000, Kentucky, Oregon, Connecticut, and Washington were among the states that had mandated outcomes, while other states had developed outcomes as guidelines for the curriculum. Washington, for example, developed Essential Academic Learning Requirements that all students must meet. The requirements are organized around four over-arching goals:

Students will be able to

1. Read with comprehension, write with skill, and communicate effectively and responsibly in a variety of ways and settings
2. Know and apply the core concepts and principles of mathematics; social, physical and life sciences; civics, history, and geography; arts; and health and fitness
3. Think analytically, logically, and creatively, and integrate experiences and knowledge to form reasoned judgments and solve problems
4. Understand the importance of work and how performance, effort and decisions directly affect future career and educational opportunities

Assessments to measure students' mastery of the Essential Academic Learning Requirements occur at the fourth-, seventh-, and tenth-grade levels. Initially, the assessments were available for voluntary use by schools; by 2008, however, all of the assessments will be required.

What Are Some Current Subject-Area Trends?

The final section of this chapter examines briefly some of the current trends and issues regarding what is taught in elementary, middle, junior high, and high schools. See Appendix 10.1 for selected subject-area references for curriculum planning and see the Teacher's Resource Guide section "Free Curriculum Materials" on this book's website for information on obtaining free curriculum materials.

Appendix 10.1

Weblink 10.1

Reading and Writing

The importance of attaining a minimum level of literacy in our society cannot be underestimated; the language arts are the tools through which students learn in nearly all other areas of the curriculum. Most students who are deficient in reading and writing skills are at a significant disadvantage when it comes to seeking employment or additional education.

The teaching of reading at all levels should focus on acquiring basic comprehension skills and learning to appreciate literature in its various forms: novels, essays, poetry, short stories, and so on. Reading teachers, however, are currently far from united as to how these aims should be realized. Does instruction in phonics enhance reading comprehension? Is a whole-language approach to the teaching of reading superior to teaching isolated decoding and comprehension skills? Should children be taught the alphabet before learning to read? Although media coverage frequently dichotomizes the teaching of reading between the phonics approach and the whole-language approach, Cheeks, Flippo, and Lindsey (1997, 130) contend that "this polarization is more political than representative of the real issues. Those who advocate for whole language do not believe that phonics is not important. Instead they argue about how it should be presented to students."

The following comments by a first-grade teacher reflect the position that many teachers have taken regarding the "reading wars": "I don't think there is one best method of teaching reading or one best program. What I have done over my twenty-seven years is pick what I think works and incorporate it" (Smolkin 1999, 1A). The eclectic approach to teaching reading is also advocated by the International Reading Association, which stated that "there is no single method or single combination of methods that can successfully teach all children to read. Therefore, teachers must be familiar with a wide range of methods for teaching reading and a strong knowledge of the children in their care so they can create the appropriate balance of methods needed for each child" (International Reading Association 1999). As part of a trend to "deescalate" the reading wars, then, many schools that emphasized a whole-language approach during the 1990s, began to shift to a "balanced" approach at the start of the new decade (see Figure 10.5).

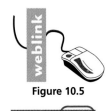

Figure 10.5

Video 10.1

Advocates of the **whole-language approach** believe that reading is part of general language development, not an isolated skill students learn apart from listening, speaking, and writing. Teachers in whole-language classrooms seldom use textbooks; instead, young students write stories and learn to read from their writing, and older students read literature that is closely related to their everyday experiences.

Literature-based reading instruction is important. The 1998 National Assessment of Educational Progress (NAEP) in reading, given to fourth- and eighth-, and twelfth-grade students. provided insight into the methods the fourth- and eight-grade teachers used to teach reading. Among the fourth-grade teachers, 57 percent used books (novels, poetry, and nonfiction) every day, while 25 percent used books once or twice a week; among the eighth-grade teachers, 53 percent used books every day, while 27 percent used them once or twice a week (National Assessment of Educational Progress 1999). Results from the 1998 NAEP showed that about 62 percent of fourth-grade students, 74 percent of eighth-grade students, and 77 percent of twelfth-grade students were at or above the "basic" level in reading.

During the last two decades, several new approaches have been incorporated into the language arts curriculum. Many English teachers have reduced the amount of time spent on grammar, electing instead to teach grammar as needed within the context of a writing program. English teachers also have generally broadened their view of literature to include more contemporary forms of writing and the literary contributions of minority or ethnic writers. Teaching in the English classroom now frequently includes such techniques as creative writing, drama, journal writing, guided fantasy exercises, and group discussions. In addition, many teachers are using computers to explore new ways to teach students reading and writing. For example, the 1998 NAEP revealed that about 42 percent of fourth-grade teachers and 20 percent of eighth grade teachers used computer software for reading instruction, and about 60 percent of both fourth-grade and eighth-grade teachers had students use computers to write compositions.

After three years of collaborative development, the International Reading Association and the National Council of Teachers of English released voluntary national standards for English-language arts in 1996. Debate over these standards continues to stimulate discussion and debate about the goals of language arts instruction.

Based on their review of literacy research, Cheeks, Flippo, and Lindsey (1997, 83–84) recommend that teachers do the following to develop children's language abilities.

1. Allow many opportunities for social imaginative play and other verbal peer interaction, which enhance language and cognitive development.
2. Develop learning activities that integrate listening, speaking, reading, and writing (oral and written language).
3. Use art, music, and drama activities to further develop language opportunities.
4. Read many books and stories to children every day.
5. Choose books and stories that you believe will be of high interest to children and will further stimulate their interest in reading books.
6. Give children opportunities to respond to the books and stories you read.
7. Reread favorite stories as often as children request them.
8. Give children opportunities to retell and/or act out stories in their own words after listening to you read them.
9. Give children many opportunities to make their own books. Children can dictate stories as the teacher writes the stories down in the children's own words. Children also can write their own books using scribble writing, pictures, and invented spellings to tell their stories in their own words.
10. Give children many opportunities to share with others the stories they write.
11. Accept "less than perfect" readings, retellings, writing, and other literacy attempts for all children.
12. Provide classroom activities and an environment that enhances the idea that literacy is part of communication and that meaning is essential for communication to take place.

Mathematics

Since it began working on the *Standards 2000* project, a set of preK–12 standards to be released in spring 2000, the National Council of Teachers of Mathematics (NCTM) has made it clear that basic mathematical skills for the new century should consist of more than computation skills. *Standards 2000* emphasizes five mathematical content standards (number and operation; patterns, functions, and algebra; geometry and spatial sense; measurement; and data analysis, statistics, and probability) that students should study with increasing breadth and depth as they move through the grades. In addition, *Standards 2000* emphasizes five mathematical processes through which students should acquire and use their mathematical knowledge: problem solving, reasoning and proof, communication, connections, and representation (National Council of Teachers of Mathematics 1998).

During the 1990s, mathematics programs, from the elementary through secondary levels, still tended to focus on the mechanical acquisition of skills. Some people believed that efforts to increase the mathematics and science competencies of students were not succeeding because textbooks were measuring low-level skills such as memorization—not the higher-order reasoning and problem-solving skills students need. For example, *A Splintered Vision: An Investigation of U.S. Science and Mathematics Education* (1996), a report by the U.S. Department of Education and the International Institute of Education, asserted that publishers included shallow analyses of many different topics to appeal to as many school districts as possible. Compared to the mathematics curricula of other nations, the report asserted, the U.S. curriculum in mathematics is "a mile wide and an inch deep." More recently, the American Association for the

Table 10.3

Advancement of Science conducted a rigorous analysis of thirteen middle school mathematics textbooks and found nine to be "unsatisfactory"; moreover, the four "satisfactory" texts were not widely used (American Association for the Advancement of Science 1999). Table 10.3 presents the "good news" and "bad news" about middle-level mathematics texts.

What is needed is **problem-centered learning,** in which students work in small groups on problems that have many or open-ended solutions. Rather than memorizing facts, working on sets of problems in textbooks, and competing against their classmates, students discover concepts, solve problems similar to those they will encounter in life, and learn to cooperate in small groups. For example, one mathematics-reform group developed a curriculum unit on testing blood for diseases that asks students to use quadratic and cubic equations to decide when to pool samples of blood rather than test each sample individually (Viadero 1996, 33). The use of manipulative materials such as Cuisinnaire rods, balance beams, counting sticks, and measuring scales also has positive effects on students' achievement in mathematics. For instance, Washington State University researcher David Slavit (1998, 280) found that "combining hands-on, visually based activities with mathematical discussions [can increase] students' structural understanding of the geometric concepts of similarity and congruence. Observing students perform these activities confirmed . . . the educational importance of 'doing' mathematics."

Science and Technology

Perhaps more than any other area of the curriculum, the teaching of science in the United States has come under increasingly critical scrutiny. On the elementary level, the science curriculum consists of assorted science-related topics: animals, plants, seasons, light, sound, heat, weather, magnets, the stars and planets, basic electricity, nutrition, oceanography, and so on. These topics are often restudied in greater depth at the middle or junior high level in courses variously titled Earth Science, General Science, Physical Science, or Life Science. At the high school level, students typically may

In what ways might these students be meeting curriculum goals of the National Assessment of Educational Progress in Science?

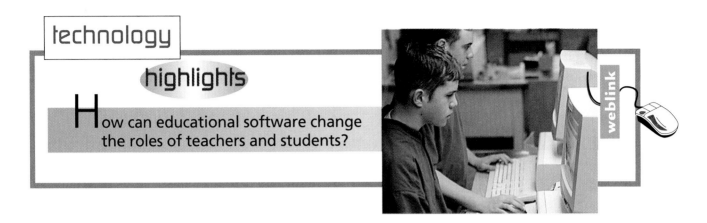

technology

highlights

How can educational software change the roles of teachers and students?

select from only a limited number of basic science courses: Biology, Chemistry, Physical Science, Anatomy and Physiology, and Physics. Many high schools do, however, distinguish between science courses that are applied (for the noncollege-bound) and those that are academic.

Several leading science educators and national committees have recommended changes in the science curriculum. Nearly all stress the need for students to learn more science and to acquire scientific knowledge, skills, and processes through an inquiry, discovery, or problem-centered method. The teacher's primary role is to guide students in their search for knowledge rather than to act solely as a source of information and/or right answers.

To assess students' achievement in science, for example, the 1996 National Assessment of Educational Progress (NAEP) in Science included a "Knowing and Doing Science" dimension that focused on the following goals:

- Students should acquire a rich collection of scientific information that will enable them to move from simply being able to provide reasonable interpretations of observations to providing explanations and predictions.
- Appropriate to their age and grade level, students will be assessed on their ability to acquire new information, plan appropriate investigations, use a variety of scientific tools, and communicate the results of their investigations.
- By grade 12, students should be able to discuss larger science- and technology-linked problems not directly related to their immediate experience. Examples include waste disposal, energy uses, air quality, water pollution, noise abatement, and the trade-offs between the benefits and adverse consequences of various technologies (National Assessment of Educational Progress 1996).

Similarly, the American Association for the Advancement of Science issued a set of "benchmarks" based on Project 2061 (2061 refers to the year Halley's comet returns). The Association recommended (1) integrating science and mathematics with other disciplines, (2) preparing students to become inquirers and critical thinkers rather than sources of right answers, and (3) focusing on the contributions science can make to current social issues—population growth, environmental pollution, waste disposal, energy, and birth control. The Association's *Atlas of Science Literacy: Mapping K–12 Learning Goals* illustrates the connections among the benchmarks through the use of "strand maps" in nine areas: seasons, gravity, water cycle, changes in matter, energy, methods in science, proportional reasoning, mental health, and feedback and control (Association for the Advancement of Science 2000). Figure 10.6 presents a strand map for gravity.

Figure 10.6

Social Studies

Goals for the social studies lack the precision that we find in other subject areas. Consider, for example, Charles Beard's comment in 1938 that the social studies aim at the "creation of rich and many-sided personalities, equipped with practical knowledge and inspired by ideals so that they can make their way and fulfill their mission in a changing society which is part of a world complex" (1938, 179). Or the current position of the National Council for the Social Studies (NCSS) that the aim of the social studies is to "teach students the content knowledge, intellectual skills, and civic values necessary for fulfilling the duties of citizenship in a participatory democracy."

Or finally, the following ten "strands" from the NCSS's (1994) *Expectations of Excellence: Curriculum Standards for Social Studies:*

1. Culture and cultural diversity
2. Human beings' views of themselves over time
3. People, places, and environments
4. Individual development and identity
5. Interactions among individuals, groups, and institutions
6. How structures of power, authority, and governance are changed
7. The production, distribution, and consumption of goods and services
8. Relationships among science, technology, and society
9. Global interdependence
10. Citizenship in a democratic society

The content of traditional social studies courses has remained comparatively unchanged during the last decade. Trends include fewer offerings in ancient history and civics and more offerings in psychology, economics, world cultures, and marriage and the family. Experimental courses or units in subjects such as African American studies, Latino and Hispanic culture, and women's history have been criticized variously as gratuitous, distorting, misrepresentative, ethnocentric, or defamatory. As you read in Chapter 7, the development of a truly multicultural curriculum is a subject of debate. In spite of such debate, however, a Public Agenda survey study of native-born and foreign-born parents' beliefs on whether a set of "American values" should be taught in the schools concluded that

> [There is] a clear-eyed patriotism among parents of all backgrounds; a deep belief that the United States is a unique nation, while acknowledging its faults. Parents want the schools to face those faults, but not to dwell on them—the parents we surveyed want history taught with fairness to all groups, but recoil from strategies that they feared might encourage divisiveness (Public Agenda 1998).

The National Center for History in the Schools at UCLA became embroiled in controversy in 1994 when it issued a set of voluntary U.S. and world history standards. The Council for Basic Education and other groups believed that the standards' authors were overly concerned about including the stories of minorities and women and the discrimination they experienced, with the result that they omitted significant historical figures and positive features of the United States and the West. Others complained that the new standards were "politically correct" to the extent that they contained an anti-Western bias. With input from two independent, bipartisan national review panels appointed by the Council for Basic Education; 33 national education organizations; and more than 1,000 educators, the National Center for History rewrote the standards and released the revised edition in 1996 with endorsements from several groups that had criticized the previous standards.

Foreign Languages

As we become increasingly aware of our interconnectedness with other nations, the small number of students who study foreign languages at the elementary through secondary levels is alarming. Support for foreign languages increased briefly immediately following Russia's launching of Sputnik in 1957, but foreign language enrollments declined dramatically during the 1960s and 1970s.

Audio Clip 10.2

Currently, about 40 percent of high school students enroll in a foreign language course (National Center for Education Statistics 1999), though the majority enroll in one of only three languages: Spanish, French, or German. Only a few schools in the country offer a course in the world's first and third most commonly spoken languages—Mandarin and Hindi. To enhance foreign language instruction in the United States in an era of expanding global interdependence, several states have developed guidelines for foreign language study, and government and private groups are working cooperatively with foreign language organizations to promote the need for foreign language study.

In *Standards for Foreign Language Learning: Preparing for the 21st Century*, the American Council on the Teaching of Foreign Languages (1996) asserted that:

> Language and communication are at the heart of the human experience. The United States must educate students who are linguistically and culturally equipped to communicate successfully in a pluralistic American society and abroad. This imperative envisions a future in which ALL students will develop and maintain proficiency in English and at least one other language, modern or classical. Children who come to school from non-English backgrounds should also have opportunities to develop further proficiencies in their first language.

To reach this goal, the Council recommended that foreign language instruction focus on the following "five C's of foreign language education":

Communication: Communicate in languages other than English
Cultures: Gain knowledge and understanding of other cultures
Connections: Connect with other disciplines and acquire information
Comparisons: Develop insight into the nature of language and culture
Communities: Participate in multilingual communities at home and around the world (American Council on the Teaching of Foreign Languages 1996)

Rarely are students introduced to foreign language study at the optimal time for learning a second language—as early as second grade. The first year of a foreign language, usually Spanish or French, is sometimes offered at the middle school or junior high school level. Students typically study the first part of Spanish I, for example, in the sixth or seventh grade and complete the course next year. As high school freshmen, then, they are ready for Spanish II.

Some schools have broadened their foreign language offerings to include such languages as Russian, Japanese, and Chinese. At a few schools, foreign language study has even become a central part of the curriculum. La Salle Language Academy in Chicago, for example, provides its K–8 students daily instruction in French, Spanish, Italian, or German. In addition, parents are encouraged to take special morning or evening language classes, and seventh- and eighth-grade students may participate in a foreign-exchange program.

The Arts

More than any other area of the curriculum, the arts have held an insecure position. When schools have faced budgetary cutbacks or pressure to raise scores on basic skills

Audio Clip 10.3

tests, a cost-conscious public has often considered the elimination of music and art. Near the end of the 1990s, however, the position of the arts in the curriculum seemed more secure. For example, in 1998 the White House held a special event, "Recognizing the Power of the Arts in Education," and the national *Arts Report Card* was published, asserting that "As a means of encountering the world around us, the arts offer a unique combination of intellectual, emotional, imaginative, and physical experiences. The arts as a means of expression are especially important in the context of current educational reform." In addition, "hard" evidence on the importance of the arts began to appear in the media, academic journals, and various national reports. *Arts Education: Basic to Learning,* a report by the Northwest Regional Educational Laboratory, pointed out that:

- In 1995 College Board testing, students who studied the arts for at least four years score 59 points higher on the verbal portion of the SAT, and 44 points higher on math, than students with no experience or coursework in the arts.
- According to a 1997 report from the Department of Education, "Children naturally sing, dance, draw, and role-play in an effort to understand the world around them and communicate their thoughts about it. A growing body of evidence demonstrates that when their caretakers engage them in these activities early in life on a regular basis, they are helping to wire the children's brains for successful learning."
- In studies at [the] University of California at Irvine, IQ scores go up among college students who listen to classical recordings immediately before testing—a phenomenon nicknamed the "Mozart Effect."
- Arts education programs are related to safer and more orderly school environments.
- Schools with strong arts programs report better attendance, increased graduation rates, improved multicultural understanding, greater community support, invigorated faculty, and the development of higher-order thinking skills, creativity, and problem-solving ability among students.
- The arts serve students with special needs, including those who are in danger of falling through the cracks of the educational system and allow success "for people who have been defined as failures" (Northwest Regional Educational Laboratory, 1999, 5).

Typically, elementary art and music are limited to one period a week, and this instruction is given either by regular teachers or by special teachers who travel from school to school. In addition, most elementary students have occasional opportunities to use crayons, watercolors, clay, and other art materials as they learn in other subject areas. And, from time to time, many children even have the opportunity to experience dance, puppetry, role-playing, pantomime, and crafts.

At the middle and junior high level, instruction in art and music becomes more structured, as well as more voluntary. Students may choose from band, chorus, arts, and crafts. At the high school level, art and music are usually offered as electives. Depending on the school's resources, however, students frequently have a wide assortment of classes to choose from: jazz band, glee club, band, orchestra, drama, chorus, photography, sculpture, ceramics, and filmmaking, to name a few. In addition, middle school and high school students may receive instruction in practical arts, such as sewing, cooking, woodworking and metalworking, automotive shop, print shop, and courses teaching agricultural knowledge and skills. A noteworthy trend is for students of both sexes to take courses in all the practical arts rather than follow traditional sex-role stereotypes; that is, you increasingly find boys and girls both in the kitchen and in the garage.

Art education in U.S. schools began to receive considerable attention when the Getty Education Center for the Arts, funded by the J. Paul Getty Trust, began to call for a "discipline-based" approach to art education. **Discipline-based art programs** emphasize art-making, art criticism, art history, and aesthetics. The Getty Institute has also spearheaded five major efforts to influence the quality of art education in the schools:

- Public advocacy for the value of art in education
- Professional development programs for school administrators and teachers
- Development of the theoretical bases of discipline-based art education
- Development of model programs to demonstrate discipline-based art education in the classroom
- Development of discipline-based curricula

In 1996, the Getty Institute and the College Board launched "The Role of the Arts in Unifying the High School Curriculum," a five-year research and development project to study how the arts can unify the school curriculum across all subject areas. Five high schools, including arts magnet and comprehensive high schools from rural and urban areas in Massachusetts, New Mexico, Texas, Maryland, and Washington, were selected to develop and test model curricula to integrate the arts with subjects such as history, literature, language, and science. Project teams at these schools will share their work with other schools over online school networks.

Physical Education

The ultimate aim of physical education is to promote physical activities that develop a desire in the individual to maintain physical fitness throughout life. More specifically, the National Association for Sport and Physical Education has stated that a physically educated student:

1. Demonstrates competency in many movement forms and proficiency in a few movement forms
2. Applies movement concepts and principles to the learning and development of motor skills
3. Exhibits a physically active lifestyle
4. Achieves and maintains a health-enhancing level of physical fitness
5. Demonstrates responsible personal and social behavior in physical activity settings
6. Demonstrates understanding and respect for differences among people in physical activity settings
7. Understands that physical activity provides opportunities for enjoyment, challenge, self-expression, and social interaction (National Association for Sport and Physical Education 1999)

In addition to their participation in activities, students in physical education programs may receive instruction in health and nutrition, sex education, and driver education.

At one time, physical education programs consisted largely of highly competitive team sports. Many children, less aggressive and competitive than their peers, did not do well in such programs and experienced a lowered sense of self-esteem. Gradually, instructors began to offer activities designed to meet the needs and abilities of all students, not just the athletically talented. In addition to traditional team sports such as football, baseball, and basketball, and individual sports such as swimming and wrestling, many students in grades K–12 may now participate in a broad array of physical activities, including aerobics, archery, badminton, dodgeball, folk and square dancing, gymnastics, handball, hockey, table tennis, golf, racquetball, shuffleboard, skating, volleyball, soccer, and yoga.

In addition to becoming more sensitive to the needs and abilities of individual students, physical education programs were required by law to provide more opportunities for female students. In 1972, Congress enacted Title IX of the Education Amendments Act, which said, "No person in the United States shall, on the basis of sex, be excluded from participation in, be denied benefits of, or be subjected to discrimination under any education or activity receiving federal financial assistance." Following Title IX, girls became much more involved in school athletic programs. The National Federation of State High School Associations, for example, found that 1.85 million young women participated in high school athletics in 1980–81 compared to only 240,000 in 1970–71. In 1999, the National Center for Education Statistics reported that more than 30 percent of female high school seniors participated in school-sponsored athletic activities.

Vocational-Technical Education

In addition to their academic (or college preparatory) curricula, many comprehensive high schools offer programs in vocational-technical education, and some high schools offer only a vocational-technical program. **Vocational-technical education** programs vary from those that actually prepare students to take jobs in business and industry after graduation to those that merely introduce students to career possibilities.

Prior to the 1990s, programs to prepare students for particular jobs or provide them with the basic skills and career awareness to enter the world of work were referred to, generally, as *vocational education*. Since vocational students in comprehensive high schools often have lower achievement levels than students in nonvocational programs, vocational education in the United States has had an "image problem." For example, "Vocational Education's Image for the 21st Century," a position paper by the ERIC Clearinghouse on Adult, Career, and Vocational Education, asserted that "Leaders of the new school reform movement do not give it [vocational education] high priority. They assume that it is separate from general education, has little educational value, and should be replaced by a predominantly academic curriculum. At best, vocational courses are expected to provide students who are not college bound with minimal training for low-status jobs at entry level" (Catri 1999, 1).

In response to such perceptions, many states and school districts changed the name of their vocational education systems and redesigned their curricula during the 1990s. Also, the major professional association for vocational educators, the American Vocational Association, changed its name to the Association for Career and Technical Education in 1999. The most common reason for these changes was public image, "negative baggage" associated with the word *vocational* (Ries 1997).

In the mid 1990s, many high schools formed partnerships with the private sector and began to develop tech-prep and school-to-work programs to address current and future needs in industry. **Tech-prep programs** enable students to prepare for the world of work by spending time at local businesses and industries during their last two years in high school. Thus students acquire their vocational training in actual on-the-job settings rather than in a high school, and they learn to transfer the knowledge and skills learned at school to the job setting. Under a provision of the Carl D. Perkins Vocational and Technical Education Act which became law in 1999, some high schools have worked with community colleges and businesses to develop tech-prep programs that high school juniors and seniors complete at a community college.

School-to-work programs prepare students to enter two-year postsecondary schools or various types of postsecondary training programs. For example, the first author of this text and a colleague helped teachers at Rogers High School in Spokane, Washington, redesign the curriculum according to five "career pathways": Business and Marketing, Communications and Arts, Science and Nature, Health and Human Services, and Industry and Technology. As part of this new "real-world" curriculum, all students would select a career pathway and take courses that prepare them to pursue the pathway at the "entry," "skilled/technical," or "professional" levels after graduation. Within the Business and Marketing pathway, for example, a student at the entry level would take courses to prepare to become a cashier or salesperson; a student at the professional level would take courses appropriate for an eventual career as an accountant or business executive. In addition, students could select from pathway-appropriate opportunities for internships, summer work, and job shadowing.

As the United States continues to be concerned about its productivity compared with other nations, and as employers continue to expect schools to graduate students who have mastered the basic skills and learned how to learn, it seems likely that vocational-technical education will continue to be an important part of the school curriculum. Through school–business partnerships such as the one at Rogers High, a new definition of vocational-technical education will be forged—one based on new, rigorous standards cooperatively developed by educators and employers from various industrial sectors.

SUMMARY

What Is Taught in Schools? (p. 276)

How Is the School Curriculum Developed? (p. 279)

What Reform Efforts Have Affected the Curriculum? (p. 283)

What Are Some Current Subject-Area Trends? (p. 289)

KEY TERMS AND CONCEPTS

Go to the website for interactive flashcards.

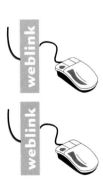

APPLICATIONS AND INTERACTIVITIES

Go to the website for interactive assignments in the following areas:

Teacher's Journal

Teacher's Database

Observations and Interviews

Professional Portfolio

Name _____ **Date** _____

For each question, write in the blank the answer you believe is correct.

10.1 The _____ curriculum refers to what a school intends to teach students.

10.2 The behaviors, attitudes, and knowledge that the culture of the school unintentionally teaches students are known as the _____ curriculum.

10.3 The intellectual processes and content that schools do not teach have been called the _____ curriculum.

10.4 Music, drama, sports, and student government are a few examples of school-sponsored activities that may be perceived as additions to the academic curriculum and are known as _____ activities or programs.

10.5 At the _____-level, curriculum decisions are made that apply to groups of students in a particular school or classroom.

10.6 A curriculum that draws from several subject areas and focuses on a theme or concept rather than on a single subject is known as an _____ curriculum.

10.7 In the seventeenth and eighteenth centuries, the primary aim of the curriculum was to train students in _____ beliefs and practices.

10.8 In the 1920s, the Progressive Education Association called on elementary-level curriculum developers to create curricula that were based on the needs and _____ of all students.

10.9 The performance-based curriculum approach focuses on assessing students' _____ of a set of rigorous learning goals or outcomes.

10.10 _____-prep programs allow students to prepare for the world of work by spending time at local businesses and industries during their last two years in high school.

Answers are available on the FlexChoice website at www.ablongman.com/parkayflex.

 www.ablongman.com/parkayflex

Name _____

Keep this checklist at your computer as a reminder to read and complete the chapter features and activities located on the FlexChoice website at www.ablongman.com/parkayflex.

**Date
Completed**

_____ ❏ **PreTest with Answers**

_____ ❏ **Audio Clip 10.1:** Thinking Over the Opening Vignette

_____ ❏ **Professional Reflection:** Identifying kinds of curriculum

_____ ❏ **Table 10.1:** Percentage of public school seniors participating in selected extracurricular activities by socioeconomic status (SES) of student and affluence of school, 1992

_____ ❏ **Table 10.2:** What content is essential for the curriculum?

_____ ❏ **Figure 10.1:** Two dimensions of curriculum planning

_____ ❏ **Figure 10.2:** Who do you think best controls the content of the school curriculum?

_____ ❏ **Figure 10.3:** Influences on the school curriculum

_____ ❏ **Case to Consider:** Ms. Hyman's ESL Writing Lesson

_____ ❏ **Figure 10.4:** A chronology of major emphasis in the school curriculum

_____ ❏ **Where Do You Stand?:** Is raising national educational standards an effective way to improve education?

_____ ❏ **Appendix 10.1:** Selected Subject-Area References for Curriculum Planning

_____ ❏ **Weblink 10.1:** Free Curriculum Materials

_____ ❏ **Figure 10.5:** A "balanced" approach to teaching reading and writing

_____ ❏ **Video 10.1:** Whole Language in Action

_____ ❏ **Table 10.3:** The "good news" and the "bad news" about middle-level mathematics textbooks

_____ ❏ **Technology Highlights:** How can educational software change the roles of teachers and students?

_____ ❏ **Figure 10.6:** Atlas of Science Literacy: Strand Map for Gravity

_____ ❏ **Audio Clip 10.2:** Learning a Foreign Language

_____ ❏ **Audio Clip 10.3:** The Value of the Arts

_____ ❏ **Summary**

_____ ❏ **Key Terms and Concepts**

_____ ❏ **Applications and Interactivities:** Teacher's Journal

_____ ❏ **Applications and Interactivities:** Teacher's Database

_____ ❏ **Applications and Interactivities:** Observations and Interviews

_____ ❏ **Applications and Interactivities:** Professional Portfolio

_____ ❏ **PostTest with Answers**

11

Teaching
with Technology

*Media and technologies [may] greatly
expand the range of teaching,
learning, and communication
modalities available to teachers and
students, but at bottom their only
value is in helping us to do other
things well—engage students deeply
in a topic, help them take more
responsibility for their learning, help
them learn to communicate clearly
about their work and their ideas.*
—Cornelia Brunner and William Tally
The New Media Literacy Handbook, 1999

1. How are educational technologies influencing schools?

2. What technologies are available for teaching?

3. How do teachers use computers and the Internet?

4. What are the effects of technology on learning?

5. Should technology be at the forefront of efforts to improve schools in the United States?

6. What barriers limit the integration of technology into schools?

At James Madison High School in New York City, tenth-grade students, mostly African American and Latino, file into a networked computer lab and find seats at large new monitors and keyboards. Outside, in the hallways, in the stairwells, and in the foyers, the school resembles a minimum-security-prison facility, with metal detectors at the doors, a police substation located off the foyer, and security guards who move through the halls breaking up small groups of students who are avoiding classes by lounging on stairs and in rest rooms. James Madison is a large school in a middle-income neighborhood, but nearly all the students are poor and working-class. Drugs and violence are a recurrent problem. The computer lab, however, is a relative haven: it is quiet here, and as students enter their names into the computer, they find that the software program greets them warmly by name, remembers exactly where they were when they left off the day before with their work, and gently guides them through well-designed exercises in biology, algebra, and American history, praising successful answers and offering patient prompting and another chance—without a hint of judgment—when they miss an answer. The teacher, who monitors the students' individual workstations from a central machine of his own, moves around the room, helping students with technical problems, finding files, and printing. The students work well and mostly silently until the bell rings fifty minutes after they entered the room. Then they

AUDIO

Audio Clip 11.1

file out to return to their regular classrooms where, despite some dedicated teachers, the crowded, noisy, and sometimes intimidating teaching conditions will ensure that they remain relatively anonymous, and will have little contact with challenging material. In the chaotic context of James Madison, technology is the vehicle of a more individualized, effective—and possibly humane—instruction than students might otherwise get.

At the Richmond Academy, a private school across town from James Madison, ninth-graders file into their social studies classroom and, before class begins, log on to one of six workstations at tables against the walls. They argue noisily about what they are finding as they unearth an archaeological site in ancient Greece. The students have been working on the computer-based archaeology simulation for about three weeks, and teams of students are each responsible for excavating one of four separate quadrants of the site. It is a welcome break for the ninth-graders, who in their other classes spend much of their time taking lecture notes and learning to parse sophisticated texts as part of their college-prep curriculum. Here they are "digging up" pottery shards, fragments of weapons, pieces of masonry, and bits of ancient texts, and trying to identify and interpret each artifact in order to fit it into their emerging picture of the site as a whole. In their research the students visit local museums, consult reference works on Greek history, art, and architecture, and ask other teachers in the school to help translate texts. Cleverly, the students' teachers have filled the site with ambiguous evidence, so that some teams find a preponderance of data suggesting the site was a temple, while others find artifacts mostly suggesting it was a battlefield. In weekly meetings the teams present their latest findings to the rest of the class, and a hot debate ensues as the amateur archaeologists struggle to reconcile the fragmentary and ambiguous data. On this day the classroom is active and noisy, yet controlled, as students take turns at the computer, graph their findings on large wall-charts, call across the room to ask if anyone has a spearhead to compare with one just found, and argue about whose final interpretation of the site will best explain the bulk of the evidence (Brunner and Tally 1999, 23–25).

Source: From *The New Media Literacy Handbook: An Educator's Guide to Bringing New Media into the Classroom,* by Cornelia Brunner and William Tally. Copyright 1999 by Cornelia Brunner and William Tally. Used by permission of Doubleday, a division of Random House, Inc.

Name _____ **Date** _____

For each question, circle the letter of the answer you believe is correct. Then read the chapter to learn more about these topics.

11.1 Critics of television assert that all of the following are accurate descriptions of the effect of too much television on learners *except*
A. Helps to dispel sexual and ethnic stereotypes.
B. May retard growth and development.
C. Promotes passivity in the young.
D. May be linked to learning disorders.

11.2 Use of Channel One in schools is controversial because
A. It promotes the sale of commercial products.
B. It will not service its products, resulting in increased costs to schools.
C. Its 20-minute news broadcasts take too much time from the school day.
D. Very few schools are willing to renew their contracts with this company.

11.3 Computer-assisted instruction (CAI) relies on computer programs that provide students with
A. A highly competitive and public learning environment.
B. Structured drill-and-practice exercises.
C. Fast-paced study programs inappropriate to slow learners.
D. In-school entertainment, e.g., games and puzzles.

11.4 All of the following are characteristics of computer simulations except
A. Model complex events.
B. Are useful only with the youngest students.
C. Provide feedback on the consequences of student decisions.
D. Require students to make critical decisions.

11.5 According to the TLC survey, the most powerful variable in predicting how likely teachers are to use the Internet is
A. How many daily lessons they must plan.
B. Access to computers at school when no computer is available at home.
C. How electronically connected teachers are at school and at home.
D. The number of teachers with whom e-mail messages are exchanged.

11.6 All of the following statements about ACOT (Apple Classrooms of Tomorrow) are true *except*
A. ACOT students went on to college at much higher rates than non-ACOT students.
B. ACOT students routinely employed inquiry and collaboration.

C. ACOT teachers worked more as mentors and less as presenters of information.
D. ACOT students scored significantly higher on tests than did non-ACOT students.

11.7 In examining the ACOT project, Schwartz and Beichner (1999) suggest that to avoid careful analysis of the ACOT findings would be to accept that technology in education is
A. Little more than the latest fad.
B. The final major revolution in teaching and learning.
C. Of little value.
D. A panacea when it is not.

11.8 According to *The Technology Literacy Challenge*, the key to integrating technology into the classroom is
A. High quality software.
B. Multimedia computers.
C. Upgrading teacher training.
D. Connection to the Internet.

11.9 As reported by Goldberg (1998), if technologies are to be introduced into schools, what must teachers do first?
A. Prepare students emotionally for their introduction to advanced technology.
B. Determine whether they wish to work with PCs or Macintosh equipment.
C. Ensure that the electrical and other infrastructure components of the school will support advanced technology.
D. Consider how technology will be used to enhance learning.

11.10 All of the following are uses of home–school communication systems *except*
A. Posting of grades on the Internet.
B. Absence and tardy parent notification.
C. Invitations to school events.
D. Teacher reminders for assignments/activities.

Answers are available on the FlexChoice website at **www.ablongman.com/parkayflex.**

In the two contrasting settings above, students are using up-to-date computers in very different ways. The teacher at James Madison High uses computers to present information to students systematically and efficiently; in effect, the computers are an *instructional delivery system*. The instructors at Richmond Academy use computers to stimulate students' higher order thinking, creativity, and problem solving as they evaluate complex, often ambiguous material; here, computers are a *catalyst for group investigation and inquiry*. Although these two examples are strikingly different, they are similar in that teachers at both schools are using the computer as a "tool" to achieve their educational goals and to create particular kinds of learning environments. The computer-based curriculum at James Madison enables the teacher to provide students with a structured, sequential way to acquire information, and the computers provide students with immediate feedback in a nonthreatening manner. Computers serve an entirely different purpose at Richmond—here, computers enable the teachers to create a rich, stimulating environment that fosters collaboration, inquiry, and decision making.

How Are Educational Technologies Influencing Schools?

Carol Gilkinson's classroom looks like those of talented teachers everywhere—lively, filled with displays of students' work, photos of field trips, and information-filled posters. A closer look, however, reveals how computers have transformed teaching and learning in her classroom. Several computers in the room allow students to communicate via the Internet with other students in Germany, Holland, Russia, and Australia. Gilkinson's students also use child-oriented "search engines" like *Yahooli*gans! and KidsLink to search for information about whales, the Brazilian rain forest, or the planet Mars on the World Wide Web. They go to "chat rooms" or "newsgroups" for children, where they can "talk" to other children around the world or participate in various global networking projects for children.

Gilkerson's classroom and the James Madison High and Richmond Academy classrooms featured in this chapter's opening scenario are representative of how recently developed technologies have transformed the learning environments in thousands of schools around the country. Moreover, the pace of change shows no signs of letting up—as one technology expert said, "We may well assume that we haven't seen anything yet. [If] present trends continue, it seems not unreasonable to expect that digital technologies will have an impact on our classrooms proportionate to that of writing and the printing press" (Withrow 1997, 4). Similarly, one of the nation's foremost futurists, Marvin Cetron, has predicted that "Computers will free educators to adopt much more sophisticated, effective, and rewarding styles of teaching. Future teachers will be facilitators, monitors, and catalysts, rather than lecturers and taskmasters" (Cetron 1997, 19–20).

Technology and the Challenge to Schools

The Internet, the World Wide Web, and related telecommunications technologies have the potential to transform teaching and learning. However, one of the education issues for the twenty-first century is how committed are teachers, administrators, policymakers, parents, and the general public to enabling students to realize the full impact that technology can have on their learning? As Howard Mehlinger (1996, 403) says, the future of schools may depend on their response to this challenge.

> The genie is out of the bottle. It is no longer necessary to learn about the American War of Independence by sitting in Mrs. Smith's classroom and hearing her version of it. There are more powerful and efficient ways to learn about the Revolutionary War, and they are all potentially under the control of the learner. Either schools will come to terms with this fact, or schools will be ignored.

Additionally, educators must develop new assessment techniques to evaluate students' learning that occurs through the use of advanced telecommunications like the Internet and the World Wide Web. The number of correct responses on homework, quizzes, and examinations will no longer suffice to measure students' learning. "If teachers want students to be able to use ditto masters, then they shouldn't spend thousands of dollars on systems that support computer-assisted instruction. If teachers want to reinforce their didactic role and their role as information providers, then they should also leave computers alone" (Morton 1996, 419).

In its *School Technology and Readiness Report,* the CEO Forum on Education and Technology (1999) called on teachers to incorporate technologies to create "new learning environments" that enable students to develop higher-order thinking skills to research, analyze, and creatively solve problems in the future. The following chart contrasts the "traditional" and "new" learning environments envisioned by the Forum.

Traditional Learning Environment	New Learning Environment
Teacher-centered instruction	→ Student-centered learning
Single-sense stimulation	→ Multisensory stimulation
Single-path progression	→ Multipath progression
Single medium	→ Multimedia
Isolated work	→ Collaborative work
Information delivery	→ Information exchange
Passive learning	→ Active/exploratory/inquiry-based learning
Factual, knowledge-based	→ Critical thinking and informed decision making
Reactive response	→ Proactive/planner action
Isolated, artificial context	→ Authentic, real-world context

When you think about your future as a teacher who will be expected to use technology to create a "new learning environment," you may find that future at once exciting and intimidating, enticing and threatening. You may ask, will I be ready to meet the challenge of integrating technologies into my teaching? In a very real sense, it is in the hands of people like you to develop new ways to use new technologies in the classrooms of tomorrow. The following Professional Reflection is designed to help you begin the process of planning for that future.

Professional Reflection   **How technically proficient are you?**

What Technologies Are Available for Teaching?

To enhance their classroom instruction, today's teachers can draw from a dazzling array of technological devices. Little more than a decade ago, the technology available to teachers who wished to use more than the chalkboard was limited to an overhead projector, a 16-mm movie projector, a tape recorder, and, in a few forward-looking school districts, television sets. Today, teachers and students use ever-more-powerful desktop and laptop computers with built-in modems, faxes, and CD-ROM players; videodisc players; camcorders; optical scanners; speech and music synthesizers; laser printers, digital cameras, and LCD projection panels. In addition, they use sophisticated software for web browsing, e-mail, word processing, desktop publishing, presentation graphics, spreadsheets, databases, and multimedia applications.

Although the array of currently available technology for the classroom is dazzling, Marvin Cetron predicts that future technologies will be even more impressive. He contends that by 2010 an "Information Appliance" (IA) "should be on the desks of most American students."

> The IA will be a computer, a fax machine, and a copier. Its 20 by 30 inch flat color screen will be half multimedia display and half picture-phone. Two buttons will set it to translate automatically among any of nine common languages, enabling users who don't speak the same language to communicate.
>
> This new one-box-does-all data center will handle all our information and communication needs. Radio, 500 television channels (many designed for the classroom), e-mail, Web access, and all forms of personal computing will come through the IA. Aimed at consumers, its controls will be simple enough for small children to use. And because it will contain more raw computing power than today's top-of-the-line PCs, it will run educational software as sophisticated as any now available for multi-user classroom systems (Cetron 1997, 21).

While the term *educational technology* is usually taken to mean computers in the classroom, many different forms of technology have influenced education in the United States. If we broadly define **educational technology** as inventions that enable teachers to reach their goals more effectively, it is clear that for some time teachers have been integrating into their classrooms many forms of educational technology, from the humble chalkboard to the overhead projector. One technology that has had a long and perhaps controversial history in education is television.

The Television Revolution

The television revolution in the United States began with great optimism. David Sarnoff, who founded NBC and introduced the first color television at the New York World's Fair in 1939, confidently predicted that television was "destined to provide greater knowledge to larger numbers of people, truer perception of the meaning of current events, more accurate appraisal of men in public life, and a broader understanding of the needs and aspirations of our fellow human beings" (Sarnoff 1940). Since that time, television has become an omnipresent feature of life in the United States, and its effects—both positive and negative—on all facets of American life are still being studied and debated, and for good cause. Children spend an estimated equivalent of two months of the year watching television. The typical child between six and eleven years of age watches about twenty-seven hours a week; and, by the time they graduate from high school, young people have watched an average of 22,000 hours of television (Shenk 1998).

Critics of television point out that it encourages passivity in the young, may be linked to increases in violence and crime, often reinforces sexual and ethnic stereotypes, retards growth and development, and may be linked to learning disorders. Psychologist Jerome Singers contends that "most [heavy-viewing] kids show lower information, lower reading recognition or readiness to reading, [and] lower reading levels; [and they] tend to show lower imaginativeness and less complex language usage" (quoted in Shenk 1998, 61). Some say that television robs children of the time they need to do homework, to read and reflect, and to build bonds with family members and others through interaction.

However, television can enhance students' learning. Excellent educational programs are aired by the Public Broadcasting Service and by some cable and other commercial networks. Television has also had a positive impact on how students are taught in schools. With the increased availability of video equipment, many schools have begun to have students produce their own television documentaries, news programs, oral histories, and dramas. Many schools have closed-circuit television systems that teachers use to prepare instructional materials for students in the district, and many districts have **distance learning networks** that use two-way, interactive telecommunications to provide enrichment instruction to students in remote areas or staff development to teachers.

Channel One   One of the most controversial uses of television in the schools is Channel One, started by Christopher Whittle in 1990. Watched daily by about eight million teenagers in more than 12,000 public and private schools in nearly every state, **Channel One** is a twelve-minute news broadcast, with two minutes of commercials for which advertisers pay as much as $200,000 per thirty-second time slot (Walsh, 1999a). On agreeing to show Channel One programs to most students on 90 percent of school days (students may opt out of viewing), schools receive the program free, including $25,000 worth of equipment (a satellite dish, two video cassette recorders, nineteen-inch color monitors mounted throughout the school, and internal wiring) that is regularly serviced at no charge. According to the Channel One Network, 99 percent of schools choose to renew their three-year contract to carry Channel One, and the Network has received numerous awards and aired more than $70 million worth of public service announcements. Moreover, the Network points out, schools are encouraged to use the equipment for other educational purposes such as viewing programs on the Learning Channel, CNN, the Discovery Channel, and C-Span; producing student news shows; conducting teacher in-service programs; and making daily announcements.

The Channel One contributions to education notwithstanding, professional associations such as the National Education Association, educational leaders, and politicians have maintained that advertisements have no place in the classroom. At a 1999 Senate committee hearing, consumer advocate Ralph Nader labeled Channel One "the most brazen marketing ploy in the history of the United States" and cited "parental neglect and the delinquency of school boards" as key reasons for the network's popularity (Walsh, 1999e). According to William Hoynes, a sociology professor at Vassar College, the primary goal of Channel One is not to inform students but to assemble a vast "teen market" and then sell high-priced advertising slots (Hoynes 1998). His analysis of Channel One programs led him to conclude that they were "fundamentally commercial" and their educational value "highly questionable."

The Computer Revolution

At Franklin Park Magnet School, a science-technology-environment-math magnet school in Lee County, Florida, students routinely experience learning via computer-based multimedia. Each morning students broadcast *FPM News* live from the school's television studio, which is controlled by a computer that allows students to produce professional-quality video shows with video fades, wipes, and special effects. Teachers have computer workstations with overhead projectors and LCD (liquid crystal display) projection panels, and their students work at individual computer workstations. According to teacher Sandi Agle, FPM students are learning essential computer skills: "In the future, these students will be using similar computer tools, not paper, to disseminate information" (Poole 1995, 354).

Although personal computers may not have transformed all schools so that all students have learning experiences like those at FPM, computers have had a significant impact on education. Like the dawn of the television era sixty years earlier, the widespread availability of personal computers has been heralded as a technological innovation that will change the teaching–learning process. As Bill Gates, founder of Microsoft, predicted in *The Road Ahead* (Gates, Myhrvold, and Rinearson 1996), "I expect education of all kinds to improve significantly within the next decade . . . information technology will empower people of all ages, both inside and outside the classroom, to learn more easily, enjoyably, and successfully than ever before."

Computers and Instruction   Since the early 1980s, the use of computers to enhance instruction has grown steadily. Two of the more common approaches are computer-assisted instruction (CAI) (sometimes called computer-*aided* instruction) and computer-managed instruction (CMI). **Computer-assisted instruction (CAI)** relies on computer programs that provide students with highly structured drill-and-practice exercises or tutorials. Research has shown CAI to be effective with at-risk students and students with disabilities because it accommodates their special needs and instruction is appropriately paced (Bialo 1989; Jones 1994; Kozma et al. 1992; Norris 1994; Signer 1991). Moreover, CAI can provide students with a more positive, supportive environment

These students, like those at Franklin Park Magnet School in Lee County, Florida, are broadcasting a live program from their school's television studio. How have the television revolution and the computer revolution changed education for the better? For the worse?

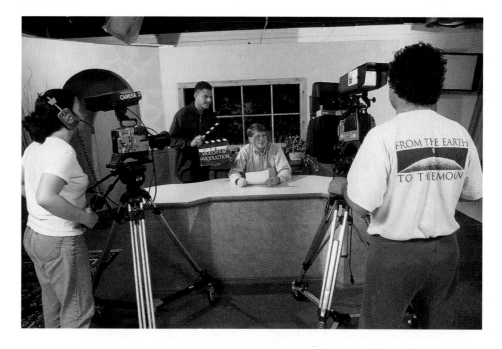

for learning; students can avoid embarrassment since their inevitable mistakes while learning are not exposed to peers. Figure 11.1 presents several additional student-centered and technology-centered advantages of CAI.

Computer-managed instruction (CMI) relies on programs that evaluate and diagnose students' needs and then, based on that assessment, guide them through the next steps in their learning. CMI also records students' progress for teachers to monitor. This chapter's opening scenario, for example, began with a glimpse of how CMI is delivered at James Madison High School. CAI and CMI can result in reduced teacher–student interactions, if the teacher interprets his or her role as primarily that of record keeper or manager. On the other hand, CAI and CMI can enhance teacher–student interactions: "Freed from the necessity of conducting routine drills and performing many management duties, the teacher has more time to be the vital human link between student and knowledge. The computer does not supplant teachers; it supports them" (Bitter and Pierson 1999, 249).

Figure 11.1

An increasingly popular approach to computer-based instruction is computer-enhanced instruction (CEI). Unlike CAI and CMI, **computer-enhanced instruction (CEI)** is less structured and more inquiry-oriented. For example, the archeological inquiries conducted by Richmond Academy students in this chapter's opening scenario illustrate CEI. Unlike CAI or CMI, teachers in CEI play a critical role in facilitating interactions between computer and student—teachers "are [essential] to the learning process, because simply seating students in front of their computers to surf the Net will not result in the same learning curve as when teachers assign well-designed projects in which students use the Net to gather information" (Kirkpatrick and Cuban 1998).

Some schools are using another inquiry-oriented approach to enhancing instruction with computers—the microcomputer-based laboratory (MBL), sometimes called CBL (computer-based laboratory). Through probes and sensors attached to computers, **microcomputer-based laboratories (MBL)** enable students to measure and graph data such as light, sound temperature, voltage, skin resistance, magnetic field, and heat flow. Students can gather data in the school laboratory or use a battery-operated interface to gather data in the field. For example, Concord Consortium, a nonprofit research and development organization dedicated to developing new ways to use technology in teaching, has developed MBL curriculum materials that enable students to learn about rain forests by using a sensor to gather local data for such variables as humidity, light, dissolved oxygen in rivers and streams, and acid rain. Students then compare local data with those obtained in an actual rain forest.

The "Magic" of Media

Personal computers have so revolutionized the instructional media available to teachers that today it is no exaggeration to refer to the "magic" of media. Carol Gilkerson, a Christa McAuliffe Educator, describes how instructional media have transformed her teaching:

> One of the chief strengths of using technology in the classroom is that it enables me to adapt my instruction to the individual needs and learning styles of the students. As computer activities can be tailored to student needs, the class becomes more student centered. CD-ROM, videodisc, and captioned instructional television present information visually and allow students to learn complex material more easily.

Some of the most exciting forms of media magic involve CD-ROMs, videodiscs, and interactive multimedia. Recent advances in computer technology have made it possible for students to become much more active in shaping their learning experiences. On a four-inch **CD-ROM,** they can access the equivalent of about 270,000 pages of text, about nine hundred 300-page books; or on a twelve-inch **videodisc** they can access the equivalent of about 54,000 photographic slides. Computer-supported **interactive multimedia** allow students to integrate information from huge text, audio, and video libraries.

Hypermedia   Systems consisting of computer, CD-ROM drive, videodisc player, video monitor, and speakers now allow students to control and present sound, video images, text, and graphics with an almost limitless array of possibilities. Students who use such hypermedia systems, the most familiar of which is the World Wide Web, can follow their curiosity, browse through enormous amounts of information, and develop creative solutions for multidimensional, real-life problem situations. On-line databases in many fields are changing the way students conduct library research, as more computerized reference works—such as directories, dictionaries, and encyclopedias—become available.

The term **hypermedia** refers to documents composed of text, audio, and visual information stored in a computer and accessed by the user in a nonlinear fashion. "Rather than reading an information space sequentially in a pre-determined order, a user of [hypermedia] explores the information space in his or her own order, usually based on his or her interests" (Schwartz and Beichner 1999, 56), with the computer used to "link" related segments of information into larger "webs" or networks. A hypermedia system is an effective learning tool because it allows students to actively construct their own learning experiences based on their interests, preferences, and learning styles.

Figure 11.2

Household water use simulator from *Exploring the Nardoo*
Source: Interactive Multimedia Learning Laboratory, Faculty of Education, University of Wollongong, Wollongong, New South Wales, Australia. Used with permission.

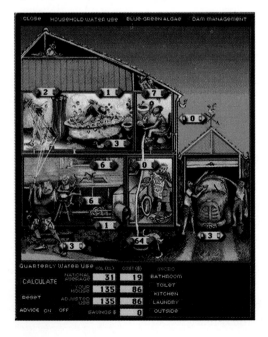

Computer Simulations   For students, computer simulations can be engaging and very motivational. Simulations model complex, multidimensional events in the real world and can range from the lemonade stand that elementary school students plan and run vicariously, practicing basic arithmetic and problem-solving skills, to a mock trial, which Harvard Law students can participate in via videodisc and computer. As learners work their way through a simulation, they make decisions at critical points, enter their decisions into the computer, and then receive feedback on the consequences of those decisions.

Currently available **computer-based simulations** provide students with contextually rich learning experiences, from visiting the great museums of the world, to exploring the bottom of the Pacific Ocean, to experiencing what it was like to be a pioneer setting out in a wagon train from St. Louis to the coast of Oregon. Figure 11.2, for example, shows a household water use simulator from *Exploring the Nardoo,* a CD-ROM program that focuses on a range of water management investigations related to the Nardoo, an imaginary river in Australia. The Nardoo program, developed by the Interactive Multimedia Learning Laboratory at the University of Wollongong in Australia, requires students to solve problems, measure, synthesize data, and communicate findings as they "conduct" research at the Water Research Centre. After students enter the number of baths, showers, toilet flushes, dish washings, car washes, and so on a hypothetical family uses per day, the simulator calculates the family's water usage and compares it with national averages. Students then implement various water-saving strategies throughout the household and rerun the simulation to determine the amount of water saved.

keepers of the
dream

Kristi Rennebohm Franz
Technology and Multicultural Educator

"...learning with the children."

Home–School Communication Systems Computer-based home–school communication systems such as the Phone Master Notification System are helping busy teachers and parents exchange information. By interfacing a computer program with its computer-based student records, Georgetown Middle School in Georgetown, Kentucky, enables teachers to use a "Talking Gradebook" to communicate students' progress to parents. Or, by using a touchtone phone and entering a teacher's room number, Georgetown students and parents can access homework assignments, test scores, and current grades. Increasingly, schools are using sophisticated **home–school communication systems** to strengthen their educational programs. Some communication systems even include a "tip line" that uses voice disguising to provide students with an anonymous, safe way to provide tips to help reduce school violence. Schools are also using home–school communication systems to disseminate the following kinds of information:

absence and tardy parent notification
invitations to school events
teacher reminders for assignments/activities
reminders to vote on bond issues
congratulatory calls

PTA/PTO information
school cancellations, early dismissals
lunch menus
bus schedules
club information

The Internet

Observers estimate that the amount of information in the world doubles every 900 days (Bitter and Pierson 1999); the **Internet,** consisting of thousands of interconnected computers around the globe, and the **World Wide Web** (the most popular "entrance" to the Internet) make available to teachers and students much of this information. As Table 11.1 shows, the size of the World Wide Web has increased exponentially since 1995. In addition, newsgroups and chat rooms on the Internet enable teachers and students to communicate with people around the world.

Newsgroups Through **newsgroups,** students can create electronic bulletin boards of their own and discuss topics of mutual interest with students at other schools, in the same community, or around the world. Messages are "posted" on the bulletin board for others to read at their convenience. When students "surf" into a newsgroup, they will find messages arranged by subject and author, with responses listed beneath the original message.

Chat rooms Students can also participate in "live" discussions held in a **chat room.** Chat rooms use Internet Relay Chat (IRC) technology and allow users to participate in live, on-line, typed discussions. In some chat rooms, students can talk to on-line experts in a wide array of fields and receive immediate responses to their questions.

AUDIO
Audio Clip 11.2

weblink

Table 11.1

technology

highlights

Can the Internet enhance school–home communication and parental involvement?

KIDLINK, a well-known chat room for children ages 10 to 15, is carefully monitored and open only to registered users. The goal of KIDLINK is to promote global dialogue among young people, and students must answer four questions when they register: (1) "Who am I?" (2) "What do I want to be when I grow up?" (3) "How do I want the world to be better when I grow up?" and (4) "What can I do now to make this happen?" Teacher-leaders of KIDLINK organize and monitor numerous projects; for example, the ongoing Family History Project has the following goals:

- To bring history alive for students by assisting them in learning how their family participated in "real" history
- To learn how previous generations actually lived, values they had, customs they practiced, and so on
- To promote creative writing skills
- To develop research and note-taking skills by "digging" around in the family tree
- To learn about other cultures by sharing with each other on the Kidproj list (an e-mail list of participants)
- To increase computer skills by using word processors, perhaps drawing or graphics programs, e-mail, listserves, and the WWW
- To learn more about community resources in individual geographical areas (Schwartz and Beichner 1999, 119–120).

Videoconferencing   Video conferences can be held over the Internet if users have video cameras connected to their computers and C-U SeeMe, PictureTel, or similar software installed. For example, recall how students of first-grade teacher Kristi Rennebohm Franz (featured in this chapter's "Keepers of the Dream") participated in a video conference with their teacher while she attended an international conference in Budapest. As with any educational technology, care must be taken that **videoconferencing** is more than a "high tech" way for teachers to lecture to passive students at other locations. "Videoconferencing best supports meaningful learning by helping diverse learners to collaborate and converse with each other in order to solve problems and construct meaning" (Jonassen, Peck, and Wilson 1999, 82)

How Do Teachers Use Computers and the Internet?

As the preceding section illustrates, a dazzling array of technologies is available for teachers to use in the classroom. However, the availability and use of these tools for teaching and learning are two different matters. To what extent and how are teachers actually using new technologies? How useful do they find them? To answer these questions, the U.S. Department of Education sponsored the Teaching, Learning, and Computing (TLC) survey which gathered data from three groups: (1) a nationally representative sample of approximately 2,250 fourth- through twelfth-grade teachers at public and private schools throughout the country, (2) 1,800 teachers at "high-end" technology schools and schools participating in national or regional educational reform programs, and (3) 1,700 principals and school-level technology coordinators (Anderson and Ronnkvist 1999; Becker 1999; Ravitz, Wong, and Becker 1999).

Preparing Lessons

The Internet has been termed "the world's largest library," and, as such, it can be a remarkable resource for planning lessons. According to the TLC survey, 28 percent of teachers use the Internet weekly or more often to gather information and resources on the Internet for their teaching, and 40 percent do so occasionally. Among teachers who have access to the Internet at school as well as at home, 46 percent report weekly or more frequent use. In Washington State's Kent School District, for instance, teachers learn to use the district's Teacher's Toolbox website (see Figure 11.3) where they share lesson plans and gather information on students' progress in other classes. Kent teachers also use the Toolbox to complete previously onerous paperwork online and to sign up for in-service training.

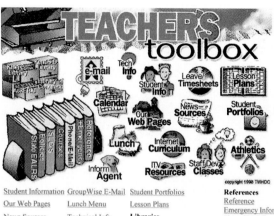

Teachers' Toolbox Class Web Page

Figure 11.3

Teacher's Toolbox, Kent School District

Note: EALRS = Essential Academic Learning Requirements
SLOS = Student Learning Objectives
ITV = Instructional Television (PBS Online)
Leave/Effective Ed = (leave and professional development balances, electronic timesheets)

Source: Kent School District, Kent, Washington. © The Michael Hren Design Company. Used with permission.

Weblink 11.1

Communicating with Other Educators

Compared to their use of the Internet to prepare lessons and gather resources, teachers use the Internet less often to communicate with other educators, according to the TLC survey. Only 16 percent of teachers used e-mail to communicate with teachers in other schools, and 23 percent did so occasionally. However, "by far the most important variable in predicting teachers' Internet use is the teacher's level of classroom connectivity" (Becker 1999, 29). For example, a comparison of e-mail use between teachers who had Internet access at home and at school with teachers who had access only at home revealed that teachers with classroom access were *three times as likely* to e-mail teachers at other schools. Not surprisingly, if teachers don't have ready access to the Internet during their daily professional lives, their use of e-mail is less frequent.

Although efforts to integrate technology into schools require information about the extent of teachers' access to and use of the Internet, it is important to ask whether teachers believe the Internet is a valuable tool for teaching. In response to this question, TLC survey data revealed that 49 percent of teachers believe that having a computer with e-mail capabilities on their own desk is "essential," and, similarly, 47 percent believe having Web access in the classroom is "essential." In addition, another 38 percent believe e-mail access is "valuable," and 41 percent believe Web access is "valuable." These results seem to counter the observation that "a lot of teachers say, '[Technology] is one more thing on my plate and I don't know how it will help me'" (Ortiz 1999).

Posting Information and Student Work on the Web

In addition to using e-mail to communicate with other educators, 18 percent of teachers posted information, professional opinions, or student work at least once on the Web. For instance, as with the use of e-mail, the likelihood of teachers posting information, opinions, or student work was strongly related to connectivity in the classroom. As classroom access to the Internet continues to increase, teachers' use of the Internet to communicate with other educators and to post material will also increase. Many school districts have taken steps to increase teacher professional communications via the Internet. As part of a "Reinventing Education" grant program, teachers in the San Jose Unified School District keep journals of their progress at integrating technology into instruction, and they share these with other teachers online. To ensure that teachers use their training in technology, the principal of Philadelphia's Hill-Freedman Middle School accepts lesson plans only by e-mail and posts daily announcements exclusively on the Internet (CEO Forum on Education and Technology 1999).

Facilitating Students' Learning via Computers and Cyberspace

Table 11.2

Video 11.1

In previous sections of this chapter, we have seen several examples of how teachers are using computers and the Internet to enhance students' learning. Table 11.2, based on TLC survey data, documents the extent of this usage and shows that a significant percentage of teachers are involving their students in an array of computer-based and online activities. After word processing and use of CD-ROM references, "research" on the Web is the most common teacher-directed use of computers by students. As with teachers' use of the Internet, student use is directly related to classroom connectivity; among teachers with modems in the classroom, almost half had students use Web search engines on at least three occasions. Moreover, teachers whose classrooms had direct high-speed connections instead of modem connections were 25 percent more likely to have students search the Web ten or more times.

Few teachers have students use the Internet to communicate with others, to collaborate on projects with classes at other schools, and to publish on the Web. The TLC survey revealed that about 5 percent of teachers have students involved in beyond-the-classroom projects and Web publishing, and by spring 1998, more than 70,000 teachers had helped students post their work on the Web (Ravitz, Wong, and Becker 1999). One example of a collaborative Web-based project is ThinkQuest at Lakeland High School in New York state. As their winning entry for a college scholarship contest, Lakeland students and a faculty sponsor developed a Web site to help others learn. Though she thought a computer teacher should oversee the project, the music teacher and band director who reluctantly agreed to be faculty sponsor found the project professionally energizing:

> At first I just wanted to give the team feedback. Then the kids' excitement and motivation got to me—they were doing extraordinary academic work and loving it. I discovered a whole new way to research, learn, and use technology. The kids taught

me so much and as they did, they grew intellectually and socially. This has truly been one of the most rewarding and authentic professional development experiences of my career (CEO Forum on Education and Technology 1999).

What Are the Effects of Computer Technology on Learning?

The use of computers and other technologies in schools has grown enormously since the early 1980s, and, as a director of the North Central Regional Education Laboratory noted, "For policymakers, the honeymoon for technology is over. They are starting to say, 'Show us the results'" (Williams 1999). In addition to information about the effects of technology on learning, there is a realization that "no one knows for certain [h]ow it is used" or "how much it is used" (Mehlinger 1996, 403). Since educational technology is a tool to help teachers teach more effectively, how it is used is critical. For example, one science teacher might use computers primarily for student drills on science terminology, while another science teacher might have students use computer simulations to determine the impact of urbanization on animal populations. The lack of information about how technology is being used in the schools aside, research results are just now beginning to appear on the long-term effects of technology on learning.

Apple Classrooms of Tomorrow Project (ACOT)

One of the most informative research studies is based on the Apple Classrooms of Tomorrow (ACOT) project launched in seven K–12 classrooms in 1986. Participating students and teachers each received two computers—one for school and one for home. Eight years later, study results indicated that all ACOT students performed as well as they were expected without computers, and some performed better. More important, perhaps, "the ACOT students routinely and without prompting employed inquiry, collaboration, and technological and problem-solving skills" (Mehlinger 1996, 405). Also, 90 percent of ACOT students went on to college after graduating from high school, while only 15 percent of non-ACOT students did. Furthermore, the behavior of ACOT teachers also changed—they worked "more as mentors and less as presenters of information" (Mehlinger 1996, 404).

An additional positive finding of the ACOT study was how teachers gradually began to use the computers in new ways in the classroom. "When [ACOT] teachers were able to move past that pervasive teacher-centered view of education, students and teachers, as communities of learners, were able to benefit from the range of individual areas of expertise represented by the entire group" (Bitter and Pierson 1999, 43). Teachers rearranged their classrooms to enable students to work collaboratively on projects, and they frequently made arrangements for students who wished to stay after school to work on multimedia projects. Frequently, "Students and teachers collaborated together, with the students often in the role of expert or resource person" (Schwartz and Beichner 1999, 33–34).

Integrating Technology   Teacher participants in the ACOT study were volunteers, many of whom had little experience with educational technology. As with teachers learning any new instructional strategy, the ACOT teachers frequently struggled to adjust to their new computer-filled rooms. Researchers found that the teachers progressed through five distinct stages as they integrated the technology into their teaching (Sandholtz, Ringstaff, and Dwyer 1997).

1. *Entry stage*—For many teachers, this was a period of painful growth and discomfort; learning to use computers presented challenges similar to those faced by beginning teachers.
2. *Adoption stage*—Becoming more proactive toward the challenge of integrating computers, teachers began to teach students how to use the computers and software.
3. *Adaptation stage*—Teachers turned from teaching the technology to using the technology as a tool to teach content.
4. *Appropriation stage*—Teachers moved from merely accommodating computers in their daily routines to personally exploring new teaching possibilities afforded by the technology.
5. *Invention stage*—Eager to move beyond teacher-centered instruction, teachers began to collaborate with peers in developing authentic, inquiry-oriented learning activities.

As informative as the ACOT study has been, it is important to remember that the project was funded by a computer manufacturer; thus, the outcomes might have been influenced by commercial bias and/or the expectation that computers *could not* have had anything other than a significant positive influence on teaching and learning. In fact, Schwartz and Beichner (1999, 34) suggest that the ACOT project "epitomizes what might be termed the 'Emperor's New Clothes' perspective on technology in education. [To] take the ACOT reports at face value would be to accept the notion that technology is the panacea that education has been searching for for ages."

Findings from Other Research Studies

A powerful way to determine whether certain educational practices actually influence students' learning is to conduct *meta-analyses,* that is, to "take the findings from single studies and calculate a way to compare them with each other. The goal is to synthesize the findings statistically and determine what the studies reveal when examined all together" (Kirkpatrick and Cuban 1998). One such meta-analysis reviewed the results of 133 research studies on educational technology from 1990 through 1994. The results of that study follow:

- Educational technology has a significant positive impact on achievement in all subject areas, across all levels of school, and in regular classrooms as well as those for special-needs students.
- Educational technology has positive effects on student attitudes.
- The degree of effectiveness is influenced by the student population, the instructional design, the teacher's role, how students are grouped, and the levels of student access to technology.
- Technology makes instruction more student-centered, encourages cooperative learning, and stimulates increased teacher–student interaction.
- Positive changes in the learning environment evolve over time and do not occur quickly (Mehlinger 1996, 405).

Another meta-analysis conducted by Heather Kirkpatrick and Larry Cuban (1998) at Stanford University also addressed the complications and difficulties involved in determining the effects of computers on learning, particularly when much of the research in that area is methodologically flawed. Research studies, they pointed out, "are of little use unless they elaborate the children's ages, the subject, the software used, the kinds of outcomes that were sought, and how the study was done." With these limitations in mind, the following is a brief summary of Kirkpatrick and Cuban's findings:

1. Seven of the single studies of elementary and secondary students yielded positive findings related to achievement and attitude change, while seven studies yielded negative or mixed findings.
2. Ten of the single studies on the effectiveness of computers to teach in core areas such as mathematics, reading, science, and social studies yielded results ranging from very positive to "cautiously negative."
3. Ten meta-analyses found higher levels of student achievement in computer-using classrooms.
4. Five meta-analyses found that student attitudes improved and students learned more in less time in computer-using classrooms.

On the basis of their meta-analysis of the research, much of it considered methodologically flawed due to a lack of scientific controls, Kirkpatrick and Cuban conclude that "we are unable to ascertain whether computers in classrooms have in fact been or will be the boon they have promised to be."

These students receive immediate feedback and reinforcement, are more engaged and motivated, and are acquiring important twenty-first century workplace skills by using computers at school. Should computers and other technology be at the forefront of efforts to improve schools?

The ambiguities of research on computer-based instruction aside, it is clear that educational technology *can* have positive effects on learning and teaching, and indications are that technology will influence all aspects of education even more in the twenty-first century. Thus the question to be asked about the effectiveness of educational technology is not, "Is it effective?" Instead, the question should be, . . . "How and under what circumstances does educational technology enhance students' learning?" As more funds are made available to purchase hardware and software, train teachers, and provide technical support, the benefits of classroom media magic will become even more widespread.

Should Technology Be at the Forefront of Efforts to Improve Schools in the United States?

Daily, the mass media feature stories on schools and classrooms that have been transformed through the use of computer-based modes of teaching and learning. Additional reports appear regularly describing the development of new technologies that hold further promise for the improvement of education in the United States. The advantages outlined in these reports include:

- Systematic, well-structured, and consistent lessons
- The ability of students to pace their learning
- The ability of teachers to accommodate their students' varied learning styles and preferred paces of learning

- Opportunities for students in rural and remote areas to interact with students and teachers in diversely populated urban and suburban areas
- Increased record-keeping efficiency, which allows teachers to spend more time with students
- Immediate feedback and reinforcement for students
- Improved student engagement and motivation that result from learning materials with color, music, video, and animated graphics
- More effective assessment of students' learning
- Cost effectiveness
- The acquisition of computer literacy skills needed for the twenty-first century workplace

For several years, some people have been questioning the role of technology in improving schools in the United States. An *Atlantic Monthly* cover story titled "The Computer Delusion" even suggested that spending money on computers in the classroom was a form of "malpractice" (Oppenheimer 1997). Some critics, like Stanford professor Larry Cuban, believe it is misguided to assume that teaching will benefit from the use of computers, as have other forms of work:

> The essence of teaching is a knowledgeable, caring adult building a relationship with one or more students to help them learn what the teacher, community, and parents believe to be important. It is an intertwining of emotional and intellectual bonds that gives a tone and texture to teaching and learning unlike what occurs in other work environments. The lure of higher productivity in teaching and learning via computer technologies, however, has seduced reformers to treat teaching like other forms of labor that gained productivity after automation (Cuban 1999a).

Elsewhere, Cuban (1999b) suggests several seldom-considered factors that might account for why the increase in available educational technologies is not reflected in more effective use of technology in the classroom:

- *Contradictory advice from experts*—During the last two decades, Cuban points out, teachers have been presented with an "ever-shifting menu of advice" about what computer skills to teach students, ranging from how to program computers in the 1980s to how to do hypertext programming or HTML in the 1990s.
- *Intractable working conditions*—While technology has transformed most workplaces, conditions of teaching have changed little. As "people for whom rollerblades would be in order to meet the day's obligations," Cuban says, teachers are hard pressed to find time and energy to integrate new technologies into their teaching.
- *The inherent unreliability of the technology*—Software malfunctions, servers that crash, and the continual need for computers with more memory and speed are among the problems Cuban notes.
- *Policymakers' disrespect for teachers' opinions*—Teachers are seldom consulted about which machines and software are most appropriate and reliable for their teaching.

Other critics, like *Chicago Tribune* columnist Bob Greene, are clear about the place of computers in the classroom: "The key to helping the next generation of American children be bright, literate, intellectually self-sufficient, steeped in the most important areas of knowledge? It all comes down to computers in the classroom. Get rid of them" (Greene 1999). Critics like Greene believe that computers can have a dampening effect on the intellectual development of children, not unlike television, and should not be used extensively in the classroom until the high school level. As Greene puts it: "We are not doing [children] any favors by plopping them in front of yet another set of screens and programming them to tap and stare away."

Lastly, many critics are concerned about what they view as tremendous pressure, much of it coming from technology-oriented corporations, for schools to "go online." As the daily fabric of our lives becomes increasingly shaped by sophisticated technologies and as a disconcerting number of politicians, business leaders, parents, and others continue to proclaim loudly that the United States is falling behind many other countries in educational attainment, technology is mistakenly touted as the "magic bullet," the panacea to turn the schools around.

Are schools falling prey to a tremendous computer-oriented "hype" encouraged by technology corporations, big business, and ambitious superintendents who want their districts to be ahead in the race for the latest technology, and politicians promoting the latest "quick fix" for education? What will be the consequences for the many schools that have cut art, music, and physical education classes to purchase computers? Will computer technology help the United States develop the kind of students and citizens the nation needs? Is there a "fit" between the undeniable power of computers and the educational goals we seek? Are there more cost-effective ways to achieve these educational goals? These are among the difficult questions that are being addressed as the role of technology in educational reform is being debated.

The Opposition:
Computers *Will Not* Improve Education

Among the first to question the role of technology in the classroom was Clifford Stoll, one of the pioneers of the Internet. In *Silicon Snake Oil: Second Thoughts on the Information Highway* (1996, 127), Stoll points out that "Our schools face serious problems, including overcrowded classrooms, teacher incompetence, and lack of security. Local education budgets hardly cover salaries, books, and paper. Computers address none of these problems. They're expensive, quickly become obsolete, and drain scarce capital budgets. Yet school administrators want them desperately." Similarly, David Shenk concludes his book, *Data Smog: Surviving the Information Glut* (1998, 220), with eight "Principles of Technorealism" endorsed by several of the nation's leading experts on technology; principle No. 5 states:

> **Wiring the schools will not save them.**
>
> The problems with America's public schools—disparate funding, social promotion, bloated class size, crumbling infrastructure, lack of standards—have almost nothing to do with technology. Consequently, no amount of technology will lead to the educational revolution prophesied by President Clinton and others. The art of teaching cannot be replicated by computers, the Net, or by "distance learning." These tools can, of course, augment an already high quality educational experience. But to rely on them as any sort of panacea would be a costly mistake.

Similarly, others critics have cautioned the public against pushing schools into the computer revolution. A sampling of their comments follow:

> Penetration of the education market with computer-based technology has depended more on effective conditioning of the market through a barrage of advertising and ideology than on the effectiveness of the technologies themselves (Noble 1996, 20).

where do you stand?

Is the use of technology in schools overemphasized?

Weblink 11.2

"Optimistic" is probably the kindest word to describe the current status of educational computing in the United States. The good examples [aren't] always easy to find and [are] far outnumbered by the bad ones (Healy 1998, 78).

I do not go as far back as the radio and Victrola, but I am old enough to remember when 16-millimeter film was to be the sure-cure. Then closed-circuit television. Then 8-millimeter film. Then teacher-proof textbooks. Now computers. I know a false god when I see one (Postman, 1995).

The Advocates:
Computers *Will* Improve Education

Despite media stories and articles critical of the call for more computers in schools, enthusiasm for technology in schools remains strong. For example, in an MCI nationwide poll in 1998, almost 60 percent of the public answered "a great amount" when asked, "How much do you think computers have helped improve student learning?" (Trotter 1998, 6). Following are a few representative comments that rebut arguments against computers in the schools.

> It has become fashionable to say that computers in education are a bust. [However,] the new media can positively change the role of the teacher and student, shifting education from broadcast to interactive learning. When done effectively, [the] results are dramatic (Tapscott July 6, 1999).

> There are real dangers in looking to technology to be the savior of education. But it won't survive without the technology (Jane David, Apple consultant, quoted in Oppenheimer 1997).

> Industrial Age educators will fight Information Age education tooth and nail. [However], in the long run they will probably do no more than slow the implementation of an emerging and vastly improved educational system. Not only is the encroachment of information technology into children's lives inevitable, but it is critical to their future—and ours (Snider 1996).

What Barriers Limit the Integration of Technology into Schools?

Figure 11.4

In his 1996 State of the Union address, President Clinton stated that "every classroom in America must be connected to the information superhighway with computers and good software and well-trained teachers." Toward that end, he launched the President's Educational Technology Initiative, which included "four pillars" of "The Technology Literacy Challenge" (see Figure 11.4). Today, the four pillars of that challenge provide an appropriate framework for examining the nation's progress toward its educational technology goals.

Pillar 1: Access to Technology for All Students

The Technology Literacy Challenge, U.S. Department of Education publication to promote the President's Educational Technology Initiative (1996a), was clear about the importance of access to technology: *"Computers become effective instructional tools only if they are readily accessible by students and teachers"* (italics in original). However, the CEO Forum on Education and Technology reported that by 1998 only 24 percent of schools had reached a "High Tech" or "Target (advanced) Tech" level of effectiveness at integrating technology, while more than half of 79,415 K–12 schools were "Low Tech" (see Figure 11.5). Access to technology in the six percent of schools at the "Target Tech" level fit the following profile.

Figure 11.5

- *Ubiquitous access to modern computers*—Student-to-computer ratio of 3:1. Student-to-multimedia capable computer ratio of 3:1.
- *New technology*—Eighty-one percent of all computers have processors equal to or greater than an Intel 386.
- *Ubiquitous Internet access*—Ninety-five percent of these schools have Internet access.
- *Prevalent networked computers*—Eighty-nine percent of these schools have access to one or more LANs (Local Area Networks).

Anderson and Ronnkvist (1999) reported the results of a survey by Quality Education Data to identify "high-end technology schools." Technology-intensive schools were defined as having all three of the following: (1) a student–computer ratio of 6:1 or less, (2) at least 25 percent of computers equipped with CD-ROM drives for multimedia, and (3) a moderate or high-speed Internet access. Using these criteria, Anderson and Ronnkvist found that only 25 percent of K–12 schools were "technology-intensive." High schools were more technology-intensive (31 percent), compared to middle schools (29 percent), and elementary schools (22 percent). The survey also revealed that about half of the nation's K–12 schools had outdated computers—as the survey report put it: "To run multimedia applications efficiently, a Pentium or Power Macintosh is needed, but only 45 percent of the school inventory consist[ed] of those computers. [So], using contemporary standards for home and office computers, over half of the computers[were] out of date" (Anderson and Ronnkvist 1999, 5).

On the positive side, Figure 11.5 shows that schools have made significant progress in their technological capabilities between 1997 and 1998, and this trend is continuing. In fact, Anderson and Ronnkvist (1999, 6) believe that schools overall are doing a good job of updating their computers. "[The] typical school acquires roughly 20 or more computers per year on the average. [Only] six years ago, the obsolete equipment made it seem doubtful that U.S. schools could keep up with the rapid pace of computing technology. The latest data suggest that schools are doing an impressive job of catching up."

The Teacher's Resource Guide section "The CEO Forum on Education and Technology's STaR Assessment of a School's Effectiveness at Integrating Technology into the Teaching and Learning Process" on this book's website, presents an assessment instrument developed by the CEO Forum that yields an approximate measure of a school's access to technology and its effectiveness at integrating technology into the teaching and learning process. The assessment score, ranging from "Low Tech" to "Target Tech," is based on five categories: hardware, connectivity to the Internet, quality of software programs, professional development for teachers, and integration and use of technology.

Weblink 11.3

Funding for Computers and Technical Support   To enable schools to participate more fully in the computer revolution, some school districts have passed bond measures to fund educational technology, and New Jersey and a few other states have adopted long-term budgets for computers and technical support. In Milwaukee, a comprehensive technology plan calls for all 156 buildings in the school system to be networked and for a mini-network, a printer, a television, and a multimedia teacher workstation in every classroom by 2002. In Cleveland, a state program has provided every primary grade classroom with three multimedia computers and each teacher with a laptop computer (Harrington-Lueker 1999).

Although schools are getting more computer hardware, most cannot afford to hire sufficient support staff for technology. About 30 percent of schools employ a full-time coordinator of technology, about 40 percent employ a part-time coordinator, and about 30 percent have no on-site technical support personnel (Furger 1999). As a result, most schools rely on central district personnel or computer-savvy teachers for support.

At urban schools, the ability to narrow what has been termed the **"digital divide"** between poor and more affluent schools is often limited by enormous obstacles, including "limited resources, low expectations, overwhelming poverty, teacher contracts, entrenched bureaucracies, political infighting, and the sheer size of these districts" (Williams 1999). *Barriers and Breakthroughs: Technology in Urban Schools,* a 1999 study by the Education Writers Association, revealed that, while most urban districts have "lighthouse" schools in which sophisticated technologies are fully integrated into the curriculum, they also have schools with woefully limited technologies. The national ratio of students to multimedia computers is about 8:1; however, in Chicago, the ratio is 16:1; Cleveland, 15:1; Detroit, 13:1; and Milwaukee 10:1 (Harrington-Lueker 1999).

Commercial Computer Labs   Confronted with limited budgets to purchase computers, many public and private schools are accepting "free" computer labs (complete with software, training, and maintenance) from companies such as California-based ZapMe. In exchange, schools agree that classes will use the labs at least four hours a day and that students will be exposed to on-screen advertisements that run continuously in a 2″ × 4″ box in a bottom corner of the screen, changing every fifteen seconds. In addition, schools agree to allow ZapMe and its for-profit partners to use the labs for computer training and related activities.

Each ZapMe lab consists of fifteen Pentium II PCs, seventeen-inch monitors, pre-installed software selected by ZapMe, a laser printer, and a high-speed satellite connection to the Internet. The PCs have no diskette drives or CD-ROM drives, thus preventing schools from using other software with the lab. The ZapMe labs, which the company predicted would number 2,000 at the end of 1999 (*PC World* 1999a), have led some critics to compare the labs to the controversial Channel One.

Table 11.3

Unequal Access to Technology   Although schools are making substantial gains in making technology available to students, a significant "digital divide" is evident when access to computers is compared to minority-group status, family income, and gender. Table 11.3 shows that between 1984 and 1997 African American and Latino students were consistently less likely than their white peers to use a computer at school or at home. In addition, research by Quality Education Data revealed that schools with fewer than 1 percent minority students enroll an average of 6.8 students per computer, whereas schools with more than 90 percent minority students enrolled an average of 10.7 students per computer (Furger 1999). A study of computers in schools by Anderson and Ronnkvist (1999) also found a similar relationship between access to computers and minority-group membership; however, the pattern was found to be "uneven" and not as significant as the relationship between computer access and family income.

Table 11.3 also shows consistent disparities over the years between access to computers and family income. Similarly, the Anderson and Ronkvist (1999) study, which used federal Chapter 1 funding as a measure of the socioeconomic status of a school and ZIP codes as a measure of community income, found a connection between access to computers and family income; however, on several indicators the gap was rather small and uneven (e.g., students per computer, percent with high-speed access, and percent with an Internet server). Nevertheless, as *The Technology Literacy Challenge* stated, "It will take careful planning to make certain that, in our reach for technological literacy, schools in all types of communities—middle income, lower-income, and better-off communities—have access to up-to-date technology in their classrooms."

Discrepancies in access to computers are also related to gender. In *Does Jane Compute?: Preserving Our Daughter's Place in the Cyber Revolution*, Roberta Furger (1998), a columnist and contributing editor at *PC World* magazine, estimates that only 16 percent of children and youth online are girls. In a chapter titled "Jane@Home," Furger suggests that boys get the largest share of family computing time. She also cites the lack of software based on girls' interests and even harassment in some male-dominated online forums. In "Jane@School," Furger contends that girls have less access to computers and receive less encouragement to pursue computer-related careers. Furger also suggests that boys tend to regard the computer as a toy, whereas girls regard it as a tool.

Some schools are taking steps to encourage girls to explore and learn with technology. Schools in Palos Park, Illinois, for example, developed a program called Girls and Technology: Skills, Computers, Awareness, and Peer Empowerment (GATSCAPE). Sixth-, seventh-, and eighth-grade girls at all levels of computer literacy get unrestricted access to technology during classes and after school. As they acquire new skills with technology, the girls are encouraged to pass on these skills to other girls formally and informally (CEO Forum on Education and Technology 1999).

Pillar 2: Internet Access for All Schools

Internet access, according to *The Technology Literacy Challenge*, is a vital part of a school's capacity to benefit from the vast resources found in cyberspace: "*Connections to networks, especially the Internet, multiply the power and usefulness of computers as learning tools by putting the best libraries, museums, and other research and cultural resources at our students' and teachers' fingertips*" (italics in original). In 1995, President Clinton created the **National Information Infrastructure (NII)** to encourage all schools, libraries, hospitals, and law enforcement agencies to become connected to the "information superhighway." At that time, schools in the United States were hardly ready to "go online"; 50 percent of schools had Internet access, but only 8 percent of all classrooms had access (see Figure 11.6). Four years later, the percentage of schools with Internet access had risen to 89 percent, and the percentage of classrooms with access had risen to 51 percent. In 1998, to provide funds to help schools and libraries connect to the Internet, the federal government launched **E-Rate,** a controversial program that provides discounts on telecommunications services and wiring to schools and libraries. With increased purchasing power from the E-rate program, schools can purchase improved telephone service and greater bandwidth, thus allowing more data to travel across wires for Internet and e-mail use. Currently, E-rate discounts are financed by fees the Federal Communications Commission (FCC) collects from telecommunications companies. Since some companies pass these costs on to consumers, critics claim that the FCC has imposed an illegal tax on telephone users. By fall 1999, E-Rate had helped more than 30,000 schools and libraries connect to the Internet (*PC World* 1999b).

Though many schools continue to report barriers to either the acquisition or the use of advanced telecommunications, schools have made steady progress toward

Figure 11.6

overcoming these barriers, as evidenced, perhaps, by *FamilyPC* magazine's launching in 1999 an annual list of the "Top 100 Wired High Schools" in the nation.

Pillar 3: Quality Educational Software

As *The Technology Literacy Challenge* made clear, for students and teachers to benefit from Information Age technology, high quality software, not just the latest hardware, must be readily available: *"Software and on-line learning resources can increase students' learning opportunities, but they must be high quality, engaging, and directly related to the school's curriculum"* (italics in original). Since computers first began to be used extensively in education in the 1980s, inadequacy of software has been a common criticism. By the turn of the century, the situation had not changed much: "Though schools have increased their outlays for software, their choices are few and far between when it comes to superior programs designed specially for classroom use" (Furger 1999). Some programs tend to deemphasize humanistic, holistic, and open-ended fields of knowledge, which are not easily quantified. Others are merely electronic page-turners, known as "drill-and-kill" software, that simply transfer textbooks or workbooks to the computer monitor, as Clifford Stoll, author of *Silicon Snake Oil*, suggests in the following:

> I find plenty of educational software that teaches factoids in arithmetic and geography, almost nothing about electricity, plumbing, or chemistry. What's there is uninspired—they work remarkably like flash cards. Many other programs just dilute minor educational messages with nifty graphics and squiggly sounds. I can't understand why students put up with such stuff (Stoll 1996, 139).

Of the bestselling program for teaching arithmetic, Stoll says:

> A poorly animated green spaceman and little blue robot accompany a tedious drill-and-practice program. It's little more than a stack of arithmetic flash cards accompanied by bleeping sounds. Instead of teaching the meaning of numbers, the software rewards kids for answering questions like 5 + 4 =? Kids see it as an imitation PacMan. Arithmetic becomes an ersatz game (Stoll 1996, 139).

These negative appraisals of educational software aside, promising efforts are being made to upgrade the quality of educational software. For example, the International Society for Technology in Education, the largest teacher-based organization devoted to disseminating effective methods for using educational technology and developer of national "Technology Foundation Standards" for preK–12 students, is working with teachers around the country to identify high-quality software to meet their curriculum goals. Steadily, new, more powerful hypermedia learning software programs are appearing that present students with problems to solve that are interesting, multifaceted, and embedded in real-world contexts. For example, the *Astronomy Village: Investigating the Universe*, developed by the National Aeronautics and Space Administration (NASA) and available at a modest cost, promotes ninth and tenth grade students' learning within a virtual observatory community (see Figure 11.7) that includes extensive multimedia resources and sophisticated exploration tools. The *Astronomy Village* requires that teams of three students select one of the following ten investigations, develop a plan, and carry it out.

- *Search for a Supernova*—Uses neutrino data to locate a supernova
- *Looking for a Stellar Nursery*—Views Omega nebula using different wavelengths

- *Variable Stars*—Identifying a Cepheid variable star in another galaxy
- *Search for Nearby Stars*—Movement of stars' positions as Earth circles sun
- *Extragalactic Zoo*—Different galaxies and clusters
- *Wedges of the Universe*—Viewing depths of space in two wedges of sky
- *Search for a "Wobbler"*—Looking for stars that wobble in their motion
- *Search for Planetary Building Blocks*—Examines Orion nebula for proplanetary disks
- *Search for Earth-Crossing Objects*—Looks for asteroids that cross Earth's path
- *Observatory Site Selection*—Selects a site for an observatory (Jonassen, Peck, and Wilson 1999, 94–95).

Included as part of the *Astronomy Village* are a star life-cycle simulator, orbital simulator, and 3D star simulator. In addition, the student teams can use the program's digitized video clips, images from the Hubble space telescope and other instruments, audio clips of astronomers discussing their work, and book chapters, NASA publications, and articles from astronomy journals and magazines. To help you evaluate computer-based instructional materials, Appendix 11.1 presents "Criteria for Evaluating Software Programs," and Appendix 11.2 presents "Criteria for Evaluating World Wide Web Sites."

Figure 11.7

The Astronomy Village: Investigating the Universe
Source: NASA Classroom of the Future, National Aeronautics and Space Administration (NASA) and Wheeling Jesuit University, Wheeling, WV. Copyright 1999 by Wheeling Jesuit University/NASA Classroom of the Future. All Rights Reserved.

Appendix 11.1   Appendix 11.2

Pillar 4: Teacher Training in Technology

Using technology to enhance students' learning requires more than investing in the latest hardware, software, and connectivity to the Internet. In the words of *The Technology Literacy Challenge*, "*Upgrading teacher training is key to integrating technology into the classroom and to increasing student learning*" (italics in original). E-mailing students, parents, and peers; conducting classroom demonstrations augmented with multimedia; using presentation graphics to address students' varied learning styles; and designing lessons that require students to use the Internet as a resource for inquiry should be second nature for teachers. Just as new technological skills are needed in the workplace—the number of jobs requiring a high level of information technology skills is expected to double between 1996 and 2006 (CEO Forum on Education and Technology 1999)—a high degree of technological literacy is needed in the classroom. Thus acquiring proficiency in the ever-evolving array of technologies should be an important part of professional development for new and veteran teachers. However, teachers frequently complain of a lack of training in how to use technology to reach their curriculum goals. Only 20 percent of teachers believe they are well prepared to integrate educational technology into the curriculum, and among the teachers who seek training in technology, 50 percent pay for their training with their own money (CEO Forum on Education and Technology 1999). On average, only 9 percent of a school district's technology budget is spent on teacher training, less than one-third of the U.S. Department of Education's recommendations (Furger 1999).

Although survey data indicate that about half of teachers have participated in technology-related staff development, those training sessions often tend to emphasize the basics of computer use rather than how to integrate technology with instruction in their subject matter (Ravitz, Wong, and Becker 1999). Moreover, 38 percent of teachers reported that at least once a month they needed help integrating computers into their lessons, but only 15 percent reported that they "always" get that help and only 12 percent more say such help is "mostly" available.

In addition, teachers have similar experiences related to technical support to keep computers working and software programs functioning properly. Forty-six percent of teachers say they need technical help at least once a month, and only 31 percent of these teachers say that such help is "always" or "mostly" available when they need it. After technical help is given, about one-third of teachers say the help was "excellent" or "very good," one-third say it was "good," and the remaining third say it was "fair" or "poor."

In response to the uneven quality of professional development and technical support, several state departments of education, school districts, and individual schools are taking steps to ensure that teachers have the help they need to fully integrate technology into their teaching.

By 1999, half of the states plus the District of Columbia required computer education for licensure (CEO Forum on Education and Technology 1999). In North Carolina, for example, all new teachers must take an examination to demonstrate their mastery of basic technology competencies in the following nine areas:

- Computer operation skills
- Setup, maintenance, and troubleshooting
- Word processing/introductory desktop publishing
- Spreadsheet/graphing
- Databases
- Networking
- Telecommunications
- Media communications (including image and audio processing)
- Multimedia integration

In addition, North Carolina is one of two states (along with Vermont) that require new teachers to develop a portfolio demonstrating mastery of "advanced" technology competencies, which is evaluated by public school and university faculty chosen by the new teacher's preservice program. The advanced competencies reflect the ability to use multiple forms of technology as they relate to the following four dimensions of learning:

- Curriculum
- Subject-specific knowledge
- Design and management of learning environments/resources
- Child development, learning, and diversity

In addition, teachers applying for five-year license renewal in North Carolina must have thirty to fifty hours of technology training.

At the school district level, creative approaches are extending teachers' technological literacy. For example, the board of education in Baldwin Park, California, leased 900 notebook computers and gave them to teachers and administrators in all of the district's 21 schools (Caterinicchia 1999).

Teacher-education programs also will play a key role in preparing technologically competent teachers to fill the roughly two million teaching vacancies the National Center for Education Statistics has projected between 1998 and 2008. However, as the CEO Forum on Education and Technology stated in its *School Technology and Readiness Report* released in 1999: "America's schools of education have only just begun to focus on preparing their students [to] understand, access, and bring technology-based experiences into the learning process." For example, according to the Milken Exchange on Education Technology's report *Will New Teachers Be Prepared to Teach in a Digital Age?*, less than half of student teachers routinely use technology during their field experience, and less than half of field experience supervisors or cooperating teachers can advise them on how to integrate technology into the curriculum (Milken Exchange on Education Technology 1999).

To ensure that preservice teachers possess the ability to integrate technology into the classroom, the National Council for the Accreditation of Teacher Education (NCATE) has developed technology-related guidelines that teacher-education programs must meet as a criterion for accreditation (National Council for the Accreditation of Teacher Education 1997a). Also, many teacher-education programs have taken innovative steps such as the following to ensure that their graduates possess the ability to integrate technology into the classroom.

- At Washington State University, identified as the nation's "most-wired" public university (Yahoo Internet Life 1999), students develop an online portfolio of literacy strategies that are critiqued by teachers around the state.
- At the University of Virginia, students use the Internet to link with students at eleven other universities to analyze case studies based on commonly occurring problems in classrooms; students also write their own cases and post them on the Web.
- At San Diego State University, student teachers, along with classroom teachers and school administrators, participate in a weekly "Multimedia Academy" taught by university staff and former student teachers.
- At the University of Northern Iowa, students learn from television-mediated observations of "live" classrooms at a P–12 laboratory school and conduct question-answer sessions with the laboratory school teachers.
- At Indiana University, students, as well as visitors from around the world, learn about educational technology at the Center for Excellence in Education, a new state-of-the-art facility with 700 computers, an "enhanced technology suite," a building-wide video distribution system, and a two-way video distance-learning classroom.
- At Boise State University, students complete a fifteen-hour technology fieldwork internship in a public school classroom with a teacher who effectively integrates technology into the curriculum.

In spite of considerable progress, much remains to be done before *The Technology Literacy Challenge* issued in 1996 will become a reality. "Current applications only scratch the surface of the capabilities that the world-wide digital communications infrastructure will eventually provide for teachers and their students" (Becker 1999, 32). Schools will need extensive support as they continue striving to establish the "four pillars" of technology. Teachers, professional associations, the private sector, state and federal governments, and local communities must continue to work together to enable classroom "media magic" to enhance every student's learning. (To assist you

Weblink 11.4

in contributing to this effort, see the Teacher's Resource Guide section "Selected Resources for Integrating Technology into Instruction" on this book's website.)

Fortunately, teachers, along with others who have an interest in education, are becoming more sophisticated in understanding the strengths and limitations of technology as a tool to promote learning. They know full well that "If [they] bring in these technologies and don't think ahead to how they'll be used to promote learning and the acquisition of skills, then the only thing that will change in school is the electric bill" (educational technology expert quoted in Goldberg 1998). They also know that, like another educational tool—the book—the computer *can* be a powerful, almost unlimited medium for instruction and learning, if they carefully reflect on *how* it will further the attainment of the goals and aspirations they have for their students.

SUMMARY

How Are Educational Technologies Influencing Schools? (p. 306)

What Technologies Are Available for Teaching? (p. 307)

How Do Teachers Use Computers and the Internet? (p. 314)

What Are the Effects of Computer Technology on Learning? (p. 317)

Should Technology Be at the Forefront of Efforts to Improve Schools in the United States? (p. 319)

What Barriers Limit the Integration of Technology into Schools? (p. 322)

KEY TERMS AND CONCEPTS

Go to the website for interactive flashcards.

APPLICATIONS AND INTERACTIVITIES

Go to the website for interactive assignments in the following areas:

Teacher's Journal

Teacher's Database

Observations and Interviews

Professional Portfolio

Handout Master M11.1

Name _____ **Date** _____

For each question, write in the blank the answer you believe is correct.

11.1 Two-way, interactive telecommunications that provide enrichment instruction to students in remote areas or staff development to teachers are known as _____ learning networks.

11.2 Channel _____ presents to school children a twelve-minute news broadcast with two minutes of commercial advertising each school day.

11.3 Computer-_____ instruction relies on computer programs that provide students with highly structured drill-and-practice exercises or tutorials.

11.4 Computer-_____ instruction relies on programs that evaluate and diagnose students' needs and, based on that assessment, guide students through the next steps in their learning.

11.5 The term _____ refers to documents composed of text, audio, and visual information stored in a computer and accessed by users in a nonlinear fashion.

11.6 According to a recent survey, few teachers use e-mail to communicate with other _____.

11.7 One of the most informative research studies of technology in schools is based on the _____ Classrooms of Tomorrow project begun in 1986.

11.8 When researchers construct a viable way to compare findings from single studies to other studies of similar phenomena, the process is known as _____-analyses.

11.9 President Clinton's "Technology Literacy Challenge" featured four pillars of challenge, including modern computers, connected classrooms, educational software, and well prepared _____.

11.10 As a way of ensuring that preservice teachers possess the ability to integrate technology into the classroom, the National Council for the Accreditation of Teacher Education (NCATE) has developed _____ that teacher-education programs must meet as a criterion for accreditation.

Answers are available on the FlexChoice website at www.ablongman.com/parkayflex.

 www.ablongman.com/parkayflex

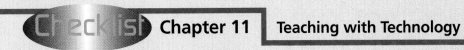

Name _____

Keep this checklist at your computer as a reminder to read and complete the chapter features and activities located on the FlexChoice website at www.ablongman.com/parkayflex.

**Date
Completed**

_____ ❑ **PreTest with Answers**

_____ ❑ **Audio Clip 11.1:** Thinking Over the Opening Vignette

_____ ❑ **Professional Reflection:** How technically proficient are you?

_____ ❑ **Figure 11.1:** Advantages of computer-assisted instruction (CAI)

_____ ❑ **Keepers of the Dream:** Kristi Rennebohm Franz

_____ ❑ **Audio Clip 11.2:** History of the Internet

_____ ❑ **Table 11.1:** Growth of the Internet and the World Wide Web

_____ ❑ **Technology Highlights:** Can the Internet enhance school–home communication and parental involvement?

_____ ❑ **Weblink 11.1:** Teacher's Toolbox, Kent School District

_____ ❑ **Table 11.2:** Percent of teachers having their students use different types of software by grade level

_____ ❑ **Video 11.1:** Technology and Students with Special Needs

_____ ❑ **Where Do You Stand?:** Is the use of technology in schools overemphasized?

_____ ❑ **Weblink 11.2:** GlobaLearn

_____ ❑ **Figure 11.4:** The Technology Literacy Challenge

_____ ❑ **Figure 11.5:** Level of school technology and readiness (STaR)

_____ ❑ **Weblink 11.3:** The CEO Forum on Education and Technology's STaR Assessment of a School's Effectiveness at Integrating Technology into the Teaching and Learning Process

_____ ❑ **Table 11.3:** Percentage of students who used a computer at school and/or home, by current grade level, race-ethnicity, and family income: 1984, 1989, 1993, and 1997

_____ ❑ **Figure 11.6:** Internet access in public schools

_____ ❑ **Appendix 11.1:** Criteria for Evaluating Software Programs

_____ ❑ **Appendix 11.2:** Criteria for Evaluating World Wide Web Sites

_____ ❑ **Weblink 11.4:** Selected Resources for Integrating Technology into Instruction

_____ ❑ **Summary**

_____ ❑ **Key Terms and Concepts**

_____ ❑ **Applications and Interactivities:** Teacher's Journal

_____ ❑ **Applications and Interactivities:** Teacher's Database

_____ ❑ **Applications and Interactivities:** Observations and Interviews

_____ ❑ **Applications and Interactivities:** Professional Portfolio

_____ ❑ **Handout Master M11.1:** Selected Resources for Integrating Technology into Instruction

_____ ❑ **PostTest with Answers**

part four

Your Teaching Future

dear mentor

**On Being Involved in
Your Educational Community**

Dear Mentor,

I am in the process of completing my degree and earning my teaching credential. I have always been active in the social issues of my community. How can I, as a teacher, be active in my school's decisions about education reform? What opportunities should I look for?

Sincerely,
Sara Waltmire

Dear Sara,

I, too, have been involved consistently in the social issues of my community. When I started teaching, I wanted to bring those issues into my school. I have come up with some pretty unusual math lessons on community, diversity, and other social issues. I also saw opportunities for students to be involved in serving others. We started a community service club and planned activities with a local food bank and a children's hospital. A few months after the club began, I learned a valuable lesson: One of the students who had taken the lead in organizing and supporting the club's activities was in much need of help herself. Her family was in financial and personal turmoil. Sometimes she had to look after herself. But still, she managed to be a good student.

Because my life had been sheltered from many of the realities of the world, I did not realize that the people who needed help weren't just "out there" somewhere but were also right inside my classroom. Problems at home are not left outside school on the steps; they travel with the student and impact everything that happens in that child's life and education. All children, whatever challenges life has put in their path, deserve a safe place to learn and construct their understanding of the world. I began to realize that changing what went on in my classroom alone was not enough. If I wanted to create real change, I had to become involved in reforming education on a wider plane.

First, I began participating on a district Pre-Algebra committee whose goal was to get input about what was working and what was not from as many teachers as possible. I was concerned that I did not have much to offer. However, on that committee I found other teachers who confront many of the same problems I did, and who wanted to make a change. We wrote a new curriculum to address the varied learning styles of our students. Participating in this project led to more projects and more people who are working to improve education.

Join in a committee, a project, or a seminar. Speak out at every chance you get. Be an advocate for kids. Sooner than you think, you will have more opportunities to serve and people asking you to help than you will have time for. One thing of which I am certain—that has been proven to me time and again—is that teachers are the most creative, devoted, and caring people you will meet. In my travels, I have met teachers from all over the United States, and I have been amazed by the different challenges we face. At the same time, if I talk with them at length, I discover that underneath it all, we are faced with many of the same challenges. We are a great community of educators working together on the critical assignment of educating children and youth.

Sincerely,

Diane Crim, Math Teacher
1999 Utah Teacher of the Year

12

Teachers as Educational Leaders

As a fledgling teacher I saw the principal come to the veteran teachers on an informal basis to get their opinions on administrative and curricular decisions. The principal knew the best way to determine how policy affects students was to ask the person who was most directly involved with students—the classroom teacher. I was very fortunate to have a forward-thinking principal who embraced the concept of site-based decision making.

—a North Carolina teacher
Teachers Leading the Way: Voices from the National Teacher Forum,
U.S. Department of Education, April 1998

focus questions

1. To what extent is teaching a full profession?

2. What is professionalism in teaching?

3. To what professional organizations do teachers belong?

4. How do teachers help shape education as a profession?

5. What new leadership roles for teachers are emerging?

6. How do teachers contribute to educational research?

7. How are teachers involved in school restructuring and curriculum reform?

It is November of your fifth year of teaching, and you are attending a meeting of the steering committee for a statewide teacher network launched that September. The state department of education divided the state into twelve regions, and you were elected by your peers to be the network leader for your region. The network is based on the premise that teachers should have opportunities to participate in, and to lead, professional development activities of their own choosing, such as curriculum workshops, leadership institutes, internships, and conferences.

Audio Clip 12.1

The purpose of this two-day meeting at the state capitol is to begin the process of designing a series of two-week summer institutes for teachers. The institutes will be invitational; and institute "fellows" will be selected by the steering committee after an extensive application and interview process. One institute will be held in each region throughout the state, and teachers will receive a $600 stipend plus expenses for attending. To disseminate the knowledge and skills they acquire and to further develop their leadership abilities, the institute fellows will design and deliver staff development programs at their home schools.

The committee chair, a teacher from a school in the state's largest city, has just laid out the group's task for the next two days. "By the end of the day tomorrow, we need to have identified which institutes will be offered in each region. Also, we need to have a 'game plan' for how each of you will facilitate the development of the summer institute in your region."

"Well, the way I see it," says the teacher next to you, "the institutes should accomplish at least two major purposes. First, they should provide teachers with ways to increase their effectiveness in the classroom by acquiring new strategies and materials. Second, and just as important, the institutes should give teachers opportunities to play key leadership roles in school reform efforts around the state."

"That's right," says another teacher. "Teachers should recognize that the institutes give them a voice and meaningful opportunities to function as professionals."

"What I like about the institutes," says the teacher across the table from you, "is that they give teachers a chance to break out of the role of passively *receiving* in-service training. It's no different for teachers than it is for students —we learn best by actively shaping our learning environment and constructing meaning."

As several members of the group, including you, nod in agreement, you reflect on what you've just heard. What does it really mean to be a professional? What are the characteristics of a profession, and to what extent does teaching reflect those characteristics? What new leadership roles for teachers are emerging? What leadership roles will you play in educational reform?

Name _____ Date _____

For each question, circle the letter of the answer you believe is correct. Then read the chapter to learn more about these topics.

12.1 It has been suggested that professionals in the United States will begin to look more and more alike. For example, doctors are accepting more regulation and school teachers
A. Are on a fast track to match their salaries within one decade.
B. Will quickly move to both higher salaries and more autonomy.
C. Are similarly coming under more stringent controls.
D. Will slowly break out of long-established bureaucratic hierarchies.

12.2 As principals respond to increasing pressure to become more effective at facilitating collaborative, emergent approaches to leadership, teachers should receive
A. Higher salaries.
B. Greater degrees of self-governance.
C. Less control over the curriculum.
D. Collective bargaining.

12.3 Grant and Murray (1999) argue that all of the following are likely true of teachers *except*
A. There is a body of pedagogical content knowledge specific to the work of teachers.
B. Teachers have genuine expertise in their subject matter.
C. Teachers will acknowledge the greater curricular expertise of administrators.
D. Teachers will no longer allow administrators to view themselves as an exclusive class of experts.

12.4 All of the following are key dimensions of professionalism in teaching *except*
A. Professional involvement.
B. Professional behavior.
C. Compliant behavior.
D. Lifelong learning.

12.5 The presidents of the NEA and AFT agreed that all of the following are assaults on public education except
A. Busing.
B. Voucher plans.
C. Charter schools.
D. Privatization.

12.6 Each of the following "clusters" represents areas of reform within which teachers may find opportunities to shape policies in the future *except*
A. Reforms in salaries and benefits awarded to teachers.
B. Organizational reform of schools.

C. Reforms in assessing students' learning.
D. Reforms in teaching as a profession.

12.7 All of the following are unique roles of a mentor *except*
A. The role is clearly defined and written in a comprehensive plan.
B. The role has the potential to change the quality of life.
C. The role is mutually recognized by student and teacher.
D. The role develops naturally.

12.8 The largest professional organization for teachers in the United States is the
A. American Federation of Teachers.
B. National Education Association.
C. American Federation of Educators.
D. American Education Association.

12.9 A significant difference between the National Education Association (NEA) and the American Federation of Teachers (AFT) is that
A. Membership in the AFT is not open to administrators.
B. The AFT does not organize teachers around various educational issues.
C. The AFT does not participate in the development of educational policies.
D. The AFT does not support collective bargaining.

12.10 What single factor appears most likely to prevent the NEA and the AFT from merging into one large teacher organization?
A. NEA's policy allowing administrators to join the association.
B. AFT's support of strikes.
C. NEA's failure to win higher salaries for teachers.
D. AFT's connected with organized labor.

Answers are available on the FlexChoice website at www.ablongman.com/parkayflex.

Educational reform, as the preceding scenario illustrates, is continuing to change dramatically what it means to be a teacher. State-sponsored teacher networks, the professionalization of teaching, shared decision making, peer review, and mentor teacher programs are just a few of the changes that are providing unprecedented opportunities for teachers to assume new leadership roles beyond the classroom. In addition, as Joseph Murphy points out in "Reconnecting Teaching and School Administration: A Call for a Unified Profession," approaches to educational leadership are becoming more collaborative and participatory:

> The hierarchical, bureaucratic organizational structures that have defined schools over the past 80 years are giving way to more decentralized and more professionally controlled systems that create new designs for school management. In these new postindustrial educational organizations, there are important shifts in roles, relationships, and responsibilities: traditional patterns of relationships are altered, authority flows are less hierarchical, role definitions are both more general and flexible, leadership is connected to competence for needed tasks rather than to formal position, and independence and isolation are replaced by cooperative work (Murphy, April 1999).

We have referred to teaching as a **profession** throughout this book; however, if we compare teaching with other professions—law and medicine, for example—we find some significant differences. As a result of these differences, current opinion is divided as to whether teaching actually is a full profession. Some have labeled teaching a *semi*-profession (Etzioni 1969), an *emerging* profession (Howsam et al. 1976), an *uncertain* profession (Powell 1980), an *imperiled* profession (Duke 1984; Sykes 1983; Freedman, Jackson, and Botes 1983; Boyer 1990), an *endangered* profession (Goodlad 1983b), and a *not-quite* profession (Goodlad 1990)!

To What Extent Is Teaching a Full Profession?

We use the terms *professional* and *profession* quite frequently, usually without thinking about their meanings. Professionals "possess a high degree of specialized *theoretical knowledge,* along with methods and techniques for applying this knowledge in their day-to-day work. . . . [and they] are united by a high degree of in-group solidarity, stemming from their common training and common adherence to certain doctrines and methods" (Abrahamsson 1971, 11–12).

From several sociologists and educators who have studied teaching come additional characteristics of occupations that are highly professionalized, summarized in Figure 12.1. Before reading further, reflect on each characteristic and decide whether it applies to teaching. Then, continue reading about the extent to which teaching satisfies each of these commonly agreed-upon characteristics of full professions. Do our perceptions agree with yours?

Figure 12.1

Institutional Monopoly of Services

On one hand, teachers do have a monopoly of services. As a rule, only those who are certified members of the profession may teach in public schools. On the other hand, the varied requirements we find for certification and for teaching in private schools weaken this monopoly. In addition, any claim teachers might have as exclusive providers of a service is further eroded by the practice of many state systems to approve temporary, or emergency, certification measures to deal with teacher shortages—a move that establishes teaching as the only profession that allows noncertified individuals to practice the profession. The National Commission on Teaching and America's Future (1996), for example, reported that more than 25 percent of the nation's teachers were not fully licensed, and about one-fourth of the high school teachers surveyed lacked a minor degree in their primary field of instruction. Furthermore, a decline of inadequately licensed teachers seems unlikely, given the U.S. Department of Education's projection that more than two million teachers would be needed between 1999 and 2009.

Perhaps the most significant argument against teachers claiming to be the exclusive providers of a service, however, is the fact that a great deal of teaching occurs in informal, nonschool settings and is done by people who are not teachers. Every day, thousands of people teach various kinds of how-to-do-it skills: how to water-ski, how to make dogs more obedient, how to make pasta from scratch, how to tune a car's engine, and how to meditate.

Teacher Autonomy

In one sense teachers have considerable autonomy. They usually work behind a closed classroom door, and only seldom is their work observed by another adult. In fact, one of the norms among teachers is that the classroom is a castle of sorts, and teacher privacy a closely guarded right. Although the performance of new teachers may be observed and evaluated on a regular basis by supervisors, veteran teachers are observed much less frequently, and they usually enjoy a high degree of autonomy.

Teachers also have extensive freedom regarding how they structure the classroom environment. They may emphasize discussions as opposed to lectures. They may set certain requirements for some students and not for others. They may delegate responsibilities to one class and not another. And, within the guidelines set by local and state authorities, teachers may determine much of the content they teach.

There are, however, constraints placed on teachers and their work. Teachers, unlike doctors and lawyers, must accept all the "clients" who are sent to them. Only infrequently does a teacher actually "reject" a student assigned to him or her.

Teachers must also agree to teach what state and local officials say they must. Moreover, the work of teachers is subject to a higher level of public scrutiny than that found in other professions. Because the public provides "clients" (students) and pays for schools, it has a significant say regarding the work of teachers. Nevertheless, it has been suggested that some "leveling" of professions will occur in the United States during the early twenty-first century: "More of the work of the traditional high-status professions, particularly medicine, will occur in bureaucratic or large organizational settings under the watchful eye of managers. [While] doctors are accepting more and more regulation, the school teachers . . . will slowly break out of long-established bureaucratic hierarchies and share more of the autonomy previously enjoyed by members of the high-status professions" (Grant and Murray 1999, 231–32).

Years of Education and Training

As sociologist Amitai Etzioni (1969) points out in his classic discussion of the "semi-professions," the training of teachers is less lengthy than that required for other professionals—lawyers and physicians, for example. The professional component of teacher education programs is the shortest of all the professions—only 15 percent of the average bachelor's degree program for a high school teacher is devoted to professional courses. However, as we learned in Chapter 2, several colleges and universities have begun five-year teacher education programs. Similarly, in its comprehensive report, *What Matters Most: Teaching for America's Future,* the National Commission on Teaching and America's Future (1996) recommended that teacher education be moved to the graduate level. If the trend toward five-year and graduate-level teacher education programs continues, the professional status of teaching will definitely be enhanced.

In most professions, new members must undergo a prescribed induction period. Physicians, for example, must serve an internship or residency before beginning practice, and most lawyers begin as clerks in law firms. In contrast, teachers usually do not go through a formal induction period before assuming full responsibility for their work. Practice teaching comes closest to serving as an induction period, but it is often relatively short, informal, and lacking in uniformity. As the National Commission on Teaching and America's Future (1996) noted, "Our society can no longer accept the [s]ink-or-swim induction [of teachers]."

Provision of Essential Service

Although it is generally acknowledged that teachers provide a service that is vital to the well-being of individuals and groups, the public does need to be reminded of this fact from time to time. This importance was driven home on a large scale during the early 1980s when several reports calling for school reform linked the strength of our country to the quality of its schools. In a sense, it is no exaggeration to say that teaching is a matter of life and death:

> every moment in the lives of teachers and pupils brings critical decisions of motivation, reinforcement, reward, ego enhancement and goal direction. Proper professional decisions enhance learning and life; improper decisions send the learner towards incremental death in openness to experience and in ability to learn and contribute. Doctors and lawyers probably have neither more nor less to do with life, death, and freedom than do teachers (Howsam et al. 1976, 15).

Degree of Self-Governance

The limited freedom of teachers to govern themselves has detracted from the overall status of the profession. In many states, licensing guidelines are set by government officials who may or may not be educators; and at the local level, decision-making power usually resides with local boards of education, largely made up of people who have never taught. As a result, teachers have had little or no say over what they teach, when they teach, whom they teach, and, in extreme instances, *how* they teach.

However, recent efforts to empower teachers and to professionalize teaching are creating new roles for teachers and expanded opportunities to govern important aspects of their work. At schools throughout the country, teachers are having a greater voice in decisions related to curriculum development, staffing, budget, and the day-to-day operation of schools. Table 12.1, for example, compares public- and private-school teachers' and principals' perceptions of teacher influence or control over discipline policies, in-service programs, curricula, textbook selection, selection of content, and teaching techniques. Although teachers and principals differ significantly in the amount of influence

weblink

Table 12.1

or control they believe teachers have, teachers should experience greater degrees of self-governance as principals respond to increasing pressure to become more effective at facilitating collaborative, emergent approaches to leadership (Parkay, Shindler, and Oaks 1997). As Gerald Grant and Christine Murray point out in *Teaching in America: The Slow Revolution* (1999, 217), "schoolteachers can assert that they have genuine expertise in their subject matter and that there is a body of pedagogical content knowledge that is specific to their work. Most important, they are no longer willing to let the administrators define themselves as the exclusive class of experts controlling either the content of the curriculum or decisions about who is fit to teach it."

Professional Associations

Teachers, like other professionals, have formed a number of vocational associations that are vitally concerned with issues such as admission to the profession, educational standards, examinations and licensing, career development, ethical and performance standards, and professional discipline. It is clear, though, that the more than 500 national teacher organizations have not progressed as far as other professions have in gaining control of these areas.

Professional Knowledge and Skills

Professionals are granted a certain status because they possess knowledge and skills not normally held by the general public. Within the profession of teaching, however, the requirements for membership are less precise. In spite of the ongoing efforts of educational researchers, there is less than unanimous agreement on the knowledge and skills considered necessary to teach. This lack of agreement is reflected in the varied programs at the 1,300 or so colleges and universities that train teachers.

During the last ten years, the National Board for Professional Teaching Standards (NBPTS) has made significant progress toward clarifying the knowledge base for teaching. As you learned in Chapter 2, the NBPTS (the majority of whose members are teachers) offers board certification to teachers who possess a high level of NBPTS-identified knowledge and skills. By the start of 2000, the NBPTS had granted national certification to about 2,000 teachers, and the Board planned to certify 100,000 teachers by 2006.

Level of Public Trust

The level of trust the public extends to teachers as professionals varies greatly. On the one hand, the public appears to have great confidence in the work that teachers do. Because of its faith in the teaching profession, the public invests teachers with considerable power over its children. For the most part, parents willingly allow their children to be molded and influenced by teachers, and this willingness must be based on a high degree of trust. In addition, most parents expect their children to obey and respect teachers.

Though all professions have some members who might be described as unprofessional, teaching is especially vulnerable to such charges. The sheer size of the teaching force makes it difficult to maintain consistently high professional standards. Moreover, teaching is subject to a level of public scrutiny and control that other, more established, professions traditionally have not tolerated. However, the era of widespread public trust may be running out for these other professions as well. Mushrooming malpractice suits against doctors, for example, may be a sign that here, too, public confidence has significantly eroded.

Prestige, Benefits, and Pay

As mentioned in Chapter 1, teachers are viewed as having higher social status than most of the population; however, this higher status is based on level of education attained rather than wealth. Thus teachers have not received salaries in keeping with other professions requiring approximately the same amount of schooling. Nevertheless, there is significant support for reducing the salary gap—on the 1999 Phi Delta Kappa/ Gallup Poll, 62 percent of the respondents favored increased pay for *all* teachers; 90 percent favored increased pay for teachers who "demonstrate high performance"; and 63 percent favored tax credits for high-performing teachers (Rose and Gallup 1999).

What Is Professionalism in Teaching?

The current goal among teachers, teacher educators, policymakers, and the general public is to make teaching a full profession. Toward this end, teachers are willing to take risks and learn new roles as they press for greater self-governance, better working conditions, and increased financial rewards. In addition, teachers are acquiring the analytical skills needed to understand and provide leadership for the complex processes of educational reform. The following sections look at the three key dimensions of professionalism in teaching presented in Figure 12.2: professional behavior, life-long learning, and involvement in the profession.

Figure 12.2

Professional Behavior

The professional teacher is guided by a specific set of values. He or she has made a deep and lasting commitment to professional practice. He or she has adopted a high standard of professional ethics and models behaviors that are in accord with that code of ethics. The professional teacher also engages in serious, reflective thought about how to teach more effectively. Moreover, he or she does this while teaching, continually examining experiences to improve practice.

Reflection-in-Action   Donald Schön (1983, 1987, and 1991) has described this professional behavior as **reflection-in-action**, and he describes how a teacher might use it to solve a problem in the classroom:

> An artful teacher sees a child's difficulty in learning to read not as a defect in the child but as a defect "of his own instruction." And because the child's difficulties may be unique, the teacher cannot assume that his repertoire of explanations will suffice, even though they are "at the tongue's end." He must be ready to invent new methods and must "endeavor to develop in himself the ability of discovering them" (1983, 66).

The professional teacher Schön describes makes careful, sensitive observations of classroom events, reflects on the meaning of those observations, and then decides to act in a certain way. Steven Lacy, selected by the Walt Disney Company as the Outstanding General Elementary Teacher for 1994–95, describes the reflective decision-making process this way:

> Our effectiveness as teachers is not reflected in the materials and structures of our pedagogy as much as it is in the countless decisions we make every day, decisions that are made in an instant. [D]o I help him with that problem or let him struggle? Do I pursue her question or stick with the lesson? Does this behavior need to be punished or ignored? Does this composition need to be criticized or praised (Levey 1996, 2–3)?

Becoming a Mentor Because of their positions and their encounters with young people, teachers may find opportunities to become mentors to some of their students. Accepting this responsibility is another example of professional behavior. The role of **mentor** is unique in several ways. First, mentorship develops naturally and is not an automatic part of teaching, nor can it be assigned to anyone. True mentorships grow from teaching relationships and cannot be artificially promoted. Second, the role of mentor is a *comprehensive* one: Mentors express broad interest in those whom they mentor. Third, the role of mentor is *mutually* recognized by student and teacher; both realize that their relationship has a special "depth." Fourth, the role of mentor is significant and has the potential to change the quality and direction of students' lives. And fifth, the opportunity to work with a mentor is free, what Gehrke (1988) terms the mentor's "gift of care."

The longer you teach, the more you will encounter opportunities for mentorships to develop, discovering that you can mentor less experienced teachers and student teachers as well as students. The rewards that come from the unique role of mentor are among the most satisfying.

What characteristics distinguish teaching as a profession? What characteristics might distinguish this teacher as a professional?

AUDIO

Audio Clip 12.2

Lifelong Learning

The professional teacher is dedicated to continuous learning—both about the teaching-learning process and about the subject taught. No longer is it sufficient for career teachers to obtain only a bachelor's degree and a teaching certificate. Rather, teachers are lifelong members of learning communities.

Several states have mandated continuing education for teachers. The content of the curriculum as well as methods and materials for teaching that content are changing so rapidly that teachers must be involved in continuous learning to maintain their professional effectiveness. In addition, we feel that teachers must practice what they preach. A teacher who is not continuously learning raises serious questions for students: If it's not important for our teachers to learn, why should we? The attitude toward learning that teachers model for students may be as important as the content they teach.

Many opportunities are available for teachers to learn new knowledge and skills. Nearly every school district makes provisions for in-service training or staff development. Topics can range from classroom-focused issues such as authentic assessment, using the Internet, classroom management, integrated curricula, or learning styles to schoolwide management issues such as restructuring, shared governance,

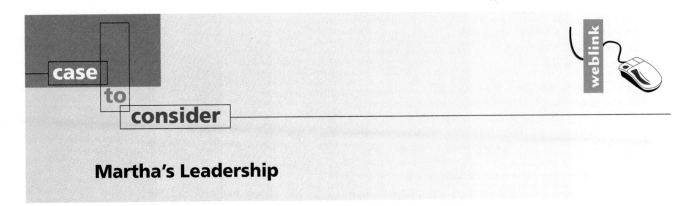

case
to
consider

Martha's Leadership

or school–community partnerships. Beyond these in-service opportunities, professional teachers actively seek additional avenues for growth, as this teacher observes during her fourth year of teaching: "After realizing what it could mean to work with colleagues and support colleagues in their work, I began arranging my own 'in-service' opportunities in my building and in the professional community. Even though I am a young teacher, I learned that I too am responsible for continuing my own learning in my profession" (Visconti 1996, 154).

Many teachers have attained National Board Certification, a professional growth experience several Board-certified teachers describe this way:

■ "One of the best professional development experiences—it gave me lots of self-confidence."
■ "The certification process was a real eye-opener. I realized I've done an awful lot—the process helps document your accomplishments."
■ "It was like the final stages of a major graduate course or a cumulative comprehensive exam or thesis."
■ "The certification process far exceeds everything I've ever done, including my M.A."
■ "The certification process was more focused than a master's program and more valuable because it was what I was really doing in the classroom" (Rotberg, Futrell, and Lieberman, 1998, 463).

Learning to Become a Leader For professional teachers, an important goal of life-long learning is to acquire leadership skills. Successful educational reform in the twenty-first century will require teacher participation in leadership. In fact, it is quite possible that "schools of the [twenty-first] century will be run by teams of teachers who [have] the tools, incentives, and leadership they need to accomplish their jobs" (Gerstner et al. 1994, 169). One such school is Anzar High School in California, which operates under a team leadership model, *without* a principal. According to Anzar High teachers, after the school opened in 1994, they "had to develop personal and interpersonal sensibilities in order not to re-create the same kind of hierarchical system with which we were familiar and comfortable" (Barnett, McKowen, and Bloom 1998, 48). The success of the team leadership model is the result of teachers' commitment to the "Anzar Communication Guidelines":

■ I commit to practice these guidelines.
■ We are all part of the same team; we collectively own the problems, and we collectively solve them.
■ We will allow conflict/differing ideas to exist.
■ We will help and support others.
■ I will be honest (Barnett, McKowen, and Bloom 1998, 48–49).

Involvement in the Profession

Today's teachers realize that they have the most important role in the educational enterprise and that, previously, they have not had the power they needed to improve the profession. Therefore, they are taking an increasingly broader view of the decisions that, as professionals, they have the right to make, as this elementary teacher points out:

> One of the problems is legislative people deciding what the education reforms should be and how they should be handled. I think it entails a lack of trust in the teachers by these authorities, and I think it's passed on to the public by the authorities. . . . Every time they start reforming education, they start reforming the teachers. For example, there's all the talk about competency testing and we're going to get rid of all the bad teachers. Teachers have the feeling that they're talking about all of us. We sometimes are used as public relations by authorities. And then often they take credit for what we do (Godar 1990, 264).

Across the country, professional teachers are deeply involved with their colleagues, professional organizations, teacher educators, legislators, policy makers, and others in a push to make teaching more fully a profession. Through their behaviors and accomplishments, they are demonstrating that they are professionals, that the professional identity of teachers is becoming stronger. During the last decade, for example, teachers have become more involved in teacher education reform, teacher certification, and professional governance. And, through the efforts of scores of teacher organizations, teachers have also made gains in working conditions, salaries, and benefits.

To What Professional Organizations Do Teachers Belong?

The expanding leadership role of teachers has been supported through the activities of more than 500 national teacher organizations (*National Trade and Professional Associations of the United States* 1999). These organizations and the scores of hardworking teachers who run them support a variety of activities to improve teaching and schools. Through lobbying in Washington and at state capitols, for example, teacher associations acquaint legislators, policymakers, and politicians with critical issues and problems in the teaching profession. Many associations have staffs of teachers, researchers, and consultants who produce professional publications, hold conferences, prepare grant proposals, engage in school improvement activities, and promote a positive image of teaching to the public. In the quest to improve the professional lives of all teachers, two national organizations have led the way: the National Education Association (NEA) and the American Federation of Teachers (AFT). These two groups have had a long history of competition for the allegiance of teachers.

The National Education Association

Membership in the **National Education Association (NEA),** the oldest and largest of the two organizations, includes both teachers and administrators. Originally called the National Teachers Association when it was founded in 1857, the group was started by forty-three educators from a dozen states and the District of Columbia (West 1980, 1).

The NEA has affiliates in every state plus Puerto Rico and the District of Columbia, and its local affiliates number more than 13,000. About two-thirds of the teachers in this country belong to the NEA. More than 78 percent of NEA's 2.4 million members are teachers; about 12 percent are guidance counselors, librarians, and administrators; almost 3 percent are university professors; about 2 percent are college and university students; about 3 percent are support staff (teacher aides, secretaries, cafeteria workers, bus drivers, and custodians); and about 2 percent are retired members.

To improve education in this country, the NEA has standing committees in the following areas: affiliate relationships, higher education, human relations, political action, teacher benefits, and teacher rights. These committees engage in a wide range of activities, among them preparing reports on important educational issues, disseminating the results of educational research, conducting conferences, working with federal agencies on behalf of children, pressing for more rigorous standards for the teaching profession, helping school districts resolve salary disputes, developing ways to improve personnel practices, and enhancing the relationship between the profession and the public.

Currently, more than two-thirds of states have passed some type of collective bargaining laws that apply to teachers. There is little uniformity among these laws, with most of the thirty-one states permitting strikes only if certain conditions have been met. The NEA has gone on record as supporting a federal statute that would set up uniform procedures for teachers to bargain with their employers.

The NEA continues today to focus on issues of concern to teachers, primarily in the area of professional governance. Efforts are being made to broaden teachers' decision-making powers related to curriculum, extracurricular responsibilities, staff development, and supervision. To promote the status of the profession, the NEA conducts annual research studies and opinion surveys in various areas and publishes *NEA Today,* the *NEA Research Bulletin,* and its major publication, *Today's Education.*

The American Federation of Teachers

The **American Federation of Teachers (AFT)** was founded in 1916. Three teachers' unions in Chicago issued a call for teachers to form a national organization affiliated with organized labor. Teacher unions in Gary, Indiana; New York City; Oklahoma; Scranton, Pennsylvania; and Washington, D.C., joined the three Chicago unions to form the AFT.

The AFT differs from the NEA in that it is open only to teachers and nonsupervisory school personnel. The AFT is active today in organizing teachers, collective bargaining, public relations, and developing policies related to various educational issues. In addition, the organization conducts research in areas such as educational reform, bilingual education, teacher certification, and evaluation, and also represents members' concerns through legislative action and technical assistance.

The AFT has more than one million members who are organized through 2,265 local affiliates. The AFT is affiliated with the American Federation of Labor–Congress of Industrial Organizations (AFL-CIO), which has over thirteen million members. To promote the idea that teachers should have the right to speak for themselves on important issues, the AFT does not allow superintendents, principals, and other administrators to join. As an informational brochure on the AFT states, "Because the AFT believes in action—in 'getting things done' rather than issuing reports, letting someone else do the 'doing'—a powerful, cohesive structure is necessary."

Unlike the NEA, the AFT has been steadfastly involved throughout its history in securing economic gains and improving working conditions for teachers. Though the AFT has been criticized for being unprofessional and too concerned with bread-and-butter issues, none other than the great educator and philosopher John Dewey took out the first AFT membership card in 1916. After twelve years as a union member, Dewey made his stance on economic issues clear:

It is said that the Teachers Union, as distinct from the more academic organizations, overemphasizes the economic aspect of teaching. Well, I never had that contempt for the economic aspect of teaching, especially not on the first of the month when I get my salary check. I find that teachers have to pay their grocery and meat bills and house rent just the same as everybody else (Dewey 1955, 60–61).

Traditionally, the AFT has been strongest in urban areas. Today, the AFT represents teachers not only in Chicago and New York but in Philadelphia, Washington, D.C., Kansas City, Detroit, Boston, Cleveland, and Pittsburgh. NEA membership has tended to be suburban and rural. The NEA has always been the larger of the two organizations, and it is presently more than twice the size of its rival.

A Merger between the NEA and AFT?

Over the years, the differences between the NEA and the AFT have become less apparent. Collective bargaining and the use of strikes, long opposed by the NEA, are now used by both organizations. The major difference between the two groups now is the AFT's affiliation with organized labor, a relationship that has led to public disaffection in some areas.

Many people within both the NEA and the AFT believe that the interests of teachers and students could best be served through a merger of the two organizations. One national teachers' union with enormous political strength is the goal. In 1968, Charles Cogen, president of the AFT, proposed a merger with the NEA. In the AFT's publication, *The American Teacher*, Cogen wrote:

> There is no use denying that the AFT and the NEA are engaged in dire competition for the membership of the teachers of America. But we must do this without giving aid and power to the governmental authorities, boards of education, and superintendents with whom we are contending. And then, let us keep the door open; let us look forward to the day when AFT-NEA unity may become a reality. Heaven knows, we fully need a strong, unified, militant, and labor-oriented teachers' union to fight the great battles that lie ahead.

The NEA, however, declined the AFT's invitation to explore that possibility and proposed instead that the AFT drop its AFL-CIO affiliation and join the NEA. A few local affiliates, however, did go on to merge.

Another attempt was made to merge in 1973–74. After several months of talks, however, the possibility of a merger was abandoned. Once again, the NEA cited the AFT's insistence on AFL-CIO affiliation as the major stumbling block.

In early 1998, a "conceptual agreement" to merge the organizations was announced by the presidents of the NEA and the AFT. The presidents cited an "assault" on public education in the form of voucher plans, charter schools, and other approaches to school privatization as a primary reason to merge (Bradley 1998a). The proposal to merge was ultimately rejected that summer in a vote by NEA and AFT members; however, in Minnesota, the AFT and NEA affiliates merged to become the nation's only state organization made up of members of both national teachers' unions.

Other Professional Organizations

In addition to the NEA and AFT, teachers' professional interests are represented by more than 500 other national organizations. Several of these are concerned with improving the quality of education at all levels and in all subject areas. **Phi Delta Kappa (PDK)**, for example, is a professional and honorary fraternity of educators concerned with

where do you stand?

Do teachers' unions have a positive effect on education?

Weblink 12.1
Weblink 12.2

Appendix 12.1

enhancing quality education through research and leadership activities. Founded in 1906, Phi Delta Kappa now has a membership of 166,000. Members, who are graduate students, teachers, and administrators, belong to one of more than 666 chapters. To be initiated into Phi Delta Kappa, one must have demonstrated high academic achievement, have completed at least fifteen semester hours of graduate work in education, and have made a commitment to a career of educational service. Phi Delta Kappa members receive *Phi Delta Kappan,* a journal of education published ten times a year.

Another example is the **Association for Supervision and Curriculum Development (ASCD)**, a professional organization of teachers, supervisors, curriculum coordinators, education professors, administrators, and others. The ASCD is interested in school improvement at all levels of education. Founded in 1921, the association has a membership of 150,000. ASCD provides professional development experiences in curriculum and supervision, disseminates information on educational issues, and encourages research, evaluation, and theory development. ASCD also conducts several National Curriculum Study Institutes around the country each year and provides a free research information service to members. Members receive *Educational Leadership,* a well-respected journal printed eight times a year. ASCD also publishes a yearbook, each one devoted to a particular educational issue, and occasional books in the area of curriculum and supervision.

In addition, as you will see in Appendix 12.1 many professional associations exist for teachers of specific subject-areas, such as mathematics, English, social studies, music, physical education, and so on, as well as for teachers of specific student populations, such as exceptional learners, young children, and students with limited English proficiency.

What New Leadership Roles for Teachers Are Emerging?

Teachers' roles are changing in fundamental and positive ways at the beginning of the twenty-first century. Greater autonomy and an expanded role in educational policymaking has led to "unprecedented opportunities for today's teachers to extend their leadership roles beyond the classroom" (Gmelch and Parkay 1995, 48). To prepare for this future, today's teachers will need to develop leadership skills to a degree not needed in the past.

Teacher Involvement in Teacher Education, Certification, and Staff Development

Teacher input into key decisions about teacher preparation, certification, and staff development is on the rise. Through their involvement with professional development schools and the National Board for Professional Teaching Standards (see Chapter 2), state professional standards boards (see Chapter 2), and scores of local, state, and national education committees, teachers are changing the character of pre- and in-service education.

For example, in 1992, the National Board for Professional Teaching Standards (NBPTS) established a network designed to allow nearly 7 percent of the nation's 2.5 million teachers to participate in field-testing various components of the NBPTS certification system. The NBPTS allocated $1 million to teachers, in the form of honoraria, for helping to field-test the NBPTS assessment materials. In commenting on the teachers' role in the field-test network, the NBPTS vice-president for assessment and research said, "Teachers are indispensable for the development of these assessments. We need their real-world perspective" (National Board for Professional Teaching Standards 1992, 3).

Teachers who have received National Board Certification are recognized as professionals not only in their schools, but also in their districts and beyond. For example, after receiving Board Certification, these teachers had the following professional opportunities:

- Helene Alolouf (Early Adolescence/English Language Arts certificate) of Yonkers, New York, was invited to teach at the Manhattanville Graduate School of Education as an adjunct professor.
- Sandra Blackman (Early Adolescence/English Language Arts certificate) of San Diego, California, was promoted to resource teacher for the Humanities Departments for fifty-five schools, where she provides staff development for a standards-based system.
- Edward William Clark Jr. (Early Childhood/Generalist certificate) of Valley, Alabama, helped the State Department of Education and the Alabama Education Association develop National Board Certification training modules to assist Alabama teachers with National Board Certification.
- Linda Lilja (Middle Childhood/Generalist certificate) of Scranton, Kansas, was invited to serve as a member of the task force for the National Teachers Hall of Fame.
- Donna W. Parrish (Early Adolescence/Generalist certificate) of Shelby, North Carolina, was appointed curriculum specialist at a middle school.

Teacher-Leaders

As the titles of the following books published during the 1990s suggest, the term **teacher-leader** has become part of the vocabulary of educational reform:

- *Awakening the Sleeping Giant: Leadership Development for Teachers* (Katzenmeyer and Moller 1996).
- *Collaborative Leadership and Shared Decision Making: Teachers, Principals, and University Professors* (Clift et al. 1995).
- *Educating Teachers for Leadership and Change* (O'Hair and Odell 1995).
- *A Handbook for Teacher Leaders* (Pellicer and Anderson 1995).
- *Teachers as Leaders: Evolving Roles* (Livingston 1992).
- *Teachers as Leaders: Perspectives on the Professional Development of Teachers* (Walling 1994).
- *Who Will Save Our Schools?: Teachers as Constructivist Leaders* (Lambert et al 1996).

"In their new leadership roles, teachers are being called upon to form new partnerships with business and industry; institutions of higher education; social service agencies; professional associations; and local, state, and federal governmental agencies. In this new role, teachers will be the key to promoting widespread improvement of our educational system" (Gmelch and Parkay 1995, 50–51). A brief look at the professional activities of Sandra MacQuinn, a teacher-leader who worked with the first author and a colleague on a major restructuring effort at Rogers High School in

technology

highlights

Bobcats

Kristin Hatcher

How are teachers playing a leadership role in the development and
dissemination of multimedia
software?

Weblink 12.3

Spokane, Washington, illustrates the wide-ranging roles of a teacher-leader. In addition to teaching, here are just a few of MacQuinn's leadership activities while serving as liaison and on-site coordinator of a school-university partnership between Rogers High School and Washington State University's College of Education:

- Writing grant proposals for teacher-developed projects
- Helping other teachers write grant proposals
- Facilitating the development of an integrated school-to-work curriculum
- Preparing newsletters to keep faculty up-to-date on restructuring
- Organizing and facilitating staff development training
- Developing connections with area businesses and arranging "job shadowing" sites for students
- Working with a community college to create an alternative school for Rogers High students at the college
- Scheduling substitute teachers to provide Rogers teachers with release-time to work on restructuring
- Making presentations on the Rogers High restructuring at state and regional conferences
- Arranging for Rogers students to visit Washington State University (WSU)
- Meeting with the principal, assistant principals, WSU professors, and others to develop short- and long-range plans for implementing site-based management; chairing meetings of the site-based council, the restructuring steering committee, and other restructuring-related committees.

At West Forest Intermediate School in Opelika, Alabama, which has several schools within a school, teachers have the following roles: coordinator of special education services and lead teacher, coordinator of the media center responsible for schoolwide implementation of technology, and director of the school's whole-language program (Gerstner et al. 1994). At a Florida elementary school with a shared decision making (SDM) form of governance, teachers work on committees that make hiring, budget, and school policy decisions. In the words of one teacher at that school: "I'm not just a teacher in a classroom, I am a member of an organization, a company that helps to run the school. I'm not just alone in my room" (Ross and Webb 1995, 76).

Figure 12.3

Dimensions of Teacher Leadership beyond the Classroom

Figure 12.3 illustrates ten dimensions of teacher leadership beyond the classroom. The many teachers whom we have assisted on school restructuring projects during the last few years have used these skills to reach an array of educational goals. Clearly, these teachers have modeled what Rallis (1990, 193) terms "an elevated conception of teaching."

At schools around the country, teachers and principals are using a "collaborative, emergent" approach to leadership; that is, the person who provides leadership for a particular schoolwide project or activity may or may not be the principal or a member of the administrative team (Parkay, Schindler and Oaks, 1997). Such schools are characterized by a "higher level of professional community" (Newmann and Wehlage 1995). They are similar to the schools Wohlstetter (1995, 24) identified as having successfully implemented school-based management (SBM): "[They] had principals who played a key role in dispersing power. [T]he principals were often described as facilitators and managers of change." In addition, teachers who accept the challenge of becoming teacher-leaders and redefining their roles to include responsibilities beyond the classroom recognize the importance of five principles Michael Fullan and Andy Hargreaves present in their book, *What's Worth Fighting For in Your School?* (1996); they use these principles to guide their professional actions (see Figure 12.4).

Figure 12.4

Professional Reflection   **Working with principals**

How Do Teachers Contribute to Educational Research?

Today's teachers play an increasingly important role in educational research. By applying research to solve practical, classroom-based problems, teachers validate the accuracy and usefulness of educational research and help researchers identify additional areas to investigate. As consumers of educational research, teachers improve their teaching, contribute to educational reform, and enhance the professional status of teaching.

In addition, increasing numbers of teachers are becoming competent researchers in their own right and making important contributions to our understanding of teaching and learning. Prior to the mid 1980s, teachers were the missing "voice" in educational research. However, as teachers and staff developers Holly and McLoughlin (1989, 309) noted more than a decade ago, "We've moved from research on teachers to research with teachers and lately to research by teachers." Since their observation, we have seen the emergence of the **teacher-researcher,** the professional teacher who conducts classroom research to improve his or her teaching.

Part of being a professional is the ability to decide *how* and *when* to use research to guide one's actions. For example, Emmerich Koller, a teacher of German at a suburban high school, describes in an article he wrote for the book *Teachers Doing Research: Practical Possibilities* (Burnaford, Fischer, and Hobson 1996) how he experimented with new teaching methods based on the latest findings from brain research and "accelerated learning," a strategy for optimizing learning by integrating conscious and unconscious mental processes. After determining how and when to put that research into practice, he commented, "At age 50, after 27 years of teaching, I have found something that has made teaching very exciting again" (Koller 1996, 180).

This teacher is conducting classroom research on the ways students come to understand a problem and to apply appropriate problem-solving skills. What are several ways the teacher might use this research as a professional?

Sources of Educational Research

Appendix 12.2

Research findings are reported in scores of educational research journals (see Appendix 12.2). In addition, there are several excellent reviews of research with which you should become familiar during your professional preparation, such as the third edition of the *Handbook of Research on Teaching* (published by Macmillan, 1986), a project sponsored by the American Educational Research Association. Its more than 1,000 pages synthesize research in several areas, including research on teaching at various grade levels and in various subject areas. Other comprehensive, authoritative reviews of research you might wish to consult include the following:

- *Encyclopedia of Educational Research,* 6th ed., four volumes (Macmillan, 1992)
- *Handbook of Research on the Education of Young Children* (Macmillan, 1993)
- *Handbook of Research on Mathematics Teaching and Learning* (Macmillan, 1992), sponsored by the National Council of Teachers of Mathematics
- *Handbook of Research on Multicultural Education* (Macmillian, 1995)
- *Handbook of Research on Music Teaching and Learning* (Macmillan, 1992), sponsored by the Music Educators National Conference
- *Handbook of Research on Science Teaching and Learning* (Macmillan, 1994), sponsored by the National Science Teachers Association
- *Handbook of Research on Social Studies Teaching and Learning* (Macmillan, 1991), sponsored by the National Council for the Social Studieshool Mathematics, and High School Mathematics (Macmillan, 1993), three volumes
- *Handbook of Research on Teaching the English Language Arts* (Macmillan, 1991), sponsored by the International Reading Association and the National Council of Teachers of English
- *Handbook of Research on Teaching Literacy through the Communicative and Visual Arts (Macmillan, 1997)*
- *Research Ideas for the Classroom: Early Childhood Mathematics, Middle School Mathematics, and High School Mathematics* (Macmillan, 1993), three volumes sponsored by the National Council of Teachers of Mathematics

Government Resources for Research Application

The federal government supports several efforts designed to help teachers improve their practice through the application of research findings. In 1966, three agencies were created to support and disseminate research: **Educational Resources Information Center (ERIC), Research and Development Centers,** and **Regional Educational Laboratories.** ERIC is a national information system made up of sixteen **ERIC Clearinghouses** and several adjunct clearinghouses—all coordinated by the central ERIC agency in Washington, D.C. (see the Teacher's Resource Guide section "Educational Resources Information Center (ERIC) Clearinghouses" on this book's website). The ERIC system, available in most college and university libraries, contains descriptions of exemplary programs, the results of research and development efforts, and related information that can be used by teachers, administrators, and the public to improve education. Each Clearinghouse specializes in one area of education and searches out relevant documents or journal articles that are screened according to ERIC selection criteria, abstracted, and indexed.

Weblink 12.4

Within the **Office of Educational Research and Improvement (OERI)** in Washington, D.C., the Office of Research (formerly the National Institute of Education) maintains fourteen research centers at universities around the country (see the Appendix "Selected National Educational Research and Improvement [OERI] Centers"on this book's website). The centers are devoted to high-quality, fundamental research at every level of education, with most of the research done by scholars at the host university. Among the areas these centers focus on are the processes of teaching and learning, school organization and improvement, the content of education, and factors that contribute to (or detract from) excellence in education.

OERI also houses Programs for the Improvement of Practice (PIP), which support exemplary projects at the state and local levels. PIP also maintains nine regional educational laboratories and sponsors a number of Assistance Centers (see the Appendix "Department of Education Regional Assistance Centers" on this book's website). Each laboratory serves a geographic region and is a nonprofit corporation not affiliated with a university. Laboratory staff work directly with school systems, state educational agencies, and other organizations to improve education through the application of research findings.

Conducting Classroom Action Research

More than three decades ago, Robert Schaefer (1967, 5) posed the following questions in *The School as the Center of Inquiry:*

> Why should our schools not be staffed, gradually if you will, by scholar-teachers in command of the conceptual tools and methods of inquiry requisite to investigating the learning process as it operates in their own classroom? Why should our schools not nurture the continuing wisdom and power of such scholar-teachers?

Schaefer's vision for teaching has become a reality. Today, thousands of teachers are involved in action research to improve their teaching. Using their classrooms as "laboratories," these teacher-researchers are systematically studying the outcomes of their teaching through the application of various research methods. In addition, they are disseminating the results of their research at professional conferences and through publications, including *Teacher as Researcher,* a journal edited, written, and published by teachers.

Simply put, **action research** is the classroom-based study by teachers, individually or collaboratively, of how to improve instruction. As in the *reflection-in-action* approach described earlier in this chapter, action research begins with a teacher-identified question, issue, or problem. How can I more effectively motivate a group of students? How do students experience the climate in my classroom? What factors limit parental participation in our school? How can our department (or teacher team) become more collegial? How does computer use in the foreign language classroom affect students' oral communication? Identification of the question to be investigated via action research is a critical step, as the staff development coordinator at an urban elementary school points out:

> As a member of the school leadership team responsible for staff development, I helped guide the process of designing and carrying out the [action research] projects. One of the major challenges in conducting action research projects for this particular group of teachers was the first step: defining the question or problem to be studied. The delicate part of the facilitator's role for this part of action research is to guide teachers toward questions that accurately represent their real concerns and to help them articulate questions in ways that clarify the important elements. If action research is to be useful and engaging, then questions must focus on significant issues related to the success of students within the classroom (Mills 2000, 130).

Action research is also "a natural part of teaching. [T]o be a teacher means to observe students and study classroom interactions, to explore a variety of effective ways of teaching and learning, and to build conceptual frameworks that can guide one's work.

This is a personal as well as a professional quest, a journey toward making sense out of and finding satisfaction in one's teaching. It is the work of teacher-researchers" (Fischer 1996, 33).

Action research can be used to study almost any dimension of teaching and learning. At the beginning of the action research cycle, Mills (2000, 41) suggests developing an "action plan" consisting of these steps:

■ Write an area-of-focus statement.
■ Define the variables.
■ Develop research questions.
■ Describe the intervention or innovation.
■ Describe the membership of the action research group.
■ Describe negotiations that need to be undertaken.
■ Develop a timeline.
■ Develop a statement of resources.
■ Develop data collection ideas.

Figure 12.5

Figure 12.5 presents a "taxonomy" of data collection techniques for action research.

Not surprisingly, becoming a teacher-researcher is hard work, given the daily demands of teaching itself. However, more schools are redefining the teacher's role to include doing action research. These schools realize that action research can provide data on the effectiveness of educational programs, enhance student learning, and energize teachers for professional growth. Four teachers who are members of the Action Research Laboratory at Highland Park High School near Chicago comment on the benefits of action research:

> By far the most rewarding part of working on an action research team was the opportunity to learn and grow with a small group of teacher colleagues. This experience of mutual commitment provided a wonderful staff development experience; by working with these colleagues consistently throughout the year, we were able to explore new ideas and take risks in the classroom with a type of "safety net" in place. For that reason alone, as well as our desire to explore the new questions and challenges raised by our research, we will continue to conduct action research into the effectiveness of our teaching and grading practices (Mills 2000, 97).

How Are Teachers Providing Leadership for School Restructuring and Curriculum Reform?

Today's teachers welcome opportunities to provide leadership for school restructuring and curriculum reform. Although teachers may have played a limited role in school governance in the past, there are currently many opportunities for teachers to become educational leaders beyond the classroom. Figure 12.6 presents five clusters of educational reform, each of which will offer teachers opportunities to shape policies during the twenty-first century.

Figure 12.6

Leadership and Collaboration for School Reform

The key to successful school restructuring and curriculum reform is teacher leadership and collaboration. At the 1998 National Teacher Forum on Leadership, sponsored by the U.S. Department of Education, participating teachers identified the following ways in which teachers can lead and collaborate for school reform. To illustrate each form of leadership, we provide one example from among the thousands of teachers exercising similar leadership.

Participating in professional teacher organizations—As President of the Wisconsin Science Teachers' Association, Sharon Nelson worked with the National Science Teachers Association, Goals 2000, to disseminate national science education standards in her state.

Taking part in school decisions—Melisa Hancock, an elementary school teacher in Kansas, became a clinical instructor at Kansas State University and played a key role in engineering a partnership with the university that led to her school becoming a professional development school.

Defining what students need to know and be able to do—Delaware teacher Jan Parsons was one of several teachers who took leadership roles on Delaware commissions that wrote standards for mathematics, science, social studies, and language arts; teachers also wrote and piloted new statewide assessments in line with the new standards.

Sharing ideas with colleagues—Tom Howe and other Wisconsin teachers developed a "Share Net Program" which allows teachers to make formal presentations to their peers on effective instructional practices.

Being a mentor to new teachers—Science teacher Fie Budzinsky serves as a Teacher Mentor for the State of Connecticut; Budzinsky had, in turn, been mentored earlier in her career by Dick Reagan, another science teacher.

Helping to make personnel decisions—North Carolina teacher Mary Ostwalt served on a selection committee formed to replace a teacher who resigned; other teachers in her district serve on selection committees for the hiring of new principals.

Improving facilities and technology—Ray Hasart and other teachers were the driving force behind the creation of a new $3.5 million technology facility at a Redmond, Oregon, high school; the facility is visited regularly by people throughout the West Coast.

Working with parents—Martina Marquez and a team of colleagues in New Mexico visit Native American villages and surrounding communities to disseminate math and reading activities parents can do with their children.

Creating partnerships with the community—North Carolina teacher Scott Griffin became a member of his community's volunteer fire department and spearheaded the redesign of the fire safety curriculum presented at schools in the community.

Creating partnerships with businesses and organizations—Georgia teacher Stephanie Blakney took the lead in developing a systemwide Partnership with Education program that led to the creation of a food bank and the Atlanta Coca-Cola Bottling Company "adopting" her school.

Creating partnerships with colleges and universities to prepare future teachers—Former Kansas Teacher of the Year Christy McNally and other award-winning teachers organized a partnership with teacher education programs throughout Kansas.

Becoming leaders in the community—Teacher Jacqueline Omland is President of the Legion auxiliary in Aberdeen, South Dakota, and a colleague is Chairman of the Legion.

Becoming politically involved—Washington State teacher Ivy Chan served as treasurer for a person who ran for State Superintendent of Public Instruction.

Leading efforts to make teachers more visible and communicate positive information—High school teacher Larry Torres started a weekly news column in his New Mexico community paper that focuses on positive articles about education; the column has now expanded to a full page.

Collaborative School Reform Networks

Many teachers are involved in restructuring and curriculum change through their schools' participation in collaborative networks for reform. Networks provide teachers with training and resources for restructuring, and they create opportunities for teachers at network schools to help teachers at nonnetwork schools with their restructuring efforts. Among the many collaborative reform networks are the Coalition of Essential Schools, the National Network for Educational Renewal, Accelerated Schools, and state-based networks, such as the League of Professional Schools.

Coalition of Essential Schools The **Coalition of Essential Schools (CES)**, started in 1984 by Theodore R. Sizer at Brown University, is a network of more than 1,000 schools and 24 regional support centers. The regional centers, with the support of CES National, coach schools through a systematic process of change at the school site. No two Coalition schools are alike; each develops an approach to restructuring suited to its students, faculty, and community. However, the efforts of Coalition schools to restructure are guided by ten Common Principles (see Appendix 12.3) extrapolated from Sizer's (1997a, 1997b, 1997c; Sizer and Sizer 1999) books on redesigning U.S. schools and the beliefs that top-down, standardized solutions to school problems don't work and that teachers must play a key role in the operation of their schools. Recently, the Coalition organized resource centers so teachers at Coalition schools can provide non-Coalition schools with restructuring assistance.

Appendix 12.3

National Network for Educational Renewal The Center for Educational Renewal at the University of Washington created the **National Network for Educational Renewal (NNER)** to encourage new opportunities for teachers to become involved in school restructuring, curriculum reform, and the preparation of teachers. Members of the NNER include 33 colleges and universities that collaborate with more than 100 school districts and nearly 500 partner schools. The NNER is based on 19 postulates for reforming teacher education that John Goodlad presented in *Educational Renewal: Better Teachers, Better Schools* (1994). For a school to become a member of the NNER, its teachers must demonstrate that they "understand their appropriate role in site-based management and school renewal" (Goodlad 1994, 89).

Accelerated Schools Stanford economist Henry M. Levin has developed a nationwide network of **accelerated schools** that provide enriched, rigorous curricula to "speed up" the learning of students at risk. Instead of placing at-risk students into remedial classes, accelerated schools provide students with challenging learning activities traditionally reserved for gifted and talented students. Accelerated Schools are based on the belief that teachers—in collaboration with administrators, parents, and community members—must be able to make important educational decisions, take responsibility for implementing those decisions, and take responsibility for the outcomes of those decisions. The National Center for the Accelerated Schools Project at Stanford operates twelve regional Accelerated Schools Satellite Centers across the country. The satellite centers provide assistance to teachers and administrators who wish to restructure their schools according to the accelerated schools model.

State-Based Educational Partnerships Many states have established state-based partnerships between a state university or college and a coalition of public schools. Several of these partnerships are patterned after the League of Professional Schools started by Carl Glickman at the University of Georgia. The overall goal of the League is to improve student learning by using shared governance and action research to focus on instructional and curricular issues. Following guidelines Glickman has outlined in

Renewing America's Schools: A Guide for School-Based Action (1993) and Revolutionizing America's Schools (1998), League schools usually begin the restructuring process by developing a covenant, a set of mutually agreed on beliefs about how students learn best, and a charter, a set of democratically developed guidelines for how shared governance will operate at the school. Presently, nearly 100 League schools exchange resources and ideas and support one another in their restructuring efforts.

SUMMARY

To What Extent Is Teaching a Full Profession? (p. 340)

What Is Professionalism in Teaching? (p. 344)

To What Professional Organizations Do Teachers Belong? (p. 347)

What New Leadership Roles for Teachers Are Emerging? (p. 350)

How Do Teachers Contribute to Educational Research? (pp. 353)

How Are Teachers Providing Leadership for School Restructuring and Curriculum Reform? (p. 356)

KEY TERMS AND CONCEPTS

Go to the website for interactive flashcards.

APPLICATIONS AND INTERACTIVITIES

Go to the website for interactive assignments in the following areas:

Teacher's Journal

Teacher's Database

Observations and Interviews

Professional Portfolio

Handout Master M12.1
Handout Master M12.2

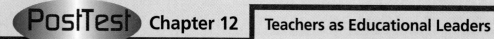

Name _____ **Date** _____

For each question, write in the blank the answer you believe is correct.

12.1 The limited freedom of teachers to _____ themselves has detracted from the overall status of the teaching profession.

12.2 During the last decade, the National Board for Professional Teaching Standards (NBPTS) has made progress toward clarifying the _____ base for teaching.

12.3 The higher social status teachers enjoy is based on level of _____ rather than wealth.

12.4 The professional teacher is guided by a specific set of _____.

12.5 Because teaching brings teachers and students into close contact, teachers may find opportunities to become _____ to some of their students.

12.6 Teachers normally have many opportunities to learn new knowledge and skills through in-service training or staff _____.

12.7 For all professional teachers, an important goal of lifelong learning is the acquisition of _____ skills.

12.8 The oldest and largest association for teachers and administrators in the United States is the National _____ Association.

12.9 Founded in 1916, the American _____ of Teachers is affiliated with the AFL-CIO and has more than one million members.

12.10 In early 1998, a "conceptual agreement" to _____ the NEA and AFT was announced by their respective presidents.

Answers are available on the FlexChoice website at www.ablongman.com/parkayflex.

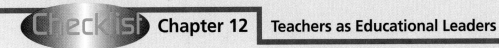

Name _____

Keep this checklist at your computer as a reminder to read and complete the chapter features and activities located on the FlexChoice website at www.ablongman.com/parkayflex.

Date
Completed

_____ ❑ **PreTest with Answers**

_____ ❑ **Audio Clip 12.1:** Thinking Over the Opening Vignette

_____ ❑ **Figure 12.1:** Does teaching meet the criteria for a profession?

_____ ❑ **Table 12.1:** Percentages of teachers and principals who report that teachers have a "good deal of influence" or "control" over school and classroom decisions, by control of school

_____ ❑ **Figure 12.2:** Professionalism in teaching

_____ ❑ **Audio Clip 12.2:** Teacher Collaboration through Mentoring

_____ ❑ **Case to Consider:** Martha's Leadership

_____ ❑ **Where Do You Stand?:** Do teachers' unions have a positive effect on education?

_____ ❑ **Weblink 12.1:** National Education Association

_____ ❑ **Weblink 12.2:** American Federation of Teachers

_____ ❑ **Appendix 12.1:** Sampler of Professional Organizations for Teachers

_____ ❑ **Technology Highlights:** How are teachers playing a leadership role in the development and dissemination of multimedia software?

_____ ❑ **Weblink 12.3:** HyperStudio

_____ ❑ **Figure 12.3:** Ten dimensions of teacher leadership beyond the classroom

_____ ❑ **Figure 12.4:** Five principles that guide the actions of teacher-leaders

_____ ❑ **Professional Reflection:** Working with principals

_____ ❑ **Appendix 12.2:** Selected Education Journals

_____ ❑ **Weblink 12.4:** Educational Resources Information Center (ERIC) Clearinghouses

_____ ❑ **Figure 12.5:** Action research data collection techniques (The Three Es)

_____ ❑ **Figure 12.6:** Opportunities for teacher leadership in school restructuring and curriculum reform

_____ ❑ **Appendix 12.3:** Coalition of Essentials Schools: Ten Common Principles

_____ ❑ **Summary**

_____ ❑ **Key Terms and Concepts**

_____ ❑ **Applications and Interactivities:** Teacher's Journal

_____ ❑ **Applications and Interactivities:** Teacher's Database

_____ ❑ **Applications and Interactivities:** Observations and Interviews

_____ ❑ **Handout Master M12.1:** Observing a School–Community Partnership

_____ ❑ **Handout Master M12.2:** Evaluating the Effectiveness of a School–University Partnership

_____ ❑ **Applications and Interactivities:** Professional Portfolio

_____ ❑ **PostTest with Answers**

13

Your First Teaching Position

What I've found very helpful is to get in touch with all my kids' parents right after the first day. I tell them a bit about how I run my class, what we're going to do that year, and how pleased I am to have their child in my room. I keep it upbeat, very positive. We're going to have a great year!

— A first-grade teacher

focus questions

1. How will you become certified or licensed to teach?

2. Where will you teach?

3. How will you find your first teaching job?

4. What can you expect as a beginning teacher?

5. How can you become a part of your learning community?

6. How can you participate in teacher collaboration?

7. How will your performance as a teacher be evaluated?

Your spring student teaching seminar ended minutes ago; now you and three other students are seated in the faculty–student lounge enjoying sodas and talking about finding a job.

"What was the interview like?" you ask one of your classmates, upon learning that he interviewed yesterday for a position at an urban school.

Audio Clip 13.1

"Yeah, tell us," another student adds. "I'm really anxious about interviewing. I don't know what to expect. There're so many things they could ask."

"Well, I was interviewed by the principal and two people from the district office—I think they were in personnel. At first, they asked questions like the ones we used in our seminar role plays: 'Why do you want to teach? What are your weaknesses? Use five adjectives to describe yourself.'"

"What else?" you ask, anxious to complete a mental image of the interview process so you'll be ready for your first interview next week.

"They asked me to describe a student teaching lesson that went well," he continues. "After I did that, one of them asked 'How could the lesson have been better—either for the entire class or for a certain student?' That one took some thinking."

As he goes on to reconstruct his response, you imagine how you would answer the same question.

Moments later, he says, "Then, one that really surprised me came when I was asked 'What would you do if your principal told you to discontinue a classroom activity because it was too noisy and left a mess for the custodians to clean up? But, the activity really involved the kids and they learned a lot.'"

He pauses for a sip of soda and then continues, "Another one was, 'Give us an example of a principle that guides your teaching.'"

Impressed with the district's ability to pose challenging questions, you again imagine how you would respond.

A few minutes later, another student asks, "What about portfolios? Did they spend much time looking at yours?"

"Did they ever!" your classmate exclaims. "With my application materials I included a portfolio on CD-ROM; plus I gave them the web address for my portfolio. They were pretty impressed. It was obvious that they had looked at just about everything in the portfolio. They asked all kinds of questions. Half the questions were about how to make a digital portfolio. But they also really wanted to see things that were related to how much my students learned while I was student teaching."

With the mention of portfolios, you're reminded of tomorrow's computer lab workshop on how to create an electronic portfolio. Hopefully, you'll have a portfolio on CD-ROM that you can take to your first job interview next week. In addition, you wonder what else you should do to prepare for the interview and what steps you can follow to increase your chances of finding the best possible teaching position.

Name _____ **Date** _____

For each question, circle the letter of the answer you believe is correct. Then read the chapter to learn more about these topics.

13.1 Approximately how many people have been licensed through alternative certification programs since 1983?
A. 100,000.
B. 70,000.
C. 90,000.
D. 80,000.

13.2 Based on interview data, all of the following statements are true about the impact of parental involvement on students *except*
A. Significant parental involvement results in fewer grade repetitions.
B. Significant parental involvement results in higher levels of student achievement.
C. Significant parental involvement results in slightly less participation in extracurricular activities.
D. Significant parental involvement results in fewer suspensions and expulsions.

13.3 The Florida Performance Measurement System is an example of
A. A standardized measure of student academic achievement.
B. A quantitative approach to teacher evaluation.
C. An alternative certification program.
D. A long-term program for training school administrators.

13.4 The Praxis Series: Professional Assessments for Beginning Teachers includes assessments of all the following *except*
A. Classroom performance.
B. Academic (basic) skills.
C. Subject matter knowledge.
D. Leadership skills.

13.5 Leo is preparing to take the National Teacher Examination for his initial teaching certification. This test will assess his
A. Interpersonal skills.
B. Basic skills, general knowledge, and professional knowledge.
C. Judgment abilities.
D. Area of specialization.

13.6 In analyzing the job market for teachers in all regions of the country during the next decade the outlook is
A. Less than favorable.
B. Favorable.
C. Unchanged.
D. Dismal.

13.7 Between now and the year 2006, enrollment in elementary schools is expected to
A. Increase.
B. Slightly decrease.
C. Experience a major decline.
D. Remain the same.

13.8 All of the following are general purposes of the interview process *except*
A. Provides an opportunity for the district to determine race and areas of disability.
B. Gives the person being interviewed the opportunity to ask questions.
C. Enables the district to gather information on potential success.
D. Enables the district to gather more information.

13.9 Which of the following is *not* a standard procedure after accepting an offer for a teaching position?
A. To notify other districts to which you have applied that you have accepted a position elsewhere.
B. To return a letter of confirmation.
C. To return the signed contract to the district.
D. To use that offer as a base of negotiation with other districts.

13.10 Research indicates that the more parents are involved in their children's education
A. The more trouble they are for teachers.
B. The higher the drop out rate.
C. The more shy the child will be.
D. The higher the achievement of the students.

Answers are available on the FlexChoice website at www.ablongman.com/parkayflex.

On completion of your teacher education program, you will still have several important steps to take before securing your first teaching position. Preparing well for these steps will go a long way toward helping you begin teaching with confidence.

It is natural that you feel both excited and a bit fearful when thinking about your first job. While taking the courses required in your teacher education program, you probably feel secure in your role as a student; you know what is expected of you. As a teacher, however, you will assume an entirely new role—a role that requires some time before it becomes comfortable. The aim of this chapter, then, is to help make the transition from student to professional teacher a positive, pleasant one. We first look at the steps you can take to become certified or licensed to teach and to identify current trends related to teacher supply and demand.

How Will You Become Certified or Licensed to Teach?

State certification is required for teaching in the public schools, and in many private schools as well. In some cases, large cities (e.g., Chicago, New York, Buffalo) have their own certification requirements that must be met. And certain local school districts have additional requirements, such as a written examination, before one can teach in those districts.

A **teaching certificate** is actually a license to teach. The department of education for each of the fifty states and the District of Columbia sets the requirements for certification. A certificate usually indicates at what level and in what content areas one may teach. One might, for example, be certified for all-level (K–12) physical education or art, secondary English, elementary education, or middle-level education. In 1999, thirty-two states offered certification for teaching at the middle school or junior high level—an increase from 1987, when twenty-six states offered such certification. In addition, a certificate may list other areas of specialization, such as driver's training, coaching, or journalism. If you plan to go into nonteaching areas such as counseling, librarianship, or administration, special certificates are usually required.

State Certification Requirements

In order for a person to receive a teaching certificate, all states require successful completion of an approved teacher education program that culminates with at least a bachelor's degree. To be approved, programs must pass a review by the state department of education approximately every five years. In addition to approval at the state level, most of the nearly 1,300 programs in the nation have regional accreditation, and more than 500 voluntarily seek accreditation by the **National Council for Accreditation of Teacher Education (NCATE)** (1999). Currently, all states require an average of six to eight semester credits of supervised student teaching. Alabama, Colorado, Idaho, Indiana, Nevada, New York, and Virginia require a master's degree for advanced certification; and Arizona, Maryland, Montana, Oregon, and Washington require either a master's degree or a specified number of semester credits after certification (Tryneski 1999). Additional requirements may also include U.S. citizenship, an oath of loyalty, fingerprinting, or a health examination.

A few states, including Iowa, North Carolina, New Mexico, and Oklahoma, waive state licensing requirements for teachers certified by the National Board for Professional Teaching Standards (NBPTS). Other states, including Massachusetts and Ohio, accept NBPTS certification as an alternative to their own requirements. For a current listing of state and local action supporting NBPTS certification, call the NBPTS at (800)-22TEACH.

Nearly all states now require testing of teachers for initial certification. States use either a standardized test (usually the National Teacher Examination [NTE] or Praxis) or a test developed by outside consultants. Areas covered by the states' tests usually include basic skills, professional knowledge, and general knowledge. Many states also require an on-the-job performance evaluation for certification (see Table 13.1).

Table 13.1

There is a trend away from granting teaching certificates for life. Some states, for example, issue three- to five-year certificates, which may be renewed only with proof of coursework completed beyond the bachelor's degree. And, amid considerable controversy, Arkansas, Georgia, and Texas have enacted testing for **recertification** of experienced teachers.

Certification requirements differ from state to state, and they are frequently modified. To remain up-to-date on the requirements for the state in which you plan to teach, it is important that you keep in touch with your teacher placement office or certification officer at your college or university. You may also wish to refer to *Requirements for Certification for Elementary and Secondary Schools* (The University of Chicago Press), an annual publication that lists state-by-state certification requirements for teachers, counselors, librarians, and administrators. Or, you may contact the teacher certification office in the state where you plan to teach (see Appendix 13.1, for a "Directory of State Teacher Certification Offices in the United States").

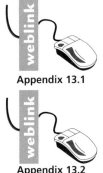

Appendix 13.1

Currently, forty-four states are members of the **Interstate Certification Agreement Contract,** a reciprocity agreement whereby a certificate obtained in one state will be honored in another (see Appendix 13.2). If you plan to teach in a state other than the one in which you are currently studying, you should find out whether both states share a reciprocity agreement.

Appendix 13.2

About 362,000 teachers, many of whom are noncertified, teach in America's growing system of private, parochial, for-profit, and charter schools (National Center for Education Statistics, 1998b). Private and parochial schools supported largely by tuition and gifts, and for-profit schools operated by private educational corporations, usually have no certification requirements for teachers. Also, teacher-created and teacher-operated charter schools, though they are public, are often free of state certification requirements. A school's **charter** (an agreement between the school's founders and its sponsor—usually a local school board) may waive certification requirements if the school guarantees that students will attain a specified level of achievement.

What are some alternatives for becoming certified or licensed to teach? What are some current trends in certification and what conditions might account for those trends?

Alternative Certification

Despite the national movement to make certification requirements more stringent, concern about meeting the demand for 2.2 million new teachers during the first decade of the twenty-first century and attracting minority-group members into the teaching profession has resulted in increasing use of alternative teacher certification programs. In 1983, only eight states offered alternatives; by 1998, forty-one states had alternative routes to certification (Feistritzer 1999).

Alternative certification programs are designed for people who already have at least a bachelor's degree in a field other than education and want to become licensed to teach. It is estimated that about 80,000 people have been licensed through alternative certification programs since 1983 (Feistritzer 1999). Most alternative certification programs are collaborative efforts among state departments of education, teacher education programs in colleges and universities, and school districts. For example, Washington State University, in collaboration with area school districts, has a federally funded program to prepare paraprofessional educators (teachers' aides, for example) in southwest Washington to become bilingual/ESL teachers. According to the National Center for Education Information, which has studied alternative certification trends since the 1980s, effective alternative teacher certification programs include the following components:

- [Candidates demonstrate a] strong academic coursework component.
- The [programs] are field-based, . . . individuals get into classrooms early in their training.
- Teacher candidates work with a qualified mentor teacher.
- Candidates usually go through their programs in cohorts, not as isolated individuals (Feistritzer 1999).

All but two states may grant certification to those who do not meet current requirements. About half of the states may even give a substandard credential to those who hold less than a bachelor's degree. In response to occasional shortages of teachers in particular subject and grade-level areas, many state systems approve temporary measures such as **emergency certification.** Nationwide, more than 12 percent of newly hired teachers enter the profession without any training at all, and another 15 percent enter without having fully met state standards, according to the National Commission on Teaching and America's Future.

Emergency certification is strongly resisted by professional teacher organizations and several state departments of education. New York, for example, decreed that under-performing schools in the state would not be allowed to hire teachers with temporary licenses as of fall 1999, and the practice would be eliminated altogether by fall 2003 (Bradley 1999). Teachers on provisional certificates in Maryland, the majority of whom teach poor and minority children, no longer can continue teaching indefinitely on a provisional certificate; they must pass the state's teacher test within two years and complete academic coursework within four years (Bradley 1999). Though strongly resisted by professional teacher organizations, alternative certification is likely to become even more widespread in the event of a teacher shortage.

The Praxis Series

Thirty-five of the forty-three states that include tests as part of their certification process require completion of the **Praxis Series: Professional Assessments for Beginning Teachers** developed by Educational Testing Service (ETS) in consultation with teachers, educational researchers, the National Education Association, and the American Federation of Teachers. The Praxis Series (*praxis* means putting theory into practice) enables states to create a system of tests that meet their specific licensing requirements.

The Praxis Series, which replaced the National Teacher Examination in the mid-1990s, consists of three components:

Praxis I: Academic skills assessments—Praxis I covers the "enabling skills" in reading, writing, and mathematics that all teachers need, regardless of grade or subject taught. Two formats, computer-based and pencil-and-paper, are available for the Praxis I assessment, which is given early in a student's teacher education program. To help students pass Praxis I, ETS offers online practice test items and, for students who need help in improving basic academic skills, LearningPlus, an interactive computer software program that provides instruction and diagnostic placement tests in reading, writing, and mathematics.

Praxis II: Subject assessments—Praxis II measures teacher education students' knowledge of the subjects they will teach. In most cases, Praxis II tests are taken on completion of an undergraduate program. The tests, available in more than seventy subject areas, have a core content module required by every state, with the remaining modules selected on an individual basis by the states. Each state can base its assessment on multiple-choice items or on candidate-constructed-response modules. In addition, Praxis II includes the Principles of Learning and Teaching (PLT) test and the Professional Knowledge test; each is a two-hour test to assess teachers' professional knowledge. The PLT is available in three versions: K–6, 5–9, and 7–12.

Praxis III: Classroom performance assessments—Praxis III is a performance-based assessment system, not a test. Developed after extensive job analyses, reviews of research, and input from educators, Praxis III involves the assessment of actual teaching skills of the beginning teacher. The assessments focus on the four domains of the Praxis Framework for Teaching as presented in Chapter 9 (see Figure 9.5): planning and preparation, the classroom environment, instruction, and professional responsibilities. In addition, Praxis III assesses the teacher's sensitivity to developmental levels and cultural differences among students. In-class assessments and pre- and post-observation interviews conducted by trained state and local personnel are the main components of Praxis III. The observations are supplemented by work samples—for example, lesson plans. Following Praxis III assessments, which normally are completed by the end of the first year of teaching, the state makes a decision about whether to grant a license to teach.

Where Will You Teach?

When you think ahead to a career in teaching, two questions you are likely to ask yourself are, How hard will it be to find a job? And, Where will I teach? From time to time, **teacher supply and demand** figures have painted a rather bleak picture for those entering the teaching profession. At other times, finding a position in a preferred location has been relatively easy.

After the U.S. Department of Education announced in 1999 that more than two million teachers would be needed during the next decade, a debate ensued about whether, in fact, the nation would soon face a critical teacher shortage. Citing statistics related to higher student enrollments resulting from the "baby boom echo" (a 1980s increase in births similar to the "baby boom" that occurred after World War II), increased immigration, teacher retirements, fewer college students going into teaching, and increased employment opportunities for women and minorities in other fields, some observers predicted a teacher shortage "crisis." Others, however, predicted that a teacher shortage would not develop. They pointed to a leveling off, and then slight decline, of school enrollments during the first decade of the new century and the fact that many "new" teachers would actually be former teachers coming back into the profession.

Despite the difficulty of predicting trends in teacher supply and demand, it is clear that even during times of teacher surplus, talented, qualified teachers are able to find jobs. Teaching is one of the largest professions in the United States; out of a national population of about 273 million, more than 53 million attended public and private elementary and secondary schools in fall 1999, where they were taught by approximately 3.2 million teachers (National Center for Education Statistics 1999). By 2009, enrollments are expected to total approximately 54.5 million students, who will be taught by approximately 3.5 million teachers (National Center for Education Statistics 1999). Within such a large profession, annual openings resulting from retirements and career changes alone are sizable.

A Favorable Job Market

Although the need for new teachers is difficult to determine, most analysts predict a favorable job market for teachers in all regions of the country during the early twenty-first century. Enrollments in public and private elementary and secondary schools are expected to continue to increase into the next century and surpass the previous high set in 1971. Elementary school enrollment is expected to reach 38 million by the year 2008, while secondary school enrollment is expected to reach 16.2 million. However, as Figure 13.1 shows, not all sections of the country will experience equivalent growth in public school K–12 enrollments during this period, and the greatest enrollment increases will be at the high school level.

Figure 13.1

Demand by Specialty Area and Geographic Region

The ease with which you will find your first teaching position is also related to your area of specialization and to the part of the country where you wish to locate. In 1999, for example, job seekers able to teach bilingual education or special education were in an especially favorable position. Also, the West had the greatest overall demand for teachers, followed by Alaska, the Great Plains/Midwest, and the South Central Region. For current employment opportunities according to speciality area and geographic region and for other job-search resources, check the following publications by the American Association for Employment in Education (820 Davis Street, Suite 222, Evanston, IL 60201-4445, (847) 864-1999). Be aware, however, that the Association does not provide placement services nor does it maintain lists of vacancies.

- *AAEE Annual: The Job Search Handbook for Educators* (Supply-demand data, interview techniques, résumé advice, and other job-search suggestions, $8.00).
- *Guide to Services and Activities for Teacher Employment* (Employment assistance services, career fair dates, contacts, teacher certification reciprocity among

states, vacancy listing information, candidates' computer data banks, and other resources, $8.00).

■ *AAEE Directory of Public School Systems in the United States* (Names, addresses, and phone numbers of contact persons, district size, school grade levels, and other information, $70.00 for complete directory; from no charge to $12.00 for individual state directories).

When considering supply and demand estimates, remember that jobs are to be had in oversupplied areas. Job hunting will be more competitive, though, and you may have to relocate to another region of the country.

Other Career Opportunities for Teachers

There are also a great many nonteaching jobs in education and education-related fields, such as principal, assistant principal, librarian, and counselor. In addition, there are many jobs that, although removed from the world of the classroom, would nevertheless enable you to use your teaching skills.

The following outline lists several places other than schools where individuals with teaching backgrounds are often employed. The number of education-related careers is likely to increase in the coming decades.

Industry
■ Publishers
■ Educational materials and equipment suppliers
■ Specialized educational service firms
■ Communications industries
■ Research and development firms
■ Management consulting firms
■ Education and training consultants
■ Educational divisions of large corporations—Xerox, IBM, CBS, General Electric, Westinghouse, etc.

Government
■ Federal agencies—U.S. Office of Education, Bureau of Prisons, Department of Labor, Office of Economic Opportunity, Department of Justice, Department of Health, Education and Welfare, etc.
■ Federal programs—Bureau of Indian Affairs Schools, Bureau of Prisons Schools, Job Corps, Overseas Dependent Schools, Peace Corps, Teacher Corps, Upward Bound, VISTA, etc.
■ Regional educational networks—Research and development centers, regional educational laboratories, sixteen clearinghouses of the Educational Resources Information Center (ERIC), etc.
■ Jobs in state departments of education

Education-Related Associations
■ Research centers and foundations
■ Professional associations—National Council of Teachers of English, National Association of Mathematics Teachers, National Education Association, American Federation of Teachers, Phi Delta Kappa, Kappa Delta Pi, Educational Testing Service, etc.

Community Organizations

- Community action programs—Upward Bound, neighborhood health centers, legal services, aid to migrant workers, etc.
- Social service agencies—United Fund agencies, Boy Scouts, Girl Scouts, YMCAs and YWCAs, settlement houses, boys' and girls' clubs, etc.
- Adult education centers
- Museums
- Hospitals

Appendix 13.3

Figure 13.2

How Will You Find Your First Teaching Job?

During the last year of your teacher education program, you will probably become increasingly concerned about finding a teaching position. The "Job Search Timetable Checklist" presented in Appendix 13.3 may help you plan your job search. Also, Figure 13.2 presents an overview of the data and impressions that more than 200 school hiring officials consider most important when they are considering first-time teachers for employment. In the remainder of this section we discuss five critical steps in that sequence: finding out about teaching vacancies, preparing a résumé, writing letters of inquiry and letters of application, being interviewed, and selecting a position.

Finding Out about Teaching Vacancies

Your college or university probably has a **placement service** designed to help graduates find jobs. On a regular basis, placement offices usually publish lists of vacancies, which are posted and, in many cases, mailed to students who have registered with the office and set up a credentials file. In addition, you can use the Internet to connect with other universities that have accessible online placement services.

A **credentials file** (known as placement papers at some institutions) usually includes the following: background information on the applicant, the type of position sought, a list of courses taken, performance evaluations by the applicant's cooperative teacher, and three or more letters of recommendation. With each job application, the candidate requests that his or her credentials be sent to the appropriate person at the school district, or the school district itself may request the applicant's papers. Placement offices usually charge a small fee for each time a candidate's papers are sent out.

A job announcement describes the position and its requirements and provides the name and address of the individual to contact at the school district. For each position you are interested in, send a letter of application to the appropriate person along with your résumé. In addition, you may have your placement office send your credentials file. Placement offices also frequently set up on-campus interviews between candidates and representatives of school district personnel departments.

State department of education employment offices help teachers locate positions. Like college and university placement offices, states publish lists of job openings, which are then distributed to registered candidates. Because most of these states will assist out-of-state candidates, you can register in more than one state.

Personal networking will play an important role in landing the right job. Let people know you are looking for a job—friends, teachers at schools you've attended, faculty at the school where you student teach, and people you meet at workshops and conferences. Also, with access to the Internet, you can conduct a global job search and even make your résumé available to millions of people. The following noncommercial Internet sites can be helpful in your job search efforts:

- School district websites
- State departments of education websites
- *Project Connect*—After obtaining a free user name and password, you can search teaching vacancies on the Web and post information about yourself, sponsored in part by the American Association for Employment in Education.
- *America's Job Bank*—A comprehensive, free job-search service linked to 2,000 state employment offices.

Preparing Your Résumé

A **résumé** presents a concise summary of an individual's professional experiences, education, and skills. Résumés must be typed and preferably no longer than one page, two pages at most. Though there is no right way to prepare a résumé, it should present—in a neat, systematic way—key information that will help an employer determine your suitability for a particular position. Because your résumé will most likely be your first contact with an employer, it must make a good impression.

Ordinarily, a résumé contains the following information:

- Personal data
- Education
- Certificates held
- Experience
- Activities and interests
- Honors and offices held
- Professional memberships
- References

Figure 13.3 is a résumé prepared by Linda M. Rodriguez that you can use as a model. To prepare an effective résumé, read "Résumé Advice for Educators" in Appendix 13.4.

Figure 13.3

Appendix 13.4

Writing Letters of Inquiry and Applications

As a job seeker, you will most likely have occasion to write two kinds of letters: letters of inquiry and letters of application. A **letter of inquiry** is used to determine if a school district has, or anticipates, any teaching vacancies. This type of letter states your general qualifications and requests procedures to be followed in making a formal application (see Figure 13.4). A letter of inquiry should also include your résumé as well as a self-addressed, stamped envelope for the school district's convenience. Be prepared not to receive a reply for each letter of inquiry you send out. Many school districts are unable to respond to all inquiries.

A **letter of application** (often called a cover letter) indicates your interest in a particular position and outlines your qualifications for that job. As most districts have several vacancies at any given time, it is important that the first sentence of your letter refer to the specific position for which you are applying. The body of the letter should then highlight why you would be an excellent choice to fill that position. Also, inform the reader that your credentials file will be sent on request or is being sent by your placement office. Close the letter by expressing your availability for an interview (see Figure 13.5).

Figure 13.4

Figure 13.5

Participating in a Job Interview

The interview is one of the most important steps in your search for an appropriate position. As the dialogue in the scenario at the beginning of this chapter suggests, school district representatives may ask a wide range of questions, both structured and open-ended.

In some districts, you might be interviewed by the principal only; in others, the superintendent, the principal, and the department chairperson might interview you; and in still others, classroom teachers might interview you. Regardless of format, the interview enables the district to obtain more specific information regarding your probable success as an employee, and it gives you an opportunity to ask questions about what it is like to teach in the district. By asking questions yourself, you demonstrate your interest in working in the district. The Teacher's Resource Guide section "Sample Interview Questions for Candidates to Ask" on this book's website presents seventeen questions you can ask, and Appendix 13.5 presents "Critical Information to Know about School Districts," which can be used to formulate questions. In addition, at some point in the interview process you may wish to present brief highlights from your professional portfolio. Or, if you have created Internet and/or CD-ROM versions of your portfolio, you could give the hiring offical(s) the URL for the portfolio or a copy of the CD-ROM itself.

What questions might you be asked in an interview for a teaching position? What questions should you have about the teaching position? about the school?

Weblink 13.1

Appendix 13.5

Accepting an Offer

One day you are notified that a school district would like to hire you. Your job search efforts have paid off! In the competition for positions, you have been successful. However, accepting your first teaching position is a major personal and professional step. Before signing a contract with a district, you should carefully consider job-related questions such as the following:

- In regard to my abilities and education, am I suited to this position?
- Would I like to work with this school's students, administrative staff, and teachers?
- Is the salary I am being offered sufficient?
- Will this position likely be permanent?
- Would I like to live in or near this community?
- Would the cost of living in this community enable me to live comfortably?
- Are opportunities for continuing education readily available?

If you accept the offer, you will need to return a signed contract to the district along with a short letter confirming your acceptance. As a professional courtesy, you should notify other districts to which you have applied that you have accepted a position elsewhere. The following Professional Reflection can help you identify the type of school that would be most satisfying for your first teaching position.

Professional Reflection   **What elements are essential for your job satisfaction?**

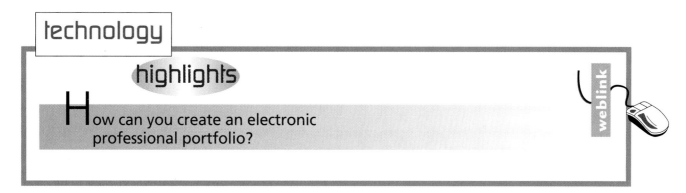

technology

highlights

How can you create an electronic professional portfolio?

Weblink 13.2

AUDIO

Audio Clip 13.2

What Can You Expect as a Beginning Teacher?

Once you accept the professional challenge of teaching, it is important to prepare well in advance of the first day of school. In addition to reviewing the material you will teach, you should use this time to find out all you can about the school's students, the surrounding community, and the way the school operates. Also reflect on your expectations.

The First Day

The first day of school can be both exciting and frightening, as the following veteran teacher acknowledges; however, if the teacher is well prepared, he or she can use anxiety to set a positive tone for the rest of the school year:

> The anxiety level for both teachers and students about [the] first day is high. Taking advantage of these feelings can make for a good beginning.

> Students like to have guidelines on how the class will be run as well as what is expected of them academically. I always begin by welcoming the students into my class and immediately giving them something to do. I hand them their textbook and an index card. On the card, they write their name, address, telephone number, and book number.

> While the students are filling out their cards and looking at the textbook, I set up my seating chart and verify attendance. Within ten minutes of meeting the students, I begin my first lesson. By keeping clerical chores to a minimum, I try to have more time on task. After a closure activity, somewhere in the middle of the class period I take a few minutes to explain how their grade will be determined, the rules of the class, and when extra help sessions are available.

> Next, we deal with some curriculum content, and then I make a homework assignment. I tell the students that any homework assignment will be written on the chalkboard every day in the same location.

> Setting high standards on the first day makes the following days easier. We will always need to monitor and adjust, but this will be within the framework set on the first day (Burden and Byrd 1999, 177).

Creating a pleasant, learning-oriented climate on the first day, as this teacher has done, will contribute greatly to your success during the first year. On the first day, students are eager to learn and are hopeful that the year will be a productive one. In addition, nearly all students will be naturally receptive to what you have to say. To them, you are a new, unknown quantity, and one of their initial concerns is to find out what kind of a teacher you will be. It is therefore critical that you be well organized and ready to take charge.

Advice from Experienced Teachers

In our work with schools and teachers, we have gathered recommendations on preparing for the first day from experienced K–12 teachers in urban, suburban, and rural schools. Teachers' recommendations focus on planning, establishing effective management practices, and following through on decisions.

> There are little things you can do, such as having a personal note attached to a pencil welcoming each child. You may want to do a few little tricks in science class or read them your favorite children's story. But, don't put all your energy into the first day and have that day be the highlight of the year. Be well prepared and have plenty of things to do. Don't worry if you don't get everything done. Remember, you have all year.
>
> —Middle school science teacher

> It really helps on the first day to have plenty of material to cover and things to do. I'd recommend taking the material you plan to cover that day and doubling it. It's better to have too much than to run out. What you don't use the first day, you use the next. It takes a while to get a feeling for how fast the kids are going to go.
>
> —Third-grade teacher

> The first day is a good time to go over rules and procedures for the year. But don't overdo it. Be very clear and specific about your expectations for classroom behavior.
>
> —Sixth-grade teacher

> From the beginning, it's important to do what you're there to do—that's teach. Teach the class something, maybe review material they learned last year. That lets them know that you're in charge, you expect them to learn. They'll look to you for direction—as long as you give it to them, you're fine.
>
> —Junior high language arts teacher

How Can You Become a Part of Your Learning Community?

Your success in your first year of teaching will be determined by the relationships you develop with the pupils, their families, your colleagues, school administrators, and other members of the school community. All of these groups contribute to your effectiveness as a teacher, but the relationships you establish with students will be the most important (and complex) you will have as a teacher.

Relationships with Students

The quality of your relationships with students will depend in large measure on your knowledge of students and commitment to improving your interactions with them. As one teacher put it:

Students respond to praise, compliments, and encouragement. I must know the subject matter, but also have a lot of patience, mental energy, and selflessness. I have found that you have to be encouraging even to the most negative students, or they can make your life miserable. Even though you might know the subject matter, you will not be a successful teacher if you can't motivate your students by talking with them, not at them (Burden and Byrd 1999, 290).

Your relationships with students will have many dimensions. Principally, you must see that each student learns as much as possible; this is your primary responsibility as a professional teacher. You will need to establish relationships with a great diversity of students based on mutual respect, caring, and concern. Without attention to this personal realm, your effectiveness as a teacher will be limited. In addition, teachers are significant models for students' attitudes and behaviors.

Relationships with Colleagues and Staff

Each working day, you will be in close contact with other teachers and staff members. As the experience of the following teacher suggests, it will definitely be to your advantage to establish friendly, professional relationships with them:

> I was on a staff with a group of teachers who really supported me. They made it a part of their day to come into my room and see how I was doing and to share things. They made it easy to ask questions and work with them. They started me on the track of cooperating with other teachers and sharing my successes and failures with them.

> They did such a good job of taking care of each other that my needs were always met. I had plenty of supplies, counseling help, administrative help. The school was a community. Anything I needed to be successful was provided.

During your first few months at the school, it would be wise to communicate to colleagues that you are willing to learn all you can about your new job and to be a team player. In most schools it is common practice to give junior faculty members less desirable assignments, reserving the more desirable ones for senior faculty. By demonstrating your willingness to take on these responsibilities with good humor and to give them your best effort, you will do much to establish yourself as a valuable faculty member. Appendix 13.6, "Negotiating a School's Culture: A Political Roadmap for the First-Year Teacher," provides additional suggestions for developing collaborative relationships with colleagues and staff.

Appendix 13.6

Your colleagues may also appreciate learning from you about new approaches and materials—if you share in a manner that doesn't make others feel inferior. The following comments by a high school department chair, for example, illustrate a first-year Spanish teacher's positive influence on others:

> She won the respect of all her colleagues in the school who have dealt with her almost immediately, not because she's so competent in Spanish and not because she's so competent as a teacher, but because she handles everything with such sensitivity and sensibleness.

> Because of the way she operates—which is quietly but effectively—she has raised the whole tenor of expectations in the department. We have some very fine faculty in Spanish, but I would speculate they don't see their group self-image as intellectuals but rather as "people people." Because of what Elizabeth has brought to the school: the knowledge about how to use computers, her knowledge of foreign language oral proficiency, her knowledge of Spanish film and Spanish authors,

she has kind of lifted everybody up and helped her colleagues see themselves in a little bit different light and to improve professionally (Dollase 1992, 49).

It is important that you get along with your colleagues and contribute to a spirit of professional cooperation or **collegiality** in the school. Some you will enjoy being around; others you may wish to avoid. Some will express obvious enthusiasm for teaching; others may be bitter and pessimistic about their work. Be pleasant and friendly with both types. Accept their advice with a smile, and then act on what you believe is worthwhile.

Relationships with Administrators

Pay particular attention to the relationships you develop with administrators, department heads, and supervisors. Though your contacts with them will not be as frequent as with other teachers, they can do much to ensure your initial success. They are well aware of the difficulties you might encounter as a first-year teacher, and they are there to help you succeed.

The principal of your new school will, most likely, be the one to introduce you to other teachers, members of the administrative team, and staff. He or she should inform you if there are assistant principals or department heads who can help you enforce school rules, keep accurate records, and obtain supplies, for example. The principal may also assign an experienced teacher to serve as a mentor during your first year. In addition, your principal will indicate his or her availability to discuss issues of concern, and you should not hesitate to do so if the need arises.

Relationships with Parents

Developing positive connections with your students' parents can contribute significantly to students' success and to your success as a teacher. In reality, teachers and parents are partners—both concerned with the learning and growth of the children in their care. As U.S. Secretary of Education Richard Riley pointed out, "Parents, teachers and school officials working closely together are proven ingredients for success in our nation's schools" (Riley 1999). Unfortunately, research indicates that mothers typically spend less than Riley's recommended 30 minutes per day talking with or reading to their children, and fathers spend less than 15 minutes. The time parents spend interacting with their children differs as much as five times from family to family (Sadker and Sadker 1994).

Audio Clip 13.3

Figure 13.6

It is important that you become acquainted with parents at school functions, at meetings of the Parent–Teacher Association or Organization (PTA or PTO), at various community events, and in other social situations. To develop good communication with parents, you will need to be sensitive to their needs, such as their work schedules and the language spoken at home.

By maintaining contact with parents and encouraging them to become involved in their children's education, you can significantly enhance the achievement of your students. Figure 13.6, based on interviews with the parents and guardians of almost 17,000 K–12 students, shows that parental involvement is associated with higher levels of student achievement, more positive attitudes toward school, greater participation in extracurricular activities, fewer suspensions and expulsions, and fewer grade repetitions. In light of such significant findings, it is important that you be willing to

Should teachers be required to make home visits?

take the extra time and energy to pursue strategies such as the following for involving parents:

- Ask parents to read aloud to the child, to listen to the child read, and to sign homework papers.
- Encourage parents to drill students on math and spelling and to help with homework lessons.
- Encourage parents to discuss school activities with their children and suggest ways parents can help teach their children at home. For example, a simple home activity might be alphabetizing books; a more complex one would be using kitchen supplies in an elementary science experiment.
- Send home suggestions for games or group activities related to the child's schoolwork that parent and child can play together.
- Encourage parents to participate in school activities such as a sports booster club, career day, and music and drama events.
- Involve parents in their children's learning by having them co-sign learning contracts and serve as guest speakers.

The Goals 2000: Educate America Act funded parent resource centers in twenty-eight states (see the Teacher's Resource Guide section "Parent Information and Resource Centers" on this book's website). To help families get involved in their children's learning, these centers offer training for parents, hotlines, mobile training teams, resource and lending libraries, support groups, and referral networks. The U.S. Department of Education also sponsors the Partnership for Family Involvement in Education, designed to help students act as a link between their teachers and schools and their families and communities. (For information, call 1-800-USA-LEARN.)

Weblink 13.3

Family involvement resources are also available on the Internet through the National Parent Information Network (NPIN), a project sponsored by the ERIC system. (For information, call (800) 583-4135.) NPIN resources include information for parents on child development, testing, working with teachers, and home learning activities. AskERIC Question & Answer Service provides forums for parents and teachers to address mutual concerns, listings of useful and inexpensive learning materials, and descriptions of model parent involvement programs. Other online resources for parental involvement in schools can be obtained from the Consortium for School Networking.

Community Relations

Communities provide significant support for the education of their young people and determine the character of their schools. In addition, communities often help their schools by recruiting volunteers, providing financial support for special projects, and operating homework hotline programs. For example, school–community partnerships have been formed through "The Employer's Promise," a national effort to involve communities in supporting the family's central role in children's learning:

- John Hancock Financial Services sponsors "Kids-to-Go," a program of day-long supervised activities for employees' school-age children during school holidays in Boston.
- Southern California Edison supports the Parent Institute for Quality Education, which has trained 7,500 parents from East Los Angeles to participate actively in their children's education.
- Hewlett-Packard staggers start times for employees who volunteer at the corporation's on-site elementary school and accommodates the schedules of employees with school-age children.
- American College Testing's "Realize the Dream" program provides workshops and resources to involve parents in their children's education.

How Can You Participate in Teacher Collaboration?

The relationships that build a learning community involve **collaboration**—working together, sharing decision making, and solving problems. As a member of a dynamic, changing profession, your efforts to collaborate will result in an increased understanding of the teaching–learning process and improved learning for all students. By working with others on school governance, curriculum development, school–community partnerships, and educational reform, you will play an important role in enhancing the professional status of teachers.

The heart of collaboration is meaningful, authentic relationships among professionals. Such relationships, of course, do not occur naturally; they require commitment and hard work. Friend and Bursuck (1999, 72–74) have identified seven characteristics of collaboration which are summarized in the following:

- Collaboration is voluntary; teachers make a personal choice to collaborate.
- Collaboration is based on parity; all individuals' contributions are valued equally.
- Collaboration requires a shared goal.
- Collaboration includes shared responsibility for key decisions.
- Collaboration includes shared accountability for outcomes.
- Collaboration is based on shared resources; each teacher contributes something—time, expertise, space, equipment, or other resource.
- Collaboration is emergent; as teachers work together, the degree of shared decision making, trust, and respect increases.

Schools that support the essential elements of collaboration are collegial schools "characterized by purposeful adult interactions about improving schoolwide teaching and learning" (Glickman, Gordon, and Ross-Gordon 1998, 5–6). In the following, we examine four expressions of teacher collaboration: peer coaching, staff development, team teaching, and co-teaching.

Peer Coaching

Experienced teachers traditionally help novice teachers, but more formal peer coaching programs extend the benefits of collaboration to more teachers. **Peer coaching** is an arrangement whereby teachers grow professionally by observing one another's teaching and providing constructive feedback. The practice encourages teachers to learn together in an emotionally safe environment. According to Bruce Joyce and Marsha Weil (2000, 440), peer coaching is an effective way to create communities of professional educators, and all teachers should be members of coaching teams:

> If we had our way, *all* school faculties would be divided into coaching teams— that is, teams who regularly observe one another's teaching and learn from watching one another and the students. In short, we recommend the development of a "coaching environment" in which all personnel see themselves as coaches.

Through teacher-to-teacher support and collaboration, peer coaching programs improve teacher morale and teaching effectiveness.

Staff Development

Increasingly, teachers are contributing to the design of staff development programs that encourage collaboration, risk-taking, and experimentation. Some programs, for example, give teachers the opportunity to meet with other teachers at similar grade levels or in similar content areas for the purpose of sharing ideas, strategies, and solutions to problems. A day or part of a day may be devoted to this kind of workshop or idea exchange. Teachers are frequently given released time from regular duties to visit other schools and observe exemplary programs in action.

One example of a collaborative staff development program is Project MASTER (Mathematics and Science Teachers Education Renewal), developed by the Chicago public schools. Groups of eight teachers (four in mathematics and four in science) from ten high schools form collegial support groups or professional cadres at their schools. A department chair or lead teacher heads the mathematics and science cadres at each school. Participants read and discuss educational research, attend workshops, and form peer coaching groups. The groups also receive training in conferencing skills, classroom observation and data collection, and analysis of instruction. Participants visit other Project MASTER schools to exchange ideas and to practice coaching and instructional analysis skills. As the following comments by participants indicate, collaboration is a powerful catalyst for professional growth and change:

What are some forms of professional collaboration in which you will participate as a teacher? In what types of co-teaching arrangements might these teachers cooperate?

> The project strengthened my understanding of instructional leadership and my own instructional leadership skills. The focus was on improving instruction, and I became more aware of certain aspects of teaching through observation (Ponticell, Olson, and Charlier 1995, 104).

> We have a chance to share, to get together with each other as a staff; this helped us become a team and help each other (103).

Team Teaching

In **team teaching** arrangements, teachers share the responsibility for two or more classes, dividing up the subject areas between them, with one preparing lessons in mathematics, science, and health, for instance, while the other plans instruction in reading and language arts.

The division of responsibility may also be made in terms of the performance levels of the children, so that, for example, one teacher may teach the lowest- and highest-ability reading groups and the middle math group, while the other teaches the middle-ability reading groups and the lowest and highest mathematics groups. In many schools, team teaching arrangements are so extensive that children move from classroom to classroom for forty- to fifty-minute periods just as students do at the high school level.

The practice of team teaching is often limited by student enrollments and budget constraints. As integrated curricula and the need for special knowledge and skills increase, however, the use of collegial support teams (CSTs) will become more common. A **collegial support team (CST)** provides teachers with a "safe zone" for professional growth, as one teacher commented:

> [The CST] allows me much discretion as to the areas I'd like to strengthen. Therefore, I am truly growing with no fear of being labeled or singled out as the "teacher who is having problems." I am aware of problem spheres and I work to correct these with the aid of my colleagues (Johnson and Brown 1998, 89).

The members of a team make wide-ranging decisions about the instruction of students assigned to the team, such as when to use large-group instruction or small-group instruction, how teaching tasks will be divided, and how time, materials, and other resources will be allocated.

Co-Teaching

In **co-teaching** arrangements, two or more teachers, such as a classroom teacher and a special education teacher or other specialist, teach together in the same classroom. Co-teaching builds on the strengths of two teachers and provides increased learning opportunities for all students (Friend and Bursuck 1999). Typically, co-teaching arrangements occur during a set period of time each day or on certain days of the week. Among the several possible co-teaching variations, Friend and Bursuck (1999) have identified the following:

- *One teach, one support*—one teacher leads the lesson; the other assists.
- *Station teaching*—the lesson is divided into two parts; one teacher teaches one part to half of the students while the other teaches the other part to the rest. The groups then switch and the teachers repeat their part of the lesson. If students can work independently, a third group may be formed, or a volunteer may teach at a third station.
- *Parallel teaching*—a class is divided in half, and each teacher instructs half the class individually.
- *Alternative teaching*—a class is divided into one large group and one small group. For example, one teacher may provide remediation or enrichment to the small group, while the other teacher instructs the large group.

How Will Your Performance as a Teacher Be Evaluated?

Most teachers are evaluated on a regular basis to determine whether their performance measures up to acceptable standards, if they are able to create and sustain effective learning environments for students. Performance criteria used to evaluate teachers vary and are usually determined by the school principal, district office, the school board, or a state education agency. In most schools, the principal or a member of the leadership team evaluates teachers.

Teacher evaluations serve many purposes: to determine whether teachers should be retained, receive tenure, or be given merit pay. Evaluations also help teachers assess their effectiveness and develop strategies for self-improvement. National studies indicate that "teachers want to be observed more, they want more feedback, and they want to talk more with other professionals about improving learning for their students" (Glickman, Gordon, and Ross-Gordon 1998, 313).

Quantitative and Qualitative Evaluation

Typically, supervisors use quantitative or qualitative approaches (or a combination) to evaluate teachers' classroom performance. **Quantitative evaluation** includes pencil-and-paper rating forms the supervisor uses to record classroom events and behaviors objectively in terms of their number or frequency. For example, a supervisor might focus on the teacher's verbal behaviors—questioning, answering, praising, giving directions, and critiquing. The Florida Performance Measurement System (FPMS) discussed in Chapter 2 is an example of a quantitative approach to teacher evaluation; (see Appendix 2.1 for the "Screening/Summative Observation Instrument" used by the FPMS).

Appendix 2.1

Qualitative evaluation, in contrast, includes written, open-ended narrative descriptions of classroom events in terms of their qualities. These more subjective measures are equally valuable in identifying teachers' weaknesses and strengths. In addition, qualitative evaluation can capture the complexities and subtleties of classroom life that might not be reflected in a quantitative approach to evaluation.

Clinical Supervision

Many supervisors follow the four-step **clinical supervision** model in which the supervisor first holds a preconference with the teacher, then observes in the classroom, analyzes and interprets observation data, and finally holds a postconference with the teacher (Anderson and Snyder 1993; Goldhammer, Anderson, and Krajewski 1993; Pajak 1993; Smyth 1995; Acheson and Gall 1997). During the preconference, the teacher and supervisor schedule a classroom observation and determine its purpose and focus and the method of observation to be used. At the postconference, the teacher and supervisor discuss the analysis of observation data and jointly develop a plan for instructional improvement.

Fulfilling the clinical supervision model is difficult and time-consuming, and time-pressed administrators must often modify the approach. For example, Kim Marshall, principal at a Boston elementary school with thirty-nine teachers, makes four random, unannounced five-minute visits to classrooms each day. This schedule allows him to observe every teacher during a two-week period, and each teacher about 19 times during a year. To make the most of his five-minute classroom visits, he follows these guidelines:

- Be a perceptive observer in order to capture something interesting and helpful to say during the feedback session.
- Give teachers a mixture of praise, affirmation, suggestions, and criticism.
- When sharing critical observations with teachers, be tactful and nonthreatening but totally honest.
- Use good judgment about when to deliver criticism and when to hold off (Marshall 1996, 344).

keepers of the
dream

Mary Lynn Peacher
The Teacher with Heart
1999 National Teacher of the Year Finalist

*"... all children
are special."*

Regardless of the approach a school district will use to evaluate your performance as a beginning teacher, remember that evaluation will assist your professional growth and development. Experienced teachers report that periodic feedback and assistance from knowledgeable, sensitive supervisors is very beneficial; such evaluation results in "improved teacher reflection and higher-order thought, more collegiality, openness, and communication, greater teacher retention, less anxiety and burnout, greater teacher autonomy and efficacy, improved attitudes, improved teaching behaviors, and better student achievement and attitudes" (Glickman, Gordon, and Ross-Gordon 1998, 317).

SUMMARY

KEY TERMS AND CONCEPTS

Go to the website for interactive flashcards.

APPLICATIONS AND INTERACTIVITIES

Go to the website for interactive assignments in the following areas:

Teacher's Journal

Teacher's Database

Observations and Interviews

Professional Portfolio

Weblink 13.4
Weblink 13.5
Weblink 13.6
Weblink 13.7
Weblink 13.8

Handout Master M13.1
Handout Master M13.2
Handout Master M13.3

Name _____ **Date** _____

For each question, write in the blank the answer you believe is correct.

13.1 A teaching _____ is actually a license to teach.

13.2 All states require an average of six to eight semester credits of supervised _____ teaching.

13.3 Currently, forty-four states are members of the _____ Certification Agreement Contract whereby a certificate obtained in one state is honored in another.

13.4 Persons who hold at least a bachelor's degree in a field other than education can in some states seek _____ certification.

13.5 Thirty-five of the forty-three states that require tests as part of their certification process require one or more of the _____ tests developed by Educational Testing Service (ETS).

13.6 U.S. Secretary of Education Richard W. Riley has observed the "_____, teachers, and school officials working closely together are proven ingredients for success in our nation's schools."

13.7 Building a learning community involves _____—working together, sharing decision making, and solving problems.

13.8 The process by which teachers grow professionally by observing one another's teaching and providing constructive feedback is known as peer _____.

13.9 In _____ teaching, teachers share responsibility for two or more classes.

13.10 Many supervisors adopt the four-step _____ supervision model involving a preconference, observation, analysis and interpretation, and a postconference.

Answers are available on the FlexChoice website at www.ablongman.com/parkayflex.

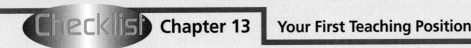
Name _____

Keep this checklist at your computer as a reminder to read and complete the chapter features and activities located on the FlexChoice website at www.ablongman.com/parkayflex.

Date
Completed

_____ ❑ **PreTest with Answers**
_____ ❑ **Audio Clip 13.1:** Thinking Over the Opening Vignette
_____ ❑ **Table 13.1:** States requiring testing for initial certification for teachers, by authorization, year enacted, year effective, and test used: 1990 and 1998
_____ ❑ **Appendix 13.1:** Directory of State Teacher Certification Offices in the United States
_____ ❑ **Appendix 13.2:** Parties to the Interstate Certification Agreement Contract
_____ ❑ **Figure 13.1:** Percent change in grades K–12 enrollment in public schools, by state: Fall 1996 to Fall 2008
_____ ❑ **Appendix 13.3:** Job Search Timetable Checklist
_____ ❑ **Figure 13.2:** Moving from "candidate" to "teacher"
_____ ❑ **Figure 13.3:** Résumé
_____ ❑ **Appendix 13.4:** Résumé Advice for Educators
_____ ❑ **Figure 13.4:** Letter of inquiry
_____ ❑ **Figure 13.5:** Letter of application
_____ ❑ **Weblink 13.1:** Sample Interview Questions for Candidates to Ask
_____ ❑ **Appendix 13.5:** Critical Information to Know about School Districts
_____ ❑ **Professional Reflection:** What elements are essential for your job satisfaction?
_____ ❑ **Technology Highlights:** How can you create an electronic professional portfolio?
_____ ❑ **Weblink 13.2:** Seventh-grade teacher Kelly Mandia's electronic teaching portfolio
_____ ❑ **Audio Clip 13.2:** An Alternative Way to Begin Teaching
_____ ❑ **Appendix 13.6:** Negotiating a School's Culture: A Political Roadmap for the First-Year Teacher
_____ ❑ **Audio Clip 13.3:** Reading to Children
_____ ❑ **Figure 13.6:** Student outcomes, by level of parental involvement in school and which parent is involved: Students in grades K–12 in two-parent families, 1996
_____ ❑ **Where Do You Stand?:** Should teachers be required to make home visits?
_____ ❑ **Weblink 13.3:** Parent Information and Resource Centers
_____ ❑ **Keepers of the Dream:** Mary Lynn Peacher
_____ ❑ **Summary**
_____ ❑ **Key Terms and Concepts**
_____ ❑ **Applications and Interactivities:** Teacher's Journal
_____ ❑ **Applications and Interactivities:** Teacher's Database
_____ ❑ **Weblink 13.4:** National Association for State Boards of Education (NASBE)
_____ ❑ **Weblink 13.5:** National Association of State Directors for Teacher Education and Certification (NASDTEC)
_____ ❑ **Weblink 13.6:** National Board for Professional Teaching Standards (NBPTS)
_____ ❑ **Weblink 13.7:** National Council for Accreditation of Teacher Education (NCATE)
_____ ❑ **Weblink 13.8:** U.S. Department of Education's National Center for Education Statistics (NCES)
_____ ❑ **Applications and Interactivities:** Observations and Interviews
_____ ❑ **Handout Master M13.1:** Developing and Conducting a Survey 1
_____ ❑ **Handout Master M13.2:** Developing and Conducting a Survey 2
_____ ❑ **Handout Master M13.3:** Qualitative Observation Log
_____ ❑ **Applications and Interactivities:** Professional Portfolio
_____ ❑ **PostTest with Answers**

14

Education Issues for the Twenty-First Century

At the turn of the century, more and more educators are working in a world of intensifying and rapid change. . . . New technologies, greater cultural diversity, the skills called for in a changing economy, restructured approaches to administration and management, and a more sophisticated knowledge-base about teaching and learning, are all pulling students and their teachers in new directions.

— Mission Statement excerpt
International Centre for Educational Change
Ontario Institute for Studies in Education
University of Toronto

Audio Clip 14.1

1. What knowledge and skills will prepare students for a global information age?

2. How can schools and teachers provide an outstanding education for all learners?

3. How can community-based partnerships address social problems that hinder students' learning?

4. How will the privatization movement affect equity and excellence in education?

5. What can teachers and schools learn from international education?

6. What is our vision for the future of education?

How will education change during the twenty-first century? What new school–community linkages will help schools meet the needs of all learners? In what ways will teachers' professional lives become more collaborative and oriented toward systemwide reform? How likely is it that, as a teacher, you will have experiences similar to the following?

After a short drive through early-morning traffic less heavy than usual, you arrive at school in time for a 7:30 A.M. meeting of your school's Teacher Leadership Team (TLT), a group that makes curricular and instructional decisions for the school. The TLT also works directly with the school's Site-Based Council (SBC), which makes budget, personnel, and other policy decisions. SBC members include three teachers, the principal, five community members, and two professors from a nearby university.

Like most schools around the country, the changing demographics of the nation are reflected in an increasingly diverse student population at your school. About 15 percent of students are from families who live below the poverty line, and one in eight students is identified as limited-English speaking. According to a district survey, students represent eighteen different languages. Overall, students at your school score in the top percentiles on state and national standardized tests; 80 percent of students go on to college, and 15 percent enroll in other forms of postsecondary programs. Within the last five years, the school has been designated twice by the state as a Blue Ribbon school.

With a few minutes before the meeting begins, you enter the classroom of another TLT member. Both of you were selected to be part of a nationwide network of teachers who will field test an interactive computer simulation developed by an instructional technology laboratory at a major university. Last week you both received the beta-test (trial) software, field-test guidelines, and registration materials for a four-day preparatory workshop to be held at the university. The university is paying for travel plus expenses, as well as providing a stipend.

"Well, did you have a chance to try out the software?" you ask upon entering the room. "I did last night, and it looks pretty impressive. I'm anxious to see what the kids think."

"I haven't had a chance yet; I've been preparing for this morning's TLT meeting," your friend says, pausing momentarily as she staples handouts arranged in neat stacks on top of her desk. Last spring she was elected to be one of the school's two curriculum coordinators. At today's TLT meeting, she and the other coordinator are presenting a model for schoolwide curriculum integration. "What do we have to do as field testers?" she asks, continuing with her stapling task. "I just glanced at the field-test guidelines."

"Well, actually quite a lot, but I think it'll be interesting," you say. "The lab wants us to use the software every day for three weeks. Also, collect student performance data on a regular basis and samples of students' work. Plus, students will complete a survey at the beginning and at the end of the field test. That's about it . . . oh, I forgot, they want us to do some student interviews . . . there's a set of constructivist-oriented questions we're supposed to use. Basically, the lab wants us to develop a picture of students' problem-solving strategies as they work through the simulation."

"That does sound interesting," your friend says.

"Right. Well, I better get out of here and let you finish getting ready for the TLT meeting," you say.

Walking down the hallway to the conference room, you think about how satisfying it is to teach at your school. Teachers are hard-working and share a strong commitment to good teaching and to building a collegial professional community. Ample leadership opportunities, common planning periods, stimulating colleagues who are professionally involved, and solid support from the district and community are just a few of the factors that make working conditions at your school very positive.

Name _____ **Date** _____

For each question, circle the letter of the answer you believe is correct. Then read the chapter to learn more about these topics.

14.1 To solve problems of poverty, discrimination, violence, crime, and so forth, students will need to do all of the following *except*
A. Become politically active.
B. Become socially compliant.
C. Become socially aware.
D. Become skilled in conflict resolution strategies.

14.2 According to RCM Research Corp. (1998), how time is used by schools often has less to do with what is best for students than with what other factor?
A. Availability of school district resources.
B. The demands of extracurricular programs.
C. Administrative convenience.
D. The needs of an agrarian economy.

14.3 After-school educational and recreational programs are designed to do all of the following *except*
A. Provide children with supervision when they might be involved in anti-social activities.
B. Provide carefully controlled experiences that inhibit socialization.
C. Provide enrichment experiences to widen children's perspectives.
D. Improve the academic achievement of children not achieving at their potential during regular school hours.

14.4 Opponents of turning the operation of public schools over to private, for-profit companies claim that
A. These companies are placing academic demands on students that are too rigorous.
B. Doing so might work and that would embarrass the public schools.
C. Public schools are already money-making.
D. Profit, rather than student achievement, is the real driving force behind such schools.

14.5 By 1999 Edison Schools, Inc. had become the largest company involved in
A. The in-service training of teachers.
B. For-profit management of schools.
C. The production of materials used in public schools.
D. Providing security for both public and private schools.

14.6 In comparing U.S. and Japanese education, Harry Wray (1999) concluded that Japan's system of national examinations
A. Are far superior to their U.S. counterparts.
B. Reinforce excessive conformity and passivity.

C. Are more closely correlated with a variety of learning styles than comparable examinations in the United States.
D. Motivate student interest in learning.

14.7 Compared to teachers in Japan, the United Kingdom, Italy, and Germany, the Organization for Economic Co-operation and Development (1995) reports that U.S. teachers have
A. More opportunities for consultation with parents and other teachers.
B. Won greater respect from the public.
C. Less time for planning and more classes to teach.
D. Fewer classroom management challenges.

14.8 In comparing the experiences of beginning teachers in the United States to those of beginning teachers in other countries, the Department of Education and the Education Forum of APEC (1997) found all of the following to be true *except*
A. Novice teachers in other countries are not expected to do the same work as experienced teachers without significant support.
B. Novice teachers in the United States are nurtured and not left to flounder on their own.
C. Beginning teachers in the United States too infrequently work in a culture of shared responsibility and support.
D. Beginning teachers in other countries experience purposive and valued induction programs.

14.9 In the future, students will need to be able to analyze unfamiliar situations and use trial-and-error methods to gather and evaluate data. These skills are examples of
A. Moral and ethical orientation.
B. Aesthetics awareness.
C. Global awareness.
D. Literacy in language, mathematics, and science.

14.10 Our nation's schools will need to become more technologically rich and teachers more technologically sophisticated to fulfill the educational priority for
A. New technological skills.
B. Conservation skills.
C. Lifelong, self-directed learning.
D. Critical thinking.

Answers are available on the FlexChoice website at www.ablongman.com/parkayflex.

Though no one has an educational crystal ball that can give a totally accurate glimpse of how the profession of teaching will evolve during the twenty-first century and how students will be taught, powerful forces are shaping schools and teaching in the directions just outlined. Moreover, thousands of teachers are collaborating and playing key leadership roles in shaping that future; and, today, hundreds of schools have professional communities identical to that described in the preceding scenario. We believe that the conditions under which teachers will work in this century will provide a dramatic contrast to those that many teachers experienced throughout much of the previous century. Isolation, lack of autonomy and self-governance, and few chances for professional growth are being replaced by collaboration, empowerment, stronger professionalism, and opportunities to provide leadership for educational change.

What Knowledge and Skills Will Prepare Students for a Global Information Age?

Figure 14.1

What knowledge and skills will students need to succeed in a global information age? Teachers in every generation have asked that question. At the beginning of the twenty-first century, the answer is confounded by conflicting theories, expectations, and values. One thing everyone agrees on, however, is that increasing cultural diversity in the United States and other countries and increasing global economic interdependence will call for communication and cooperation skills. People will need to be able to live together well and use environmental resources wisely. To equip students to do this, teachers will need to dedicate themselves to ensuring that all students develop knowledge, skills, attitudes, and values in nine key areas (see Figure 14.1). Though these nine areas of learning will not be all that students will need, learning in these areas will best enable them to meet the challenges of the future.

Literacy in Language, Mathematics, and Science

To solve the problems of the future, students will need to be able to write and speak clearly and succinctly. To access critical information from enormous data banks, they will need to be able to read complex material with a high degree of comprehension. Moreover, the continued development of "user-friendly" technologies such as voice-activated computers and reading machines will not reduce the need for high-level language arts literacy. As Sue Walters, a junior high school teacher in Kennebunk, Maine, told the prestigious Council of 21, a group of leaders in business, government, and education chaired by Senator John Glenn: "Reading, writing, and math are needed for continued learning and should not be lost in our race toward the future" (American Association of School Administrators 1999, 29). Students will also need to be able to apply mathematical and scientific concepts to solve new problems. For example, they will need to be able to analyze unfamiliar situations, pose appropriate questions, use trial-and-error methods to gather and evaluate relevant data, and summarize results.

New Technological Skills

Students of the future will also need to attain high levels of skill in computer-based technologies. To teach students skills in accessing the vast stores of information that computers routinely handle today, our nation's schools will become more technologically rich and teachers more technologically sophisticated. No longer able to resist the "irresistible force" of Information Age technology (Mehlinger 1996), schools will join the larger society where "the computer is a symbol of the future and all that is good about it" (Morton 1996, 417). In such an environment, students will not only learn to use computers as "tools" to access information—they will use computers to communicate worldwide and to generate creative solutions to real-world problems.

Problem Solving, Critical Thinking, and Creativity

Audio Clip 14.2

Students of the future will need to be able to think rather than to remember. Although the information that students learn in schools may become outdated or useless, the thinking processes they acquire will not. These processes focus on the ability to find, obtain, and use information resources for solving problems or taking advantage of opportunities. Students will need to learn how to cope with change, how to anticipate alternative future developments, how to think critically, and how to analyze and synthesize large amounts of complex data.

Forecasts about the future share one thing in common—they place a priority on creative thinking to solve future problems. The acquisition of structured bodies of knowledge, while important, is not sufficient preparation for the future. Students must learn to think creatively to solve unforeseen problems. Students who are stretched to develop their creativity today will become the adults who invent ways to solve tomorrow's problems.

Can creative thinking be taught? William J. J. Gordon (1968, 1971a, 1971b, 1975), who has devoted his career to the study of creativity, believes it can. Gordon developed synectics, a teaching method based on the thinking process that is designed to "teach" creativity through the use of metaphor and analogy. **Synectics** is based on the assumptions that (1) creativity is important; (2) creativity is not mysterious; (3) in all fields, creative invention draws from the same underlying intellectual processes; and (4) the creativity of individuals and groups is similar (Joyce, Weil, and Calhoun 2000).

What knowledge and skills for the twenty-first century does this learning activity support? What else will students need to know and be able to do in the future?

Social Awareness, Communication Skills, and Team Building

Tomorrow's students must be able to communicate with people from diverse cultures. The ability to create a better world in the future, then, will surely depend on our willingness to celebrate our rich diversity through the kind of communication that leads to understanding, friendly social relations, and the building of cohesive teams. "[T]he classroom should be a laboratory for collaborative decision making and team building" (Uchida, Cetron, and McKenzie 1996, 8).

An important lesson for students will be to learn that poverty, discrimination, violence, crime, and unequal opportunities, wherever they occur, affect us all. To solve these and other social problems, students will need to become socially aware, politically active, and skilled in conflict resolution strategies.

Global Awareness and Conservation Skills

Tomorrow's students will need to recognize the interconnectedness they share with all countries and with all people. Our survival may depend on being able to participate intelligently in a global economy and respond intelligently to global threats to security, health, environmental quality, and other factors affecting the quality of human life. The curriculum of the future must emphasize cultural diversity, interdependence, respect for the views and values held by others, an orientation toward international cooperation for resolving global issues, and practical knowledge and skills on, for example, the conservation of natural energy resources.

Health and Wellness Education

With ever-increasing health care costs, the spread of diseases such as AIDS, increased risks of cancer, and longer life spans, it is imperative that students of the future acquire appropriate knowledge, skills, and attitudes in the area of health education. To live healthy lives, then, students of tomorrow will need consumer education to select from among an increasingly complex array of health care services. In addition, they will need to be able to make informed choices among alternatives for the prevention or treatment of problems relating to substance abuse, nutrition, fitness, and mental health. Sex education, still a matter for debate in some communities, seems more critical today than at any time in the past.

Moral and Ethical Orientation

Audio Clip 14.3

The school culture and the curriculum reflect both national and community values. The traditional practice of using values-clarification activities in the classroom, however, has been criticized by some for promoting relativism at the expense of family values or religious doctrines. Yet, as we witness the effects of violence in schools, gang warfare, racial violence, sexual exploitation of children, drunk driving, white-collar crime, false advertising, unethical business practices, excessive litigation, and so on, many citizens are calling for schools to pay more attention to issues of public morality and ethical behavior. "[T]o survive and prosper in the twenty-first century, students will need self-discipline, which entails an ethical code and the ability to set and assess progress toward their own goals" (Uchida, Cetron, and McKenzie 1996, 17). In response to harassment and intimidation that can lead to violence in the hallways, for example, many schools have implemented anger management programs similar to the Second Step program created by the Seattle-Based Committee for Children. According to a teacher at a school that begins the year with Second Step lessons for all students, "We have created a culture in our school that says we all recognize that some things just aren't accepted" (Gutloff 1999).

Aesthetics Awareness

Another challenge for teachers and schools is to encourage creativity and greater appreciation for the arts. Many observers of U.S. education point out that emotional, spiritual, aesthetic, and reflective, or meditative, dimensions of life receive less emphasis than analytical thinking and practical life skills. Although literature and drama are standard fare in curricula, most students know little, for example, about music, painting, and sculpture. Public school students are rarely taught art history or principles of design or other criteria for evaluating creative works. As a result, students may lack the concepts and experiences that lead to an appreciation of beauty and the development of aesthetic judgment.

Lifelong, Self-Directed Learning

The key educational priority that should guide teachers of the future is to create within each student the ability, and the desire, to continue self-directed learning throughout his or her life.

It has often been said that one of the primary purposes of schooling is for students to learn how to learn. In a world characterized by rapid social, technological, economic, and political changes, all persons must take responsibility for their own learning. Career changes will be the norm, and continuing education over a lifetime will be necessary.

How Can Schools and Teachers Provide an Outstanding Education for All Learners?

Although we don't know exactly how teaching will change during the twenty-first century, we do know that teachers will continue to have a professional and moral obligation to reach all learners, many of whom will be from environments that provide little support for education. Imagine, for example, that one of your students is Dolores, described in the following scenario.

> Fifteen-year-old Dolores and her twin brother, Frank, live with their mother in a housing project in a poor section of the city. Their mother divorced her third husband two years ago, after she learned that he had been sexually abusing Dolores. Since then, Dolores's mother has been struggling to make ends meet with her job as a custodian at a hospital. Two evenings a week, she goes to a neighborhood center to learn English. She hopes to become proficient enough in English to get a job as a secretary.

> Dolores wishes her mother and Frank didn't fight so much. The fights usually revolve around Frank missing school and his drinking. Just last night, for example, Frank came home drunk and he and his mother got into another big fight. When she accused him of being involved in a street gang, Frank stormed out and went to spend the night at his cousin's apartment two blocks away.

> At 6:30 that morning, Dolores awoke just as her mother left for work. The hinges on the apartment door, painted over by a careless maintenance worker, creaked loudly as she closed the door behind her. Dolores felt reassured by the sound of her mother locking the dead bolt—the apartment beneath them had been burglarized last week. Like Frank, she wasn't getting along well with her mother lately, so it would be nice to have the apartment to herself while she got ready for school.

> Dolores got up slowly, stretched, and looked around the cluttered livingroom of the one-bedroom apartment. Her mother slept in the bedroom, and Frank, when he wasn't out all night or at his cousin's, slept on the other couch in the living room.

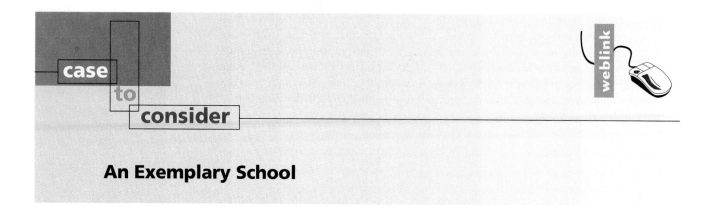

case to consider

weblink

An Exemplary School

She had trouble sleeping last night. Now that it was winter, the radiator next to the beige couch on which she slept clanked and hissed most of the night. Also, she was worried—two weeks ago a doctor at the neighborhood clinic confirmed that she was pregnant. Yesterday, she finally got up enough courage to tell her boyfriend. He got angry at her and said he "wasn't gonna be no father."

Dolores knew she ought to be seeing a doctor, but she dreaded going to the clinic alone. Her mother took a day off from work—without pay—when she went two weeks ago. Right after that, her mother complained about missing work and said, "Don't expect me to take off from work every time you go to the clinic. You should have thought about that before you got in trouble."

Later that morning, Dolores is in your class, sitting in her usual spot in the middle of the back row. While your students work on an in-class writing assignment, you glance at Dolores and wonder why she hasn't been paying attention during the last few weeks like she usually does. At that moment, Dolores, wearing the same clothes she wore yesterday, stifles a yawn.

As you continue to move about the room, checking on students' progress and answering an occasional question, you wonder if you should talk with Dolores after class. You don't want to pry into her life outside of school, but you're worried about what might be causing her to act differently.

Although the family will continue to remain a prominent part of our culture, evidence indicates that many children, like Dolores and Frank, live in families that are under acute stress. Soaring numbers of runaway children and cases of child abuse suggest that the family is in trouble. In addition, teachers will continue to find that more and more of their students are from families that are smaller, have working mothers, have a single parent present, or have unrelated adults living in the home.

Equity for All Students

A dominant political force in the twenty-first century will be continued demands for equity in all sectors of U.S. life, particularly education. For example, the constitutionality of school funding laws will be challenged where inequities are perceived, and tax reform measures will be adopted to promote equitable school funding. Classroom teachers will continue to be held accountable for treating all students equitably.

In Chapter 7, you learned about the importance of preparing multicultural instructional materials and strategies to meet the learning needs of students from diverse cultural, ethnic, and linguistic backgrounds. In Chapter 8, you learned how to create an inclusive classroom to meet the needs of all students, regardless of their developmental levels, intelligences, abilities, or disabilities. In addition, you should create a learning environment in which high-achieving and low-achieving students are treated the same. Thomas Good and Jere Brophy (2000) reviewed the research in this area and found that several teacher behaviors indicated unequal treatment of students. The behaviors identified include waiting less time for them to answer questions, interacting with them less frequently, giving less feedback, calling on them less often, seating them farther way, failing to accept and use their ideas, smiling at them less often, making less eye contact, praising them less, demanding less, grading their tests differently, and rewarding inappropriate behaviors.

Effective teachers establish respectful relationships with *all* students; they listen to them; they give frequent feedback and opportunities to ask questions; and they demand higher-level performance. In their assessment of student's learning, they give special attention to the questions they ask of students. Research indicates that most questions teachers ask are **lower-order questions,** those that assess students' abilities to recall specific information. Effective teachers, however, also ask **higher-order questions** that demand more critical thinking and answers to questions such as, Why? What if . . . ? In addition, to reach all learners and prepare them for the future, effective teachers provide students with active, authentic learning experiences.

Active, Authentic Learning

Since the 1970s, educational researchers have increased our understanding of the learning process. Though learning theorists and researchers disagree about a definition for *learning,* most agree that **learning** "occurs when experience causes a relatively permanent change in an individual's knowledge or behavior" (Woolfolk 1998, 204). Research into multiple intelligences and multicultural learning modes has broadened our understanding of this definition of learning. In addition, research in the fields of neurophysiology, neuropsychology, and cognitive science will continue to expand our understanding of how people think and learn.

Our growing understanding of learning indicates that all students learn best when they are actively involved in authentic activities that connect with the "real world." Small-group activities, cooperative learning arrangements, field trips, experiments, and integrated curricula are among the instructional methods you should incorporate into your professional repertoire.

How Can Community-Based Partnerships Address Social Problems That Hinder Students' Learning?

Earlier in this book, we examined social problems that affect schools and place students at risk of dropping out: poverty, family stress, substance abuse, violence and crime, teen pregnancy, HIV/AIDS, and suicide (see Chapter 4). We also looked at intervention programs schools have developed to ensure the optimum behavioral, social, and academic adjustment of at-risk children and adolescents to their school experiences: peer counseling, full-service schools, school-based interprofessional case management, compensatory education, and alternative schools and curricula. Here, we describe

Figure 14.2

innovative, community-based partnerships that some schools have developed recently to prevent social problems from hindering students' learning.

The range of school-community partnerships found in today's schools is extensive. For example, as the "Interactive Organizational Model" in Figure 14.2 illustrates, Exeter High School in suburban Toronto has developed partnerships with 13 community organizations and more than 100 employers. Through Exeter's Partners in Learning program, business, industry, service clubs, and social service agencies make significant contributions to students' learning.

The Community as a Resource for Schools

To assist schools in addressing the social problems that impact students, many communities are acting in the spirit of a recommendation made by Ernest Boyer: "Perhaps the time has come to organize, in every community, not just a *school* board, but a *children's* board. The goal would be to integrate children's services and build, in every community, a friendly, supportive environment for children" (Boyer 1995, 169). In partnerships between communities and schools, individuals, civic organizations, or businesses select a school or are selected by a school to work together for the good of students. The ultimate goals of such projects are to provide students with better school experiences and to assist students at risk.

Civic Organizations   To develop additional sources of funding, many local school districts have established partnerships with community groups interested in improving educational opportunities in the schools. Some groups raise money for schools. The American Jewish Committee and the Urban League raised funds for schools in Pittsburgh, for example. Other partners adopt or sponsor schools and enrich their educational programs by providing funding, resources, or services.

Volunteer Mentor Programs   Mentorship is a trend in community-based partnerships today, especially with students at risk. Parents, business leaders, professionals, and peers volunteer to work with students in neighborhood schools. Goals might include dropout prevention, high achievement, improved self-esteem, and healthy decision making. Troubleshooting on lifestyle issues often plays a role, especially in communities plagued by drug dealing, gang rivalry, casual violence, and crime. Mentors also model success.

Some mentor programs target particular groups. For instance, the Concerned Black Men (CBM), a Washington, DC–based organization with fifteen chapters around the country, targets inner-city African American male youth. More than 500 African American men in diverse fields and from all walks of life participate as CBM mentors to students in area schools. Their goal is to serve as positive adult male role models for youth, many of whom live only with their mothers or grandmothers and lack male teachers in school. To date, CBM has given cash awards and scholarships to more than 4,000 youth selected on the basis of high academic achievement, motivation, leadership in academic and nonacademic settings, and community involvement.

Corporate-Education Partnerships   Business involvement in schools has taken many forms, including, for example, contributions of funds or materials needed by a school, release time for employees to visit classrooms, adopt-a-school programs, cash grants for pilot projects and teacher development, educational use of corporate facilities and expertise, employee participation, student scholarship programs, and political lobbying for school reform. Extending beyond advocacy, private sector efforts include job initiatives for disadvantaged youths, inservice programs for teachers, management training for school administrators, minority education and faculty development, and even construction of school buildings.

Business-sponsored school experiments focus on creating model schools, laboratory schools, or alternative schools that address particular local needs. In Minneapolis, for example, the General Mills Foundation has provided major funding to create the Minneapolis Federation of Alternative Schools (MFAS), a group of several schools designed to serve students who have not been successful in regular school programs. The goals for students who attend MFAS schools include returning to regular school when appropriate, graduating from high school, and/or preparing for postsecondary education or employment.

In addition to contributing more resources to education, chief executive officers and their employees are donating more time; 83 percent of the top managers surveyed by a recent *Fortune* poll said they "participate actively" in educational reform, versus 70 percent in 1990. At Eastman Kodak's Rochester, New York, plant, for example, hundreds of employees serve as tutors or mentors in local schools. In some dropout prevention programs, businessmen and businesswomen adopt individual students, visiting them at school, eating lunch with them once a week, meeting their families, and taking them on personal field trips.

Schools as Resources for Communities

A shift from the more traditional perspective of schools needing support from the community to meet the needs of students whose lives are impacted by social problems is the view that schools should serve as multipurpose resources *for* the community. By focusing not only on the development of children and youth, but on their families as well, schools ultimately enhance the ability of students to learn. As Ernest Boyer (1995, 168) put it, "No arbitrary line can be drawn between the school and life outside. Every [school] should take the lead in organizing a *referral service*—a community safety net for children that links students and their families to support agencies in the region—to clinics, family support and counseling centers, and religious institutions."

Beyond the School Day Many schools and school districts are serving their communities by providing educational and recreational programs before and after the traditional school day and during the summers. Increasingly, educational policymakers recognize that the traditional school year of approximately 180 days is not the best arrangement to meet students' learning needs. As the RCM Research Corporation, a nonprofit group that studies issues in educational change, points out: "Historically, time has been the glue that has bonded the traditions of our public school system—i.e., the Carnegie units, equal class periods, no school during summer months, 12 years of schooling, etc.—and, as a result, the use of time has become sacrosanct, 'We have always done it this way!' How time is used by schools often has more to do with administrative convenience than it does with what is best educationally for the student" (RCM Research Corporation 1998).

Proposals for year-round schools and educationally oriented weekend and after-school programs address the educational and developmental needs of students impacted by social problems. According to the San Diego–based National Association for Year-Round Education, more than 2,800 public schools now extend their calendars into the summer, and more than two million students go to school year-round. In Austin, Texas, for example, schools can participate in an Optional Extended Year (OEY) program that allows them to provide additional instruction in reading and mathematics to students at risk of being retained a grade. Schools participating in OEY can choose from among four school day options: (1) extended day, (2) extended week, (3) inter-session of year-round schools, and (4) summer school (Idol 1998; Washington 1998). Futurist Marvin Cetron predicts that, soon, "schools will educate and train both children and adults around the clock: the academic day will stretch to seven hours for children; adults will work a 32-hour week and prepare for their next job in the remaining time" (Uchida, Cetron, and McKenzie 1996, 35).

Programs that extend beyond the traditional school day also address the needs of parents and the requirements of the work world. More than two million elementary-age, "latchkey" children come home to an empty home every afternoon, according to Census Bureau figures. As an elementary teacher in Missouri said, "Many of my students just hang around at the end of every day. They ask what they can do to help me. Often there's no one at home, and they're afraid to go home or spend time on the streets" (Boyer 1995, 165).

After-school educational and recreational programs are designed to (1) provide children with supervision at times when they might become involved in antisocial activities, (2) provide enrichment experiences to widen children's perspectives and increase their socialization, and (3) improve the academic achievement of children not achieving at their potential during regular school hours (Fashola 1999). Ernest Boyer argued that schools should adapt their schedules to those of the workplace so that parents could become more involved in their children's education, and that businesses, too, should give parents more flexible work schedules. Drawing on the model of Japan, Boyer suggested that the beginning of the school year could be a holiday to free parents to attend opening day ceremonies and celebrate the launching and continuation of education in the same way that we celebrate its ending.

For several years, the After-School Plus (A+) Program in Hawaii has operated afternoon enrichment programs from 2:00 to 5:00 for children in kindergarten through sixth grade. The children, who are free to do art, sports, drama, or homework, develop a sense of *ohana,* or feeling of belonging (Cohen 1990, 1). Since the mid-1970s, schools in Buena Vista, Virginia, have operated according to a Four Seasons Calendar that includes an optional summer enrichment program. Buena Vista's superintendent estimates that the district saves more than $100,000 a year on retention costs; though some students take more time, they are promoted to the next grade (Boyer 1995).

Although some research indicates that extended school days and school calendars have a positive influence on achievement (Gandara and Fish 1994; Center for Research on Effective Schooling for Disadvantaged Students 1992), the Center for Research on the Education of Students Placed at Risk (CRESPAR) at Johns Hopkins University concluded that "there is no straightforward answer to the question of what works best in after-school programs" (Fashola 1999). According to CRESPAR, few studies of the effects of after-school programs on measures such as achievement or reduction of antisocial behavior meet minimal standards for research design. Nevertheless, CRESPAR found that after-school programs with stronger evidence of effectiveness had four elements: training for staff, program structure, evaluation of program effectiveness, and planning that includes families and children (Fashola 1999).

Social Services   In response to the increasing number of at-risk and violence-prone children and youth, many schools are also providing an array of social services to students, their families, and their communities. The following comments by three female students highlight the acute need for support services for at-risk youth who can turn to aggression and violence in a futile attempt to bolster their fragile self-esteem and to cope with the pain in their lives. All three girls have been involved in violent altercations in and around their schools, and all three frequently use alcohol and illegal drugs.

Fifteen-year-old "Mary" has been physically abused by both her father and mother, and she was raped when she was fourteen. "Linda," also fifteen years old, was sexually molested during a four-year period by a family acquaintance, and she endures constant physical and psychological abuse from her father. Fourteen-year-old "Jenny" is obsessed with death and suicide, and she aspires to join a gang.

> When you're smoking dope, you just break out laughing, you don't feel like punching people because it's just too hard. It takes too much. . . . You're mellow. . . . You just want to sit there and trip out on everybody. . . . It's even good for school work. When I used to get stoned all the time last year, I remember, I used to sit in class and do my work because I didn't want the teacher to catch me, and this year I'm getting failing marks 'cause I'm not doing my work 'cause I'm never stoned (Mary).

> I just know I got a lot of hatred. . . . And there's this one person [Jenny], and it just kinda happened after she mouthed me off, I was just like totally freaked with her and now I just want to slam her head into something. I wanna shoot her with a gun or something. I wanna kill her. . . . If I could get away with it I'd kill her. I wouldn't necessarily kill her, but I'd get her good. I just want to teach her a lesson. I'd beat the crap out of her. She's pissed me off so badly. I just want to give her two black eyes. Then I'd be fine. I'd have gotten the last word in (Linda).

> I like fighting. It's exciting. I like the power of being able to beat up people. Like, if I fight them, and I'm winning, I feel good about myself, and I think of myself as tough. . . . I'm not scared of anybody, so that feels good. My friends are scared of a lot of people, and I go "Oh yeah, but I'm not scared of them." . . . All these people in grade eight at that junior high are scared of me, they don't even know me, and they're scared of me. It makes me feel powerful (Jenny) (Artz 1999, 127, 136, 157).

In Chapter 4, we looked at how full-service schools provide educational, medical, social and/or human services, and how the school-based interprofessional case management model uses case managers to deliver services to at-risk students and their families. Although many believe that schools should not provide such services, an increase in the number of at-risk students like Mary, Linda, and Jenny suggest that the trend is likely to continue, with more schools following the lead of schools in Charlotte-Mecklenburg, North Carolina; Seattle; and Palm Beach County, Florida. Charlotte-Mecklenburg schools organized a Children's Services Network, "which brings together all of the community agencies concerned with children, coordinates the services, increases support, and prepares a report card on progress" (Boyer 1995, 169). In Seattle, a recent referendum required that a percentage of taxes be set aside to provide services to elementary-age children. And Palm Beach County officials created the Children's Services Council to address sixteen areas, from reducing the dropout rate to better child care. From parent support groups, to infant nurseries, to programs for students with special needs, the council has initiated scores of projects to benefit the community and its children.

How Will the Privatization Movement Affect Equity and Excellence in Education?

One of the most dramatic reforms in American education during the last decade has been the development of charter schools and for-profit schools, both of which were developed to provide an alternative to the perceived inadequacies of the public schools. On many different levels—governance, staffing, curricula, funding, and accountability— the **privatization movement** is a radical departure from schools as most people have known them.

Charter Schools

In 1991, Minnesota passed the nation's first charter school legislation calling for up to eight teacher-created and -operated, outcome-based schools that would be free of most state and local rules and regulations. When the St. Paul City Academy opened its doors in September 1992, it became the nation's first charter school.

Charter schools are independent, innovative, outcome-based, public schools. "The charter school concept allows a group of teachers, parents, or others who share similar interests and views about education to organize and operate a school. Charters can be granted by a local school district, by the state, or by the national government. In effect, charter schools offer a model for restructuring that gives greater autonomy to individual schools and promotes school choice by increasing the range of options available to parents and students within the public schools system" (Wohlstetter and Anderson 1994, 486). As of late 1999, thirty-six states, Puerto Rico, and the District of Columbia had adopted charter school legislation; and 1,700 charter schools were open (White House Press Release 1999). Charter schools in Arizona range from those focusing on the fine arts to charter schools in remote regions of the state that serve Native American communities.

To open a charter school, an original charter (or agreement) is signed by the school's founders and a sponsor (usually the local school board). The charter specifies the learning outcomes that students will master before they continue their studies. Charter schools, which usually operate in the manner of autonomous school districts (a feature that distinguishes them from the alternative schools that many school districts operate), are public schools and must teach all students. If admission requests for a charter school exceed the number of available openings, students are selected by drawing.

Because charter schools are designed to promote the development of new teaching strategies that can be used at other public schools, they can prove to be an effective tool for promoting educational reform and the professionalization of teaching in the future. Moreover, as Milo Cutter, one of the two teachers who founded St. Paul City Academy points out, charter schools give teachers unprecedented leadership opportunities and the ability to respond quickly to students' needs:

> [We had] the chance to create a school that takes into account the approaches we know will work. We listen to what the students want and need, because we ask them. And each day we ask ourselves if we are doing things the best way we can. We also have the flexibility to respond. We can change the curriculum to meet these needs as soon as we see them. Anywhere else it would take a year to change. It is much better than anything we have known in the traditional setting (North Central Regional Education Laboratory 1993, 3).

Murnane and Levy (1996) suggest that charter schools are "too new to have a track record," and they should not be seen as a "magic bullet" that will dramatically, and with little effort, improve students' achievement. In addition, they suggest four questions that observers should pose to determine whether individual charter schools promote both equity and excellence.

- Does the charter school commit itself to a goal, such as mastery of critical skills for all its students, or will it emphasize other goals?
- Does the charter school commit itself to serve a fair share of the most difficult-to-educate children, and does it have a strategy for attracting such children—or will it discourage applications from such children?
- Does the charter school's contract with the school district provide enough time and enough financial support for the school to persevere and learn from the mistakes that are inevitable in any ambitious new venture?

■ Does the charter school commit itself to providing information about student achievement that will allow parents to make sound judgments about the quality of the education their children are receiving (Murnane and Levy 1996, 113)?

For-Profit Schools

One of the most controversial educational issues for the twenty-first century is the practice of turning the operation of public schools over to private, for-profit companies. Advocates of **privatization** believe privately operated schools are more efficient; they reduce costs and maximize "production"—that is, student achievement. Opponents, however, are concerned that profit, rather than increasing student achievement, is the real driving force behind **for-profit schools**. Figure 14.3, for example, shows that for-profit education companies had revenues of $82 billion in 1998, a 25 percent increase over 1997; and revenues were projected to reach $99 billion in 1999 and $123 billion in 2000. Critics of for-profit schools are also concerned that school districts may not be vigilant enough in monitoring the performance of private education companies.

Figure 14.3

Concerned about the slow pace of educational reform in the United States, Christopher Whittle, the originator of Channel One, launched the $3 billion Edison Project in 1992—an ambitious plan to develop a national network of more than 1,000 for-profit secondary schools by 2010. As of 1999, the Edison Project, now named Edison Schools, Inc., had become the largest company involved in the for-profit management of schools, and it managed seventy-seven public schools attended by 37,000 students nationwide (Walsh 1999b).

In 1999, Edison Schools, Inc. reported that achievement was steadily moving upward at the "vast majority" of Edison schools. At seventeen of the Edison schools that had been able to establish achievement trends, fourteen had records the company labeled "positive" or "strongly positive," and three had records that were labeled "weak" (Walsh 1999b). However, in a report analyzing the results reported by Edison the previous year, the American Federation of Teachers claimed that the company exaggerated achievement gains at many schools and downplayed negative results at others. "On the whole, Edison results were mediocre," the report claimed (American Federation of Teachers 1998a).

Another approach to for-profit schools was developed by Education Alternatives, Inc. (EAI), a company that negotiates with school districts to operate their public schools. Participating school districts give the company the same per-pupil funding to operate the school that the district would have used. The company, using its own curricula and cost-saving techniques, agrees to improve student performance and attendance in return for the opportunity to operate schools at a profit. Education Alternatives, Inc., which began operating its first for-profit school in Dade County, Florida, in 1991, became the first private company to run an entire school district when the Duluth, Minnesota, School Board awarded the company a three-month contract in 1992 to serve

where do you stand?

Is privatization an effective way to improve education in the United States?

technology highlights

How does the United States compare to other countries regarding the importance of information technology in the curriculum?

weblink

Figure 14.4

as interim superintendent for the district. In Baltimore and Hartford, Connecticut, where EAI operated several schools in the mid-1990s, critics challenged the achievement gains the company reported and accused the company of mismanaging finances. After numerous disputes over the management of schools, both school systems eventually terminated their contracts with the company. In 1999, EAI moved its headquarters from Bloomington, Minnesota, to Scottsdale, Arizona, and became the Tesseract Group, Inc. At that time, the company operated forty schools serving more than 6,000 students.

What Can Teachers and Schools Learn from International Education?

The world has truly become smaller and more interconnected as telecommunications, cyberspace, and travel by jet bring diverse people and countries together. As we continue to move closer together, it is clear that education is crucial to the well-being of every country and to the world as a whole. "For teachers, on whom the quality of education ultimately depends, the challenges and opportunities the twenty-first century will bring are remarkably similar worldwide, and there is much the U.S. can learn from other countries about the conditions that promote the ability of teachers and students to deal with that future" (Parkay and Oaks 1998). For example, an observation in a *Bangkok Post* editorial on the need to prepare Thai youth for a changing world echoes calls for educational reform in the United States: "The country's policy planners [s]hould seriously review and revamp the national education system to effectively prepare our youths [for] the next century" (Sricharatchanya 1996, 15). Similarly, a community leader's comments about educating young substance abusers in Bangkok's Ban Don Muslim community could apply to youth in scores of American communities: "We are in an age of cultural instability. Children are exposed to both good and bad things. [I]t's hard to resist the influences and attitudes from the outside world that are pulling at the children's feelings" (Rithdee 1996, 11). Lastly, the curriculum goals at Shiose Junior High School in Nishinomiya, Japan, are based on Japan's fifteenth Council for Education and would "fit" American junior high schools as well; according to principal Akio Inoue (1996, 1), "Students will acquire the ability to survive in a changing society, that is, students will study, think and make judgments on their own initiative. It is also important that we provide a proper balance of knowledge, morality, and physical health, and that we nurture humanity and physical strength for that purpose." As a result of the universal challenges that confront educators, we are entering an era of increasing cross-national exchanges that focus on sharing resources, ideas, and expertise for the improvement of education worldwide.

Comparative Education

As the nations of the world continue to become more interdependent, policies for educational reform in the United States will be influenced increasingly by **comparative education,** the study of educational practices in other countries. Comparative education studies show how school systems in other countries work and how American students compare with students in other countries on certain measures of schooling and achievement. In addition, research in comparative education enables professionals to share information about successful innovations internationally. Teachers can collaborate on global education projects and test change models that other countries have used to help match educational and societal needs and goals.

International Comparisons of Achievement   The first **International Assessment of Educational Progress (IAEP)** in 1991 revealed that the achievement levels of U.S. students were often below those of students from other countries. Subsequent IAEP comparisons have shown some improvement in the rankings of American students in mathematics and science. Figure 14.5(a), for example, based on the **Third International Mathematics and Science Study (TIMSS)** sponsored by the International Association for the Evaluation of Educational Achievement (1997a, 1997b), shows how the mathematics and science achievement levels of fourth-grade U.S. students compare with those of students from several other countries. However, as Figure 14.5(b) shows, the relative standing of U.S. students in these subject areas was significantly lower by the final year of secondary school. Gains in literacy, however, have been more significant; for example, *A First Look—Findings from the National Assessment of Educational Progress* reported that U.S. fourth-graders ranked second in 1995 on a thirty-two-nation survey of reading skills.

Figure 14.5

Since the publication of *A Nation at Risk* in 1983, there has been an unbroken trend for the media and some observers of U.S. education to decry the perceived poor performance of U.S. students on international comparisons of achievement. A closer examination of international comparisons, however, reveals the seldom-reported fact that the United States's position in country-by-country rankings is based on *aggregate* achievement scores—in other words, achievement scores of all students are used to make the comparisons. Not taken into account is the United States's commitment to educating all students (not just the academically able or those from home environments that encourage education), the widely varying quality of U.S. schools, and differences in students' *opportunity to learn* the content covered in achievement tests. That is, when only the top students of each country are compared, the rankings of U.S. students improve dramatically. As David Berliner and Bruce Biddle point out in *The Manufactured Crisis: Myths, Fraud, and the Attack on America's Public Schools* (1995, 52), "If one actually looks at and thinks about the comparative evidence, [o]ne discovers that it does not confirm the myth of American educational failure. Indeed, it suggests that in many ways American education stands head and shoulders above education in other countries."

To illustrate their point, Berliner and Biddle summarize Ian Westbury's (1992) analysis of data from the International Association for the Evaluation of Educational Achievements' (IEA) Second International Mathematics Study, which purported to show U.S. eighth-graders significantly behind their Japanese peers in mathematics achievement. Westbury noted that Japanese eighth-grade students were *required* to take courses that covered algebra, while U.S. students typically take such courses a year or two later. When Westbury compared the achievement of U.S. and Japanese students who had taken prealgebra and algebra, the achievement of U.S. students matched or exceeded that of Japanese students (see Figure 14.6).

Figure 14.6

Berliner and Biddle (1995, 63) go on to offer these cautions about interpreting cross-national studies of educational achievement.

- Few of those studies have yet focused on the unique values and strengths of American education.
- Many of the studies' results have obviously been affected by sampling biases and inconsistent methods for gathering data.
- Many, perhaps most, of the studies' results were generated by differences in curricula—in opportunities to learn—in the countries studied.
- Aggregate results for American schools are misleading because of the huge range of school quality in this country—ranging from marvelous to terrible.
- The press has managed to ignore most comparative studies in which the United States has done well.

A National Curriculum?   Decisions about the operation of schools in the United States are made largely at the district or individual school level. However, in some countries (Japan, Korea, and England, for example) education is centralized and teachers follow a standardized national curriculum. Since the first International Assessment of Educational Progress (IAEP) in 1991 revealed that the achievement levels of U.S. students are often below that of students from other countries (many of which have national curricula), some have proposed a **national curriculum** for the United States. Proposals for a national curriculum are also supported by the public. On the last Gallup Poll of the Public's Attitudes toward the Public Schools that asked for opinions about a national curriculum and national examinations, 46 percent believed they were "very important" and 27 percent "quite important" (Elam and Rose 1995, 48).

Although there is widespread support for national examinations and a national curriculum, there is also widespread opposition to such a system. For example, in his comparative study of U.S. and Japanese education, Harry Wray (1999, 137) concluded that Japan's system of national examinations "reinforce[s] excessive conformity, passivity, standardization, anxiety, group consciousness, and controlled education." Furthermore, Wray goes on to say, "Excessive emphasis on passing entrance examinations plays a contributing role in killing most students' interest in studying and scholarship after entering a university, especially for those outside the science, engineering, and medical areas. Students exhausted by the dehumanizing methodology lose motivation and curiosity" (Wray 1999, 138). Additionally, national examinations have been criticized because they encourage students to take a narrow view of learning and they tend to emphasize lower-order thinking skills that can be assessed easily by pencil-and-paper measures. As one Japanese university student confided to Wray: "In elementary school we had many occasions to give our opinions; however, after we entered junior high school, we did not get such opportunities because all the studies are for high school entrance examinations, and all the studies in high school are for university entrance examinations. One who is considered 'intelligent' is one who can get good grades, not those who have their own opinions" (Wray 1999, 137).

Lessons from Other Countries

The previous comments about Japanese education aside, U.S. educators can learn a great deal from their colleagues around the world regarding what works and what doesn't work in other countries. When considering the possibility of adopting practices from other countries, however, it is important to remember that educational practices reflect the surrounding culture. When one country tries to adopt a method used elsewhere, a lack of support from the larger society may doom the new practice to failure. In addition, it is important to realize that the successes of another country's educational system may require sacrifices that are unacceptable to our way of life. Nevertheless, there are many practices in other countries that American educators and policymakers should consider.

Support for Teachers and Teaching   In many other countries, teachers and the profession of teaching receive a level of societal support that surpasses that experienced by teachers in the United States. For example, teachers in many countries are accorded greater respect than their U.S. counterparts; and, as Figure 14.7 shows, the salary range (as a ratio of per-capita Gross Domestic Product) for teachers in Japan, the UK, Italy, and Germany is significantly greater than it is for U.S. teachers.

Figure 14.7

In addition, most U.S. teachers have about one hour or less per day for planning, and U.S. high school teachers teach about thirty classes a week, compared with twenty by teachers in Germany and fewer than twenty by Japanese teachers (U.S. Department of Education and International Institute on Education 1996). "[T]his leaves them with almost no regular time to consult together or learn about new teaching strategies, unlike their peers in many European and Asian countries where teachers spend between 15 and 20 hours per week working jointly on refining lessons, coaching one another, and learning about new methods" (National Commission on Teaching and America's Future 1996, 14).

The National Commission on Teaching and America's Future (1996) also found that other countries invest their resources in hiring more teachers, who comprise about 60 to 80 percent of total staff compared to only 43 percent in the United States (see Figure 14.8). In the United States, the Commission (1996, 15) noted that in U.S. schools "too many people and resources are allocated to activities outside of classrooms, sitting on the sidelines rather than the front lines of teaching and learning." Many other countries also invest more resources in staff development and beginning teacher support programs than U.S. schools. A joint report by the U.S. Department of Education and the Education Forum of APEC (Asia-Pacific Economic Cooperation) nations indicated that the experiences of beginning teachers in other countries are more positive than those of their U.S. counterparts for the following reasons:

Figure 14.8

1. New teachers are viewed as professionals on a continuum, with increasing levels of experience and responsibility; novice teachers are not expected to do the same job as experienced teachers without significant support.
2. New teachers are nurtured and not left to "flounder on their own"; interaction with other teachers is maximized.
3. Teacher induction is a purposive and valued activity.
4. Schools possess a culture of shared responsibility and support, in which all or most of the school's staff contributes to the development and nurturing of the new teacher.
5. Assessment of new teachers is downplayed (U.S. Department of Education 1997).

Parental Involvement   The powerful influence of parental involvement on students' achievement is well documented (Booth and Dunn 1996; Buzzell 1996; ERIC Clearinghouse 1993; Epstein 1992). Japan probably leads the world when it comes to parental involvement in education. Japanese mothers frequently go to great lengths to ensure that their children get the most out of the school's curriculum. The *kyoiku mama* (literally, education mother) will tutor her child, wait for hours in lines to register her child for periodic national exams, prepare healthy snacks for the child to eat while studying, forgo television so her child can study in quiet, and ensure that her child arrives on time for calligraphy, piano, swimming, or martial arts lessons. Though few U.S. parents might wish to assume the role of the *kyoiku parent,* it seems clear that U.S. students would benefit from greater parental involvement.

Pressure to Excel   There have been many calls to make U.S. schooling more rigorous—a longer school calendar, longer school days, more homework, and harder examinations, for example, have all been proposed. These changes, it is assumed, would increase student achievement and find favor with the majority of the public that wants greater academic rigor in the schools. More often than not, Japan, Korea, and other Asian countries are held up as models for the direction U.S. education should take.

But should U.S. schools be patterned after schools in these countries? Several of those who have studied and experienced Asian schools are beginning to think not. For example, Paul George (1995), who studied the Japanese public school his son attended for two years, reports in *The Japanese Secondary School: A Closer Look* that large numbers of students, deprived of sleep from having attended *jukus* (cram schools) to do well on college entrance exams, waste time in school, having been told by their *juku* instructors not to pay attention to their teachers. Additionally, a teacher of English in rural Japan reports that 70 percent of students at her school attend *jukus* and frequently are awake past midnight (Bracy 1996). According to Gerald Bracey (1996, 128), if U.S. parents want their children to achieve at the level of Asian students, which is often only a few percentage points higher on standardized examinations, they must understand the sacrifices made by Asian students and their parents and be prepared to adhere to these guidelines:

1. [W]hen their children come home from public school, they should feed them and then ship them off to a private school or tutor until 10 P.M.; most youngsters, both elementary and secondary, will need to go to school all day on Sunday, too.
2. [They should] spend 20 to 30 percent of their income on [a]fter-school schools.
3. [W]hen their children turn four, they should take them on their knees and tell them, "You are big boys and girls now, so you need to start practicing for college entrance examinations" (Bracey 1996, 128).

In addition, U.S. students would need to realize that "if they sleep four hours a night, they will get into college, but if they sleep five hours a night, they won't; they must study instead" (Bracey 1996, 128).

What Is Our Vision for the Future of Education?

Imagine that it is the year 2020, and we are visiting Westside Elementary school, a school in a medium-sized city in a midwestern state. All of the teachers at Westside have been certified by the National Board for Professional Teaching Standards (NBPTS). The salaries of the board-certified teachers are on a par with those of other professionals with comparable education and training. About half of the fifty-five teachers at Westside have also earned the advanced professional certificate now offered by the NBPTS. These teachers are known as lead teachers and may earn as much as $125,000 per year. Westside has no principal; the school is run by an executive committee of five lead teachers elected by all teachers at the school. One of these lead teachers is elected to serve as committee chair for a two-year period. In addition, the school has several paid interns and residents who are assigned to lead teachers as part of their graduate-level teacher-preparation program. Finally, teachers are

assisted by a diagnostician; hypermedia specialist; computer specialist; video specialist; social
worker; school psychologist; four counselors;
special remediation teachers in reading, writing,
mathematics, and oral communication; bilingual
and ESL teachers; and special-needs teachers.

Westside Elementary operates many programs
that illustrate the close ties the school has developed
with parents, community agencies, and businesses.
The school houses a daycare center that provides
after-school employment for several students from
the nearby high school. On weekends and on Monday, Wednesday, and Friday evenings the school is
used for adult education and for various community group activities. Executives from three local
businesses spend one day a month at the school visiting with classes and telling students about their
work. Students from a nearby college participate in
a tutoring program at Westside, and the college has
several on-campus summer enrichment programs
for Westside students.

What vision of the school of
the future does this photograph suggest? What might
you add to the image to
achieve a broader perspective
on tomorrow's teachers and
learners?

Westside has a school-based health clinic that offers health care services and a counseling center that provides individual and family counseling. In addition, from time to
time Westside teachers and students participate in service-learning activities in the
community. At the present time, for example, the fifth-grade classes are helping the
city develop a new recycling program.

All the facilities at Westside—classrooms, library, multimedia learning center,
gymnasium, the cafeteria, and private offices for teachers—have been designed to
create a teaching/learning environment free of all health and safety hazards. The cafeteria, for example, serves meals based on findings from nutrition research about
the best foods and methods of cooking. The school is carpeted, and classrooms are
soundproofed and well lit. Throughout, the walls are painted in soft pastels taste-
fully accented with potted plants, paintings, wall hangings, and large murals depicting life in different cultures.

The dress, language, and behaviors of teacher, students, and support personnel at
Westside reflect a rich array of cultural backgrounds. In the cafeteria, for example, it
is impossible not to hear several languages being spoken and to see at least a few students and teachers wearing non-Western clothing. From the displays of students'
work on bulletin boards in hallways and in classrooms, to the international menu offered
in the cafeteria, there is ample evidence that Westside is truly a multicultural school
and that gender, race, and class biases have been eliminated.

Each teacher at Westside is a member of a teaching team and spends at least part
of his or her teaching time working with other members of the team. Furthermore, teachers determine their schedules, and every effort is made to assign teachers according to
their particular teaching expertise. Students attend Westside by choice for its excellent
teachers; its curricular emphasis on problem solving, human relations, creative thinking, and critical thinking; and its programs for helping at-risk students achieve academic success.

Instruction at Westside is supplemented by the latest technologies. The school
subscribes to several computer databases and cable television services, which teachers
and students use regularly. The hypermedia learning center has an extensive collection
of CD-ROMs and computer software, much of it written by Westside teachers. The

center also has virtual-reality interactive videodisc systems, workstations equipped with the latest robotics, and an extensive lab with voice-activated computers. The computer-supported interactive multimedia in the center use the CD-ROM format and the more advanced Integrated Services Digital Network (ISDN) delivery system based on the optical fiber.

Every classroom has a video camera, fax machine, hypermedia system, and telephone that, in addition to everyday use, are used frequently during satellite video teleconferences with business executives, artists, scientists, scholars, and students at schools in other states and countries. Westside Elementary's technological capabilities permit students to move their education beyond the classroom walls, as they determine much of how, when, where, and what they learn.

Tomorrow's Teacher

Teaching and the conditions under which teachers work may change in some fundamental and positive ways during the next two decades. Teaching will become increasingly professionalized, for example, through such changes as more lengthy and rigorous preprofessional training programs, salary increases that put teaching on a par with other professions requiring similar education, and greater teacher autonomy and an expanded role for teachers in educational policy making. There will be more male teachers who are African Americans, Hispanic and Latino, or members of other minority groups. There will be greater recognition for high-performing teachers and schools through such mechanisms as merit pay plans, master teacher programs, and career ladders. Tomorrow's teachers will achieve new and higher levels of specialization. The traditional teaching job will be divided into parts. Some of the new jobs may be the following:

- Learning diagnostician
- Researcher for software programs
- Courseware writer
- Curriculum designer
- Mental health diagnostician
- Evaluator of learning performances
- Evaluator of social skills
- Small-group learning facilitator
- Large-group learning facilitator
- Media-instruction producer
- Home-based instruction designer
- Home-based instruction monitor

Though we cannot claim to have handed you an educational crystal ball so that you can ready yourself for the future, we hope you have gained both knowledge and inspiration from our observations in this chapter. Certainly, visions of the future, such as the one of Westside Elementary, will not become a reality without a lot of dedication and hard work. The creation of schools like Westside will require commitment and vision on the part of professional teachers like you.

weblink

Professional Reflection **What does the future hold for education in your state?**

SUMMARY

What Knowledge and Skills Will Prepare Students for a Global Information Age? (p. 392)

How Can Schools and Teachers Provide an Outstanding Education for All Learners? (p. 395)

How Can Community-Based Partnerships Address Social Problems That Hinder Students' Learning? (p. 397)

How Will the Privatization Movement Affect Equity and Excellence in Education? (p. 401)

What Can Teachers and Schools Learn from International Education? (p. 404)

What Is Our Vision for the Future of Education? (p. 408)

KEY TERMS AND CONCEPTS

Go to the website for interactive flashcards.

APPLICATIONS AND INTERACTIVITIES

Go to the website for interactive assignments in the following areas:

Teacher's Journal

Teacher's Database

Observations and Interviews

Professional Portfolio

Weblink 14.1
Weblink 14.2
Weblink 14.3
Weblink 14.4

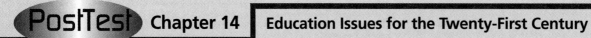
Name _____ **Date** _____

For each question, write in the blank the answer you believe is correct.

14.1 In the future, students wanting to access critical information from enormous data banks will need the capability to read complex material with a high degree of _____.

14.2 Students of the future will need to know how to _____ rather than remember.

14.3 The ability to communicate with persons from _____ cultures will be critically important in the future.

14.4 A primary goal for every teacher in the future should be to create within each student the ability, and the desire, to continue self-directed _____ throughout his or her life.

14.5 When experience causes a relatively permanent change in a person's knowledge or behavior, _____ is said to have taken place.

14.6 Some have suggested that every school should organize a _____ service through which a community safety net for children links students and their families to support agencies in the area.

14.7 Independent, innovative, outcome-based, public schools are known as _____ schools.

14.8 Those who support the _____ of schools believe privately operated schools are more efficient than traditional public schools.

14.9 The study of education practices in the United States and other countries is known as _____ education.

14.10 It is likely that the future will see greater numbers of _____ teachers who are members of minority groups.

Answers are available on the FlexChoice website at www.ablongman.com/parkayflex.

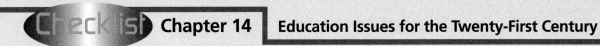

Chapter 14 | **Education Issues for the Twenty-First Century**

Name _____

Keep this checklist at your computer as a reminder to read and complete the chapter features and activities located on the FlexChoice website at www.ablongman.com/parkayflex.

Date
Completed

_____ ❑ **PreTest with Answers**
_____ ❑ **Audio Clip 14.1:** Thinking Over the Opening Vignette
_____ ❑ **Figure 14.1:** Educational priorities for the future
_____ ❑ **Audio Clip 14.2:** Critical Thinking Skills
_____ ❑ **Audio Clip 14.3:** Teaching Values
_____ ❑ **Case to Consider:** An Exemplary School
_____ ❑ **Figure 14.2:** Exeter High School interactive organizational model
_____ ❑ **Figure 14.3:** Big business—revenues for the education industry
_____ ❑ **Where Do You Stand?:** Is privatization an effective way to improve education in the United States?
_____ ❑ **Technology Highlights:** How does the United States compare to other countries regarding the importance of information technology in the curriculum?
_____ ❑ **Figure 14.4:** The importance of information technology and technical studies: An international perspective
_____ ❑ **Figure 14.5:** Nations' average mathematics and science performance compared with the United States
_____ ❑ **Figure 14.6:** Japanese and American achievement scores for students age 13—from The Second International Mathematics Study of the IEA
_____ ❑ **Figure 14.7:** Ratio of teacher salaries (starting and maximum) per-capita GDP by education level and career point
_____ ❑ **Figure 14.8:** Comparisons of educational staff by function
_____ ❑ **Professional Reflection:** What does the future hold for education in your state?
_____ ❑ **Summary**
_____ ❑ **Key Terms and Concepts**
_____ ❑ **Applications and Interactivities:** Teacher's Journal
_____ ❑ **Applications and Interactivities:** Teacher's Database
_____ ❑ **Weblink 14.1:** U.S. Department of Education
_____ ❑ **Weblink 14.2:** National Center for Education Statistics
_____ ❑ **Weblink 14.3:** National Assessment of Educational Progress (IAEP)
_____ ❑ **Weblink 14.4:** Third International Mathematics and Science Study (TIMSS)
_____ ❑ **Applications and Interactivities:** Observations and Interviews
_____ ❑ **Applications and Interactivities:** Professional Portfolio
_____ ❑ **PostTest with Answers**

References

Abrahamsson, B. (1971). *Military professionalization and political power*. Stockholm: Allmanna Forlagret.

Acheson, A. A., and Gall, M. D. (1997). *Techniques in the clinical supervision of teachers: Preservice and inservice applications*, 4th ed. New York: Longman.

*Ackerman, R. H., Moller, G., and Katzenmeyer, M. (eds.). (1996). *Every teacher as a leader: Realizing the potential of teacher leadership*. San Francisco: Jossey-Bass.

Acton v. Vernonia School District, 66 F.3d 217 (9th Cir. 1995); 115 S. Ct. 2386 (1995).

*Adler, M. (1982). *The paideia proposal: An educational manifesto*. New York: Macmillan.

*Adler, M. (1984). *The paideia program: An educational syllabus*. New York: Macmillan.

Aiken, W. M. (1942). *The story of the Eight-Year Study*. New York: Harper and Row.

Alali, A. A. (ed.). (1995). *HIV and AIDs in the public schools: A handbook for curriculum development, teacher education, and the placement of affected students, with a directory of resources*. Jefferson, NC: McFarland.

Alan Guttmacher Institute. (1999). *Teenage pregnancy: Overall trends and state-by-state information*. New York: Alan Guttmacher Institute.

*Alexander, C. J. (1998). Studying the experiences of gay and lesbian youth. *Journal of Gay and Lesbian Social Services*, 8.

Alfonso v. Fernandez, 606 N. Y. S.2d 259 (N. Y. App. Div. 1993).

Alvin Independent School District v. Cooper, 404 S. W.2d 76 (Tex. Civ. App. 1966).

*American Association for the Advancement of Science. (1999). *Middle grades mathematics textbooks: a benchmark-based evaluation*. New York: Oxford University Press, 1999.

*American Association for the Advancement of Science. (2000). *Atlas of science literacy goals: mapping K–12 learning goals*. New York: Oxford University Press.

*American Association of School Administrators. (1999). *Preparing schools and school systems for the 21st century*. Arlington, VA: American Association of School Administrators.

American Association of University Women (AAUW). (1991). *Shortchanging girls, shortchanging America*. Washington, DC: American Association of University Women.

American Association of University Women (AAUW). (1992). *How schools shortchange girls: The AAUW report*. Researched by The Wellesley College Center for Research on Women. Washington, DC: AAUW Educational Foundation.

American Association of University Women (AAUW). (1993). *Hostile hallways: The AAUW survey on sexual harassment in America's schools*. New York: Louis Harris and Associates.

American Council on the Teaching of Foreign Languages. (1996). *Standards for foreign language learning: Preparing for the 21st century*. Lawrence, KS: American Council on the Teaching of Foreign Languages.

*American Federation of Teachers. (1998a). *Student achievement in Edison schools: Mixed results in an ongoing experiment*.

Washington, DC: American Federation of Teachers.

*American Federation of Teachers. (1998b). *Teacher salaries in the 100 largest cities, 1996–97*. Washington, DC: American Federation of Teachers.

*American Federation of Teachers. (1999a). [Online]. AFT on the issues: Vouchers and the accountability dilemma. http://www. aft.org [1999, July]

*American Federation of Teachers. (1999b). *Teaching as a career: From the American Federation of Teachers*. Washington, DC: American Federation of Teachers. http://www. aft.org/pr/teaching.htm

*American School Board Journal. (1998, December). School leaders focus on standards and achievement, A13–A15.

*Anderson, J. D. (1997). Supporting the invisible minority. *Educational Leadership, 54*. 65–68.

*Anderson, J. P., Floisand, B., Martinez, D., and Robinson, D. P. (1997). Horizonte—where students come first. *Educational Leadership, 54*(7), 50–52.

*Anderson, R. E., and Ronnkvist, A. (1999). The presence of computers in American schools. The University of California, Irvine, and the University of Minnesota, Center for Research on Information Technology and Organizations.

*Anderson, R. H., and Snyder, K. J. (eds.). (1993). *Clinical supervision: Coaching for higher performance*. Lancaster, PA: Technomic.

*Anderson, R. J., Keller, C. E., and Karp, J. M. (eds.) (1998). *Enhancing diversity: Educators with disabilities*. Washington, DC: Gallaudet University Press.

*Annie E. Casey Foundation. (1999). *Kids count data book, 1999*. Baltimore, MD: Annie E. Casey Foundation.

Anyon, J. (1996). Social class and the hidden curriculum of work. In E. Hollins (ed.). *Transforming curriculum for a culturally diverse society*. Mahwah, NJ: Lawrence Erlbaum, 179–203.

Application of Bay v. State Board of Education, 233 Ore. 609, 378 P.2d 558 (1963).

Aristotle. (1941). *Politics* (Book VIII). In Richard McKeon (ed.). *The basic works of Aristotle*. New York: Random House.

Aronson, E., and Gonzalez, A. (1988). Desegregation, jigsaw, and the Mexican-American experience. In P. A. Katz, and D. A. Taylor (eds.). *Eliminating racism: Profiles in controversy*. New York: Plenum Press.

*Artz, S. (1999). *Sex, power, and the violent school girl*. New York: Teachers College Press.

Ashton-Warner, S. (1963). *Teacher*. New York: Simon and Schuster.

*Asian Americans/Pacific Islanders in Philanthropy. (1997). *An invisible crisis: The educational needs of Asian Pacific American youth*. New York: Asian Americans/Pacific Islanders in Philanthropy.

Astuto, T. (ed.). (1993). *When teachers lead*. University Park, PA: University Council for Educational Administration.

Baker, K. A. (1991). *Bilingual Education*. Bloomington, IN: Phi Delta Kappa.

*Ballantine, J. H. (1997). *The sociology of education: A systematic analysis*, 4th ed. Upper Saddle River, NJ: Prentice Hall.

Banks, C. A. M. (1997, Spring). The challenges of national standards in a multicultural society. *Educational Horizons*, 126–32.

*Banks, J. A. (1993, September). Multicultural education: Development, dimensions, and challenges. *Phi Delta Kappan*, 22–28.

Banks, J. A. (1997). *Teaching strategies for ethnic studies*, 6th ed. Boston, Allyn and Bacon.

*Banks, J. A. (1999). *An introduction to multicultural Education*, 2nd ed. Boston: Allyn and Bacon.

Banks, J. A., and Banks, C. A. (eds.). (1997). *Multicultural education: Issues and perspectives*, 3rd ed. Boston: Allyn and Bacon.

Barbin v. State, 506 So. 2d 88 (1st Cir. 1987).

*Barnett, D., McKowen, C., and Bloom, G. (1998). A school without a principal. *Educational Leadership, 55*(7), 48–49.

*Barrett, H. (2000, April). Create your own electronic portfolio (using off-the-shelf software). *Learning and Leading with Technology*.

Barth v. Board of Education, 490 N.E. 2d 77 (Ill.app. 186 Dist. 1986).

Battles v. Anne Arundel County Board of Education, 904 F. Supp. 471 (Md. 1995), aff'd, 95 F.3d 41 (4th Cir. 1996).

Beard, C. (1938). *The nature of the social sciences*. New York: Charles Scribner.

*Becker, H. J. (1999). *Internet use by teachers: Conditions of professional use and teacher-directed student use*. The University of California, Irvine, and The University of Minnesota, Center for Research on Information Technology and Organizations.

Bell, T. H. (1986, March). Education policy development in the Reagan administration. *Phi Delta Kappan*, 487–93.

*Bennett, C. I. (1999). *Comprehensive multicultural education: Theory and practice*, 4th ed. Boston: Allyn and Bacon.

*Bennett, L. (1997). Break the silence: Gay and straight students in Massachusetts team up to make a difference. *Teaching Tolerance, 6*, 24–31.

Bennett, W. (1987). *James Madison High School: A curriculum for American students*. Washington, DC: U.S. Department of Education.

Berliner, D. C., and Biddle, B. J. (1995). *The manufactured crisis: Myths, fraud, and the attack on America's public schools*. Reading, MA: Addison-Wesley Publishing Company.

*Bernstein, B. B. (1996). *Pedagogy, symbolic control and identity: Theory, research, critique (critical perspectives on literacy and education)*. New York: Taylor and Francis.

Besner, H. F., and Spungin, C. I. (1995). *Gay and lesbian students: Understanding their needs*. Washington, DC: Taylor and Francis.

*Bialo, E. (1989). Computers and at-risk youth: A partial solution to a complex problem. *Classroom Computer Learning, 9*(4), 48–55.

Bielaska v. Town of Waterford, 491 A. 2d 1071 (Conn. 1985).

*Bitter, G. G., and Pierson, M. E. (1999). *Using technology in the classroom*. Boston: Allyn and Bacon.

Bloom, B. S. (1981). *All our children learning: A primer for parents, teachers, and other educators*. New York: McGraw-Hill.

Board of Education, Sacramento City Unified School District v. Holland, 786 F. Supp. 874 (ED Cal. 1992).

References marked with asterisks are new to this edition.

*Board of Education of Oklahoma City Public Schools v. Dowell, 498 U.S. 237, 249–50 (1991).

Boleman, L. G., and Deal, T. E. (1994). *Becoming a teacher leader: From isolation to collaboration.* Thousand Oaks, CA: Corwin Press.

Booth, A., and Dunn, J. F. (eds.). (1996). *Family–school links: How do they affect educational outcomes?* Mahwah, NJ: Lawrence Erlbaum Associates, Publishers.

Borich, G. D. (1996). *Effective teaching methods,* 3rd ed. Englewood Cliffs, NJ: Merrill.

Boyer, E. (1990). Teaching in America. In M. Kysilka (ed.). *Honor in Teaching: Reflections.* West Lafayette, ID: Kappa Delta Pi.

Boyer, E. (1995). *The basic school: A community for learning.* Princeton, NJ: The Carnegie Foundation for the Advancement of Teaching.

Boyer, E. L. (1983). *High school: A report on secondary education in America.* New York: Harper.

Bracy, G. W. (1993). "Now then, Mr. Kohlberg, about moral development in women . . . " In G. Hass, and F. W. Parkay. (eds.). *Curriculum planning: A new approach,* 6th ed. Boston: Allyn and Bacon, 165–66.

Bracey, G. W. (1996, October). The sixth Bracey report on the condition of public education. *Phi Delta Kappan,* 127–38.

*Bracey, G. W. (1999, March). Getting along without national standards. *Phi Delta Kappan,* 80(7), 548–50.

*Bradley, A. (1997, April 30). Staying in the game. *Education Week on the Web.*

*Bradley, A. (1998a, February 4). Unions agree on blueprint for merging. *Education Week on the Web.*

*Bradley, A. (1998b, September 9). New teachers are hot commodity. *Education Week on the Web.*

*Bradley, A. (1999, April 2). Crackdown on emergency licenses begin as teacher shortage looms. *Education Week on the Web.*

Brameld, T. (1956). *Toward a reconstructed philosophy of education.* New York: Holt, Rinehart and Winston.

Brameld, T. (1959). Imperatives for a reconstructed philosophy of education. *School and Society,* 87.

Brown, F. B., Kohrs, D., and Lanzarro, C. (1991). The academic costs and consequences of extracurricular participation in high school. Paper presented at the Annual Meeting of Educational Research Association.

Brown, M. E. (1994). *Computer simulation: Improving case study methods for preservice and inservice teacher education.* ERIC Document Reproduction Services No. ED371–730.

Brown v. Board of Education of Topeka, Kansas, 347, U.S. 483, 74 S. Ct. 686 (1954).

Brown v. Board of Education of Topeka, Kansas, 349, U.S. 294, 75 S. Ct. 753 (1955).

Brown v. Hot, Sexy and Safer Productions, Inc., 68 F. 3d 525 (1st Cir. 1995), cert. denied, 116 S. Ct. 1044 (1996).

*Bruner, C., and Bennett, D. (1997). Technology and gender: Differences in masculine and feminine views. *NASSP Bulletin,* 81, 46–51.

Bruner, J. S. (1960). *The process of education.* New York: Random House.

*Brunwer, C. and Tally, W. (1999). *The new media literacy handbook: An educator's guide to bringing new media into the classroom.* New York: Anchor Books.

*Bryk, A. S., Sebring, P. B., Kerbow, D., Rollow, S., and Easton, J. Q. (1998). *Charting Chicago school reform: Democratic localism as a lever for change.* Boulder, CO: Westview Press.

*Bucky, P. A. (1992). *The private Albert Einstein.* Kansas City: Andrews and McMeel.

Burch v. Barker, 651 F. Supp. 1149 (W. D. Wash. 1987).

Burch v. Barker, 861 F. 2d 1149 (9th Cir. 1988).

*Burden, P. R., and Byrd, D. M. (1999). *Methods for effective teaching,* 2nd ed. Boston: Allyn and Bacon.

Burnaford, G., Fischer, J., and Hobson, D. (1996). *Teachers doing research: Practical possibilities.* Mahwah, NJ: Lawrence Erlbaum Associates.

Burton v. Cascade School Dist. Union High School No. 5, 512 F.2d 850 (9th Cir. 1975).

*Button, H. W., and Provenzo, E. G. (1989). *History of education and culture in America,* 2nd ed. Englewood Cliffs, NJ: Prentice Hall.

Buzzell, J. B. (1996). *School and family partnerships: Case studies for regular and special educators.* Albany, NY: Delmar Publishers.

*Calkins, L. (1991). *Listening between the lines.* Portsmouth, NH: Heinemann.

Campbell, D. M., Cignetti, P. B., Molenyzer, B. J., Nettles, D. H., and Wyman, Jr., W. M. (1996). *How to develop a professional portfolio: A manual for teachers.* Boston: Allyn and Bacon.

Cantor, L. (1989). Assertive Discipline—more than names on the board and marbles in a jar. *Phi Delta Kappan,* 71(1), 57–61.

Carmichael, L. B. (1981). *McDonogh 15: The making of a school.* New York: Avon Books.

*Carnegie Council on Adolescent Development. (1989). *Turning points: Preparing American youth for the 21st century.* New York: Carnegie Council on Adolescent Development.

Carnegie Council on Adolescent Development. (1995). *Great transitions: Preparing adolescents for a new century.* New York: Carnegie Council on Adolescent Development.

Carroll, J. (1963). A model of school learning. *Teachers College Record,* 64.

*Caterinicchia, D. (1999, June 18). Teachers' limited tech know-how prompts laptop lease. *CNN Interactive.*

*Catri, D. B. (1999). *Vocational education's image for the 21st century.* Columbus, OH: Center on Education and Training for Employment, Ohio State University.

*Cawelti, G. (1999). *Portraits of six benchmark schools: Diverse approaches to improving student achievement.* Arlington, VA: Educational Research Service.

Center for Research on Effective Schooling for Disadvantaged Students. (1992). Helping students who fall behind, Report No. 22. Baltimore, MD: The Johns Hopkins University.

*Center for the Study and Prevention of Violence, University of Colorado at Boulder. (1998). [Online]. Response to the Columbine school incident. http://www.colorado.edu/cspv [1999, April 21].

*Centers for Disease Control and Prevention. (1998a). Characteristics of health education among secondary schools—school health education profiles, 1996. Atlanta, GA: Centers for Disease Control and Prevention.

*Centers for Disease Control and Prevention. (1998b). *Youth risk behavior surveillance—United States, 1997.* Atlanta, GA: Centers for Disease Control and Prevention.

*CEO Forum on Education and Technology. (1999). *School Technology and Readiness Report.* Washington, DC: CEO Forum on Education and Technology.

*Cetron, M. (1997). Reform and tomorrow's schools. *TECHNOS,* 61, 19–22.

*Chase, B. (1997, October 15). Restoring the impulse to dream: The right to a quality public education. *Vital Speeches of the Day,* 20–23.

*Chase, B. (1999). Teachers lead the fight for innovation and investment in public education. In J. W. Noll (ed.). *Taking sides: Clashing views on controversial issues* 10th ed. Guilford, CT: McGraw–Hill.

Chaskin, R. J., and Rauner, D. M. (1995, May). Youth and caring: An introduction. *Phi Delta Kappan.*

*Chavkin, N. F., and Gonzalez, D. L. (1995). Forging partnerships between Mexican American parents and schools. *ERIC Digest.*

Cheeks, E. H., Flippo, R. F., and Lindsey, J. D. (1997). *Reading for success in elementary schools.* Madison, WI: Brown and Benchmark.

*Child Care Bureau. (1997). *Out–of–school time: School–age care.* Washington, DC: U.S. Department of Health and Human Services, Child Care Bureau.

Chubb, J. E., and Moe, T. (1990). *Politics, markets and America's schools.* Washington, DC: Brookings Institution.

*Clift, R. T., et al. (1995). *Collaborative leadership and shared decision making: Teachers, principals, and university professors.* New York: Teachers College Press.

*Clinton, B. (1999, May 19). White House press briefing.

*Codell, E. R. (1999). *Educating Esmé.* Chapel Hill, NC: Algonquin Books.

Cohen, D. (1990, March 14). Hawaii program for after–school care irks private firms. *Education Week.*

Cohen, S. (ed.) (1974). *Massachusetts School Law of 1648. Education in the United States.* New York: Random House.

Cohn, M. M., and Kottkamp, R. B. (1993). *Teachers: The missing voice in education.* Albany, NY: State University of New York Press.

*Coladarci, T., and Cobb, C. D. (1996). Extracurricular participation, school size, and achievement and self-esteem among high school students: A national look. *Journal of Research in Rural Education,* 12(2), 92–103.

Coleman, J. S., Campbell, E. Q., Hobson, C. J., McPartland, J., Mood, A. L., Weinfeld, F. D., and York, R. L. (1966). *Equality of educational opportunity.* Washington, DC: U.S. Government Printing Office.

*Comber, C., et al. (1997). The effects of age, gender and computer experience upon computer attitudes. *Educational Research,* 39, 123–33.

Combs, A. (1979). *Myths in education: Beliefs that hinder progress and their alternatives.* Boston: Allyn and Bacon.

*Comer, J. P. (1997). *Waiting for a miracle: Why schools can't solve our problems—and how we can.* New York: Dutton.

*Committee for Economic Development. (1994). *Putting learning first: Governing and managing schools for high achievement.* New York: Research and Policy Committee, Committee for Economic Development.

*Cookson, P. W., Jr., and Shroff, S. M. (1997). Recent experience with urban school choice plans. *ERIC/CUE Digest, 127.*

Cornbleth, C. (1990). *Curriculum in context.* London: the Falmer Press.

Cornfield v. Connsolidated High School District No 230, F.2d 1316 (7th Cir. 1993).

Costa, A. L. (1984). A reaction to Hunter's knowing, teaching, and supervising. In P. L. Hosford (ed.). *Using what we know about teaching.* Alexandria, VA: Association for Supervision and Curriculum Development.

Coughlin, E. K. (1993, March 24). Sociologists examine the complexities of racial and ethnic identity in America. *Chronicle of Higher Education.*

Counts, G. (1932). *Dare the school build a new social order?* New York: The John Day Company.

Csikszentmihalyi, M., and McCormack, J. (1986, February). The influence of teachers. *Phi Delta Kappan,* 415–19.

*Cuban, L. (1997, August 10). Unless teachers get involved, wiring schools just enriches computer makers. *The Los Angeles Times.*

*Cuban, L. (1999a, January). High-tech schools, low-teach teaching. *The Education Digest.*

*Cuban, L. (1999b, August 4). The technology puzzle: Why is greater access not translating into better classroom use? *Education Week,* 47, 68.

Curtis v. School Committee of Falmouth, 652 N.E. 2d 580 (Mass. 1995), *cert. denied,* 116 S. Ct. 753 (1996).

*Curwin, R., and Mendler, A. (1989, March). We repeat, let the buyer beware: A response to Canter. *Educational Leadership,* 46(6), 83.

Curwin, R. and Mendler, A. (1988, October) Packaged discipline programs: Let the buyer beware. *Educational Leadership,* 46(6), 68–71.

Cziko, G. A. (1992, March). The evaluation of bilingual education: From necessity and probability to possibility. *Educational Researcher,* 10–15.

Daniels, C. B. (1984). Quality of educational materials: A marketing perspective. In F. W. Parkay, S. Obrien, and M. Hennesey, (Eds). *Quest for quality: Improving basic skills instruction in the 1980s.* Lanham, MD: University Press of America.

Danzberger, J. P. (1994a, January). Governing the nation's schools: The case for restructuring local school boards. *Phi Delta Kappan,* 67–73.

Danzberger, J. P. (1994b, January). School board reform in West Virginia. *Phi Delta Kappan.*

*Darling-Hammond, L. (1993). Progress toward professionalism in teaching. In G. Cawelti (ed.). *Challenges and achievements of American education: The 1993 yearbook of the Association for Supervision and Curriculum Development.* Washington, DC: Association for Supervision and Curriculum Development.

*Darling-Hammond, L. (1999). Educating teachers for the next century: Rethinking practice and policy. In G. A. Griffin (ed.). *The education of teachers: Ninety–eighth year-*

book of the National Society for the Study of Education.* Chicago: University of Chicago Press.

*Darling-Hammond, L., Wise, A. E., and Klein, S. P. (1995). *A license to teach: Building a profession for 21st–century schools.* Boulder, CO: Westview Press.

*Davis, G. A., and Rimm, S. B. (1998). *Education of the gifted and talented, 4th ed.* Boston: Allyn and Bacon.

Davis v. Meek, 344 F. Supp. 298 N.D. Ohio (1972).

Davis v. Monroe County Board of Education, Supp. 97–843. Georgia (1999).

*Davitt, J. (1997, January 3). The ultimate good shepherd. *Times Educational Supplement.*

*Deal, T. E., and Peterson, K. D. (1999). *Shaping school culture: The heart of leadership.* San Francisco: Jossey–Bass Publishers.

Dean v. Board of Education, 523 A. 2d 1059 (Md. App. 1987).

*Department of Health and Human Services. (1999). *Profile of homelessness in America.* Washington, DC: Department of Health and Human Services.

Dewey, J. (1900). *The school and society.* Chicago: University of Chicago Press.

Dewey, J. (1902). *The child and the curriculum.* Chicago: University of Chicago Press.

Dewey, J. (1916). *Democracy and education: An introduction to the philosophy of education.* New York: Macmillan.

Dewey, J. (1955). Quoted in *Organizing the teaching profession: The story of the American Federation of Teachers.* Glencoe, IL: The Commission on Educational Reconstruction.

*Dobbs, S. M. (1998). *Learning in and through arts: A guide to discipline-based art education.* Los Angeles: Getty Education Institute for the Arts.

Doe v. Renfrow, 635F.2d 582 (7th Cir. 1980), cert. denied, 451 U.S. 1022, rehearing denied, 101 S. Ct. 3015 (1981).

Dollase, R. H. (1992). *Voices of beginning teachers: Visions and realities.* New York: Teachers College Press.

Doyle, W. (1986). Classroom organization and management. In M. Wittrock (ed.). *Handbook of research on teaching, 3rd ed.* New York: Macmillan.

Dryfoos, J. G.(1994). *Full-service schools: A revolution in health and social services for children, youth, and families.* San Francisco: Jossey-Bass.

*Dryfoos, J. G. (1998). *Safe passage: Making it through adolescence in a risky society.* New York: Oxford University Press.

Duffy, G., and Roehler, L. (1989). The tension between information-giving and mediation: Perspectives on instructional explanation and teacher change. In J. Brophy (Ed.). *Advances in research on teaching,* Vol. 1. Greenwich, CT: JAI Press.

Duke, D. L. (1984). *Teaching—the imperiled profession.* Albany, NY: State University of New York Press.

Durlak, J. A. (1995). *School-based prevention programs for children and adolescents.* Thousand Oaks, CA: Sage Publications.

*Dykgraaf, C. L., and Kane, S. (1998, October). For-profit charter schools: What the public needs to know. *Educational Leadership,* 56(2), 51–53.

*Economist. (1999a, January 16). A contract on schools: Why handing education over to companies can make sense.

*Economist. (1999b, January 16). Reading, writing, and enrichment: Private money is pouring into American education—and transforming it.

Edelman, M. W. (1993). *The measure of our success: A letter to my children.* New York: Harper Perennial.

*Edelman, M. W. (1997, November 9). Young families shut out of the American dream. *Seattle Times,* B5.

*Education Week (1996a, January 10). Studies seek to adjust for pay variables.

*Education Week. (1996b, April 24). Virginia governor victorious in rejecting Goals 2000.

*Education Week. (1997). *Staying in the game.*

*Education Week. (1998, September 9). New teachers are hot commodity.

*Education Week. (1999a, March 31). N.M. governor digs in his heels on vouchers.

*Education Week. (1999b, April 14). States increasingly flexing their policy muscle.

*Education Week. (1999c, May 5). Battle over principals in Chicago: Administration vs. local councils.

*Education Week. (1999d, May 26). Clinton ESEA plan targets accountability.

*Education Week. (1999e, June 2). Substituting the privilege of choice for the right to equality.

*Education Week on the Web. (1999, July 29). Issue paper: Privatization of public education.

Educational Testing Service. (1995, Spring). Bringing volunteers into teacher education programs. *ETS Policy Notes,* 8–9.

*Edwards, A. T. (1997). Let's stop ignoring our gay and lesbian youth. *Educational Leadership,* 54.

Edwards, P., and Young, L. (1992). Beyond parents: family, community, and school involvement. *Phi Delta Kappan,* 74(1), 72, 74, 76, 78, 80.

Edwards v. Aguillard, 482 U.S. 578(1987).

*Ehrenreich, B. 1989. *Fear of falling: The inner life of the middle class.* New York: Harper Perennials.

Eisner, E. (1994). *The educational imagination: On the design and evaluation of school programs,* 3rd ed. New York: Macmillan.

*Eisner, E. W. (1998). *The kind of schools we need: Personal essays.* Portsmouth, NH: Heinemann.

Elam, S. M., and Rose, L. C. (1995, September). The 27th annual Gallup poll of the public's attitudes toward the public schools. *Phi Delta Kappan,* 41–56.

Elam, S. M., Rose, L. C., and Gallup, A. (October 1993). The 25th annual Phi Delta Kappa Gallup Poll of the public's attitudes toward the public schools. *Phi Delta Kappan,* 137–52.

Elam, S. M., Rose, L. C., and Gallup, A. (1994, September). The 26th annual Phi Delta Kappan/Gallup Poll of the public's attitudes toward the public schools. *Phi Delta Kappan,* 41–56.

*Emerson, R., Fretz, R., and Shaw, L. (1995). Writing ethnographic field notes. Chicago: University of Chicago Press.

Engel v. Vitale, 370 U.S. 421 (1962).

*Epstein, J. (1995, May). School/family/community partnerships: Caring for the children we share. *Phi Delta Kappan,* 76(9), 701–12.

Epstein, J. L. (1992). School and family partnerships. In M. C. Alkin (Ed.). *Encyclopedia of educational research,* 6th ed. New York: Macmillan.

ERIC Clearinghouse. (1993). *Value search: Parent involvement in the educational process.* Eugene, OR: ERIC Clearinghouse on Educational Management.

Erikson, E. H. (1963). *Childhood and society.* New York: W. W. Norton.

*Erikson, E. H. (1997). *The life cycle completed: Extended version with new chapters on the ninth stage of development by Joan M. Erikson.* New York: W.W. Norton and Company.

*Esbensen, F., and Osgood, D.W. (1997). *National evaluation of G.R.E.A.T. research in brief.* Washington, DC: U.S. Department of Justice, Office of Justice Programs, National Institute of Justice, NCJ 167264.

*Essex, N. L. (1999). *School law and the public schools: A practical guide for educational leaders.* Boston: Allyn and Bacon.

Etzioni, A. (1969). *The semi-professions and their organization: Teachers, nurses, social workers.* New York: Free Press.

Etzioni, A. (1999, June 9). The truths we must face to curb youth violence. *Education Week on the Web.*

Evertson, C. M., Emmer, E. T., Clements, R. S., and Worsham, M. E. (1997). *Classroom management for elementary teachers,* 4th ed. Boston: Allyn and Bacon.

Fagen v. Summers, 498 P.2d 1227 (Wyo. 1972).

*Fashola, O. (1999). *Review of extended-day and after-school programs and their effectiveness.* Johns Hopkins University: Center for Research on the Education of Students Placed at Risk.

*Feistritzer, E. (1999, May 13). Teacher quality and alternative certification programs. Testimony before the House Committee on Education and the Workforce. Washington, DC.

*Feldhusen, J.F. (1997). Educating teachers for work with talented youth. In N. Colangelo and G. A. Davis (Eds.) *Handbook of gifted education.* Boston: Allyn and Bacon.

Felsenthal, H. (1982, March). Factors influencing school effectiveness: An ecological analysis of an "effective" school. Paper presented at the Annual Meeting of the American Educational Research Association, New York.

*Ferguson, A., Barovick, H., et al. (1999, May 24). Character goes back to school. *Time,* 153, 68–69.

Fischer, J. C. (1996). Open to ideas: Developing a framework for your research. In G. Burnaford, J. Fischer, and D. Hobson, (Eds.). *Teachers doing research: Practical possibilities.* Mahwah, NJ: Lawrence Erlbaum Associates, Publishers.

Fischer, L., and Sorenson, G. P. (1996). *School law for counselors, psychologists, and social workers, 3rd ed.* White Plains, NY: Longman.

Franklin, B. (1931). Proposals relating to the education of youth in Pennsylvania. In Thomas Woody (Ed.), *Educational views of Benjamin Franklin.* New York: McGraw–Hill.

Franklin v. Gwinnett County Public Schools, 112 S. Ct. 1028 (1992).

Franz, K. R. (1996, Autumn). Toward a critical social consciousness in children: multicultural peace education in a first grade classroom. *Theory into Practice,* 35(4), 264–70.

Freedman, S., Jackson, J., and Botes, K. (1983). Teaching: An imperiled profession. In L. Shulman, and G. Sykes, (Eds.). (1983). *Handbook of teaching and policy.* New York: Longman.

Freeman v. Pitts, 503 U.S. 467 (1992).

*Friend, M., and Bursuck, W. D. (1999). *Including students with special needs: A practical guide for classroom teachers,* 2nd ed. Boston: Allyn and Bacon.

*Frost, D. (1997). *Reflective action planning for teachers: A guide to teacher-led school and professional development.* London: D. Fulton Publishers.

Fuligni, A. J., and Stevenson, H. W. (1995). Home environment and school learning. In Lorin W. Anderson (Ed.), *International encyclopedia of teaching and teacher education,* 2nd ed. Oxford: Pergamon, 378–82.

*Fullan, M., and Hargreaves, A. (1996). *What's worth fighting for in your school?* New York: Teachers College Press.

*Fuller, B., Burr, E., Huerta, L., Puryear, S., and Wexler, E. (1999). *School choice: Abundant hopes, scarce evidence on results.* University of California–Berkeley and Stanford University: Policy Analysis for California Education.

*Furger, R. (1998). *Does Jane compute? Preserving our daughters' place in the cyber revolution.* New York: Warner Books.

*Furger, R. (1999, September). Are wired schools failing our kids? *PC World.*

*Gaddy, B. B., Hall, W. W., and Marzano, R. J. (1996). *School wars: Resolving our conflicts over religion and values.* San Francisco: Jossey-Bass Publishers.

*Gagné, R. M. (1974). *Essentials of learning for instruction.* Hinsdale, IL: Dryden.

*Gagné, R. M. (1977). *The conditions of learning,* 3rd ed. New York: Holt, Rinehart and Winston.

Gallup, G. H. (1975, September). The 7th annual Gallup poll of the public's attitudes toward the public schools. *Phi Delta Kappan,* 227–41.

Gandara, P., and Fish, J. (Spring 1994). Year-round schooling as an avenue to major structural reform. *Educational Evaluation and Policy Analysis,* 16.

*Garbarino, J. (1999). *Lost boys: Why our sons turn violent and how we can save them.* New York: Free Press.

Gardner, H. (1983). *Frames of mind.* New York: Basic Books.

Gardner, H. (1995, November). Reflections on multiple intelligences: Myths and messages. *Phi Delta Kappan,* 200–03, 206–09.

*Gardner, H. (1999). *The disciplined mind: What all students should understand.* New York: Simon and Schuster.

*Gates, B., Myhrvold, N., and Rinearson, P. M. (1996). *The road ahead.* New York: Penguin.

Gaylord v. Tacoma School District No. 10, 88 Wa. 2d 286, 599 P.2d 1340 (1977).

Gehrke, N. (1988, Summer). Toward a definition of mentoring. *Theory Into Practice,* 190–94

*Gehrke, N. J., and Romerdahl, N. S. (1997). *Teacher leaders: Making a difference in schools.* West Lafayette, IN: Kappa Delta Pi.

George, P. (1995). *The Japanese secondary school: A closer look.* Columbus, OH: National Middle School Association; and Reston, VA: National Association of Secondary School Principals.

*Gerber, S. B. (1996). Extracurricular activities and academic achievement. *Journal of Research and Development in Education,* 30(1), 42–50.

Gerstner, L. V., Semerad, R. D., Doyle, D. P., and Johnston, W. B. (1994). *Reinventing education: Entrepreneurship in America's public schools.* New York: Dutton.

Gilligan, C. (1993). *In a different voice: Psychological theory and women's development.* Cambridge, MA: Harvard University Press.

Gipp, G. (1979, August-September). Help for Dana Fast Horse and friends. *American Education,* 15.

*Giroux, H. A. (1999, Winter). Schools for sale: Public education, corporate culture, and the citizen-consumer. *The Educational Forum,* 63(2), 140–49.

*Glasser, W. R. (1997, April). A new look at school failure and school success. *Phi Delta Kappan,* 596–602.

*Glasser, W. R. (1998a). *Quality school,* 3rd ed. New York: Harper Perennial.

*Glasser, W. R. (1998b). *The quality school teacher: Specific suggestions for teachers who are trying to implement the lead-management ideas of the quality school.* New York: Harper Perennial.

*Glasser, W. R. (1998c). *Choice theory: A new psychology of personal freedom.* New York: HarperCollins.

*Glasser, W. R., and Dotson, K. L. (1998). *Choice theory in the classroom.* New York: Harper Perennial.

*Glickman, C. D. (1993). *Renewing America's schools: A guide for school-based action.* San Francisco: Jossey-Bass.

*Glickman, C. D. (1998). *Revolutionizing America's schools.* San Francisco: Jossey-Bass.

*Glickman, C., Gordon, S. P., and Ross-Gordon, J. M. (1998). *Supervision of instruction: A developmental approach,* 4th ed. Boston: Allyn and Bacon.

Gmelch, W. H., and Parkay, F. W. (1995). Changing roles and occupational stress in the teaching profession. In M. J. O'Hair, and S. J. Odell (Eds.). *Educating teachers for leadership and change: Teacher education yearbook III.* Thousand Oaks, CA: Corwin Press, 46–65.

Godar, J. (1990). *Teachers talk.* Macomb, IL: Glenbridge Publishing.

*Goldberg, D. (1998). Does technology make the grade? *Family Circle PC World.*

Goldhammer, R., Anderson, R. H., and Krajewski, R. J. (1993). *Clinical supervision: Special methods for the supervision of teachers,* 3rd ed. Fort Worth, TX: Harcourt Brace Jovanovich.

Goleman, D. (1997). *Emotional intelligence.* New York: Bantam Books.

*Goleman, D. (1998). *Working with emotional intelligence.* New York: Bantam Books.

*Good, T. E., and Brophy, J. E. (1997). *Looking in classrooms,* 7th ed. New York: Longman.

*Good, T. E., and Brophy, J. E. (2000). *Looking in classrooms,* 8th ed. Boston: Pearson Publishing.

*Good, T. E., and Grouws, D. (1979). The Missouri mathematics effectiveness project: An experimental study in fourth-grade classrooms. *Journal of Educational Psychology,* 71, 355–62.

Goodlad, J. I. (1983a, April). What some schools and classrooms teach. *Educational Leadership,* 8–19.

Goodlad, J. (1983b, Spring). Teaching: An endangered profession. *Teachers College Record,* 575–78.

Goodlad, J. (1990). *Teachers for our nation's schools.* San Francisco: Jossey-Bass.

Goodlad, J. (1994). *Educational renewal: Better teachers, better schools*. San Francisco: Jossey-Bass.

Gordon, W. J. J. (1968). *Making it strange, Books 1 and 2*. Evanston, IL: Harper and Row.

Gordon, W. J. J. (1971a). *Invent-o-rama*. Cambridge, MA: Porpoise Books.

Gordon, W. J. J. (1971b). *What color is sleep?* Cambridge, MA: Porpoise Books.

Gordon, W. J. J. (1975). *Strange and familiar, Book 1*. Cambrdige, MA: Porpoise Books.

Goss v. Lopez, 419 U.S. 565 (1975).

*Grant, C. A. (1978). Education that is multicultural: Isn't that what we mean? *Journal of Teacher Education, 29*(5), 45–58.

Grant, C. A. (1994, Winter). Challenging the myths about multicultural education. *Multicultural Education*, 4–9.

*Grant, G., and Murray, C. E. (1999). *Teaching in America: The slow revolution*. Cambridge, MA: Harvard University Press.

Grant, P. G., Richard, K. J., and Parkay, F. W. (1996, April). *Using video cases to promote reflection among preservice teachers: A qualitative inquiry*. Paper presented at the Annual Meeting of the American Educational Research Association, New York.

*Greene, B. (1999, July 7). A 21st century idea for schools: Log off and learn. *Chicago Tribune*, Sec. 2, p. 1.

Greene, M. (1995). What counts as philosophy of education? In Wendy Kohli (Ed.). *Critical conversations in philosophy of education*. New York: Routledge.

Griego-Jones, T. (1996). Reconstructing bilingual education from a multicultural perspective. In C. A. Grant, and M. L. Gomez (Eds.), *Making schooling multicultural: Campus and classroom*. Englewood Cliffs, NJ: Merrill.

*Griffin, G. A. (1999). Changes in teacher education: Looking to the future. In G. A. Griffin (Ed.). *The education of teachers: Ninety–eighth yearbook of the National Society for the Study of Education* (pp. 1–28). Chicago: University of Chicago Press.

*Grossman, D., and Siddle, P. (1999). Combat. In L. Kurtz (ed.). *The encyclopedia of violence, peace, and conflict*. San Diego: Academic Press.

*Guskey, D. (1996, March). "Uniform" improvement? *Education Digest*.

*Gutloff, K. (1999, October). Anger in the halls. *NEA Today*, 8–9.

Haberman, M. (1995, June). Selecting "star" teachers for children and youth in urban poverty. *Phi Delta Kappan*, 777–81.

*Haberman, M. (1996). Selecting and preparing urban teachers. In J. Sikula (Ed.). *The second handbook of research on teacher education* (pp. 747–60). New York: Macmillan.

*Hadderman, M. (1998). Charter schools. *ERIC Digest*, 118.

*Hale-Benson, J. E. (1986). *Black children: Their roots, culture, and learning styles*. Baltimore, MD: Johns Hopkins University Press.

*Hallahan, D. P., and Kauffman, J. M. (2000). *Exceptional children: Introduction to special education*, 8th ed. Boston: Allyn and Bacon.

*Hamburg, D. A. (1997). Toward a strategy for healthy adolescent development. *American Journal of Psychiatry, 154*(6), 6–12.

*Hammett, R. F. (1997). Computers in schools: White boys only? *English Quarterly 28*,1.

*Hankins, K. H. (1998). Cacophony to Symphony: Memoirs in Teacher Research. *Harvard Educational Review, 68*(1), 80–95.

Hansen, D. T. (1995). *The call to teach*. New York: Teachers College Press.

*Hardman, M. L., Drew, C. J., and Egan, M. W. (1999). *Human exceptionality: Society, School, and family*, 6th ed. Boston: Allyn and Bacon.

*Harrington-Lueker (ed.). (1999). *Barriers and breakthroughs: Technology in urban schools*. Washington, DC: Education Writers Association.

Hazelwood School District v. Kuhlmeier, 56 U.S.L.W. 4079, 4082 (1988); 484 U.S. 260, 108 S. Ct. 562 (1988).

Health. (June 1999). New York: Family Media, Inc.

*Healy, J. M. (1998). *Failure to connect: How computers affect our children's minds—for better and worse*. New York: Simon and Schuster.

*Heath, S. B. (1983). *Ways with words*. Cambridge: Cambridge University Press.

Hedges, L. V. (1996). Quoted in Hedges finds boys and girls both disadvantag-ed in school. *Education News*. The Department of Education, University of Chicago.

Heinich, R., Molenda, M., and Russell, J. D. (1993). *Instructional media and the new technologies of instruction*, 4th ed. New York: Macmillan.

*Hendrie, C. (1999, May 5). Battle over principals in Chicago: Admistration vs. local councils. *Education Week on the Web*.

*Henriques, M. E. (1997, May). Increasing literacy among kindergartners through cross-age training. *Young Children*, 42–47.

Henry, E., Huntley, J., McKamey, C., and Harper, L. (1995). *To be a teacher: Voices from the classroom*. Thousand Oaks, CA: Corwin Press.

Henry, M. (1993). *School cultures: Universes of meaning in private schools*. Norwood, NJ: Ablex.

Henry, M. E. (1996). *Parent–school collaboration: Feminist organizational structures and school leadership*. Albany, NY: State University of New York Press.

Herbert, B. (1993, June 27). Listen to the children. *New York Times*, OP–ED.

*Herndon, J. (1969). *The way it spozed to be*. New York: Bantam Books.

Hess, G. A., Jr. (1995). *Restructuring urban schools: A Chicago perspective*. New York: Teachers College Press.

Hirshfelder, A. B. (1986). *Happily may I walk: American Indians and Alaska Natives today*. New York: Charles Scribner.

*Hoff, D. (1999, January 13). With 2000 looming, chances of meeting national goals iffy. *Education Week on the web*.

*Hole, S. (1998). Teacher as rain dancer. *Harvard Educational Review, 68*(3), 413–21.

Holland, A., and Andre, T. (1987, Winter). Participation in extracurricular activities in secondary schools. *Review of Educational Research*, 437–466.

Holly, M. L., and McLoughlin, C. (eds.). (1989). *Perspectives on teacher professional development*. New York: Falmer Press.

The Holmes Group. (n.d.). *Tomorrow's schools: Principles for the design of professional development schools*. East Lansing, MI: Holmes Group.

Holmes, M., and Weiss, B. J. (1995). *Lives of women public schoolteachers: Scenes from American educational history*. New York: Garland.

*Holmes Partnership. (1999). *Origins of the Holmes Partnership (1987–1997)*. Auburn, AL: Holmes Partnership.

*Holt, J. (1964). *How children fail*. New York: Delta.

Holt v. Shelton, 341 F. Supp. 821 (M.D. Tenn. 1972).

*Holt–Reynolds, D. (1999). Good readers, good teachers? Subject matter expertise as a challenge in learning to teach. *Harvard Educational Review, 69*(1), 29–50.

*Hopkins, B. J., and Wendel, F. C. (1997). *Creating school-community-business partnerships*. Bloomington, IN: Phi Delta Kappa Educational Foundation.

Hortonville Joint School District No. 1 v. Hortonville Education Association, 426 U.S. 482, 96 S. Ct. 2308 (1976).

Howsam, R. B., Corrigan, D. C., Denemark, G. W., and Nash, R. J. (1976). *Educating a profession*. Washington, DC: American Association of Colleges for Teacher Education.

*Hoynes, W. (1998, Summer). News for a teen market: The lessons of Channel One. *Journal of Curriculum and Supervision*, 339–56.

*Hoyt, W. H. (1999). An evaluation of the Kentucky Education Reform Act. In *Kentucky Annual Economic Report 1999*. Lexington, KY: University of Kentucky, Center for Business and Economic Research, 21–36.

Huling-Austin, L. (1990). Teacher induction programs and internships, In W. R. Houston (ed.), *Handbook of research on teaching*. New York: Macmillan.

Hun-Choe. (1996, November 15). Bringing the cane down on school bullies. *Bangkok Post*, 8.

*Hunter, M. (1994). *Enhancing teaching*. New York: Macmillan.

*Hurwitz, S. (1999, April). New York: Can Rudy Crew hang tough on vouchers and pull off a turnaround in the nation's biggest school system? *The American School Board Journal*, 36–40.

Hutchins, R. M. (1963). *A conversation on education*. Santa Barbara, CA: Fund for the Republic.

Hyman v. Green, 403 N.W. 2d 597 (Mich. App. 1987).

*Idol, L. (1998). Optional extended year program, Feedback, Publ. No. 97.20. Austin Independent School District, TX, Office of Program Evaluation.

Igoa, C. (1995). *The inner world of the immigrant child*. New York: Lawrence Erlbaum Associates, Publishers.

Imber, M., and van Geel, T. (1993). *Education law*. New York: McGraw–Hill, Inc.

Immediato v. Rye Neck School Dist., 73 F.3d 454 (2d Cir. 1996).

*Indiana University. (1999, February). *IU school of education programs offer life-changing experiences*. Bloomington, IN: Indiana University, Office of Communication and Marketing.

*Inger, M. (1991). Improving urban education with magnet schools. *ERIC/CUE Digest*, 76.

Ingraham v. Wright, 430 U.S. 651 (1977).

Inoue, A. (1996, October 10). *Creating schools with special characteristics*. Paper presented at the eighth Washington State University

College of Education/Nishinomiya Education Board Education Seminar. Washington State University, Pullman.

*International Association for the Evaluation of Educational Achievement. (1997a). *Mathematics achievement in the primary school years: IEA's third international mathematics and science study*. Amsterdam, Netherlands: International Association for the Evaluation of Educational Achievement.

*International Association for the Evaluation of Educational Achievement. (1997b). *Science achievement in the primary school years: IEA's third international mathematics and science study*. Amsterdam, Netherlands: Author International Association for the Evaluation of Educational Achievement.

*International Reading Association. (1999, April). *Using multiple methods of beginning reading instruction*. Newark, DE: International Reading Association.

Jackson, P. (1990). *Life in classrooms*. New York: Teachers College Press.

*Jacobson, L. (1996, November 22). Gay student to get nearly $1 million in settlement. *Education Week on the Web*.

Jeglin v. San Jacinto Unified School District, 827 F. Supp. 1459 (Cal. 1993).

*Jencks, C., and Phillips, M. (eds.). (1998). *The black–white test score gap*. Washington, DC: Brookings Institution Press.

*Jencks, C., et al. (1972). *Inequality: A reassessment of the effect of family and schooling in America*. New York: Basic Books.

*Jenkinson, E. B. (1995). Myths and misunderstandings surround the schoolbook protest movement. *Contemporary Education, 66*(2), 70–73.

*Jensen, E. (1998). *Teaching with the brain in mind*. Alexandria, VA: Association for Supervision and Curriculum Development.

Jersild, A. (1955). *When teachers face themselves*. New York: Teachers College Press.

*Johnson, D. W., and Johnson, R. T. (1999). *Learning together and alone: Cooperative, competitive, and individualistic learning*, 5th ed. Boston: Allyn and Bacon.

Johnson, J., and Immerwahr, J. (1994). *First things first: What Americans expect from the public schools, a report from Public Agenda*. New York: Public Agenda.

Johnson, J., and Yates, J. (1982). *A national survey of student teaching programs*. DeKalb, IL: Northern Illinois University, Teaching Programs. Eric Document Reproduction Services No. ED 232–963.

Johnson, M. (1926). The educational principles of the School of Organic Education, Fairhope, Alabama. In G. M. Whipple, (Ed.). *The twenty–sixth yearbook of the National Society for the Study of Education*. Bloomington, IL: Public School Publishing Company.

*Johnson, M. J., and Brown, L. (1998). Collegial support teams. In D. J. McIntyre, and D. M. Byrd (Eds.) *Strategies for career-long teacher education: Teacher education yearbook VI*. Thousand Oaks, CA: Corwin Press.

*Jonassen, D. H., Peck, K. L., and Wilson, B. G. (1999). *Learning with technology: A constructivist perspective*. Upper Saddle River, NJ: Merrill.

*Jones, J. (1994). Integrated learning systems for diverse learners. *Media and Methods 31*(3).

*Jones, J. M. (1981). The concept of racism and its changing reality. In B. D. Bowser and R. G. Hunt (eds.). *Impacts of racism on white Americans*. Beverly Hills, CA: Sage.

*Jordan, K. M., Vaughan, J.S., and Woodworth, K. J. (1997). I will survive: Lesbian, gay, and bisexual youths' experience of high school. *Journal of Gay and Lesbian Social Services, 7*, 17–33.

*Jordan, W. J., and Nettles, S. M. (1999). *How students invest their time out of school: Effects on school engagement, perceptions of life chances, and achievement*. Baltimore, MD: Center for Research on the Education of Students Placed at Risk.

*Joyce, B., Weil, M., and Calhoun, E. (2000). *Models of teaching*, 6th ed. Boston: Allyn and Bacon.

*Karp, J. M., and Keller, C. E. (1998). Preparation and employment experiences of educators with disabilities. In R. J. Anderson, C. E. Keller, and J. M. Karp, (Eds.). *Enhancing diversity: Educators with disabilities*. Washington, DC: Gallaudet University Press.

Karr v. Schmidt, 401 U.S. 1201, 91 S. Ct. 592, 27 L. Ed.2d 797 (1972).

*Katzenmeyer, G. M., and Moller, G. (1996). *Awakening the sleeping giant: Leadership development for teachers*. Thousand Oaks, CA: Corwin Press.

*Kavarsky, M. (1994). Salome Urena Middle Academies. *Journal of Emotional and Behavioral Problems, 3*(3), 37–40.

*Keller, C. E., Anderson, R. J., and Karp, J. M. (1998). Introduction in R. J. Anderson, C. E. Keller, J. M. and Karp, (Eds.). *Enhancing diversity: Educators with disabilities*. Washington, DC: Gallaudet University Press.

*Keresty, B., O'Leary, S., and Wortley, D. (1998). *You can make a difference: A teacher's guide to political action*. Portsmouth, NH: Heinemann.

*Kerr, S. T. (1999). Visions of sugarplums: The future of technology, education, and the schools. In *Issues in curriculum: A selection of chapters from past NSSE yearbooks: Ninety–eighth yearbook of the National Society for the Study of Education, Part II*. Chicago: University of Chicago Press.

King, S. H. (1993, Summer). The limited presence of African-American teachers. *Review of Educational Research*.

*Kirkpatrick, H., and Cuban, L. (1998). Computers make kids smarter—right? *TECHNOS Quarterly 7*(2), 26–31.

*Kleinfeld, J. (1998). *The myth that schools shortchange girls: Social science in the service of deception*. Washington, DC: Women's Freedom Network.

Knezevich, S. J. (1984). *Administration of public education: A source book for the leadership and management of educational institutions, 4th ed*. New York: Harper and Row.

*Knupfer, N. N. (1998). Gender divisions across technology advertisements and the WWW: Implications for educational equity. *Theory into Practice 37*, 1, 54–63.

*Kohl, H. R. (1967). *36 children*. New York: Signet.

Kohlberg, L. (2000). The cognitive-developmental approach to moral education. In F. W. Parkay, and G. Hass, (Eds.). *Curriculum planning: A contemporary approach*, 7th ed. Boston: Allyn and Bacon, 136–48.

*Kohn, A. (1997, February). How not to teach values: A critical look at character education. *Phi Delta Kappan*, 428–39.

Koller, E. (1996). Overcoming paradigm paralysis: A high school teacher revisits foreign language education. In G. Burnaford, J. Fischer, and D. Hobson, (Eds.). *Teachers doing research: Practical possibilities*. Mahwah, NJ: Lawrence Erlbaum Associates.

*Kotlowitz, A. (1991). *There are no children here: The story of two boys growing up in the other America*. New York: Doubleday.

Kounin, J. (1970). *Discipline and group management in classrooms*. New York: Holt, Rinehart and Winston.

*Kozma, R., et al. (1992). Technology and the fate of at-risk students. *Education and Urban Society 24*(4), 440–53..

*Kozol, J. (1967). *Death at an early age*. Boston: Houghton Mifflin.

Kozol, J. (1991). *Savage inequalities: Children in America's schools*. New York: Crown Publishers.

Krizek v. Cicero–Stickney Township High School District No. 201, 713 F. Supp. 1131 (1989).

*Krogh, S. L. (2000). Weaving the web. In F. W. Parkay, and G. Hass, (Eds.). *Curriculum planning: A contemporary approach*, 7th ed. Boston: Allyn and Bacon, 338–41.

*Ladson-Billings, G. (1994). *The dreamkeepers: Successful teachers of African American children*. San Francisco: Jossey-Bass.

*Lambert, L., et al. (1996). *Who will save our schools?: Teachers as constructivist leaders*. Thousand Oaks, CA: Corwin Press.

*LaMorte, M. W. (1999). *School law: Cases and Concepts*, 6th ed. Boston: Allyn and Bacon.

Larry, P. v. Riles, 793 F.2d 969 (9th Cir. 1984).

Lau v. Nichols, 414 U.S. 563 (1974).

Lee, V. E., Chen, X., and Smerdon, B. A. (1996). *The influence of school climate on gender differences in the achievement and engagement of young adolescents*. American Association of University Women.

Lemon v. Kurtzman, 403 U.S. 602, 91 S. Ct. 2105, 291 L. Ed.2d 745 (1971).

Levey, S. (1996). *Starting from scratch: One classroom builds its own curriculum*. Portsmouth, NH: Heinemann.

Levine, D. U., and Levine, R. F. (1996). *Society and education*, 9th ed. Boston: Allyn and Bacon.

Levy, F. (1996, October). What General Motors can teach U.S. schools about the proper role of markets in education reform. *Phi Delta Kappan*, 108–14.

*Lewis, A. (1992). Helping young urban parents educate themselves and their children. *ERIC/CUE Digest, 85*.

*Lewis, J. F. (1995, September). Saying no to vouchers: What is the price of democracy? *NASSP Bulletin*, 45–51.

*Lewis, R. B., and Doorlag, D. H. (1999). *Teaching special students in general education classrooms*, 5th ed. Upper Saddle River, NJ: Merrill.

*Lickona, T. (1993). The return of character education. *Educational Leadership, 51*(3), 6–11.

Lickona, T. (1998, February). A more complex analysis is needed. *Phi Delta Kappan*, 449–54.

Lieberman, A. (1990). Foreword. In S. Mei–ling Yee, (Eds.).*Careers in the classroom: When teaching is more than a job. New York: Teachers College Press.

*Lieberman, M. (1997). The teachers unions: How the NEA and AFT sabotage reform and hold students, parents, teachers, and taxpayers hostage to bureaucracy. New York: Free Press.

*Lightfoot, S. L. (1982). The good high school: Portraits of character and culture. New York: Basic Books.

Lindsay, D. (1996, March 13). N.Y. bills give teachers power to oust pupils. Education Week.

Livingston, C. (ed.). (1992). Teachers as leaders: Evolving roles. Washington, DC: National Education Association.

*Locilento v. John A. Coleman Catholic High School, 523 N.Y.S. 2d 198 (A.D. 3d Dept. 1987).

Louis Harris and Associates. (1990). The Metropolitan Life survey of the American teacher 1990: New teachers: Expectations and ideals. New York: Louis Harris and Associates.

Louis Harris and Associates. (1991). The Metropolitan Life survey of the American teacher, 1991: Coming to terms—teachers' views on current issues in education. New York: Louis Harris and Associates.

Louis Harris and Associates. (1995). The Metropolitan Life survey of the American teacher, 1984–1995: Old problems, new challenges. New York: Louis Harris and Associates.

*Louis Harris and Associates. (1997). The Metropolitan Life survey of the American teacher, 1997: Examining gender issues in public schools. New York: Louis Harris and Associates.

*Macías, R. F., et al. (1998). Summary report of the survey of the states limited English proficient students and available educational programs and services, 1996–97. Washington, DC: National Clearinghouse for Bilingual Education.

*MacLeod, J. (1995). Ain't no makin' it: Aspirations and attainment in a low–income neighborhood. Boulder, CO: Westview Press.

MacNaughton, R. H., and Johns, F. A. (1991, September). Developing a successful schoolwide discipline program. NASSP Bulletin, 47–57.

*Madaus, G. F. (1999). The influence of testing on the curriculum. In M. J. Early and K. J. Rehage (eds.). Issues in curriculum: A selection of chapters from past NSSE yearbooks: Ninety-eighth yearbook of the National Society for the Study of Education, Part II (pp. 73–111). Chicago: University of Chicago Press.

*Mahoney, J., and Cairns, R. B. (1997). Do extracurricular activities protect against early school dropout? Developmental Psychology, 33(2), 241–53.

Mailloux v. Kiley, 323 F., 448 F.2d 1242 Supp. 1387, 1393 (1st Cir. 1971).

Mann, H. (1868). Annual reports on education. In Mary Mann (Ed.). The life and works of Horace Mann, vol. 3. Boston: Horace B. Fuller.

Mann, H. (1957). Twelfth annual report. In Lawrence A. Cremin (Ed.). The republic and the school: Horace Mann on the education of free men. New York: Teachers College Press.

*Mann, L. (1998, Summer). Getting global with technology. Curriculum Update.

Manning, M. L., and Baruth, L. G. (1996). Multicultural education of children and adolescents. Boston: Allyn and Bacon.

*Manzo, K. K. (1999, June 2). States setting strategies to reduce mistakes in textbooks. Education Week on the Web..

Marcus v. Rowley 695 F.2d 1171 (9th Cir. 1983).

*Marks, H. M., Newmann, F. M., and Gamoran, A. (1996). Does authentic pedagogy increase student achievement? In F. M. Newmann, et al. (Eds). Authentic achievement: Restructuring schools for intellectual quality. San Francisco: Jossey-Bass Publishers, 49–76.

Marshall, K. (1996, January). How I confronted HSPS (hyperactive superficial principal syndrome) and began to deal with the heart of the matter. Phi Delta Kappan, 336–45.

Maslow, A. (1954). Motivation and personality. New York: Basic Books.

Maslow, A. (1962). Toward a psychology of being. New York: Basic Books.

*McCarthy, M. M., Cambron-McCabe, N. H., and Thomas, S. B. (1998). Public school law: Teachers' and students' rights, 4th ed. Boston: Allyn and Bacon.

*McGhan, B. (1997, Winter). Compulsory school attendance: An idea past its prime? The Educational Forum, 134–39.

Mehlinger, H. D. (1996, February). School reform in the Information Age. Phi Delta Kappan, 400–07.

*Mental Health in Schools Center. (1998). Restructuring boards of education to enhance effectiveness in addressing barriers to student learning: A Center report. University of California–Los Angeles: Mental Health in Schools Center. Eric Document No. ED 423–479.

*Miami Herald. (1999, April 26). It's clear sailing for school vouchers: Legislators agree on tuition plan.

*Milken Exchange on Education Technology. (1999). Will new teachers be prepared to teach in a digital age? A national survey on information technology in teacher education. Santa Monica, CA: Milken Exchange on Education Technology.

*Mills, G. E. (2000). Action research: A guide for the teacher researcher. Upper Saddle River, NJ: Merrill.

*Missouri v. Jenkins, 515 U.S. 70 (1995).

*Modi, M., Konstantopoulos, S., and Hedges, L. V. (1998). Predictors of academic giftedness among U.S. high school students: Evidence from a nationally representative multivariate analysis. Paper presented at the Annual Meeting of the American Educational Research Association, San Diego. Eric Document No. ED422-356.

*Molino, F. (1999). My students, my children. In M. K. Rand, and S. Shelton-Colangelo, (Eds.). Voices of student teachers: Cases from the field. (pp. 55–56). Upper Saddle River: Merrill.

Montagu, A. (1974). Man's most dangerous myth: The fallacy of race, 5th ed. New York: Oxford University Press.

Moore, D. R. (1992). Voice and choice in Chicago. In W. H. Clune, and J. F. Witte (eds.). Choice and control in American education: Volume II. The practice of choice, decentralization and school restructuring. Philadelphia: Falmer Press.

*Moore, J. P., and Terrett, C. P. (1999). Highlights of the 1997 national youth gang survey. Fact sheet. Washington, DC: U.S. Department of Justice, Office of Justice Programs, Office of Juvenile Justice and Delinquency Prevention.

Moran v. School District No. 7, 350 F. Supp. 1180 (DC Mont. 1972).

*Moreno, N. P. (1999, July). K–12 science education reform—A primer for scientists. Bioscience, 49(7), 569–577.

Morris, J. E., and Curtis, K. E. (1983, March/April). Legal issues relating to field-based experiences in teacher education. Journal of Teacher Education, 2–6.

Morris, V. C., and Pai, Y. (1994). Philosophy and the American school: An introduction to the philosophy of education. Lanham, MD: University Press of America.

Morrison v. State Board of Education, 82 Cal. Rptr. 175, 461 P.2d 375 (Cal. 1969).

Morton, C. (1996, February). The modern land of Laputa: Where computers are used in education. Phi Delta Kappan, 416–19.

Moyers, B. D. (1989). A world of ideas: Conversations with thoughtful men and women. New York: Doubleday.

Mozert v. Hawkins County Board of Education, 827 F.2d 1058 (6th Cir. 1987), cert. denied, 484 U.S. 1066 (1988).

*Murphy, J. (1999, April). Reconnecting teaching and school administration: A call for a unified profession. Paper presented at the Annual Meeting of the American Educational Research Association, Montreal.

*Murray v. Pittsburgh Board of Public Education, 919 F. Supp. 838 (Pa. 1996).

*Nash, R. J. (1997). Answering the "virtuecrats": A moral conversation on character education. New York: Teachers College Press.

*Nathan, J. (1998, March). Heat and light in the charter school movement. Phi Delta Kappan, 79(7), 499–505.

National Assessment of Educational Progress (NAEP). (1996). Measuring essential learning in science. Washington, DC: National Assessment Governing Board, U.S. Department of Education.

*National Assessment of Educational Progress (NAEP). (1999). The nation's report card. Washington, DC: Office of Educational Research and Improvement.

*National Association for Sport and Physical Education. (1999). National standards for physical education. Reston, VA: National Association for Sport and Physical Education.

*National Association for Year–Round Education. (1999). History of year–round education. San Diego, CA: National Association for Year–Round Education. http://www.nayre.org.

National Board for Professional Teaching Standards. (1992, June 22). Press release. Detroit: National Board for Professional Teaching Standards.

*National Board for Professional Teaching Standards. (1994). Toward high and rigorous standards for the teaching profession. National Board for Professional Teaching Standards.

National Board for Professional Teaching Standards. (1995). An invitation to national board certification. Detroit: National Board for Professional Teaching Standards.

National Center for Education Statistics. (1980). High school and beyond study. Washington, DC: National Center for Education Statistics.

National Center for Education Statistics (1995). Public school teacher cost differences across the United States. Washington, DC: National Center for Education Statistics.

*National Center for Education Statistics (1998a). *The condition of education 1998*. Washington, DC: National Center for Education Statistics.

*National Center for Education Statistics (1998b). *Private school universe survey, 1995–96*. Washington, DC: National Center for Education Statistics.

*National Center for Education Statistics. (1999). *Digest of education statistics 1998*. Washington, DC: U.S. Department of Education, Office of Educational Research and Improvement.

*National Clearinghouse on Child Abuse and Neglect. (1998). *Child maltreatment 1996: Reports from the states to the National Child Abuse and Neglect data system*. Washington, DC: U.S. Government Printing Office.

*National Commission on Civic Renewal. (1998). *A Nation of Spectators*. College Park, MD: National Commission on Civic Renewal.

*National Commission on Excellence and Education. (1983). *A nation at risk: The imperative for educational reform*. Washington, DC: U. S. Government Printing Office.

National Commission on Teaching and America's Future. (1996). *What matters most: Teaching for America's future*. New York: National Commission on Teaching and America's Future.

*National Council for Accreditation of Teacher Education (NCATE). (1997a). *Standards for accreditation of teacher education*. Washington, DC: National Council for Accreditation of Teacher Education (NCATE).

*National Council for Accreditation of Teacher Education (NCATE). (1997b). *Standards, procedures, and policies for the accreditation of professional education units*. Washington, DC: National Council for Accreditation of Teacher Education (NCATE).

*National Council for Accreditation of Teacher Education (NCATE). (1999). *NCATE: Did you know?* Washington, DC: National Council for Accreditation of Teacher Education (NCATE).

National Council for the Social Studies. (1994). *Expect excellence: Curriculum standards for the social studies*. Washington, DC: National Council for the Social Studies.

*National Council of Teachers of Mathematics. (1998). *Principles and standards for school mathematics: Discussion draft*. Reston, VA: National Council of Teachers of Mathematics.

*National Education Association. (1997). *NEA Research: Status of the American public school teacher, 1995–96: Highlights*. Washington, DC: National Education Association.

*National Education Goals Panel. (1998). *The national education goals report: Building a nation of learners, 1998*. Washington, DC: U.S. Government Printing Office.

*National Education Goals Panel. (1999). National Education Goals Panel recommends that goals be renamed "America's Education Goals" and continue beyond the year 2000. Press Release, National Education Goals Panel.

*National Governors' Association. (1998, November 4). Press release.

*National Institute for Mental Health. (1999). *Suicide fact sheet*. Washington, DC: National Institute for Mental Health.

*National Joint Committee on Learning Disabilities. (1997). *Operationalizing the NJCLD definition of learning disabilities for ongoing assessment in schools*. Rockville, MD: National Joint Committee on Learning Disabilities.

*National Trade and Professional Associations of the United States, 34th ed. (1999). B. Downs, S. E. White, and A. G. Wood, (Eds.). New York: Columbia Books, Inc.

*Neill, A. S. (1960). *Summerhill: A radical approach to child rearing*. New York: Hart.

*Nelson, J. L., Carlson, K., and Palonsky, S. B. (2000). *Critical issues in education: A dialectic approach*, 4th ed. New York: McGraw-Hill.

New Jersey v. Massa, 231 A.2d 252, N.J. Sup. Ct. (1967).

New Jersey v. T.L.O., 221 Cal. Rptr. 118, 105 S. Ct. 733 (1985).

*Newmann, F. M., et al.(eds). (1996). *Authentic achievement: Restructuring schools for intellectual quality*. San Francisco: Jossey-Bass.

Newmann, F. M., and Wehlage, G. G. (1995). *Successful school restructuring: A report to the public and educators by the Center on Organization and Restructuring of Schools*. Madison, WI: University of Wisconsin, Center on Organization and Restructuring of Schools.

Nieto, S. (1992). *Affirming diversity: The sociopolitical context of multicultural education*. White Plains, NY: Longman.

*Noble, D. (1996, November). Mad rushes into the future: The overselling of educational technology. *Educational Leadership*, 18–23.

Noddings, N. (1992). *The challenge to care in schools: An alternative approach to education*. New York: Teacher's College Press.

Noddings, N. (1995, May). Teaching themes of care. *Phi Delta Kappan*, 76(9), 675–79

*Noll, J. W. (ed.). (1999). *Taking sides: Clashing views on controversial educational issues*, 10th ed. Guilford, CT: McGraw-Hill.

*Norris, C. (1994). Computing and the classroom: Teaching the at–risk student. *Computing Teacher* 21(5), 12, 14.

North Central Regional Educational Laboratory. (1993). *Policy briefs, report 1, 1993*. Elmhurst, IL: Author.

*Northwest Regional Educational Laboratory. (1999). *Arts education: Basic to learning*. Portland: Northwest Regional Educational Laboratory.

Null v. Board of Education, 815 F. Supp. 937 (W. Va. 1993).

Oberti v. Board of Education of the Borough of Clementon School District, 789 E. Supp. 1322 (D. N.J. 1992)

*Odden, A., and Busch, C. (1998). *Financing schools for high performance: Strategies for improving the use of educational resources*. San Francisco: Jossey–Bass.

O'Hair, M. J., and Odell, S. J. (eds.). (1995). *Educating Teachers for Leadership and Change: Teacher education yearbook III*. Thousand Oaks, CA: Corwin Press, Inc.

Ohman v. Board of Education, 301 N.Y. 662, 93 N.E. 2d 927 (1950).

*Okrent, D. (1999, May 10). Raising kids online: What can parents do? *Time*, 38–43.

*Olsen, L. (1997). *Made in America: Immigrant students in our public schools*. New York: New Press.

*Oppenheimer, T. (1997, July). The computer delusion. *The Atlantic Monthly*, 45–62.

O'Reilly, R. C., and Green, E. T. (1983). *School law for the practitioner*. Westport, CN: Greenwood Press.

*Orfield, G. and Yun, J. T. (1999). *Resegregation in American schools*. Cambridge, MA: Harvard University, the Civil Rights Project.

*Ortiz, M. G. (1999, April 19,). Urban schools lag in technology. *Detroit Free Press*.

*Ozmon, H. W., and Craver, S. M. (1999). *Philosophical foundations of education*, 6th ed. Upper Saddle River, NJ: Merrill.

Pajak, E. (1993). *Approaches to clinical supervision: Alternatives for improving instruction*. Norwood, MA: Christopher-Gordon.

*Paliokas, K. L., and Rist, R. C. (1996, April 3). School Uniforms: Do they reduce violence —or just make us feel better? *Education Week*, 61(7), 46–49.

Pang, V. O. (1994, December). Why do we need this class: Multicultural education for teachers. *Phi Delta Kappan*.

Parkay, F. W. (Summer 1988). Reflections of a protégé. *Theory into Practice*, 195–200.

*Parkay, F. W., and Hass, G. (2000). *Curriculum planning: A contemporary approach*, 7th ed. Boston: Allyn and Bacon.

*Parkay, F. W., and Oaks, M. M. (1998, April 15). *Promoting the professional development of teachers: What the U.S. can learn from other countries*. Paper presented at the Annual Meeting of the American Educational Research Association, San Diego.

Parkay, F. W., Shindler, J., and Oaks, M. M. (1997, January). Creating a climate for collaborative, emergent leadership at an urban high school: Exploring the stressors, role changes, and paradoxes of restructuring. *International Journal of Educational Reform*, 64–74.

*Parkay, F. W., Potisook, P., Chantharasakul, A., and Chunsakorn, P. (1999). *New roles and responsibilities in educational reform: A study of Thai and U.S. principals' attitudes toward teacher leadership*. Kasetsart University, Bangkok: Center for Research on Teaching and Teacher Education.

*Parker, L., and Shapiro, J. P. (1993). The context of educational administration and social class. In C. A. Capper (Ed.). *Educational administration in a pluralistic society* (pp.36–65). Albany, NY: State University of New York Press.

PASE (Parents in Action on Special Education) v. Hannon, No. 74C3586, U.S. District Court for the Northern District of Illinois, Eastern Division, 506 F. Supp. 831; 1980 U.S. Dist.

Patchogue–Medford Congress of Teachers v. Board of Education of Patchogue–Medford Union Free School District, 70 N.Y. 2d 57, 510 N.E. 2d 325 (1987).

PC World. (1999a, September). "Free" computer labs saddle kids with on–screen commercials.

PC World. (1999b, September). Schools may lose cheap Internet access.

*Pellicer, L.O., and Anderson, L. W. (1995). *A handbook for teacher leaders*. Thousand Oaks, CA: Corwin Press.

Peter Doe v. San Francisco Unified School District, 131 Cal. Rptr. 854 (1976).

*Piirto, J. (1999). *Talented children and adults: Their development and education*. Upper Saddle River, NJ: Merrill.

*Pipho, C. (1999, February). The profit side of education. *Phi Delta Kappan*, 80(6), 421–22.

*Pitton, D. E. (1998). *Stories of student teaching: A case approach to the student teaching experience*. Upper Saddle River, NJ: Merrill.

Ponticell, J. A., Olson, G. E., and Charlier, P. S. (1995). Project MASTER: Peer coaching and collaboration as catalysts for professional growth in urban high schools. In M. J. O'Hair, and S. J. Odell, (Eds.). *Educating teachers for leadership and change: Teacher education yearbook III.* Thousand Oaks, CA: Corwin Press, 96–116.

Poole, B. J. (1995). *Education for an information age: Teaching in the computerized classroom.* Madison, WI: Brown and Benchmark.

*Popham, W. J. (1999, May 12). Commentary: Assessment apathy. *Education Week on the Web.*

Portner, J. (1999, May 12). Schools ratchet up the rules on student clothing, threats. *Education Week on the Web.*

Posner, G. J. (1993). *Field experience: A guide to reflective teaching,* 3rd ed. New York: Longman.

*Postman, N. (1995, October 9). Virtual students, digital classroom. *The Nation.*

Powell, A. G. (1980). *The uncertain profession: Harvard and the search for educational authority.* Cambridge, MA: Harvard University Press.

Power, E. J. (1982). *Philosophy of education: Studies in philosophies, schooling, and educational policies.* Englewood Cliffs, NJ: Prentice Hall.

Public Agenda. (1994). *First things first: What Americans expect from the public schools.* New York: Public Agenda.

*Public Agenda. (1998). *A lot to be thankful for: What parents want children to learn about America.* New York: Public Agenda.

*Public Agenda. (1999). *Reality check: The status of standards reform..* New York: Public Agenda.

Rallis, S. F. (1990). Professional teachers and restructured schools: Leadership challenges. In B. Mitchell, and L. L. Cunningham, (Eds.). *Educational leadership and changing contexts of families, communities, and schools* (89th NSSE yearbook). Chicago: University of Chicago Press.

*Rand, M. K., and Shelton–Colangelo, S. (1999). *Voices of Student Teachers: Cases from the Field.* Upper Saddle River, NJ: Merrill.

Ravitch, D. (1983). *The troubled crusade: American education, 1945–1980.* New York: Basic Books.

*Ravitch, D. (1990). Multiculturalism: E pluribus plures. *American Scholar, 59*(3), 337–55.

*Ravitch, D. (1997, December). The fight for standards. *Forbes, 160*(13), 106.

*Ravitz, J. L., Wong, Y. T., and Becker, H. J. (1999). Report to participants. The University of California, Irvine, and The University of Minnesota: Center for Research on Information Technology and Organizations.

Ray v. School District of DeSoto County, 666 F. Supp. 1524 (M. D. Fla. 1987).

*RCM Research Corporation. (1998). *Time: Critical issues in educational change.* Portsmouth, NH: RCM Research Corporation.

*Renzulli, J. S. (1998). The three–ring conception of giftedness. In S. M. Baum, S. M. Reis, and L. R. Maxfield, (Eds.). *Nurturing the gifts and talents of primary grade students.* Mansfield Center, CT: Creative Learning Press.

Rice, R., and Walsh, C. E. (1996). Equity at risk: The problem with state and federal education reform efforts. In C. Walsh (Ed.). *Education reform and social change: Multicultural voices, struggles, and visions.* Mahwah, NJ: Lawrence Erlbaum Associates, Publishers.

Rickover, H. G. (1959). *Education and freedom.* New York: E. P. Dutton.

Rickover, H. G. (1983, February 3). Educating for excellence. *Houston Chronicle.*

*Ries, E. (1997). To "V" or not to "V": For many the word "vocational" doesn't work. *Techniques 72*(8), 32–36.

*Riley, R. W. (1998, August 19). Research shows teachers, schools work hard on parental involvement; parents want even more partnerships. Press release. Washington, DC.

*Rippa, S. A. (1997). *Education in a free society: An American history,* 8th ed. New York: Longman.

*Ripple, R. E., and Rockcastle, V. E. (Eds.). (1964). *Piaget rediscovered: A report of the conference on cognitive studies and curriculum development.* Ithaca, NY: Cornell University, School of Education.

Rithdee, K. (1996, November 3–9). Fighting drugs with faith. *The Bangkok Post Sunday Magazine.*

Roberts v. City of Boston, 59 Mass. (5 Cush.) 198 (1850).

Robinson, G. E., and Protheroe, N. (1994, September). Local school budget profiles study. *School Business Affairs,* 31–32, 34–40.

Rogers, C. (1961). *On becoming a person.* Boston: Houghton Mifflin.

Rogers, C. (1974). *Freedom to learn.* Columbus, OH: Merrill.

Rogers, C. (1982). *Freedom to learn in the eighties.* Columbus, OH: Merrill.

*Rogers, K. (1991). *The relationship of grouping practices to the education of the gifted and talented learner.* Storrs, CT: University of Connecticut, National Research Center on the Gifted and Talented.

Romans v. Crenshaw, 354 F. Supp. 868 (S.D. Tex. 1972).

*Romer, R. (2000). Today standards—tomorrow success. In F. W. Parkay, and G. Hass, (Eds.). *Curriculum planning: A contemporary approach,* 7th ed. Boston: Allyn and Bacon, 314–17.

*Rose, L. C., and Gallup, A. M. (1998, September). The 30th annual Phi Delta Kappa/Gallup poll of the public's attitudes toward the public schools. *Phi Delta Kappan,* 41–56.

*Rose, L. C., and Gallup, A. M. (1999). The 31st annual Phi Delta Kappa/Gallup poll of the public's attitudes toward the public schools. *Phi Delta Kappan, 81*(1), 41–56.

*Rose, L. C., Gallup, A. M., and Elam, S. M. (1997, September). The 29th annual Phi Delta Kappa/Gallup poll of the public's attitudes toward the public schools. *Phi Delta Kappan,* 41–56.

Rosenshine, B. (1988). Explicit teaching. In D. Berliner and B. Rosenshine (eds.), *Talks to teachers.* New York: Random House.

*Rosenshine, B. (1995). Advances in research on instruction. *The Journal of Educational Research, 88*(5), 262–268.

Rosenshine, B., and Stevens, R. (1986). Teaching functions. In Merlin C. Wittrock (Ed.). *Handbook of research on teaching,* 3rd ed. New York: Macmillan.

*Rosenshine, B., Meister, C., and Chapman, S. (1996). Teaching students to generate questions: A review of the intervention studies.

Review of Educational Research, 66(2), 181–221.

Ross, D. D., and Webb, R. B. (1995). Implementing shared decision making at Brooksville Elementary School. In A. Lieberman (Ed.). *The work of restructuring schools: Building from the ground up.* New York: Teachers College Press.

Rossell, C. H. (1990, Winter). The research on bilingual education. *Equity and Choice,* 29–36.

*Rotberg, I. C., Futrell, M. H., and Lieberman, J. M. (1998). National board certification: Increasing participation and assessing impacts. *Phi Delta Kappan, 79*(6), 462–466.

*Rothstein, R. (1998, May). Bilingual education: The controversy. *Phi Delta Kappan,* 672, 674–678.

*Ruenzel, D. (1999, April). Pride and prejudice. *Teacher Magazine on the Web.*

Sadker, M., and Sadker, D. (1994). *Failing at fairness: How our schools cheat girls.* New York: Touchstone.

Sallie Mae Corporation. (1995). *A report from the 1994 Sallie Mae symposium on quality education.* Washington, DC: Sallie Mae Corporation.

*Salovey, P., and Sluyter, D. J. (eds.). (1997). *Emotional development and emotional intelligence: Educational implications.* New York: Basic Books.

*Sandholtz, J. J., Ringstaff, C., and Dwyer, D. C. (1997). *Teaching with technology: Creating student-centered classrooms.* New York: Teachers College Press.

*Sarason, S. B. (1997). *How schools might be governed and why.* New York: Teachers College Press.

*Sarnoff, D. (1940). Foreword to L. R. Lohr. *Television broadcasting.* New York: McGraw-Hill.

Sartre, Jean-Paul. (1972). Existentialism. In John Martin Rich (ed.). *Readings in the philosophy of education.* Belmont, CA: Wadsworth.

Schaefer, R. (1967). *The school as the center of inquiry.* New York: Harper and Row.

Schaill v. Tippecanoe School Corporation, 864 F.2d 1309 (7th Cir. 1988).

*Schifter, D. (ed.). (1996). *What's happening in math class? Envisioning new practices through teacher narratives, vol. 1.* New York: Teachers College Press.

Schmidt, P. (1991, February 20). Three types of bilingual education effective, E. D. study concludes. *Education Week on the Web.*

Schmuck, R. A., and Schmuck, P. A. (1997). *Group processes in the classroom,* 7th ed. Madison, WI: Brown and Benchmark.

Schnaiberg, L. (1995, November 1). Record increase in special-education students reported. *Education Week on the Web.*

Schnaiberg, L. (1996, June 12). Staying home from school. *Education Week on the Web.*

*Schneider, R. B. and Barone, D. (1997, spring). Cross-age tutoring. *Childhood Education,* 136–143.

Schön, D. (1983). *The reflective practitioner: How professionals think in action.* New York: Basic Books.

Schön, D. (1987). *Educating the reflective practitioner: Toward a new design for teaching and learning in the professions.* San Francisco: Jossey-Bass.

Schön, D. (1991). *The reflective turn: Case studies in an on educational practice.* New York: Teachers College Press.

School District of Abington Township v. Schempp, 374 U.S. 203, 83 S. Ct. 1560, 10 L.Ed. 2d 844 (1963).

*Schwartz, J. E., and Beichner, R. J. (1999). *Essentials of educational technology*. Boston: Allyn and Bacon.

*Schwartz, W. (1995, December). Opportunity to learn standards: Their impact on urban education. *ERIC/CUE Digest*, 110.

*Schwebel, A. J., et al. (1996). *The student teacher's handbook*, 3rd ed. Mahwah, NJ: Lawrence Erlbaum Associates.

Scopes, J. (1966). *Center of the storm*. New York: Holt, Rinehart, and Winston.

Scoville v. Board of Education of Joliet Township High School District 204, cert. denied, 400 U.S. 826, 91 S. Ct. 51 (1970); 425 F.2d 10 (7th Cir. 1971).

Sears, J. T. (1991). Educators, homosexuality and homosexual students: Are personal feelings related to professional beliefs? *Journal of Homosexuality*, 22.

*Shade, B. J. (1982). Afro-American cognitive style: A variable in school success? *Review of Educational Research 52,2*, 219–238.

Shanley v. Northeast Independent School District, 462 F.2d 960 (5th Cir. 1972).

Sharan, Y., and Sharan, S. (1989/1990, December/January). Group investigation expands cooperative learning. *Educational Leadership*, 17–21.

*Shenk, D. (1998). *Data smog: Surviving the information age*. New York: HarperEdge.

Sheuerer, D., and Parkay, F. W. (1992). The new Christian right and the public school curriculum: A Florida report. In J. B. Smith, and J. G. Coleman, Jr. (Eds.). *School library media annual: 1992*, vol. 10. Englewood, CO: Libraries Unlimited.

Shoop, R. J., and Dunklee, D. R. (1992). *School law for the principal: A handbook for practitioners*. Boston: Allyn and Bacon.

*Sigalit, U., and Van Lehn, K. (1995). STEPS: A simulated, tutorable physics student. *Journal of Artificial Intelligence in Education*, 6(4), 405–37.

*Signer, B. (1991). CAI and at–risk minority urban high school students. *Journal of Research on Computing in Education*, 24(2).

Simonetti v. School District of Philadelphia, 308 Pa Super. 555, 454 A. 2d 1038 (Pa. Super. 1982).

Singer, A. (1994, December). Reflections on multiculturalism. *Phi Delta Kappan*, 284–88.

*Sizer, T. (1997a). *Horace's compromise: The dilemma of the American high school*, 3rd ed. Boston: Houghton Mifflin.

*Sizer, T. (1997b). *Horace's school: Redesigning the American high school*. Boston: Houghton Mifflin.

*Sizer, T. (1997c). *Horace's hope: What works for the American high school*. Boston: Houghton Mifflin.

*Sizer, T. and Sizer, N. (1999). *The students are watching: Schools and the moral contract*. Boston: Beacon Press.

Skinner, B. F. (1972). Utopia through the control of human behavior. In J. M. Rich (Ed.). *Readings in the philosophy of education*. Belmont, CA: Wadsworth.

*Slavin, R. E. (2000). *Educational psychology: Theory and practice*, 6th ed. Boston: Allyn and Bacon.

*Slavit, D. (1998). Above and beyond AAA: The similarity and congruence of polygons.

Mathematics Teaching in the Middle School, 3(4), 276–280.

*Sleeter, C. E. (1999). Curriculum controversies in multicultural education. In M. J. Early and K. J. Rehage (eds.). *Issues in curriculum: A selection of chapters from past NSSE yearbooks: Ninety-eighth yearbook of the National Society for the Study of Education* (pp. 257–280). Chicago: University of Chicago Press.

*Smith, D. D. (1998). *Introduction to special education: Teaching in an age of challenge*, 2nd ed. Boston: Allyn and Bacon.

Smith, K. B., and Meier, K. K. (1995). *The case against school choice: Politics, markets, and fools*. Armonk, NY: M.E. Sharpe.

*Smith, M. S., Stevenson, D. L., and Li, C. P. (1998, November). Voluntary national tests: Helping schools improve instruction and learning in reading and math. *Phi Delta Kappan*, 41–56.

Smith v. Archbishop of St. Louis, 632, S.W. 2d 516 (Mo. app. 1982).

Smith v. Board of School Commissioners of Mobile County, 655 F. Supp. 939 (S. D. Ala.), rev'd, 827 F.2d 684 (11th Cir. 1987).

*Smolkin, R. (1999, February 27–28). The reading debate rages. *Moscow-Pullman Daily News*, 1A, 10A.

*Smyth, J. W. (1995). *Clinical supervision: Collaborative learning about teaching*. New York: State Mutual Book and Periodical Service.

*Snider, J. H. (1996, May–June). Education wars: The battle over information-age technology. *The Futurist*, 24–29.

Sommers, C. H. (1994). *Who stole feminism?: How women have betrayed women*. New York: Simon and Schuster.

Sommers, C. H. (1996, June 12). Where the boys are. *Education Week on the Web*.

*Sosniak, L. A. (1999). Professional and subject matter knowledge for teacher education. In G. A. Griffin (ed.). *The education of teachers: Ninety-eighth yearbook of the National Society for the Study of Education*. Chicago: University of Chicago Press.

Sowell, E. J. (1996). *Curriculum: An integrative introduction*. Boston: Allyn and Bacon.

Splintered vision (A): An investigation of U.S. science and mathematics education. (1996). Washington, DC: U.S. Department of Education and Internation al Institute on Education.

Spokesman Review. (1993, June 4). Harassment claims vex teachers.

*Spring, J. (1997). *The American school 1642–1996*, 4th ed. New York: McGraw Hill.

*Spring, J. (1998). *Conflict of interests: The politics of American education*, 3rd ed. Boston: McGraw Hill.

Spring, J. (1999). *American education*, 8th ed. New York: McGraw–Hill.

Sricharatchanya, P. (1996, November 5). Education reforms are also crucial. *Bangkok Post*.

St. Michel, T. (1995). *Effective substitute teachers: Myth, mayhem, or magic?* Thousand Oaks, CA: Corwin Press.

Stahl v. Cocalico School District, 534 A. 2d 1141 (Pa. Cmwlth. 1987).

Stanford, B. H. (1992). Gender equity in the classroom. In D. A. Byrnes and G. Kiger (Eds.), *Common bonds: Anti–bias teaching in a diverse society*. Wheaton, MD: Association for Childhood Education International.

State v. Rivera, 497 N. W.2d 878 (Iowa 1993).

Station v. Travelers Insurance Co., 292 So.2d 289 (La. Ct. App. 1974).

*Steinberg, A. (1999, March/April). The human cost of over-reliance on tests. *Harvard Education Letter*.

Steinberg, L., Dornbusch, S., and Brown, B. (1996) *Beyond the classroom: Why school reform has failed and what parents need to do*. New York: Simon and Schuster.

Sternberg, R. J. (1996, March). Myths, countermyths, and truths about intelligence. *Educational Researcher*, 11–16.

*Stoll, C. (1996). *Silicon snake oil: Second thoughts on the information highway*. New York: Anchor.

Stover, D. (1992, March). The at-risk kids schools ignore. *The Executive Educator*, 28–31.

*Sue, D. W., and Sue, D. (1999). *Counseling the culturally different: Theory and practice*, 3rd ed. New York: Wiley.

Sullivan v. Houston Independent School District, 475 F.2d 1071 (5th Cir. 1969), cert. denied 414 U.S. 1032 (1969).

*Swisher, K., and Deyhle, D. (1987). Styles of learning and learning styles: Educational conflicts for American Indian/Alaskan Native youth. *Journal of Multilingual and Multicultural Development*, 8(4).

Sykes, G. (1983, October). Contradictions, ironies, and promises unfulfilled: A contemporary account of the status of teaching. *Phi Delta Kappan*, 87–93.

*Tapscott, D. (1999, July 6,). Kids, technology and the schools. *Computerworld*.

Teach for America. (1999). About us. New York: Teach for America. http://www.teachforamerica.org

Teacher Centers of New York State. (1999) What is a teacher center? http://www.tier.net/tcenters/class.htm.

Tellijohann, S. K., and Price, J. H. (1993). A qualitative examination of adolescent homosexuals' life experiences: Ramifications for secondary school personnel. *Journal of Homosexuality*, 26.

Terman, L. M., and Oden, M. H. (1947). The gifted child grows up. In L. M. Terman (Ed.). *Genetic studies of genius*, vol. 4. Stanford, CA: Stanford University Press.

Terman, L. M., and Oden, M. H. (1959). The gifted group in mid–life. In L. M. Terman (Ed.). *Genetic studies of genius*, vol. 5. Stanford, CA: Stanford University Press.

Terry, W. (1993, February). Make things better for somebody. *Parade Magazine*.

Terman, L. M., Baldwin, B. T., and Bronson, E. (1925). Mental and physical traits of a thousand gifted children. In L. M. Terman (ed.). *Genetic studies of genius*, vol. 1. Stanford, CA: Stanford University Press.

Thelen, H. A. (1960). *Education and the human quest*. New York: Harper and Row.

Thelen, H. A. (1981). *The classroom society: The construction of educational experience*. London: Croom Helm.

Tinker v. Des Moines Independent Community School District, 393 U.S. 503 (1969).

*Tombari, M. L., and Borich, G. D. (1999). *Authentic assessment in the classroom: Applications and practice.*. Upper Saddle River, NJ: Merrill.

Tozer, S. E., Violas, P. C., and Senese, G. (1993). *School and society: Educational practice as social expression*. New York: McGraw-Hill.

*Trotter, A. (1998, October 1). A question of effectiveness. *Education Week on the Web.*

Trueba, H. T., Cheng, L. R. L., and Kenji, I. (1993). *Myth or reality: Adaptive strategies of Asian Americans in California.* Washington, DC: Falmer Press.

*Tryneski, J. (Ed.). (1999). *Requirements for certification of teachers, counselors, librarians, administrators for elementary and secondary schools: Sixty–fourth ed., 1999–2000.* Chicago: University of Chicago Press.

Tyler, R. (1949). *Basic principles of curriculum and instruction.* Chicago: University of Chicago.

U.S. Census Bureau. (1993, September). *We the . . . first Americans.* Washington, DC: U.S. Census Bureau.

*U.S. Census Bureau. (1998). *Statistical abstract of the United States 1998.* Washington, DC: U.S. Census Bureau.

*U.S. Census Bureau. (1999). *The Asian and Pacific Islander population in the United States: March 1997.* Washington, DC: U.S. Census Bureau.

*U.S. Department of Education. (1996a). *Getting America's students ready for the 21st century: Meeting the technology literacy challenge.* Washington, DC: U.S. Department of Education.

*U.S. Department of Education. (1996b). *Manual on school uniforms.* Washington, DC: U. S. Department of Education.

*U.S. Department of Education. (1996c). *The technology literacy challenge.* Washington, DC: U.S. Department of Education.

*U.S. Department of Education. (1997). *From students of teaching to teachers of students.* Washington, DC: U.S. Department of Education.

*U.S. Department of Education (1998). *Twentieth annual report to Congress on the implementation of the Individuals with Disabilities Education Act: To assure the free appropriate public education of all children with disabilities.* Washington, DC: U.S. Department of Education.

*U.S. Department of Education. (1999a). [Online]. Safe schools, healthy schools: Remarks as prepared for delivery by U.S. Secretary of Education Richard W. Riley. http://www.ed.gov/Speeches/04–1999/990430.html [1999, April 30].

*U.S. Department of Education. (1999b). *Schools with IDEAs that work.* Washington, DC: U.S. Department of Education.

U.S. Department of Education and International Institute on Education. (1996). *A splintered vision: An investigation of U.S. science and mathematics education.* Washington, DC.

*U.S. Department of Health and Human Services. (1998, October 27). *Improving Head Start: A success story.* Washington, DC: U.S. Department of Health and Human Services.

U.S. Department of Justice. (1996). *1995 national youth gang survey.* Washington, DC: U.S. Department of Justice.

U.S. Government Printing Office. (1990). *Who's Minding the Kids?.* Washington, DC: U.S. Government Printing Office.

Uchida, D., Cetron, M., and McKenzie, F. (1996). *Preparing students for the 21st century.* Arlington, VA: American Association of School Administrators.

Unified School Dist. No 241 v. Swanson, 717 P.2d 526 (Kan. App. 1986).

*United Press International. (1998, November 15). Teachers may soon make $100,000.

The University of Memphis. (1994/95, Winter). Technology provides field experiences. *Perspectives.* Memphis: University of Memphis, College of Education.

Uribe, V., and Harbeck, K. M. (1991). Addressing the needs of lesbian, gay and bisexual youth. *Journal of Homosexuality, 22.*

Utay, C., and Utay, J. (1997). Peer–assisted learning: The effects of cooperative learning and cross–age peer tutoring with word processing on writing skills of students with learning disabilities. *Journal of Computing in Childhood Education, 8.*

*Valenza, J. K. (1997). Girls + technology = turnoff? *Technology Connections, 3.*

Van Lehn, K. (1994). Applications of simulated students: An exploration. *Journal of Artificial Intelligence in Education, 5*(2).

van Manen, M. (1991) *The tact of teaching: The meaning of pedagogical thoughtfulness.* Albany, NY: State University of New York Press.

*Vaughn, S., Bos, C. S., and Schumm, J. S. (1997). *Teaching mainstreamed, diverse, and at-risk students in the general education classroom.* Boston: Allyn and Bacon.

Venezky, R. L. (1992). Textbooks in school and society. In P. W. Jackson (Ed.). *Handbook of research on curriculum.* New York: Macmillan.

Viadero, D. (1996, May 8). Math texts are multiplying. *Education Week.*

*Viadero, D. (1999, January). [Untitled article]. *Education Week, 10*(4), 23.

Visconti, K. (1996). Stay in or get out? A "twenty–something" teacher looks at the profession. In G. Burnaford, J. Fischer, and D. Hobson, (Eds.). *Teachers doing research: Practical possibilities.* Mahwah, NJ: Lawrence Erlbaum Associates.

*Vygotsky, L. S. (1978). *Mind in society: The development of higher mental process.* Cambridge, MA: Harvard University Press.

*Vygotsky, L. S. (1986). *Thought and language.* Cambridge, MA: MIT Press.

*Walberg, H. J., and Greenberg, R. C. (1997, May). Using the learning environment inventory. *Educational Leadership,* 45–47.

Walberg, H. J., and Niemiec, R. P. (1994, May). Is Chicago school reform working? *Phi Delta Kappan,* 713–715.

Walberg, H. J., and Niemiec, R. P. (1996, May 22). Can the Chicago reforms work? *Education Week on the Web.*

Waller, W. (1932). *The sociology of teaching.* New York: Wiley.

Walling, D. R. (ed.). (1994). *Teachers as leaders: Perspectives on the professional development of teachers.* Bloomington, IN: Phi Delta Kappa Educational Foundation.

*Walsh, M. (1999a, April 2). Conservatives join effort to pull the plug on Channel One. *Education Week on the Web.*

*Walsh, M. (1999b, April 14). Most Edison schools report rise in test scores. *Education Week on the Web.*

*Walsh, M. (1999c, May). Two reports offer bright outlook for education industry. *Education Week, 18*(36), 5.

*Walsh, M. (1999d, May 5).Shootings raise host of legal questions. *Education Week on the Web.*

*Walsh, M. (1999e, May 26). Nader, Schlafly lambaste Channel One at Senate hearing. *Education Week on the Web.*

*Walsh, M. (1999f, September 8). Edison Project, now Edison Schools Inc., plans to go public. *Education Week on the Web.*

*Walters, L. S. (1999, January/February). What makes a good school violence prevention program? *Harvard Education Letter.*

*Walthers, K. (1995, September). Saying yes to vouchers: Perception, choice, and the educational response. *NAASP Bulletin,* 52–61.

*Washington State Department of Health, Non–Infectious Disease and Conditions Epidemiology Section. (1994). *Youth violence and associated risk factors: An epidemiological view of the literature.* Olympia, WA: Washington State Department of Health, Non–Infectious Disease and Conditions Epidemiology Section.

*Washington, W. (1998). Optional extended year program feedback. Austin Independent School District, TX, Department of Accountability, Student Services, and Research.

Wasserman, S. (1994, April). Using cases to study teaching. *Phi Delta Kappan,* 602–11.

*Webb, L. D., Metha, A., and Jordan, K. F. (1999). *Foundations of American education,* 3rd ed. Englewood Cliffs, NJ: Prentice Hall.

Wechsler, D. (1958). *The Measurement and appraisal of adult intelligence,* 4th ed. Baltimore: Williams and Wilkins.

*Weidmer, T. L. (1998). Digital portfolios: Capturing and demonstrating skills and levels of performance. *Phi Delta Kappan, 79*(8), 586–589.

West, A. M. (1980). *The National Education Association: The power base for education.* New York: Free Press.

West v. Board of Education of City of New York, 187 N. Y. S.2d 88 8 A.D. 2d 291 (N.Y. App. 1959).

*White House Press Release. (1999). President Clinton releases $100 million in grants to support public charter schools. Washington, DC: White House.

*White, K. A. (1997). A matter of policy. *Education Week on the Web.* http://www.edweek.org/sreports/tc/policy/po–n.htm

*Whitely, B. E. (1997). Gender differences in computer–related attitudes and behavior: A meta–analysis. *Computers in Human Behavior, 13.*

*William Randolph Hearst Foundation. (1999). *United States Senate Youth Program Survey.* San Francisco: William Randolph Hearst Foundation.

*Williams, J. (1999, April 18). Urban schools' obstacles hindering technology. *Milwaukee Journal Sentinel.*

Willig, A. C. (1987, Fall). Examining bilingual education research. *Review of Educational Research,* 363–376.

*Willingham, W. W., and Cole, N. S. (1997). *Gender and fair assessment.* Mahwah, NJ: Lawrence Erlbaum Associates.

*Wirt, F. M., and Kirst, M. W. (1997). *The political dynamics of American education.* Berkeley: McCutchan Publishing Corporation.

*Withrow, F. B. (1997). Technology in education and the next twenty-five years. *T.H.E. Journal, 2411,* 59–61.

Wohlstetter, P. (1995, September). Getting school-based management right: What works and what doesn't. *Phi Delta Kappan,* 22–24, 26.

Wohlstetter, P., and Anderson, L. (1994, February). What can U.S. charter schools learn from England's grant-maintained schools? *Phi Delta Kappan,* 486–491.

*Wolfe, D. T., and Antinarella, J. (1997). *Deciding to lead: The English teacher as reformer.* Portsmouth, NH: Boynton Cook Publishers.

*Wolfgang, C. H. (1999). *Solving discipline problems: Methods and models for today's teachers,* 4th ed. Boston: Allyn and Bacon.

Woolfolk, A. E. (1995). *Educational psychology,* 6th ed. Boston: Allyn and Bacon.

*Woolfolk, A. E. (1998). *Educational psychology,* 7th ed. Boston: Allyn and Bacon.

*Wray, H. (1999). *Japanese and American education: Attitudes and practices.* Westport, CT: Bergin and Garvey.

*Yahoo Internet Life. (1999). America's 100 most wired colleges.

Yamamoto, K., Davis, O. L. Jr., Dylak, S., Whittaker, J., Marsh, C., and van der Westhuizen, P C. (Spring 1996). Across six nations: Stressful events in the lives of children. *Child Psychiatry and Human Development,* 139–150.

*Young, C. (1999). *Ceasefire! Why women and men must join forces to achieve true equality.* New York: Free Press.

Zehm, S. J., and Kottler, J. A. (1993). *On being a teacher: The human dimension.* Newbury Park, CA: Corwin Press.

Zucker v. Panitz, 299 F. Supp. 102 (DCS.D. N.Y. 1969).

*Zukowski, V. (1997, Fall). Teeter–totters and tandem bikes: A glimpse into the world of cross–age tutors. *Teaching and change,* 71–91.

Glossary

A

Academic freedom: the right of teachers to teach, free from external constraint, censorship, or interference.

Academic learning time: the amount of time students spend working on academic tasks with a high level of success (80 percent or higher).

Academies: early secondary schools with broader and more practical curricula than those found in grammar schools of the previous era.

Accelerated schools: a national network of schools that provide enriched, rigorous curricula to "speed up" the learning of students at risk.

Accountability: the practice of holding teachers responsible for adhering to high professional and moral standards and creating effective learning environments for all students.

Action research: classroom-based study, by teachers, of how to improve their instruction.

Aesthetics: the branch of axiology concerned with values related to beauty and art.

Afrocentric schools: schools that focus on African American history and cultures for African American pupils.

Aims of education: what a society believes the broad, general purposes of education should be—for example, socialization, achievement, personal growth, and social improvement.

Allocated time: the amount of time teachers allocate for instruction in various areas of the curriculum.

Alternative certification: a provision allowing people who have completed college but not a teacher education program to become certified teachers.

Alternative school: a small, highly individualized school separate from a regular school; designed to meet the needs of students at risk.

Amendments to the Individuals with Disabilities Education Act (IDEA 97): amendments to IDEA that emphasize educational outcomes for students with disabilities and provide greater access through changes in eligibility requirements, IEP guidelines, public and private placements, student discipline guidelines, and procedural safeguards.

American Federation of Teachers (AFT): a national professional association for teachers, affiliated with the AFL-CIO.

Assertive discipline: an approach to classroom discipline requiring that teachers establish firm, clear guidelines for student behavior and follow through with consequences for misbehavior.

Assessment: the process of gathering information related to how much students have learned.

Assistive technology: technological advances (usually computer-based) that help exceptional students learn and communicate.

Association for Supervision and Curriculum Development (ASCD): a professional organization for educators interested in school improvement at all levels.

Attention deficit disorder (ADD): a learning disability characterized by difficulty in concentrating on learning.

Attention deficit hyperactivity disorder (ADHD): a learning disability characterized by difficulty in remaining still so that one can concentrate on learning.

Authentic assessments: an approach to assessing students' learning that requires them to solve problems or work on tasks that approximate as much as possible those they will encounter beyond the classroom.

Authentic learning tasks: learning activities that enable students to see the connections between classroom learning and the world beyond the classroom.

Axiology: the study of values, including the identification of criteria for determining what is valuable.

B

Back-to-basics movement: a movement begun in the mid-1970s to establish the "basic skills" of reading, writing, speaking, and computation as the core of the school curriculum.

Behaviorism: a philosophical orientation based on behavioristic psychology that maintains that environmental factors shape people's behavior.

Between-class ability grouping: the practice of grouping students at the middle and high school levels for instruction on the basis of ability or achievement, often called *tracking*.

Bicultural: the ability to function effectively in two or more linguistic and cultural groups.

Bilingual education: a curriculum for non-English-speaking and English-speaking students in which two languages are used for instruction and biculturalism is emphasized.

Block grants: a form of federal aid given directly to the states, which a state or local education agency may spend as it wishes with few limitations.

Block scheduling: a high school scheduling arrangement that provides longer blocks of time each class period, with fewer periods each day.

Brown v. Board of Education of Topeka: a 1954 landmark court case rejecting the "separate but equal" doctrine used to prevent African Americans from attending schools with whites.

Buckley Amendment: a 1974 law, the Family Educational Rights and Privacy Act, granting parents of students under eighteen and students over eighteen the right to examine their school records.

Burnout: an acute level of stress resulting in job dissatisfaction, emotional and physical exhaustion, and an inability to cope effectively.

C

Caring classroom: a classroom in which the teacher communicates clearly an attitude of caring about students' learning and their overall well-being.

Categorical aid: state-appropriated funds to cover the costs of educating students with special needs.

CD-ROM: a small plastic disk (usually 4.72 or 5.25 inches in diameter) that holds 600 or more megabytes of information that can be read by a computer.

Censorship: the act of removing from circulation printed material judged to be libelous, vulgar, or obscene.

Channel One: a controversial twelve-minute news broadcast, including two minutes of commercials, aired daily in more than 12,000 public and private schools; schools receive Channel One programs, equipment, and service free of charge upon agreeing to show the programs to students.

Character education: an approach to education that emphasizes the teaching of values, moral reasoning, and the development of "good" character.

Charter: an agreement between a charter school's founders and its sponsors specifying how the school will operate and what learning outcomes students will master.

Charter schools: independent schools, often founded by teachers, that are given a charter to operate by a school district, state, or national government, with the provision that students must demonstrate mastery of predetermined outcomes.

Chat rooms: Internet sites where students can participate in on-line discussions by typing in their comments and questions.

Chief state school officer: the chief administrator of a state department of education and head of the state board of education, often called the commissioner of education or superintendent of public instruction.

Choice theory: an approach to classroom management, developed by psychiatrist William Glasser, based on a belief that students will usually make good choices (i.e., behave in an acceptable manner) if they experience success in the classroom and know that teachers care about them.

Classroom climate: the atmosphere or quality of life in a classroom, determined by how individuals interact with one another.

Classroom culture: the "way of life" characteristic of a classroom group; determined by the social dimensions of the group and the physical characteristics of the setting.

Classroom management: day-to-day teacher control of student behavior and learning, including discipline.

Classroom organization: how teachers and students in a school are grouped for instruction and how time is allocated in classrooms.

Clinical supervision: a four-step model supervisors follow in making teacher performance evaluations.

Coalition of Essential Schools: a national network of public and private high schools that have restructured according to nine common principles.

Code of ethics: a set of guidelines that defines appropriate behavior for professionals.

Cognitive development: the process of acquiring the intellectual ability to learn from interaction with one's environment.

Cognitive science: the study of the learning process that focuses on how individuals manipulate symbols and process information.

Collaboration: the practice of working together, sharing decision making, and solving problems among professionals.

Collaborative consultation: an approach in which a classroom teacher meets with one or more other professionals (such as a special educator, school psychologist, or resource teacher) to focus on the learning needs of one or more students.

Collective bargaining: a process followed by employers and employees in negotiating salaries, hours, and working conditions; in most states, school boards must negotiate contracts with teacher organizations.

Collegial support team (CST): a team of teachers—created according to subject area, grade level, or teacher interests and expertise—who support one another's professional growth.

Collegiality: a spirit of cooperation and mutual helpfulness among professionals.

Committee of Fifteen: an NEA committee that recommended an academically oriented elementary curriculum (1895).

Committee of Ten: an NEA committee that recommended an academically rigorous curriculum for high school students (1893).

Common schools: free state-supported schools that provide education for all students.

Comparative education: the comparative study of educational practices in different countries.

Compensatory education programs: federally funded educational programs designed to meet the needs of low-ability students from low-income families.

Computer-assisted instruction (CAI): the use of computers to provide individualized drill-and-practice exercises or tutorials to students.

Computer-based simulations: computer programs that present the user with multifaceted problem situations similar to those they will encounter in real life.

Computer-enhanced instruction (CEI): the use of computers to provide students with inquiry-oriented learning experiences such as simulations and problem-solving activities.

Computer-managed instruction (CMI): the use of computers to evaluate and diagnose students' learning needs and record students' progress for teachers to monitor.

Concrete operations stage: the stage of cognitive development (seven to eleven years of age) proposed by Jean Piaget in which the individual develops the ability to use logical thought to solve concrete problems.

Constructivism: a psychological orientation that views learning as an active process in which learners *construct* understanding of the material they learn—in contrast to the view that teachers transmit academic content to students in small segments.

Constructivist teaching: a method of teaching based on students' prior knowledge of the topic and the processes they use to *construct* meaning.

Cooperative learning: an approach to education in which students work in small groups, or teams, sharing the work and helping one another complete assignments.

Copyright laws: laws limiting the use of photocopies, videotapes, and computer software programs.

Core curriculum: a set of fundamental courses or learning experiences that are part of the curriculum for all students at a school.

Corporal punishment: physical punishment applied to a student by a school employee as a disciplinary measure.

Cost of living: the amount of money needed, on average, for housing, food, transportation, utilities, and other living expenses in a given locale.

Co-teaching: an arrangement whereby two or more teachers teach together in the same classroom.

Credentials file: a file set up for students registered in a teacher placement office at a college or university, which includes background information on the applicant, the type of position desired, transcripts, performance evaluations, and letters of recommendation.

Cross-age tutoring: a tutoring arrangement in which older students tutor younger students; evidence indicates that cross-age tutoring has positive effects on the attitudes and achievement of tutee and tutor.

Cultural identity: an overall sense of oneself, derived from the extent of one's participation in various subcultures within the national macroculture.

Cultural pluralism: the preservation of cultural differences among groups of people within one society. This view is in contrast to the melting-pot theory, which says that ethnic cultures should melt into one.

Culture: the way of life common to a group of people; includes knowledge deemed important, shared meanings, norms, values, attitudes, ideals, and view of the world.

Curriculum: the school experiences, both planned and unplanned, that enhance (and sometimes impede) the education and growth of students.

D

Dame schools: colonial schools, usually held in the homes of widows or housewives, for teaching children basic reading, writing, and mathematical skills.

Democratic classroom: a classroom in which the teacher's leadership style encourages students to take more power and responsibility for their learning.

Departmentalization: an organizational arrangement for schools in which students move from classroom to classroom for instruction in different subject areas.

Desegregation: the process of eliminating schooling practices based on the separation of racial groups.

"Digital divide": inequities in access to computer technology that are related to minority-group status, family income, and gender.

Direct instruction: a systematic instructional method focusing on the transmission of knowledge and skills from the teacher to the students.

Discipline-based art programs: art education in which students learn art production, art criticism, art history, and aesthetics.

Discovery learning: an approach to teaching that gives students opportunities to inquire into subjects so that they "discover" knowledge for themselves.

Dismissal: the involuntary termination of a teacher's employment; termination must be made for a legally defensible reason with the protection of due process.

Distance learning: the use of technology such as video transmissions that enables students to receive instruction at multiple, often remote, sites.

Distance learning networks: two-way, interactive telecommunications systems used to deliver instruction to students at various locations.

Diversity: differences among people in regard to gender, race, ethnicity, culture, and socioeconomic status.

Due process: a set of specific guidelines that must be followed to protect individuals from arbitrary, capricious treatment by those in authority.

E

Education Consolidation and Improvement Act (ECIA): a 1981 federal law giving the states a broad range of choices for spending federal aid to education.

Education for All Handicapped Children Act (Public Law 94-142): a 1975 federal act that guarantees a free and appropriate education to all handicapped children (often referred to as the mainstreaming law or Public Law 94-142).

Educational malpractice: liability for injury that results from the failure of a teacher, school, or school district to provide a student with adequate instruction, guidance, counseling, and/or supervision.

Educational philosophy: a set of ideas and beliefs about education that guide the professional behavior of educators.

Educational reform movement: a comprehensive effort made during the 1980s and into the 1990s to improve schools and the preparation of teachers.

Educational Resources Information Center (ERIC): a national information system made up of sixteen clearinghouses that disseminate descriptions of exemplary programs, results of research and development efforts, and related information.

Educational technology: computers, software, multimedia systems, and advanced telecommunications systems used to enhance the teaching-learning process.

Eight-Year Study: an experiment in which thirty high schools were allowed to develop curricula that did not meet college entrance requirements (1932-1940).

Elementary and Secondary Education Act: part of President Lyndon B. Johnson's Great Society Program, this act allocated federal funds on the basis of the number of poor children in school districts.

Emergency certification: temporary, substandard certification requirements set by a state in response to a shortage of teachers.

Emotional intelligence: a level of awareness and understanding of one's emotions that allows the person to achieve personal growth and self-actualization.

Entitlements: federal programs to meet the educational needs of special populations.

Epistemology: a branch of philosophy concerned with the nature of knowledge and what it means to know something.

E-rate: a controversial program that uses fees from telecommunications companies to provide discounts on telecommunications services and wiring to schools and libraries.

ERIC Clearinghouses: sixteen Educational Resources Information Center Clearinghouses that disseminate descriptions of exemplary educational programs, the results of research and development efforts, and related information.

Essentialism: formulated in part as a response to progressivism, this philosophical orientation holds that a core of common knowledge about the real world should be transmitted to students in a systematic, disciplined way.

Ethical dilemmas: problem situations in which an ethical response is difficult to determine; that is, no single response can be called "right" or "wrong."

Ethics: a branch of philosophy concerned with principles of conduct and determining what is good and evil, right and wrong, in human behavior.

Ethnic group: individuals within a larger culture who share a racial or cultural identity and a set of beliefs, values, and attitudes and who consider themselves members of a distinct group or subculture.

Ethnicity: a shared feeling of common identity that derives, in part, from a common ancestry, common values, and common experiences.

Evaluation: making judgments about, or assigning a value to, measurements of students' learning.

Exceptional learners: students whose growth and development deviate from the norm to the extent that their educational needs can be met more effectively through a modification of regular school programs.

Existentialism: a philosophical orientation that emphasizes the individual's experiences and maintains that each individual must determine his or her own meaning of existence.

Expenditure per pupil: the amount of money spent on each pupil in a school, school district, state, or nation; usually computed according to average daily attendance.

Explicit curriculum: the behavior, attitudes, and knowledge that a school intends to teach students.

Extracurricular/cocurricular programs: school-sponsored activities students may pursue outside of, or in addition to, academic study.

F

Fair use: the right of an individual to use copyrighted material in a reasonable manner without the copyright holder's consent, provided that use meets certain criteria.

Female seminaries: schools established in the early nineteenth century to train women for higher education and public service outside the home.

Field experiences: opportunities for teachers-in-training to experience firsthand the world of the teacher, by observing, tutoring, and instructing small groups.

For-profit schools: schools that are operated, for profit, by private educational corporations.

Formal operations stage: the stage of cognitive development (eleven to fifteen years of age) proposed by Jean Piaget in which cognitive abilities reach their highest level of development.

Formative evaluation: an assessment, or diagnosis, of students' learning for the purpose of planning instruction.

Freedom of expression: freedom, granted by the First Amendment to the Constitution, to express one's beliefs.

Fringe benefits: benefits (i.e., medical insurance, retirement, and tax-deferred investment opportunities) that are given to teachers in addition to base salary.

Full inclusion: the policy and process of including exceptional learners in general education classrooms.

Full-funding programs: state programs to ensure statewide financial equity by setting the same per-pupil expenditure level for all schools and districts.

Full-service schools: schools that provide students and their families with medical, social, and human services in addition to their regular educational programs.

G

Gender bias: subtle bias or discrimination on the basis of gender; reduces the likelihood that the target of the bias will develop to the full extent of his or her capabilities.

Gender-fair classroom: education that is free of bias or discrimination on the basis of gender.

G.I. Bill of Rights: a 1944 federal law that provides veterans with payments for tuition and room and board at colleges and universities and special schools; formally known as the Servicemen's Readjustment Act.

Gifted and talented: exceptional learners who demonstrate high intelligence, high creativity, high achievement, or special talent(s).

Goals 2000: Educate America Act: a comprehensive funding program to help schools achieve a set of eight national goals emphasizing student achievement, effective learning environments, professional development for teachers, and parental involvement.

Grievance: a formal complaint filed by an employee against his or her employer or supervisor.

Group investigation: an approach to teaching in which the teacher facilitates learning by creating an environment that allows students to determine what they will study and how.

H

Hidden curriculum: the behaviors, attitudes, and knowledge the school culture unintentionally teaches students.

Hierarchy of needs: a set of seven needs, from the basic needs for survival and safety to the need for self-actualization, that motivate human behavior.

Higher-order questions: questions that require the ability to engage in complex modes of thought (synthesis, analysis, and evaluation, for example).

Holmes Group: a group of ninety-six colleges of education that prepared *Tomorrow's Teachers*, a 1986 report calling for all teachers to have a bachelor's degree in an academic field and a master's degree in education.

Holmes Partnership: a consortium of professional organizations—including the Holmes Group, the National Board for Professional Teaching Standards, the National Education Association, and the American Federation of Teachers—committed to the reform of teacher education.

Home-school communication systems: computer-based systems that allow schools to disseminate information to parents and, in turn, enable parents to communicate directly with school personnel.

Horn book: a copy of the alphabet covered by a thin transparent sheet made from a cow's horn.

Humanism: a philosophy based on the belief that individuals control their own destinies through the application of their intelligence and learning.

Humanistic psychology: an orientation to human behavior that emphasizes personal freedom, choice, awareness, and personal responsibility.

Hypermedia: an interactive instructional system consisting of a computer, CD-ROM drive, videodisc player, video monitor, and speakers. Hypermedia systems allow students to control and present sound, video images, text, and graphics in an almost limitless array of possibilities.

I

Inclusion: the practice of integrating all students with disabilities into general education classes.

Indian Education Act of 1972 and 1974 Amendments: a federal law and subsequent amendment designed to provide direct educational assistance to Native American tribes and nations.

Individual racism: the prejudicial belief that one's ethnic or racial group is superior to others.

Individualized education plan (IEP): a plan for meeting an exceptional learner's educational needs, specifying goals, objectives, services, and procedures for evaluating progress.

Individuals with Disabilities Education Act (IDEA): a 1990 federal act providing a free, appropriate education to disabled youth between three and twenty-one years of age. IDEA superseded the earlier Education for all Handicapped Children Act (Public Law 94-142).

Induction programs: programs of support for beginning teachers, usually during their first year of teaching.

Information processing: a branch of cognitive science concerned with how individuals use long- and short-term memory to acquire information and solve problems.

Inquiry-based curriculum: a curriculum that teaches not only the content but also the thought processes of a discipline.

Inquiry learning: an approach to teaching that gives students opportunities to explore, or *inquire* into, subjects so that they develop their own answers to problem situations.

Inservice workshops: on-site professional development programs in which teachers meet to learn new techniques, develop curricular materials, share ideas, or solve problems.

Institution: any organization a society establishes to maintain, and improve, its way of life.

Institutional racism: institutional policies and practices, intentional or not, that result in racial inequities.

Instructional goals: general statements of purpose that guide schools and teachers as they develop instructional programs.

Integrated curriculum: a school curriculum that draws from two or more subject areas and focuses on a theme or concept rather than on a single subject.

Intelligence: the ability to learn; the cognitive capacity for thinking.

Interactive multimedia: computer-supported media that allow the user to interact with a vast, nonlinear, multimedia database to combine textual, audio, and video information.

Interactive teaching: teaching characterized by face-to-face interactions between teachers and students in contrast to preactive teaching.

Internet: a set of interconnected computer networks created for the rapid dissemination of vast amounts of information around the world.

International Assessment of Educational Progress (IAEP): a program established in 1991 for comparing the achievement of students in the United States with that of students from other countries.

Internship programs: programs of assistance and training for beginning teachers, usually for those who have not gone through a teacher education program.

Interstate Certification Agreement Contract: a reciprocity agreement among approximately thirty states whereby a teaching certificate obtained in one state will be honored in another.

Interstate New Teacher Assessment and Support Consortium (INTASC): an organization of states established in 1987 to develop performance-based standards for what beginning teachers should know and be able to do.

J

Job analysis: a procedure for determining the knowledge and skills needed for a job.

K

Kentucky Education Reform Act (KERA): comprehensive school-reform legislation requiring all Kentucky schools to form school-based management councils with authority to set policies in eight areas.

Kindergarten: a school for children before they begin formal schooling at the elementary level; based on the ideas of German educator Friedrick Fröebel, *kindergarten* means "garden where children grow."

Knowledge base: the body of knowledge that represents what teachers need to know and be able to do.

L

Language-minority students: students whose language of the home is a language other than English.

Latchkey children: children who, because of family circumstances, must spend part of each day unsupervised by a parent or guardian.

Latin grammar school: colonial schools established to provide male students a precollege education; comparable to today's high schools.

Learning: changes in behavior the individual makes in response to environmental stimuli; the acquisition and organization of knowledge and skills.

Learning disability (LD): a limitation in one's ability to take in, organize, remember, and express information.

Learning objectives: specific, measurable outcomes of learning that students are to demonstrate.

Learning styles: cognitive, affective, and physiological behaviors through which an individual learns most effectively; determined by a combination of hereditary and environmental influences.

Least restrictive environment: an educational program that meets a disabled student's special needs in a manner that is identical, insofar as possible, to that provided to students in general education classrooms.

Lemon test: a three-part test, based on *Lemon v. Kurtzman*, to determine whether a state has violated the separation of church and state principle.

Letter of application: a letter written in application for a specific teaching vacancy in a school district.

Letter of inquiry: a letter written to a school district inquiring about teaching vacancies.

Limited English proficiency (LEP): a designation for students with limited ability to understand, read, or speak English and who have a first language other than English.

Local school council: a group of community members that is empowered to develop policies for the operation of local schools.

Local school district: an agency at the local level that has the authority to operate schools in the district.

Logic: a branch of philosophy concerned with the processes of reasoning and the identification of rules that will enable thinkers to reach valid conclusions.

Lower-order questions: questions that require students to recall specific information.

M

Magnet school: a school offering a curriculum that focuses on a specific area such as the performing arts, mathematics, science, international studies, or technology. Magnet schools, which often draw students from a larger attendance area than regular schools, are frequently developed to promote voluntary desegregation.

Mainstreaming: the policy and process of integrating disabled or otherwise exceptional learners into regular classrooms with nonexceptional students.

Massachusetts Act of 1642: a law requiring each town to determine whether its young people could read and write.

Massachusetts Act of 1647: a law mandating the establishment and support of schools; often referred to as the Old Deluder Satan Act because education was seen as the best protection against the wiles of the devil.

Mastery learning: an approach to instruction based on the assumptions that (1) virtually all students can learn material if given enough time and taught appropriately and (2) learning is enhanced if students can progress in small, sequenced steps.

McGuffey readers: an immensely popular series of reading books for students in grades one through six, written in the 1830s by Reverend William Holmes McGuffey.

Measurement: the gathering of data that indicate how much students have learned.

Mentor: a wise, knowledgeable individual who provides guidance and encouragement to someone.

Mentoring: an intensive form of teaching in which a wise and experienced teacher (the mentor) inducts a student (the protégé) into a professional way of life.

Metaphysics: a branch of philosophy concerned with the nature of reality.

Microcomputer-based laboratories (MBL): the use of computers to gather and then analyze data that students have collected in a school laboratory or in the field.

Microteaching: a brief, single-concept lesson taught by a teacher education student to a small group of students; usually designed to give the education student an opportunity to practice a specific teaching skill.

Minorities: groups of people who share certain characteristics and are smaller in number than the majority of a population.

Modeling: the process of "thinking out loud" which teachers use to make students aware of the reasoning involved in learning new material.

Modes of teaching: different aspects of the teaching function—for example, teaching as a way of being, as a creative endeavor, as a live performance, and so on.

Montesorri Method: a method of teaching, developed by Maria Montessori, based on a prescribed set of materials and physical exercises to develop children's knowledge and skills.

Moonlight: to hold a second job to increase one's income.

Moral reasoning: the reasoning process people follow to decide what is right or wrong.

Morrill Land-Grant Act: an 1862 act that provided federal land that states could sell or rent to raise funds to establish colleges of agriculture and mechanical arts.

Multicultural curriculum: a school curriculum that addresses the needs and backgrounds of all students regardless of their cultural identity and includes the cultural perspectives, or "voices," of people who have previously been silent or marginalized.

Multicultural education: education that provides equal educational opportunities to all students—regardless of socioeconomic status; gender; or ethnic, racial, or cultural backgrounds—and is dedicated to reducing prejudice and celebrating the rich diversity of American life.

Multiculturalism: a set of beliefs based on the importance of seeing the world from different cultural frames of reference and valuing the diversity of cultures in the global community.

Multiple intelligences: a perspective on intellectual ability, proposed by Howard Gardner, suggesting that there are at least seven types of human intelligence.

N

A Nation at Risk: a 1983 national report critical of American education.

National Assessment of Educational Progress (NAEP): an ongoing, large-scale national testing program to assess the effectiveness of education in the United States.

National Board for Professional Teaching Standards (NBPTS): a board established in 1987 that began issuing professional certificates in 1994-95 to teachers who possess extensive professional knowledge and the ability to perform at a high level.

National Council for Accreditation of Teacher Education (NCATE): an agency that accredits, on a voluntary basis, almost half of the nation's teacher education programs.

National curriculum: a standardized curriculum set at the national level and delivered to students at all schools throughout the country. Usually, countries with national curricula have nationwide testing to assess students' mastery of the curriculum.

National Defense Education Act: a 1958 federally sponsored program to promote research and innovation in science, mathematics, modern foreign languages, and guidance.

National Education Association (NEA): the oldest and largest professional association for teachers and administrators.

National Governor's Association: an association of state governors that influences policies in several areas, including teacher education and school reform.

National Information Infrastructure (NII): a federal plan to create a telecommunications infrastructure linking all schools, libraries, hospitals, and law enforcement agencies to the Internet and the World Wide Web.

National Network for Educational Renewal: a national network of colleges and universities that collaborate with school districts and partner schools to reform education according to nineteen postulates in John Goodlad's *Teachers for Our Nation's Schools.*

Negligence: failure to exercise reasonable, prudent care in providing for the safety of others.

Newsgroups: Internet sites where students can post and exchange information on electronic bulletin boards.

Nondiscrimination: conditions characterized by the absence of discrimination; for example, employees receive compensation, privileges, and opportunities for advancement without regard for race, color, religion, sex, or national origin.

Normal schools: schools that focus on the preparation of teachers.

Null curriculum: the intellectual processes and subject content that schools do not teach.

O

Observations: field experiences wherein a teacher education student observes a specific aspect of classroom life such as the students, the teacher, the interactions between the two, the structure of the lesson, or the setting.

Office of Educational Research and Improvement (OERI): a federal agency that promotes educational research and improving schools through the application of research results.

Open-space schools: schools that have large instructional areas with movable walls and furniture that can be rearranged easily.

Opportunity to learn (OTL): the time during which a teacher provides students with challenging content and appropriate instructional strategies to learn that content.

Outcome-based education: an educational reform that focuses on developing students' ability to demonstrate mastery of certain desired outcomes or performances.

Outcome-based teacher education: an approach to teacher education emphasizing outcomes (what teachers should be able to do, think, and feel) rather than the courses they should take.

P

Parochial schools: schools founded on religious beliefs.

Pedagogical content knowledge: the knowledge accomplished teachers possess regarding how to present subject matter to students though the use of analogies, metaphors, experiments, demonstrations, illustrations, and other instructional strategies.

Peer coaching: an arrangement whereby teachers grow professionally by observing one another's teaching and providing constructive feedback.

Peer counseling: an arrangement whereby students, monitored by a school counselor or teacher, counsel one another in such areas as low achievement, interpersonal problems, substance abuse, and career planning.

Peer-mediated instruction: approaches to teaching, such as cooperative learning and group investigation, that utilize the social relationships among students to promote their learning.

Peer-tutoring: an arrangement whereby students tutor other students in the same classroom or at the same grade level.

Perennialism: a philosophical orientation that emphasizes the ideas contained in the Great Books and maintains that the true purpose of education is the discovery of the universal, or perennial, truths of life.

Performance assessment: the process of determining what students can *do* as well as what they know.

Performance-based education: an educational reform that focuses on developing students' ability to demonstrate mastery of certain desired performances or outcomes.

Performance-based teacher education: an approach to teacher education emphasizing performances (what teachers should be able to do, think, and feel) rather than the courses they should take.

Personal-development view: the belief that teachers become more effective by increasing their self-knowledge and developing themselves as persons.

Phi Delta Kappa: a professional and honorary fraternity of educators with 650 chapters and 130,000 members.

Placement service: a school, government, or commercial service that matches job applicants with job openings and arranges contacts between employers and prospective employees.

Portfolio assessment: the process of determining how much students have learned by examining collections of work that document their learning over time.

Practicum: a short field-based experience during which teacher education students spend time observing and assisting in classrooms.

Praxis Series: Professional Assessments for Beginning Teachers: a battery of tests available to states for the initial certification of teachers. Consists of assessments in three areas: academic skills, knowledge of subject, and classroom performance.

Preactive teaching: the stage of teaching when a teacher prepares to teach or reflects on previous teaching experiences in contrast with interactive teaching.

Preoperational stage: the stage of cognitive development (two to seven years of age), proposed by Jean Piaget, in which the individual begins to use language and symbols to think of objects and people outside of the immediate environment.

Primer: a book with very explicit religious and moral messages about the proper conduct of life that colonial children used to learn to read.

Privatization movement: Umbrella term for reform initiatives that seek to run public schools as private enterprises.

Problem-centered learning: an approach to instruction in which students work in small groups on problems that have many or open-ended solutions.

Problem-solving orientation: an approach to teaching that places primary emphasis on the teacher's role as a decision maker and problem solver.

Profession: an occupation that requires a high level of expertise, including advanced study in a specialized field, adherence to a code of ethics, and the ability to work without close supervision.

Professional development schools (PDS): schools that have formed partnerships with a college or university for the purpose of improving the schools and contributing to the improvement of teacher preparation programs. Activities at a PDS may include collaborative research, team teaching, demonstration lessons by teacher education faculty, and various professional growth opportunities for teachers and teacher educators.

Professional empowerment: a trend for teachers to have expanded opportunities to make decisions that affect their professional lives.

Professional portfolio: a collection of various kinds of evidence (e.g., projects, written work, and video demonstrations of skills) documenting the achievement and performance of individuals in an area of professional practice.

Professional standards boards: state agencies to regulate and improve the professional practice of teachers, administrators, and other education personnel.

Progressive movement: a movement during the 1920s and 1930s to create schools that emphasized democracy, children's interests and needs, and closer connections between school and community.

Progressivism: a philosophical orientation based on the belief that life is evolving in a positive direction, that people may be trusted to act in their own best interests, and that education should focus on the needs and interests of students.

Property taxes: local taxes assessed against real estate and, in some areas, against personal property such as cars, household furniture and appliances, and stocks and bonds.

Prosocial values: values such as honesty, patriotism, fairness, and civility that promote the well-being of a society.

Psychosocial crisis: a life crisis at one of eight different stages of growth and development. According to psychologist Erik Erikson, individuals must resolve each crisis to reach the next stage.

Psychosocial development: the progression of an individual through various stages of psychological and social development.

Q

Qualitative evaluation: the appraisal of teacher performance through the use of written, open-ended descriptions of classroom events in terms of their qualities.

Quantitative evaluation: the appraisal of teacher performance by recording classroom events in terms of their number or frequency; for example, teacher verbal behaviors such as questioning, praising, or critiquing.

R

Race: a concept of human variation used to distinguish people on the basis of biological traits and characteristics.

Reading and writing schools: colonial schools, supported by public funds and fees paid by parents, that used a religiously oriented curriculum to teach boys reading and writing skills and, to a lesser degree, mathematics.

Realities of teaching: actual conditions teachers face in the classroom; the demands as well as the rewards.

Recertification: the practice in some states of requiring experienced teachers to undergo periodic testing to maintain their teaching certificates.

Redistricting: the practice of redrawing district boundaries to equalize educational funding by reducing the range of variation in the ability of school districts to finance education.

Reflection: the process of thinking carefully and deliberately about the outcomes of one's teaching.

Reflection-in-action: the process of engaging in serious, reflective thought about improving one's professional practice while one is engaged in that practice.

Reflective teaching log: a journal of classroom observations in which the teacher education student systematically analyzes specific episodes of teaching.

Regional Educational Laboratories: nine federally supported, nonprofit agencies that serve a region of the country and work directly with educators to improve schools.

Regional Educational Service Agency (RESA): a state educational agency that provides supportive services to two or more school districts; known in some states as education service centers, intermediate school districts, multicounty education service units, board of cooperative educational services, or educational service regions.

Relevancy-based curriculum: a curriculum that is relevant to students' needs, interests, and concerns about social issues.

Reorganization of Secondary Education: an NEA commission that recommended a high-school curriculum based on individual differences (1913).

Research and Development Centers: fourteen federally supported, university-based centers, each conducting research and development activities in a different area of education.

Research-based competencies: specific behaviors that educational research has identified as characteristic of effective teachers.

Restructuring: reorganizing how schools are controlled at the local level so that teachers, principals, parents, and community members have greater authority.

Résumé: a concise summary of an individual's professional experiences and education.

S

Scaffolding: an approach to teaching based on the student's current level of understanding and ability; the teacher varies the amount of help given (e.g., clues, encouragement, or suggestions) to students based on their moment-to-moment understanding of the material being learned.

School-based interprofessional case management: an approach to education in which professionally trained case managers work directly with teachers, the community, and families to coordinate and deliver appropriate services to at-risk students and their families.

School-based management: various approaches to school improvement in which teachers, principals, students, parents, and community members manage individual schools and share in the decision-making processes.

School-based teacher education: a model of teacher preparation through which professional coursework is presented on-site at a school, usually to students who have a bachelor's degree.

School board: the primary governing body of a local school district.

School choice: various proposals that would allow parents to choose the schools their children attend.

School culture: the collective "way of life" characteristic of a school; a set of beliefs, values, traditions, and ways of thinking and behaving that distinguish it from other schools.

School restructuring: approaches to school improvement that change the way students are grouped for instruction, uses of classroom time and space, instructional methods, and procedures for decision making and governance.

School-to-work programs: educational programs, often developed collaboratively by schools and industry, that emphasize the transfer of knowledge and skills learned at school to the job setting.

School traditions: those elements of a school's culture that are handed down from year to year.

School-within-a-school: an alternative school (within a regular school) designed to meet the needs of students at risk.

Scientific management: the application of management principles and techniques to the operation of big business and large school districts.

Search and seizure: the process of searching an individual and/or his or her property if that person is suspected of an illegal act; reasonable or probable cause to suspect the individual must be present.

Self-assessment: the process of measuring one's growth in regard to the knowledge, skills, and attitudes possessed by professional teachers.

Self-contained classroom: an organizational structure for schools in which one teacher instructs a group of students (typically, twenty to thirty) in a single classroom.

Service learning: an approach to teaching in which students participate in community-based service activities and then reflect on the meaning of those experiences.

Sex-role socialization: socially expected behavior patterns conveyed to individuals on the basis of gender.

Sex-role stereotyping: beliefs that subtly encourage males and females to conform to certain behavioral norms regardless of abilities and interests.

Sexual harassment: unwanted and unwelcome sexual behavior directed toward another person, whether of the same or opposite sex.

Social reconstructionism: a philosophical orientation based on the belief that social problems can be solved by changing, or *reconstructing,* society.

Socratic questioning: a method of questioning designed to lead students to see errors and inconsistencies in their thinking, based on questioning strategies used by Socrates.

Special education: a teaching specialty for meeting the special educational needs of exceptional learners.

Stages of development: predictable stages through which individuals pass as they progress through life.

State aid: money given by a state to its cities and towns to provide essential services, including the operation of public schools.

State board of education: the highest educational agency in a state, charged with regulating the state's system of education.

State department of education: the branch of state government, headed by the chief state school officer, charged with implementing the state's educational policies.

Stereotyping: the process of attributing behavioral characteristics to all members of a group; formulated on the basis of limited experiences with and information about the group, coupled with an unwillingness to examine prejudices.

Student-centered curriculum: curricula that are organized around students' needs and interests.

Student diversity: differences among students in regard to gender, race, ethnicity, culture, and socioeconomic status.

Student-mobility rates: the proportion of students within a school or district who move during an academic year.

Student variability: differences among students in regard to their developmental needs, interests, abilities, and disabilities.

Students at risk: students whose living conditions and backgrounds place them at risk for dropping out of school.

Students with disabilities: students who need special education services because they possess one or more of the following disabilities: learning disabilities, speech or language impairments, mental retardation, serious emotional disturbance, hearing impairments, orthopedic impairments, visual impairments, or other health impairments.

Subject-centered curriculum: a curriculum that emphasizes learning an academic discipline.

Substitute teaching: Temporary teachers who replace regular teachers absent due to illness, family responsibilities, personal reasons, or professional workshops and conferences.

Successful schools: schools characterized by a high degree of student learning, results that surpass those expected from comparable schools, and steady improvement rather than decline.

Summative evaluation: an assessment of student learning made for the purpose of assigning grades at the end of a unit, semester, or year and deciding whether students are ready to proceed to the next phase of their education.

Superintendent: the chief administrator of a school district.

Synectics: a method for "teaching" creativity through the use of metaphors and analogies.

T

Teach for America: a program that enables recent college graduates without a teaching certificate to teach in districts with critical shortages of teachers and, after taking professional development courses and supervision by state and school authorities, earn a teaching certificate.

Teacher accountability: society's expectations that teachers will adhere to high professional and moral standards and create effective learning environments for all students.

Teacher centers: centers where teachers provide other teachers with instructional materials and new methods and where teachers can exchange ideas.

Teacher-leader: a teacher who assumes a key leadership role in the improvement and/or day-to-day operation of a school.

Teacher-researcher: a teacher who regularly conducts classroom research to improve his or her teaching.

Teacher–student ratio: a ratio that expresses the number of students taught by a teacher.

Teacher supply and demand: the number of school-age students compared to the number of available teachers; may also be projected based on estimated numbers of students and teachers.

Teachers' thought processes: the thoughts that guide teachers' actions in classrooms. These thoughts typically consist of thoughts related to planning, theories and beliefs, and interactive thoughts and decisions.

Teaching certificate: a license to teach issued by a state or, in a few cases, a large city.

Teaching contract: an agreement between a teacher and a board of education that the teacher will provide specific services in return for a certain salary, benefits, and privileges.

Teaching simulations: an activity in which teacher education students participate in role-plays designed to create situations comparable to those actually encountered by teachers.

Team teaching: an arrangement whereby a team of teachers teaches a group of students equal in number to what the teachers would have in their self-contained classrooms.

Tech-prep programs: an arrangement that enables students to prepare for the world of work by spending time at local businesses and industries during their last two years in high school; students learn to transfer knowledge and skills learned at school to the job setting.

Tenure: an employment policy in which teachers, after serving a probationary period, retain their positions indefinitely and can be dismissed only on legally defensible grounds.

Third International Mathematics and Science Study (TIMSS): an international assessment of mathematics and science achievement among fourth-, eighth-, and twelfth-grade students in forty-one nations.

Time on task: the amount of time students are actively and directly engaged in learning tasks.

Title IX: a provision of the 1972 Education Amendments Act prohibiting sex discrimination in educational programs.

Tort liability: conditions that would permit the filing of legal charges against a professional for breach of duty and/or behaving in a negligent manner.

Tyler rationale: a four-step model for curriculum development in which teachers identify purposes, select learning experiences, organize experiences, and evaluate.

V

Vertical equity: an effort to provide equal educational opportunity within a state by providing different levels of funding based on economic needs within school districts.

Videoconferencing: the use of computer-mounted video cameras to conduct two-way interactive conferences over the Internet.

Videodisc: a twelve-inch plastic disk, each side of which holds about thirty minutes of motion video, or 54,000 frames of video; each frame can be frozen with a high degree of clarity.

Vocational-technical education: schooling that prepares students for particular jobs or provides them with the basic skills and career awareness needed to enter the world of work.

Voucher system: funds allocated to parents that they may use to purchase education for their children from public or private schools in the area.

W

Whole-language approach: the practice of teaching language skills (listening, reading, and writing) as part of students' everyday experiences rather than as isolated experiences.

Within-class ability grouping: the practice of creating small, homogeneous groups of students within a single classroom for the purpose of instruction, usually in reading or mathematics, at the elementary level.

Women's Educational Equity Act (WEEA): a 1974 federal law that guarantees equal educational opportunity for females.

World Wide Web (WWW): the most popular connection to the Internet; composed of home pages which users access through browser programs such as Netscape Communicator, Microsoft Internet Explorer, or America Online.

Name Index

Abrahamsson, B., 340
Acheson, A. A., 383
Addams, J., 82–83
Adler, M., 67, 89
Aiken, W. M., 286
Alali, A. A., 174–175
Alexander, C. J., 212
Alolouf, H., 351
Anderson, J. D., 212
Anderson, J. P., 268
Anderson, L., 402
Anderson, L. W., 351
Anderson, R. E., 315, 323, 324–325
Anderson, R. H., 383
Anderson, R. J., 11–12
Andre, T., 278
Andrews, R., 176
Angelou, M., 186, 267
Anyon, J., 102–103
Aristotle, 98
Aronson, E., 198
Artz, S., 401
Ashton-Warner, S., 86, 246

Bagley, W. C., 68
Baker, K. A., 205
Baldwin, B. T., 229
Ballantine, J. H., 105
Banks, J. A., 191, 194, 196, 198, 201, 203–204, 206–207, 208, 253–254
Barnett, D., 346
Barone, D., 264
Baruth, L. G., 203
Beard, C., 294
Becker, H. J., 315, 316, 328, 329
Beecher, C., 79
Beichner, R. J., 166, 312, 314, 317, 318
Bennett, C. I., 193, 195, 196, 198, 199, 200, 202, 203, 204, 212
Bennett, W., 89, 139
Bennett, W. J., 288
Berliner, D. C., 145, 195, 405–406
Bernstein, B. B., 192
Besner, H. F., 116, 212
Bialo, E., 310
Biddle, B. J., 145, 195, 405–406
Bigler, P., 2
Binet, A., 226
Bitter, G. G., 311, 313
Bitterwolf, C., 24
Black, H. L., 169, 178
Blackman, S., 351
Blakney, S., 357
Bloom, B. S., 261
Bloom, G., 346
Blow, S., 82
Booth, A., 407
Borich, G. D., 248, 250, 257, 266
Bos, C. S., 237

Botes, K., 340
Boyer, E., 89, 281, 340, 398–401
Bracey, G. W., 223, 408
Bradley, A., 11, 349, 368
Brameld, T., 69–70
Bronson, E., 229
Brophy, J. E., 248, 253, 255, 256, 257, 397
Brown, B., 263
Brown, F. B., 278
Brown, L., 197, 382
Brown, M. E., 43
Bruner, C., 302, 304
Bruner, J. S., 287–288
Bryan, W. J., 161
Bryk, A. S., 133
Bucky, P. A., 7–8
Budzinsky, F., 357
Burden, P. R., 244, 375, 377
Burnaford, G., 353
Burr, E., 286
Bursuck, W. D., 236, 238–239, 380, 382
Busch, C., 141, 143
Bush, G., 98, 139
Button, H. W., 75, 77, 78, 81, 82
Buzzell, J. B., 407
Byrd, D. M., 244, 375, 377

Cairns, R. B., 278
Calhoun, E., 260, 263, 393
Calkins, L., 29
Cambron-McCabe, N. H., 155, 156, 160, 164
Campbell, D. M., 49
Campbell, E. Q., 195
Cantor, L., 259
Carlson, K., 65
Carmichael, L. B., 6
Carroll, J., 261
Caterinicchia, D., 328
Catri, D. B., 298
Cetron, M., 306, 308, 393, 394, 400
Challenger, J., 10
Chan, I., 357
Chang, L., 236–237
Chantharasakul, A., 14–15
Chapman, S., 35
Charlier, P. S., 381
Chaskin, R. J., 251
Cheeks, E. H., 290, 291
Chen, X., 177, 210
Cheng, L. R. L., 205
Chubb, J. E., 145
Chunsakorn, P., 14–15
Cignetti, P. B., 49
Clark, E. W., Jr., 351
Clements, R. S., 257, 258
Clift, R. T., 351
Clinton, B., 98, 113–114, 119, 140, 143, 170–171, 322
Cobb, C. D., 278
Codell, E. R., 246, 248
Cogen, C., 349
Cohen, D., 400
Cohen, S., 75

Subject Index

Chicago Board of Education, 236
Chicago public schools, 132–134, 381
Chicago School Reform Act, 133–134
Chicanos, 199
Chief state school officer, 137–138
Child abuse/neglect, 114, 166
Child and the Curriculum, The (Dewey), 83–84
Child Care Bureau, 112
Child-centered teaching, 68–69, 84
Child development. *See* Development, stages of
Childhood and Society (Erikson), 222
Child-oriented reform efforts, 284–285
Child-oriented "search engines," 306
Children
    desire to work with, 6–7
    latchkey, 112, 225, 400
    Puritan view of, 73, 75
Children's Defense Fund, 110–111
Children's Services Council, 401
Children's Services Network, 401
Chinese immigrants, 201–202
Choice theory, 256
Church
    church and state, separation of, 178–179
    reform efforts and, 283–284
Citizenship, 98, 283–284
City-as-School, 119
Civic community, education to create and maintain, 100–101
Civic organizations, 398
Civil Rights Act (1964)
    Title VII of, 157
Civil rights movement, 197–198
Classical (type S) conditioning, 71
Class meetings, 266–267
Classroom
    caring, 251–252
    culture of, 107, 248–251
    democratic, 24, 256
    ethical dilemmas in, 155
    gender-fair, 211–212
    inclusive, 238–241
    observing in, 41–42
    self-contained, 106
Classroom action research, 355–356
Classroom aides, 43
Classroom climate, 248–251
Classroom dynamics, 250–251
Classroom experiences, learning to teach from, 42–43
Classroom learning environment, 244–271
    caring classroom, 251–252
    classroom organization, 252–255
    creating positive, 251–255
    culture of classroom, 107, 248–251
    physical environment, 252
Classroom management, 12–13, 255–260
    democratic classroom, 24, 256
    developing your own approach to, 259–260
    effective responses to student behavior, 258–260
    preventive planning, 256–258
Classroom organization, 252–255
Classroom performance assessments (Praxis III), 369

Climate, classroom, 248–251
Clinical supervision, 383–384
Coaching, peer, 380–381
Coalition of Essential Schools (CES), 358
Cocurricular/extracurricular programs, 278
Code of ethics, 154–155
Cognitive development model, 220–222, 233
Cognitive science, 72
Collaboration
    participating in teacher, 380–382
    for school reform, 356–357
"Collaborative, emergent" approach to leadership, 352–353
Collaborative consultation, 238–239
Collaborative school reform networks, 358–359
Colleagues
    observation of, 33
    relationships with, 33, 377–378, 393–394
Collective bargaining, 160, 349
College Board, 296, 297
Colleges and universities
    land-grant, 80
    partnerships with, 357
Collegiality, 108, 378
Collegial support team (CST), 382
Colonial era (1620–1750), education in, 72–76, 283–284
Columbia Teachers College, Project Synergy at, 233
Columbine High School shootings, 113–114, 170, 223–224
Commercial computer labs, 324
Commissioner of education. *See* Chief state school officer
Commission on Reorganization and Secondary Education, 285
Committee for Economic Development, 116
Committee of Fifteen, 285
Committee of Ten, 284–285
Common School Journal, The, 79
Common schools, state-supported, 78–80, 81
Communication
    based on constructive assertiveness, 258–259
    home–school systems of, 313
    with other educators, using Internet for, 315–316
Communication skills, 250, 393–394
Community(ies)
    becoming leader in, 357
    creating partnerships with, 357, 379–380, 397–401
    need for support of, 13–14
    as resource for schools, 398–399
    schools as resources for, 399–401
    sense of, 108
Community environments, schools and, 104–105
Community organizations, career opportunities in, 372
Community relations, 379–380
Community service program, 399–400
Comparative education, 405–406
Compensatory education programs, 118–119
Competencies, 21–22
    research-based, 36
Competent parties to teaching contract, 157
Compressed video technology, interactive, 41
Compulsory education, 75, 80–83, 284

National Information Infrastructure (NII), 325
National Institute for Mental Health, 115
National Joint Committee on Learning Disabilities, 230
National Network for Educational Renewal (NNER), 358
National Parent Information Network (NPIN), 379
National Research Center on Gifted and Talented Education, 231–232, 233
National Science Teachers Association (NSTA), 354, 357
National Task Force on Learning Style and Brain Behavior, 228
National Teacher Examination (NTE), 367
National Teacher Forum on Leadership (1998), 356–357
National Teachers Association. *See* National Education Association (NEA)
National Trade and Professional Associations of the United States, 347
Nation at Risk, A, 21, 38–39, 89, 405
Nation of Spectators, A (National Commission on Civil Renewal), 223
Nation Prepared, A, 38
Native Americans, education for, 75–76, 84–85, 202–204
Naturalist intelligence, 227
NBPTS. *See* National Board for Professional Teaching Standards (NBPTS)
Needs
    choice theory on, 256
    hierarchy of, 224
    learning. *See* Learning needs
Negligence, tort liability for, 164–165
Networking, job search and personal, 372–373
Networking computer programs, 167
Network software license, 167
New England Primer, 74
New Jersey v. Massa, 179
New Jersey v. T.L.O., 172
Newsgroups, 313
New York City school system, 129, 131, 146
New York City School Volunteer Program, 8–9
Ninth Amendment, 159–160
Nondiscrimination
    students' rights to, 174–175
    teachers' rights to, 157
Nonteaching tasks, time spent at, 14
Normal schools, 79–80
Northwest Regional Educational Laboratory, 296
Null curriculum, 277–278
Null v. Board of Education, 180

Oberti v. Board of Education of the Borough of Clementon School District, 235
Objectives, learning, 265
Observation
    in classrooms, 41–42
    of colleagues, 33
Observation instruments, 42
Occupational therapist, collaborative consultation with, 239
Offer and acceptance
    of job, 374
    of teaching contract, 157
Office of Economic Opportunity, local programs administered through, 142–143
Office of Educational Research and Improvement (OERI), 354–355

Ohman v. Board of Education, 165
Old Deluder Satan Act (1647), 75
On Being a Teacher (Zehm and Kottler), 24, 36
Open-space schools, 106
Operant (type R) conditioning, 71
Operating budget, school district, 142
Opportunities
    career, 371–372
    job, 11–12
    teaching as opportunity to serve, 24
Opportunity to learn (OTL), 255, 405
Optional Extended Year (OEY) program, 399–400
Organization, classroom, 252–255
Organizational structures of schools districts, 129
Organization for instruction, 257–258
Origin of Species (Darwin), 83
Orthopedic impairment, 230
Outcome-based education, 36–37, 289
Outcomes, unpredictability of, 15–17

Pacific Islanders, education of, 200–202
Paideia Proposal (Adler), 89
Paperwork, 14
Parallel teaching, 382
Parent Advisory Council (PAC), 131
Parent Institute for Quality Education, 379
Parents
    concerns for educational policies, 128
    condom-distribution programs and consent of, 175, 179
    control of schools and, 87–88, 131
    educational attainment of, 102
    home school rights, 177–178
    involvement of, 99, 378–379, 407–408
    legal rights of, 168–175
    "parent-rights" cases involving religious expression, 179
    support of, need for, 13–14
    voucher system and, 146
    working with, 239–240, 357
Parent-Teacher Association (PTA), 13–14, 131, 378
Parent-Teacher Organization (PTO), 13, 131, 378
Parochial schools, 73, 367
Partnership for Family Involvement in Education, 379
Partnerships
    addressing social problems, 398–399
    with businesses and organizations, 298–299, 357
    with colleges and universities, 357
    with community, 357, 379–380, 397–401
    corporate-education, 146–147, 398–399
    with parents, 239–240, 357
    school-based interprofessional case management, 118
    state-based educational, 358–359
    teacher–student, need for, 18
PASE v. Hannon, 227
Patchogue-Medford Congress of Teachers v. Board of Education of Patchogue-Medford Union Free School District, 173
Pay, 9–10, 344
Pedagogical content knowledge, 34
Pedagogy, emphasis on authentic, 109
Peer coaching, 380–381
Peer counseling, 117
Peer-mediated instruction, 263–264
Peer sexual harassment, 177–178

Road Ahead, The (Gates, Myhrvold, and Rinearson), 310
Roberts v. City of Boston, 76
Role models, 18–19, 261–262
"Role of the Arts in Unifying the High School Curriculum, The" (R&D project), 297
Romans v. Crenshaw, 174
Roosevelt, Franklin, 201
Rules and consequences "face," 260
Rules and procedures, establishing, 257
Rural schools, 104

Safety in schools, 99, 114. See also Violence
St. Paul City Academy, 402
Salaries, 9–10, 344
Salary gap, 344
Sales taxes, 142
Sallie Mae Corporation, 104–105, 238
Salome Urena Middle Academy (SUMA), 118
Same-sex harassment, 177–178
San Antonio Independent School District v. Rodriguez, 144
San Diego State University, 329
San Francisco Board of Education, 201
San Francisco Unified School District, 165–166
SAT scores, 211, 296
Savage Inequalities (Kozol), 104, 143–144
SAVe (Suspension Avoidance Vehicle), 119
Scaffolding, 262
Schaill v. Tippecanoe School Corporation, 173
School(s). See also Control of schools, struggle for; Social problems affecting schools
    accelerated, 358
    alternative, 119–120, 174, 233, 286–287, 399
    career opportunities in and outside, 369–372
    changing population of, 190–191
    charter, 367, 402–403
    colonial, 72–76, 283–284
    community as resource for, 398–399
    compulsory education and, effect on, 80–83
    culture of, 105–106, 394
    Dame, 74
    describing, 101–103
    ethical dilemmas in, 155
    exemplary, 401–404
    expanded role for, in teacher education, 39
    for-profit, 403–404
    full-service, 117–118, 401
    influence of educational technology on, 306–307
    lighthouse, 324
    magnet, 146, 233, 297
    normal, 79–80
    open-space, 106
    parochial, 73, 367
    private, 170, 367
    professional development (PDSs), 39, 51–52
    progressive, 83–85, 286–287
    reform efforts and, 284–285
    as resources for communities, 399–401
    security measures in, 114
    social class and, 102–103
    as social institutions, 103–107
    successful, characteristics of, 107–109
    year-round, 9, 400
School and Society, The (Dewey), 83

School as the Center of Inquiry, The (Schaefer), 355
School-based interprofessional case management, 118
School-based management (SBM), 132–134, 353
School-based teacher education, 46–47
School board, 129–130
School choice, 145
School completion, Goals 2000 goal for, 98–99
School desegregation, 85–86, 197–198
School District of Abington Township v. Schempp, 178–179
School districts
    legal rights of, 175–180
    local, 129
    operating budget, average allocation of, 142
School governance. See Control of schools, struggle for
School organizational capacity, greater, 109
School prayer, 178–179
School psychologist, collaborative consultation with, 239
School readiness, 98
School records, privacy of, 173–174, 235
School reform, leadership and collaboration for. See also Reform, educational
School restructuring, 109, 132
School Safety Check Book (NEA), 114
School shootings, 113–114, 170, 223–224
Schools with IDEAs That Work (USDE), 239–240
School Technology and Readiness Report (CEO Forum), 307, 329
School-to-work programs, 298–299
School traditions, 106
School violence. See Violence
School Wars, 131
School-within-a-school, 119
Science
    current trends in curriculum for, 292–293
    Goals 2000 goal for, 99
    literacy in, 392
Scientific management, 81
Scoville v. Board of Education of Joliet Township High School District 204, 169
Screening of teacher education candidates, 99
Search and seizure, reasonable, 172–173
"Search engines," child-oriented, 306
Seating arrangements, 252
Seattle-Based Committee for Children, Second Step program created by, 394
Second International Mathematics Study, 405
Secular humanism, 70–71, 161–162
Security, job, 10–11
Segregation, 75–76, 85–86, 197–198
Self-actualization, 71, 100
Self-assessment, 50–51
Self-contained classroom, 106
Self-directed study, 233
Self-esteem, 267–268
Self-governance, degree of, 342–343
Self-knowledge, 32–33, 35–36, 72
Seminaries, female, 77
Sensorimotor intelligence, 221
Separation of church and state, 178–179
Serious emotional disturbance (SED), 230
Serrano v. Priest, 144
Service learning, 100–101
Service profession, teaching as, 8–9, 24